The Economics of East Asian Integration

In memory of the late Dr Hadi Soesastro and the late Dr Koji Nishikimi

The Economics of East Asian Integration

A Comprehensive Introduction to Regional Issues

Edited by

Masahisa Fujita

President, Research Institute of Economy, Trade and Industry, Professor, Konan University and Professor, Kyoto University, Japan

Ikuo Kuroiwa

Director General, Development Studies Center, IDE-JETRO, Japan

Satoru Kumagai

Director, Economic Integration Studies Group, Inter-disciplinary Studies Center, IDE-JETRO, Japan

Edward Elgar
Cheltenham, UK • Northampton, MA, USA

© Institute of Developing Economies (IDE), JETRO 2011

Published by
Edward Elgar Publishing Limited
The Lypiatts
15 Lansdown Road
Cheltenham
Glos GL50 2JA
UK

Edward Elgar Publishing, Inc.
William Pratt House
9 Dewey Court
Northampton
Massachusetts 01060
USA

A catalogue record for this book
is available from the British Library

Library of Congress Control Number: 2010941495

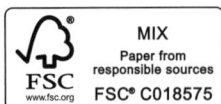

FSC
MIX
Paper from
responsible sources
www.fsc.org   FSC® C018575

ISBN 978 0 85793 011 8 (cased)

Typeset by Servis Filmsetting Ltd, Stockport, Cheshire
Printed and bound by MPG Books Group, UK

Contents

Contributors

Mitsuyo Ando, Associate Professor of International Economics, Faculty of Business and Commerce, Keio University.

Biswa Nath Bhattacharyay, Lead Professional and Adviser to Dean, Asian Development Bank Institute (ADBI), Tokyo and Lead Professional, Asian Development Bank (ADB), Manila.

Christopher Findlay, Professor and Head of School, School of Economics, Faculty of the Professions, The University of Adelaide.

Masahisa Fujita, President, Research Institute of Economy, Trade and Industry; Professor, Konan University; Professor, Kyoto University.

Toshitaka Gokan, Visiting Researcher, The Center for Operations Research and Econometrics, Université catholique de Louvain, Belgium.

Nobuaki Hamaguchi, Professor, Research Institute for Economics and Business Administration, Kobe University.

Daisuke Hiratsuka, Director-General, Research Planning Department, IDE-JETRO.

Masayoshi Honma, Professor, Graduate School of Agricultural and Life Sciences, University of Tokyo.

Nobuhiro Horii, Associate Professor, Faculty of Economics, Kyushu University.

Ikumo Isono, Research Fellow, Bangkok Research Center, IDE-JETRO.

Kentaro Kawasaki, Associate Professor, Faculty of Business Administration, Toyo University.

Ho Yeon Kim, Professor, School of Economics, Sungkyunkwan University.

Michikazu Kojima, Director, Inter-disciplinary Studies Center, IDE-JETRO.

Hosaki Kono, Visiting Scholar, Department of Economics, Harvard University.

Kensuke Kubo, Honorary Visiting Scientist, Planning Unit, Indian Statistical Institute.

Satoru Kumagai, Director, Inter-disciplinary Studies Center, IDE-JETRO.

Ikuo Kuroiwa, Director General, Development Studies Center, IDE-JETRO.

Tomohiro Machikita, Research Fellow, Inter-disciplinary Studies Center, IDE-JETRO.

Etsuyo Michida, Research Fellow, Inter-disciplinary Studies Center, IDE-JETRO.

Koji Nishikimi, Director, Inter-disciplinary Studies Center, IDE-JETRO.

Eiji Ogawa, Professor, Hitotsubashi University Graduate School of Commerce and Management.

Jiro Okamoto, Visiting Fellow, Crawford School of Economics and Government, ANU College of Asia and the Pacific, The Australian National University.

Wei Zhao, Director, Institute of International Economics, Zhejiang University.

Preface

This book originated from the international joint research project on economic integration in East Asia conducted by the Institute of Developing Economies, JETRO (IDE-JETRO), Japan for the fiscal years 2007–08. This research project investigated various issues related to the economic integration such as institution building of FTAs, production networks and location choice of MNEs, R&D and innovation, infrastructure development and transport cost, international migration and service trade, monetary integration, and regional disparity and poverty. It also examined energy, environment, and agricultural issues.

After encountering difficulties with import-substitution policies, East Asian economies changed their policy orientation and liberalized trade and investment. As a result, *de facto* integration preceded *de jure* integration especially in export-oriented industries, where import tariffs on intermediate inputs were eliminated on the condition that all such outputs are exported abroad. Furthermore, rapid progress in transport and communication technology – as well as vigorous infrastructure development in this region – significantly reduced trade and transport costs. In *de jure* integration, an important turning point came with the signing of the AFTA agreement in 1992, and *de jure* integration has gained momentum as other East Asian countries have followed suit in signing free trade agreements with intra-regional as well as extra-regional countries. *De jure* integration promotes free movement not only of goods, but also of services, capital, and natural persons. Thus it is expected to have a significant impact on economic activities in the region.

With these perceptions in mind, we have attempted in this book to provide a common knowledge base of economic integration in East Asia for both academics and practitioners in the region. Each chapter contains both ample data and analyses from solid viewpoints. Anyone who has interest in this topic will find rich information not only on his or her own field but also on neighbouring fields. Various topics are further explored in box articles in several chapters, and undergraduate students should discover much of interest.

Although this is intended to be a 'textbook' on the topic, it also contains a strong message. It is our hope that after reading through the book, readers will understand how important it is for East Asia to be a single integrated region and eventually to become the 'world innovation centre' in addition to further developing as the 'world manufacturing center'.

The process of economic integration in East Asia is progressing day by day, and in this sense, the present book should be updated accordingly. We would appreciate readers' comments. We are grateful to all the participants in the project for their valuable inputs.

Finally, we are sorry to inform you that Hadi Soesastro, Senior Economist and the former Executive Director of the Centre for Strategic and International Studies (CSIS), Jakarta, passed away on 4 May 2010. He was one of Indonesia's most prominent economists as well as one of the intellectual founders of regionalism in Southeast Asia. We actually tried to ask him to contribute a chapter to this volume but his health condition made it difficult to accept our invitation.

It should also be added that our colleague Koji Nishikimi initially organized this project. However, as his health did not allow him to continue the assignment, his role was taken over by Ikuo Kuroiwa. It is with deep regret that we report that Nishikimi, who was an excellent economist as well as our beloved friend, passed away on 23 January 2010. Needless to say, this volume would not have been possible without his important contributions. We would like to extend our deepest condolences to the families of Hadi Soesastro and Koji Nishikimi.

Masahisa Fujita, Ikuo Kuroiwa and Satoru Kumagai
August 2010

Introduction

Masahisa Fujita, Ikuo Kuroiwa and Satoru Kumagai

After encountering difficulties with import-substitution policies, East Asian economies endeavored to liberalize trade and investment, and progress was made toward economic integration in the region. In particular, *de facto* integration preceded *de jure* integration in exported-oriented industries, where import tariffs on intermediate inputs were eliminated on condition that all such outputs were exported abroad. At the same time, rapid progress in transport and communication technology – as well as in infrastructure improvement – significantly reduced trade and transport costs, and thus facilitated the dispersion of economic activities throughout the region, so that latecomer countries could join the production networks organized by multinational enterprises (MNEs).

In a previous stage of industrial development, dense industrial agglomerations were created in advanced East Asian countries, such as Japan and the Asian Newly Industrializing Economies (NIEs). However, when companies were faced with rising wages and congestion in agglomerated areas, declining trade and transport costs facilitated relocation of labor-intensive industries to lower-wage countries, initially in Southeast Asia and then, after economic liberalization, to China and Vietnam. This catching-up process summarizes the industrial development of East Asia, where production networks have continuously expanded into less developed regions in tandem with newly created industrial agglomerations.

It is often claimed that the regional economy of East Asia has been integrated through market forces, with little support from formal institutional arrangements. However, this situation began to change when the ASEAN Free Trade Area (AFTA) was launched in 1993 with the aim of removing trade barriers throughout the region. *De jure* integration has gained momentum since the Singapore–Japan Free Trade Agreement (FTA) came into effect in 2002. Subsequently ASEAN's bilateral FTA with China was formally launched in 2005, and the ASEAN–Korea and ASEAN–Japan FTAs took effect in 2007 and 2008 respectively. Furthermore, ASEAN has taken a further step forward, transforming itself from a mere free trade area into the ASEAN Economic Community (AEC), which could enhance the free movement of goods, services, investment, capital, and skilled labor, and could contribute to the formation of a single market as well as a single production base in an increasingly competitive international market. The AEC is scheduled to be established by 2015.

Meanwhile the Asian financial crisis of 1997 triggered the spread of regional frameworks for financial cooperation, such as the Chiang Mai Initiative (CMI), the Asian Bond Market Initiative (ABMI), and the Asian Bond Fund (ABF). In the CMI, Japan, China and Korea joined in a regional currency swap arrangement with ASEAN to stabilize the regional economy, while the ABMI and the ABF aim to develop efficient and liquid bond markets in Asia, enabling better utilization of Asian savings for Asian investment. They also aim to mitigate currency and maturity mismatches in the financing of Asian borrowers, which was once considered a major cause of the Asian financial crisis.

As noted above, East Asian economic integration has made progress in both *de facto* and *de jure* terms. Considering the continuing trend toward lowering trade and transport costs, as well as the increasing number of free trade agreements and other regional cooperation frameworks, economic integration seems likely to advance further. However, today's East Asian economy has faced serious challenges that cover a number of areas and which call for concerted efforts by all the East Asian economies. In particular, the following issues should be addressed to enhance economic integration and growth in a sustainable manner.

1. The spatial structure of the East Asian economies has been strongly affected by decreasing trade and transport costs. The spatial structure – as well as the mechanics of East Asian economic integration – needs to be explained by consistently resorting to a comprehensive analytical framework. It is important to indicate the relationship between transport costs and industrial location. In particular, it is critically important to demonstrate how declining transport costs facilitate the dispersion of industrial activities, so that less developed economies may obtain opportunities to attract investment and participate in production networks organized by MNEs.

2. It is a well-known fact that economic integration in East Asia has been propelled by the activities of MNEs. MNEs have established production networks which are helpful to strengthen the competitiveness of the East Asian economies. However, rising wages in East Asia have made it necessary to search for success factors other than abundant labor and an investor-friendly investment climate. In this regard, technological progress has become a factor of key importance, especially for higher income East Asian countries. In the medium and long term,

East Asia needs to become an innovation center rather than a factory of the world.

3.   Agriculture often constitutes a stumbling block that needs to be overcome for integration to make progress. Similarly, international integration of the service sector and the labor market, as well as monetary integration, involve a variety of sensitive and difficult problems. These problems need to be examined carefully if feasible solutions are to be found.

4.   Formal institutions, such as the WTO and FTAs, eliminate cross-border barriers against trade in goods, services, labor, and investment. It follows that further integration will require strengthening of formal institutions. Similarly, efficient transportation and logistics services are key drivers of economic integration. It is thus very important to work out the best solutions for strengthening formal institutions as well as for improving efficiency in transportation and logistics services.

5.   Economic integration may give rise to negative side effects, including regional inequality and increased poverty in parts of the integrated economy. These effects should be identified and appropriate measures taken to address them. In addition, energy and environmental issues are becoming increasingly serious. Coordinated efforts are necessary to realize sustainable growth and development in East Asia.

Although no easy solutions can be expected, these problems require special attention. Each chapter in this book tries to capture essential features of these problems and attempts to draw some policy implications. In broad terms, the book has the following features:

*   The book is intended for policy makers, practitioners, academics, and students who are involved or interested in economic integration in East Asia. Thus the book avoids technical details, but interested readers may find the references in each chapter helpful for pursuing in-depth study.
*   The book deals with economic integration of the East Asian countries, comprising the ten ASEAN countries – Brunei, Indonesia, Malaysia, the Philippines, Singapore, Thailand, Cambodia, Lao PDR, Myanmar, and Vietnam – plus three Northeast Asian countries – China, Japan, and the Republic of Korea (that is, ASEAN+3). But some chapters include India, Australia, and New Zealand as well (that is, ASEAN+6). Other combinations of countries are referred to in some of the chapters, depending on the purposes of the analysis or the availability of the data.

● The book is composed of five parts (Parts I–V), with each part dealing with specific topics of East Asian integration mentioned above. Below is an overview of each chapter.

PART I   FACTS AND THEORIES

Part I (Chapters 1–3) introduces facts and theories relating to East Asian integration. Many statistics and data are presented to give an introductory view of the progress of East Asian integration. The chapters in this section show that integration has already played a pivotal role in the economic development of each East Asian economy. An analytical framework of East Asian integration is provided, relying on the theories of New Economic Geography (NEG). NEG illuminates consistently the impacts of declining transport costs on the spatial structure of the integrating East Asian economy. NEG is referred to frequently in other parts of the book.

Chapter 1 provides a brief history of economic development in East Asia and gives an overview of the basic economic profile of each country. We then take a closer look at the structure of intra-regional trade with particular reference to production networks in the electronics and automobile industries. We point out that East Asia is nowadays functioning as a factory of the world, importing raw materials from outside the region, trading intermediate goods within the region, and then exporting final products to overseas destinations, and especially to the United States and the European Union (EU). East Asia may have become one of the world's most industrialized regions as a result, but its vulnerability arising from over-reliance on the United States and the EU has emerged since the beginning of the world economic crisis in 2008. In this context, it is becoming increasingly important to create final demand within the region big enough to absorb the bulk of the final products that the region manufactures.

Chapters 2 and 3 provide a basic framework for analyzing the extent to which economic integration contributes to industrial development in East Asia. In order to examine the major effects of integration on resource allocation and economic disparities, we take a close look at how economic integration creates forces of agglomeration and dispersion. We find that progress toward economic integration first accelerates industrial agglomeration in certain areas and/or countries of the integrated region. However, further progress toward integration may trigger a leap-out of the agglomerated industries and consequently bring about a shift from agglomeration toward concentrated dispersion. This process of concentrated dispersion tends to spur the governments of integrated countries into excessive competition for luring footloose industries. Such governments need to adopt effective policy coordination, including coordinated types of assistance for the development of the Least Developed Countries (LDCs) within the integrated region.

PART II INTEGRATION (1): PRODUCTION NETWORKS AND INNOVATION

Part II (Chapters 4–6) deals with issues relevant to production networks and innovation. It is often said that East Asian economies have been integrated and have achieved rapid economic growth by participating in production networks organized by MNEs. It is nevertheless important to examine the multifaceted impact of MNEs on the host country economies. This part of the book also deals with productivity growth and innovation. These issues are crucially important when considering success factors for future economic development in East Asia.

Chapter 4 discusses international production and distribution networks in East Asia. The effective utilization of international production and distribution networks has been one of the key elements underlying East Asia's high performance in the last decade or so. This chapter sheds light on the production networks that have rapidly developed in East Asia since the 1990s and gives a detailed account of their main characteristics and mechanisms, using finely disaggregated international trade data and micro-data relating to MNEs, that is, Japanese and American firms operating in the region. The production networks that can be seen mainly in the machinery industries in East Asia are distinctive as regards their significance in each economy, their geographical extensiveness involving many countries at different income levels, and their sophistication in both intra-firm and arm's-length relationships. To further activate fragmentation and to take advantage of the forces that are globalizing corporate activities for economic development, the key policy at government level is to host network-forming Foreign Direct Investment (FDI) and to promote agglomeration by implementing various measures that facilitate trade and FDI. A deliberate effort to reduce service link costs is also beneficial, as is effective utilization of FTAs and Regional Trade Agreements (RTAs).

In Chapter 5, the authors examine the positive and negative roles that MNEs play in host countries. Previous studies have confirmed that East Asian countries have enjoyed the benefits brought by MNEs in the form of faster economic growth, larger trade surpluses and smoother technology transfer. The negative effects, by comparison, have been rather mild.

Discussions of related theories and the MNEs' location choices in East Asia are also presented in this chapter, followed by a review of the path to prosperity taken by Korea and a survey of representative Korean firms which managed to become MNEs in the course of that process. In their march toward foreign expansion, Korean firms have responded particularly well to policies at home and in host countries.

Chapter 6 examines the productivity growth experience of the East Asian countries and India, and discusses possible explanations for various national experiences. An overview of labor productivity and total factor productivity reveals that growth has been uneven among Asian countries, especially following the currency crisis of 1997–98. One possible explanation is that China and India, which have been experiencing positive growth in the new millennium, have maintained high levels of research and development (R&D) spending relative to their GDPs. One of the factors that stimulate local R&D is reform of the intellectual property protection system. Patent reform, greater R&D spending, and higher rates of patenting have been highly correlated in East Asia and India, to the extent that in some technology fields, East Asia is now a major center of knowledge creation. However, an assessment of the overall effect of patent reform on economic development requires further investigation.

PART III INTEGRATION (2): AGRICULTURE, SERVICES, LABOR, AND MONEY

This part of the book (Chapters 7–10) focuses on issues relevant to agriculture, service trade liberalization, international labor migration, and monetary integration. Agriculture often becomes a stumbling block that hinders economic integration, but the difficulties posed by the agricultural sector must be overcome if a more integrated East Asia is to be created. Similarly, service trade liberalization should be encouraged. International labor migration involves complex issues, but its causes and consequences should be clarified to draw out some policy implications. On the other hand, regional monetary and financial cooperation, which was launched after the Asian currency crisis, is expected to evolve into a more rigid form of policy coordination.

Chapter 7 discusses agricultural issues related to East Asia's economic integration. Agriculture comprises an important part of GDP and in some countries accounts for a significant proportion of exports, and thus contributes to the economy of the East Asian region. Currently, intra-regional agricultural trade accounts for about 30% of total imports in the region, and trade in farm products displays a large potential for expanding intra-regional trade. Stringent agricultural protection measures remain in place in Japan and Korea, and some developing countries in the region are enforcing heavier agricultural protection, which may impede the elimination of all tariffs for economic integration. When considering the treatment of agriculture in the process of economic integration, it is useful to review the FTAs and Economic Partnership Agreements (EPAs) that have been concluded so far. It is important to fully incorporate the agricultural sector in the process of economic integration while arranging for it to be treated differently from other sectors. It would be desirable to establish a forum on agricultural partnership in East Asia, to discuss agricultural issues comprehensively on a multi-country basis.

Chapter 8 has a particular focus on the extent of international integration in the service sector. The author shows how an open service sector performs better on its own and how it can contribute to better performance in other parts of the economy, which in turn may lead to greater integration of other sectors of the economy as well. The significance of the sector in the economy is reviewed, and the phenomenon of the rising share of services in output is discussed. There then follows a discussion of the nature of trade and investment in services, and of barriers to trade in services. The significance of these barriers and progress on liberalization in East Asia is reviewed. The last section outlines some future steps that could support a services reform program.

Chapter 9 outlines a fundamental framework for interpreting the causes and consequences of international migration and presents some current evidence concerning the international migration of high-skilled and low-skilled workers in East Asia. This chapter also identifies some implications of the relationship between economic integration and immigration. In order to understand the causes and consequences of international migration, two mechanisms linking migration and economic integration are presented: namely (1) selectivity and sorting effects of out-migration in sending countries; (2) diversity-based international knowledge production and 'brain circulation' as consequences of immigration. In addition, this chapter discusses some implications of enhancing innovation capacity with a view to creating a world innovation center via economic integration and labor mobility.

Chapter 10 explains the costs and benefits of monetary integration, discusses theories and empirical studies on Optimum Currency Areas (OCAs), and examines the implications of the Asian currency crisis of 1997 for increased monetary integration and the possible formation of a currency union. The double mismatch of financial institutions' balance sheets in terms of maturity and currency has been identified as a factor that increased the severity of the Asian currency crisis of 1997. In response to this, the monetary authorities of the East Asian countries launched three kinds of initiative in the 2000s: the Chiang Mai Initiative, the Asian Bond Market Initiative, and the Asian Bond Fund. These initiatives are regarded as the first steps toward regional monetary and financial cooperation in East Asia, and have opened the way for the development of regional monetary coordination, leading to possible regional monetary integration in the future.

PART IV   DRIVERS OF INTEGRATION

Part IV (Chapters 11–14) discusses the drivers of East Asian integration. There are two kinds of drivers of economic integration. One is the formal institutions which eliminate barriers not only against trade in goods but also against trade in services and investment. The other is a rapid decline in trade and communication costs resulting from technological progress and infrastructure improvement. These issues are discussed comprehensively, and some policy recommendations are presented.

Chapter 11 reviews the historical development of institution building in East Asia and discusses the prospects for the future. After the Second World War, the central theme of the newly independent states became the maintenance of national sovereignty, territorial integrity and policy autonomy, and economic integration was not sought until the 1990s. Economic globalization and the end of the Cold War encouraged ASEAN members to form AFTA, which served as a precedent for the subsequent East Asian economic integration processes. The Asian financial crisis, along with other factors such as the stagnation of Asia-Pacific Economic Cooperation (APEC) and World Trade Organization (WTO) activities, acted as a trigger for East Asian regionalism in the form of the ASEAN+3 process. Since the turn of the century, a number of initiatives, agreements and frameworks have proliferated in and around East Asia. At this point in time, it seems that economic integration in the region is better understood when the processes are viewed as a whole, and when due recognition is given to their distinctive flexible, inclusive and multi-layered nature.

Chapter 12 discusses the recent development in institution and policy coordination in East Asia, with particular focus on the ASEAN+6 grouping (ASEAN plus China, Japan, the Republic of Korea, India, Australia and New Zealand). The increase in intra-regional trade has been driven by ongoing transactions in parts and components. This reflects policy efforts to exempt import tariffs on intermediate inputs when used for exported-oriented industries, such as electronics. On the other hand, tariffs on consumer goods are still high. In recent years, although FTAs have proliferated, the utilization rates of tax privileges under FTAs have not been particularly significant. In particular, small and medium enterprises (SMEs) have not obtained benefits from FTAs. Moreover, region-wide FTAs cannot solve the 'spaghetti bowl' problem, which is likely to persist as long as each country freely sets its own tariff rates and lists for exclusions from tariff elimination. The way to escape from this trap is to eliminate tariffs on all manufactured products. The elimination of most-favored nation (MFN) tariffs under the WTO should be actively pursued.

Chapter 13 discusses transport costs, which are one of the key factors in economic integration. Freight transport in East Asia has been developing extremely rapidly in recent decades. Transport networks, which vary in routes, modes, speed and quality, have evolved to offer faster, more extensive and more accurate services to meet industry needs. On the other hand, there are several unsolved bottlenecks remaining in East Asia, where there are great differences in transport development. To identify the remaining bottlenecks, it is necessary to determine what factors affect transport costs and trade patterns. This chapter also discusses how transport networks have been improved in East Asia.

Chapter 14 discusses the challenges and issues of infrastructure development for East Asia's economic integration. Infrastructure development, especially of the cross-border variety, is an essential determinant of successful economic integration in East Asia. The effective development of cross-border infrastructure is crucial for sustaining rapid growth in East Asia, particularly in narrowing the gap among the region's economies. This could be 'hard' infrastructure or physical connectivity, as well as the harmonization and refinement of existing policies, rules and regulations, also regarded as 'soft' (or facilitating) infrastructure. Cross-border infrastructure development provides access to a larger market and to production networks, particularly for landlocked and isolated countries. Infrastructure development can accelerate economic integration in East Asia insofar as physical linkages can come to terms with diversity, and particularly geographical diversity. Improving connectivity can bring large welfare gains through increased market access, reduced trade costs and more efficient energy production and use. Infrastructure can bind the countries of East Asia to a commitment to stimulate economic activity through a sharing of scarce resources and by ensuring the symmetric distribution of regional infrastructure costs and benefits across participating countries, thereby contributing to the emergence of an integrated Asia.

PART V   COHESION AND SUSTAINABILITY

Part V (Chapters 15–18) focuses on issues related to cohesion and the sustainability of the integrating East Asian economies. If only a part of each country is incorporated into regional integration, leaving other parts behind, policies of economic integration may widen regional inequalities rather than reduce them. Poverty may also increase in sectors of the economy that are negatively affected by integration. On the other hand, energy supply and environmental management are becoming crucially important in ensuring the sustainability of the integrating economy. Regional cooperation is indispensable for tackling such increasingly difficult challenges.

Chapter 15 investigates the relationship between economic integration and regional disparities in East Asia. Income inequalities across countries are tending to become less pronounced in East Asia, especially in those countries which are more open to regional integration of trade and investment. On the other hand, regional inequalities within each country are increasing because of the tendency toward industrial agglomeration. Because of low labor mobility and the poor absorptive capacity of the urban sector due to lack of adequate infrastructure, existing agglomerations in several countries are too small to enable people in poor regions to migrate out of poverty, and the result is persistent and exacerbated regional income inequality.

In Chapter 16, the relationship between poverty and economic integration is discussed. Theoretically, economic integration can be expected to facilitate agglomeration and concentrated dispersion, resulting in the urbanization of some rural areas and the creation of new opportunities for employment and economic activity. These forces will in due course vitalize the regional economy and can eventually contribute to poverty reduction. However, it cannot be guaranteed that all poor people will be able to participate in this process. Empirical evidence suggests that even in East Asia, trade expansion and FDI inflow have not yet contributed to poverty alleviation. Although economic integration does not appear to affect poverty rates in aggregate, it is bound to create losers and winners. The chapter discusses measures for making economic integration more supportive of the poor and less harmful for the losers in the integration process.

Chapter 17 explores the issue of whether energy supply will become a bottleneck that hampers rapid economic growth in East Asia and, if that is the case, what kinds of measures should be taken in the region. In particular, regional energy cooperation is crucial for sustainable development in East Asia. The author analyzes the issues relevant to regional energy cooperation, such as the energy structure of East Asia, the ongoing progress of energy cooperation, the drastic changes in the energy market and their impacts, and the frictions involved in energy use in East Asia. In the context of these analyses, the need for energy cooperation is discussed.

Chapter 18 analyzes the impacts of economic integration on environmental issues. Ensuring that the environmental consequences of economic integration are as benign as possible is of key importance to sustainable development in East Asia. While the openness of economies in East Asia is often found to reduce local pollution such as sulfur dioxide, adverse effects can be seen in other areas such as global warming, deforestation and the emission of hazardous waste. This chapter reviews studies on the impact of trade on the environment and discusses linkages between openness and the environment. It is suggested that, as a precautionary measure, trade should be monitored carefully to avoid a possible adverse impact on the environment. To draw lessons for Asia, this chapter summarizes what the European Union (EU) and the North American Free Trade Agreement (NAFTA) have achieved so far in environmental management.

The book concludes with a chapter that explores the important challenges facing East Asian integration. The chapter attempts to present policy options, and indicates the directions that have to be followed to address these challenges.

PART I

Facts and Theories

1. A history of *de facto* economic integration in East Asia

Ikuo Kuroiwa and Satoru Kumagai

1.1 INTRODUCTION

This chapter overviews the progress of *de facto* economic integration, or in other words, the evolving structure of production and trade in East Asia.[1] Firstly, a brief history of industrial development in East Asia is provided with a focus on industrial policy. Secondly, key statistics are furnished to give readers basic information, through an overview of the economies in the region. Thirdly, the trade structure of East Asia is examined with a focus on production networks in the electronics and automobile industries. Fourthly, drivers of economic integration are examined with reference to trade policy and tariff rates as well as freight costs. It is of great interest to explore how production networks have evolved in East Asia and why East Asia was able to become the manufacturing factory of the world; however, in the face of the current global economic crisis, a need has arisen to transform the East Asian economy, and this is discussed in the conclusion of the chapter.

1.2 INDUSTRIAL DEVELOPMENT IN EAST ASIA

Only half a century ago, East Asia was generally seen as a region of 'poverty' and 'stagnation'. Now, East Asia has transformed itself into the 'growth center' of the world, recording a high economic growth rate well above the world average for decades. Some people regard this as a 'miracle', and it was a favorite theme of argument for economists in the 1990s and thereafter (World Bank 1993, Krugman 1994, Stiglitz and Yusuf 2001).

Economic development in East Asia is characterized by the sequential 'take-off'[2] of member countries. The multi-tiered economic development in East Asia is often referred to as the 'flying geese' pattern of economic development (Figure 1.1, Box 1.1). Although the shape of the figure appears to have changed in recent years, the model is a fine illustration of the historical development of East Asian economies up through the 1990s.

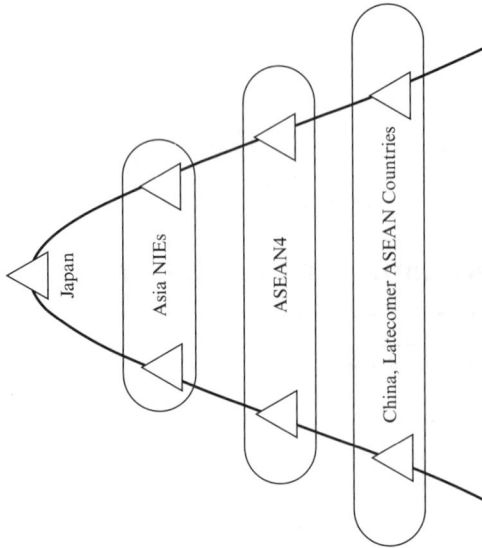

Source: Authors.

Figure 1.1   'Flying geese' pattern of economic development in East Asia

Figure 1.2 shows the time of take-off for each country. Although there are various definitions of economic take-off, it is defined herein as the time when manufacturing exports compose half or more of the total exports in each country. The time of take-off may be early or late, depending on factors inherent in each country; in particular, the timing of the transition from a planned economy to a market economy and from an import-substitution policy to an export-oriented policy seems to be crucial. In any case, the figure clearly indicates the existence of the flying geese pattern in the sequence of economic development in East Asia.[3]

The sequence of economic take-off was as follows. Japan succeeded first in modernizing its economy following the Meiji Restoration during the latter half of the 19th century. Japan continued to develop its economy during the next century, despite the interruption of World War II, and became virtually the sole developed country in Asia in the 1960s (Correspondents of Economist 1963: see also Table 1.1 for post-World War II industrial policy in East Asia).

The second wave of industrialization in East Asia took place in the Asian NIEs known as the four 'dragons' or 'tigers' (Taiwan, Korea, Hong Kong and Singapore) from the 1950s to the 1970s. These countries were swift to switch from a traditional import substitution policy to an

BOX 1.1   THE 'FUNDAMENTAL' FLYING GEESE
MODEL

The concept of the flying geese model was originally developed
by Akamatsu (1935, 1937, 1962). It is somewhat surprising that
the flying geese model mentioned in this section is derived from
the older 'original' flying geese model presented by Akamatsu
(1935). In fact, the model started as a 'one-country one-product'
model that explains the historical pattern of development of an
industry in a country from the viewpoints of import, export and
production of one specific product. Akamatsu himself explains this
basic pattern as follows:

> Wild geese fly in orderly ranks forming an inverse V, just as airplanes
> fly in formation. This flying pattern of wild geese is metaphorically
> applied to the below-figured three time-series curves, each denoting
> import, domestic production, and export of manufactured goods in less
> advanced countries. (Akamatsu 1962, p.11)

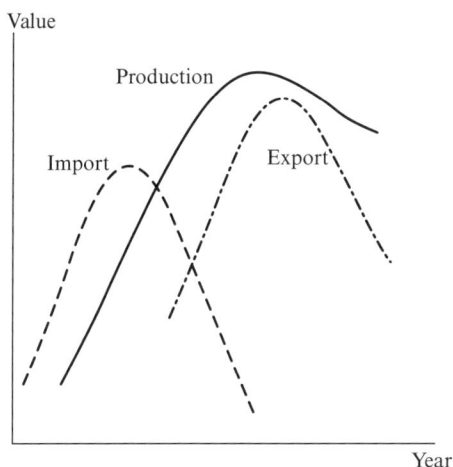

*Box Figure 1.1   Akamatsu 'fundamental' flying geese pattern of
economic development*

The figure that Akamatsu mentions is precisely like Box Figure
1.1. Although it does not resemble flying geese as much as Figure
1.1, it actually is the origin of the flying geese pattern of economic

development. Akamatsu (1962, p.12) called this the 'fundamental wild-geese-flying pattern'.

It is regrettable for Akamatsu that he lumped together various models under the name of 'flying geese' in his grand theory of the history of world economic development. As Figure 1.1 more closely resembles the pattern of flying geese and is so popular now, it overshadows the Box Figure 1.1 version of the theory, although this 'fundamental' model contains many still unanswered research questions, such as why so many industries trace the 'fundamental' flying geese pattern and what the mechanism behind it is. For more information about the flying geese model, see Kojima (2000).

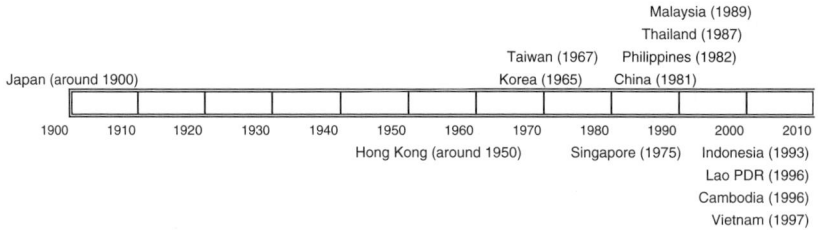

Source: Compiled from various sources by the authors.

Figure 1.2   Time of 'take-off' in East Asia

export-oriented industrialization policy, and they succeeded in translating their economies into industrialized economies (Vogel 1991).

The third wave of industrialization occurred in the leading ASEAN countries (Malaysia, Thailand, the Philippines and Indonesia) in the 1980s. They followed the success of the 'four tigers' and emulated the export-oriented industrialization policy (Leipziger and Thomas 1997); however, one difference is that the leading ASEAN countries have been more dependent on foreign direct investment to propel their industrialization process (Bende-Nabende 1999).

The fourth wave of industrialization in the 1990s was led by China, which had industrialized itself by the 1980s, when its opening up to the world economy was accelerated after the famous southern tour by Deng Xiaoping in 1992. Vietnam, one of the newcomer ASEAN countries, followed suit and successfully reformed its economy through 'Doi Moi'

Table 1.1   Evolution of industrial policies in East Asia, 1950s–1990s

Economy	1950s	1960s	1970s	1980s	1990s
Japan	1950–58 IS	1959– EO	1967– Liberali- zation	Mid 1980s Deregu- lation	Inter- national- ization
China		1965–76 Defense/ industry (heavy industria- lization)	1977–78 Plant impor- tation	1980s Coastline liberali- zation (light indus- tries)	1990s Infra- structure High technology
Hong Kong (China)	1950– EO (laissez-faire, education, infrastructure, institutional support)		1979– Improved institutional support for industry		1990s Upgraded support for technology
Korea, Republic of		1961–72 EO	1973–79 EO IS (heavy industry)	1980– Liberali- zation (trade, invest- ment, finance)	1990s Deregu- lation since mid-1980s (innovation- oriented)
Taiwan	1953–57 IS	1958–80 EO			1986– Liberali- zation
Singapore	1950s IS (while still part of Malaya)	1960s-1980s EO			1990s Strategic indepen- dence (high technology and services) Regionali- zation
Malaysia	1950–70 Moderate IS Added EO		1971–85 Continued IS EO		1986– Liberali- zation
Thailand		1961–71 IS	1971–86 IS (capital goods, beginning in 1981)		1986– EO Techno- logy- incentive Industries Some EO

Table 1.1   (continued)

Economy	1950s	1960s	1970s	1980s	1990s
Indonesia		1967–73 Stabiliza-tion Beginning IS	1974–85 Strong IS		1986– Liberali-zation EO
Philippines	1950– IS	Continued IS		1980s Liberali-zation (poli-tical instab-ility)	1990s Continued liberali-zation (streng-thened political stability)

Note: IS import substitution, EO export orientation

Source: Pangestu (2002), Table 17.1.

(renovation), and currently, the wave of industrialization in East Asia has reached Lao PDR and Cambodia.

1.3   KEY STATISTICS ON EAST ASIA

Although most countries in East Asia have now successfully launched their economic development and the newcomers seem to be quickly catching up to the leaders, huge gaps remain among the countries in their levels of economic development. Moreover, East Asia encompasses countries with very different characteristics, as shown by the statistics below.

1.3.1   Population

East Asia is one of the world's most populous regions, but the countries in East Asia vary significantly in their population (Figure 1.3). China has the largest population of any country in the world, with 1.3 billion, which represents more than 60% of the East Asian population. Indonesia is the second largest, at 219 million, with the world's fourth largest population. Six fairly populous countries follow, namely Japan, the Philippines, Vietnam, Thailand, Myanmar and Korea,[4] with populations of 48 million to 128 million each. The remaining seven countries are less populous,

1,400

1307.6

1,200

1,000

800

600

400

200

219.2

127.8

85.3 83.2

65.1 55.4 48.1

26.0 22.8 13.8 6.8 5.9 4.3 0.4

0

China Indonesia Japan* Philippines Vietnam Thailand Myanmar Korea Malaysia Taiwan Cambodia Hong Kong Lao PDR* Singapore Brunei

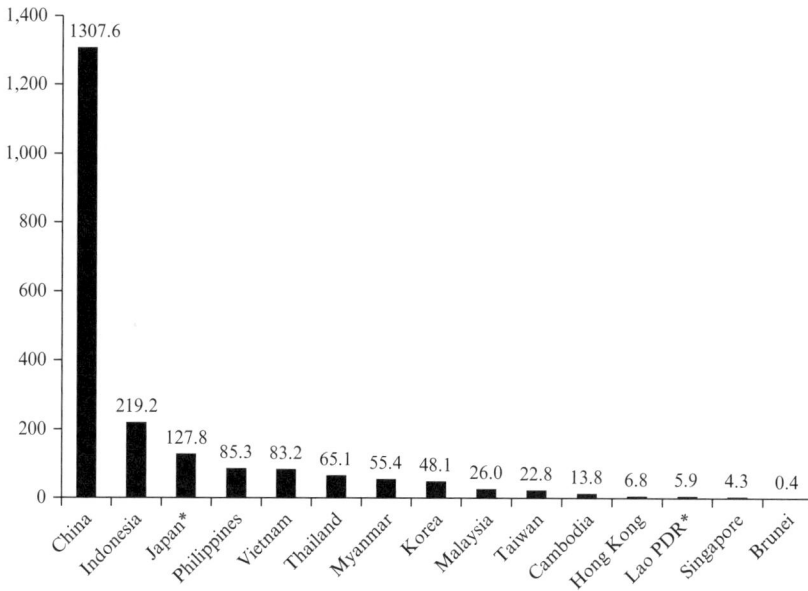

Note: * is an estimation.

Source: World Economic Outlook 2008, IMF.

Figure 1.3 Population, 2005 (millions)

although Malaysia, with a current population of 26 million, may enter the fairly populous group in the latter half of the 21st century.[5]

The total population of East Asia is 2,072 million, which is 4.4 times larger than that of the EU25 (456 million as of 2004). Only 6 out of 25 EU countries have a larger population than Malaysia; in other words, compared with the EU25, East Asia as a group is composed of larger countries.

Regarding the spatial distribution of population, a notable change is the rapid urbanization of East Asia. In 2005, 21% of East Asia's population resided in 182 urban agglomerations with populations greater than 750,000; this ratio has increased steadily from 8% in 1955, when only 35 such agglomerations existed (Hamaguchi 2009).

Population size and urbanization significantly affects the development of industry. For instance, the industries with increasing returns to scale (IRS) technologies tend to agglomerate in large countries where a large home market exists (see Chapters 2 and 3). Therefore, large countries may have an advantage over small countries when it comes to the development of industries such as automobiles. Given this, small countries

Latecomer
ASEAN
China   ASEAN
9%   0%

ASEAN4
+Brunei

NIEs
13%

Japan
71%

(1990)

Latecomer
ASEAN
1%

China
25%

ASEAN4
+Brunei

Japan
50%

NIEs
16%

(2005)

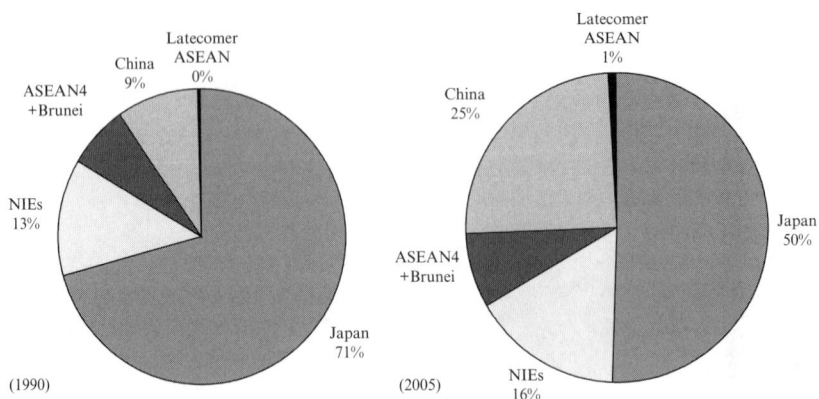

Source: World Economic Outlook 2008, IMF.

Figure 1.4   Sizes of East Asian economies

should target the industries in which IRS technologies are less significant or specialize in sub-sectors in which even small players can carve out a niche; it should be noted that deepening integration will enable small countries to benefit from specialization and scale economies that would otherwise be achievable only in far larger countries (World Bank 2009).

1.3.2   Size of Economies

The total nominal GDP of East Asian economies was US$8,529 billion in 2005, which is about two-thirds of that of the EU25 (US$13,075 billion) and NAFTA (US$13,439 billion). The relative sizes of East Asian economies are changing rapidly (Figure 1.4). In 1990, Japan made up 71% of the regional GDP. In 2005, the share of Japan's economy in the region had declined to 50%, and China's share increased from 9% to 25%. It is readily apparent that Japan and China will be the two dominant economies in the region for the next few decades.

Figure 1.5 shows the average growth rate of GDP for each group of countries. It clearly reveals that Japan, the lead goose, has decelerated, and in a somewhat similar position are Asian NIEs and ASEAN4, although they are still maintaining a moderate growth rate. On the other hand, China and newcomer ASEAN countries, the trailing geese, are now enjoying an era of high economic growth. As a result, the income gap between countries has shrunk due to economic integration in the region, but there still remains a significant disparity in East Asia.[6]

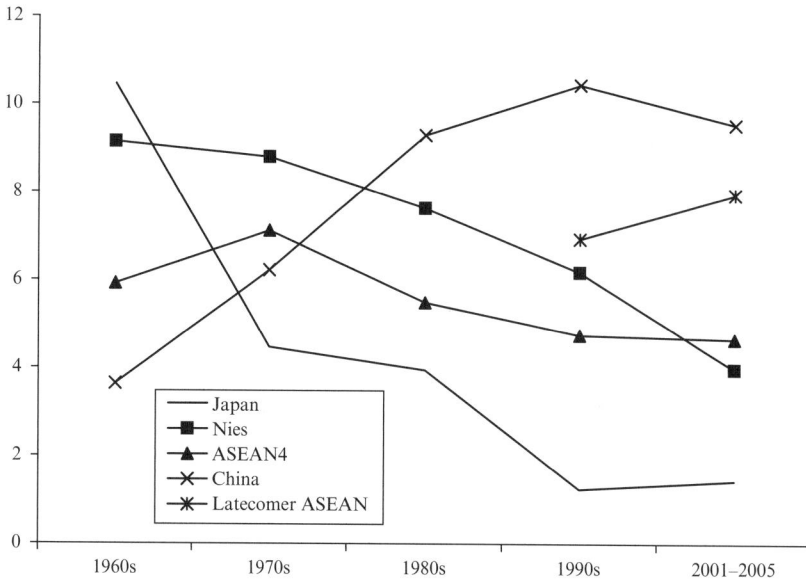

Source: World Development Indicators and National Statistics, Taiwan.

Figure 1.5   Growth rate in real GDP (%)

1.3.3   Disparities Between Countries

The difference in nominal GDP per capita between Myanmar and Japan is surprisingly large, at 1:162 in 2005 (Figure 1.6). In the case of the EU25, the difference between Latvia, (US$6,955) and Luxembourg (US$80,423) is only 1:12. The huge difference in nominal GDP per capita in East Asia gives multinational enterprises (MNEs) a strong incentive to extend their operations into different countries according to the wage level, which is highly correlated with the nominal GDP per capita. As shown in Chapter 4, fragmentation was a key factor in promoting economic integration in East Asia, and fragmentation has proliferated in this region because of its diversity and heterogeneity.

1.3.4   Disparities Within a Country

East Asia is a growth center of the world. However, the growth is not evenly distributed geographically. Within the region, some countries are much more prosperous than other countries, and within a country, some cities/regions attract the bulk of investment and grow rapidly while other

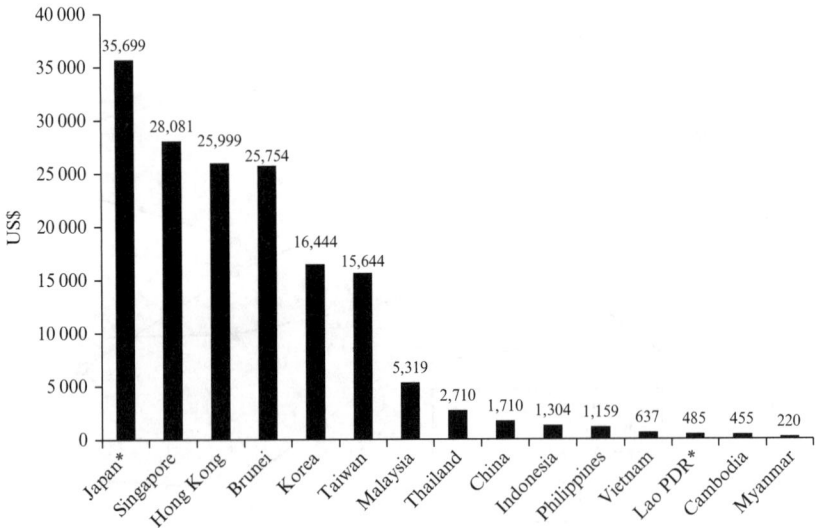

Note: * is an estimation.

Source: World Economic Outlook 2008, IMF.

Figure 1.6   Nominal GDP per capita (2005)

cities/regions are left behind. Uneven growth and economic disparities is one of the characteristics of East Asian economies, and it is becoming an increasingly urgent issue.

China is a typical example of such geographically uneven growth within a country (see Chapter 15). Coastal provinces have a strong advantage over inland provinces in terms of transport costs, especially when the market is abroad. Transport cost is likewise an issue for landlocked countries such as Lao PDR. Thus in inland areas, it is extremely important to develop an excellent transport network in order to narrow the development gap within individual countries as well as between countries.

1.4   EAST ASIA AS THE 'WORLD'S FACTORY': EVOLUTION OF PRODUCTION NETWORKS

1.4.1   Overview

The distinguishing feature of economic integration in East Asia is the fact that the largest force driving the regional integration is economic, rather than political, factors. Although ASEAN, which is now positioned at the center of East Asian regional integration, was founded in 1967 as a result of the international conflicts and security concerns of the member countries at that time, the regional cooperation schemes initiated by ASEAN evolved to focus the main thrust of their effort on economic issues, especially starting in the mid 1970s (Low 2004).

Economic integration in East Asia has progressed according to the *de facto* mode rather than the *de jure* mode. Although FTAs and EPAs have proliferated in recent years, East Asia long enjoyed 'virtual free trade' under certain circumstances, which was enabled by the unilateral establishment of Export Processing Zones (EPZs) and Free Trade Zones (FTZs). The first of these in the region was instituted in 1966 at Kaohsiung, Taiwan, and then they spread to other countries (Figure 1.7). Multinational enterprises (MNEs) utilized these EPZs/FTZs in the region and enjoyed virtual free trade in the production of goods that were exported to third countries.[7] Corresponding to the establishment of EPZs/FTZs in East Asia, the US has reduced the tariff on re-imported half-finished semiconductors. This ensures semiconductor-specific virtual free trade. The Japanese government also adopted a similar policy (Rasiah 1988).

While we identify EPZs/FTZs as a 'pull' factor for pro-trade FDI, a critical 'push' factor is the Plaza Accord of 1985. To address the rapid appreciation of home currencies against the US dollar, MNEs in Japan and Asian NIEs rushed to invest in other countries, especially in Southeast Asia, in order to utilize the host countries as export bases. As a result of the pro-trade FDI, which is one of the largest driving forces of *de facto* integration in this region, intra-regional trade in East Asia surged from US$126 billion in 1985 to US$1,650 billion in 2006, an increase by a factor of 13.1. During the same period, intra-regional trade in NAFTA and in the EU25 increased by a factor of 6.0 and 6.1, respectively. As a result, the volume of intra-regional trade in East Asia was almost double that of NAFTA and was equivalent to 60% of that in the EU25 in 2006 (Figure 1.8).

The structure of intra-regional trade in East Asia has also changed dramatically in the past two decades. In 1985, primary goods (SITC-0 to SITC-4) accounted for 40% of total intra-regional trade. In 2006, machinery and transport equipment (SITC-7) claimed the largest share (51.1%), while primary goods accounted for only 12.7% of total intra-regional trade. During the same period, the structure of intra-regional trade in two other regions, NAFTA and the EU25, did not change significantly. Only East Asia experienced a major change in the composition of intra-regional trade, from a trade structure dominated by primary goods to one dominated by manufactured goods, thereby narrowing the gap with the other two regions.

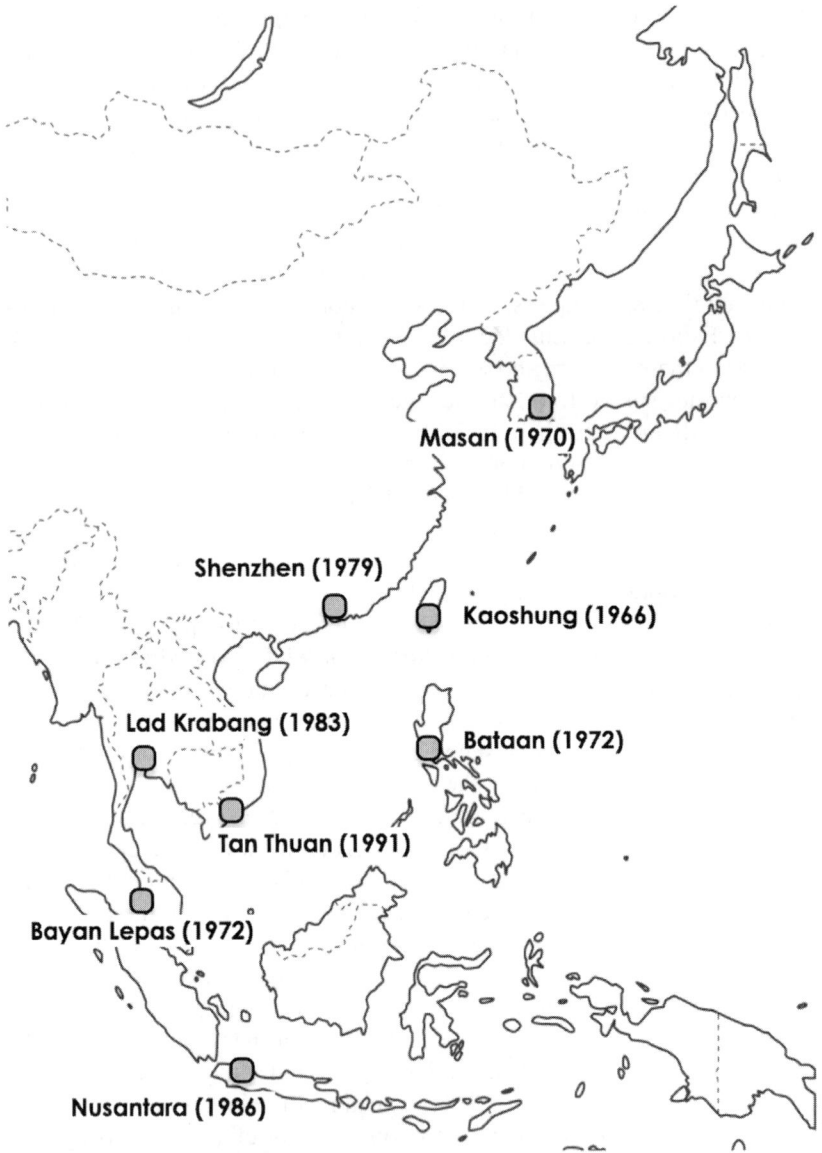

Masan (1970)

Shenzhen (1979)

Kaoshung (1966)

Lad Krabang (1983)

Bataan (1972)

Tan Thuan (1991)

Bayan Lepas (1972)

Nusantara (1986)

Source: Compiled from various sources by the authors.

Figure 1.7   Country-first FTZs/EPZs in East Asia

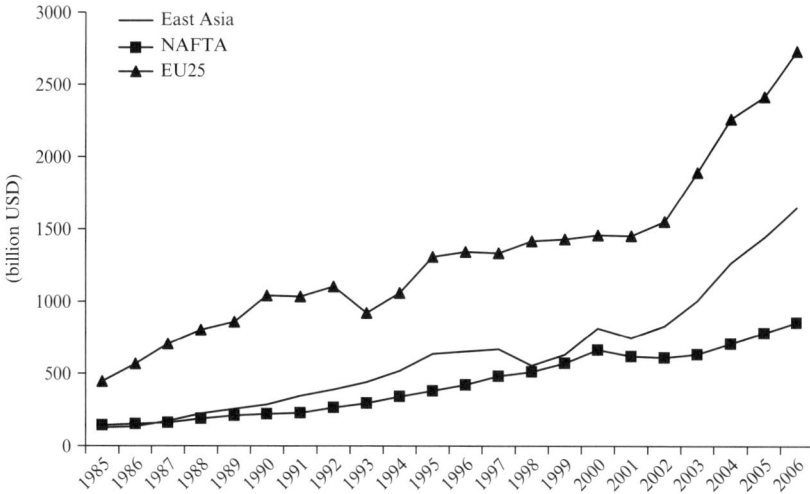

Source: COMTRADE.

Figure 1.8 Volume of intra-regional trade

Although the share of manufactured goods has increased sharply and the structure of intra-regional trade in East Asia appears to have become similar to that in the EU25 and NAFTA, the similarity is only superficial. From other perspectives, they remain significantly different.

In brief, intra-regional trade in East Asia is led by production goods, while that in the EU is more balanced between consumption goods and production goods. Figure 1.9 shows the trade flow among East Asia, the EU25, NAFTA and the rest of the world (ROW) by type of goods based on the RIETI-TID classification reconfigured from BEC (basic economic classification),[8] namely, (a) primary goods, (b) processed goods, (c) parts and components, (d) capital goods and (e) consumption goods. Figure 1.9(a) shows that ROW exported primary goods to the other three regions. Among them, East Asia imported the largest amount of primary goods (US$380.3 billion), while the bilateral trade of primary goods among the three regions was quite small.

Figure 1.9(b) shows that the intra-regional trade of processed goods (for example, steel and chemical products) in East Asia was twice as large as that in NAFTA, but only 55% of that in the EU25. ROW also exported a large amount to other regions, especially to the EU25. The relatively large amount of transactions between ROW and the EU25 is explained by the

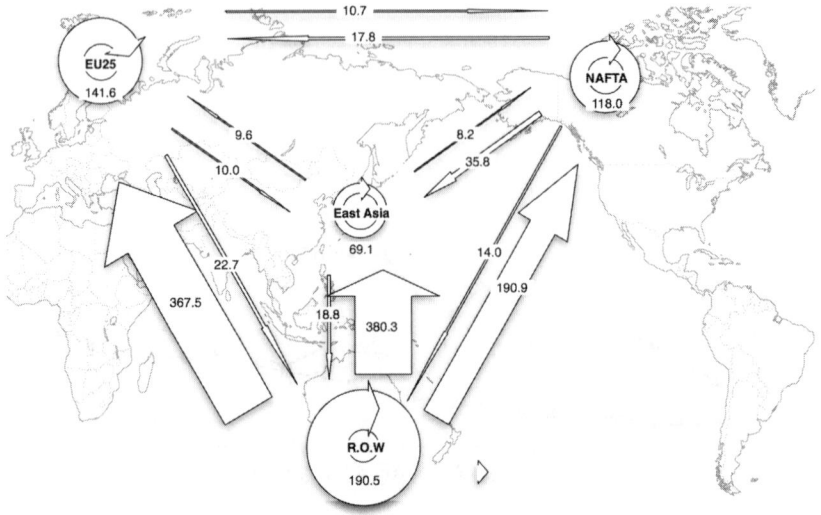

Figure 1.9(a)   The world trade of primary goods, 2006 (US$ billion)

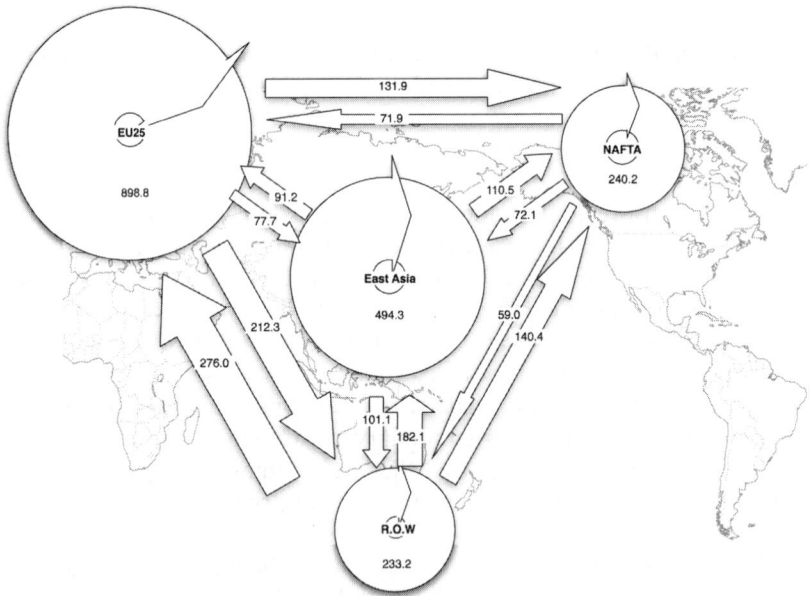

Figure 1.9(b)   The world trade of processed goods, 2006 (US$ billion)

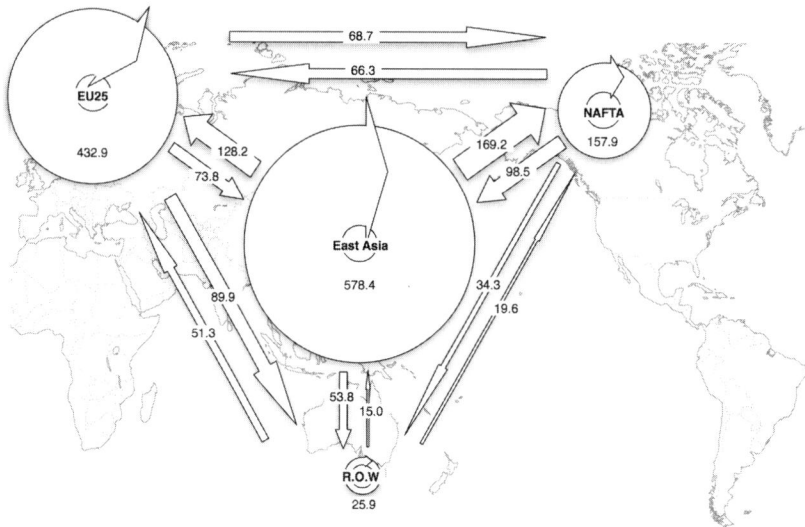

Figure 1.9(c)   The world trade of parts and components, 2006 (US$ billion)

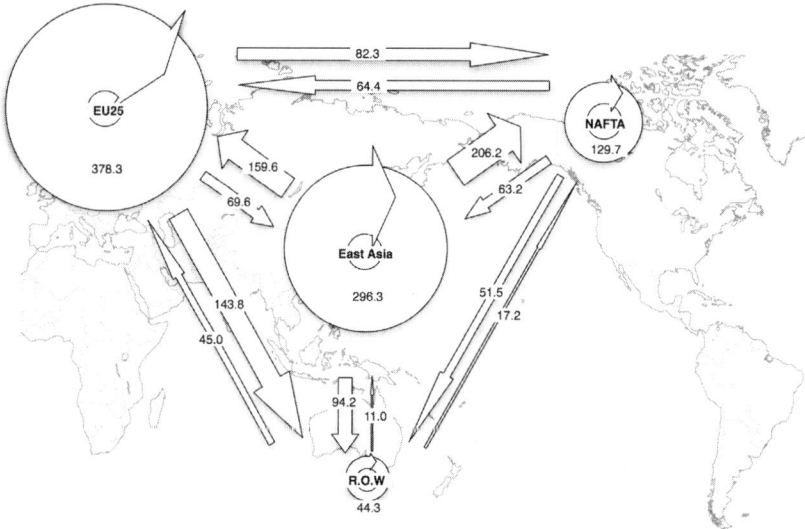

Figure 1.9(d)   The world trade of of capital goods, 2006 (US$ billion)

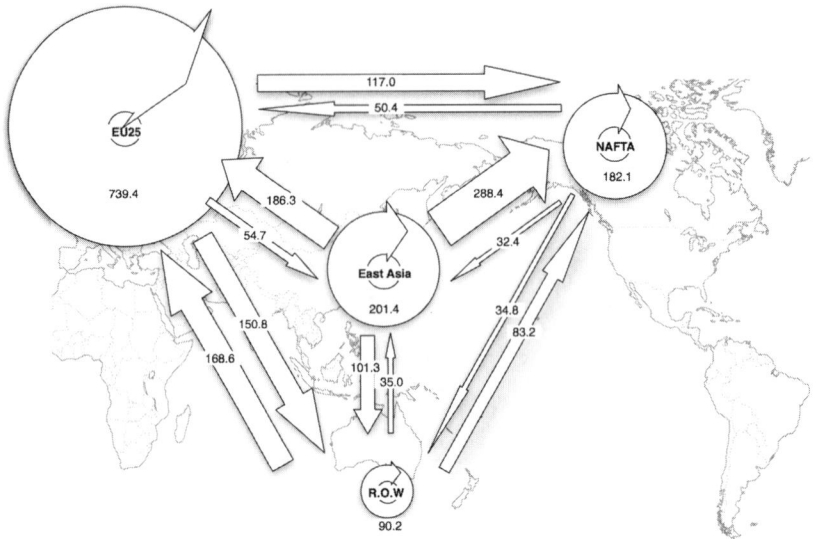

Note: The classification is based on RIETI-TID, reconfigured from BEC, as follows: primary goods (BEC 111, 21, 31), basic material (BEC 121, 22, 32), parts and components (BEC 42, 53), capital goods (BEC 41, 521), consumption goods (BEC 112, 122, 51, 522, 61, 62, 63).

Source: COMTRADE.

Figure 1.9(e)   The world trade of consumption goods, 2006 (US$ billion)

active trade between the EU25 and the rest of Europe, which is classified as part of ROW.

Figure 1.9(c) reveals that the intra-regional trade of parts and components in East Asia was the largest in the world, amounting to US$578.4 billion. In addition, East Asia exported considerable amounts of parts and components to the EU25 and NAFTA, recording a trade surplus of US$54.4 billion and US$70.7 billion, respectively.

Figure 1.9(d) shows that the intra-regional trade of capital goods in East Asia was relatively sizeable, but less than that in the EU25. However, East Asia exported significant amounts of capital goods to the EU25 and NAFTA, posting trade surpluses of US$90.0 billion and US$143.0 billion, respectively.

Figure 1.9(e) shows that the intra-regional trade of consumption goods in the EU25 was the largest of any region (US$739.4 billion). In the case of East Asia, intra-regional trade was US$201.4 billion, while exports to the

EU25 and NAFTA were US$186.3 billion and US$288.4 billion, respectively. As a result, East Asia recorded huge trade surpluses in consumption goods trade with the EU25 and NAFTA, amounting to US$131.6 billion and US$256 billion, respectively. The inactivity seen in intra-regional trade of consumption goods in East Asia was partly due to the sluggish trade of passenger cars; the intra-regional trade of passenger cars in East Asia (US$7.5 billion) was only a little over 10% of that in NAFTA (US$70.6 billion) and 3.9% of that in the EU25 (US$192.5 billion).

From these figures, especially Figures 1.9(a), (c), and (e), the following tendencies are clearly observable. Firstly, East Asia imported an enormous amount of primary goods from ROW. Secondly, East Asia traded parts and components actively within the region, and considerable amounts of them were exported to the EU25 and NAFTA. Thirdly, the intra-regional trade of consumption goods was not particularly active in East Asia. Instead, East Asia exported large amounts of consumption goods to NAFTA and the EU25, recording a huge trade surplus.

The main destinations of consumption goods exported from East Asia were NAFTA (37%) and the EU25 (24%), with East Asia absorbing only a quarter of the consumption goods exported from East Asian countries. In contrast, the EU25 and NAFTA absorbed 70% and 60%, respectively, of the exports from countries within their own regions.

The above facts suggest that East Asia is functioning as a 'factory' or a 'production base' for the world (Box 1.2). The region's production-oriented trade structure seems to reflect the policy orientation in East Asia, where some countries established EPZs/FTZs to promote exports by removing import tariffs on exports to third countries, while protecting their domestic markets by imposing high tariffs on imports.

East Asia's production-oriented trade structure has made great contributions to the industrial development in the region by involving the liberalizing East Asian economies in the region's production networks. In the following sections, the spatial linkages of the electronics and automobile industries (Figure 1.10) are introduced to illustrate the expanding production networks in East Asia (Figure 1.11).

Spatial linkages

With the acceleration of production fragmentation (or the expansion of production networks), a part of the production process that was previously undertaken by domestic industry relocates to another country, and the different processes of production are linked through intermediate goods trade. Thus, inter-industrial relationships are strengthened across borders, and industrial output in one country is affected by other countries to a greater extent than in the past.

BOX 1.2   AN EVOLVING WORLD FACTORY

East Asia is now functioning as a 'factory', and it is increasingly adopting the just-in-time mode of production. Two trends are revealed by analysis using the gravity equation, which explains the volume of trade between any two countries surprisingly well. As the original gravity equation in physics explains the magnitude of the gravitational force between two masses as the product of their masses times the gravitational constant, divided by the square of the distance between them, the gravity equation in international trade predicts that the volume of trade between two countries is proportional to the product of their GDPs and inversely proportional to the distance between them.

Deardorff (1995) specified the standard gravity equation as

$$T_{ij} = A \frac{Y_i Y_j}{D_{ij}} \tag{1.1}$$

where T_{ij} denotes the value of the trade between countries i and j, Y_i and Y_j denote the GDPs of each country, D_{ij} is the distance between them, and A is a constant. In empirical studies, equation (1.1) is usually estimated in its log linear form as

$$\log(T_{ij}) = \alpha + \beta_1 \log(Y_i) + \beta_2 \log(Y_j) + \beta_3 \log(D_{ij}) + \varepsilon_{ij} \tag{1.2}$$

For Box Figure 1.2, the following equation is estimated.

$$\log(T_{ijt}) = \alpha_t + \beta_{1t} cty_i + \beta_{2t} ptn_j + \beta_{3t} \log(D_{ij}) + \beta_{3t} adj_{ij} + \varepsilon_{ij} \tag{1.3}$$

where cty_i is the country dummy for country i and ptn_j is the country dummy for country j. These two dummies are expected to absorb all country specific factors affecting bilateral trade volume, including GDP. adj_{ij} is the dummy that takes 1 if countries i and j share a common border.

The distance elasticity of trade proposed in Box Figure 1.2 is β_{3t} from 1985 to 2006.

This analysis reveals two facts. First, the gravity, that is, the distance elasticity of trade volume, is consistently lower in East Asia than in the EU25 (Box Figure 1.2). This may be because of the difference in the modes of trade. In East Asia, the main modes of trade are air and sea, while in the EU25 the main mode is land.

The cost of land transport increases in direct proportion to the distance, while the cost of air and sea transport is determined by various factors and is less elastic for distance.

Secondly, in both East Asia and the EU, distance elasticity of trade volume has been increasing over the last two decades, as a trend. This means that countries tend to trade with nearer countries more than before. We can imagine some reasons behind this

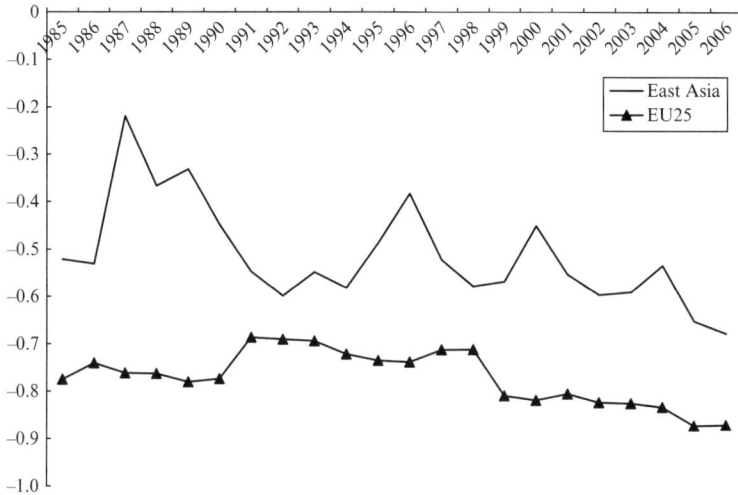

Source: Calculated from COMTRADE by authors.

Box Figure 1.2 The distance elasticity of the volume of intra-regional trade

tendency. It could be because the decrease in transport costs enables trading of what were once non-tradable goods from nearby countries. For instance, some fresh vegetables are now imported from neighboring countries. It is also conceivable that time-to-delivery has become increasingly important, such that factories try to procure goods as much as possible from nearer countries. Considering the production-oriented trade structure in East Asia, the latter scenario is the more plausible one for intra-regional trade in East Asia; that is, the just-in-time mode of production is evolving to integrate cross-border transactions.

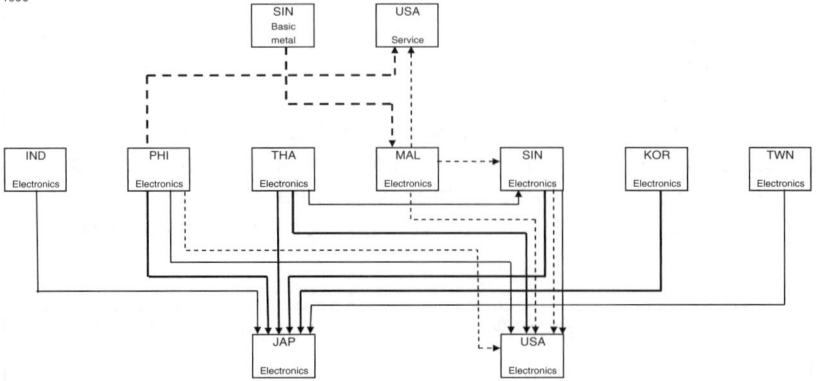

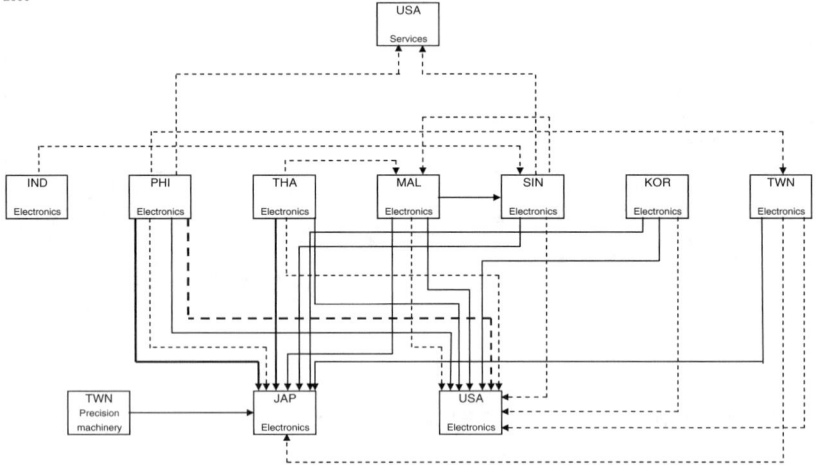

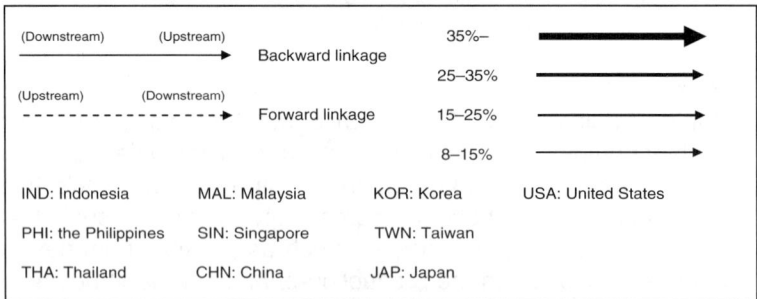

Source: Asian International Input–Output Table (1990, 2000).

Figure 1.10(a)   Spatial linkages of the electronics sector

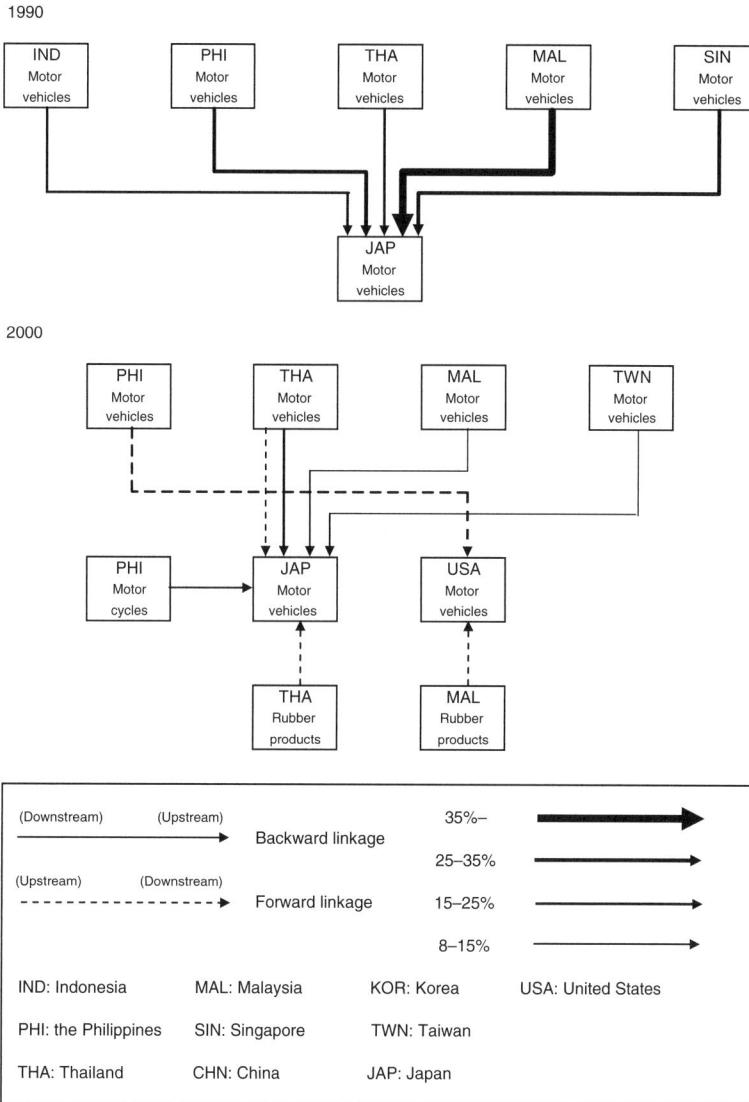

Source: Asian International Input–Output Table (1990, 2000).

Figure 1.10(b)   Spatial linkages of the automotive sector

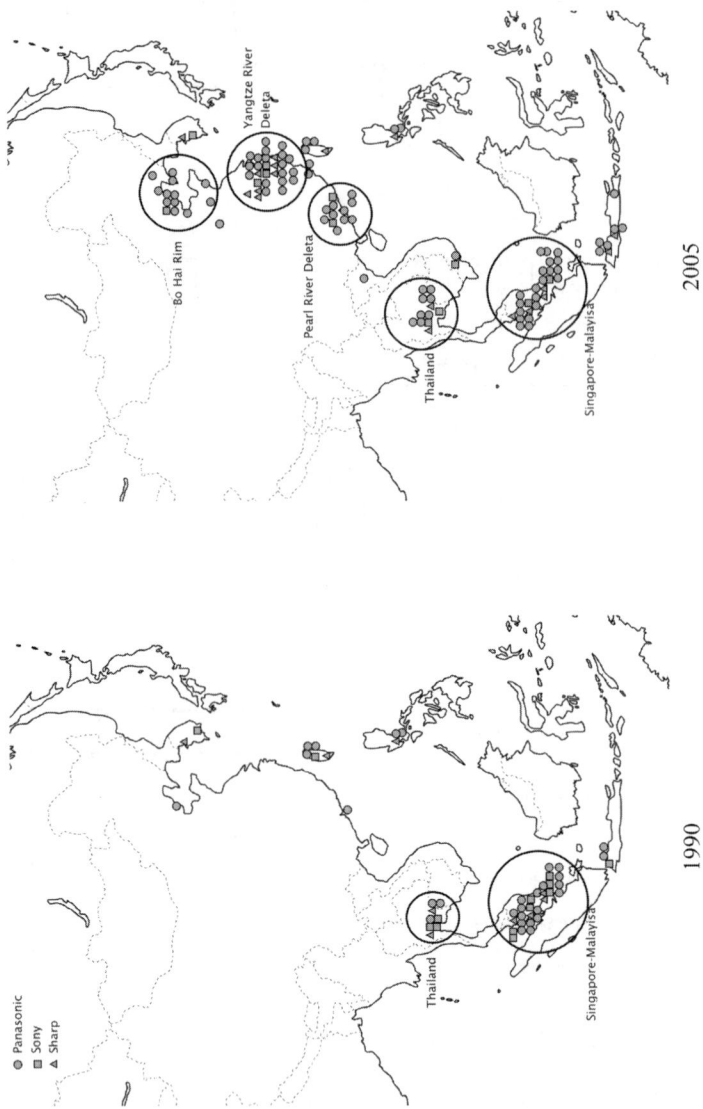

Source: Toyo Keizai (1994 and 2006).

Figure 1.11(a) Location of the affiliates of Japanese MNEs in the electronics sector (1990 and 2005)

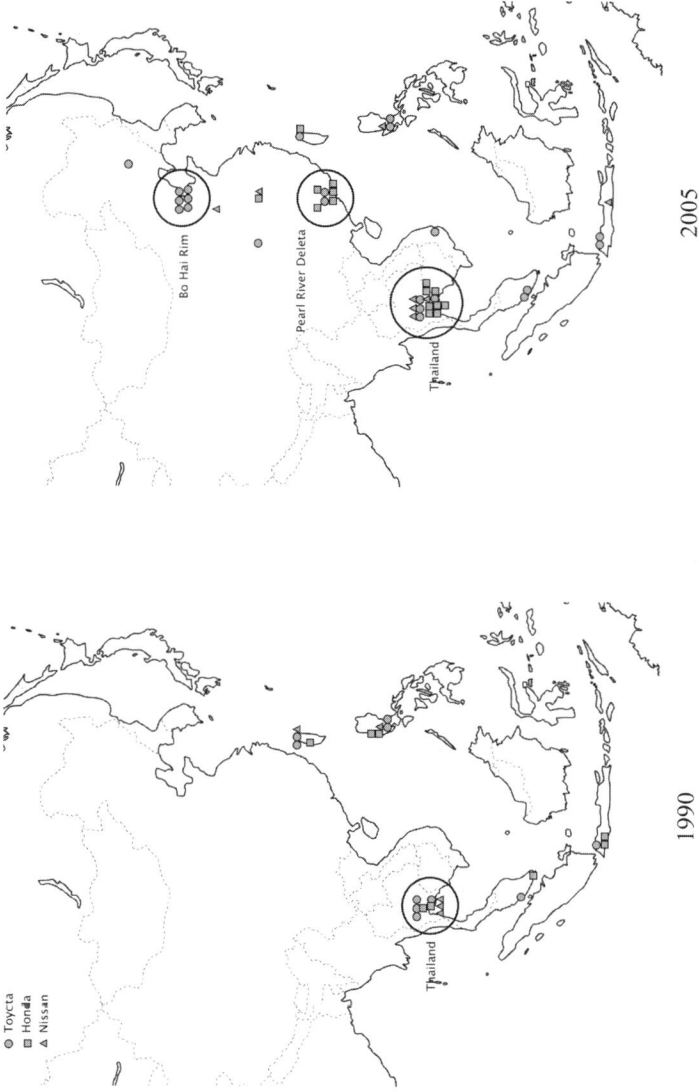

Legend:
- Toyota
- Honda
- Nissan

1990

2005

Bo Hai Rim

Pearl River Deleta

Thailand

Source: Toyo Keizai (1994, 2006).

Figure 1.11(b)   Location of the affiliates of Japanese MNEs in the automotive sector (1990 and 2005)

In this book, this kind of inducement mechanism for production is referred to as 'spatial linkage'. There are two types of spatial linkage effects – backward and forward. Suppose that, as a result of production fragmentation, inputs produced in Country A are utilized by an industry in Country B. Then, as the industrial output in Country B increases, the demand for its inputs will increase, leading to an increase in the industrial output in Country A through the spatial backward linkage effects. On the other hand, an increase in the industrial output in Country A will increase the production capacity of the downstream industry and thereby induce an increase in the industrial output in Country B through the spatial forward linkage effects.

1.4.2 Spatial Linkages of the Electronics Sector

Figure 1.10(a) indicates the pairs of strong spatial linkages in the electronic sector in eight East Asian countries (five ASEAN countries plus China, Korea, and Taiwan), Japan and the US for 1990 and 2000. Note that spatial linkages indicate the strength of repercussive effects across borders, and the spatial linkages that appear in the figure are only those where output of the recipient industry (of repercussive effects) increased by more than 8% of the output of the inducing industry; extremely strong spatial linkages are indicated by bold lines.[9]

Figure 1.10(a) shows that there was strong interdependency between the industries across borders, and an extensive production network for the electronics industry was already established in 1990. In particular, the electronics sectors in Indonesia, the Philippines, Thailand and Singapore as well as in Korea and Taiwan had strong backward linkage effects on Japan and the US, whereas Japan and the US did not have such linkage effects (due to high self-sufficiency of their economies). On the other hand, the electronics sectors in the Philippines, Malaysia and Singapore exerted strong forward linkage effects on the US electronics and service sectors. This suggests that the production networks of the electronics sector expanded rapidly with industries in Japan, the rest of East Asia and the US, respectively, located in the upstream, midstream and downstream of roundabout production processes. At the same time, in East Asia, strong spatial linkages can be seen only between Singapore and Thailand and between Singapore and Malaysia, while other linkages were relatively weak.

In 2000, the spatial backward linkage effects on Japan became weaker in several countries, while such a clear tendency cannot be seen in the linkages with the US. The spatial forward linkage effects on the US electronics industry were strengthened, and so were the forward linkage effects on the Japanese electronics industry, especially from the Philippines and Taiwan.

Furthermore, many East Asian economies strengthened their spatial forward linkages with each other, so that the structure of interdependency became more complex and broad-based.

It should be noted that a dense production network has been formed in East Asia due to the strong export orientation of the electronics industry. Moreover, the electronics industry was able to expand its production networks thanks to low transport costs relative to its value.

The development of production networks can be observed from the increasing number of locations of foreign affiliates of Japanese MNEs in 1990 and 2005 (Figure 1.11(a)). In 1990, factories of three major Japanese MNEs were mainly located in Singapore and Malaysia with some in Thailand. In 2005, three more agglomerations had emerged in China, specifically in the Bo Hai Rim, the Yangtze River Delta and the Pearl River Delta.

It is noteworthy that these MNEs attracted a great number of suppliers and led to the formation of competitive industrial clusters; that is to say, industrial clusters developed in tandem with the expansion of production networks. This occurred because rising wages and congestion in agglomerated areas induced the dispersion of industries – which was facilitated by declining trade and transport costs – but dispersed industries again created agglomerations at new production sites (see the mechanism of the 'concentrated dispersion' in Chapters 2 and 3). This is a fine illustration of how industries in high income countries (that is, Japan and Asian NIEs) relocated to low income countries (in Southeast Asia and China) and of how waves of industrialization have spread throughout the region.

1.4.3   Spatial Linkages of the Automobile Sector

Figure 1.10(b) shows that, in 1990, the automobile industry in the five Southeast Asian countries had strong backward linkage effects on the Japanese automobile industry, and no other industries had such strong spatial linkage effects. Thus, the structure of spatial linkages was quite simple. In 2000, the spatial backward linkage effects on Japan declined drastically, and a new form of interdependency emerged, including strong spatial forward linkage effects of the Thai and Philippine automobile industries on the Japanese and the US automobile industries; the rubber industries in Thailand and Malaysia also had strong forward linkage effects on the Japanese and US automobile industries.

In the automobile sector, the one-sided dependency on inputs from the Japanese automobile industry declined considerably, and the production network in the automobile industry expanded into the neighboring Southeast Asian countries. The catalyst seems to have been trade liberalization within ASEAN, which was accelerated by the Brand-to-Brand Complementation (BBC) Scheme, ASEAN Industrial Cooperation (AICO) Scheme, and ASEAN Free Trade Area (AFTA).

However, the production network in the automobile industry was far more geographically confined than in the electronics industry, due to the protectionist policies in the host countries. Furthermore, high transport costs and strong agglomeration economies – as well as the local content requirement policy in the host countries – contributed to the increasing local content of the automobile industry, so that its dependency on imported inputs from other East Asian countries did not increase as much as in the electronics industry (Kuroiwa 2008).

The difference between the production networks of the electronics sector and the automobile sector is reflected in the location of foreign affiliates of three major Japanese automobile MNEs in 1990 and 2005 (Figure 1.11(b)). In 1990, a relatively small agglomeration of Japanese automobile factories developed in Thailand. In 2005, two more agglomerations emerged in China, namely in the Bo Hai Rim and the Pearl River Delta, and by this time, the agglomeration in Thailand had also grown considerably larger. Nonetheless, the factories of the automobile industry tend to agglomerate in a smaller number of areas than do those in the electronics industry due to strong agglomeration economies.

1.5   DRIVERS OF ECONOMIC INTEGRATION IN EAST ASIA

As described in Chapter 4, economic integration in East Asia has been driven by the expansion of production networks. The new economic geography theory indicates that fragmentation – as well as industry agglomeration, in its own manner – is caused by declining transport costs (see Chapters 2 and 3). In particular, fragmentation is sensitive to transport costs, and the rapid decline in transport costs was crucial to the expansion of production networks. Below, we focus on two factors that affect transport costs, namely freight costs and tariff rates.

1.5.1   Drivers of Integration

Freight costs
One of the main drivers of East Asia's trade growth has been declining transport costs. Asia has one of the lowest freight costs among all developing regions (Figure 1.12) and one of the most developed transportation infrastructures.

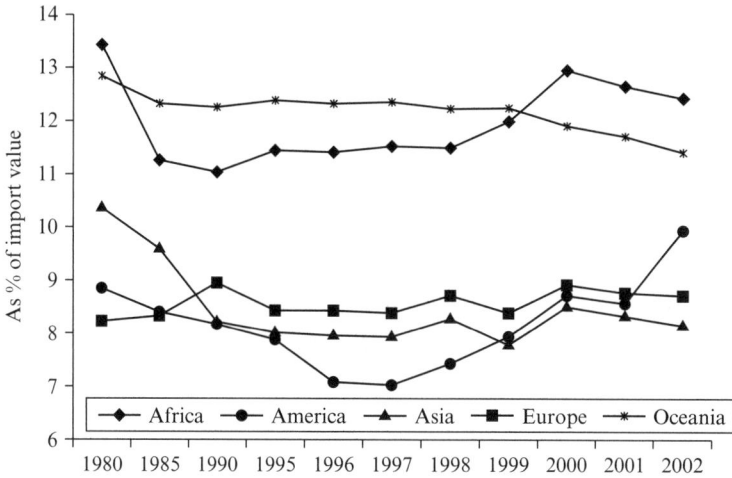

Source: Review of Maritime Transport, UNCTAD, various years.

Figure 1.12   Freight costs of developing countries among regions

Lowering of transport costs has been complemented by the advances in supply chains and logistics. In particular, the rising efficiency of air cargo transport and supply chain management, which enables just-in-time production and delivery with very thin inventory, was crucially important in East Asia, especially for electronics.

Tariff rates
Figure 1.13 presents the trends in tariff rates, weighted by trade volume for East Asian economies during 1990 and 2006. A downtrend in overall tariff rates can be observed in East Asia. In particular, China and Thailand reduced their tariff rates significantly in the 1990s. Other countries also reduced their tariff rates steadily, and the trade-weighted average tariff rates in East Asia are now less than 5%, except for the newer ASEAN countries.[10]

Intra-regional tariff rates, on the other hand, have been reduced more rapidly due to free trade agreements. For example, the ASEAN6 countries – comprising Brunei Darussalam, Indonesia, Malaysia, the Philippines, Singapore and Thailand – pledged to eliminate all tariffs by 2010, whereas the newer members – Cambodia, Lao PDR, Myanmar and Vietnam – pledged to eliminate all tariffs by 2015; as a result, tariffs among ASEAN members have been eliminated for 63.42% of the IL (inclusion list) products, with the average tariff brought down from

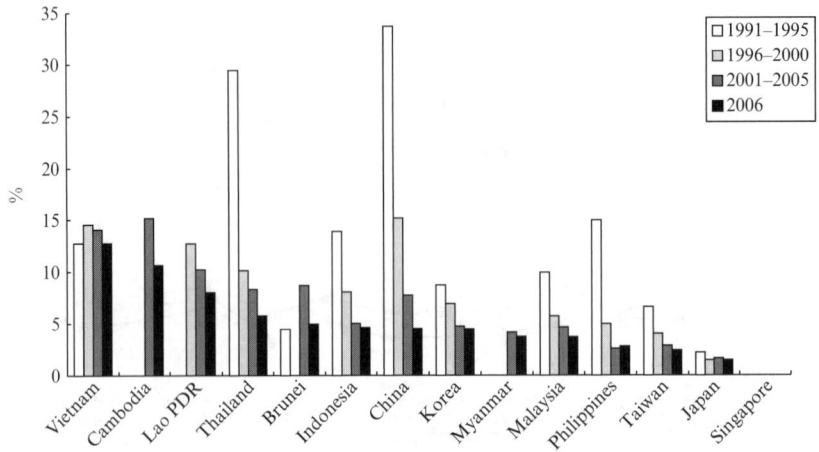

Note: The tariff rate is effective applied rate, which is the tariff rate actually applied to imported goods from the world, weighted by import value from each country.

Source: TRAINS database, UNCTAD.

Figure 1.13   Average tariff rates in East Asia

12.76% in 1993 to 1.95% in 2008 (40th ASEAN Economic Ministers Meeting, 2008).

Figure 1.14 shows effective tariff rates for intra-regional trade in East Asia in 2006. The figure clearly indicates that intra-regional trade of consumption goods was the most discriminated against in East Asia, with effective tariff rates on intermediate goods and capital goods being significantly lower than those on consumption goods. This tariff structure is clearly reflected in the trade structure seen in Figure 1.9(a)–(e): intra-regional trade predominates in production goods, especially parts and components, while intra-regional trade of consumption goods is suppressed by high tariff rates.

1.5.2 Trade Policy and Tariff Rates

The electronics and automobile industries show contrasting trade patterns, although both have played crucial roles in industrial development in East Asia. Below, these two industries are examined from the viewpoint of trade policy. We will demonstrate that different approaches to trade policy are clearly reflected in the contrasting trade patterns of these two industries.

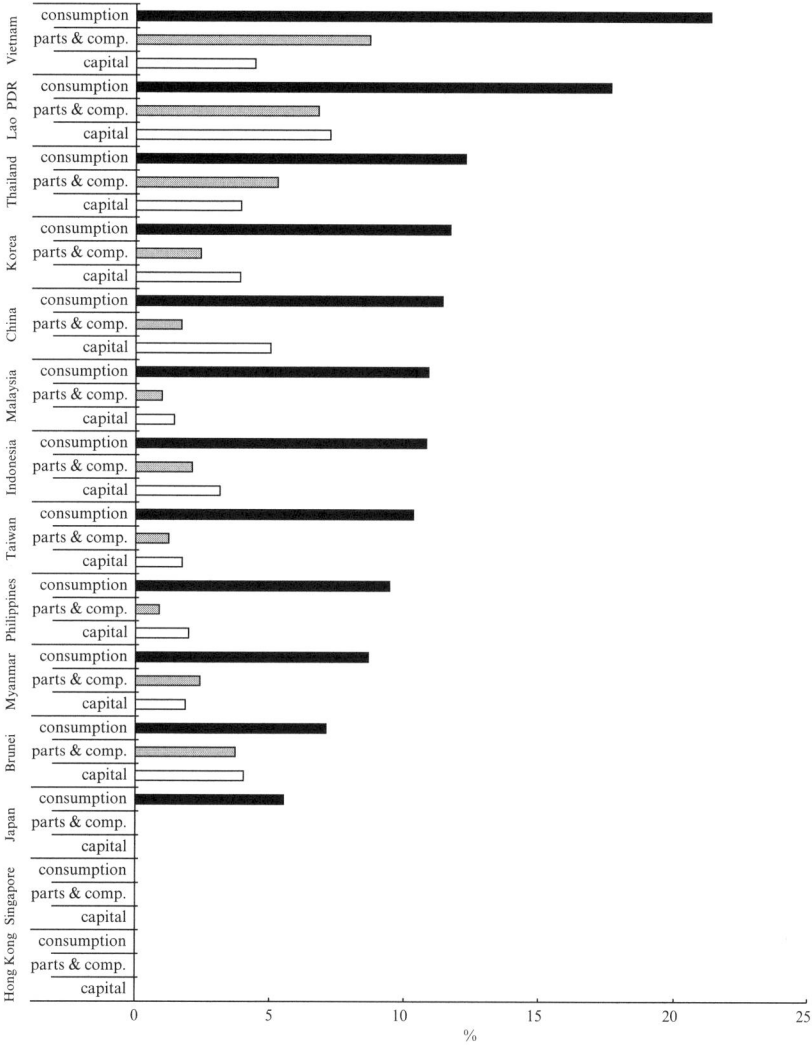

Note: The tariff rate is effective applied rate, which is the tariff rate actually applied to imported goods from East Asian countries, weighted by import value from each country.

Source: TRAINS database, UNCTAD.

Figure 1.14 Average effective tariff rate of intra-regional trade in East Asia (2006)

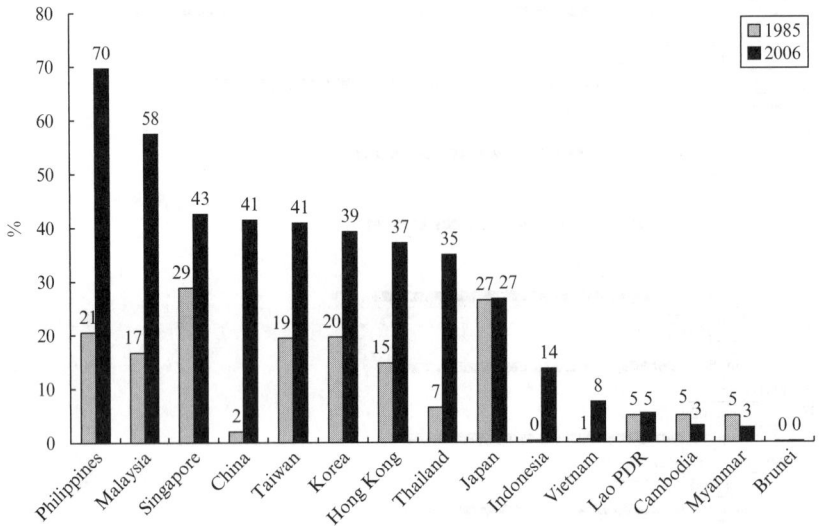

Source: COMTRADE.

Figure 1.15   Share of electronics in total export

Electronics sector

Figure 1.15 presents the share of electronics in the total exports of each country. In half of the East Asian countries, the share of electronics exceeds 30% and has shown significant increases over the past two decades; in particular, the Philippines indicates an extremely high share of electronics, at 70%, followed by Malaysia, Singapore, and China.

The tariff rates on the electronics sector were relatively low and were further reduced during the 1990s (Figure 1.16). However, the electronics sector had been virtually liberalized before the tariff rates declined. In the 1960s, the electronics industry was invited to East Asia to address high unemployment in the host countries. To promote this industry, East Asian countries established EPZs/FTZs and set the tariff rates either to zero or at a very low level, and home countries such as the US and Japan reduced their import tariffs on goods processed offshore, creating a 'virtual free trade' environment for the export-oriented electronics sector. In the case of Penang, Malaysia, for example, the state government attracted mainly US semiconductor companies (Rasiah 1988), and they have expanded their operations up to the present day, making Penang a 'Silicon Island'. Political intentions also matched the needs of MNEs

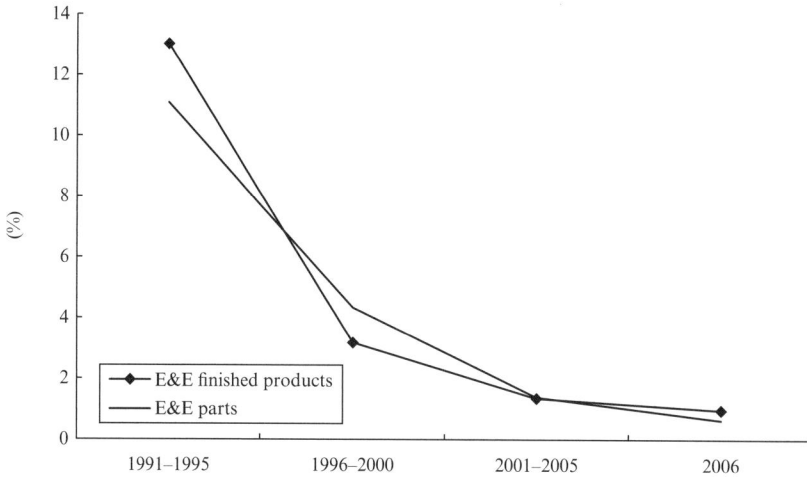

Note: Average effectively applied weighted tariff rate of intra-regional trade in East Asia.

Source: TRAINS database, UNCTAD.

Figure 1.16   Average tariff rates of electronics sector in East Asia

following the Plaza Accord in 1985, and electronics trade in East Asia increased significantly.

Automobile sector
However, the above-mentioned 'virtual free trade' applied only to export-oriented industries, and many industries remained protected by high tariffs. A notable example is the automobile sector, which was highly protected by tariffs and non-tariff barriers (NTBs) to foster 'national' automobile industries until recently (Figure 1.17).

The trade in automobile parts and vehicles has increased as a result of economic cooperation, especially in ASEAN, which has implemented various trade schemes to enhance the intra-ASEAN trade in the automobile sector from time to time (Table 1.2). It appears that intra-ASEAN trade in the automobile sector has responded in a fairly direct manner to the trade liberalization schemes (Figure 1.18). The increased trade in auto parts during the first half of the 1990s was a consequence of the BBC Scheme, while the increase in the latter half of the 1990s was due to the AICO Scheme. The rapid increase in the trade of both finished cars and parts after 2003 was clearly induced by AFTA.[11]

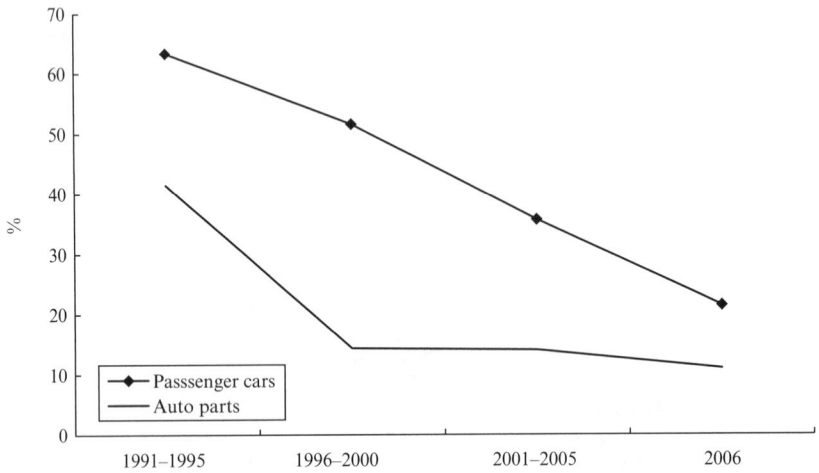

Note: Average effectively applied weighted tariff rate of intra-regional trade in East Asia.

Source: TRAINS database, UNCTAD.

Figure 1.17   Average tariff rates of automotive sector in East Asia

Table 1.2   The history of trade liberalization of automotive sector in ASEAN

Scheme	Period	Summary
Brand to Brand Complementation (BBC)	1988–	50% off the tariff on automotive parts, limited to the companies who own brand
ASEAN Industrial Cooperation (AICO)	1996–	Tariff of 0–5% on automotive parts, limited to companies who have more than 30% ASEAN capital participation
ASEAN Free Trade Area (AFTA)	2003–	Tariff of 0–5% on both automotive parts and finished cars

1.6   CONCLUSION

As described above, production networks have expanded in East Asia through the activities of MNEs, and industrial clusters have developed in tandem with the expansion of production networks. East Asian

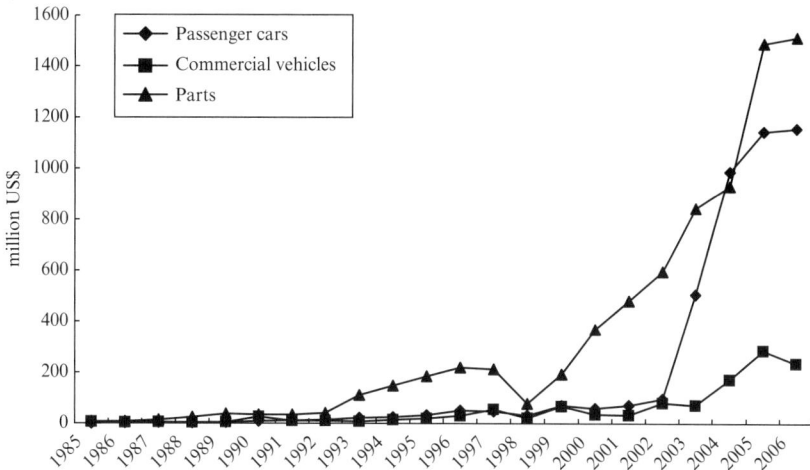

Source: COMTRADE.

Figure 1.18   Intra-ASEAN trade in automotive sector

economies, especially less developed economies, could develop their industries by participating in such networks.

As shown in the electronics and automobile industries, the geographical spread of production networks as well as the location of industries clearly reflect the attributes of each industry, especially agglomeration economies and transport costs. At the same time, they are crucially influenced by the trade policy of each economy. Considering the continuing trend toward lowering tariff rates, as well as the increasing number of free trade agreements, the production networks led by MNEs will continue to expand, covering a greater number of less developed economies in the region and strengthening the competitiveness of the East Asian economy as a whole.

On the other hand, the global economic and financial crisis has revealed the vulnerability of the East Asian economy. As shown above, East Asia has heavily depended on the US and EU markets, especially for final products, and thus, in the face of the current economic crisis that has hit these economies seriously, its production networks worked to its disadvantage and stifled industrial development. Today, there exists an extremely urgent need to create final demand in the region to absorb a larger portion of the products of East Asia. To achieve this, economic integration is expected to play a critical role. Free trade agreements must eliminate trade barriers in the region not only for intermediate inputs but also for consumption goods and capital goods. Financial cooperation schemes, such as the Asian Bond

Market Initiative and the Asian Bond Fund, are effective for developing the Asian bond market. Infrastructure projects, especially cross-border transport infrastructure, would be helpful for creating integrated markets in the region. Private investment would also be attracted if infrastructure and other facilities were set up to improve the investment environment. These schemes are instrumental for mobilizing East Asian savings for East Asian investment, thus narrowing the savings–investment gap.

East Asia is facing a new challenge, and transformation from being the 'world's factory' is necessary for continued economic growth. Economic integration is expected to play a pivotal role in transforming East Asia.

Achievement of a more balanced and secure economy will require coordinated efforts by all members in the region. In particular, free trade agreements and other regional cooperation frameworks will play a pivotal role.

NOTES

1. Note that in this chapter, 'East Asia' consists of ASEAN10, China, Korea, Japan and Taiwan.
2. 'Take-off' is the term used by Rostow (1960) for the transitional period that separates modern society from traditional society.
3. Actually, the Akamatsu flying geese model is a building block in his larger theory of historical development of the global economy, driven by countries' iterant 'heteronization' and 'homogenization'. His theory is meticulous and descriptive (see Akamatsu 1962) but not integrated in the theories of mainstream international economics. Kojima (1960) offered the explanation that the accumulation of capital (the Heckscher-Ohlin factor) is the fundamental driving force of the flying geese model. Kojima (2000) further mentioned the Ricardian advantage of learning-by-doing and economies of scale as a driving force. Fujita and Mori (1999) attempted to reproduce the multi-country, multi-product flying geese pattern of economic development using a simulation model of spatial economics, or new economic geography.
4. The population of Korea is 48 million and is expected to decrease in the future; North Korea has a population of 23 million.
5. The United Nations Population Fund (UNFPA) forecasts that Malaysia's population will reach about 40 million in 2050.
6. The World Development Report for 2009 shows that incomes diverged sharply in East Asia from 1950 to 1970 but converged after this period. This convergence occurred because of the market policies in China and Vietnam as well as economic integration in East Asia (World Bank 2009).
7. For a comprehensive analysis of Asian FTZs/EPZs, see Amirahmadi and Wu (1995).
8. For the detailed classification, see the note in Figure 1.9.
9. For details concerning the methodology, see Kuroiwa (2008).
10. Although the tariff rate in Myanmar is relatively low, the country adopts various trade-controlling measures, including a two-tier exchange market. Therefore, the actual trade barriers in Myanmar may be the highest in East Asia.
11. As mentioned in Chapter 13 of this volume, these free trade schemes in ASEAN have always been under-utilized, especially by small and medium firms. On the other hand, MNCs, which can afford to pay the administrative costs to apply the free trade schemes, benefit from them.

REFERENCES

Akamatsu, Kaname (1935), 'Waga kuni yomo kogyohin no boueki susei', *Shogyo Keizai Ronso*, **13**, 129–212.
Akamatsu, Kaname (1937), 'Waga kuni keizai hatten no sougou bensyoho', *Shogyo Keizai Ronso*, **15**, 179–210.
Akamatsu, Kaname (1962), 'Historical pattern of economic growth in developing countries', *The Developing Economies*, **1**, 3–25.
Amirahmadi, Hooshang and Weiping Wu (1995), 'Export processing zones in Asia', *Asian Survey*, **35**.
Bende-Nabende, Anthony (1999), *FDI, Regionalism, Government Policy, and Endogenous Growth: A comparative study of the ASEAN-5 economies, with development policy implications for the least developed countries*, Aldershot: Ashgate.
Correspondents of Economist (1963), *Consider Japan*, London: Gerald Duckworth. (http://www.normanmacrae.com/CJ/consider_japan1.html)
Deardorff, Alan V. (1995), 'Determinants of bilateral trade: does gravity work in a neoclassical world?', NBER Working Paper Series, no. 5377.
Fujita, Masahisa and Tomoya Mori (1999), 'A flying geese model of economic development and integration: evolution of international economy a la East Asia', Discussion Paper 493.
Hamaguchi, Nobuaki (2009), 'Regional integration, agglomeration, and income distribution in East Asia', in Yukon Huang and Alessandro Magnoli Bocchi (eds), *Reshaping Economic Geography in East Asia*, Washington DC: World Bank.
Kojima, Kiyoshi (1960), 'Capital accumulation and the course of industrialisation, with special reference to Japan', *Economic Journal, LXX*, 757–68.
Kojima, Kiyoshi (2000), 'The "flying geese" model of Asian economic development: origin, theoretical extensions, and regional policy implications', *Journal of Asian Economics*, **11**, 375–401.
Krugman, Paul (1994), 'The myth of Asia's miracle', *Foreign Affairs*, **73**(6), 72–8.
Kuroiwa, Ikuo (2008), 'Cross-border production networks in Southeast Asia', in I. Kuroiwa and M.H. Toh (eds), *Production Networks and Industrial Clusters: Integrating Economies in Southeast Asia*, Singapore: Institute of Southeast Asian Studies.
Leipziger, Danny M. and Vinod Thomas (1997), 'An overview of country experience', in Danny M. Leipziger (ed.), *Lessons from Asia*, Ann Arbor: University of Michigan Press.
Low, Linda (2004), *ASEAN Economic Co-operation and Challenges*, Singapore: ISEAS.
Pangestu, Mari (2002), 'Industrial policy and developing countries', in Bernard Hoekman, Aaditya Matto and Philip English (eds), *Development, Trades and the WTO: A Handbook*, Washington, DC: World Bank.
Rasiah, Raja (1988), 'The semiconductor industry in Penang: implications for the New International Division of Labor (NIDL) theories', *Journal of Contemporary Asia*, **18**(1), 24–46.
Rostow, Walt Whitman (1960), *The Stages of Economic Growth: A Non-Communist Manifesto*, Cambridge: Cambridge University Press.
Stiglitz, Josef E. and Shahid Yusuf (2001). *Rethinking the East Asia Miracle*, New York: Oxford University Press.

Vogel, Ezra F. (1991), *The Four Little Dragons: The Spread of Industrialization in East Asia*, Cambridge: Harvard University Press.

World Bank (1993), *The East Asian Miracle: Economic Growth and Public Policy*, Oxford: Oxford University Press.

World Bank (2009), *World Development Report: Reshaping Economic Geography*, Washington DC: World Bank.

2. Analytical framework for East Asian integration (1): industrial agglomeration and concentrated dispersion

Koji Nishikimi and Ikuo Kuroiwa

2.1 INTRODUCTION

The past few decades have seen economic integration in East Asia progress significantly on both *de facto* and *de jure* bases. Such integration generally encourages trade and investment in the integrated region and leads to a dynamic evolution in the intra- and inter-regional structure of production advantages. Each country's potentials for industrialization and economic development are thus significantly affected by the integration progress.[1] In this chapter and the next, we provide a framework for analyzing the influences of economic integration on industrial development in the integrated countries from the viewpoint of new economic geography (or spatial economics).

The recent progress in industrialization in East Asia has been closely associated with the development of industrial agglomerations. The self-reinforcing mechanism of agglomeration growth enables the rapid and spontaneous process of industrial development. In drawing a blueprint for economic integration, therefore, the effective utilization of agglomeration economies constitutes a critical factor for the successful industrial development of each member country. In this chapter, we examine the individual causes of agglomeration economies and explore the major influences of economic integration.

The remainder of this chapter is organized as follows. In the next section, we overview the two economic forces of dispersion and agglomeration, which exert crucial influences on industrial location. Influenced by these forces, an industrial cluster having substantially grown may become saturated and start to disperse again to other regions that have good logistic connections with the present cluster. This process of concentrated dispersion gives a typical picture of industrial development accompanying the economic integration in East Asia. Section 2.3 explains the chief mechanisms that create the agglomeration forces, because the latter generally emerge from more complex processes than the dispersion forces. We briefly examine the theoretical models that explain how industrial location is affected by the regional market size, degree of input–output linkage, structure of the transport network, and so on. In Section 2.4, we examine the possible consequences of economic integration on industrial location in the integrated region. In particular, we discuss the effects of a reduction in international trade and transport costs and enhancement of production factor mobility, which serve as the major drivers of economic integration, especially in its early stages. Section 2.5 presents concluding remarks.

2.2   DISPERSION, AGGLOMERATION AND CONCENTRATED DISPERSION OF INDUSTRIES: THE MAIN PERSPECTIVE

Industrial production is generally affected by various regional conditions such as the availability and local prices of inputs including skilled/unskilled labor, qualified materials, and competent business services, as well as good access to sizable markets. Each firm thus examines these local conditions closely in order to choose its optimal production location. If there are no agglomeration economies, whereby these appeal factors are reinforced by a concentrated location of producers, industries may well be dispersed across regions – for instance, labor-intensive industries like garment manufacturing scatter over low-wage regions, while resource-intensive industries such as mineral refineries tend to operate near the material sites. In this case, the industrial location closely reflects the regional structure of comparative advantage, and changes as the endowment structure evolves over time.

In contrast, if there are significant agglomeration economies at work, the industrial location may appear to be lumpy – firms are likely to cluster in a limited number of attractive regions, leaving others sparse. In this case, the centripetal force of the agglomeration economies dominates the centrifugal force provided by low wages and/or rents in sparse regions (dispersion force). Classical examples of such agglomeration include the automobile industry clustered in Detroit, USA and Aichi, Japan; financial services in New York, London, Frankfurt and Tokyo; IT industries in Silicon Valley, and so on. More recently, a growing number of industrial agglomerations have also been arising in the emerging countries of East Asia – for instance, the pickup truck cluster in Thailand, the IT cluster in

- **Dispersion force**   ⇐   local factor price, competition in local market, etc.
- **Agglomeration force**   ⇐   firm level IRS, local externalities (spillover effects), etc.

Concentrated dispersion

Progress in agglomeration   ⇒   ⎰ Saturation (wage↑, rent↑)
                       ⇒   ⎨ Sprawl to the neighboring area
                            ⎩ Leap-out to the remote area linked by logistic networks

                 ⇓   (incl. fragmentation)
       Formation of a new agglomeration at a remote area

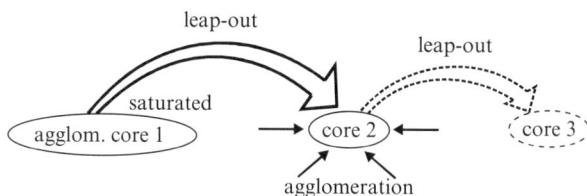

Source: Authors.

Figure 2.1   *Dispersion, agglomeration and concentrated dispersion*

Malaysia, the mobile phone cluster in Beijing-Tianjin, as well as the huge multi-industry agglomerations in the Zhu Jiang (Pearl River) and Chang Jiang (Pearl River) and Chang Jiang deltas.

The remarkable growth of East Asian industries in recent years has been closely associated with the development and evolution of industrial agglomerations. As will be discussed in detail in the next section, there are several causes and mechanisms of agglomeration formation, but regardless of circumstances, the agglomeration economies usually arise in industries characterized by increasing returns to scale (IRS) at the firm level and/or in those carrying the local externality among neighboring firms. The agglomeration tendency of IRS industries, however, does not imply that they are never influenced by dispersion forces. In fact, they will leave the agglomerated area once they find that external wages and rents are sufficiently low *vis-à-vis* the centripetal effects of the agglomeration economies. It is often observed that a saturated agglomeration area sprawls over neighboring regions. If some remote regions are connected with the agglomerated core via an efficient logistic network, the agglomeration may leap out along the network, while the industrial structure of the existing core evolves – for example, from simple manufacturing to R&D activities. This evolutionary process of sprawling/leaping of an agglomeration is called 'concentrated dispersion', as shown in Figure 2.1.[2] The concentrated dispersion of industrial location will be discussed in details in Sections 2.4 and 3.2 (in the next chapter).

2.3   ORIGINS OF AGGLOMERATION ECONOMIES

There are several sources of agglomeration economies,[3] and different sources basically lead to different types of agglomeration. For example, simple home market effects (as explained in 2.3.1) tend to bring about a single-industry agglomeration, while the hub formation effect (2.3.4) may lead to a multi-industry agglomeration. Likewise, the vertical linkage effect (2.3.2) may encourage the formation of a full-set agglomeration from up- to downstream production processes, which is often observed in an automobile cluster, whereas information spillover effects (2.3.5) may cause an agglomeration of related industries such as clusters of IT and bio-medical science (BMS). In either case, however, agglomeration economies arise from the interaction between transport costs and scale economies at the firm level or from the local externality among neighboring firms. In the following section, we scrutinize each cause of agglomeration economies.

2.3.1   Home Market Effect

The primal source of the agglomeration force is provided by the home market effect (HME), which was first shown by Krugman (1980) to be a determinant of the international trade pattern of the IRS industries and was then incorporated into spatial economic analysis by Fujita (1988) and Krugman (1991a). Figure 2.2 shows a typical process through which the HME emerges in an IRS industry, *M*, that produces differentiated goods. When market demand for *M* (in all varieties) grows, each firm increases its production (as shown by arrow (1) in Figure 2.2), and some new firms enter the market and produce new varieties of *M* (arrow (2)). Following this, because of the scale economies in *M*-production, the production increase in individual firms raises their productivity (lowers their average production cost) (arrow (3)), which yields more profit to the firms and/or lowers the price of each variety of *M* (arrows (4)). This profit increase stimulates more firms to enter the *M*-market, and it provides consumers with a wider variety of *M*-goods (arrow (5)). Both the variety increase and the price reduction raise the real income of consumers (arrow (6)) and consequently further enlarge the *M*-market by attracting more consumers to that market (arrow (7)).[4] On the whole, a country with a large domestic market tends to carry a disproportionately large (in

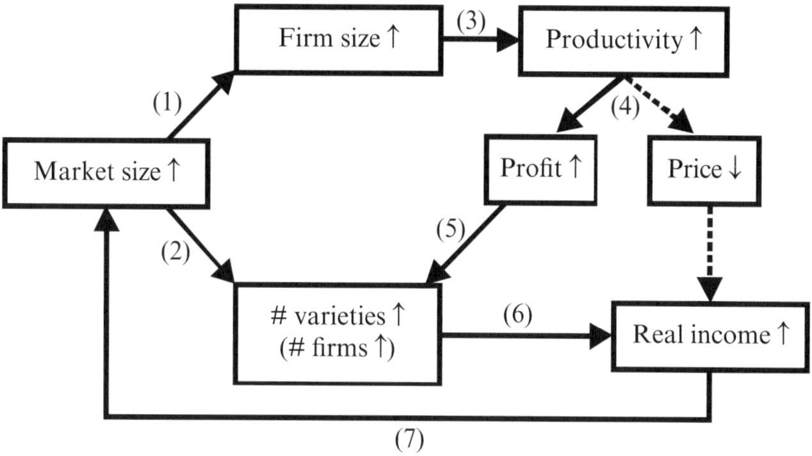

Note: The dotted arrows are not effective in the Dixit and Stiglitz (1977) framework, in which the effect of productivity growth is completely absorbed by the increase in product variety.

Source: Authors.

Figure 2.2 Home market effect

both variety and quantity) IRS sector and exports those IRS products to small countries.

If international trade incurs significant transport costs, the above-noted circular causation of HME will result in the concentrated location of IRS firms in countries where a large market exists. Baldwin et al. (2003) construct a theoretical model of Figure 2.2 to show that *M*-sector in a large country achieves higher operating profit and thus attracts a disproportionately large amount of global capital.[5] In other words, with significant costs for international trade, IRS industries tend to agglomerate in large countries where a large home market exists.

2.3.2 Vertical Linkage of Industries

A circular causation similar to the HME may emerge in vertically linked sectors where the intermediate goods are produced by upstream IRS firms/plants and delivered to downstream firms/plants at a significant transport cost. A typical example may be given by the automobile industry, which is associated with a large number of upstream sectors supplying various heavy and precisely elaborated parts, including

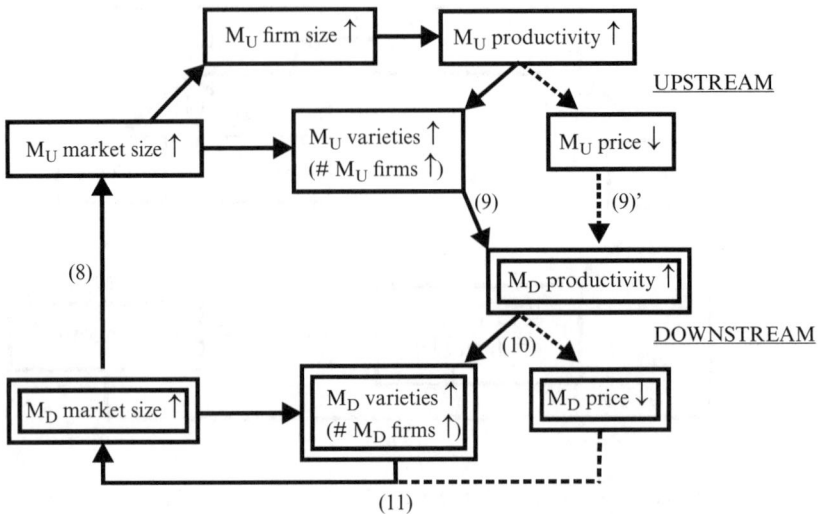

Note: The dotted arrows are not effective in the Dixit and Stiglitz (1977) framework in which the effect of productivity growth is completely absorbed by the increase in product variety.

Source: Authors.

Figure 2.3   Vertical linkage and agglomeration force

engines, transmissions, bodies, electronic devices, and so on. Figure 2.3 shows the basic framework of the vertical linkage model developed by Krugman and Venables (1995), Venables (1996) and Fujita and Hamaguchi (2001). They assume that the entire process of production of the M-good is comprised of the upstream (M_U) and downstream (M_D) processes, where both processes of production are characterized by IRS.[6] An expansion of the final product market (M_D market; for example, motor car market) induces an increase in the production of the intermediate good (M_U; for example, car bodies) (arrow (8)), which brings an increase in M_U variety (wider variation in body design and color, for example) and a decrease in M_U price, due to the IRS property of M_U production (via a mechanism analogous to the HME). These changes in the upstream sector then improve the profitability of the downstream sector (arrows (9) and (9)'), which in turn increases the variety of M_D (a wider range of car models) and decreases the price of M_D, again due to the IRS property of the downstream sector (arrow (10)). This results in a further expansion of the M_D market, which sets in motion the circular causation (arrow (11)).

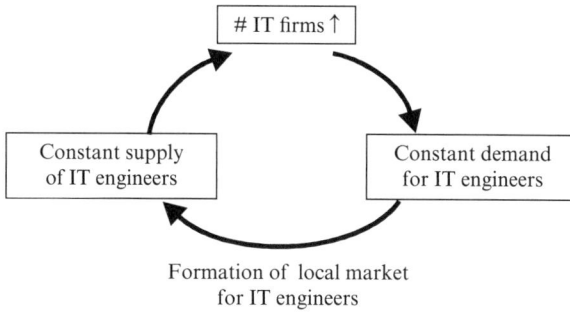

Source: Authors.

Figure 2.4 Input market effect (case of IT engineers)

2.3.3 Formation of a Specific Input Market

If production in an industry requires a specific input, the producers may gain the benefits of clustering via establishing a local market for that input. For example, IT firms need to employ engineers acquainted with advanced IT technology, but the demand of individual firms may fluctuate too much to absorb a constant supply of expert engineers. However, if a sufficient number of IT firms locate together in a given area and pool their demand for experts, they may succeed in setting up a constant local market of IT experts in that area.[7] If such a market appears, it will attract both special engineering workers seeking IT jobs and IT firms seeking good experts. This results in a circular causation between the establishment of a specific input market and the formation of industrial agglomeration, as illustrated in Figure 2.4.

2.3.4 Hub Formation

The formation of transport hubs provides another source of agglomeration economies. The basic mechanism of hub-formation originates from scale economies in transportation (rather than manufacturing production), which have been stimulated by the development of large-sized and high-speed carriers. Scale economics in transportation provide an incentive for collective transport, and this leads to the development of transport network systems with trunk routes and the hub-spoke structure of transportation.

Figure 2.5 shows a possible development process of a transport hub. Consider an initial situation with three location sites, *A*, *B* and *C*, where *B* and *C* are situated in a symmetric state – the two sites have an equal number of firms in production and transport the same volume of goods

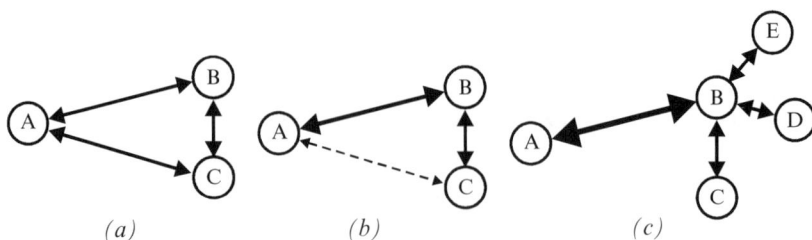

Source: Authors.

Figure 2.5   Formation of transport hub

between A and each of them (along routes A–B and A–C), as shown
by panel (a). Suppose now that the number of firms in B incidentally
increases. This leads to an increase in transport volume (panel (b)) and,
due to scale economies in transport, a decline in the transport cost between
A and B. In addition, by pooling the individual demand for transport,
the increase of firms in B allows the operation of a regular liner service
between A and B, which also substantially reduces the transport cost.
If the transport cost along route A–B decreases sufficiently to offset the
cost of B–C transport, traders in C will use the indirect transport route,
A–B–C, rather than the direct route, A–C. The link between A and B will
thus become a trunk route along which more frequent transport is served
at a lower cost. Moreover, other neighboring countries may also start
using this trunk route, and eventually, a hub-spoke structure of transportation emerges, as illustrated in panel (c).

Once a hub-spoke structure arises in a transportation network, the hub
will attract many producers and consumers with its significant transport
advantages, that is, the hub effect, which will trigger a reciprocal reinforcement process between industrial agglomeration and transport development, as shown in Figure 2.6.[8] It should be noted here that a transport
hub is apt to attract a wide range of industries that need efficient and
frequent transportation. Accordingly, the hub formation effect, unlike the
other causes of agglomeration, may trigger an agglomeration of diversified industries that have few production/transaction linkages between
each other. Moreover, even constant-returns-to-scale (CRS) plants such
as garment factories may trigger the formation of a hub agglomeration in
a rural small town – the new plants create a transport network to convey
their materials, workers, and outputs, the transport development attracts
more firms to that town, which, in turn, yields further demand for freight
and passenger transportation. This process of hub-formation with CRS
industries suggests a sequential development strategy for small economies,

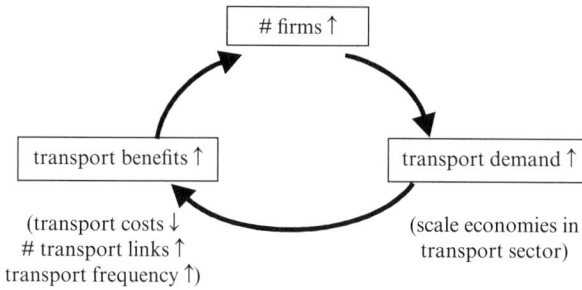

Source: Authors.

Figure 2.6   Hub formation effect

where the agglomeration development based on IRS industries is hardly applicable due to their small home market. Those small economies may start by fostering conventional CRS industries, such as apparel, footwear, food products, and other resource-processing industries, or even a tourism industry. When they successfully attain the critical amount of transport demand needed to create a hub, they can then upgrade the industries to those with greater economies of scale, such as electronics and machinery.

2.3.5   Spillover of Technological/Market Information

Industrial agglomeration can also be caused by the local spillover of information.[9] Up-to-date knowledge of technology and market trends often plays a key role in many spheres of business. Such knowledge and information tend to spill over from one producer to another through direct business contacts, the close monitoring of rival firms and other daily contacts, all of which should be easily implemented if the interested producers operate together in one area.[10] The high availability of up-to-date information lowers the setup costs of opening a business and encourages the entry of new firms into that area. This facilitates a circular causation between local knowledge spillover and the agglomeration of related industries, as shown by Figure 2.7.[11]

2.4   LOCATION EFFECTS OF ECONOMIC INTEGRATION

How does economic integration affect the location of industries? Does it make them more agglomerated or dispersed? As economic integration

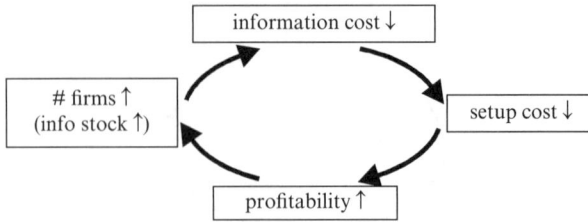

Source: Authors.

Figure 2.7   Knowledge spillover and agglomeration

is normally accompanied by trade facilitation and factor mobilization among the integrated countries, in this section we consider these questions for each of those factors.

2.4.1   Lowering of Trade and Transport Costs

First let us consider the effects of a reduction in trade costs. International trade entails various kinds of costs, including transport costs (pecuniary and time costs), policy barriers (tariff and non-tariff), contract enforcement costs, local distribution costs (wholesale and retail charges), information costs, and so on. Estimating the *ad valorem* tax equivalent value of those trade costs, Anderson and Wincoop (2004) report that trade costs, broadly defined, vary widely across countries and products, and may amount on average to as much as 170% of production costs.[12] Trade liberalization accompanying the process of economic integration reduces the trade costs in most of the categories noted above, and thus significantly affects the pattern of industrial location and international trade among the countries concerned.

A reduction in trade costs, broadly defined, allows firms to consider more aspects of a production advantage rather than of transportation when determining their production sites. Since a production advantage is mainly derived from the two factors of low resource costs and agglomeration merits, a firm's location decision will become more sensitive to both due to trade facilitation. Consequently, in general, trade liberalization may result in either the dispersion or agglomeration of industry.[13] However, because agglomeration tends to raise local wages and rents, agglomeration having substantially expanded will tend to be dispersed again; that is, concentrated dispersion will occur, as explained in Section 2.2 (see also Figure 2.8).

Puga (1999) shows how this process of concentrated dispersion is

1. Reduction of Trade/Transport Costs

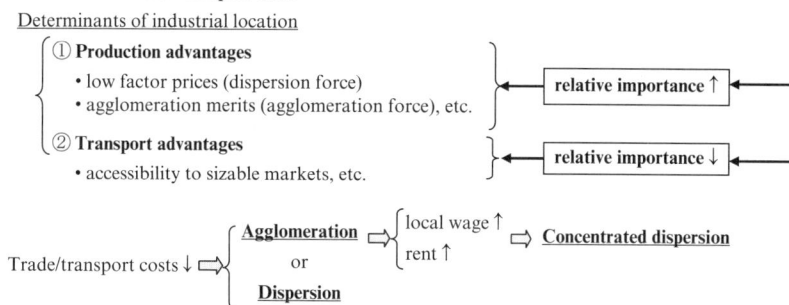

Determinants of industrial location

⎧ ① **Production advantages**
⎪   • low factor prices (dispersion force)
⎨   • agglomeration merits (agglomeration force), etc.
⎪
⎩ ② **Transport advantages**
    • accessibility to sizable markets, etc.

relative importance ↑

relative importance ↓

Trade/transport costs ↓ ⟹ ⎰ **Agglomeration** ⟹ ⎰ local wage ↑ ⟹ **Concentrated dispersion**
                        ⎱ or   ⎱ rent ↑
                          Dispersion

2. Enhancement of Factor Mobility

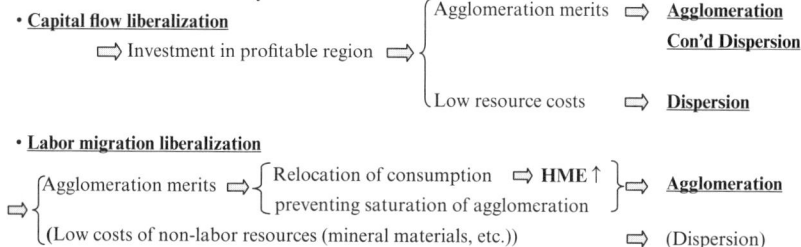

• **Capital flow liberalization**

⟹ Investment in profitable region ⟹ ⎰ Agglomeration merits ⟹ **Agglomeration**
                                                              Con'd Dispersion
                                   ⎱ Low resource costs ⟹ **Dispersion**

• **Labor migration liberalization**

⟹ ⎰ Agglomeration merits ⟹ ⎰ Relocation of consumption ⟹ HME ↑ ⎱ ⟹ **Agglomeration**
   ⎱   ⎱ preventing saturation of agglomeration ⎰
     (Low costs of non-labor resources (mineral materials, etc.))   ⟹ (Dispersion)

Source: Authors.

Figure 2.8   Location effects of economic integration

derived by trade liberalization between two countries, assuming decreasing returns in the agricultural sector and restrictive labor migration across the border. When trade costs become excessive, the transport advantage is put before the production advantage, so that the IRS industry operates in each country to supply consumers there, a situation of autarkic equilibrium. As trade costs decrease, the production advantage increases in importance, and firms cluster in a country in order to exploit the HME provided by the integrated market, that is, agglomeration equilibrium occurs. However, because of diminishing returns in agriculture, progress in agglomeration causes a contraction of agricultural production and hence a rise in wages in the agglomerated country. As trade costs decrease sufficiently, the wage difference between countries expands, and firms start relocating back to the low-wage country. Consequently, the IRS industry operates in both countries, that is, there is concentrated dispersion equilibrium.

This mechanism of concentrated dispersion may also promote the fragmentation of IRS industries if their production process can be split into

Table 2.1　Transport cost and location pattern

Transport cost	Home (labor-abundant)	Foreign (capital-abundant)
(1) High	M_U	M_U
	M_D	M_D
	A	A
(2) Medium		M_U
	A	M_D
		(A)
(3) Low		M_U
	M_D	
	A	(A)

Note: By assumption, the manufacturing sector, both M_U and M_D, is characterized by IRS in production, while agriculture, A, is CRS. The upstream sector, M_U, is assumed to be capital intensive, while the downstream sector is labor intensive.

Source: Summarized by authors based on Amiti (2005).

several blocks characterized by distinctive factor intensities.[14] As discussed in Chapter 1 (and examined more closely in Chapter 4), an increasing number of manufacturing firms, especially in the electronics and machinery industries, have expanded their production networks throughout East Asia, relocating the 'fragmented' production blocks to separate countries where resource endowment is suitable for their production.[15]

Amiti (2005) examines, by using a two-factor (labor, capital) and two-country (Home, Foreign) model, how the location pattern of vertically linked industries changes as the transport costs of their products decrease. She assumes (1) both upstream and downstream industries exhibit scale economies in production; (2) the downstream industry is more labor-intensive than the upstream industry; and (3) Home and Foreign are respectively labor- and capital-abundant. Table 2.1 shows the typical location patterns of the two industries. When the trade cost is sufficiently high, both countries produce various intermediate and final goods (Case (1)). As the trade cost falls, the agglomeration force intensifies, and both upstream and downstream industries relocate from Home to Foreign. Consequently, both industries are agglomerated in Foreign, and Home becomes an agrarian country (Case (2)).[16] However, if the transport cost declines further, the labor-intensive downstream industry relocates from industrialized Foreign to labor-abundant Home, and fragmentation occurs (Case (3)).

Amiti's theoretical findings hint at why MNEs in the two symbolic industries of growing East Asia, electronics and automobiles, exhibit contrasting patterns of location. As observed in Chapter 1, many electronics firms eagerly apply fragmentation and disperse their affiliated plants widely over East Asia, whereas a set of automobile plants, from up- to downstream, tend to cluster together in relatively few areas. Consequently, the local contents of inputs in their production exhibit dramatically contrasting trends, as reported in Box 2.1. As for the transport costs, electronics products are often perceived as much smaller and less costly to transport than automobile products. The results in Table 2.1 suggest that when trade costs generally decline in the process of economic integration, electronics firms are more likely to apply fragmentation than automobile firms (Case (3) in Table 2.1); note that the transportation cost comprises a major determinant of fragmentation, along with other factors discussed in Box 2.2. On the other hand, higher transport costs, as well as a stronger agglomeration force, in the automobile sector promote the vertical linkage type of industrial clustering and consequently push up the local content [Case (2)].[17]

2.4.2 Enhancement of Factor Mobility

Another pillar of economic integration is the enhanced international mobility of production factors, particularly capital and labor. As summarized in Figure 2.8, the liberalization of international capital flows encourages the flexible relocation of firms across borders to profitable sites. This makes both agglomeration and dispersion forces more effective because high profitability can be achieved in both agglomerated cores and low-wage peripheries. Lowering investment barriers may therefore encourage either the agglomeration or dispersion of industries operating in the integrated countries. In contrast, the liberalization of international labor migration encourages workers to move to high-wage regions. Wages are usually higher in industrial agglomerations than in sparse regions though there could be high-wage areas in peripheries, such as valuable mineral resource sites. Enhancement of labor mobility is therefore likely to reinforce agglomeration force, rather than dispersion force.

In addition, the liberalization of international labor migration encourages industrial agglomeration via twofold effects. First, because workers spend a large fraction of their earnings near their workplace, labor migration tends to be accompanied by an expansion of the home market in the country receiving the labor inflow. This accelerates industrial agglomeration by magnifying HME. It should be noted here that shifts of income and expenditures are not induced so much by international capital flows, since much of the capital earnings is spent in the home country rather than in the host country of investment. The second effect of labor migration is

BOX 2.1   LOCAL CONTENT OF THE AUTOMOBILE
           AND ELECTRONICS INDUSTRIES

Local content indicates the percentage of domestic inputs (materials, parts, and so on) and value added aspects (wages, profits, and so on). It thus indicates the proportion of dependency on domestic resources, while the import content (the percentage of imported inputs) represents the proportion of dependency on external resources. One of the authors calculated the local content of 27 industries in eight East Asian countries (China, Korea, Taiwan, Singapore, Malaysia, Thailand, Indonesia, and the Philippines), using the Asian International Input–Output Tables, and obtained the following findings:

1.   Many industries (22 out of 27) decreased their local content, and increased their dependency on imported inputs in 1990–2000. This phenomenon was closely associated with the progress of fragmentation, since fragmentation increases dependency on imported inputs and thus increases the share of the intermediate goods trade.
2.   The automobile industry had relatively high local content (the average local content of the eight countries was 71.1% in 1990). Moreover, among all industries the average local content of the automobile industry increased most sharply (+3.9%) in 1990–2000, while the import content from Japan (which used to be a dominant supplier of automobile parts and components) plummeted. Thus, despite a sizable decline in import content from Japan, a substantial portion of that decline was compensated for by an increase in local content, so that the industry's production network expanded only with neighboring countries, especially in ASEAN (see Figure 1.10(b)). The automobile industry increased local content because of high transport costs, just-in-time delivery, the local content requirement policy of the host country, and so on.
3.   The electronics industry already had a lower local content than the automobile industry (the average local content was 60.3% in 1990). Furthermore, the average local content of the electronics industry decreased most significantly (−5.6%) in 1990–2000, while the import content from other East Asian countries

increased substantially. Therefore, the industry's production network spread extensively throughout East Asia (see Figure 1.10(a)). The electronics industry increased import content because of low transport costs, rising efficiency in air cargo transport and supply chain management, export-oriented industrial policies, and so on (Kuroiwa 2008).

It is notable that the high and increasing trend of local content in the automobile industry as well as the low and decreasing trend of local content in the electronics industry is consistent with Amity's analysis on fragmentation and industrial agglomeration (see Cases (2) and (3) in Table 2.1).

to enable an elastic labor supply to industrial agglomerations. This prevents the saturation of agglomeration and discourages the concentrated dispersion of the agglomerated industries. In other words, industrial agglomerations tend to keep growing if international labor migration is allowed.

In East Asia, the international capital flow has been eagerly promoted in the process of globalization since the 1990s, but international labor migration, especially of unskilled labor, has been restricted to date. This, together with substantial capital inflows from the rest of the world, has probably caused the recent significant progress of concentrated dispersion in East Asia.

2.5 CONCLUDING REMARKS

Economic integration exerts two different forces on industrial location: dispersion force and agglomeration force. The dispersion force relocates industries across integrated countries according to each country's comparative advantage and achieves static efficiency in resource allocation. In contrast, the agglomeration force serves as a dynamic source of industrialization, but may also simultaneously result in economic disparities between integrated countries and among domestic regions within each country.[18] During the recent progress of industrial development in East Asia, the agglomeration force appears to be increasing in importance.

The trade and transport cost reduction and enhancement of international capital flows accompanying economic integration often accelerate

BOX 2.2   DETERMINANTS OF FRAGMENTATION

According to Lall et al. (2004), the intensity of fragmentation differs according to industry, depending on the following four factors:

- *The technical divisibility of production processes* Engineering activities like automobiles or electronics have discrete (separable) stages of production and components with differing scales, skills and technological needs, whose production can be located at different sites and under different ownership. By contrast, continuous process industries, such as chemicals, are more difficult to break up economically.
- *The factor intensity of the process*   It is only economical to relocate processes if they are labor-intensive and reduce production costs significantly by shifting to lower-wage sites. The reduction in production costs must more than offset a rise in transport and coordination costs.
- *The technological complexity of each process* Some labor-intensive processes (for example design and development) cannot be shifted to lower-wage areas with low skills and capabilities; only simpler and more stable ones can be efficiently relocated.
- *The value to weight ratio of the product*   The scope for fragmentation depends on the weight of the product relative to its value. For example lightweight and high-value products (such as semiconductors) can be shipped long distances to exploit cost differences while heavyweight and low-value ones can only be shipped to nearby areas or remain in the original producing country due to higher transport costs relative to value.

Considering the above factors, Lall et al. (2004) concluded that: (1) in high-technology industries, fragmentation is strong in electronics, (2) in medium-technology industries, fragmentation is strong in automobiles, but the weight of the product and its high basic capability requirements mean that it only extends to a few proximate, relatively industrialized locations and (3) in low-technology industries, production fragmentation is strong in clothing, footwear, sports goods and toys.

the industrial agglomeration in East Asia. However, as agglomeration cores become saturated, wages and rents start rising in those regions, which encourages leap-out (concentrated dispersion) of the clustered firms to remote areas where there is good accessibility to the existing cores. The enhancement of international labor migration, conversely, tends to discourage the concentrated dispersion of IRS firms. In East Asia, as international migration is substantially limited (compared to domestic migration), industrial clusters may well expand across countries if the latter are well connected by efficient logistic networks. In this sense, economic integration is a crucial factor in ensuring widespread industrial development throughout East Asian countries.

NOTES

1. For a comprehensive review of economic integration in Europe, North America, Asia and the world, see Baldwin and Wyplosz (2004), Jovanović (2005), OECD (1998), Fujita et al. (2008), Huang and Bocchi (2008), and World Bank (2009).
2. World Bank (2009) carries out comprehensive studies of the leaping-out process of industrial agglomeration. Moreover, the leaping-out of plant location may occur within a firm if its production activity is separable into several processes that are suitable for production in different regions. Such a firm can gain production efficiency and profitability by relocating the separated processes to suitable regions and connecting them with an efficient logistic network. This phenomenon is often called 'fragmentation' and is widely observed in recent East Asia. See also Section 2.4.1.
3. For theoretical analyses of agglomeration economies, see Krugman (1991b), Fujita et al. (1999), Fujita and Thisse (2002), Baldwin et al. (2003), Ottaviano and Thisse (2004), and others.
4. In the typical formulation by Dixit and Stiglitz (1977), the home market effect causes no change in equilibrium price. In their model, all the influences of market size difference are reflected in the number (range) of product varieties.
5. Their extended model imposes international mobility of goods and capital (in the footloose capital model), but not of labor. For details, see the footloose capital model and the constructed capital model by Baldwin et al. (2003).
6. In their formal models, for the sake of analytical simplicity, Krugman and Venables (1995) and Venables (1996) apply a plain setting where M_U and M_D are produced in the same manufacturing process. A circular causation of agglomeration economies may arise even in the case that the downstream industry is characterized by CRS production. In this case, the effects of variety increase in the downstream sector vanish, and only the price reduction effect remains at work in the M_D part of Figure 2.3.
7. This effect of demand-pooling arises from the law of large numbers, which may be classified as a kind of scale economies. The circular causation in forming input markets is caused by the interaction of this scale effect and the transport costs in input delivery.
8. For comprehensive discussion concerning hub effects, see Krugman (1993), Fujita and Mori (1996), Konishi (2000), Mori and Nishikimi (2002), Fujita and Mori (2005), and Behrens (2007).
9. Local spillover of technological information may be interpreted as a composite of IRS in production and positive costs of information transfer. Information spillover allows the common use of knowledge among producers, which yields scale economies in regional production – the average costs, including R&D, decrease in inverse proportion to regional

production. On the other hand, the locality of spillover can be interpreted as the information transfer cost discontinuously rocketing at the regional border from zero to infinity.

10. Baranes and Tropeano (2003) argue that, along with the communicative nature of information transfer, the tough competition among nearby firms tends to encourage knowledge sharing by preventing each firm from free-riding.

11. These situations were first formulated by Marshall (1920) as Marshallian externality and incorporated more recently in the framework of endogenous growth theory. This was then combined with spatial economics by Krugman (1991b), Martin and Ottaviano (1999), Baldwin et al. (2001), Baldwin et al. (2003), Baldwin and Martin (2004), Rodríguez-Clare (2007), and so on.

12. Of this 170% trade cost, 21% is attributable to transport costs (including 9% for time costs), 44% to border-related trade barriers, and 55% to retail and wholesale costs (2.7=1.21*1.44*1.55). Estimation of trade costs generally suffers from serious data limitations. In addition, there is still no established method for the indirect estimation of trade costs. For details, see Anderson and Wincoop (2004), Hummels (1999), and Bosker and Garretsen (2007).

13. For details on the locational influences of trade liberalization, see Puga (1999), Ricci (1999), Epifani (2001), Forslid and Wooton (2003), and Amiti (2005).

14. Fragmentation may be simply explained by conventional models of CRS production. For example, Deardorff (1998), Jones and Kierzkowski (2001), Arndt (2004), and Haddad (2007), using linear models of international trade, and carrying out close studies on the mechanism and economic consequences of fragmentation.

15. Theoretically speaking, under the significant influence of agglomeration economies, fragmentation may lead to a perverse pattern of plant location, such that the labor- (capital-) intensive process is located in the capital- (labor-) abundant country. Epifani (2001) shows, however, that a perverse pattern of location can be sustained in equilibrium only in the presence of: (a) small international factor abundance differences; (b) small intersectoral factor-intensity differences; (c) pronounced equilibrium scale economies; and (d) a high share of intermediates in total costs.

16. It is also possible that both upstream and downstream industries agglomerate in Home, provided some conditions are satisfied (see Amiti 2005). In this chapter, however, we only deal with the case where both industries agglomerate in Foreign.

17. When East Asian countries adopted an import substitution (IS) policy, from the 1950s to the first half of the 1980s (Table 1.1), trade and transport costs became prohibitively high so that MNEs had no choice but to set up factories in each host country to meet local final consumer demand. This is a situation similar to Case (1) in Table 2.1, although they needed to import a substantial amount of intermediate goods due to the lack of a competitive supporting industry.

18. Section 3.3 discusses the problem of regional disparities caused by agglomeration forces in more detail.

REFERENCES

Amiti, Mary (2005), 'Location of vertically linked industries: agglomeration versus comparative advantage', *European Economic Review*, **49**, 809–32.

Anderson, James E. and Eric van Wincoop (2004), 'Trade costs', *Journal of Economic Literature*, **42**, 691–751.

Arndt, Sven W. (2004), 'Trade integration and production networks in Asia: the role of China', Lowe Institute of Political Economy Working Papers.

Baldwin, Richard E. and Philippe Martin (2004), 'Agglomeration and regional growth', Chapter 60 in J. Vernon Henderson and Jean-François Thisse (eds), *Handbook of Regional and Urban Economics*, Amsterdam: Elsevier.

Baldwin, Richard E. and Charles Wyplosz (2004), *The Economics of European Integration*, New York: McGraw-Hill.

Baldwin, Richard E., Philippe Martin and Gianmarco I.P. Ottaviano (2001), 'Global income divergence, trade and industrialization: the geography of growth take-offs', *Journal of Economic Growth*, **6**, 5–37.

Baldwin, Richard E., Rikard Forslid, Philippe Martin, Gianmarco I.P. Ottaviano and Frédéric Robert-Nicoud (2003), *Economic Geography and Public Policy*, Princeton: Princeton University Press.

Baranes, Edmond and Jean-Philippe Tropeano (2003), 'Why are technological spillovers spatially bounded? A market oriented approach', *Regional Science and Urban Economics*, **33**, 445–66.

Behrens, Kristian (2007), 'On the location and lock-in of cities: geography vs transportation technology', *Regional Science and Urban Economics*, **37**, 22–45.

Bosker, Maarten and Harry Garretsen (2007), 'Trade costs, market access and economic geography: why the empirical specification of trade costs matters', CESIFO Working Paper no. 2071.

Deardorff, Alan V. (1998), 'Fragmentation in simple trade models', RSIE Discussion Paper no. 422.

Dixit, Avinash K. and Joseph E. Stiglitz (1977), 'Monopolistic competition and optimum product diversity', *American Economic Review*, **67**, 297–308.

Epifani, Paolo (2001), 'Heckscher-Ohlin and agglomeration', CESPRI Working Paper no. 126.

Forslid, Rikard and Ian Wooton (2003), 'Comparative advantage and the location of production', *Review of International Economics*, **11**, 588–603.

Fujita, Masahisa (1988), 'A monopolistic competition model of spatial agglomeration: differentiated product approach', *Regional Science and Urban Economics*, **18**, 87–124.

Fujita, Masahisa and Nobuaki Hamaguchi (2001), 'Intermediate goods and the spatial structure of an economy', *Regional Science and Urban Economics*, **31**, 79–109.

Fujita, Masahisa and Tomoya Mori (1996), 'The role of ports in the making of major cities: self-agglomeration and hub-effect', *Journal of Development Economics*, **49**, 93–120.

Fujita, Masahisa and Tomoya Mori (2005), 'Transport development and the evolution of economic geography', IDE Discussion Papers no. 21.

Fujita, Masahisa and Jacques-François Thisse (2002), *Economics of Agglomeration: Cities, Industrial Location, and Regional Growth*, Cambridge: Cambridge University Press.

Fujita, Masahisa, Paul Krugman and Anthony J. Venables (1999), *The Spatial Economy: Cities, Regions, and International Trade*, Cambridge, MA: MIT Press.

Fujita, Masahisa, Satoru Kumagai and Koji Nishikimi (eds) (2008), *Economic Integration in East Asia: Perspectives from Spatial and Neoclassical Economics*, Cheltenham, UK and Northampton, MA, USA: Edward Elgar.

Haddad, Mona (2007), 'Trade integration in East Asia: the role of China and production networks', World Bank Policy Research Working Paper, no. 4160.

Huang, Yukon and Alessandro M. Bocchi (eds) (2008), *Reshaping Economic Geography in East Asia*, Washington, DC: World Bank.

Hummels, David (1999), 'Toward a geography of trade costs', unpublished manuscript, University of Chicago.

Jones, Ronald W. and Henryk Kierzkowski (2001), 'A framework for fragmentation', Chapter 2 in Sven W. Arndt and Henryk Kierzkowski (eds), *Fragmentation: New Production Patterns in the World Economy*, Oxford: Oxford University Press.

Jovanović, Miroslav N. (2005), *The Economics of European Integration: Limits and Prospects*, Cheltenham, UK and Northampton, MA, USA: Edward Elgar.

Konishi, Hideo (2000), 'Hub cities: city formation without increasing returns', *Journal of Urban Economics*, **48**, 1–28.

Krugman, Paul (1980), 'Scale economies, product differentiation, and pattern of trade', *American Economic Review*, **70**, 950–59.

Krugman, Paul (1991a), 'Increasing returns and economic geography', *Journal of Political Economy*, **99**, 483–99.

Krugman, Paul (1991b), *Geography and Trade*, Cambridge, MA: MIT Press.

Krugman, Paul (1993), 'The hub effect or threeness in interregional trade', Chapter 3 in Wilfred J. Ethier, Elhanan Helpman and J. Peter Neary (eds), *Theory, Policy and Dynamics in International Trade*, Cambridge: Cambridge University Press.

Krugman, Paul and Anthony Venables (1995), 'Globalization and inequality of nations', *Quarterly Journal of Economics*, **110**, 857–80.

Kuroiwa, Ikuo (2008), 'Cross-border production networks in Southeast Asia', in Ikuo Kuroiwa and Toh Mun Heng (eds), *Production Networks and Industrial Clusters: Integrating Economies in Southeast Asia*, Singapore: Institute of Southeast Asian Studies.

Lall, Sanjaya, Manuel Albaladejo and Jinkang Zhang (2004), 'Mapping fragmentation: electronics and automobiles in Southeast Asia and Latin America', *Oxford Development Studies*, **32**(3), 407–32.

Marshall, Alfred (1920), *Principles of Economics*, London: Macmillan.

Martin, Philippe and Gianmarco I.P. Ottaviano (1999), 'Growing locations: industry location in a model of endogenous growth', *European Economic Review*, **43**, 281–302.

Mori, Tomoya and Koji Nishikimi (2002), 'Economy of transport density and industrial agglomeration', *Regional Science and Urban Economics*, **32**, 167–200.

OECD (1998), *Migration, Free Trade and Regional Integration in North America*, Paris: OECD Publishing.

Ottaviano, Gianmarco and Jacques-François Thisse (2004), 'Agglomeration and economic geography', in J. Vernon Henderson and Jacques-François Thisse (eds), *Handbook of Regional and Urban Economies, Volume 4: Cities and Geography*, Amsterdam: North-Holland.

Puga, Diego (1999), 'The rise and fall of regional inequality', *European Economic Review*, **43**, 303–34.

Ricci, Luca A. (1999), 'Economic geography and comparative advantage: agglomeration versus specialization', *European Economic Review*, **43**, 357–77.

Rodríguez-Clare, Andrés (2007), 'Clusters and comparative advantage: implications for industrial policy', *Journal of Development Economics*, **82**, 43–57.

Venables, Anthony (1996), 'Equilibrium location of vertically linked industries', *International Economic Review*, **37**, 341–59.

World Bank (2009), *World Development Report 2009: Reshaping Economic Geography*, Washington, DC: World Bank.

3. Analytical framework for East Asian integration (2): evolution of industrial location and regional disparity

Koji Nishikimi and Ikuo Kuroiwa

3.1 INTRODUCTION

As discussed in the preceding chapter, industrial firms are always affected by both agglomeration and dispersion forces. Under the influence of substantial agglomeration force, the circular causations of agglomeration economies may create a huge magnification effect, such that a slight difference in the initial condition among countries can grow into an immense inequality in the subsequent development performance. Under such circumstances, the long-term progress of industrialization and cluster formation can be triggered by the success of a short-term or temporary policy program to invite a critical magnitude of IRS industries. The government of each country can therefore play a crucial role in achieving economic development.

The magnification effect, on the other hand, may enlarge the economic disparities among countries that are endowed with different initial conditions. If progress in terms of economic integration brings unacceptable levels of inequality for some member countries, the integration process may hit a snag even if it promises greater benefits to the integrated region as a whole. We must thus devote sufficient care to the spatial disparity effects of economic integration.

The remainder of this chapter is organized as follows. In Section 3.2, we consider the evolutionary process from agglomeration to concentrated dispersion in detail, which was briefly described in the preceding chapter, and discuss its policy implications for East Asian economic integration. How 'concentrated dispersing' industries could be lured into a particular country is probably the greatest concern for many developing countries. However, due to the attributes of agglomeration economies, policy coordination would be needed to avoid conflicts of interest among the integrated countries. We overview the historical experiences of policy coordination among Southeast Asian countries where state-led policy coordination was taken over by the MNE-led production coordination. Section 3.3 examines how the initial distribution of industries among countries affects the process of concentrated dispersion accompanying economic integration. It is shown that progress in economic integration may deprive the integrated less developed countries (LDCs) of the development opportunities for industrialization via the so-called 'straw effect' if the integration is carried out by a set of countries exhibiting significant differences in their home market size and industrialization level. This implies the need for policies to fill the initial gaps in industrialization. Section 3.4 presents concluding remarks.

3.2 AGGLOMERATION, CONCENTRATED DISPERSION AND DEVELOPMENT COORDINATION

In this section, we examine the stability of the equilibrium location and consider what changes in economic conditions drive the evolution from agglomeration to concentrated dispersion equilibrium. To do so, we consider a simple model as follows: there are two countries, 1 and 2, between which manufacturing firms can freely relocate. Capital, K, is also freely mobile between the two countries, while the total amount of available K is set constant at $\bar{K}$. Labor, in contrast, is assumed to be immobile across the national border. Here, the industrial location is determined solely by the allocation of capital which pursues higher profitability in M-production between Countries 1 and 2.

3.2.1 Stability of Equilibrium

Suppose that the manufacturing sector, M, produces a homogeneous good, using K, L and differentiated intermediate goods, I. The intermediate goods are freely mobile within a country, but significant transport costs are incurred if they are moved across the border. To simplify the analysis, we assume constant input requirement in manufacturing – a unit of M production requires a constant unit of K, L and each variety of I. Moreover, we suppose that the number (variety) of the intermediate inputs produced in each country largely depends on the country's industrialization level, and thus the number of those inputs that need to be imported decreases as M production increases.[1]

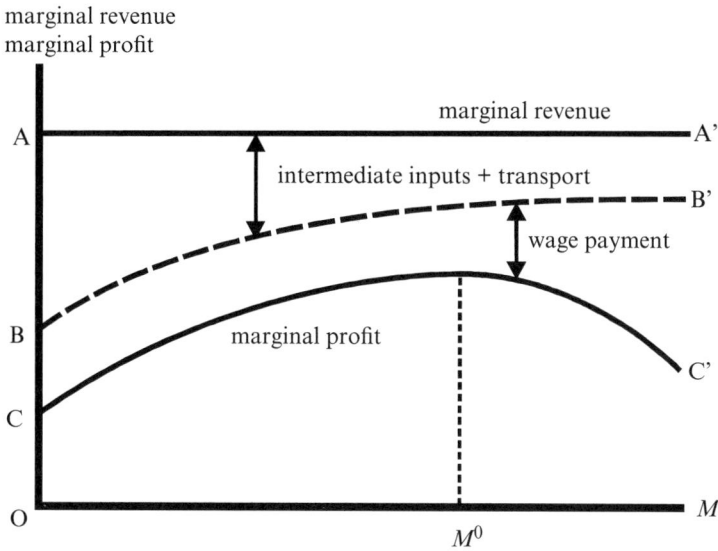

marginal revenue
marginal profit

marginal revenue   A'

intermediate inputs + transport   B'

wage payment

A

B   marginal profit

C   C'

O
M^0 M

Source: Authors.

Figure 3.1   Derivation of marginal profit curve

Because transport costs are required only for imported inputs, an increase in M production decreases the marginal costs (per unit production of M) spent on intermediate inputs (that is, costs of all variety of I plus transport costs of imported inputs), and this exerts agglomeration economies on manufacturing firms. On the other hand, a process of agglomeration increases labor demand and consequently raises wages because of immobility of labor.[2] This pushes up the labor cost per unit of M-production, which causes agglomeration (congestion) diseconomies.

Under the interactive influences of the agglomeration economies and diseconomies noted above, the manufacturing firms determine their location by comparing profitability in the two countries. Figure 3.1 shows how to derive the marginal profit curve for M-industry in a country, where marginal profit represents the increase in profit when an additional unit of M is produced. In the figure, for the sake of simplicity, it is assumed that the producer's price of M-good is constant, regardless of the output level.[3] Due to this assumption, the revenue per unit production of M is given constant at the level of the producer's price, which is given by the length of O-A in Figure 3.1. The marginal costs on intermediate and labor inputs are given, respectively, by the distances between Curve A-A' and B-B' and between B-B' and C-C'. Recall that as the production of M increases,

marginal profit

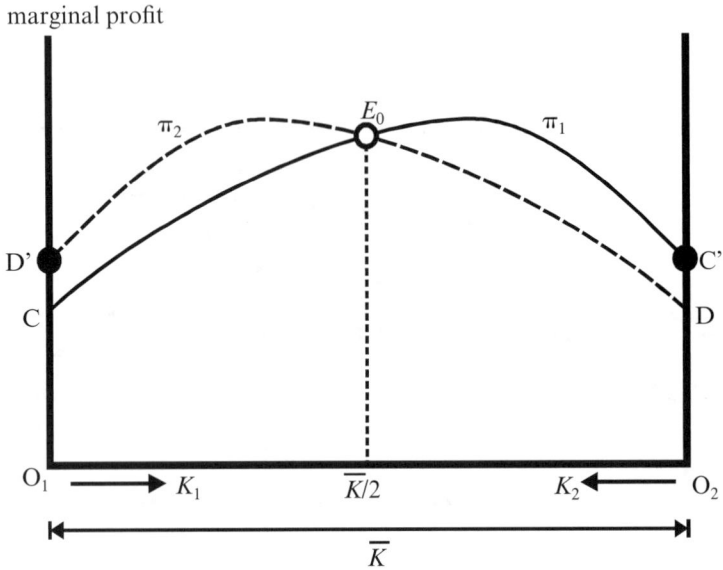

Source: Authors.

Figure 3.2   Agglomeration equilibrium

the cost of intermediate goods decreases by the effect of agglomeration economies, while the labor cost increases via congestion diseconomies. The marginal profit curve, C-C', can be derived by subtracting these input costs from the marginal revenue, A-A'. Because of the interaction of the agglomeration economies and diseconomies, the marginal profit is represented by the bell-shaped curve C-C'.

Now, consider the capital allocation between Countries 1 and 2. As a unit of M requires a constant amount of K input, the marginal profit curve can be redrawn, by converting the horizontal axis, as a function of K instead of M. Figure 3.2 depicts the marginal profit curves for the two countries, measuring Country 1's capital input, K_1, rightward from Point O_1 and Country 2's capital, K_2, leftward from O_2. In the figure, the total quantity of capital is given by the length of the horizontal axis, that is, $\overline{K}$. Here we assume that the two countries provide equal potentials for the manufacturing industry, so that the marginal profit curves, C-C' and D-D', are drawn symmetrically to each other. The marginal profit in both countries is equalized at $K_1 = K_2 = \overline{K}/2$. However, this equilibrium, E_0, is not stable – for example, a small shift of capital from Country 2 to 1 (a small move from E_0 to the right) makes M-sector in Country 1 more profitable than that in Country 2, which attracts more capital to Country 1 (note that π_1 exceeds π_2 on the right hand side of E_0). This adjustment process ceases at a complete agglomeration equilibrium, Point C', where all capital is concentrated in Country 1. Likewise, we can verify that another extreme allocation, Point D', also gives a stable equilibrium.

The situation drawn by Figure 3.2 shows two possible equilibria of complete agglomeration, at Points C' and D', only one of which, however, can be realized. This often leads to excessive competition between the governments of both countries in an attempt to lure industrial agglomeration, because it is hardly acceptable for either country for all firms to agglomerate only in the neighboring country. The excessive competition among neighboring countries sometimes triggers keen public investment in infrastructure, such as ports and manufacturing bases, to become quite decentralized. However, in the long run, most of these investments become redundant because only a few can attract a sufficient number of firms that will result in the exertion of significant economies of agglomeration.

The stability of equilibrium is largely determined by the interaction of agglomeration economies and diseconomies, which are closely associated with the technological characteristics of industry. For example, labor-intensive industries are sensitive to wage rises, hence their marginal profit is significantly affected by congestion diseconomies rather than agglomeration economies. Consequently, the marginal profit curve for labor-intensive industries tends to peak at a reduced degree of agglomeration, compared with capital- or technology-intensive industries. Similarly, congestion diseconomies become relatively large when an industry has weak agglomeration economies (for example, due to weak input–output linkages or reduced information spillover),[4] hence the marginal profit curve for such industry peaks at a smaller output level. Therefore, when congestion diseconomies are significantly strong and/or agglomeration economies are significantly weak, the marginal profit curves have flatter shapes as shown in Figure 3.3. Notice that unlike the case of Figure 3.2, the symmetric equilibrium, E_1, is stable – a small shift of capital from Country 2 to 1, for instance, makes the M-industry in Country 2 more profitable, which draws capital back to Country 2 (note that π_2 exceeds π_1 on the right hand side of E_1). Moreover, in this case, the complete agglomeration equilibria are no longer stable, so that only the concentrated dispersion equilibrium, E_1, can appear in the long term.

The above discussion concerning Figures 3.2 and 3.3 implies that industries characterized by labor-intensive and/or less IRS production, such as apparel, tend to be dispersed to the low wage regions. Moreover, if the production process of an industry can be split into several production blocks embodying different technological features as in the case of the

marginal profit

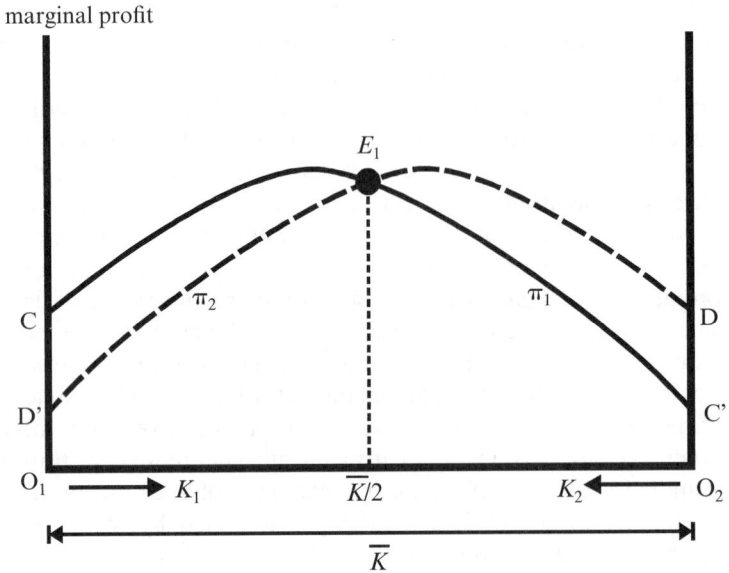

Source: Authors.

Figure 3.3   Concentrated dispersion equilibrium

electronics industry, labor-intensive and/or less IRS blocks are likely to be fragmented and leave the agglomerated high-wage regions at a relatively early stage.[5]

3.2.2   Agglomeration to Concentrated Dispersion

We now consider the changes in the economic environment that trigger an evolution from an agglomeration equilibrium to a concentrated dispersion equilibrium.

(1) Reduction in intra-regional transport costs

Let us first examine the effect of a reduction in trade and transport costs. Consider an agglomeration equilibrium where all firms in M-industry are agglomerated in Country 1. Curves C-C' and D-D' in Figure 3.4 are reproduced from Figure 3.2, and the initial equilibrium is given by point C'. Now, suppose that the trade and transport costs between the two countries are reduced substantially, the two marginal profit curves will shift upward due to the reduced transport costs of imported inputs. It should be noted, however, that the reduced transport costs are larger

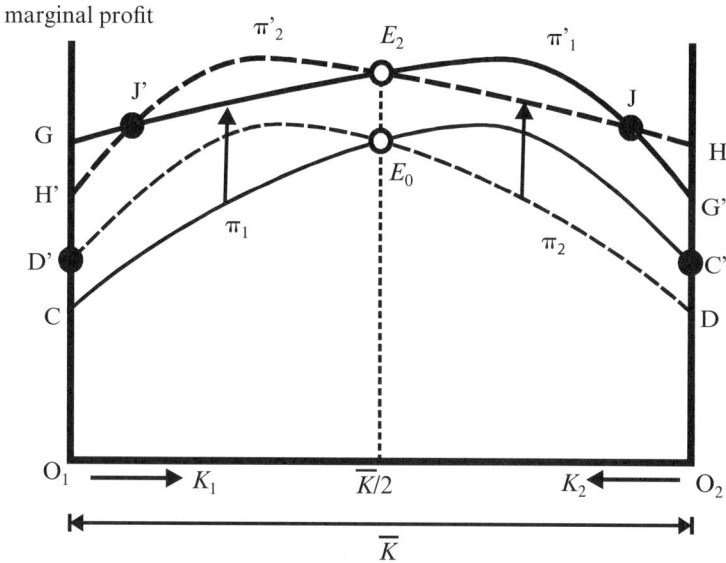

Source: Authors.

Figure 3.4 Agglomeration to concentrated dispersion (effect of a fall in trade/transport costs)

when the manufacturing production is small because a greater number (variety) of inputs need to be imported. Consequently, the marginal profit curves become flatter in the range of small K, as shown by curves G-G' and H-H'. With the new set of the marginal profit curves, G-G' and H-H', the agglomeration equilibrium is no longer stable. Instead, two stable equilibria of concentrated dispersion are available at points J and J'. In other words, a fall in trade and transport costs leads to a changeover from complete agglomeration to concentrated dispersion. It is thus vital for less developed regions to build good transport and logistics links with existing agglomeration cores, in order to stimulate the concentrated dispersion of the industries agglomerated therein.

(2) Capital increase
A similar evolution may be caused by capital accumulation in the integrated region or a global capital inflow from the third country. Figure 3.5 shows such a case, where the available capital for investment in Countries 1 and 2 increases significantly to $\overline{K}'$. The origin for Country 2, O_2, shifts to the right as $\overline{K}$ increases. If the capital increase is sufficiently

marginal profit

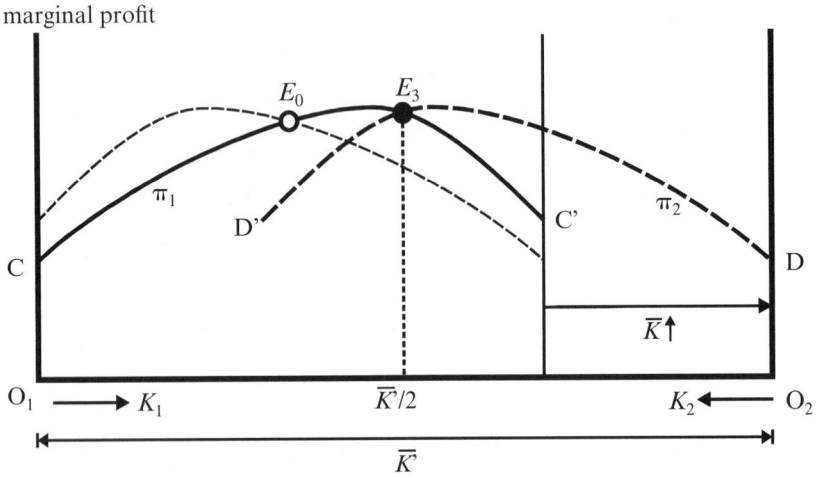

Source: Authors.

Figure 3.5   Effect of capital inflow

large, the agglomeration in Country 1 becomes saturated, and the concentrated dispersion equilibrium, E_3, will be achieved. In the continuous process of capital inflow or accumulation, the agglomeration pattern of M-industry catastrophically changes from complete agglomeration, C', to symmetric agglomeration, E_3. In the era of capital globalization in particular, the creation of attractive investment climates serves as a crucial factor for the dynamic evolution of industrial agglomeration in the integrated area.

3.2.3   Coordination Failure in Agglomeration Development: East Asian Experiences

(1) Benefits and risks of policy coordination
As we mentioned in the discussion on Figure 3.2, the agglomeration-luring game carried out by the integrated countries often triggers a prisoners' dilemma. Initially, these countries have an equal opportunity to obtain a new industrial cluster, which may be established by launching active public policies, including the construction of new infrastructure and targeted industrial promotion. However, only a few of these will succeed in fostering industrial agglomeration. In this situation, the governments of the integrated countries may well encounter a tradeoff between efficiency and equity, because improvement in overall production efficiency deprives

individual countries of equitable development opportunities.[6] To avoid the redundant investment associated with agglomeration luring, policy coordination may be needed among neighboring countries in the integrated region.

Policy coordination, however, is not a panacea for efficient resource allocation in agglomeration luring. First, there is often a serious conflict of interests among the countries involved, causing coordination to fail. Secondly, coordination may lead to allocation inefficiency. This is because, if the geographical distribution of clustering industries is determined by negotiation in an inter-government assembly, those industries are likely to be separated from market competition. This treatment would tend to spoil the industries and cause serious inefficiency in resource allocation.

In fact, ASEAN countries in the 1970s implemented policy coordination whereby heavy and chemical industries were to be set up and developed collectively within the region.[7] Since heavy and chemical industries are typical IRS industries, the local market of each ASEAN country was too small to achieve efficiency. Thus, the ASEAN countries entered into negotiations to decide which industry was to be allocated to each member country. At the same time, Preferential Trade Agreements (PTAs) were signed by these governments, so that member countries could sell their products in each other's markets and achieve efficiency by expanding production. However, they could not reach agreement on the allocation of the key industries – notably petrochemicals and steel – due to a serious conflict of interests. Moreover, only a few projects were actually implemented, all of which were business failures.[8]

In addition, the ASEAN countries tried to allocate a specific automobile parts industry to each member country in an attempt to collectively manufacture ASEAN cars.[9] However, this scheme also failed because (1) all member countries considered the automobile industry strategically important, making serious conflicts of interest unavoidable, and (2) local production in the automobile industry had already been started by MNEs – especially Japanese MNEs such as Toyota and Mitsubishi – and the scheme itself was not in their interests.

(2) From state-led policy coordination to MNE-led production coordination
As shown above, policy coordination led by the state did not work effectively due to serious conflicts of interest and allocation inefficiencies. On the other hand, the MNEs, which had already established production bases in each ASEAN country, also had an incentive to coordinate production over the whole ASEAN region and improve efficiency.

Against this backdrop, the Mitsubishi Motors Corporation (MMC) proposed the Brand to Brand Complementation (BBC) scheme in 1982, which was approved in 1988 by ASEAN governments. Under the BBC scheme, automobile MNEs are allowed to specialize in specific parts in each ASEAN country and trade them with each other at preferential tariff rates; it was also stipulated that exports and imports should be kept in balance to avoid conflicts of interest between the member countries. In this way, economies of scale were achieved for the production of large functional parts such as engines and transmissions, which generally require a minimum annual production of 150,000 to 200,000 units per model. Moreover, since these key parts bring high added value relative to transport costs, it was fairly economical to concentrate production and trade within the region. On the other hand, the assembly process does not require such economies of scale, and so can be dispersed throughout the region.[10]

Under the BBC scheme, the Philippine MMC factory was engaged in the production of transmissions, which were exported to Thailand; the Thai MMC factory was engaged in the production of truck fenders, inlet manifolds, and steering wheel core metals, which were then exported to the Philippines or Malaysia; and the Malaysian MMC factory was engaged in the production of doors, which were exported to Thailand. Other Japanese automobile companies followed suit and initiated the concentration of production and intra-regional trading of key parts. Toyota, for example, concentrated the production of manual steering gears in Malaysia; manual transmissions in the Philippines; diesel engines in Thailand; and gasoline engines in Indonesia. These parts were then traded actively among the member countries (Shimizu, 1998).

The BBC scheme was effective in achieving economies of scale and improving efficiency in production. At the same time, since the preservation of trade balance was required, serious conflicts of interest were avoided among the member countries. Furthermore, because the BBC scheme was initiated by the MNEs, it was largely in accordance with their interests, which prompted fierce competition in the international market. In fact, although the BBC scheme was later taken over by the ASEAN Industrial Cooperation (AICO) scheme and the ASEAN Free Trade Area (AFTA), users of these schemes continued to increase, especially in the automobile industry. It is also expected that the users of such schemes will spread to other industries where a region-wide market is necessary to achieve economies of scale in production.

It should be noted that the MNE-led production coordination turned out to be more effective than state-led policy coordination, and that ASEAN countries were able to adjust themselves flexibly in order to increase the competitiveness of industries.

3.3 ECONOMIC DISPARITY AND THE DEVELOPMENT OF LDCS

3.3.1 Effects of Inequality in Economic Size

The discussions in Section 3.2 suggest that in order to exploit economic integration, each country in the integrated region should develop its long-term policies, such as developing an efficient logistic network for luring the 'concentrated dispersing' IRS industries. These policies are effective particularly in cases where the integrated countries initially face similar economic conditions. Conversely, if these countries differ significantly in economic size (in income or production), which may reflect significant differences in factor endowment, technology/skill level, asset holdings, and so forth, the IRS industries may excessively agglomerate in a country with a large home market. Nishikimi (2008) examines how the industrialization paths of the integrated countries are affected by their economic size. He extends the footloose capital model of Baldwin et al. (2003) to a three-country case where Countries 1 and 2 are to be integrated, as illustrated in Figure 3.6. It is assumed, as in the model of Section 3.2.1, that capital freely flows across national borders, while labor is mobile only within a country. In the process of integration, the trade and transport costs (τ) between Countries 1 and 2 decline continuously, whereas the costs on trade between each of them and ROW are set constant at τ' ($\geq \tau$).

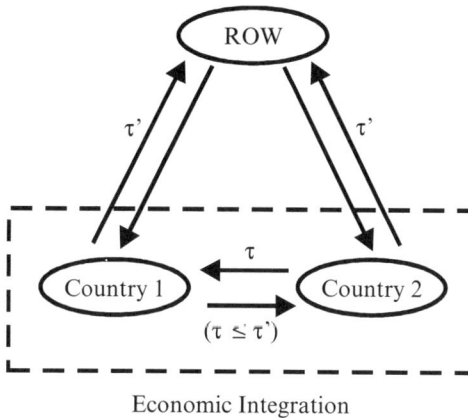

Economic Integration

Source: Nishikimi (2008).

Figure 3.6   Three-country model of economic integration

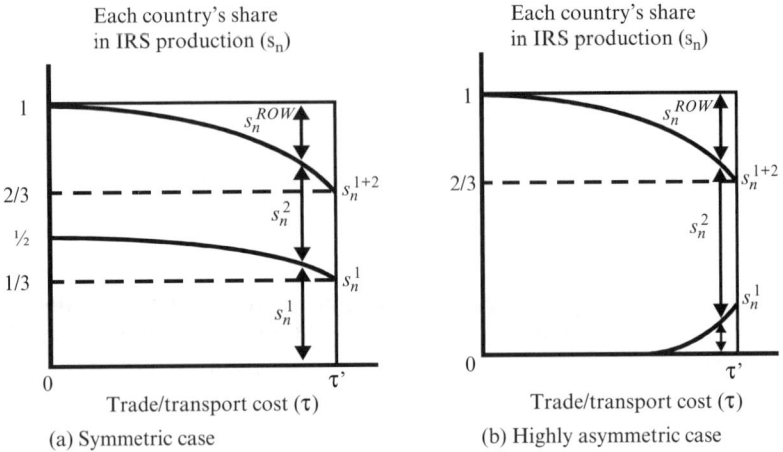

Each country's share   Each country's share
in IRS production (s_n)   in IRS production (s_n)

(a) Symmetric case   (b) Highly asymmetric case

Source: Drawn by authors based on Nishikimi (2008).

Figure 3.7   Trade/transport cost and production share

The two panels of Figure 3.7 depict the country shares of IRS industry (s^1, s^2, s^{ROW}) as a function of the intra-regional trade and transport cost, τ. Panel (*a*) shows the case where the three countries have identically sized economies (labor endowment). When trade and transport costs are all equal among the three countries (that is, $\tau=\tau'$), the three countries have identical conditions, and hence in equilibrium they have the same share of manufacturing industry (shown on the right side of panel (*a*)). As the trade and transport cost, τ, decreases in the process of economic integration, an increasing number of manufacturing firms relocate from ROW to Countries 1 and 2, because the transport facilitation within the integrated economy makes ROW relatively isolated and less attractive to global capital (due to HME). However, Countries 1 and 2 take equal shares in IRS production as they have identical conditions.[11] In this case, therefore, integration does not intensify the disparity between the integrated countries.

Integration may exacerbate the disparity between the integrated countries, in contrast, if these countries differ significantly in economic size. The right panel (*b*) of Figure 3.7 shows a case where Country 1 is much smaller than Country 2 in labor endowment and hence also IRS production, while maintaining all other assumptions the same as in the symmetric case of panel (*a*). As integration progresses (τ decreases), Country 1 loses its share of IRS manufacturing, whereas the integrated economy as a whole attracts more capital in the global market. Eventually, when $\tau = 0$, all IRS production agglomerates in Country 2. This striking result of the deindustrialization of small Country 1 is created by circular causations of HME – the large market in Country 2 attracts a large fraction of global capital, which, in turn, widens the variety of Country 2's IRS products and enlarges their market; note that the size of the home market reflects several properties of the country such as population and per capita income, which, in turn, relies on labor skill, technological level – all factors requiring relatively long periods for accumulation. If integration is carried out by widely diversified countries, the progress of integration may deprive small LDCs of their opportunities for industrial development through the straw effects noted above. In this sense, the economic integration of East Asian countries, which differ significantly in various aspects, should be carried out with special care to ensure inequality is not exacerbated.[12] Excessive expansion of economic inequality among the member countries may obstruct sustainable progress towards integration.

Furthermore, Nishikimi (2008) shows that liberalization of international trade may intensify economic disparity between domestic regions in cases where international trade takes place in particular regions equipped with ports. Trade liberalization improves the transport advantage of the port areas *vis-à-vis* inland regions, which encourages industrial agglomeration in coastal regions. Consequently, the inequalities between coastal and inland regions will expand in the process of economic integration.[13] Such a situation can be observed, especially in recent China, where the production share of eleven coastal provinces increased from 53.3% in 1990 to 61.3% in 2005, although these provinces occupy only 12.4% of the total land area of China.[14]

3.3.2 Development Strategy for LDCs

If some LDCs in the integrated countries suffer from a heavy burden of initial inequality, as discussed in the preceding section, it would be reasonable to enforce such policy measures that encourage their industrialization by filling the gaps in the initial conditions. Fujita and Mori (1996) examine the pattern of the evolution of industrial agglomeration and probe the possibility of industrialization policy by purposefully manipulating trade and transport costs. They show that the government of an LDC can foster a new cluster by increasing the international trade and transport cost, for example via trade barriers. Once the new cluster is established in that country, it then creates a lock-in effect and may remain at the same place even if the government rescinds the policy and lowers the trade cost to the previous level.[15]

However, Rodríguez-Clare (2007) cautions about the undervaluation of price distortion effects, which are caused by the strategic trade policies noted above. He argues that the agglomeration-luring policies to be enforced during the suspended period may well entail a substantial efficiency loss in resource allocation, especially for small developing countries, where the home market effect works only very weakly. In such cases, it is unrealistic to pursue the clustering potential of new industries.

Moreover, current LDCs face two important constraints on industrial policy that could have been neglected a few decades ago. These constraints are (1) shrinking policy space, and (2) the institutional capability of the state. These constraints are discussed below with particular reference to CLMV (Cambodia, Lao PDR, Myanmar, and Vietnam):

(1) Shrinking policy space

Since the late 1990s, economic reform in the less developed East Asian countries has been accelerated by their accession to the WTO and the establishment of FTAs. Myanmar, Cambodia and Vietnam joined the WTO in 1994, 2004 and 2007, respectively. Vietnam, Laos, Myanmar and Cambodia acceded to ASEAN in the second half of the 1990s. Unlike economic reform undertaken by countries at their own initiative, the forces establishing liberalization under the WTO and FTAs are formal and rule-based. Therefore, these rules are stringently enforced and policy space, which defines the range of policy choices available to member countries, is constrained accordingly. In such a context, the traditional debate concerning the efficacy of infant industry protection has become less relevant, as many of these policies are illegal under the rules of the WTO and FTAs (Bora et al., 2000; Sturgeon and Lester, 2004). Note that in addition to the ban on export promotion and import restrictions, the WTO, for example, does not allow member countries to support local suppliers through local content requirements under the TRIMs; reverse engineering and imitation have become less feasible under TRIP. Moreover, FTAs try to remove barriers related to the movement of goods, services, capital, and skilled labor across borders.

However, not all industrial policies are under these constraints. For example, active infrastructure development such as ports and economic corridors, as well as the establishment of special economic zones (SEZs) at strategically important locations, would serve as an effective measure to attract MNEs and participate in their production networks. Furthermore, latecomer countries are given additional time to open their markets; in particular, the deadline for CLMV to eliminate all tariffs under AFTA is 2015, which is five years later than that for the more advanced ASEAN countries. This time allowance may not be long enough to develop large-scale IRS industries from scratch, but it is a crucial time period to foster an existing industrial cluster to such an extent that it can exert significant lock-in effects.

(2) Institutional capability of the state

One of the important lessons learned from the public policy dispute in the 1990s was the importance of institutional capabilities. The World Bank (1993) concluded that appropriate industry-specific policy, such as directed credit, might have worked in the first-tier Asian newly industrialized economies (NIEs) – Korea and Taiwan – but the second-tier Asian NIEs – Thailand, Malaysia, and Indonesia – lacked the necessary state capabilities for active industrial policy, such as cohesive and autonomous bureaucracies and mechanisms for public and private sector consultation.[16] Thus, selective government intervention would do more harm than good there. This is because, if the state capability is too weak, selective government intervention, which gives government officials strong discretion over which industries are to be protected, may not work or may simply induce opportunistic behaviors, such as rent-seeking, and lead to allocation inefficiency. Thus, to prevent government intervention from becoming too costly, it was urged that the state's roles match its capability (World Bank, 1997); in other words, if the state capability is too weak, it should refrain from active industrial policies, especially industry-specific ones.

Although more efforts must be made to assess the state capabilities of the CLMV countries, it is still uncertain whether they are endowed with sufficiently strong institutional capabilities.[17]

In considering the efficacy of industrial policy, the above two constraints – shrinking policy space and weak state capability – are becoming increasingly important. In this respect, generic policies such as macroeconomic stability, labor market flexibility, the provision of general infrastructure (in particular transport and public utility infrastructure), free trade and open investment policies should be prioritized; in addition, building human capital and ensuring good governance (establishment of the rule of law, eradication of corruption, and so on) are particularly important to fill the initial gaps between the CLMV and other East Asian countries. These generic policies improve the overall business environment in the host country and provide the baseline for entry into production networks.

The second category of industrial policy involves measures which promote the agglomeration of specialized personnel, suppliers, and information spillover in specific industries so that industrial clusters become more competitive and sticky. These policy measures include generous tax incentives and business facilitation for specific industries, building sophisticated physical infrastructures, providing access to capital, upgrading the industry-specific skills and capacities of local suppliers, and active R&D promotion in specific industries.

These policy measures are highly selective in targeting specific industries and require greater institutional resources. It is thus more practical for the less developed Southeast Asian countries to focus on generic policies. Subsequently, as the industry becomes more mature and upgraded – and if, at the same time, the institutional capability of the state grows sufficiently – measures that promote the industrial clustering of specific industries may become more relevant.

3.4   CONCLUDING REMARKS

Under the influence of agglomeration economies, the leaders of the integrated countries often encounter a tradeoff between efficiency and equity, because the thorough pursuit of overall production efficiency may intensify the disparity between countries. In such cases, some policy coordination may be necessary to avoid conflicts of interest among the integrated countries. Southeast Asian countries have devised a coordination mechanism where the MNEs play a central role.

In particular, due attention must be paid to the initial unfavorable conditions of LDCs. The progress of integration may deprive small LDCs of the opportunities to develop IRS industries through the straw effect. Thus the governments of LDCs must elaborate their development strategies, taking special notice of the attributes of agglomeration economies; in particular, attention must be paid to circular causations of agglomeration economies which may create a huge magnification effect, and the long-run progress of industrialization and cluster formation can be triggered by the success of short-run or temporary policy programs to invite a critical magnitude of IRS industries.

In this regard, infrastructure development for transportation and telecommunication network facilities – as well as other policy measures to improve the investment climate – should be further prioritized as essential measures to attract industrial firms to their countries. This kind of generic policy may lure the 'concentrated dispersing' industries if it sets up a good access to the saturating agglomeration in neighboring countries or regions.

Furthermore, if these facilities successfully attract a significant number of firms or plants, it may lead to the creation of a transport hub. The latter then provides a source for the further agglomeration of industries, including IRS industries. Such an industrial upgrade strategy may provide a realistic scheme of industrial development for LDCs in East Asia, where the limited size of the home market may result in an initial difficulty in luring IRS industries.

At the same time, the LDCs must fully utilize their time frame to liberalize their economies, so that existing IRS industries can develop the agglomeration force to the extent that they can exert a significant lock-in effect.

NOTES

1. More generally, the total number of I-variety produced in each country should also be endogenously determined in a framework of general equilibrium. Venables (1996), Puga (1999) and Amiti (2005), for example, analyze such cases by constructing a vertical linkage model of agglomeration economies on the basis of Dixit-Stiglitz's framework and obtain similar results to ours.
2. To be strict, in order that a process of agglomeration of M-sector results in a wage rise, there has to be a sector with diminishing returns, such as the agricultural sector in Puga (1999)'s model.
3. This occurs if most of the M-products in Countries 1 and 2 are exported to the world market, which is sufficiently large, comparing to the M-production in the two countries. Puga (1999) and Amiti (2005) examine more general cases where the prices of M and I change, reflecting factor prices and transport costs.
4. For details of individual sources of agglomeration economies, see Section 2.3.
5. This process of fragmentation or concentrated dispersion brings about an evolution of the industrial structure of the agglomeration core as well. For example, the core area releases labor/land intensive activities and attracts more knowledge intensive R&D activities instead.
6. It should be noted that this problem may occur in the process of concentrated dispersion as well. 'Concentrated dispersing' firms or plants also tend to be clustered in a limited number of new sites, so that the central or local governments of the potential sites likely encounter keen competition for luring them.
7. The section on the policy coordination in ASEAN and the BBC scheme is based on Shimizu (1998).
8. This scheme was called the ASEAN Industrial Project (AIP). Under the AIP, only two urea (fertilizer) projects were carried out in Indonesia and Malaysia, but neither of them was a business success (Shimizu 1998).
9. This scheme was called the ASEAN Industrial Complementation (AIC). Under the AIC, Thailand, for example, was given exclusive privileges for manufacturing body panels for commercial vehicles (1 ton and above) and brake drums for trucks for a certain period of time. Similarly, other ASEAN countries were given privileges for manufacturing specific automobile parts, and were able to sell their products to each other at preferential tariff rates under the PTA.
10. Note that, as shown in Box 2.1, the local content of the automobile industry was high and continued to increase in many East Asian countries. However, some key parts – most notably engines and transmissions – were produced more efficiently by concentrating production within the region, because (1) these parts are subject to prominent economies of scale, and (2) the market size of each ASEAN country was not large enough for them. As a result of the concentration of production and intra-regional trading of key parts – which was facilitated by the BBC scheme, the AICO scheme, and AFTA – the automobile production network expanded regionally within ASEAN in the 1990s (see Figure 1.10 (b) in Chapter 1).

11. If three countries have identical labor endowment, the integrated economy always achieves a concentrated dispersion equilibrium because the model assumes sufficient agglomeration diseconomies. See Nishikimi (2008) and Baldwin et al. (2003) for details.

12. Among East Asian countries, to date, the inequality in GDP per capita has not shown an expanding tendency, largely due to China's and Vietnam's remarkable catch-up. The East Asian LDCs, such as Cambodia and Laos, have also significantly grown by attracting CRS industries including apparel and footwear manufacturing. By contrast, in EU-15, where most countries had already achieved a per capita GDP above US$10,000 by 1990, significant expansions of inequality have been observed – the variation coefficient of per capita GDP increased from 0.33 in 1990 to 0.38 in 2005; the max/min ratio from 4.03 to 4.09; the Herfindahl index from 0.074 to 0.076.

13. If each integrated country has a geographical composition as discussed in the text (accessible coastal and remote inland areas), integration leads to the formation of a coastal industrial belt running along countries and possibly narrowing disparity among them, while intensifying the inequality of their domestic regions. See Chapter 15 for details.

14. The eleven provinces are Beijing, Tianjin, Hebei, Shanxi, Liaoning, Shanghai, Jiangsu, Zhejiang, Shandong, Fujian and Guangdong. Chapter 15 of this volume discusses the disparity effects of economic integration more closely.

15. These kinds of policies sometimes work effectively in nurturing infant industries.

16. McKendrick et al. (2000) argue that these two sets of related institutions are important for the successful implementation of industrial policy. The bureaucracies must be cohesive and autonomous in order to avoid political intervention, especially from interest groups. The mechanism for public and private sector consultation is helpful for the government to gather information about the industry. However, it is difficult to identify correctly the current situation of the industry, and identical policies in seemingly similar situations can lead to completely different results. In particular, policy making with superficial information may lead to negative results.

17. For example, Ohno (2003) argues that Vietnam lacks the state capability for industrial policy and has made recommendations for institutional reform in the government sector.

REFERENCES

Amiti, Mary (2005), 'Location of vertically linked industries: agglomeration versus comparative advantage', *European Economic Review*, **49**, 809–32.

Baldwin, Richard E., Rikard Forslid, Philippe Martin, Gianmarco I.P. Ottaviano and Frédéric Robert-Nicoud (2003), *Economic Geography and Public Policy*, Princeton: Princeton University Press.

Bora, Bijit, Peter J. Lloyd and Mari Pangestu (2000), 'Industrial policy and the WTO', Policy Issues in International Trade and Commodities Studies Series No. 6, United Nations Conference on Trade and Development, Geneva.

Fujita, Masahisa and Tomoya Mori (1996), 'The role of ports in the making of major cities: self-agglomeration and hub-effect', *Journal of Development Economics*, **49**, 93–120.

McKendrick, David G; Richard F. Donner and Stephan Haggard (2000), *From Silicon Valley to Singapore: Location and Competitive Advantage in the Hard Disk Drive Industry*, Stanford: Stanford University Press.

Nishikimi, Koji (2008), 'Specialization and agglomeration forces of economic integration', Chapter 3 in Masahisa Fujita, Satoru Kumagai and Koji

Nishikimi (eds), *Economic Integration in East Asia: Perspectives from Spatial and Neoclassical Economics*, Cheltenham, UK and Northampton, MA, USA: Edward Elgar.

Ohno, Kenichi (2003), 'Vietnam's industrialization strategy in the age of globalization', http://www.grips.ac.jp/module/vietnam/main_en.pdf (accessed on 20 February 2008).

Puga, Diego (1999), 'The rise and fall of regional inequality', *European Economic Review*, **43**, 303–34.

Rodríguez-Clare, Andrés (2007), 'Clusters and comparative advantage: implications for industrial policy', *Journal of Development Economics*, **82**, 43–57.

Shimizu, Kazushi (1998), *Political Economy of Intra-ASEAN Economic Cooperation* (in Japanese ASEAN Ikinai Keizai Kyouryoku no Seiji Keizaigaku), Kyoto: Minerva Shobo.

Sturgeon, Timothy and Richard Lester (2004), 'The new global supply-base: new challenges for local suppliers in East Asia', in Shahid Yusuf, M. Anjum Altaf and Kaoru Nabeshima (eds), *Global Production Networking and Technological Change in East Asia*, Washington DC: Oxford University Press.

Venables, Anthony (1996), 'Equilibrium location of vertically linked industries', *International Economic Review*, **37**, 341–59.

World Bank (1993), *The East Asian Miracle: Economic Growth and Public Policy*, New York: Oxford University Press.

World Bank (1997), *World Development Report 1997: The State in a Changing World*, Washington DC: World Bank.

PART II

Integration (1): Production Networks and Innovation

4. International production/ distribution networks in East Asia

Mitsuyo Ando

4.1 INTRODUCTION

The formation of international production/distribution networks in East Asia, with extensive promotion of foreign direct investment (FDI), is an important phenomenon (see Box 4.1). The very recent and rapid development of production networks since the 1990s undermines, or at least partially nullifies, the applicability of a wide range of traditional theories and practical thought. In the context of international trade theory, the pattern of industry-wide location of production and international trade in East Asia no longer follows the typical North-South division of labor, which is explained by traditional comparative advantage theories such as the Ricardian and Heckscher–Ohlin models. International division of labor in terms of production processes (that is, fragmentation of production[1,2] (see Box 4.2)), rather than of industry level, has explosively developed in the region, particularly in machinery industries,[3] while European-type horizontal intra-industry trade has rarely emerged heretofore.[4]

International production/distribution networks have been formed in other regions in the world as well. The production networks observed mainly in machinery industries in East Asia, however, are distinctive in (i) their significance in the regional economy, (ii) their geographical extensiveness involving many countries at different income levels, and (iii) their sophistication in both intra-firm and arm's length (inter-firm) relationships (Ando and Kimura 2005).

More specifically, first and foremost, production networks have already become a substantial component of each country's economy in the Asian region.[5] No longer can each country's manufacturing activities and international trade be discussed without considering the existence of production networks.

Secondly, production networks involve a large number of countries with various income levels in the region, in contrast to networks between specific countries or between a developed country and a developing country in geographical proximity. The latter type of production network includes those in the US–Mexico nexus and those in the WE (Western Europe) – CEE (Central and Eastern Europe) nexus.[6] Cross-country differences in factor prices and other location advantages seem to be effectively utilized in the formation of vertical production chains spread out in the region (see Figure 4.1 for an illustration of typical East Asian and US–Mexico (maquila) operations).

BOX 4.1   ECONOMIC GROWTH AND MANUFACTURING COMPETITIVENESS

East Asia consists of countries at different income levels, and each of the East Asian countries has attained high economic growth (Box Table 4.1). Annual growth rates of per capita GDP in the period between 1985 and 2003, for instance, range from 3% to 8%, except in Japan and the Philippines. In the course of their economic growth, East Asian countries significantly enhanced manufacturing competitiveness. Box Table 4.2 provides the competitive industrial performance (CIP) index compiled by the United Nations Industrial Development Organization (UNIDO). The CIP index measures the ability of countries to competitively produce and export manufactured goods, based on four different aspects of competitive performance. Clearly, East Asian countries have strengthened manufacturing competitiveness since 1985, and their component indices of the CIP index are higher than the sample average in most cases.

As a comparison, we use Latin America, as Latin American countries had income levels similar to those in East Asia in the mid-1980s. Their annual per capita GDP growth rates are less than 2%, except for Chile and Costa Rica, and their manufacturing competitiveness has also stagnated or even deteriorated. Although countries in both regions had similar income levels in 1985, Latin American countries' ranking in terms of manufacturing competitiveness in 2003 lagged far behind countries in East Asia. Why has East Asia successfully continued to achieve high performance and to improve its manufacturing competitiveness so rapidly, and why have other regions such as Latin America failed to do so? One of the key elements contributing to East Asia's performance in the last decade or so has been the effective development and utilization of international production/distribution networks.

Box Table 4.1   *GDP per capita in East Asia and Latin America (constant 2000, US$)*

		GDP per capita		Annual growth (%)
		1985	2003	1985–2003
East Asia	Vietnam	202	473	4.8
	China	290	1209	8.3
	Indonesia	474	872	3.4
	Philippines	821	1043	1.3
	Thailand	956	2277	4.9
	Malaysia	2081	4033	3.7
	Korea, Rep.	4386	12245	5.9
	Singapore	10866	23619	4.4
	Hong Kong	14544	26362	3.4
	Japan	27012	37227	1.8
Latin America	Bolivia	872	1017	0.9
	Honduras	1042	1205	0.8
	Ecuador	1280	1420	0.6
	El Salvador	1585	2157	1.7
	Colombia	1627	2060	1.3
	Peru	2035	2190	0.4
	Jamaica	2246	3228	2.0
	Chile	2432	5215	4.3
	Costa Rica	2772	4225	2.4
	Brazil	3355	3733	0.6
	Panama	3371	3992	0.9
	Uruguay	4219	5495	1.5
	Venezuela	4801	3966	−1.1
	Mexico	5040	5872	0.9
	Argentina	6156	6932	0.7

Source: Data from World Bank (2009).

Box Table 4.2   Competitive Industrial Performance (CIP) index and its component indices

Country	CIP index					
	Rank			Index		
	2003	1993	1985	2003	1993	1985
East Asia						
China	27	28	61	**0.41**	**0.34**	0.02
Hong Kong	13	6	18	**0.53**	**0.58**	0.32
Indonesia	47	60	65	0.26	0.22	0.01
Japan	4	3	2	**0.72**	**0.74**	0.73
Korea, Rep.	9	17	22	**0.59**	**0.48**	0.25
Malaysia	19	20	30	**0.47**	**0.46**	0.12
Philippines	32	44	45	**0.40**	**0.27**	0.04
Singapore	1	1	6	**0.90**	**0.84**	0.59
Taiwan	10	10	19	**0.54**	**0.51**	0.29
Thailand	28	32	43	**0.41**	**0.32**	0.06
Vietnam	72	. . .	. . .	0.19	. . .	. . .
Latin America						
Argentina	60	42	29	0.23	0.27	0.12
Bolivia	99	87	69	0.10	0.11	0.01
Brazil	42	27	27	**0.29**	**0.34**	0.14
Chile	65	66	53	0.21	0.20	0.03
Colombia	82	63	49	0.17	0.21	0.04
Costa Rica	39	69	44	**0.31**	0.19	0.05
Ecuador	106	90	58	0.09	0.11	0.03
El Salvador	57	53	57	0.25	0.24	0.03
Honduras	94	93	66	0.13	0.08	0.01
Jamaica	77	68	52	0.18	0.20	0.03
Mexico	31	25	28	**0.40**	**0.39**	0.13
Panama	104	88	51	0.10	0.11	0.03
Peru	85	71	48	0.16	0.18	0.04
Uruguay	70	45	42	0.20	0.26	0.06
Venezuela	95	74	35	0.12	0.16	0.09
# of samples/ sample average	120	100		0.28	0.28	

Note: Indices higher than the sample average are highlighted in bold.

Source: Data from UNIDO (2009).

| Component indices of CIP index | | | | | | | |
| Manufacturing value added per capita index | | Manufactured exports per capita index | | Industrialization intensity index | | Industrial export quality index | |
2003	1993	2003	1993	2003	1993	2003	1993
0.04	0.02	0.01	0.00	0.80	0.74	0.81	0.60
0.13	0.18	0.89	1.00	0.25	0.39	0.86	0.74
0.03	0.02	0.01	0.01	0.51	0.48	0.52	0.37
1.00	1.00	0.10	0.13	0.78	0.83	1.00	1.00
0.42	0.25	0.11	0.08	0.87	0.76	0.96	0.81
0.14	0.10	0.11	0.09	0.76	0.85	0.89	0.78
0.02	0.02	0.01	0.00	0.57	0.54	0.99	0.49
0.61	0.50	1.00	0.97	1.00	1.00	0.97	0.90
0.39	0.31	0.17	0.18	0.70	0.75	0.91	0.80
0.10	0.08	0.03	0.03	0.68	0.51	0.81	0.67
0.01	0.00	0.00	...	0.35	...	0.41	...
0.11	0.14	0.01	0.01	0.35	0.46	0.46	0.47
0.01	0.01	0.00	0.00	0.14	0.16	0.26	0.27
0.08	0.09	0.01	0.01	0.46	0.69	0.61	0.59
0.09	0.07	0.03	0.02	0.33	0.34	0.39	0.38
0.03	0.05	0.00	0.00	0.31	0.52	0.34	0.27
0.08	0.07	0.03	0.01	0.36	0.42	0.75	0.27
0.02	0.03	0.00	0.00	0.15	0.26	0.20	0.15
0.04	0.03	0.00	0.00	0.40	0.51	0.54	0.41
0.01	0.01	0.00	0.00	0.19	0.19	0.34	0.13
0.03	0.04	0.01	0.02	0.22	0.32	0.45	0.41
0.07	0.07	0.04	0.02	0.60	0.64	0.90	0.83
0.02	0.03	0.00	0.01	0.07	0.15	0.29	0.26
0.03	0.03	0.01	0.01	0.24	0.29	0.38	0.39
0.08	0.12	0.02	0.02	0.24	0.40	0.46	0.51
0.04	0.05	0.00	0.02	0.25	0.35	0.20	0.24
0.14	0.13	0.08	0.08	0.33	0.39	0.54	0.49

BOX 4.2   TWO-DIMENSIONAL FRAGMENTATION AND ITS COST STRUCTURE

A two-dimensional framework of fragmentation and its cost structure, built on the insights of Jones and Kierzkowski (1990, 2001),
is useful in thinking of fragmentation at the country level and the
firm level together (Kimura and Ando 2005b). One axis represents
(geographical) distance between the original position before fragmentation and the new location of the fragmented production
block (Box Figure 4.1). The fragmentation is domestic when the
distance is within the national border and is cross-border/
international fragmentation when beyond the national border. The
other axis measures the degree of integration/disintegration in
terms of consolidated production; intra-firm production is at the
lower end of the axis, shifting increasingly to arm's length production toward the top. When a fragmented production block is within
the boundary of a firm, it is intra-firm fragmentation. Once it is
beyond the boundary of a firm, the relationship becomes arm's

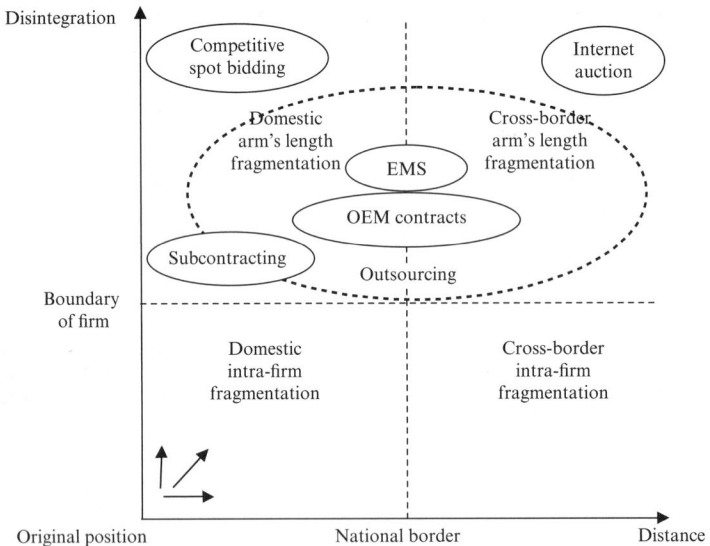

Source: Kimura and Ando (2005b).

Box Figure 4.1   Fragmentation in a two-dimensional space

length (that is, arm's length fragmentation). To put it simply, four patterns of fragmentation emerge: domestic intra-firm fragmentation, domestic arm's length fragmentation, cross-border intra-firm fragmentation, and cross-border arm's length fragmentation.

Box Table 4.3 summarizes the cost structure of two-dimensional fragmentation. The key for fragmentation, regardless of the type of fragmentation, is reduction of the costs of service links connecting fragmented production blocks. Fragmentation occurs when the service link costs are sufficiently low so as to make the total costs (production costs plus the service link costs) lower than otherwise.

Box Table 4.3   Tradeoffs in two-dimensional fragmentation

	Service link cost connecting production blocks	Production cost per se in production blocks
Fragmentation along the distance axis	*Cost due to geographical distance:* Elements (examples): transportation, telecommunications, inefficiency in distribution, trade impediments, coordination cost	*Cost reduction from location advantages:* Elements (examples): wage level, access to resources, infrastructure service inputs such as electricity, water, and industrial estates, technological capability
Fragmentation along the disintegration axis	*Transaction cost due to losing controllability:* Elements (examples): information gathering cost on potential business partners, monitoring cost, risks on the stability of contracts, immature dispute settlement mechanisms, other deficiencies in the legal system and economic institutions	*Cost reduction from (dis)internalization:* Elements (examples): availability of various types of potential business partners including foreign and indigenous firms, development of supporting industry, institutional capacity for various types of contracts, degree of incomplete information

Source: Kimura and Ando (2005b).

The process of movement up along the axis is affected significantly by the extent of industrial clustering and agglomeration (see Fujita et al. 1999 for agglomeration). One channel for the connection between fragmentation and agglomeration comes from the increasing-returns nature of service links. Service links typically have strong economies of scale so that production blocks fragmented by many firms tend to locate in certain specific places where service link costs are low. Another channel is to use arm's length fragmentation inside agglomeration. Some transactions such as procurement of customized parts and components require frequent spec changes and exact delivery timing, and thus upstream and downstream firms should locate nearby. Once the critical mass of agglomeration is formed, it becomes one of the important elements of location advantages for individual firms considering fragmentation along the distance axis. At the same time, the existence of various kinds of potential business partners generates opportunities for fragmentation along the disintegration axis. Such sophisticated networks in turn provide opportunities for indigenous firms to penetrate into production networks developed by MNEs once they gain competitiveness.

Thirdly, production networks construct efficient intra-firm and arm's length relationships that include different firm nationalities. Multinational enterprises (MNEs) as well as indigenous firms in each country appear to be forming sophisticated inter-firm relationships.

This chapter focuses on international production/distribution networks in East Asia and presents evidence concerning their features and mechanisms from both disaggregated international trade data and micro-data at the firm level.[7] The remainder of this chapter is organized as follows. Section 4.2 delineates some features of production networks in East Asia, using disaggregated international trade data. Section 4.3 presents further evidence using micro-data of MNEs, that is, Japanese firms and US firms in East Asia. Section 4.4 discusses the policy implications.

4.2   DEVELOPMENT OF INTERNATIONAL TRADE IN EAST ASIA

Machinery trade comprises a significant portion of East Asian trade. Figure 4.2 presents the share of machinery goods in total exports to

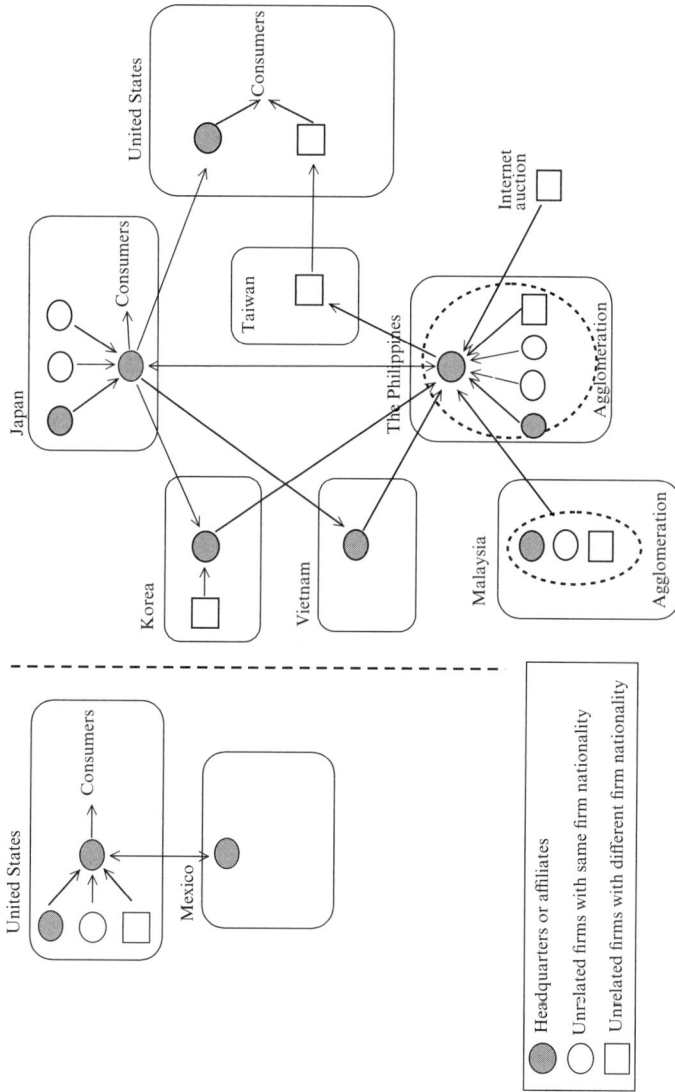

United States

Consumers

Japan

Consumers

Taiwan

The Philippines

Internet auction

Agglomeration

Korea

Vietnam

Malaysia

Agglomeration

United States

Consumers

Mexico

● Headquarters or affiliates
○ Unrelated firms with same firm nationality
□ Unrelated firms with different firm nationality

Source: Prepared by author, based on Ando and Kimura (2009).

Figure 4.1 Typical East Asian operations and maquila operations: an illustration

101

(a) In the early 1990s

2005
1990

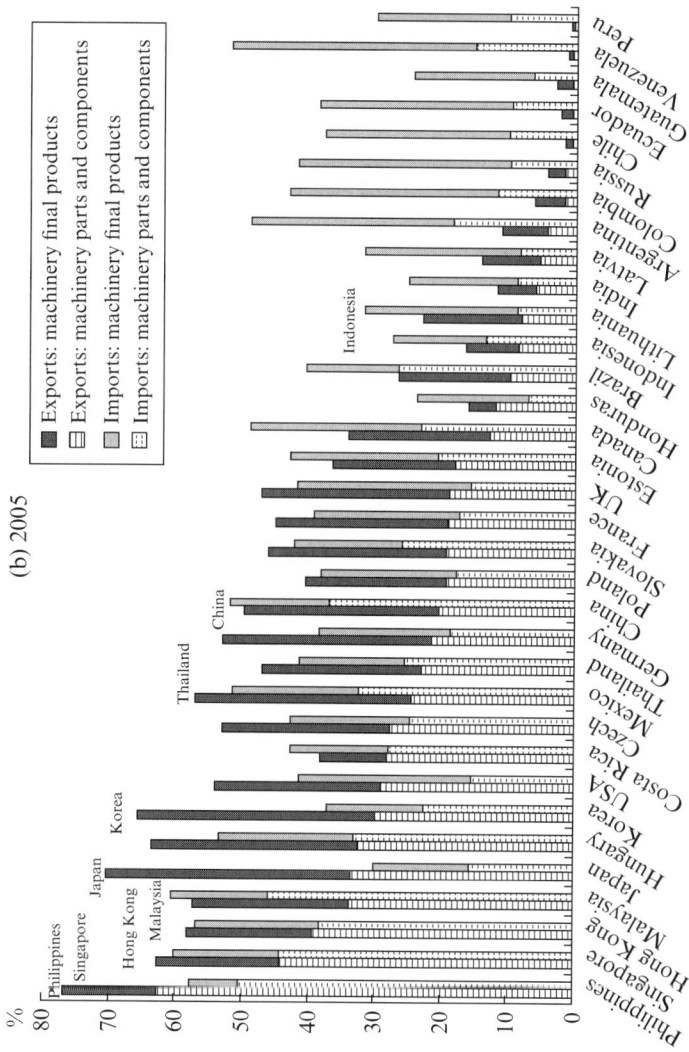

(b) 2005

Exports: machinery final products
Exports: machinery parts and components
Imports: machinery final products
Imports: machinery parts and components

Source: Author's calculation, based on UN Comtrade.

Figure 4.2 Machinery final products and parts and components: shares in total exports and imports

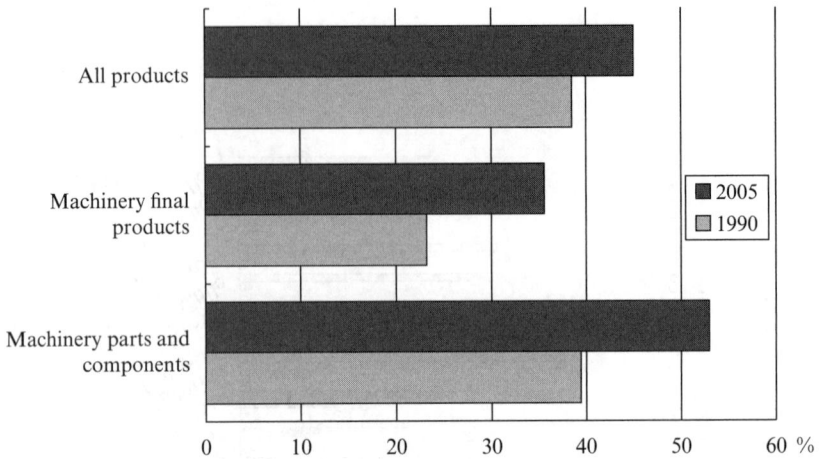

Source: Author's calculation, based on UN Comtrade.

Figure 4.3   Intra-regional export ratios in East Asia in 1990 and 2005

and imports from the world in the early 1990s (Figure 4.2a) and in 2005 (Figure 4.2b), with a distinction between machinery final products and parts and components.[8] The figure plots countries from highest to lowest export share of machinery parts and components in order to address the relative significance of machinery intermediate goods trade. In the early 1990s, most countries displaying high export shares of machinery parts and components were developed countries. In 2005, however, a number of East Asian developing countries surpassed the developed countries and stood on the left hand side. As a result, the share of machinery in total exports exceeds 50% in most East Asian countries, with the highest ratio, at close to 80%, seen in the Philippines, and the share of machinery parts and components lies roughly around 20% to 60%. The figure confirms how significant machinery industries are for each East Asian economy.

Moreover, not only exports but also imports are composed of a high share of machinery parts and components, and the shares of both were much higher in 2005 than in the early 1990s. These facts suggest the existence of active and dramatically expanding vertical back-and-forth transactions through the fragmentation of production (see Box 4.2).

A large portion of the above-mentioned machinery parts and components trade in East Asia is intra-regional (Figure 4.3). When intra-regional export shares in 1990 are compared with those in 2005, one can observe a rapid expansion of intra-regional trade particularly for machinery parts and components. The intra-regional export share was 53% in 2005, having risen from less than 40% in 1990. Considering that intra-regional export values of machinery parts and components in 2005 were 6.4 times those of 1990 in real terms, the increased intra-regional export share demonstrates how explosively and rapidly vertical back-and-forth transactions of machinery parts and components proliferated throughout the region (see Box 4.3).

Interestingly, East Asia is also gaining a position as a destination of machinery final goods. The intra-regional share for machinery final goods is still much lower than that for machinery parts and components. The portion, however, has grown from 23% to 36%. This indicates the increasing importance of East Asia as a destination of final goods, in addition to the region's importance as a manufacturing factory for the world, probably due to the increase in demand occurring concurrently with regional economic growth.

A rapid increase in intra-regional trade of machinery parts and components notably contributes to intra-regional export growth. In the period from 1990 to 2005, intra-regional exports in East Asia expanded by 3.5 times compared to 1990 (Figure 4.4). The increases in intra-regional exports of machinery parts and components and of final products explain 41% and 24% of that growth, respectively. In other words, the expanding machinery trade produced more than 60% of the intra-East Asian export growth. Corresponding figures for machinery parts and components (machinery goods including intermediate goods) are 15% (64%) for China, 42% (58%) for ASEAN4 (Indonesia, Malaysia, the Philippines, and Thailand), 56% (71%) for NIES3 (newly industrializing economies (Hong Kong, Korea, and Singapore), and 47% (58%) for Japan. Clearly, machinery trade, particularly machinery intermediate trade, is a major contributor to the development of intra-East Asian trade.

In the process of trade expansion within the region, East Asian countries have strengthened intra-regional trade relationships by increasing trade with countries that were less important trading partners in the past. Table 4.1 presents by-destination intra-East Asian export shares of China, ASEAN4, NIES3, and Japan in 1990 and 2005. As the table shows, trade relationships with China and ASEAN countries (or among ASEAN countries) in particular have intensified among East Asian countries. In particular, destination patterns of machinery parts and components significantly changed; for instance, China's shares rose from 0% to 13% for ASEAN4, from 32% to 54% for NIES3, and from 5% to 34% for Japan. Similarly, ASEAN4's shares went up from 5% to 13% for China and from 8% to 18% for ASEAN4.

BOX 4.3   A DRASTIC EXPANSION OF VERTICAL
           PARTS AND COMPONENTS TRADE IN
           EAST ASIA

Box Figure 4.2 decomposes machinery trade (exports plus imports) in 1990 and 2000 into one-way trade (inter-industry trade), vertical intra-industry, and horizontal intra-industry trade, with a distinction of machinery parts and components from machinery final products. This figure is based on the results of the following decomposition: first, export values are compared with import values for each commodity at the finely disaggregated (HS six-digit) level, and commodities with more than 10 times differences are classified into one-way trade and the remainder into intra-industry trade. Then, for commodities categorized into intra-industry trade, export-import unit price ratios are calculated to divide them into vertical intra-industry trade (with export-import unit price ratios more than a certain criterion) and horizontal intra-industry trade (with export-import unit price ratios less than that criterion).

In the 1990s, vertical transactions, particularly vertical back-and-forth transactions of parts and components in vertically fragmented production processes across borders, rather than the trade of quality-differentiated commodities, were greatly expanded

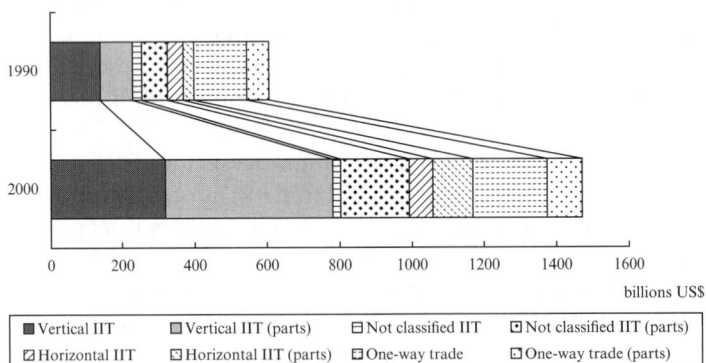

0	200	400	600	800	1000	1200	1400	1600

billions US$

■ Vertical IIT	⊞ Vertical IIT (parts)	⊟ Not classified IIT	⊡ Not classified IIT (parts)
▨ Horizontal IIT	⊠ Horizontal IIT (parts)	▢ One-way trade	▢ One-way trade (parts)

Source: Data prepared by author, based on Ando (2006).

*Box Figure 4.2   Vertical transactions of machinery parts and
                   components for East Asia*

in East Asia. Active division of labor at the production process level has stepped into the formation of international production networks in the region.

Such a trend is salient for the electric machinery sector. In the transportation equipment sector, one-way trade is still the main pattern of trade in the whole sector due to import substitution policies in many developing countries. Even in this sector, however, vigorous vertical transactions of parts and components across borders were observed in 2000, whereas they were seldom found in 1990. See Ando (2006) for the details and a discussion on changes in East Asian trade structure in the 1990s.

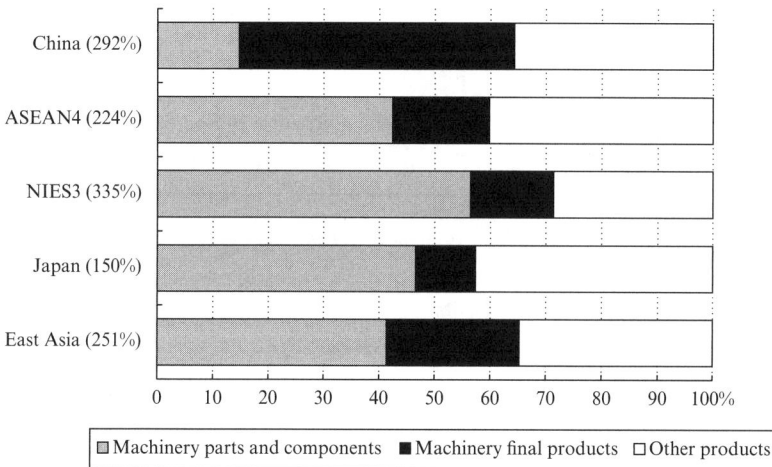

Notes: Figures in parentheses are growth rates during the period. Growth rates are on a real basis, using the US wholesale price index.

Source: Author's calculation, based on UN Comtrade.

Figure 4.4   Contribution to intra-regional export growth in 1990–2005

NIES's shares for China are outstandingly high, largely due to its heavy transactions with Hong Kong. Nonetheless, they are tending to decline. Combined with high growth rates of intra-regional trade (shown in Figure 4.3), all of these facts suggest that East Asian countries have rapidly intensified intra-regional trade activities involving various

Table 4.1   Intra East Asian exports, by destination: 1990 and 2005 (%)

Export from	to	Machinery parts and components		Machinery final goods		All products	
		1990	2005	1990	2005	1990	2005
China	ASEAN4	5	13	3	9	4	11
	NIES3	88	64	94	69	75	60
	Japan	7	24	4	22	21	29
ASEAN4	China	0	13	1	16	4	15
	ASEAN4	8	18	9	19	8	19
	NIES3	69	49	68	38	39	39
	Japan	24	21	22	27	49	28
NIES3	China	32	54	30	43	30	50
	ASEAN4	28	20	26	23	25	22
	NIES3	21	17	25	18	18	15
	Japan	19	9	19	16	27	12
Japan	China	5	34	8	32	9	34
	ASEAN4	35	26	33	21	32	23
	NIES3	60	40	59	47	59	43

Note: Figures represent the share in total intra-regional trade of an exporting country/ region for machinery parts and components, machinery final goods, or all products.

Source: Data from Author's calculation, based on UN Comtrade.

countries in the region more actively than before, rather than intensifying trade relationships with specific countries in the region such as Hong Kong or Japan.[9]

In regions other than East Asia, in contrast, higher shares of machinery trade and higher shares of machinery parts and components trade in total trade are observed for some specific countries such as the US, Mexico, Germany, France, Hungary, Czech Republic, Poland, and Slovakia (Figure 4.2). This suggests the development of production networks in machinery industries between the US and Mexico and between UK/Germany and CEE countries, but these networks do not extensively cover numerous countries in regions such as the networks in East Asia do.[10] Other countries, particularly those in Latin America (except Mexico) are found on the right hand side with far lower shares of machinery exports. In addition, the shares of machinery exports are much lower than those of imports, suggesting import-substituting operations.

Table 4.2   Sectoral composition of Japanese and US parent firms and their affiliates (%)

Industry	Shares in all industries		Shares of non-sector switching affiliates
	Number of parent firms	Number of affiliates	
Japanese all-sized parent firms investing in East Asia			
Manufacturing	**68**	**62**	**75**
Machinery (total)	34	33	73
Japanese parent firms of SMEs investing in East Asia			
Manufacturing	**65**	**60**	**87**
Machinery (total)	29	27	85
US all-sized parent firms investing in the world			
Manufacturing	**52**	**36**	
Machinery (total)	22	13	

Note: Data for Japanese and US firms are in 2000 and 1999, respectively. Shares of non-sector switching affiliates are shares of manufacturing/machinery affiliates in all affiliates in East Asia of manufacturing/machinery parent firms.

Source: Author's preparation, based on Ando et al. (2008).

4.3   DEVELOPMENT OF INTRA-REGIONAL TRANSACTIONS IN EAST ASIA AT THE FIRM LEVEL

In East Asia, effective and aggressive utilization of FDI has played a crucial role in the dramatic changes in the trade structure in the last decade or so, as described in the previous section. To shed light on features of production networks in East Asia from the viewpoint of MNEs, this section investigates Japanese and US firms' activities in East Asia by using micro data at the firm level.

Japanese manufacturing parent firms, particularly machinery parent firms, are active investors in East Asia; almost 70% of the Japanese firms with affiliates in East Asia were categorized in the manufacturing sector, and half of them were in the machinery sector in 2000 (Table 4.2). Moreover, Japanese manufacturing affiliates, regardless of the industries of their parent firms, account for over 60% of the total Japanese affiliates in the region. Clearly, manufacturing activities are dominant in East Asia in terms of both Japanese parent firms and their affiliates.

A parent firm often conducts various types of operations and establishes foreign affiliates in order to conduct subsets of those activities. Among the affiliates in East Asia of Japanese manufacturing parent firms, 75% are manufacturing affiliates (Table 4.2). That is to say, manufacturing parent firms have many affiliates in the manufacturing sector. The corresponding portion is even higher for small- and medium-sized enterprises (SMEs) engaged in manufacturing; 87% of affiliates in the region of Japanese manufacturing SMEs are engaged in manufacturing.[11] Such an investment pattern (manufacturing investment by manufacturing firms) reflects a typical strategy for firms involved in manufacturing activities, a strategy which is aimed at supplying intermediate goods for other firms and/or for their own affiliates – that is, a sort of 'vertical FDI'. Large-scale manufacturing activities by Japanese firms, particularly with active FDI by Japanese SMEs, are one of the essential components of production networking in East Asia (see Box 4.4).

US firms are in general more active in FDI in non-manufacturing, mainly in services sectors, than Japanese firms: the manufacturing (machinery) share in terms of the number of parent firms was 52% (22%) in 1999 (Table 4.2). Moreover, foreign affiliates of US firms intensively concentrate on non-manufacturing sectors; the manufacturing (machinery) share is as low as 36% (13%).

In East Asia, however, manufacturing activities in terms of sales, particularly in machinery sectors, are dominant not only among Japanese affiliates but also among US affiliates in the region. The manufacturing (machinery) share was 59% (45%) in 2004 for Japanese affiliates and 46% (30%) in 2003 for US affiliates in East Asia (Table 4.3). The corresponding shares become even higher for Japanese and US affiliates in East Asia, excluding Hong Kong (and Singapore for US affiliates) where sales by non-manufacturing affiliates are fairly large: the manufacturing (machinery) share is 65% (48%) for Japanese affiliates and 57% (39%) for US affiliates. These figures suggest that manufacturing activities by both Japanese and US firms, particularly in machinery sectors, are quite intensive in East Asia, reflecting the features of East Asian countries as host countries, although in general foreign affiliates of US firms operate more intensively in non-manufacturing sectors.

Given that Japanese and US firms' major activities in East Asia are manufacturing activities mainly in machinery sectors, let us look at their transactions within East Asia in the manufacturing/machinery sectors. Table 4.4 presents shares of (a) by-destination sales in total sales and those of (b) by-origin purchases in total purchases by Japanese machinery affiliates in East Asia (total), NIES4 (NIES3 plus Taiwan), ASEAN4, and China, with a distinction between intra-firm transactions and arm's length transactions at each destination/origin. Two interesting insights emerge.

BOX 4.4 PRODUCTION NETWORKS IN EAST ASIA AND DOMESTIC OPERATIONS IN JAPAN

The journalistic literature often claims that the globalization of corporate activities, particularly the expansion of operations in developing countries, reduces domestic corporate activities and domestic employment in the home country. However, even in the case in which FDI is pursuing inexpensive labor in developing countries, the effect of FDI on domestic operations is not necessarily negative; it depends on whether the cost reduction achieved through FDI allows the firm to strengthen its competitiveness and whether the firm maintains activities at home that are complementary to operations abroad, sometimes further shifting their activities in the domestic market to the procurement of specialized parts and components, headquarters functions, and/or new products.

The manufacturing sector in Japan displays a trend of reducing domestic employment over time. Ando and Kimura (2010), however, find that manufacturing firms that are expanding operations in East Asia are more likely to keep or sometimes even increase domestic employment than other manufacturing firms. The growth of domestic employment at globalizing manufacturing firms is higher by as much as 8% during the six years of the sample period in the analysis compared to those not expanding operations in East Asia. Manufacturing firms expanding operations in East Asia, on the other hand, seem to slightly reduce the number of domestic establishments and affiliates compared with other manufacturing firms, indicating that the expansion of operations in East Asia is used as an opportunity to reshuffle domestic corporate structure. Furthermore, firms expanding operations in East Asia tend to intensify export/import activities with East Asia relative to other regions more so than other firms, suggesting the complementarity between trade and FDI. This is another piece of supporting evidence for expanding fragmentation of production by Japanese firms and their involvement in further development of production/distribution networks in East Asia.

Table 4.3   Sales by Japanese and US affiliates in East Asia (%)

	By-sector sales shares						By-country/region shares in East Asia		
	World	East Asia	East Asia*	China	ASEAN4	NIES4	China	ASEAN4	NIES4
Japanese affiliates in East Asia in 2004									
Manufacturing	49	59	65	78	80	38	24	43	33
Machinery (total)	37	45	48	61	60	27	25	44	32
Non-manufacturing	51	41	35	22	20	62	9	15	76
Wholesale trade	43	35	29	18	16	55	9	14	78
US affiliates in East Asia in 2003									
Manufacturing	46	46	57	72	56	35	24	29	48
Machinery (total)	21	30	39	52	n.a.	n.a.	26	n.a.	n.a.
Non-manufacturing	54	54	43	28	44	65	8	19	74
Wholesale trade	25	34	18	17	14	45	7	10	83

Note: East Asia* excludes Hong Kong for Japanese affiliates and Hong Kong and Singapore for US affiliates.

Source: Data prepared by author, based on Ando et al. (2008).

Table 4.4   Intra-firm and arm's length transactions by Japanese machinery affiliates in East Asia

		East Asia		NIES4		ASEAN4		China	
		1992	2001	1992	2001	1992	2001	1992	2001
Number of affiliates		715	2121	343	644	286	791	54	552
(a) Sales									
Values (billion JPY)		5202	14826	2770	5213	2125	6399	114	2427
Share in total by destination (%)									
(i)	**Japan**	**17**	**29**	**19**	**31**	**15**	**30**	**40**	**30**
	Intra-firm	15	23	18	20	13	27	40	25
	Arm's length	2	6	1	10	2	4	0	5
(ii)	**Local**	**66**	**40**	**64**	**44**	**66**	**31**	**46**	**45**
	Intra-firm	5	5	4	5	7	7	0	4
	Arm's length	61	35	60	40	59	23	46	41
(iii)	**Other East Asia**	**9**	**20**	**10**	**14**	**10**	**25**	**11**	**18**
	Intra-firm	5	10	3	7	7	12	11	15
	Arm's length	4	10	7	8	2	13	0	4
(i+ii+iii)	**East Asia (total)**	**92**	**89**	**93**	**89**	**91**	**86**	**97**	**93**
	Intra-firm	25	39	25	32	27	46	51	44
	Arm's length	67	50	68	58	64	40	46	49

Table 4.4 (continued)

	East Asia		NIES4		ASEAN4		China	
	1992	2001	1992	2001	1992	2001	1992	2001
(b) Purchases								
Values (billion JPY)	2466	10417	1140	3733	1204	4560	54	1626
Share in total by origin (%)								
(i) **Japan**	**46**	**38**	**47**	**40**	**44**	**36**	**76**	**38**
Intra-firm	39	27	39	32	39	23	71	24
Arm's length	7	11	9	8	5	13	5	14
(ii) **Local**	**43**	**40**	**42**	**38**	**45**	**41**	**21**	**43**
Intra-firm	1	4	1	3	1	5	5	3
Arm's length	43	36	41	34	44	35	16	40
(iii) **Other East Asia**	**8**	**20**	**10**	**21**	**8**	**22**	**2**	**18**
Intra-firm	5	9	9	11	2	8	2	12
Arm's length	3	11	1	10	6	14	0	6
(i+ii+iii) **East Asia (total)**	**98**	**99**	**99**	**99**	**97**	**98**	**98**	**99**
Intra-firm	45	40	48	46	42	36	78	39
Arm's length	53	59	51	53	56	62	20	60

Note: Figures for 'Share in total by destination/origin' express sales to/purchases from each destination/origin as a percentage of total sales/purchases by Japanese affiliates in corresponding regions/countries.

Source: Data from author's preparation, based on Ando and Kimura (2009).

Firstly, their transactions with other East Asian countries (that is, East Asian countries other than Japan and the host country) have increased relatively on both the sales and purchases sides, implying the development of production networks in the 1990s. Secondly, arm's length transactions have been more actively utilized than before, reflecting development of agglomeration and supporting industry.

Regarding the first point, most of the sales and purchases by Japanese affiliates in East Asia are transactions among Japan, local market, and other East Asian countries. Moreover, the shares of transactions with other East Asian countries tend to become larger over time; in the case of the machinery industry, such transactions were 20% of sales and purchases in 2001, up from 9% of sales and 8% of purchases in 1992. Combined with an explosive increase in value of transactions, these suggest the presence and development of strong intra-regional production networks involving not only the local market but also other East Asian countries through back-and-forth transactions of intermediate goods.

As for the second point, arm's length transactions have been more actively utilized than before, particularly when selling goods to/purchasing goods from Japan and other East Asian countries. In addition, purchases from Japan by Japanese machinery affiliates in East Asia tend to be shifted to intra-firm and arm's length purchases from other East Asian countries. Purchases from Japan by Japanese manufacturing affiliates in China, above all, seem to be replaced by arm's length purchases in the local market as well as intra-firm and arm's length purchases from other East Asian countries. While intra-firm purchases from Japan as a percentage of total purchases by Japanese machinery affiliates in China decreased from 71% in 1992 to 24% in 2001, arm's length purchases in the local market increased from 16% in 1992 to 40% in 2001, eventually reaching the level of ASEAN4/NIES4. Considering the fact that operation by Japanese firms in China seriously started in the late 1990s (see the number of affiliates as well as sales in Table 4.4), such a rapid shift suggests the formation of local vertical links in agglomeration in China, reflecting the lowering of service link costs as well as more developed industrial clusters (agglomeration) involving MNEs and indigenous firms becoming more competitive than before (see Box 4.2 for the discussion on the relationship between agglomeration and arm's length fragmentation).[12]

The behavior of Japanese affiliates in East Asia in terms of international division of labor is quite similar to that of US affiliates in the region (Figure 4.5).[13] The shares of sales to investing countries (Japan/US), local markets, and other East Asian countries were 26%/27%, 46%/42%, and 19%/18% in 2001/1999 for Japanese/US manufacturing affiliates.[14] Furthermore, shares of transactions with other East Asian countries were

(a) Japanese manufacturing affiliates in East Asia

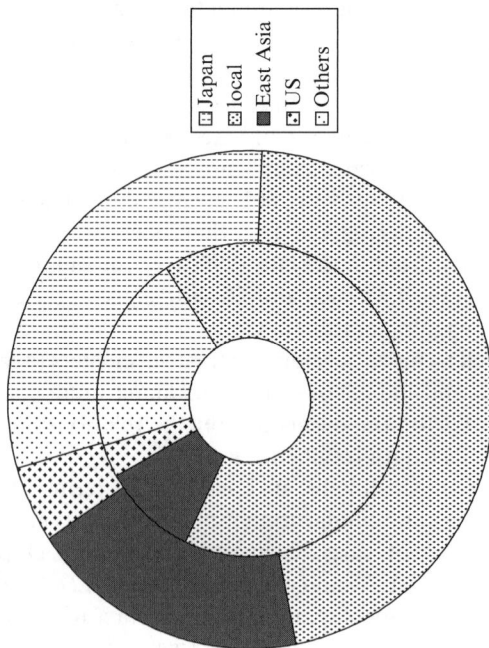

(b) US manufactuirng affiliates in East Asia

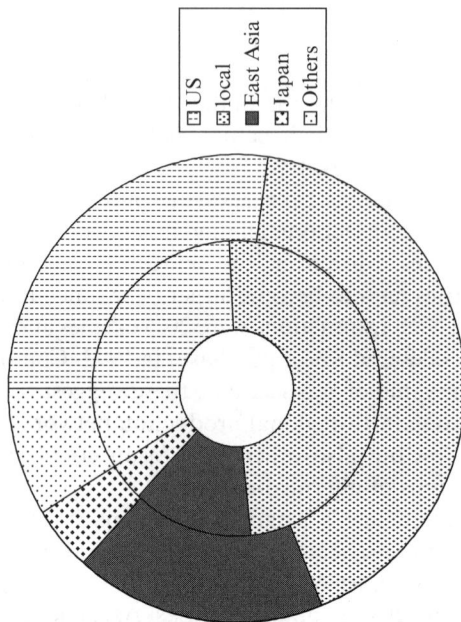

Notes: Manufacturing sectors in 1992 (inside) and 2001 (outside) for Japanese affiliates; all sectors in 1989 (inside) and manufacturing sectors in 1999 (outside) for US affiliates. 'East Asia' refers to East Asian countries other than local market and Japan.

Source: Data from Ando et al. (2008).

Figure 4.5   Patterns of sales for Japanese and US manufacturing affiliates in East Asia, by destination

Table 4.5   *Ratios of sales by Japanese and US affiliates in East Asia, by destination*

	Japanese affiliates in East Asia						
	Japan		Local		Third countries		
	(Intra-firm)		(Intra-firm)		(Intra-firm)	Other East Asia	(Intra-firm)
1992 (manu-facturing)	16	(84)	66	(6)	18	(43)	10	(45)
2001 (manu-facturing)	26	(77)	46	(11)	28	(46)	19	(44)

	US affiliates in East Asia (excl. Japan)						
	US		Local		Third countries		
	(US parent firms)		(Other US affili-ates)		(Other US affili-ates)	Other East Asia	(Other US affili-ates)
1989 (all)	24	(86)	49	(11)	27	(42)	14	(41)
1999 (all)	17	(87)	57	(11)	26	(59)	15	n.a.
1999 (manu-facturing)	27	n.a.	42	n.a.	31	n.a.	18	n.a.

Source: Data prepared by author, based on Ando et al. (2008).

19%/18% of sales in 2001/1999, having risen from 10%/14% in 1992/1989 for Japanese/US manufacturing affiliates.[15] These indicate the presence and development of strong intra-regional production networks in East Asia, regardless of firm nationalities.

Another similarity between Japanese and US affiliates in East Asia seen in behavior in transactions is the close link between geographical proximity (agglomeration) and arm's length fragmentation (see Box 4.2). The close link between distance and arm's length fragmentation here means that the closer the distance from the location of an affiliate, the more arm's length transactions tend to be utilized. Intra-firm ratios for transactions with Japan (investing country), other East Asian countries, and the local market in 2001 became smaller in the following order for Japanese manufacturing affiliates in East Asia: 77%, 44%, and 11% for sales (purchases) (Table 4.5). Interestingly, ratios of intra-firm sales (plus arm's length sales to other US firms) to the US (investing country), other East Asian countries, and the local market became smaller in the following order for US affiliates in East Asia in 1999 as well: 87%, 41% (in 1989), and 11%. These observations prove a close link between geographical proximity (agglomeration) and disintegration-type fragmentation, indicating the formation of agglomeration of fragmented production blocks, regardless of firm nationalities.

What is slightly different between Japanese and US affiliates in East Asia is the behavior in transactions within/beyond the same firm nationality. If intra-firm ratios of sales in the local market and in other East Asian countries by Japanese manufacturing affiliates are compared with ratios of sales by US affiliates to other US affiliates in the local market and in other intra-regional countries, they are more or less equal: intra-firm sales ratios of Japanese manufacturing affiliates are 11% for the local market and 44% for other East Asia, while ratios of sales to other US affiliates by US affiliates are 11% for the local market and 41% for other East Asia (Table 4.5). Considering that some portion of arm's length transactions by Japanese affiliates in East Asia are those with Japanese affiliates of other Japanese firms in the region, ratios of intra-firm sales plus sales to Japanese affiliates of other Japanese firms are certainly larger than those of sales by US affiliates to firms with the same firm nationality (that is, other US affiliates) in the local market and in other East Asian countries. This suggests that US firms in East Asia seem to utilize transactions beyond the firm nationality significantly more than Japanese firms in East Asia do.

How about transactions between the US and Mexico at the firm level? They seem to depend more on intra-firm transactions. In the case of US firms in all (manufacturing) industries, most of the sales by US affiliates in Mexico go back to the US parent: 99% in 1989 and 91% in 1999. Similarly, more than half of the sales by Japanese manufacturing affiliates in Mexico go to Japanese affiliates of the same firms located in the US, though intra-firm ratios dropped from 1992 to 2001. These suggest that production networking in the US–Mexico nexus is still dependent on intra-firm transactions, though the firms tend to utilize arm's length transactions more heavily than before.

4.4   POLICY IMPLICATIONS

This chapter has shed light on international production/distribution networks that have rapidly developed in East Asia since the 1990s and has provided evidence concerning their features and mechanisms using disaggregated international trade data and micro-data at the firm level. International production/distribution networks have been formed in other regions in the world as well. The production networks, particularly in machinery industries, in East Asia, however, are distinctive in their significance in each economy, their geographical extensiveness which involves many countries at different income levels, and their sophistication in both intra-firm and arm's length relationships. The effective development and utilization of international production/distribution networks is one of the key elements of East Asia's high performance in the last decade or so.

As discussed in Box 4.2, a crucial factor for fragmentation of production is reduction of service link costs, since fragmentation occurs when the service link costs are sufficiently low so as to make the total costs lower than otherwise. For instance, the reduction of trade barriers such as tariffs and non-tariff measures (NTMs) would reduce service link costs connecting fragmented production blocks across borders, and various trade and FDI facilitation policies would promote agglomeration and help to reduce service link costs for arm's length transactions.

East Asian countries have introduced various types of policies and measures to promote exports and FDI. One of the key measures extensively implemented in East Asia is a duty drawback system; that is, a system for refunding duties and indirect taxes on imported inputs to be used for export production. Most export-oriented MNEs pay few import tariffs on their imported intermediate goods under this system and are able to more easily spread their production processes within the region beyond national borders on the basis of cost and market considerations. In addition to the above, a representative example of the measures to promote exports and FDI is rapid construction of container yards and highway networks, which facilitate the explosive increase in container transportation. Furthermore, concentration of public resources on the development of economic infrastructure, including roads, ports, electricity, water supply, telecommunications, and industrial estate services, has helped to reduce service link costs and promote the creation of industrial clusters. The lowered service link cost enables firms to make use of differences in location advantages in countries across East Asia with widely varying income levels and development stages.

In order to further activate fragmentation and to take advantage of the forces of globalizing corporate activities for economic development, the key is to host network-forming FDI and help form agglomeration by implementing various trade and FDI facilitation measures. Intentional efforts to reduce service link costs are also effective. Furthermore, effective utilization of free trade agreements (FTAs)/regional trade agreements (RTAs) can be valuable for further activation of fragmentation. In fact, even in the transport equipment sector where import substitution policies remain in many developing countries, patterns of international division of labour have been significantly changed, partially reflecting the recently

concluded FTAs/RTAs. Going beyond the traditional infant industry protection argument, the new role of government in this era of globalization
needs to be considered.

NOTES

1. The term 'fragmentation' refers to the splitting up of a product process into two or
   more steps that lead to the same final product (Deardorff 2001). Until recently, fragmentation was primarily a domestic phenomenon. Recent developments in the world
   trading system as well as technological advances have created new opportunities for
   extending production fragmentation across national borders. See, for instance, Jones
   and Kierzkowski (1990, 2001) and Arndt and Kierzkowski (2001) for the fragmentation
   theory. Also, see Box 4.2 for two-dimensional fragmentation and its cost structure.
2. Many other terms have been used with the same meaning as, or with meanings related
   to, fragmentation. These include 'delocalization', employed by Leamer (1996), 'disintegration' (Feenstra 1998), 'intra-mediate trade' (Antweiler and Trefler 2002), 'intra-
   product specialization' (Arndt 1997), 'vertical specialization' (Yi 2003) and 'multistage
   production' (Dixit and Grossman 1982). Another term used is 'Outsourcing'.
3. Unless specified otherwise, machinery industries in this chapter basically include
   general machinery, electric machinery, transport equipment, and precision machinery,
   HS (Harmonized System) 84-92.
4. Fukao et al. (2003) provide extensive statistical data analysis of European-type horizontal intra-industry trade.
5. Although some firms in other industries such as textiles and garments also develop
   production networks, it is relevant to highlight production networks in machinery
   industries for East Asia, given their significance in each economy.
6. See, for instance, Kimura and Ando (2005a), Ando et al. (2008), and Ando and Kimura
   (2007) for a comparison of features of production networks in the US–Mexico nexus
   and WE–CEE nexus with those in East Asia.
7. Kuroiwa (2008) provides interesting findings on international production networks in
   East Asia, using the Asian International Input–Output Table.
8. See Ando and Kimura (2005) for a definition of machinery parts and components.
9. Ando and Kimura (2009) provide the results of gravity estimation on intra-East Asian
   exports, based on export values in the HS (Harmonized System) classification in real
   terms for machinery parts and components, machinery final goods and all products.
   Kimura et al. (2007), on the other hand, show results of gravity estimation of intra-
   East Asia, intra-Europe exports, and world exports based on export values at the SITC
   (Standard International Trade Classification) in nominal terms. Based on the results
   in these two studies, Ando and Kimura (2009) emphasize that trade relationships are
   even stronger in East Asia, particularly among developing countries with substantially
   weaker trade relationships in 1990, because service link costs across borders are smaller
   than in other regions.
10. Connections among CEE countries are weak, and the WE market is predominantly
    important as the sales destination of CEE operations. Proximity to the market seems to
    be crucial for selling products to the WE market, probably due to subtle taste adjust-
    ment as well as international commercial policies. See Ando and Kimura (2007) for
    more detailed analysis and discussion.
11. SMEs are herein defined as firms with regular workers numbering less than 300.
12. The rapid increase in the number of affiliates indicates there is a possibility that newly
    established affiliates have different characters and operations from existing affiliates,
    resulting in a significant change in the patterns of sales/purchases by affiliates. However,

according to interviews during factory visits in East Asia including China, the pattern discussed here seems to reflect the actual tendency.

13. Due to lack of access to raw data of US affiliates, most information on US affiliates here is from US affiliates in all industries or manufacturing sectors. In addition, only the sales side is discussed because no information is available concerning the purchase side for US affiliates.

14. Ratios for Japan and other East Asia as destinations for sales by US manufacturing affiliates are estimated by using shares of Japan and East Asia for US affiliates in all industries, shares of third countries for US affiliates in all industries, and shares of third countries for US manufacturing affiliates.

15. 14% in 1989 is the ratio of East Asia for US affiliates in all industries since the ratio is not available for US manufacturing affiliates in that year.

REFERENCES

Ando, Mitsuyo (2006), 'Fragmentation and vertical intra-industry trade in East Asia', *North American Journal of Economics and Finance*, **17** (3), 257–81.

Ando, Mitsuyo, Sven Arndt and Fukunari Kimura (2008), 'Production networks in East Asia: strategic behavior by Japanese and US firms', in Kyoji Fukao and JCER (eds), *Japanese Firms' Strategy in East Asia: A Comparison with US and European Firms* (in Japanese). The English version appeared in JCER Discussion Paper No. 103, August 2006.

Ando, Mitsuyo and Fukunari Kimura (2005), 'The formation of international production and distribution networks in East Asia', in Takatoshi Ito and Andrew K. Rose (eds), *International Trade* (NBER-East Asia seminar on economics, volume 14), Chicago: The University of Chicago Press.

Ando, Mitsuyo and Fukunari Kimura (2007), 'Fragmentation in Europe and East Asia: evidences from international trade and FDI data', in Jong-Kil Kim and Pierre-Bruno Ruffini (eds), *Corporate Strategies in the Age of Regional Integration*, Cheltenham, UK and Northampton, MA, USA: Edward Elgar, pp. 52–76.

Ando, Mitsuyo and Fukunari Kimura (2009), 'Fragmentation in East Asia: further evidences', ERIA Discussion Paper, Series No. 2009–20. See also Ando, Mitsuyo and Fukunari Kimura (2010), 'The special patterns of production and distribution networks in East Asia', in Prema-chandra Athukorala (ed.), *The Rise of Asia: Trade and Investment in Global Perspective*, London: Routledge, Chapter 3.

Ando, Mitsuyo and Fukunari Kimura (2010), 'International production/distribution networks in East Asia and domestic operations: evidences from Japanese firms', in Robert M. Stern (ed.), *Quantitative Analysis of Newly Evolving Patterns of International Trade: Fragmentation; Offshoring of Activities; and Vertical Industry Trade*, World Scientific Studies in International Economics.

Antweiler, Werner and Daniel Trefler (2002), 'Increasing returns and all that: a view from trade', *American Economic Review*, **92** (March), 93–119.

Arndt, Sven W. (1997), 'Globalization and the open economy', *North American Journal of Economics and Finance*, **8**, 71–79.

Arndt, Sven W. and Henryk Kierzkowski (2001), *Fragmentation: New Production Patterns in the World Economy*, Oxford: Oxford University Press.

Deardorff, Alan V. (2001), 'Fragmentation in simple trade models', *North American Journal of Economics and Finance*, **12**, 121–37.

Dixit, Avinash K. and Gene M. Grossman (1982), 'Trade and protection with multistage production', *Review of Economic Studies*, **59**, 583–94.

Feenstra, Robert C. (1998), 'Integration of trade and disintegration of production in the global economy', *Journal of Economic Perspectives*, **12** (Fall), 31–50.

Fujita, Masahisa, Paul Krugman and Anthony J. Venables (1999), *The Spatial Economy: Cities, Regions, and International Trade*, Cambridge: MIT Press.

Fukao, Kyoji, Hikari Ishito and Keiko Ito (2003), 'Vertical intra-industry trade and foreign direct investment in East Asia', *Journal of the Japanese and International Economies*, **17**, 468–506.

Jones, Ronald W. and Henryk Kierzkowski (1990), 'The role of services in production and international trade: a theoretical framework', in Ronald W. Jones and Anne O. Krueger (eds), *The Political Economy of International Trade: Essays in Honor of Robert E. Baldwin*, Oxford: Basil Blackwell.

Jones, Ronald W. and Henryk Kierzkowski (2001), 'A framework for fragmentation', in Sven W. Arndt and Henryk Kierzkowski (eds), *Fragmentation: New Production Patterns in the World Economy*, Oxford: Oxford University Press.

Kimura, Fukunari and Mitsuyo Ando (2005a), 'The economic analysis of international production/distribution networks in East Asia and Latin America: the implication of regional trade arrangements', *Business and Politics*, **7**(1), Article 1.

Kimura, Fukunari and Mitsuyo Ando (2005b), 'Two-dimensional fragmentation in East Asia: conceptual framework and empirics', *International Review of Economics and Finance*, **14**, 317–48.

Kimura, F., Y. Takahashi and K. Hayakawa (2007), 'Fragmentation and parts and components trade: comparison between East Asia and Europe', *North American Journal of Economics and Finance*, **18**, 23–40.

Kuroiwa, Ikuo (2008), 'Cross-border production networks in Southeast Asia: application of the international input–output analysis', in Ikuo Kuroiwa and Mun Heng Toh (eds), *Production Networks and Clusters in Integrating Southeast Asia*, Singapore: Institute of Southeast Asia (ISEAS).

Leamer, Edward E. (1996), 'The effects of trade in services, technology transfer and delocalisation on local and global income inequality', *Asia-Pacific Economic Review*, **2** (April), 44–60.

UNIDO (United Nations Industrial Development Organization) (2009), 'Industrial development scoreboard – 2007 update', available at http://www.unido.org/index.php?id=5058.

World Bank (2009), 'World Development Indicators Online', available at http://publications.worldbank.org/WDI/.

Yi, Kei-Mu (2003), 'Can vertical specialization explain the growth of world trade?', *Journal of Political Economy*, **111**, 52–102.

5. Theories on FDI and the behavior of MNEs in East Asia

Ho Yeon Kim and Toshitaka Gokan

The expanding role of foreign direct investment (FDI) in global economic development is now widely recognized. FDI emanates from location decisions of multinational enterprises (MNE) that roam across national borders to maximize their profits. Multinational production, investment and trade are becoming ever more important. As Markusen and Venables (1999) point out, the general view in the 1970s was that multinational investment was detrimental to the welfare of host economies, creating monopoly situations. In the 1990s, however, views became much more optimistic, suggesting that multinationals may stimulate development in host economies. Indeed, FDI represents the cutting edge of globalization; it conjoins a unique bundle of capital and managerial/technological knowledge.

These optimistic views are supported by the strong evidence in East Asian countries. Hong Kong, Korea, Singapore, and Taiwan all fostered export-oriented production activities which were related with MNEs, and domestic enterprises in those countries have grown to become MNEs. Korean MNEs in particular have spread not only in East Asia but also into other regions. Given these optimistic views, then, governments in potential host countries may have an interest in how MNEs choose their production sites.

In this chapter, we examine the positive and negative roles MNEs play in host countries. Our survey of related theories is complemented by a discussion of location choices of MNEs in East Asia, with a review of the path to prosperity taken by Korea as a typical example of the phenomenon we mentioned above, and a survey of representative Korean firms which managed to become MNEs in that process.

5.1   THE EFFECTS OF MNES ON THE HOST COUNTRIES

5.1.1   Macroeconomic Benefits

MNEs may contribute to economic growth, but the causality between MNEs and economic growth may be bidirectional. One direction decides the effects of MNEs on economic growth. The other direction determines whether the expected economic growth or realized economic growth entices MNEs to operate in the host countries.

MNEs may also contribute to the trade surplus. In Vietnam in 2005, the foreign investment sector constituted 15% of the GDP, and it accounted for 37.1% of total imports and 57.2% of total exports. As a result, the foreign-invested sector realized about US$5 billion in export surplus.[1] Furthermore, Nguyen and Xing (2008) show that FDI increases exports to the countries that supply FDI to Vietnam, using data on 23 countries for the period of 1990 to 2004.

Hsiao and Hsiao (2006) examined the causality among FDI, GDP and exports, from 1996 to 2004 in East Asia, and found that, as a whole, FDI promoted both GDP and exports; the exports increased GDP, and GDP raised exports to a lesser extent. That is, export-oriented FDI and export-promoting trade policies facilitated economic growth in East Asia (see Box 5.1).

At the same time, there is great variation among East Asian countries in terms of these causal relationships. For instance, Korea and Hong Kong lacked causality between them; high levels of GDP and exports attracted FDI in China; FDI promoted both economic growth and exports in Singapore; GDP and exports strengthened each other in Taiwan and Malaysia; and GDP increased exports in the Philippines. In Thailand, those relationships are more complicated: exports and FDI increased GDP, GDP weakly increased exports and FDI, and FDI weakly increased exports. Figure 5.1 presents the causalities mentioned above.

As for side effects, MNEs may harm the economies in host countries by crowding out domestic investment and increasing regional income inequality. Because the inflow of MNEs may ignite severe competition in host countries, it is thought that some local firms may be forced to leave the market. Agosin and Machado (2005), however, show that domestic investment, not only in East Asia but in other regions as well, did not suffer from crowding out nor did it enjoy an inflow due to foreign investment during 1971 to 2000. However, the situation differs depending on the countries involved. Using the data from 1980 to 1999, Kumar and Pradhan (2005) show that FDI crowded out domestic investment in the Philippines and

---

BOX 5.1   HOST COUNTRIES' BENEFITS FROM MNES AND TRADE POLICY

The effect of MNEs on economic growth hinges upon the trade policies that are adopted. East Asian countries in the 1960s and 1970s favored import substitution policies to foster their import sectors. High tariff rates protected domestic markets from international competition, but by jumping tariffs, MNEs improved the access to these segmented markets. However, policymakers shifted their trade policies from fostering the import sector to promoting exports after the 1980s. Under the new export promotion policies, MNEs operate plants to compete and cooperate in the international markets. The difference between these two policies has been clarified by econometrical analysis.

Balasubramanyam et al. (1996) compared the effects of foreign direct investments under import substitution policy and export promotion policy for the period of 1970 to 1985 in 40 countries, using categories which divide countries into two trade policy groups. In East Asia, Indonesia and the Philippines pursued import substitution policies, whereas Singapore, Hong Kong, Korea and Malaysia maintained export promotion policies. Thailand was included in both groups depending on categories. Not surprisingly, those countries which adopted an export promotion policy enjoyed higher economic growth. Furthermore, Kohpaiboon (2003) examined whether the effects of FDI on economic growth differed depending on the trade policy in Thailand during 1970 to 1999 and found that FDI promoted economic growth as the ratio of exports to gross output in the manufacturing sector increased.

Singapore, while no relation exists between the two forms of investment in China, Indonesia and Malaysia; FDI crowds in domestic investment in Korea and Thailand.

As another side effect, FDI may exacerbate regional inequalities. In China, FDI benefited the eastern and coastal regions and harmed inland areas, although FDI was advantageous to China as a whole from 2001 to 2003, as seen through panel data from 19 industries and 30 provinces (Ran et al. 2007). The calculations by Zhang and Zhang (2003) on the relative magnitude of factors causing regional inequalities during 1986 to 1998 show that domestic capital dominated, at 75%, with foreign capital

East Asia

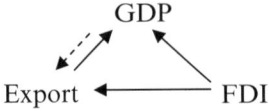

Korea and Hong Kong   **China**

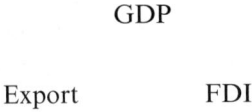   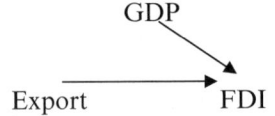

Singapore   **Taiwan and Malaysia**

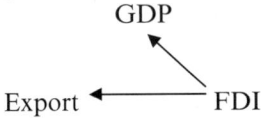   

Philippines   **Thailand**

   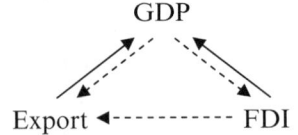

Figure 5.1   GDP, export and FDI causality

at 8.1% and foreign trade at 5.8%. Thus, foreign capital contributed to the widening of the regional inequalities, although it was not the main cause. Considering the interregional migration by millions of persons in China, Fu (2004) explained that labor migration and the clusters of regional HQs and FDI engendered an asymmetric spread of provincial GDP in China. Using Wu-Hausman statistics, the author found that migration and income inequality tend to strengthen each other.

5.1.2   Microeconomic Benefits

In transition economies, MNEs promote the system of regulations and institutions required for a market economy, encourage competition, allow variety in ownership, and improve public enterprises (Zhang 1993). Girma and Gong (2008) show from the data on China during 1999 to 2005 that state-owned enterprises (SOEs) financed by foreign entities raise labor productivity and survival anticipation. However, the opposite effects were discovered among SOEs without any foreign capital and upstream SOEs with export-oriented MNEs.

Under general circumstances, Moran (2005) classified MNEs' contributions in their host countries into three categories: primary contribution, backward linkage, and externality. As primary contributions, MNEs introduce new products, renew the quality of products and/or reduce consumer prices; MNEs use additional capital, technologies and management resources; MNEs improve the productivity of local firms; MNEs introduce local firms to new economic activities; and MNEs connect local firms to foreign markets. As backward linkages, new demand may be attached with a foreign subsidiary's coaching. Finally, as externalities, local firms can source the flow of workers who have mastered new skills and make improvements by imitation of, or competition with, MNEs; local firms may have some incentives to acquire certifications such as ISO 9000; and local firms may find new opportunities to provide their products to the other MNEs in the international market.

Given the above list, host countries may expect local firms to engage in R&D activities under the influence of MNEs. Rasiah (2003) shows that MNEs in Malaysia in 2001 possessed stronger capabilities in human resources, process technology and R&D. According to manufacturing surveys conducted in 2002 and 2003, Malaysian firms with higher foreign ownership accomplished greater innovation (Lee 2004). Even in the cases of Singapore and Penang (Malaysia), innovation-related linkages were more international than in the European cases in Barcelona, Stockholm and Vienna (Diez and Kiese 2006). The major difference between the two cases was that, although firms cooperate with customers and buyers in both cases, firms in Singapore and Penang have stronger relations with foreign affiliates.

Regarding the interaction between MNEs and local firms in Thailand, Pupphavesa and Pussarungsri (1994) found that MNEs transfer technologies to domestic firms via many channels. The most effective channel was learning facilitation through testing and diagnostic feedback on quality and/or advanced indications of future targets. Other channels also enabled direct technology transfer, for example training and advice on plant layout, or the spillover type of technology transfer, for example product design and exposure to the management of manufacturing activity.

A good example of technology transfer would be the case of AB Volvo's truck and bus plants in Xian, China. Volvo provides technology support to local suppliers and MNEs' suppliers. Both types of suppliers received the same supply of product designs and technical specifications as well as feedback on product quality. Consequently, 82% of local suppliers and 10% of MNEs' suppliers improved their operations with the assistance of Volvo (Ivarsson and Alvstam 2005).

Additionally, there is an issue surrounding the payment of less than adequate wages by MNEs. When MNEs pay higher wages, foreign entry improves the usage of the labor force. In East Asia, MNEs tend to pay higher wages than local firms in the host countries. Indonesian workers in the manufacturing sector during 1990 to 1999 enjoyed higher wages when working for MNEs than for domestic firms when compared on the basis of gender and education levels, and skilled workers earned 20% to 30% higher wages (Harrison and Scorse 2004). Lipsey and Sjoholm (2004) also found that MNEs in Indonesia paid more than 50% above the average wage at the point in time two years after taking over domestic firms, comparing employees on the basis of education level. In a survey of MNEs in Guangdong Province, China, in 1997, Liu et al. (2004) found that, when fringe benefits were included, MNEs paid higher wages than local firms. In the case of Hong Kong's garment firms in Guangdong, 76 out of 84 MNEs paid slightly more to managers than did Chinese firms. In Vietnam, Thoburn et al. (2007) report that the textile firms which are well positioned in the global production network paid workers enough (see Box 5.2).

5.2   THEORIES OF MNE FROM THE VIEWPOINT OF LOCATION[2]

5.2.1   Product Life-cycle Theory

Vernon (1966) proposed the concept of 'product cycle' to help explain the activities of US MNEs abroad. Initially, the product is produced for the home market in the home country. At a later stage of the product cycle, it is exported to other countries which are similar to the home country in their demand patterns. As demand becomes more price-elastic, as labor becomes a more important ingredient of costs, and as foreign markets expand, the incentives for locating value-adding activities on foreign soil increase. Eventually, the subsidiary can produce the products instead of importing from the parent company, and soon begins to export back to the home country.

The product life-cycle model of FDI combines Vernon's original model with the internalization theory of the multinational firm in that foreign production cannot take place unless the firm holds some monopolistic advantage. Using a sample of 36 countries, Graham (1999) found

---

BOX 5.2   DO TRADE AGREEMENTS IMPROVE LABOR CONDITIONS?

A trade agreement can improve labor conditions, as Polaski (2006) illustrates with the following anecdote. In 1999, the US–Cambodia Trade Agreement on Textiles and Apparel was rectified. A unique point is that additional quotas for accessing the US textile market were disbursed annually as incentives when labor rights in Cambodia reached certain benchmarks set by the two governments. The international labor organization (ILO) monitored the achievement of the benchmarks semiannually and reported on the labor conditions, identifying the apparel factories by name. Depending on the results of the monitoring, Cambodia received additional quotas. The additional quotas were disbursed not for each plant but for the entire country of Cambodia. In order to avoid a free rider problem, the Cambodian government limited the quotas to the plants which joined the monitoring program. Thus, all apparel firms participated in the program.

In this trade agreement, apparel firms had three incentives: direct increase of their quotas, their reputation in the eyes of other apparel firms, and their reputation in the eyes of foreign buyers. Because the ILO reported each factory's condition, foreign buyers could contract only with the factories which would not harm the MNEs' reputations. Chiu (2007) reports that improvements in Hong Kong-invested garment factories occurred due to pressure from foreign buyers. Thus, most plants followed the suggestions made by the ILO and improved the workers' labor rights, and the improved labor rights became another attraction in the Cambodian apparel industry. Polaski (2006) and Chiu (2007) suggest the applicability of this arrangement to other labor-abundant countries.

---

a positive relationship between Japan's FDI and both its imports and exports in the early 1990s. As FDI gave rise to increased movement of goods, this suggests that FDI does not necessarily provoke hollowing out or deindustrialization of the home country.

5.2.2   Flying Geese Theory

While Vernon's product cycle theory addresses the issue from the perspective of developed countries where new products are invented, the flying geese model adopts the perspective of developing countries. Originally proposed in the 1930s by Akamatsu and developed over many years (Akamatsu 1962), the flying geese theory illustrates how a new product is introduced to less developed countries via imports and how these countries acquire production techniques and become exporters. In the Asian context, the model predicts a progressive sequence of expansion in stages for any given industry, from Japan to the NIEs, followed by ASEAN, China, Vietnam and India.

Inspired by early observations, Kojima (1985) argued that FDI should occur when a country's comparative advantage in some product is eroded because FDI can deliver technology, management skills, and movable capital to the foreign sites where total production costs are lowest. Instead of replacing exports, FDI can then generate new exports to third countries or even to the home country.

Dowling and Cheang (2000) observed a flying-geese type development in East Asia during 1970 to 1995, and their findings were endorsed by Kim and Jin (2003) with more recent data. Asian countries are usually viewed as being involved in a multi-layered catching-up process of industrialization wherein Japan has supplied capital and technology through the expansion of trade and FDI, and in return, the NIEs have exported commodities to Japan in which Japan no longer has a comparative advantage. The same process has been repeated with respect to ASEAN countries. Thus, FDI has proven itself to be an effective channel for developed countries to transfer their comparative advantage to less developed countries. During the process, technology and know-how are also transferred to host economies, paving the way for peripheral countries to catch up with more industrialized regions. In East Asia, technology transfer occurred in the form of R&D spillover to overseas subsidiaries, training of local personnel and reverse engineering.

Edgington and Hayter (2000) examined the role of Japanese FDI as a catalyst for the development of the Asian electronics industry. Although there exists strong evidence in support of the overall patterns suggested by the flying geese model, the authors caution that the role of the host government's policy and local capital should not be disregarded. In any case, there is nothing automatic about moving up the value chain. In the early stage, the motivations of MNEs (to secure low-cost labor) and host countries (to develop simple skills) often overlap; however, once the host countries make a substantial move up the value chain, further transfer becomes difficult because of conflicting objectives over proprietary knowledge. Furthermore, innovations no longer emerge only in core countries, leading to orderly diffusion in a hierarchical manner; they instead appear also in countries striving to catch up.

5.2.3 Eclectic Theory

Dunning (1993, p. 90) argues that Kojima's theory fails to explain the types of trade flows that are based to a lesser extent on the distribution of factor endowments and to a greater extent on the need to exploit the economies of scale, product differentiation, and other manifestations of market failure. Dunning's (1977) eclectic theory is a consolidation of various FDI literature. It states, in short, that an 'ownership' advantage allows a firm to overcome the disadvantages of foreign location, and this may be a product or a manufacturing process to which other firms have no access (such as a patent or a trademark). Also, 'location' advantages, such as low input costs or a protective trade policy, make it more profitable to produce in a country than to export to it. Finally, 'internalization' advantages make it more desirable for a firm to undertake foreign production on its own rather than dealing with a foreign partner. Dunning (1993, p. 80) observes that at any given moment, the more a country's enterprises possess ownership advantages, the greater the incentive they have to internalize their use. They are then more likely to find it in their interest to exploit these advantages from a foreign location.

Markusen (1998) also notes that MNEs are found in industries in which knowledge capital is vital. Knowledge capital includes human capital in the form of employees, patents, proprietary knowledge on procedures, and marketing assets such as trademarks and brand names. There is often a 'public-good' property within the firm. Blueprints, chemical formulae, and reputation capital are very costly to produce, but they can be supplied at a relatively low cost to foreign production facilities without reducing the value or productivity of those assets in existing facilities.

Internalization advantages arise from the same feature of knowledge; knowledge easily transferred to foreign locations is also easily dissipated. Conversely, Markusen (1991) argues, a developing country may already possess many of the ingredients necessary to produce a particular class of goods, while lacking key technical and managerial skills. The entry of the multinational firm into such a country provides missing resources and leads to the production and export of goods that were previously imported.

5.2.4 New Trade Theory

The ideas of Dunning (1977) and Markusen (1998) are formalized with the approach used in new trade theory. Brülhart (1998) noted that new trade theory dispenses with all exogenous elements except for market size, which is determined by the size of the immobile labor force.

Inter-industry specialization leads to sectors clustering in locations which offer the best access to markets, while intra-industry specialization leads to each firm producing a unique variety of goods. The main characteristics of this theory are summarized in Navaretti and Venables (2004). As they become multinational, firms face trade-offs between costs and benefits. The costs are foregone economies of scale and economies of integration, and the benefits are better market access and cheaper production factors.

With the scale economy, the larger the output of a firm or plant is, the greater the profitability. The magnitude of scale economies increases with the size of fixed costs. As fixed costs at the plant attached to the headquarters become smaller, the merits of producing large batches fade. Thus, there is a greater probability that the firm will become multinational. When production activities are integrated, production efficiency increases. Providing counterexamples, Navaretti and Venables (2004) cite the case of reheating steel products or delayed transportation between plants. Furthermore, the lack of adequate communication between plants and headquarters may reduce the productivity of plants when production activities are physically separated, although this kind of 'diseconomy' can be somewhat mitigated with the adoption of information technologies.

Producers operate plants in other countries to save transport costs and avoid trade barriers, and so better market access from the home country may actually slow down the evolution of multinational firms. Markusen (1984) argues that multinational activity arises with moderate to high trade costs. When transport costs are low, production factors also play an important role in dictating the location of multinational firms, and differences in input costs emerge as the decisive factor for attracting multinational firms. The costs of inputs, such as wages, tend to differ across countries, and using cheaper inputs, firms can supply more affordable products.

5.2.5   New Economic Geography

During the 1990s, renewed interest in the spatial dimension of economic activities gave rise to the so-called 'new economic geography'. As Ensign (1995) observes, location theory has emphasized that production generally moves from decentralization to agglomeration as market imperfections arise. Benefits of agglomeration include economies of scale in production and localization economies due to shared inputs. By combining these concepts with transportation costs, Krugman (1991) constructed what is now known as the core-periphery model.

New economic geography treats location endogenously. Both

production factors and firms are mobile, and even market size is explained within the model. Market-size externalities and input–output linkages produce self-reinforcing agglomeration processes. As pointed out by Krugman and Hanson (1993), this NEG approach can, for example, explain the effects of trade liberalization better than international trade theory because 'the issue is not how countries will specialize, but where production will locate'.

Amiti (2005) shows that low trade costs can lead to agglomeration of both upstream and downstream firms in one country due to the benefits of close proximity, even when they differ in factor intensities. This is because the weakening of the crowding effects is greater than the weakening of the market-access and cost-of-living effects. Robert-Nicoud (2006) finds the same results with multinational firms. Furthermore, adding the dispersion effects stemming from decreasing returns to labor in agriculture, the author shows that industrial agglomeration emerges when transport costs take intermediate values. This is because the labor costs that increase with the agglomeration of production activity are dominant in the total costs of firms when the transport costs are low. When the agglomeration takes the form of FDI, Markusen and Venables (1999) argue, competition from foreign investors tends to reduce profits of local firms, while linkage to suppliers reduces input costs.

Navaretti and Venables (2004) raise the possibility that, when there are no local firms, multinational firms act as the catalyst for industrial agglomeration. Following the entry of multinational firms, there can be: (1) a large number of solely domestic firms engaged in production, or (2) a large number of domestic firms in upstream industry with a large number of multinational firms downstream. Relocating firms begin to benefit from the forward and backward linkages, and a critical mass is reached by some countries which then undergo rapid industrialization. Further growth causes the process to repeat itself. Industry thus spills over in a series of waves from one country to another.

5.3 KOREAN MULTINATIONALS

5.3.1 Characteristics of Korean FDI

Korea stands out as a unique case of a country that quickly transformed itself into a major economic power that combined an overarching government and a strong predilection toward entrepreneurship among its business people. Hanink (1994, p. 344) examines the end of the Korean War in 1953 when Korea was devastated with no capital stock. After a brief and unsuccessful attempt at an import substitution policy, the country began to adopt an outward-oriented growth policy. The government encouraged the formation of a small number of large business enterprises called *chaebol*. In addition, the government maintained low wages by suppressing labor unions. These measures came in tandem with discretionary allocation of export credit, exchange rate adjustments and the removal of tariffs on inputs to be used by exporters. Thanks to all these efforts, real per capita income began to ascend. The rest of Korea's phenomenal and compressed development is a well-known story. Korea is now a major producer of automobiles, large vessels, semiconductors and consumer electronics.

Lall (1996) offers an interesting assessment of the economic achievements made by Japan, China and Korea. First, Japan developed its ownership advantage through a deliberate strategy of: (1) keeping foreign firms out, (2) importing technology by licensing, copying and reverse engineering, and (3) developing its own research. This helped protect national enterprises and build up indigenous technology. Japan went international relatively late, and this was when its enterprises started to invest abroad in a search for low-cost locations. Over time, the pattern shifted to technologically driven FDI; activities in which Japan was losing competitiveness were relocated overseas or phased out, just as the flying geese model predicts.

China's initial isolation was stalwart, but the country has opened rapidly. The pattern of inward FDI has been shifting from simple labor-intensive operations to heavy industry aimed at the domestic market and to more complex export-oriented activities. Local firms are now more concerned about learning from MNEs and gaining access to their proprietary technologies and markets, rather than being passive recipients of capital and know-how. On the other hand, Lall (1996) notes that Korea promoted its hand-picked local firms to become giant conglomerates and forced them into high technology industries with minimal reliance on FDI. In the process, it developed the deepest and broadest base of technological capabilities anywhere in the developing world and has had the largest investment in R&D.

Lee and Slater (2007) argue that the rapid development of the NIEs has disturbed the original concept of the investment development path (IDP). MNEs from East Asia increased the outward FDI from those catching-up countries earlier than the IDP would suggest. The companies that developed technological capabilities played a major role in that process. The government protected domestic markets until the indigenous conglomerates were sufficiently powerful. Industrial upgrading took place without significant involvement of MNEs and FDI from advanced countries. The preferential industrial policies enabled Korean firms to accumulate the technological capabilities needed to go abroad.

Hobday (2001) provides a general overview of the electronics industry in Asia. For latecomers in the electronics market, the original equipment manufacture (OEM) system played an important role. OEM is a form of subcontracting where a finished product is made to the specifications of the buyer and then marketed through the buyer's distribution channels. Since buyers provided advice on the selection of equipment and training of managers and engineers, OEM aided technology transfer. In the 1960s, Korean chaebols began OEM production with Japanese companies. This enabled the firms to attain economies of scale by exporting large volumes of goods. By the late 1980s, OEM began to shift to ODM (own design and manufacture) under which the local firms acquire design capabilities by carrying out detailed product design in accordance with the general guidelines specified by the buyer.

Castley (1998) found that many of the technology import contracts of Korean firms in the 1970s included arrangements for the purchase of Japanese parts and components. In the 1980s, Korea imported the technology embodied by imported capital equipment. The increase in R&D investment, ironically, only led to an increase in dependent patterns of procurement of components and capital goods.

5.3.2 Location Choices of Korean Conglomerates in East Asia

Using province-level data, Lee and Kim (2004) have shown that Korean investment in China evolved from a cost-saving approach to one aimed at market penetration. Kang and Lee (2007) identified market size, existence of special economic zones, quality of labor and transportation infrastructure as positive factors, while labor costs and distance from Korea deter investment decisions.

In 2004, ten Korean firms were included in the 100 largest foreign companies in China. Four of them were affiliated with the LG group, and three were subsidiaries of Samsung. According to Jones and Sakong (1980, pp. 304–5), the Korean chaebol are similar to the early Meiji zaibatsu of Japan, in that control is centralized in a single dynamic individual who founds one enterprise, gets it running, passes management to a relative or associate, and moves on to something new. A major difference is that the chaebol do not operate their own banks. It is true that underpriced resources, notably credit, were channeled into a small number of chaebol throughout the development era. This is not necessarily due to political favoritism, the authors argue, but may simply reflect the fact that they have a proven track record that shows them to be capable of using the resources most efficiently. We briefly review the early development of the Samsung and Hyundai groups below.

Samsung Trading Company was established in 1948 and grew substantially during the Korean War years. Its initial growth was in import substitution of consumer goods such as sugar, flour and textiles. When imitators began to enter one market, Samsung moved on to something new, one step ahead of the crowd.[3] It then turned its eyes abroad to seek out more business opportunities. Starting with Portugal in 1982, Samsung swiftly expanded to the US, UK, Mexico, Indonesia, Turkey, Hungary, Spain, Malaysia, China and India. In 1997, Samsung and LG, another electronics giant, began to import to Korea appliances that their subsidiaries manufactured in China and Indonesia.[4]

Hyundai's initial growth also occurred during the Korean War, through the construction of army barracks and airports, and later in the housing construction boom and the international construction markets in Southeast Asia and the Middle East. Whereas Samsung concentrated on consumer goods, Hyundai has focused on heavy producers' goods such as construction, shipbuilding, machinery, and one consumer durable, automobiles. Hyundai has been the leader in the nationwide effort to move the economy into a stage of industrialization. The uncertainty of success meant that Hyundai took far more risks than Samsung and had to be far more innovative.[5] Hyundai began assembling cars under license in the 1960s. A Canadian assembly plant erected in 1989 represents its early effort toward global expansion, although the plant closed prematurely in 1994 due to sagging sales.

Below, we examine the activities of four large MNEs in more detail.

LG Electronics
Lucky Chemical Incorporated was established in 1947, and Gold Star Electronics began making radios in 1958 as a subsidiary of Lucky. The two companies merged in 1995 to become the LG group. The electronics division has ten plants in Korea employing 30,000 workers, and there are 32 plants overseas employing another 38,000. Figure 5.2 shows the location of LG affiliates worldwide, in Mexico, Brazil, UK, Poland, Egypt, Turkey, India, Thailand, Vietnam, Indonesia, China, Kazakhstan and Russia.

LG Electronics started investing in China in 1993. The initial motive was to create a production base near its home country for exports that utilized low-cost labor, rather than to make a preemptive move to acquire a huge domestic market share. This particular case renders stronger support to the product life-cycle theory than to the new trade theory. LG now has 16 plants and employs 18,000 workers in China, with all the plants

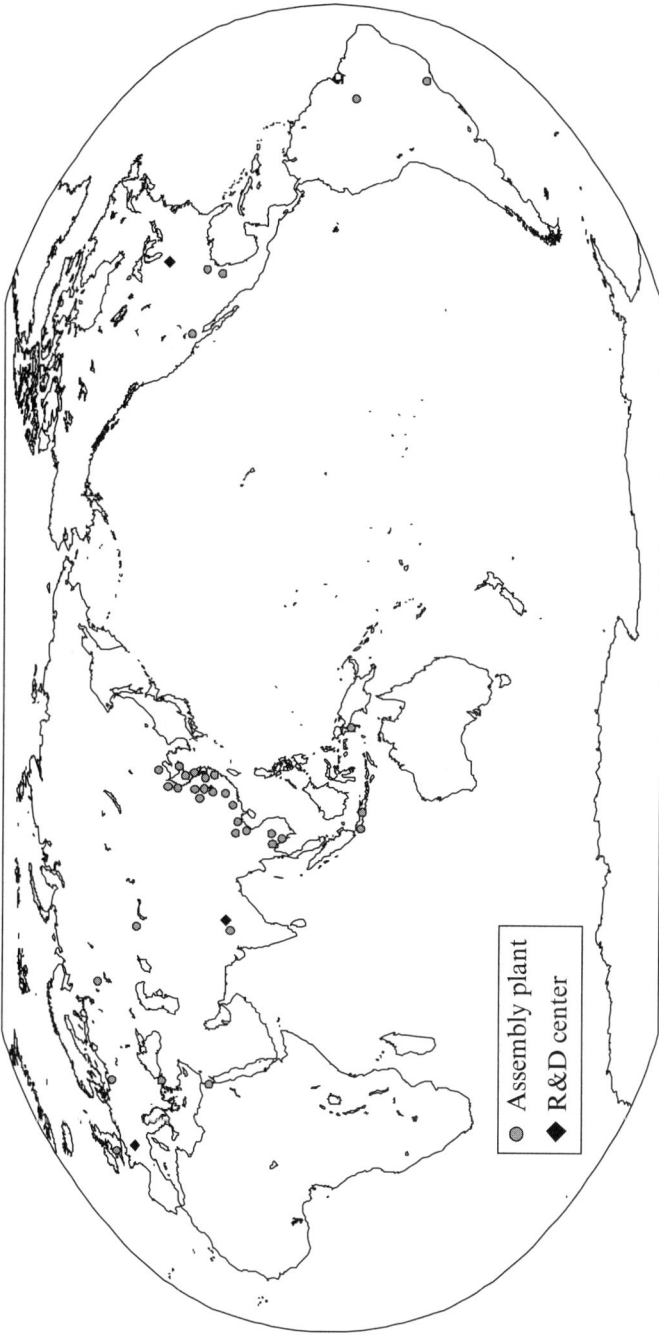

Figure 5.2   Locations of LG affiliates

located in the eastern part of the country, in Tianjin, Shanghai, Nanjing, Shenyang, Qingdao, Yantai and Hangzhou. These plants produce a full range of consumer electronics, and the company plans to expand its markets from coastal areas to inland provinces. In 1997 LG also began production in India, where it manufactures household appliances and mobile phones. The company is pursuing an extensive localization policy in order to remain competitive, with three major R&D centers in the US, Germany, and India which are developing cutting-edge technology in digital and mobile communications, and 11 small-scale R&D offices around the world.

Samsung Electronics

This group moved into the electronics business in the early 1970s with cheap television sets sold under the Sanyo label. According to Kim Y. (1998), Samsung Electronics Company (SEC) focused in the 1970s on the development of its mass production capability, using international linkages to acquire product designs and marketing outlets. Technology was supplied by Japanese electronics firms such as Sanyo and NEC. During the 1980s, OEM production was successful, but it retarded design and marketing capabilities. Efforts toward internationalization were hampered by the rigid and hierarchical organization which was unsuitable for overseas operations. In the 1990s, SEC actively pursued expansion of offshore production and improvement of R&D capabilities.

SEC is now a world-class manufacturer of displays, memory chips and mobile phones, and the success of its efforts to establish a global operation is illustrated by the high share of parts procured from abroad.[6] In addition to nine plants at home, Samsung maintains 29 manufacturing facilities in 14 countries, as shown in Figure 5.3, in the US, Mexico, UK, Spain, Hungary, Slovakia, Indonesia, Thailand, Malaysia, India, Vietnam, Philippines, China and Brazil. Samsung is known as the most successful foreign manufacturer in Malaysia, where a large complex of assembly plants and 40 suppliers, employing 8,000 workers, is turning sand into CRT tubes and then into TVs and monitors. This is compelling evidence of new economic geography at work.

Along the coastal area of China exist 12 plants. According to Yang (2004), generic parts are supplied by firms in China, while more sophisticated parts come from the global sourcing center in Hong Kong. Samsung has five regional distribution centers in China. Final products are sold in China or exported worldwide. The R&D centers try to localize their products to better serve the Chinese market. Indeed, Samsung invests heavily in research and development, operating ten R&D centers in eight different

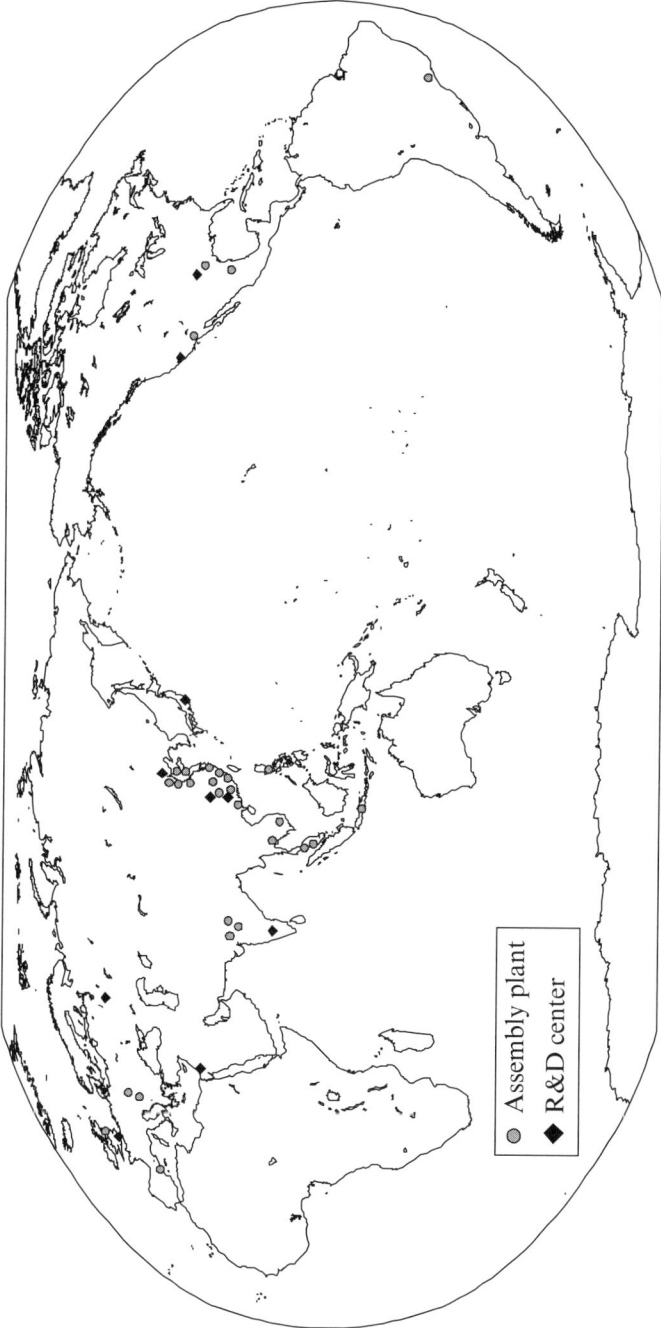

Figure 5.3 Locations of Samsung affiliates

countries. In 2007, Samsung ranked second in the number of patents registered in the US, just behind IBM.

Lee and Slater (2007) note that SEC continued bold and seemingly high-risk investment in the semiconductor technology in the mid 1990s, while Japanese and US competitors reduced their investment, and the strategy finally paid off when the industry rebounded. SEC has invested more than 20% of its net income in R&D over the years, which is the highest ratio among the major semiconductor producers. Despite SEC making headlines for outstanding performance and market value surpassing Sony's, Moon and Lee (2004) point out that SEC still needs to make more R&D investment, including investment in research facilities to remain competitive.

Hyundai Automotive

Hyundai acquired KIA Motors in 1999 to become the third largest conglomerate in Korea. Its Ulsan facility is one of the world's largest auto complexes, churning out 1.6 million cars a year. With two additional plants in Korea, the Hyundai-KIA group now exports over 2.8 million vehicles worldwide annually. The company's primary concern is with the labor union, which is notorious for its militancy, annual strikes, and demands for pay hikes well above productivity increases; recent plant openings abroad are making the workers all the more nervous. Assembly plants in Turkey and India opened in 1997 and 1998, respectively. In the US, the Alabama plant was completed in 2005, and another plant is under construction in Georgia with the prospect of sharing parts suppliers, which makes a strong case for the reasoning of the new economic geography.

The Beijing plant, which opened in 2002, is a 50:50 joint venture and employs 4,000 workers. Hyundai chose Beijing to avoid the turf of other foreign competitors in Shanghai (GM, Volkswagen), Wuhan (Citroen) and Changchun (Volkswagen). According to Yang (2004), Hyundai has 49 Korean suppliers in China. They import raw materials from Korea and supplies finished modules to the plant in Beijing, while more generic parts come from Chinese suppliers. In addition, as shown in Figure 5.4, there are assembly plants for complete knock down (CKD) kits in the 11 countries of Russia, Malaysia, Sudan, Egypt, Indonesia, China, Iran, Vietnam, Venezuela, Taiwan and Pakistan. Hyundai also operates three R&D centers, in the US, Germany and Japan.

Pohang Steel

Pohang Steel Company (POSCO) was established in 1968 as a public company and underwent a number of expansion phases. It completed two large steel mill complexes in 1992 and boasted the world's largest

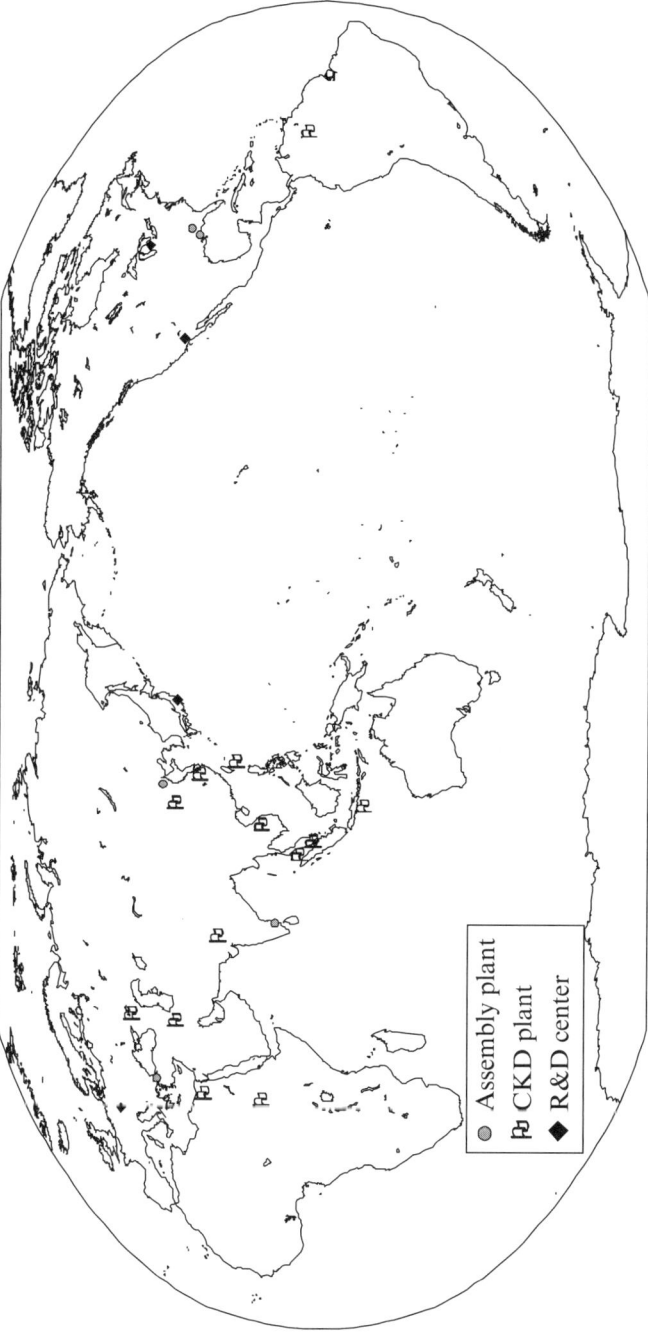

Figure 5.4   Locations of Hyundai affiliates

steel-making capacity until Mittal Steel and Arcelor merged in 1999. POSCO currently imports the majority of its iron ore from Australia and Brazil, and bituminous coal from Australia, China and Canada. Its products are in turn exported to China, Japan, the US and Southeast Asia. The company is currently trying to offset decreasing domestic sales with foreign production. It has 15 processing plants overseas, as shown in Figure 5.5, mostly in the form of joint ventures in China, Vietnam, Indonesia, Thailand, Myanmar, Malaysia, India and Brazil.

POSCO was privatized in 2000, and the transition appears to have been successful. It has been keenly interested in securing its own sources of raw materials in order to lessen its dependency on foreign vendors, and in developing new technology which requires fewer inputs. In 2005, the company struck a $12 billion deal to erect a steel mill in a seaport near Puri, India. Slated to open in 2010, the Chennai (Madras) mill is the largest single FDI project ever undertaken by a Korean firm, and it represents the biggest inward investment for India as well. The prospect of better access to local steel consumption played a major role in the selection of the location, as new trade theory dictates, and POSCO also obtained mining rights for up to 30 years to secure cheap iron ore from a nearby mine.

5.4   CONCLUDING REMARKS

In this chapter, we survey the positive and negative roles that MNEs play in host countries. We also provide a review of related theories complemented by discussion of the MNEs' location choices in East Asia, followed by a comparative analysis of the behaviors of Korean firms. Generally speaking, previous studies concur that East Asian countries enjoyed the benefits brought by MNEs in the form of faster economic growth and smoother technology transfer, while the negative effects from the MNEs were rather mild. Korean firms responded well to policies in home and host countries in their process of foreign expansion.

At the time of writing, an economic crisis of unprecedented scale is sweeping the globe. Many MNEs in Asia are experiencing difficulties, and so their FDI is also likely to shrink. Rather than being a brief interlude, the crisis may unfortunately prove to be a significant shakeout involving substantial disinvestment. Nonetheless, the role of the MNEs as catalysts of regional economic integration in East Asia is expected to grow in importance for the foreseeable future.

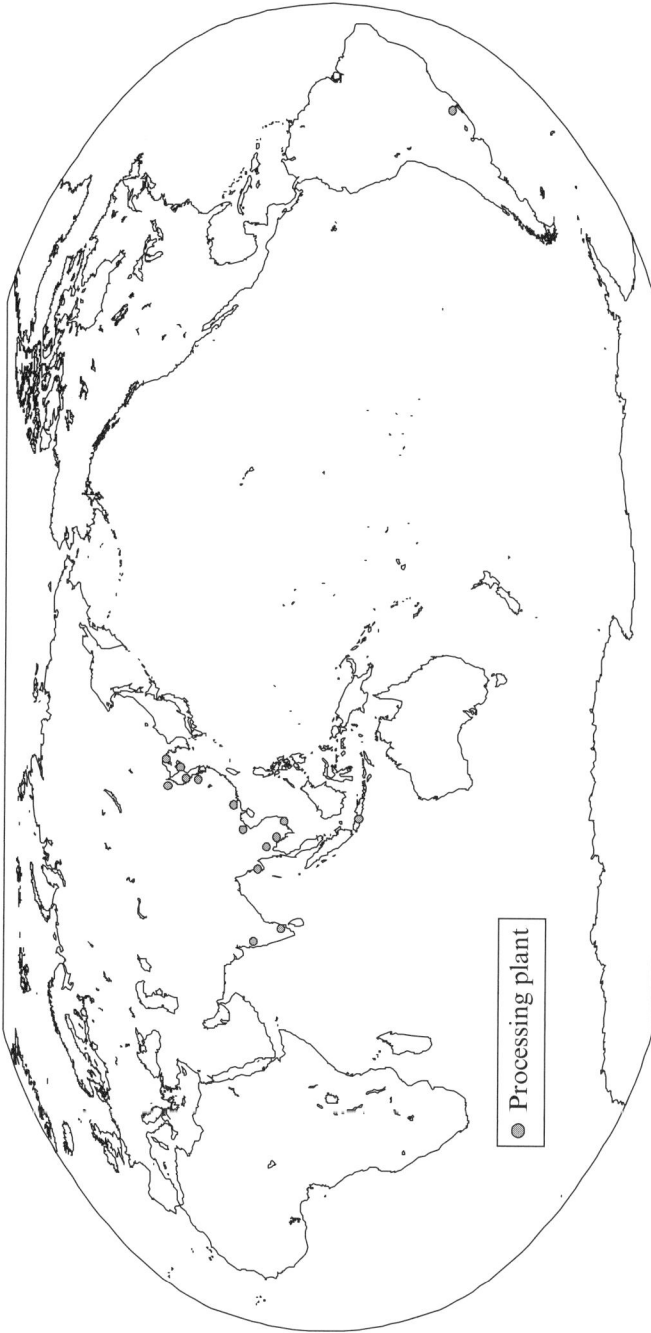

Figure 5.5   Locations of POSCO affiliates

● Processing plant

NOTES

1.　Source: Statistical Yearbook of Vietnam 2006.
2.　This section is an abridged and revised version of Kim H.Y. (2008).
3.　Jones and Sakong (1980), pp. 349–50.
4.　*Chosun Ilbo*, 2 May 1997.
5.　Jones and Sakong (1980), pp. 354–7.
6.　In 2004, Samsung plants in Korea dealt with 522 foreign firms in addition to 1,131 domestic suppliers (*Maekyung Economy*, 23 February 2005).

REFERENCES

Agosin, Manuel R. and Roberto Machado (2005), 'Foreign investment in developing countries: does it crowd in domestic investment?', *Oxford Development Studies*, **33**(2), 151–62.

Akamatsu, Kaname (1962), 'A historical pattern of economic growth in developing countries', *Developing Economies*, **1**, 3–25.

Amiti, Mary (2005), 'Location of vertically linked industries: agglomeration versus comparative advantage', *European Economic Review*, **49**, 809–32.

Balasubramanyam, V.N., M. Salisu and David Sapsford (1996), 'Foreign direct investment and growth in EP and IS countries', *Economic Journal*, **106**, 92–105.

Brülhart, Marius (1998), 'Economic geography, industry location and trade: the evidence', *World Economy*, **21**(6), 775–801.

Castley, Robert J. (1998), 'The Korean electronics industry: the Japanese role in its growth', in Chris Rowley and Johngseok Bae (eds), *Korean Businesses: Internal and External Industrialization*, London: Routledge, pp. 29–47.

Chiu, Catherine C.H. (2007), 'Workplace practices in Hong Kong-invested garment factories in Cambodia', *Journal of Contemporary Asia*, **37**(4), 431–48.

Diez, Javier R. and Matthias Kiese (2006), 'Scaling innovation in South East Asia: empirical evidence from Singapore, Penang (Malaysia) and Bangkok', *Regional Studies*, **40**(9), 1005–23.

Dowling, Malcolm and Chia Tien Cheang (2000), 'Shifting comparative advantage in Asia: new tests of the flying geese model', *Journal of Asian Economics*, **11**(4), 443–63.

Dunning, John H. (1977), 'Toward an eclectic theory of international production: some empirical tests', *Journal of International Business Studies*, **11**, 9–31.

Dunning, John H. (1993), *Multinational Enterprises and the Global Economy*, Harlow, UK: Addison-Wesley.

Edgington, David W. and Roger Hayter (2000), 'Foreign direct investment and the flying geese model: Japanese electronics firms in Asia-Pacific', *Environment and Planning A*, **32**, 281–304.

Ensign, Prescott C. (1995), 'An examination of foreign direct investment theories and the multinational firm: a business/economics perspective', in Milford B. Green and Rod B. McNaughton (eds), *Location of Foreign Direct Investment: Geographic and Business Approaches*, Aldershot: Ashgate, pp. 15–27.

Fu, Xiaolan (2004), 'Limited linkages from growth engines and regional disparities in China', *Journal of Comparative Economics*, **32**, 148–64.

Girma, Sourafel and Yundan Gong (2008), 'Putting people first? Chinese state-owned enterprises' adjustment to globalization', *International Journal of Industrial Organization*, **26**, 573–85.

Graham, Edward M. (1999), 'Foreign direct investment outflows and manufacturing trade: a comparison of Japan and the United States', in Dennis J. Encarnation (ed.), *Japanese Multinationals in Asia: Regional Operations in Comparative Perspective*, Oxford: Oxford University Press, pp. 87–99.

Hamilton, Carl and Lars E.O. Svensson (1982), 'On the welfare effects of a duty-free zone', *Journal of International Economics*, **13**(1–2), 45–64.

Hanink, Dean M. (1994), *The International Economy: A Geographical Perspective*, New York: John Wiley & Sons.

Harrison, Ann E. and Jason Scorse (2004), 'Moving up or moving out? Anti-sweatshop activists and labor market outcomes', NBER working papers 10492.

Hobday, Mike (2001), 'The electronics industries of the Asia-Pacific: exploiting international production networks for economic development', *Asian-Pacific Economic Literature*, **15**(1), 13–29.

Hsiao, Frank S. T. and Mei-Chu W. Hsiao (2006), 'FDI, exports, and GDP in East and Southeast Asia – panel data versus time-series causality analyses', *Journal of Asian Economics*, **17**, 1082–1106.

Ivarsson, Inge and Claes G. Alvstam (2005), 'Technology transfer from TNCs to local suppliers in developing countries: a survey of AB Volvo's truck and bus plants in Brazil, China, India and Mexico', *World Development*, **33**(8), 1325–44.

Jones, Leroy P. and Il Sakong (1980), *Government, Business, and Entrepreneurship in Economic Development: The Korean Case*, Council on East Asian Studies, Harvard University.

Kang, Sung Jin and Hong Shik Lee (2007), 'The determinants of location choice of South Korean FDI in China', *Japan and the World Economy*, **19**, 441–60.

Kim, Ho Yeon (2008), 'Location choices of Korean MNEs in East Asia: escaping the nutcracker', in M. Fujita, S. Kumagai, and K. Nishikimi (eds), *Economic Integration in East Asia*, Cheltenham, UK and Northampton, MA, USA: Edward Elgar, pp. 203–48.

Kim, Ho Yeon and Kyu Sung Jin (2003), 'A study on sequential changes in the industrial structure of East Asian countries' (in Korean), *Journal of Northeast Asian Economics*, **15**(2), 33–62.

Kim, Youngsoo (1998), 'Technological capabilities and Samsung Electronics' international production network in East Asia', *Management Decision*, **36**(8), 517–27.

Kohpaiboon, Archanun (2003), 'Foreign trade regimes and the FDI-growth nexus: a case study of Thailand', *Journal of Development Studies*, **40**(2), 55–69.

Kojima, Kiyoshi (1985), 'The allocation of Japanese direct foreign investment and its evolution in Asia', *Hitotsubashi Journal of Economics*, **26**, 99–116.

Krugman, Paul (1991), 'Increasing returns and economic geography', *Journal of Political Economy*, **99**(3), 483–99.

Krugman, Paul and Gordon Hanson (1993), 'Mexico-US free trade and the location of production', in Peter M. Garber (ed.), *The Mexico-US Free Trade Agreement*, Cambridge, MA: MIT Press, pp. 163–86.

Kumar, Nagesh and J. Pradhan (2005), 'Foreign direct investment, externalities and economic growth in developing countries: some empirical explorations', in Edward M. Graham (ed.), *Multinationals and Foreign Investment in Economic Development*, Basingstoke: Palgrave Macmillan, pp. 42–84.

Lall, Sanjaya (1996), 'The investment development path: some conclusions', in John H. Dunning and Rajneesh Narula (eds), *Foreign Direct Investment and Governments: Catalysts for Economic Restructuring*, London: Routledge, pp. 423–41.

Lee, Cassey (2004), 'The determinants of innovation in the Malaysian manufacturing sector: an econometric analysis at the firm level', *ASEAN Economic Bulletin*, **21**(3), 319–29.

Lee, Hong Shik and Hyuk Hwang Kim (2004), 'International investment location decisions: the case of Korean firms in China' (in Korean), *Journal of International Economic Studies*, **8**(2), 257–89.

Lee, Jaeho and Jim Slater (2007), 'Dynamic capabilities, entrepreneurial rent-seeking and the investment development path: the case of Samsung', *Journal of International Management*, **13**, 241–57.

Lipsey, Robert E. and Fredrik Sjoholm (2004), 'Foreign direct investment, education and wages in Indonesian manufacturing', *Journal of Development Economics*, **73**, 415–22.

Liu, Minzuan, Luodan Xu and Liu Liu (2004), 'Wage-related labor standards and FDI in China: some survey findings from Guangdong province', *Pacific Economic Review*, **9**(3), 225–43.

Markusen, James R. (1984), 'Multinationals, multiplant economies and the gains from trade', *Journal of International Economics*, **16**, 205–26.

Markusen, James R. (1991), 'The theory of the multinational enterprise: a common analytical framework', in Eric D. Ramstetter (ed.), *Direct Foreign Investment in Asia's Developing Economies and Structural Changes in the Asia-Pacific Region*, Boulder, CO: Westview Press, pp. 11–32.

Markusen, James R. (1998), 'Multinational firms, location and trade', *World Economy*, **21**, 733–56.

Markusen, James R. and Anthony J. Venables (1999), 'Foreign direct investment as a catalyst for industrial development', *European Economic Review*, **43**, 335–56.

Moon, Hwy Chang and Donghun Lee (2004), 'The competitiveness of multinational firms: a case study of Samsung Electronics and Sony', *Journal of International and Area Studies*, **11**(1), 1–21.

Moran, Theodore H. (2005), 'How does FDI affect host country development? Using industry case studies to make reliable generalizations', in *Does Foreign Investment Promote Development?*, Washington DC: Institute for International Economics, pp. 281–313.

Navaretti, Giorgio Barba and Anthony J. Venables (2004), *Multinational Firms in the World Economy*, Princeton, NJ: Princeton University Press.

Nguyen, Thanh Xuan and Yuqing Xing (2008), 'Foreign direct investment and exports: the experience of Vietnam', *Economics of Transition*, **16**(2), 183–97.

Polaski, Sandra (2006), 'Combining global and local forces: the case of labor rights in Cambodia', *World Development*, **34**(5), 919–32.

Pupphavesa, Wisam and Bunluasak Pussarungsri (1994), 'FDI in Thailand', Proceedings of AT9 researchers' meeting.

Ran, Jimmy, Jan P. Voon and Guangzhong Li (2007), 'How does FDI affect China? Evidence from industries and provinces', *Journal of Comparative Economics*, **35**, 774–99.

Rasiah, Rajah (2003), 'Foreign ownership, technology and electronics exports from Malaysia and Thailand', *Journal of Asian Economics*, **14**, 785–811.

Robert-Nicoud, Frederic (2006), 'Off-shoring of business services and deindustrialization: threat or opportunity – and for whom?', CEPR Discussion Paper No. 734.

Thoburn, John, Kirsten Sutherland and Nguyen Thi Hoa (2007), 'Globalization and poverty: impacts on households of employment and restructuring in the textiles industry of Vietnam', *Journal of the Asia Pacific Economy*, **12**(3), 345–66.

Vernon, Raymond (1966), 'International investment and international trade in the product cycle', *Quarterly Journal of Economics*, **80**, 190–207.

Yang, Pyung Sub (2004), *Investment Strategies of Korean Firms in China* (in Korean), Korea Institute of International Trade.

Zhang, Xiaobo and Kevin H. Zhang (2003), 'How does globalisation affect regional inequality within a developing country? Evidence from China', *Journal of Development Studies*, **39**(4), 47–63.

Zhang, Xiaoning J. (1993), 'The role of foreign direct investment in market-oriented reforms and economic development: the case of China', *Transnational Corporations*, **2**, 121–48.

6. Productivity, R&D, and intellectual property rights in East Asia and India

Kensuke Kubo

6.1 INTRODUCTION

One of the key elements of economic development is improvement in productivity – an increase in the amount of output obtainable from a given amount of input. Productivity improvement is not the only source of economic growth; per capita output – a conventional measure of economic development – can increase through the accumulation of physical capital, even if productivity remains constant. However, economists and policy-makers have recognized that the per capita level of the capital stock is constrained by the savings rate, and that a policy to increase savings has limited impact on long-run economic growth (Romer 2005).

The pattern of productivity growth varies over time periods, geographical regions, and across different types of activity. In Section 6.2, we will see how in East Asia (defined as including Southeast Asia) and India since the 1980s, the productivity growth rate in the manufacturing sector has varied widely between sub-periods, across countries, and across different industries within countries. The main objective of this chapter is to explore the factors that account for the observed differences in productivity growth.

A starting point is that in most of the developing countries of Asia, the rapid growth of manufacturing output coincided with increased participation in international transactions of finished goods, intermediate goods, and capital. This suggests the existence of a positive relationship between trade and foreign direct investment on the one hand, and productivity growth on the other. By definition, productivity growth involves changes in technology – improvements in the ways that inputs are combined to produce outputs. In the case of developing countries, a large proportion of technological change involves acquisition of existing knowledge from developed countries. Indeed, as we will see in Section 6.3, the economics literature provides evidence on how substantial amounts of knowledge have been transferred to developing countries from abroad through trade and investment channels.

Recent studies emphasize that a key to successful technology transfer is the recipient firms' capacity to absorb new knowledge. This absorptive capacity is positively correlated with the amount of knowledge-generating activities (research and development, or R&D) conducted by the recipient firms themselves (Cohen and Levinthal 1989). Thus, Section 6.3 also discusses the relationship between local R&D effort and productivity growth in developing countries.

Despite the clear evidence that local R&D generates high returns, actual expenditure on R&D in developing countries is low, even in the industrializing economies of Asia (generally less than 1% of GDP). Section 6.4 describes this fact in further detail, and discusses the reasons behind the cross-country variability in R&D expenditure.

According to recent studies, a major determinant of local R&D effort in developing countries is the level of protection afforded to intellectual property rights (Lederman and Maloney 2003). Patents and other intellectual property rights enable creators of new knowledge (such as a new product or a new manufacturing process) to gain from it, by giving them the exclusive right to use the claimed invention. It is thus possible that the rapid upgrading of intellectual property rights systems by Asian countries in recent decades has contributed significantly to the rise of local R&D. Section 6.5 briefly describes the recent evolution of patent systems in the East Asian countries and India, and shows that stronger patent systems are indeed associated with higher national R&D expenditures. Whether or not patent system reform leads to higher levels of technology transfer is an open question, however. On the one hand, firms' capacities to absorb technology may rise with the higher R&D expenditure induced by stronger patents. On the other hand, the opportunities for absorption faced by them may either increase or decrease.

Section 6.5 also examines data on patenting by Asian inventors in the US – generally considered to be a good measure of R&D output. The ratio of US patent grants to R&D expenditure has increased with the strengthening of the patent system in each country, but the evidence regarding the quality of those patents is mixed. Section 6.6 concludes the chapter by exploring the implications of the above for the productivity growth patterns of East Asia and India.

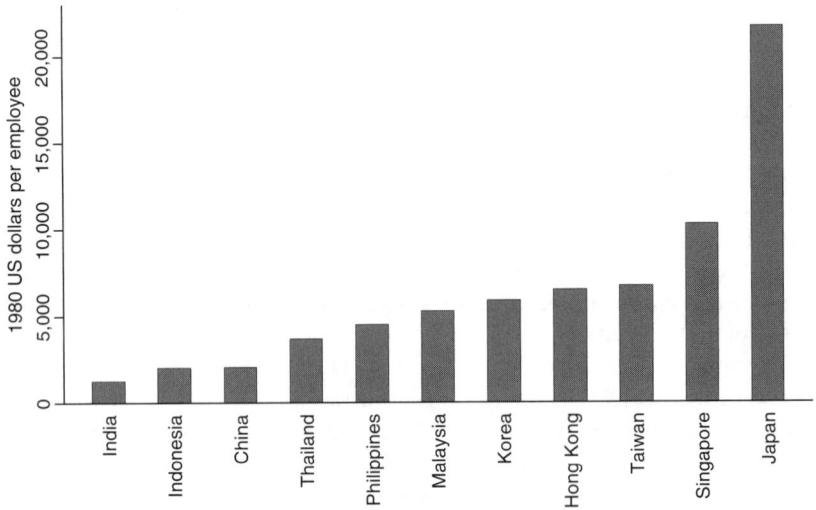

Note: Labor productivity is defined as value-added divided by the number of employees.

Source: Data was obtained from the Groningen Growth and Development Centre Sectoral Database (Timmer and de Vries 2007) and Szirmai et al. (2005).

Figure 6.1   Labor productivity in the manufacturing sector, 1980

6.2   A BRIEF LOOK AT PRODUCTIVITY GROWTH IN EAST ASIA AND INDIA

When countries of varying levels of development are compared, a general pattern emerges where the more developed countries have higher levels of productivity. Figure 6.1 compares the major industrial and industrializing countries of East Asia and India according to their labor productivity levels. Here, labor productivity is defined as the ratio of real value-added to the number of people employed, and the data is for the manufacturing sector in 1980. The observations are ordered from lowest to highest, and it is evident that the more developed economies (in terms of per-capita income), such as Japan and Singapore, tend to be located on the higher side.

Figure 6.2 shows how manufacturing labor productivity in the same countries has grown in recent decades. Excluding the Philippines during the first two periods, all of the economies experienced an expansion in labor productivity during the entire observed period. The growth of East

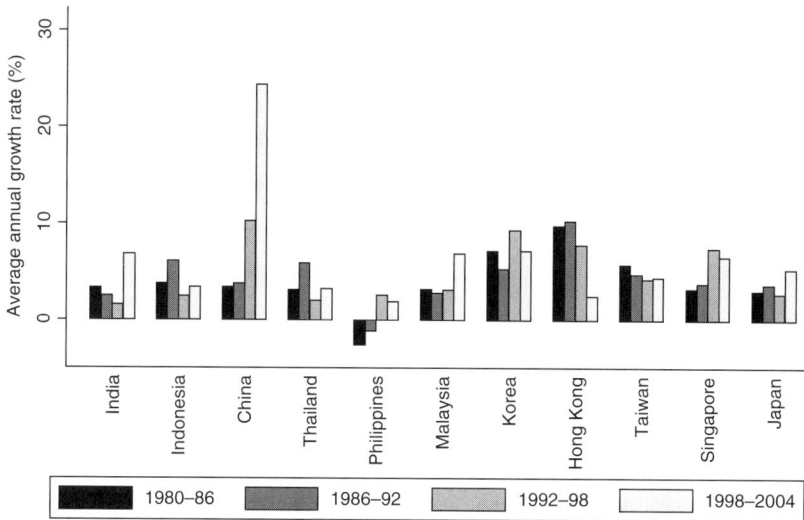

Source: Data was obtained from the Groningen Growth and Development Centre
Sectoral Database (Timmer and de Vries 2007) and Szirmai et al. (2005).

Figure 6.2   Growth of manufacturing labor productivity

Asian manufacturing during this period was defined by close economic
integration based on the development of regional production networks.
The manufacturing firms of Korea, Taiwan, and Singapore started out
as exporters of low-cost final goods in the 1970s, subcontracting from
companies in the more advanced industrialized economies. These countries gradually expanded into the business of supplying high technology
components and intermediate products, forming a key element of regional
production networks (Gill and Kharas 2007). The manufacturing industries of Malaysia, Thailand, and Indonesia began their rapid growth
in the 1980s, as did Chinese manufacturing in the 1990s, also through
participation in these regional networks. In each case, the rapid growth
of the manufacturing sector was supported by a large inflow of foreign
direct investment. Thus, part of the increase in labor productivity can be
ascribed to a rise in the ratio of capital to labor.

This suggests a shortcoming of labor productivity data: it is only a
partial measure of productivity. Value-added per worker may increase
even in the absence of productivity growth if the increase in the capital
stock is sufficiently high. Hence, an alternative measure of productivity
called 'multi-factor productivity' or 'total factor productivity' (TFP) is
often employed by economists and policy-makers. This measure takes

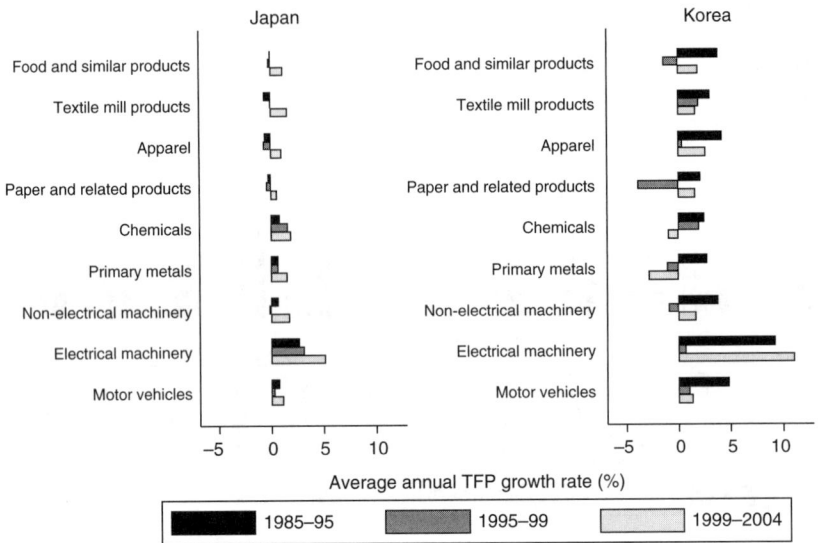

Source: Total factor productivity growth rates estimated from firm-level data by Ito et al. (2008).

Figure 6.3(a)   Total factor productivity growth at the firm level

into account not only the volume of labor input but also other inputs such as capital and raw materials. In applications where detailed firm-level information is used, TFP is expressed as the ratio between an index of gross output and a combined index of labor, capital, and material inputs. In other applications, where estimation is based on country-level or industry-level aggregate data, TFP is calculated by dividing an index of value-added by a combined index of labor and capital. An increase (decrease) in the level of TFP is then interpreted as a sign of productivity growth (deterioration).

Figure 6.3 presents the results of gross output-based TFP estimation by Ito et al. (2008), who used data on listed firms in Japan, Korea and China. In the case of Japan, TFP growth was low (negative for some industries) during the late 1980s and 1990s, but turned generally positive during 1999–2004. In Korea, TFP growth during 1985–95 was much higher than in Japan for all industries. However, some industries experienced negative TFP growth during the late 1990s – a period characterized by the Asian currency crisis of 1997–98. Several Korean industries, most notably the electrical machinery (including electronics) sector, were able to resume earlier rates of productivity growth in the subsequent period. Due to the

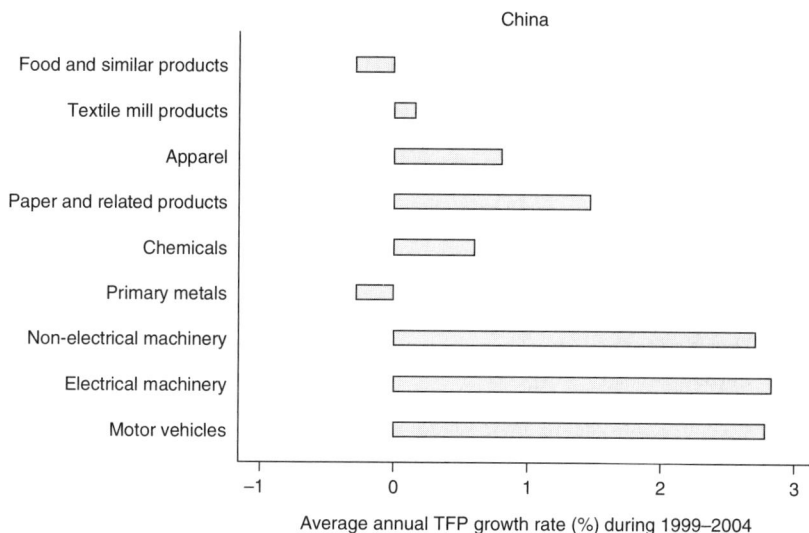

Source: Total factor productivity growth rates estimated from firm-level data by Ito et al. (2008).

Figure 6.3(b)   Total factor productivity growth at the firm level

unavailability of data, the estimates for China (Figure 6.3b) are confined to 1999–2004, where it is shown that the machinery industries experienced an impressive TFP growth rate of above 2% per year.

Figure 6.4 presents the author's estimates for TFP growth in the major industrializing economies of Southeast Asia and India. The results are based on industry-level data collected from various countries by the United Nations Industrial Development Organization (UNIDO 2006).[1] In the database, Revision 3 of the International Standard Industrial Classification (ISIC) at the 3-digit level is used to group industries. Because the value-added approach was used instead of the gross output approach, and due to the inferior quality of the data, the estimates are less precise than those in Figure 6.3. Moreover, estimates for Thailand could not be obtained because the UNIDO database does not contain sufficient information on gross fixed capital formation in Thai industries (required for constructing an estimate of the capital stock). Nevertheless, the results form a useful starting point for understanding productivity changes in the region.

The first thing to notice from Figure 6.4 is that the Southeast Asian economies experienced an almost across-the-board decrease in TFP during 1997–2003, the period immediately following the currency crisis.

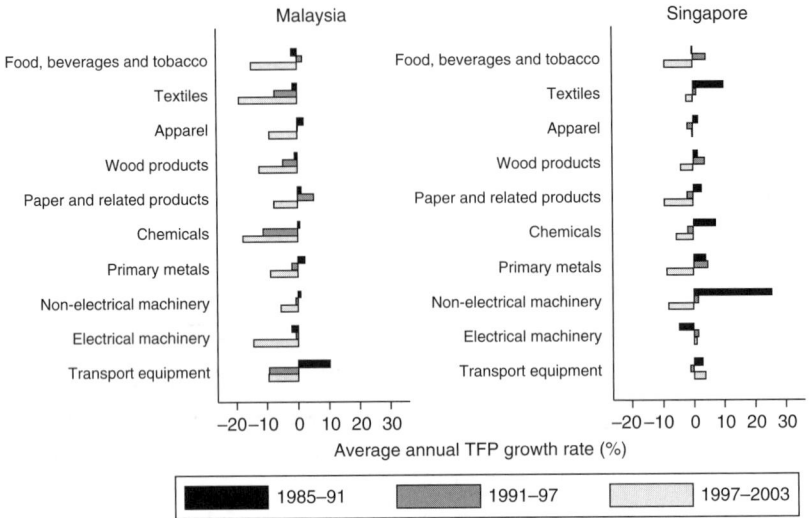

Source: Estimates of total factor productivity growth rates are based on industry-level data from United Nations Industrial Development Organization (2006).

Figure 6.4(a)   Total factor productivity growth at the industry level

Secondly, the following Southeast Asian industries experienced significantly lower productivity growth in 1991–97 than in the preceding period of 1985–91: textiles and non-electrical machinery in Singapore, transport equipment in Malaysia, and non-electrical machinery in Indonesia. It appears that a deceleration in productivity growth had begun prior to the currency crisis. Thirdly, Indian industries recorded across-the-board increases in TFP during 1997–2004, while their Southeast Asian counterparts floundered.

   The overall picture that emerges from Figures 6.2, 6.3 and 6.4 is that while most of the East Asian economies and India experienced continual growth in labor productivity during the 1980s and 1990s, the sources of that growth may have differed across periods, countries, and industries. Throughout the entire period, capital accumulation – supported by foreign direct investment – contributed to an increase in output per worker. Meanwhile, total factor productivity growth seems to have been positive only for some countries and industries in certain time periods. Particularly noteworthy is the finding that China and India experienced high rates of TFP growth during the post-Asian currency crisis years, while TFP growth in the Southeast Asian economies remained stagnant or even turned negative during the same period. On the other hand, it

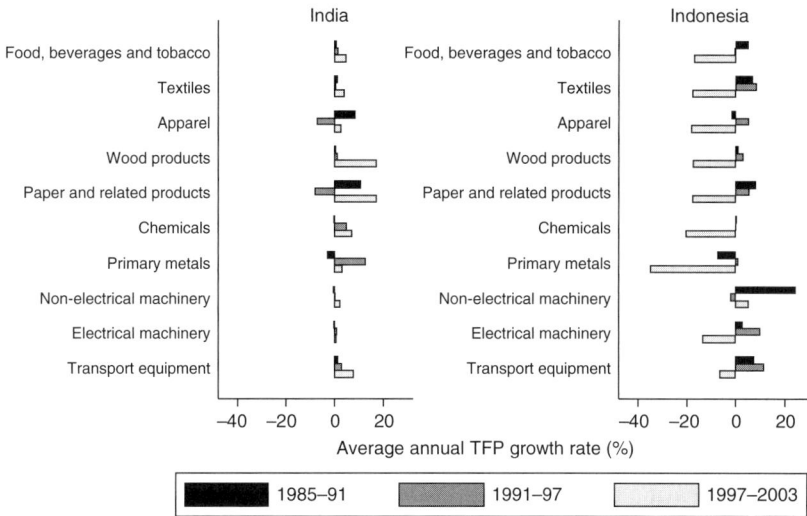

Source: Estimates of total factor productivity growth rates are based on industry-level data from United Nations Industrial Development Organization (2006).

Figure 6.4(b)   Total factor productivity growth at the industry level

should be recognized that many Southeast Asian industries – transport equipment in Malaysia, non-electrical machinery in Singapore, and non-electrical machinery in Indonesia, to name a few – experienced very high rates of TFP growth during 1985–91.

What drives the similarities and differences in productivity growth performance? How relevant is the phenomenon of economic integration in explaining the productivity growth of East Asian and Indian firms? In the next section, we begin to answer these questions by examining the various sources of technological change.

6.3   SOURCES OF TECHNOLOGICAL CHANGE

6.3.1   Import of Inputs and Technology

Perhaps the most obvious way to acquire technology from abroad is importing inputs (capital goods and intermediate materials) that embody new technology. In surveys conducted by the World Bank in Southeast Asia, one-third to one-half of the responding firms mentioned new machinery and equipment as the most important source of new technology (Gill and Kharas 2007). If imported goods are indeed an important conduit of technology flow, productivity growth in developing countries should be affected by the technology levels of the countries of origin for their imports. This idea forms the basis of the statistical investigation by Coe et al. (1997). They found that developing countries which receive a larger share of input imports from advanced countries also tend to have higher rates of productivity growth. Schiff and Wang (2006) extended the analysis of Coe et al. by using international industry-level rather than country-level data, and considering indirect as well as direct routes of technology transfer. Their results agree with those of Coe et al.: the technology levels of trading partners do matter for TFP growth.

Importing new technology in disembodied form is another common route of technology transfer. Technologies are frequently traded within and across countries in exchange for royalty payments and other forms of compensation through licensing contracts. While the uncertainties and informational asymmetries surrounding the value of new technologies can create difficulties for the pricing of licenses, firms have developed various contractual forms to facilitate trade, such as the use of running royalties instead of lump-sum payments (Gallini and Wright 1990). In a study of the impact of technology licenses on firm productivity in Chile, Alvarez et al. (2002) found that local firms that make higher licensing payments to foreign entities tend to have higher TFP growth rates. Their estimates suggest that the rate of return on licensing expenditures is around twice as high as that on physical investments. Also using Chilean data, López (2007) extended the analysis to include the effect that licensing has on local firms that are not themselves licensees of foreign technology, but are either suppliers or buyers of the licensee firms. According to his results, firms that buy inputs from an industry in which there are many licensee firms tend to experience higher TFP growth. On the other hand, firms that supply inputs to an industry with a high concentration of licensee firms do not exhibit higher growth rates.

Taken together, the empirical results on input trade and technology licensing show that the import of technology – whether embodied or not – has a significant impact on productivity growth in developing countries. It is difficult to say which of the two is more important for productivity growth in East Asia and India, as the two can be complements instead of substitutes in some situations; licensing agreements often accompany the trade of inputs. In fact, it is not only inputs and disembodied technology that move across borders and influence growth trajectories: the massive inflow of financial capital has been an important part of the Asian growth story, a topic to which we turn next.

6.3.2   Foreign Direct Investment

In a study of 69 developing countries, Borensztein et al. (1998) found that foreign direct investment (FDI) has a significantly positive impact on national growth rates, provided that the initial level of human capital in the recipient country is above a certain threshold level. The same general pattern seems to hold in the industrializing economies of East Asia, but the Indian experience, at least up to the end of the last century, has been less positive. As Ahluwalia (2002) noted, policies to promote foreign direct investment 'were expected to generate faster industrial growth and greater penetration of world markets in industrial products, but performance in this respect has been disappointing' (p. 75). This divergence in country experience suggests that the impact of FDI on productivity growth is best examined at the microeconomic level. Accordingly, Siddharthan and Lal's (2004) cross-industry analysis using firm-level data has uncovered the subtle nature of FDI-induced productivity change. Indian firms in industries with higher FDI penetration experienced faster labor productivity growth, provided that the firms had high initial productivity levels. Meanwhile, firms with lower initial productivity levels were adversely affected by FDI penetration, with a significant share of firms exiting their respective markets. This 'culling of the weak' effect may have been especially strong in India, because a large proportion of FDI into India was – and continues to be – oriented towards the domestic market. Thus, increased FDI led to stiffer competition in domestic output markets.

As regards the productivity-enhancing effect of FDI, two distinct routes can be considered: the direct effect on firms that receive the foreign capital themselves, and the indirect (or 'spillover') effect on firms that compete or trade with the foreign-owned firms. From a policy perspective, the existence (or not) of spillover effects is more important than the magnitude of direct effects. This is because the direct effects of FDI are internalized by the parties to the investment transaction, and hence the magnitude of such effects has no direct implications for policy-making. On the other hand, if spillover effects (which are essentially externalities) are found to be significant, there is some scope for policy intervention, such as subsidies for FDI, import controls on certain finished products, and local content requirements (Blalock and Gertler 2005).[2]

Nevertheless, the appropriate starting point would be to examine whether foreign capital improves the productivity of recipient firms, for otherwise there is little scope for spillovers. Arnold and Javorcik's (2005) analysis of Indonesian firms during 1983–96 examined the direct effect of FDI. They found that manufacturing plants that receive foreign capital significantly outperformed plants that remained under full domestic ownership; productivity growth in the former group exceeded growth in the latter group by 34 percentage points. Arnold and Javorcik duly take into account the possibility of 'reverse causality' – that more productive firms are likely to be targets of acquisition by foreigners – by estimating a difference-in-difference model on panel data. While the finding of a positive impact of FDI on productivity may not by itself be surprising, it is important that the magnitude of such effects has been properly documented.

A larger literature has explored the existence of spillover effects. Spillovers can be further divided into those that affect firms that compete with the foreign-owned firm (horizontal spillovers), and those that affect their suppliers and buyers (vertical spillovers). In a study on Indonesian manufacturing during 1988–96, Blalock and Gertler (2005) found evidence of vertical spillovers: local firms who supply to industries with higher FDI penetration tend to have higher productivity growth rates. Meanwhile, they found no evidence of horizontal productivity spillovers from FDI. In a separate study on Indonesia, however, the same authors showed that horizontal competitors also benefit significantly from FDI due to the increased productivity of the supplying industries (Blalock and Gertler 2007).

Recent studies on FDI spillovers have focused on the role of R&D activity conducted in the local economy. Studying the Czech manufacturing sector, Kinoshita (2001) found that horizontal spillover effects exist when the local firm invests in R&D. Alternatively, Todo and Miyamoto (2006) showed, in a sample of Indonesian firms, that horizontal spillovers do occur in industries where the foreign-owned firm conducts local R&D.

6.3.3 How Important is Local R&D?

Each of the routes of technology transfer discussed above involves some level of effort by firms located in the developing country market to make use of the new technology. When importing new technology or inputs embodying new technology, firms and individuals must expend time and effort to adapt the technology to local conditions. For example, in the agricultural seed industry, elite varieties are regularly traded across borders. Farmers and local seed companies in developing countries such as India, China, and Thailand who acquire the elite seeds then invest in 'localization' – finding the optimal cultivation technique for the newly introduced crop varieties and in many cases, breeding new varieties by crossing the imported varieties with existing local ones.[3] Such localization investments also occur in the manufacturing industries. Similarly, technology transfer through FDI (including both the direct route and spillovers) involves adoptive or absorptive effort, both at the foreign-owned plant and the domestic plants that trade or compete with it (Kinoshita 2001, Todo and Miyamoto 2006). The productivity increase gained through learning-by-exporting (for example, Bernard and Jensen 1999, Blalock and Gertler 2004) is also a result of trial-and-error and other efforts to meet the demands of overseas customers.

Since absorptive effort plays such a prominent role in the process of technology transfer, it is natural to ask how costly it is. There is no reason to assume that this cost is the same across countries and firms. In fact, Cohen and Levinthal (1989) argue that the cost of absorptive effort is lower (or inversely, absorptive capacity is higher) in firms that invest in R&D themselves. This is because such firms are better able to grasp the mechanics of the new technology and know which 'parameters' (for example, the timing of seed planting) should be adjusted in order to improve the performance of the new technology. Another benefit of having R&D experience is that it allows firms to make use of new technology based on limited information. There are situations where the relevant information concerning a new technology is not fully available, for instance when the new technology is embodied in an imported consumer product, or when information on a production process is only available in outline from published patent specifications. In such cases, firms that have scientific capabilities (gained through R&D activities) are better placed to interpolate between the limited information available, and functionalize the new technology, for example by reverse engineering a motorcycle or by theorizing about the route of synthesis of a pharmaceutical compound. There is yet another route by which local R&D effort can facilitate the transfer of new technology. Having an in-house R&D program makes it easier for local firms to attract technical and scientific personnel away from foreign-owned firms in the same industry. Such inter-firm mobility of technical personnel is an important route of productivity spillovers from FDI firms that conduct local R&D (Todo and Miyamoto 2006).

In addition to facilitating technology transfer through building up absorptive capacity, local R&D effort contributes directly to the productivity growth of local firms in developing countries. However, it is difficult to isolate the direct effect of local R&D on productivity growth from the indirect effect, partly because of the difficulty of directly measuring absorptive capacity. Thus, a good first step is to measure the overall effect of local R&D on productivity growth in developing countries. Lederman and Maloney (2003) conducted such an exercise using a dataset of 53 countries, and found that local R&D expenditures have a significantly positive effect on productivity growth. They estimate that the social rate of return on local R&D (including R&D by foreign-owned firms) is quite high, at 78% for the entire sample including developed countries. This is significantly higher than the return on capital. More importantly, this rate of return is inversely related to the income level, so that poorer countries tend to face higher social returns on R&D.

6.4 DETERMINANTS OF NATIONAL R&D EXPENDITURE

Lederman and Maloney (2003) found that less money is allocated to R&D in poorer countries, even though the social rate of return is higher there. Figure 6.5 replicates the results of Lederman and Maloney (their Figure 1b) using updated data from the United Nations Educational, Scientific, and Cultural Organization (UNESCO), focusing on the industrializing East Asian countries and India. A broad trend that can be observed from the figure is that as countries' incomes rise (in terms of higher per capita GDP), they tend to allocate a higher percentage of GDP to R&D. This movement over time is clear for the highly industrial economies of Korea, Taiwan, and Singapore. China and Malaysia have also shown a clear

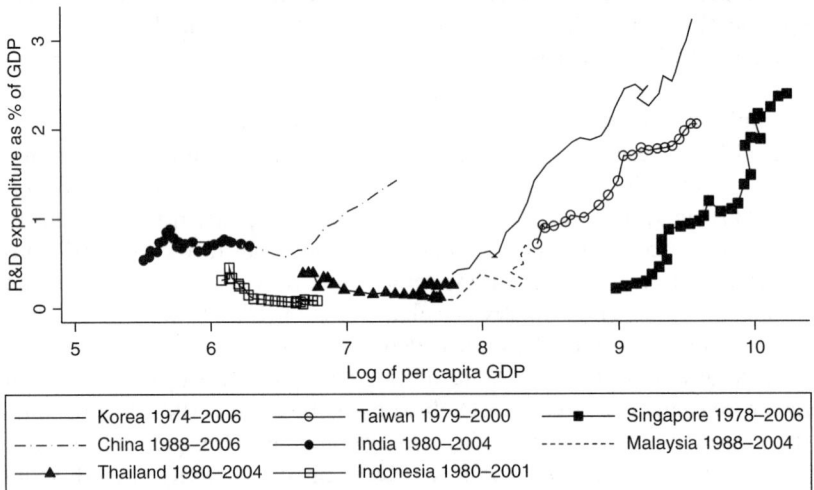

	Korea 1974–2006	—○— Taiwan 1979–2000	—■— Singapore 1978–2006
– · – · – ·	China 1988–2006	—●— India 1980–2004	-------- Malaysia 1988–2004
—▲—	Thailand 1980–2004	—□— Indonesia 1980–2001	

Notes: Per capita GDP is measured in constant (2000) US dollars. Missing values for R&D expenditure have been interpolated.

Source: Data sources are Lederman and Saenz (2005) and UNESCO Institute for Statistics S&T database.

Figure 6.5 R&D expenditure and per capita GDP

rising trend in recent years. On the other hand, the R&D-to-GDP ratio has remained stable in India, Thailand, and Indonesia.

Figure 6.5 reveals additional patterns regarding the relationship between income levels and R&D propensity. Notwithstanding their currently high R&D-GDP ratios, Korea, Taiwan, and Singapore spent relatively little on R&D in the 1970s and 1980s, when their income levels were already quite high. Interestingly, it appears that the trajectories of Korea and Thailand overlap, and so do those of Taiwan and Malaysia. On the other hand, China and India are currently spending a higher proportion of their income on R&D, relative to their per capita income levels, in comparison to the historical experience of the other Asian countries. Given the large effect of local R&D expenditure on productivity growth, it is possible that the relatively high productivity growth in China and India in recent years (see Figures 6.3 and 6.4) is partly caused by their high R&D expenditures. Conversely, the low productivity growth in the Southeast Asian economies (Figure 6.4) may partly be attributable to the comparatively low R&D spending in those countries. The fact that the trajectories of Southeast Asian countries overlap with those of Korea and Taiwan is no reason for comfort; it is possible that the level of local R&D spending that is required to maintain positive productivity growth is higher today than it was in the 1970s and 80s. This is especially likely if we accept that local R&D activity is a requirement for absorbing new technologies. Given that the new technologies available to Asian countries from abroad are becoming increasingly complex, the absorptive capacity required of developing country firms to make use of new technologies must also be growing over time.

In view of the large cross-country variation in R&D intensity, it is natural to ask what factors, besides income level, determine R&D spending levels in developing countries. Lederman and Maloney (2003) provide an answer to this through econometric analysis. Regressing the R&D-GDP ratio on various country characteristics, they found the following to be positively and significantly associated with R&D intensity: (i) financial market depth, (ii) the strength of intellectual property protection, (iii) the government's ability to mobilize resources, and (iv) the quality of domestic research institutions.

Although not included as a regressor in Lederman and Maloney, another important explanatory factor may be the availability of R&D personnel. As Figure 6.6 shows, the number of R&D personnel per million inhabitants increased as incomes rose in Korea, Taiwan, and Singapore; the same pattern appears to have started in China and Malaysia. This increase can be explained by the higher demand for scientific manpower arising from the growth in R&D spending. What is important, however, is

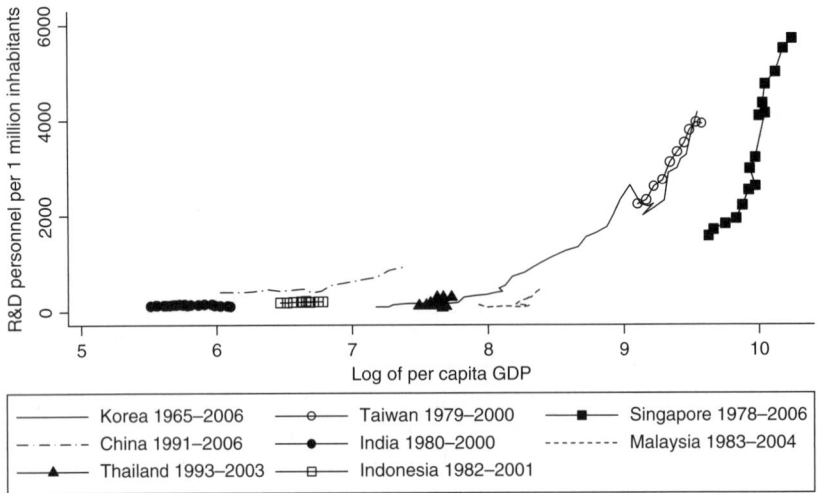

Notes: R&D personnel is defined as researchers. Per capita GDP is measured in constant (2000) US dollars. Missing values for R&D personnel have been interpolated.

Source: Data sources are Lederman and Saenz (2005) and UNESCO Institute for Statistics S&T database.

Figure 6.6   R&D personnel and per capita GDP

that the supply of R&D personnel in these countries has been able to meet the higher demand.

The expenditures shown in Figure 6.5 include both R&D conducted by local firms and that conducted by the subsidiaries of multinational firms. While the country-level data from UNESCO do not distinguish between the two types of firms, some studies have used firm-level data to characterize the R&D behavior of foreign-owned firms specifically. In one such study, Ito and Wakasugi (2007) examined the R&D location decisions of Japan-based multinational firms. They found that the overseas affiliates of Japanese multinationals are more likely to conduct R&D – and to have dedicated laboratories – in countries with abundant scientific human resources and technological knowledge, as well as strong intellectual property protection. These findings are similar to those of Lederman and Maloney for R&D in general. An additional finding by Ito and Wakasugi is that overseas affiliates with a higher propensity to export their products are more likely to conduct R&D.

6.5 PATENT SYSTEMS AND LOCAL R&D

6.5.1 Upgrading Intellectual Property Rights Systems

That stronger protection for intellectual property rights is associated with higher R&D activity should be heartening for the governments of developed countries that advocated the global harmonization of intellectual property rights systems, and worked hard to ensure that it became reality. Under the Agreement on the Trade-Related Aspects of Intellectual Property Rights (TRIPS), which was signed during the Uruguay Round negotiations of the General Agreement on Tariffs and Trade (GATT) and entered into force with the establishment of the WTO in 1995, various aspects of the intellectual property rights systems of WTO member countries were upgraded to conform to 'international standards' – often understood to mean the standards then in place in the most developed countries. Notable aspects of the TRIPS Agreement include: (i) coverage of all fields of technology, including pharmaceutical products and microorganisms, by patent protection; (ii) extension of patent terms and copyright terms to 20 years and 50 years, respectively; (iii) restrictions on the use of compulsory licensing practices by governments; and (iv) provisions to ensure that governments enforce the exclusive rights of the holders of intellectual property.

Meanwhile, various regional and bilateral trade agreements – especially those involving the United States – are being employed to buttress the commitments made under TRIPS, and in some cases, to ensure that participants upgrade their intellectual property rights systems beyond what is required by TRIPS. For example, the US–Singapore Free Trade Agreement stipulates that Singapore must provide patent term extensions in cases where the introduction of the protected product (such as a new pharmaceutical) has been delayed during the regulatory approval process ('patent term restoration'). The agreement also prevents the Singaporean drug approval agency from approving generic versions of a patented drug before all relevant patents on the original product have expired ('patent linkage regulation'). It also restricts the ability of the Singaporean government to force patent holders to grant licenses to third parties ('restriction on compulsory licensing'). The US–Vietnam Bilateral Trade Agreement also contains clauses pertaining to patent term restoration and compulsory licensing, but it does not require Vietnam to introduce patent linkage regulation (Fink and Reichenmiller 2005).

While it is difficult to quantify the characteristics of a system as complex as that of intellectual property protection, Park (2008) has constructed a comprehensive dataset of the strength of national patent systems for

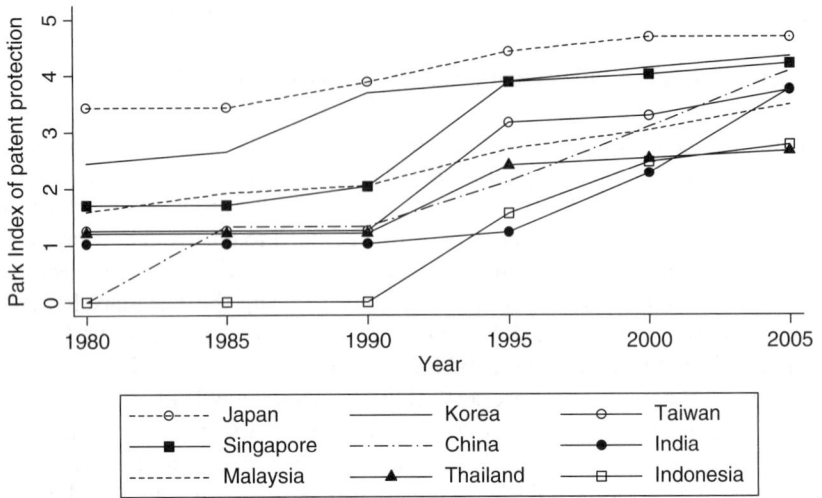

Notes: The values for China in 1980 and Indonesia in 1980–90 have been altered to zero (Park records them as missing) as those countries did not have a patent law during those years.

Source: Data source is Park (2008).

Figure 6.7 Upgrading of patent systems

122 countries over the period 1960–2005. Using his data, Figure 6.7 plots the evolution of patent systems in East Asian countries and India during 1980–2005. From this figure, it is apparent why some commentators have criticized the TRIPS Agreement as simply aligning developing countries' intellectual property systems with those of the richest economies. As Park (2008) notes, the coefficient of variation among all the countries in his dataset fell from 0.42 in 1995 to 0.27 in 2005, indicating a rapid convergence of protection levels. Of the countries shown in Figure 6.7, two (China and Indonesia) did not have any patent system in 1980. Even in countries that did have functional patent laws, large swathes of the technology space were precluded from protection until recently; patent protection for pharmaceutical products was not available in Korea until 1986, nor in India until 2005.[4]

The fact that developing countries' patent protection levels were determined somewhat exogenously through international agreements, rather than endogenously in balance with the level of development, makes it likely that the economic interests of some local firms and consumers were hurt. This is because the excludability afforded by patents generally leads

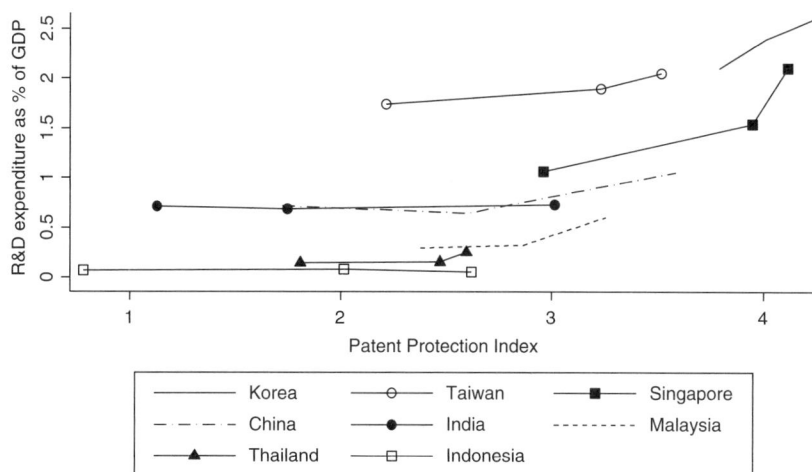

Notes: Each observation constitutes a country–time interval pair. For each country, the left-most observation corresponds to average values for both variables during the interval 1990–95, the middle observation to the averages during 1995–2000, and the right-most observation to the average during 2000–2005.

Source: The Patent Protection Index is from Park (2008), while R&D data is from Lederman and Saenz (2005) and UNESCO Institute for Statistics S&T database.

Figure 6.8   Patent system reform and R&D growth

to higher prices for new products and higher costs for using new processes. Advanced countries like Japan had ample time for adjustment and consensus building while they gradually reformed their intellectual property rights systems, so that the impacts of higher prices and costs were minimized. It is possible that many of today's developing countries have upgraded their intellectual property protection levels without sufficiently considering the effects of such a policy, or else in full knowledge of its detrimental impact but with no choice but to accede.

The policy changes do provide, however, a convenient opportunity to examine the relationship between patent strength and industrial development. Figure 6.8 plots the relationship between the strength of patent protection (as measured by the Park Index) and the R&D-GDP ratio. While country experiences vary greatly, none of the countries has significantly reduced its R&D in response to strengthened patents. In the following countries, increased patent protection is clearly associated with higher R&D intensity: Korea, Taiwan, Singapore, China, Malaysia, and Thailand. This finding is in line with the aforementioned results of Lederman and Maloney (2003), who have controlled for other observable factors. However, even in the face of such seemingly solid evidence, caution must be used in attributing the growth in R&D directly to strengthened patent rights, as the following example illustrates.

Throughout the mid- to late 1990s, Indian pharmaceutical companies rapidly increased their real R&D expenditures (Okada and Kubo 2004). At first glance, this may appear to confirm the innovation-promoting effect of stronger patents, as Indian firms foresaw that pharmaceutical product patents would be introduced in 2005. However, a closer investigation reveals that this may not necessarily have been the case. Much of the R&D conducted by Indian firms was actually targeted towards developed country markets, where their patent rights would be assured regardless of whether or not India offered protection to pharmaceuticals (Lanjouw and Cockburn 2001). Why, then, did Indian pharmaceutical firms increase their R&D as the introduction of product patents loomed nearer? A possible explanation is that by affording legal monopolies to innovative drug companies from developed countries, pharmaceutical product patents were expected to reduce the size of the domestic pharmaceutical market left open to Indian firms. Faced with this prospect, Indian firms chose to maintain profitability by exporting to the most profitable markets available to them, namely the generic pharmaceutical markets of the United States and other advanced economies (Lanjouw 1998). While the development of generic pharmaceuticals does not require as much investment in R&D as new drug development, firms in this industry nevertheless invest in R&D mainly to invent around the various patent barriers erected by brand-name drug companies (Hollis 2003). Thus, the increased R&D by Indian pharmaceutical companies during the 1990s may have reflected their willingness to export to the advanced markets, rather than to profit from patent protection at home.

Whether the effect of patent protection on local R&D is predominantly direct or indirect (as in the previous example), the fact remains that local firms do tend to become more R&D intensive under stronger protection. Thus, it is likely that firms' absorptive capacities also rise under the more stringent patent regimes. Does this mean that technology transfer will occur more rapidly? The answer is indeterminate, as changes in patent regimes affect not only firms' absorption capacities, but also the availability of technology absorption opportunities. The direction of this latter effect is not clear a priori. On the one hand, stronger patent protection has been shown to increase cross-country licensing activity as well as FDI, implying an increase in technology absorption opportunities (Fink and Maskus 2005). On the other hand, the higher coverage of technologies under stronger patent systems implies that there are fewer opportunities for imitating new technologies that are introduced through licensing or

FDI. In addition, the practice of hiring away technical personnel from foreign-owned firms will become less profitable under stronger intellectual property rights. This is because a larger proportion of the knowledge held by potential recruits is likely to be protected as intellectual property, either formally through patents or informally as trade secrets. Thus, the channel of horizontal spillovers from foreign-owned and licensee firms to local firms may be severely constricted. The net effect of stronger patent systems on the pace of technology transfer is likely to vary across industries as well as countries, and is a promising area for future research.

So far, we have only considered the effect of stronger patent protection on the productivity of individual local firms. In some countries and industries, a more pressing concern is the effect of patent reform on industry output. While stronger protection may well contribute to higher productivity growth among local firms that survive, it may be at the cost of fewer local firms operating, with a lower level of combined industry output. If this were the case, our basic premise – stated at the beginning of the chapter – that productivity growth implies economic development, breaks down.

One prominent case where firm-level productivity growth may come into conflict with industry output is the case of the Indian pharmaceutical industry. In 2005, the Indian Patent Office began examining and granting patents to (mostly foreign) pharmaceutical companies that have developed innovative new drugs. These companies are likely to supply their products to the Indian market at profit-maximizing prices, which are drastically higher than the prices that would have prevailed under competitive supply. While the actual impact of pharmaceutical product patents on prices, output, and consumer welfare has yet to be examined fully, two recent studies have estimated those effects through simulation (Chaudhuri et al. 2006, Dutta 2006). Both of these studies indicate that the benefits accruing to the innovator pharmaceutical firms (through higher prices) are far smaller than the combined loss in profits and welfare suffered by local Indian firms and consumers, respectively.

6.5.2 Characteristics of Patenting Behavior in East Asia and India

In addition to affecting the volume of R&D conducted by Asian firms, the strengthening of intellectual property rights systems may have influenced the productivity of their R&D as well as the direction of research. Figure 6.9 appears to support this view. For each country, the graph shows the number of patents granted by the US Patent and Trademark Office for every 1 million US dollars (2000 prices) spent on R&D. Following Luthria and Maskus (2004), the number of patent grants in each year is divided by

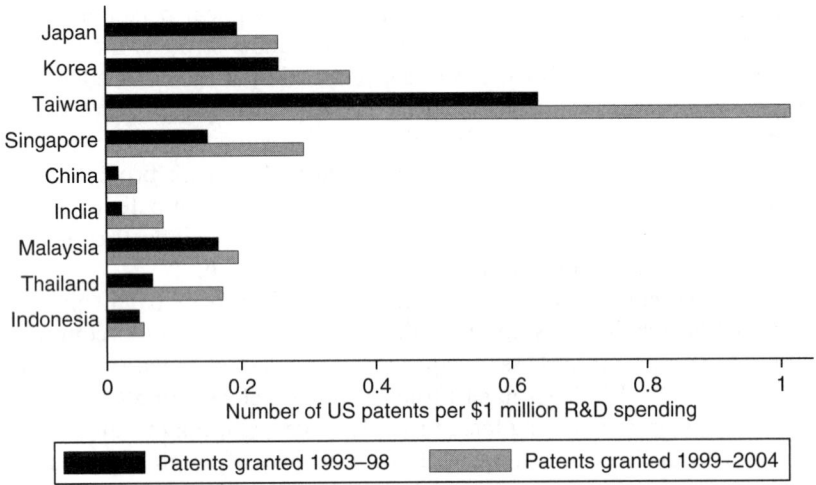

Notes: The number of US patents in each year is divided by R&D expenditure (measured in 2000 US dollars) incurred 5 years earlier. For example, patent counts for 2004 were divided by annual R&D spending in 1999.

Source: Patent data is from the NUS-MBS database, while R&D data is from Lederman and Saenz (2005).

Figure 6.9   Patent to R&D ratios

the amount of R&D spending five years prior, to take account of the lags between R&D spending, fruition of R&D effort, and patent grant. The ratios are then grouped into two six-year intervals.

It is noticeable that the patent-R&D ratio increased in all the countries. While this was a worldwide phenomenon during the 1990s, the following countries stand out for having higher rates of change: Taiwan, Singapore, China, India, and Thailand. Returning to Figure 6.7, it is seen that these very countries experienced the largest increase in the strength of patent protection between 1990 and 1995. Recalling that the R&D expenditure figures used to generate Figure 6.9 are lagged by five years, it is safe to say that the strengthening of patent systems during the early 1990s played some role in raising the patent-R&D ratio.

Some authors have interpreted the increase in the ratio between US patents and R&D expenditure as reflecting a rise in R&D productivity, induced by stronger domestic patent systems (Luthria and Maskus 2004). While this is a strong possibility, another interpretation – not necessarily conflicting – is that stronger patent laws in the domestic market induced local firms to target their R&D efforts away from home, and towards

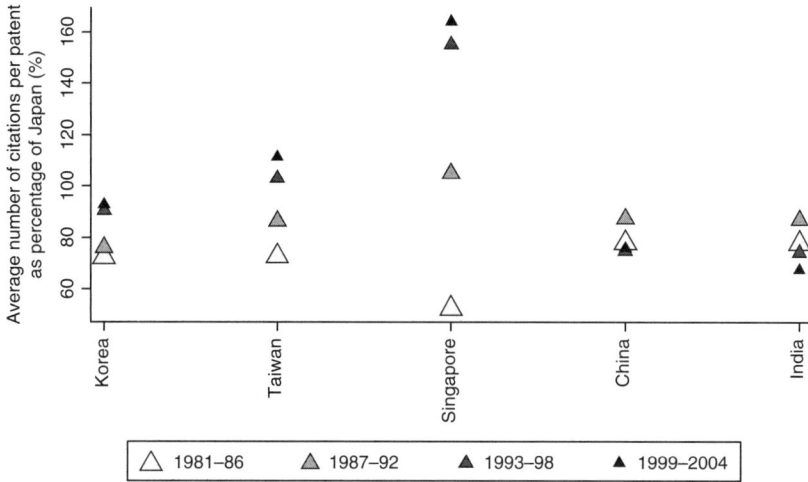

Notes: For each country, the average number of citations received per patent in each period is divided by the same figure for Japan. This circumvents the truncation problem inherent in citation count data.

Source: Patent data is from the NUS-MBS database.

Figure 6.10   Evolution of patent quality

overseas markets. This is indeed what appears to have happened in the Indian pharmaceutical industry (see Section 6.5.1), and it may also be happening, to a lesser extent, in other Asian countries.[5]

An alternative measure of R&D productivity in Asian firms is the quality of the patents that they received in the US. The quality of a patent can be proxied by the number of times it is cited by subsequent patents (Trajtenberg 1990). Figure 6.10 shows the average number of citations received by the patents granted to inventors in each country, aggregating over groups of years. It is possible to observe changes in this measure over time and across countries. It appears that patent quality in Korea, Taiwan, and especially Singapore improved during the 1990s, to the extent that the average quality in the latter two countries is higher than in Japan. On the other hand, the quality of Chinese and Indian patents has remained stable, and in the case of India, has slightly deteriorated in recent years.

Some of the cross-country differences in patent citation frequency may be due to differences in the distribution of patents over technology groups, rather than differences in inherent patent quality. Hu (2008) has shown that patents in the 'electrical and electronics' as well as the 'computers and communications' fields have a higher propensity to cite previous patents in the same field. From Figure 6.11, we find that Korea, Taiwan, and Singapore all have a high proportion of their US patent grants in these two technology areas, which automatically leads to their patents receiving a larger number of citations.

Still, the increasing rate at which Korean, Taiwanese, and Singaporean patents are cited suggests that these countries are reaching higher levels of technological sophistication. Moreover, according to estimates by Hu (2008), patents obtained by inventors in East Asian countries are increasingly citing other East Asian patents. To illustrate, suppose that there are two randomly selected US patents. If the first patent happens to belong to a Singaporean inventor, and the second to a Taiwanese inventor, then there is a 63% higher chance that the first patent cites the second patent relative to the case where both patents belong to US inventors. This and other similar results were obtained by Hu after controlling for technology field and other factors.

The rise in intra-regional patent citations not only attests to the increasing sophistication of East Asian R&D activity, but it also supports the view that East Asia is approaching a self-sufficient center of knowledge creation in some technological areas such as electronics, where intra-regional knowledge flows beget new ideas (Gill and Kharas 2007). On the other hand, the East Asian economies remain relatively weak in the 'drugs and medical' technology field, as seen in Figure 6.11. Hu, as well as Luthria and Maskus (2004), have attributed the dearth of East Asian pharmaceutical patents to the high barriers faced by newly industrializing countries when entering a highly science-driven (as opposed to engineering-driven) field. However, the fact that India has received a large proportion of its US patents in 'drugs and medical' suggests the need for an alternative explanation. It is more likely that in East Asia, the opportunities for higher education, as well as for research-oriented jobs in the private sector, are relatively more abundant in the electronics and computer-related fields.

6.6   CONCLUSION

Explaining the productivity growth experience of Asian countries is a difficult task that requires many separate studies, and this chapter merely presents a starting point for such analyses. With this caveat in mind, several findings, both from existing literature and from the simple exercises contained above, are worth reiterating. Firstly, the growth of productivity has been uneven among Asian countries, especially after the currency crisis of 1997–98. Estimates of TFP growth suggest that productivity increased in Korea, China, and India during the post-crisis years; in

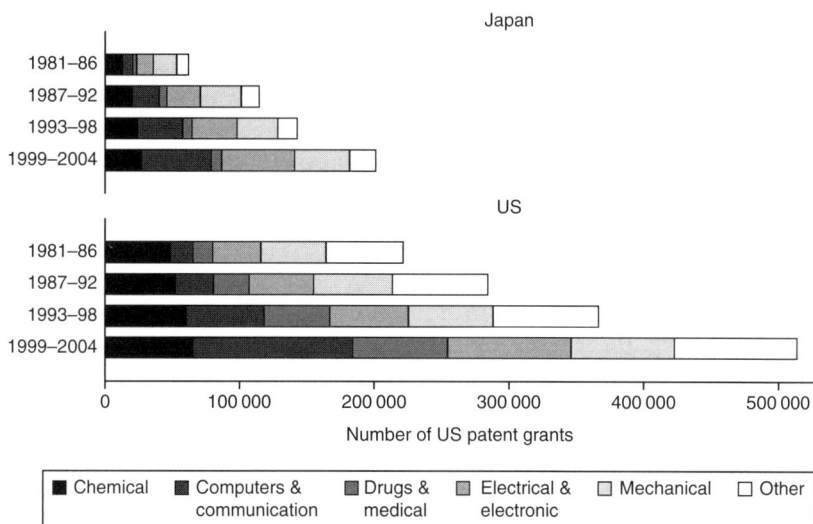

Source: Patent counts were obtained from the NUS-MBS patent database.

Figure 6.11(a)   Patent counts by technology group

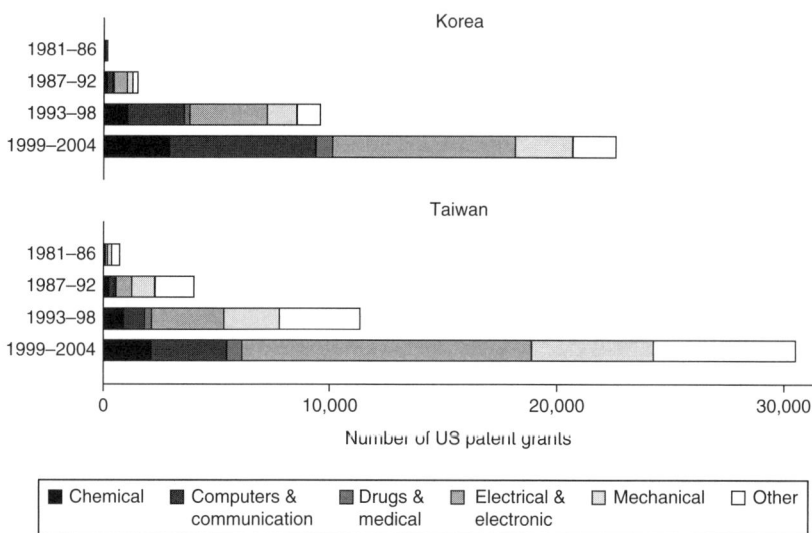

Source: Patent counts were obtained from the NUS-MBS patent database.

Figure 6.11(b)   Patent counts by technology group

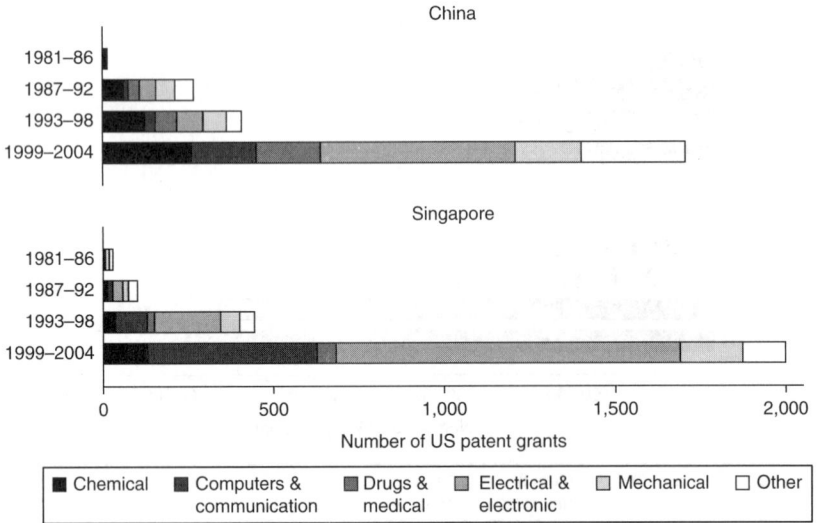

Source: Patent counts were obtained from the NUS-MBS patent database.

Figure 6.11(c)   Patent counts by technology group

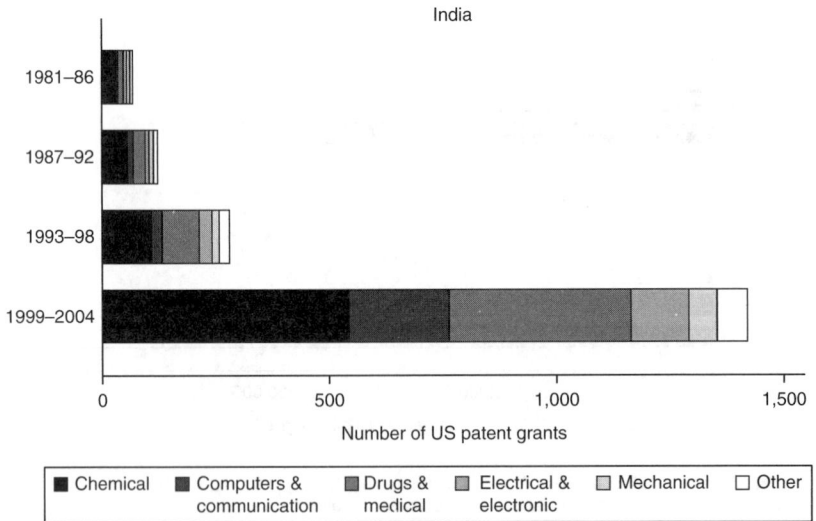

Source: Patent counts were obtained from the NUS-MBS patent database.

Figure 6.11(d)   Patent counts by technology group

the Southeast Asian economies of Singapore, Malaysia, and Indonesia, a decrease in productivity was observed.

One possible explanation for this divergence – especially between China and India on the one hand, and Malaysia and Indonesia on the other – is that R&D intensity (the ratio between R&D expenditure and GDP) is relatively high in China and India, even compared to Korea and Taiwan during the 1970s and 1980s. Local R&D appears to be important to productivity growth not only for its direct impact on innovation, but also for improving firms' capacity to absorb new technology introduced through licensing and foreign direct investment. Thus, the R&D intensive economies of China and India have been well poised to enjoy spillovers from the increasing flow of technology and capital from abroad.

Increased R&D activity in East Asia, supported in part by strengthened patent systems, has already paid a handsome dividend; the region, led by Korea and Taiwan, has become a major center of knowledge creation in certain fields such as electronics. Looking ahead, however, the strengthening of intellectual property rights may create complications. On the one hand, a stronger intellectual property rights system is associated with higher local R&D effort, licensing, and FDI in most countries. On the other hand, stronger rights may work to decrease technological absorption opportunities. The net effect of intellectual property rights reform on technology transfer is still unknown, and presents a promising avenue for further research. Perhaps more importantly, the current focus of the empirical literature on productivity growth as the ultimate outcome variable may be ill placed. As suggested by the example from the Indian pharmaceutical industry, in industries where patent protection is prevalent, higher firm-level productivity does not necessarily imply higher welfare. It may be time to widen our attention to other outcome variables such as consumer welfare.

NOTES

1. Other studies that have used the same UNIDO database to calculate TFP growth include Sun (2004) and Schiff and Wang (2006).
2. While the existence of externalities certainly justifies policy intervention, Gill and Kharas (2007) warn that too often, fiscal incentives to attract FDI become too generous and wasteful.
3. Morris (1998) provides several case studies from the international maize seed industry.
4. China introduced protection for pharmaceutical products relatively early on, in 1993. Interestingly, Japanese patent law only offered process patent protection for pharmaceuticals (like Korea before 1986 and India before 2005) until 1976.
5. In the Chinese pharmaceutical industry, despite the introduction of pharmaceutical product patents in 1993, local firms have continued to invest in R&D targeted towards

the domestic market. This is because the Chinese government developed a system of quasi-intellectual property protection for local firms. Under this system, drug companies that have created new drug formulations (such as new combinations of existing ingredients) were granted marketing exclusivity for several years. While the health and safety ramifications of such a policy should raise concerns, it seems to have achieved the goal of maintaining the profitability of local firms (Xiang et al. 2007).

REFERENCES

Ahluwalia, Montek Singh (2002), 'Economic reforms in India since 1991: has gradualism worked?', *Journal of Economic Perspectives*, **16**, 67–88.

Alvarez, Roberto, Gustavo Crespi and Joseph Ramos (2002), 'The impact of licenses on a "late starter" LDC: Chile in the 1990s', *World Development*, **30**, 1445–60.

Arnold, Jens Matthias and Beata Smarzynska Javorcik (2005). 'Gifted kids or pushy parents? Foreign acquisitions and plant performance in Indonesia', World Bank Policy Research Working Paper 3193.

Bernard, Andrew B. and J. Bradford Jensen (1999), 'Exceptional exporter performance: cause, effect, or both?', *Journal of International Economics*, **47**, 1–25.

Blalock, Garrick and Paul J. Gertler (2004), 'Learning from exporting revisited in a less developed setting', *Journal of Development Economics*, **75**, 397–416.

Blalock, Garrick and Paul J. Gertler (2005), 'Foreign direct investment and externalities: the case for public intervention', in Theodore H. Moran, Edward M. Graham and Magnus Blomström (eds), *Does Foreign Direct Investment Promote Development?*, Washington, DC: Institute for International Economics, pp. 73–106.

Blalock, Garrick and Paul J. Gertler (2007), 'Welfare gains from foreign direct investment through technology transfer to local suppliers', *Journal of International Economics*, **74**, 402–21.

Borensztein, Eduardo, José De Gregorio and Jong-Wha Lee (1998). 'How does foreign direct investment affect economic growth?', *Journal of International Economics*, **45**, 115–35.

Chaudhuri, Shubham, Pinelopi K. Goldberg and Panle Jia (2006), 'Estimating the effects of global patent protection in pharmaceuticals: a case study of quinolones in India', *American Economic Review*, **96**, 1477–514.

Coe, David T., Elhanan Helpman and Alexander W. Hoffmaister (1997), 'North-south R&D spillovers', *Economic Journal*, **107**, 134–49.

Cohen, Wesley M. and Daniel A. Levinthal (1989), 'Innovation and learning: the two faces of R&D', *Economic Journal*, **99**, 569–96.

Dutta, Antara (2006), 'Free entry in the market for drugs in India: implications for social welfare', mimeograph.

Fink, Carsten and Keith E. Maskus (2005). *Intellectual Property and Development: Lessons from Recent Economic Research*, Washington, DC: World Bank and Oxford University Press.

Fink, Carsten and Patrick Reichenmiller (2005), 'Tightening TRIPS: the intellectual property provisions of recent US free trade agreements', Trade Note 20, World Bank International Trade Department.

Gallini, Nancy T. and Brian D. Wright (1990), 'Technology transfer under asymmetric information', *RAND Journal of Economics*, **21**, 147–60.

Gill, Indermit and Homi Kharas (eds) (2007), *An East Asian Renaissance: Ideas for Economic Growth*, Washington, DC: World Bank.

Hollis, Aidan (2003), 'The anti-competitive effects of brand-controlled "pseudo-generics" in the Canadian pharmaceutical market', *Canadian Public Policy*, **24**, 21–32.

Hu, Albert Guangzhou (2008), 'Knowledge flow in East Asia and beyond', Singapore Centre for Applied and Policy Economics Working Paper No. 2008/02.

Ito, Banri and Ryuhei Wakasugi (2007), 'What factors determine the mode of overseas R&D by multinationals? Empirical evidence', *Research Policy*, **36**, 1275–87.

Ito, Keiko, Moosup Jung, Young Gak Kim and Tangjun Yuan (2008), 'A comparative analysis of productivity growth and productivity dispersion: microeconomic evidence based on listed firms from Japan, Korea, and China', Japan Center for Economic Research Discussion Paper No. 111.

Kinoshita, Yuko (2001), 'R&D and technology spillovers via FDI: innovation and absorptive capacity', CEPR Discussion Paper 2775.

Lanjouw, Jean O. (1998), 'The introduction of pharmaceutical product patents in India: "heartless exploitation of the poor and suffering?"', NBER Working Paper 6366.

Lanjouw, Jean O. and Iain M. Cockburn (2001), 'New pills for poor people? Empirical evidence after GATT', *World Development*, **29**, 265–89.

Lederman, Daniel and William F. Maloney (2003). 'R&D and development', World Bank Policy Research Working Paper 3024.

Lederman, Daniel and Laura Saenz (2005), 'Innovation and development around the world, 1960–2000', World Bank Policy Research Working Paper 3774.

López, Ricardo A. (2007), 'Foreign technology licensing, productivity, and spillovers', *World Development*, **36**, 560–74.

Luthria, Manjula and Keith E. Maskus (2004), 'Protecting industrial inventions, authors' rights, and traditional knowledge: relevance, lessons, and unresolved issues', in Kathie Krumm and Homi Kharas (eds), *East Asia Integrates: A Trade Policy Agenda for Shared Growth*, Washington, DC: World Bank and Oxford University Press, pp. 95–114.

Morris, Michael L. (ed.) (1998). *Maize Seed Industries in Developing Countries*, Boulder: Lynne Rienner Publishers and CIMMYT.

Okada, Yosuke and Kensuke Kubo (2004), 'Indo seiyaku sangyo ni okeru kenkyu kaihatsu to tokkyo shutsugan: WTO/TRIPS eno gan'I' (R&D and patent applications in the Indian pharmaceutical industry: implications for the WTO/TRIPS agreement) *Ajia Keizai*, **45**, 113–46.

Park, Walter G. (2008), 'International patent protection: 1960–2005', *Research Policy*, **37**, 761–66.

Romer, David (2005), *Advanced Macroeconomics*, McGraw-Hill.

Schiff, Maurice and Yanling Wang (2006), 'North-south and south-south trade-related technology diffusion: an industry-level analysis of direct and indirect effects', *Canadian Journal of Economics*, **39**, 831–44.

Siddharthan, N.S. and K. Lal (2004), 'Liberalisation, MNE and productivity of Indian enterprises', *Economic and Political Weekly*, **34**, 448–52.

Sun, Chia-Hung. (2004), *The Growth Process in East Asian Manufacturing Industries: A Re-examination*, Cheltenham, UK and Northampton, MA, USA: Edward Elgar.

Szirmai, Adam, Ruouen Ren and Manyin Bai (2005), 'Chinese manufacturing performance in comparative perspective, 1980–2002', Yale University Economic Growth Center Discussion Paper No. 920.

Timmer, Marcel P. and Gaaitzen J. de Vries (2007), 'A cross-country database for sectoral employment and productivity in Asia and Latin America, 1950–2005', Groningen Growth and Development Centre Research Memorandum GD-98.

Todo, Yasuyuki and Koji Miyamoto, (2006), 'Knowledge spillovers from foreign direct investment and the role of local R&D activities: evidence from Indonesia', *Economic Development and Cultural Change*, **55**, 173–200.

Trajtenberg, Manuel (1990), 'A penny for your quotes: patent citations and the value of innovations', *RAND Journal of Economics*, **21**, 172–87.

UNIDO (2006), *Industrial Statistics Database at the 3-digit level of ISIC Code (Rev. 2)*, CD-ROM.

Xiang, Anbo, Zhengjun Zhang, Xiaohong Chen, and Mariko Watanabe (2007), 'Chugoku iyakuhin sangyo: sangyo no zentaizo' (The Chinese pharmaceutical sector: overview of the industry), in Kensuke Kubo (ed.), *Nihon no jenerikku iyakuhin shijo to indo chugoku no seiyaku sangyo* (The Japanese Generic Drug Market and the Pharmaceutical Industries of India and China), Chiba: Institute of Developing Economies, Japan External Trade Organization (in Japanese).

PART III

Integration (2): Agriculture, Services, Labor, and Money

7. Agricultural issues related to East Asia's economic integration

Masayoshi Honma

7.1 INTRODUCTION

Agriculture is often considered a stumbling block that hinders economic integration. Indeed, in forming free trade areas through FTAs (free trade agreements) or EPAs (economic partnership agreements), the treatment of the agricultural sector is one of the most central issues in the negotiations, and sensitive products are excluded, or at least treated differently from other sectors in the list of tariff eliminations.

Agricultural policy is associated with a country's stage of economic development, and over the course of economic growth in a country, the agricultural policy tends to shift from exploitation to protection of agriculture (Honma and Hayami 1986, Honma 1994). In the East Asian region, which is defined here as Japan, Korea, China and ASEAN (Association of Southeast Asian Nations) countries, the stage of economic development differs by country, and thus so does agricultural policy.

It is not an easy task to harmonize agricultural policies in a region where there are both countries that export and countries that import agricultural products. As observed in the WTO (World Trade Organization) agricultural negotiations, interests among East Asian countries do not necessarily coincide with each other but are often rather sharply conflicted by agricultural issues.

Despite the difficulties, the agricultural sector should be reoriented and adjusted towards East Asian economic integration, because, if agriculture is excluded from the integration, the benefits of integration will be halved for the countries in which agriculture is an important economic sector. Also, unless agriculture is included, consumers in food importing countries will lose the opportunity to access agricultural products in the region at lower prices. Thus, all sectors should advance toward integration, if all countries are to take full advantage of it.

The purpose of this chapter is to examine the agricultural issues in order to develop a way to include the agricultural sector in the framework of

179

the integrated East Asian region. For this purpose, firstly, the structures of agriculture in the region are examined to clarify the similarities and differences among the countries in the region. Secondly, agricultural trade is investigated through examination of the performance of imports and exports in individual countries as well as the trade flows in the region. Thirdly, the levels of agricultural protection in terms of import tariffs and the nominal rate of protection are discussed. Fourthly, the treatment of agriculture in existing FTAs/EPAs is reviewed to draw lessons from past experiences. Fifthly, the direction of agricultural policy for East Asian Economic Integration is suggested, with reference to the lessons from the Common Agricultural Policy in the European Union. Finally, in the conclusion, the path toward harmonization of agricultural policy in the region for economic integration and its policy implications are discussed.

7.2   STRUCTURE OF AGRICULTURE IN EAST ASIA

It is important first to recognize how agricultural structure differs among the countries in East Asia. Table 7.1 shows basic indicators for agriculture in 11 countries in the region.[1]

Rural population comprises more than half of the total population in China and most ASEAN countries except Singapore, Malaysia and the Philippines, whereas in Japan and Korea rural population is respectively 34% and 19% of the total population. The importance of agriculture in terms of share of employment in the total economy contrasts sharply among the countries. Agricultural share in employment is only 4.6% and 8.7%, respectively, in Japan and Korea, whereas it is 44% in China and more than 40% in ASEAN countries except Singapore, Malaysia and the Philippines.

The most important resource endowment for agriculture is agricultural land. China has 112 million hectares of agricultural land, but this amounts to only 0.1 ha per capita of agricultural population because the agricultural population in rural areas is dense compared with the land resources. In this sense, China is a land-scarce country with a large agricultural population. In other words, China should absorb rural population into non-agricultural employment in order to increase labor productivity. It is noteworthy that the amount of agricultural land per capita of agricultural population is low not only in China but also in most countries in the region. Except in Malaysia which has 2.0 ha, all other ASEAN countries possess less than 1.0 ha of agricultural land per capita of agricultural population. Japan's average of 1.2 ha is rather large by Asian standards.[2]

Table 7.1 also displays the level of cereal production per hectare by

Table 7.1 *Basic indicators of agricultural structure in East Asian countries*

	Rural population (million)	Share in total population (%)	Agricultural employment (1000)	Share in total employment (%)	Agricultural land (1000ha)	Per agricultural population (ha)	Yield of cereal production (kg/ha)
Japan	43.8	34.3	2927	4.6	4714	1.2	5849
Korea	9.3	19.4	1982	8.7	1839	0.6	6238
China	784.5	60.5	–	44.1	115632	0.1	5095
Malaysia	8.4	33.8	–	14.7	7585	2.0	3321
Thailand	43.3	67.9	15178	44.4	17687	0.6	3044
Philippines	31.1	38.1	11544	37.2	10700	0.4	2916
Indonesia	115.5	53.1	41652	44.6	36500	0.4	4278
Singapore	0.0	0.0	5	0.3	1	0.2	–
Cambodia	11.4	80.9	–	60.3	3852	0.4	2231
Lao PDR	4.4	79.7	–	–	1074	0.2	3648
Vietnam	60.7	74.0	24721	59.9	8920	0.2	4641

Source: World Bank, World Development Report 2008.

Table 7.2   Economic indicators of agriculture in East Asian countries

	Agriculture value added (US$ million)	Share in total GDP (%)	Per agricultural worker (US$)
Japan	74849	1.7	19177
Korea	22416	3.7	6922
China	246982	12.7	292
Malaysia	10843	9.2	2898
Thailand	16164	10.1	554
Philippines	12949	14.7	429
Indonesia	38429	14.9	421
Singapore	93	0.1	19959
Cambodia	1710	33.7	181
Lao PDR	1157	46.8	264
Vietnam	9936	21.7	182

Source: World Bank, World Development Report 2008.

country. This figure is equivalent to land productivity and reflects the natural conditions and other inputs of agricultural production, such as labor and fertilizer per hectare. It is observed that Japan, Korea and China produce more than 5,000 kg/ha of cereals, whereas all ASEAN countries produce less than 5,000 kg/ha. This indicates that ASEAN countries have the potential to increase land productivity by using other inputs more intensively.

The importance of agricultural production is measured in terms of value added in agricultural activities. The value added in agriculture and the related indicators are presented in Table 7.2. The share of agricultural value added in the total GDP of the economy is an indicator of economic development, as described by Petty-Clark's law, which states that in the course of economic development, the weight of economic activities shifts from primary industry to secondary industry and then to tertiary industry.

Agricultural value added in Japan and Korea accounts for only 1.7% and 3.7% of the nation's GDP, respectively, whereas it is 12.7% in China and more than 10% in most ASEAN countries. Particularly in Cambodia and Lao PDR, it reaches 34% and 47%, respectively, implying that these are agriculture-based countries.

The agricultural value added per agricultural worker (shown in Table 7.2) is equivalent to labor productivity in agriculture. In Japan and Singapore, it is about US$19,000 and US$20,000, respectively, though the latter's agriculture is negligible in its economy. In Korea and Malaysia, agricultural labor productivity amounts to US$7,000 and US$3,000, respectively, but all other countries produce less than US$1,000 dollars. In China, gross national income per capita exceeded US$2,000 in 2006 (World Bank, 2007), but agricultural value added per agricultural worker remains at the low level of US$292, which is lower than that of Indonesia and the Philippines.

These statistics indicate the differences in the role of agriculture in each country. The countries in which agriculture plays an important role tend to promote agricultural exports to drive their economic growth, whereas food importing countries tend to resist freer agricultural trade because they still have a large rural population even though the share of agriculture in their economy has declined sharply, as in Japan (see Box 7.1) and Korea. This situation complicates the process of economic integration when agriculture is fully included in the integration.

7.3 STRUCTURE OF AGRICULTURAL TRADE IN EAST ASIA

The greatest impact of the integration of East Asia will be changes in agricultural trade, including reduction or elimination of tariffs and non-tariff barriers. To consider the effects of integration, it is necessary to investigate the current structure of agricultural trade in the region.

Figure 7.1 shows the value of the annual movement of all agricultural imports and exports of Japan, Korea, China and ASEAN countries (ASEAN+3) since 1980. Agricultural imports of the region amounted to US$124 billion in 2006, which accounted for 16.7% of world agricultural imports, whereas agricultural exports of the region amounted to US$81 billion in 2006, which accounted for 11.2% of world agricultural exports. As indicated in Figure 7.1, the value of both agricultural imports and exports has increased in recent years, but the share of imports has declined slightly from the mid 1990s while the share of exports has been rather stable, at around 10% of the world exports.

Table 7.3 shows the performance of agricultural trade for individual countries at four points in time since 1980 in three year averages. The largest food importer in the region is Japan, accounting for 36.1% of the total food imports of the region in 2004–06, followed by China whose imports account for 29.8% of the regional total. Japan's share declined from 51.5% in 1989–91, whereas China increased its share from 17.8% in the same period.

China is also the largest exporter of the region, accounting for 28.5% of the regional total exports in 2004–06, followed by Thailand, Indonesia and

BOX 7.1   THE POLITICAL ECONOMY OF JAPANESE AGRICULTURE: THE IRON TRIANGLE

The system of protecting the agricultural sector in Japan, which has been called the 'iron triangle', consists of the MAFF (Ministry of Agriculture, Forestry and Fisheries), the ruling LDP (Liberal Democratic Party) and JA (Japan Agricultural Cooperatives). In particular JA, like a government body, has played an important role in farm product and input marketing, treating large and small farmers equally irrespective of the size of their transactions. Under such circumstances, it has been difficult for large farmers to increase their advantage by consolidating small farms into larger operational units.

In 2007, a new agricultural policy scheme was introduced. It provides a direct payment for large-acreage farms so as to guarantee income only for those who operate farms exceeding a certain size. This program appeared to be a start in the right direction to correct the inefficient egalitarianism in Japan's agricultural policy. However, the scheme has met strong resistance, forcing compromises from the beginning. Originally, this program was designed to target mainly large, individual farmers. JA, however, was strongly opposed to such a policy targeted only at large farmers, whose numbers are small, because JA needs to maintain the high number of family farms in order to protect its political influence, particularly in the ruling LDP. In the end, political pressure from JA opened the door to direct payments to small, part-time farmers, by allowing them to participate in the program if they organize themselves into a collective farming unit.

Nevertheless, under the strong external and internal pressures favoring structural reform of agriculture so that Japan will be able to cope with globalization more positively, the iron triangle seems to be melting slightly. MAFF has gradually moved towards adopting more market-oriented policies, such as the targeted direct payment program. The ruling LDP is also experiencing a shift in the balance of its interest representation towards urban areas. Only JA remains as a gigantic stumbling block in the way of agricultural policy reform. JA should recognize the fact that large-scale, efficient farmers are beginning to exit from the JA marketing system. As their exit from JA accelerates, JA is losing its economic base.

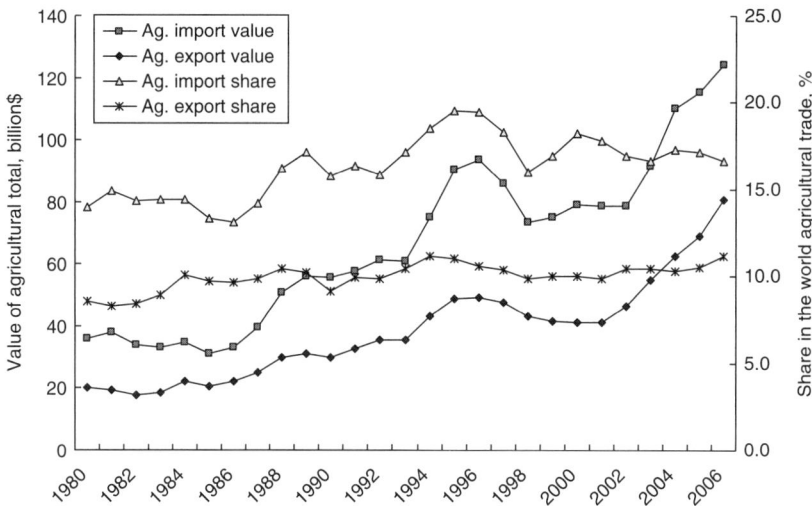

Source: FAO, FAOSTAT.

Figure 7.1   Value and share of agricultural trade of ASEAN+3

Malaysia whose shares are 16% to 19% each of the regional total. China increased its share in the 1980s when Indonesia and Malaysia lost part of their shares. On the other hand, Thailand has maintained its share at around 18% of the regional total.

It is interesting to examine the balance of agricultural trade in the region. The total balance can be calculated as the difference between agricultural exports and imports, as shown in Figure 7.1, which presents regular deficits in the region as a whole over time. The deficit was US$46 billion in 2004–06, which was the result of increases since the late 1990s. In order to see the sources of deficits in the agricultural trade balance in the region, the balance is decomposed into the four balances of Japan, Korea, China and ASEAN. The result is shown in Figure 7.2. The Japanese deficit is steadily increasing, and so is the Korean deficit slightly. ASEAN regularly records surpluses in its agricultural trade balance, and surpluses have increased in recent years. Dramatic changes have occurred in China in recent years, increasing the deficit rapidly, though China was a net food exporter in the early 1990s.

To understand the inter-dependency of agricultural trade in the East Asian region, it is important to investigate not only total agricultural trade but also trade flows. Tables 7.4 and 7.5 show the trade flows of agricultural trade among Japan, Korea, China and six ASEAN countries for 2002–04 and 2005–07.

Table 7.3 *Value of agricultural imports and exports for East Asian countries (US$ million)*

	1979–81 average		1989–91 average		1999–2001 average		2004–06 average	
	Import	Export	Import	Export	Import	Export	Import	Export
Japan	17519	908	29114	1174	35334	1898	42120	1952
Korea	3457	591	6572	1125	7963	1609	11381	2258
China	7439	4290	10096	10769	14872	12617	34734	20097
Malaysia	1339	3740	2211	4519	3851	6153	6276	11521
Thailand	557	3410	1579	5760	2644	7285	4139	13126
Philippines	623	1849	1191	1240	2550	1447	3841	2385
Indonesia	1517	2314	1755	2962	4292	4815	5440	11537
Singapore	1922	1498	3547	2668	4017	2780	5014	3536
Brunei	81	2	165	9	196	1	268	2
Cambodia	66	5	14	41	232	33	375	51
Lao PDR	32	1	13	34	75	31	159	22
Vietnam	374	95	226	667	1312	2260	2502	3740
ASEAN+3	34965	18940	56579	31141	77668	41318	116735	70622
World	244668	224033	345042	319279	439537	414409	685856	661248
Share in the world	0.143	0.085	0.164	0.098	0.177	0.100	0.170	0.107

Source: FAO, FAOSTAT.

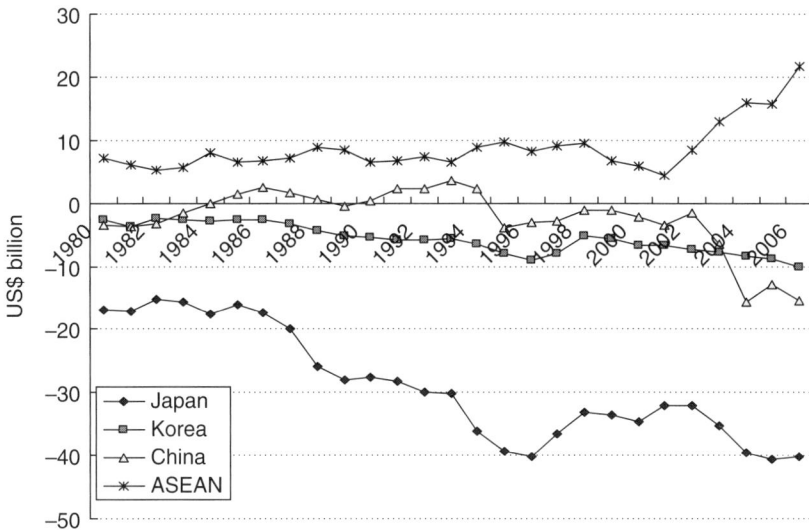

Source: FAO, FAOSTAT.

Figure 7.2   Balance of agricultural trade for ASEAN+3, UD$ billion

In the agricultural trade in 2005–07 shown in Table 7.5, the total imports of nine countries amounted US$173.2 billion, using the UN COMTRADE definition of agricultural commodities which differs from the FAO definition used in Table 7.2. Intra-regional trade of agricultural commodities amounted to US$49.3 billion, accounting for 28.4% of the total imports of nine countries in 2005–07. This amount of intra-regional trade explains 43.8% of the total agricultural exports of nine countries amounting to US$112.4 billion.

Thus, East Asian countries depend on intra-regional trade for food exports more than for food imports. In short, countries in the region import agricultural products from a wider range of suppliers in the world, but their exports target the countries in the region. This means that East Asia has the capacity to increase intra-regional trade in import markets by shifting its food supply sources from other regions to East Asia when the markets are integrated.

The regional dependency ratio is low in such markets as China, Thailand, Japan, and Indonesia, at less than 30%, while in contrast more than half the food imports of Malaysia come from East Asian countries. When exporting agricultural commodities, Korea and Singapore depend on the region, shipping more than half of their food exports to countries

Table 7.4 Trade flows of agricultural products among ASEAN+3, 2002–04 (US$ billion)

Exporter	Importer									Regional total (A)	World (B)	Regional dependency (A/B)
	Japan	Korea	China	Malaysia	Thailand	Philippines	Indonesia	Singapore	Vietnam			
Japan		364	451	37	162	31	37	89	36	1208	3049	0.396
Korea	1438		252	30	50	31	39	36	16	1894	3096	0.612
China	6727	2289		586	214	251	486	262	245	11060	21423	0.516
Malaysia	699	246	1544		316	144	323	1036	145	4452	11190	0.398
Thailand	2902	435	1246	915		198	425	368	98	6587	14451	0.456
Philippines	431	123	77	91	72		58	53	22	927	2308	0.402
Indonesia	1127	342	1064	628	105	91		583	87	4027	10274	0.392
Singapore	444	46	184	516	134	231	274		156	1986	3735	0.532
Vietnam	800	200	561	147	53	142	137	139		2178	5275	0.413
Regional total	14569	4045	5378	2950	1108	1121	1779	2565	805	34319	74802	0.459
World	59307	14246	28662	5518	5397	3215	5427	5298	2205	129276		
Regional dependency	0.246	0.284	0.188	0.534	0.205	0.349	0.328	0.484	0.365	0.265		

Source: UN, UNCOMTRADE.

Table 7.5   Trade flows of agricultural products among ASEAN+3, 2005–07 (US$ billion)

Exporter	Importer									Regional Total (A)	World (B)	Regional Dependency (A/B)
	Japan	Korea	China	Malaysia	Thailand	Philippines	Indonesia	Singapore	Vietnam			
Japan		468	916	44	216	36	44	88	64	1877	4237	0.443
Korea	1311		400	36	89	46	60	37	39	2018	3635	0.555
China	8477	3179		855	388	430	616	310	378	14633	32580	0.449
Malaysia	898	369	2962		467	236	391	1261	298	6882	16337	0.421
Thailand	3397	584	2431	1413		288	469	385	322	9289	20720	0.448
Philippines	453	183	81	97	122		80	73	54	1143	2928	0.390
Indonesia	1527	571	2381	972	117	179		989	235	6971	18463	0.378
Singapore	619	68	450	602	272	189	467		261	2928	5150	0.568
Vietnam	1105	295	1118	224	75	488	96	118		3518	8326	0.423
Regional total (A)	17787	5717	10739	4242	1746	1891	2223	3262	1650	49257	112375	0.438
World (B)	66328	18573	50080	8402	7130	4066	7726	7157	3711	173171		
Regional dependency (A/B)	0.268	0.308	0.214	0.505	0.245	0.465	0.288	0.456	0.445	0.284		

Source: UN, UNCOMTRADE.

in East Asia. More than 40% of food exports from other countries are also shipped as intra-regional trade.

Among the trade flows by country, most important is the trade flow from China to Japan, which accounts for 17.2% of the total intra-regional trade among nine countries. Others that are relatively important are the trade flows from Thailand to Japan, China to Korea, and Malaysia to China, each of which accounts for 6% to 7% of the total intra-regional trade among nine countries. All other trade flows amount to no more than 5% of the total intra-regional trade in the region.

In comparing Table 7.5 with Table 7.4, it is noted that the regional dependency ratio for imports increased slightly and that the same ratio for exports decreased marginally, though the amount of intra-regional trade itself increased substantially by 43.5% for 2002–04 to 2005–07. Looking at individual markets, imports to Thailand, the Philippines and Vietnam showed increased dependency on intra-regional trade, while Japan, Malaysia and Singapore increased the share of their exports to the countries in the region during the period.

7.4   LEVEL OF AGRICULTURAL PROTECTION IN EAST ASIA

Trade performances are not only the result of economic activities but also depend on policies, and particularly on the border measures. Table 7.6 shows the tariff rates of selected agricultural products in East Asian countries in 2005. Tariffs shown in Table 7.6 are WTO MFN based tariffs and the secondary tariffs if tariff rate quotas are applied. There are three types of tariffs that are imposed on imports: *ad valorem* duty expressed as a percentage of import price per unit, specific duty expressed as amount to pay per unit of weight, and a mixture of the two.

Table 7.6 contains all the three types of duty, so it is rather difficult make comparisons. All tariffs should be expressed using a common measure, such as *ad valorem* equivalent duties. For example, the tariff on rice in Japan, at 341 yen/kg, is equivalent to 778% in *ad valorem* duty.[3] It should be noted that tariff rates do not accurately indicate the level of protection if non-tariff barriers are also imposed.

For example, the tariff rate on rice imports in Korea is very low, but this does not mean that protection of rice is low in Korea. This country is exempted from tarification for rice and maintains a quantitative import restriction that allows minimum access for imports of rice.

Another example is the import tariff on pork in Japan. Table 7.6 shows a very low level of tariff on pork, but this applies to pork imports

Table 7.6 Tariff rates of selected agricultural products in East Asian countries in 2005 (%)

Country	Wheat	Barley	Maize	Rice	Beef	Pork	Chicken	Butter	Hen Eggs	Sugar
Japan	55y/kg	39y/kg	0	341y/kg	50	4.3	11.9	29.8%+ 985y/kg	17	35.30y/kg
Korea	1.8	324	328	5	40	22.5	18	89	27	18
China	68	3	68	68	25	20	20	23.3	21	58
Malaysia	0	0	–	40	0	0	0	2	5	0
Thailand	1.00b/kg	–	–	–	–	–	–	30	–	–
Philippines	3	–	50	50	10	40	40	7	10	50
Indonesia	0	–	0	430Rp/kg	5	5	10	5	5	700Rp/kg

Note: WTO MFN rates; secondary tariff rates if tariff rate quota is applied.

Source: APEC tariff database.

Table 7.7   Level of agricultural protection measured by nominal rate of protection (NRP) in Asian countries

Country	NRP (%)		NRP (%)	
	1980–84	2000–04	1986–88	2005–07
Japan	–	–	163	94
Korea	–	–	232	146
China	−50.8	0.9	–	–
Malaysia	−5.7	2.3	–	–
Thailand	−0.1	7.6	–	–
Philippines	0.8	27.0	–	–
Indonesia	15.3	36.5	–	–

Source: World Bank, World Development Report 2008 and ECD, PSE/CDE database 2008.

whose prices are beyond a certain level called the gate price. For imports of pork whose import prices are below the gate price, the difference between the gate price and the import price is charged as a tariff. In short, pork imports are subject to the so-called 'differential tariff' system, and imported pork cannot be sold in the Japanese market at any price less than the gate price.

While it is easily seen that high tariffs are applied mostly to products imported in Japan, Korea and China, it is desirable to compare the levels protection using a common measure. Table 7.7 shows the weighted averages of nominal rates of protection (NRP) for agricultural products in selected East Asian countries in the 1980s and the 2000s. NRP is the difference between the average price received by producers at the farm gate and the border price divided by the latter. Thus, it shows by what percentage the domestic price exceeds the border price.

NRPs for Japan and Korea are very high, with both countries maintaining a high level of agricultural protection, although NRPs declined from 163% and 232% in 1986–88 to 94% and 146% in 2005–07, respectively. Japan and Korea are known as countries which protect agriculture heavily. However, the level of agricultural protection was low (or even negative, in Korea), which means that agricultural prices were lower than the international prices and that the agricultural sector was exploited, before each country entered in its period of rapid economic growth, in the 1950s for Japan and in the 1980s for Korea (Anderson et al. 1986). One of the reasons for the rapid increase in the agricultural protection level was the need to pay the cost of structural adjustment, in the form of protecting agriculture, to moderate migration and other socioeconomic changes during the industrial growth era (Honma and Hayami 1986).

It can be noted that China shifted its NRP from a largely negative level to a positive level. As seen in Table 7.6, China's tariffs are high compared with other developing East Asian countries, within a range of 60% to 70% for grains. Also, the Philippines and Indonesia show substantial growth in agricultural protection, supporting the observation that countries' agricultural policies are switched from exploitation to protection in the course of economic development (Honma and Hayami 1986). Table 7.7 is consistent with this observation. Moreover, it is anticipated that countries will increase their level of agricultural protection as their economies continue to grow. This will make it more difficult to fully include the agricultural sector in the process of economic integration, particularly for the sensitive commodities such as rice in China, Indonesia and the Philippines.

7.5 TREATMENT OF AGRICULTURE IN PAST FTA NEGOTIATIONS

In studying the process of economic integration, it is imperative to consider the FTAs/EPAs among the countries in East Asia. Indeed, many countries in the region have established FTAs with other countries around the world, including East Asian countries. Thus, it is useful to review the treatment of the agricultural sector in previous FTA negotiations.[4] The fact of the matter is that it is almost impossible to find an existing FTA where trade in agricultural products has been treated like any other product and liberalized without exception. Even in the case of the US–Australia FTA, which is an FTA between two of the world's major exporters of agricultural products, exceptional treatment is given to certain agricultural segments and products.

Given the importance of examining how agriculture has been treated in the FTAs in the past, this section reviews the treatment of agriculture in some major FTAs in East Asia, including AFTA, CAFTA, the Japan–Mexico EPA, and Japan's EPAs with East Asian countries. It is also worthwhile to study the treatment of agriculture in the US's FTAs, in the event that East Asian integration expands to the other regions. The treatment of agriculture in FTAs involving the US is reviewed in the Appendix.

7.5.1 AFTA (ASEAN Free Trade Area)[5]

AFTA was signed in 1992 by Brunei, Indonesia, Malaysia, the Philippines, Singapore and Thailand. AFTA signaled to the rest of the world that

ASEAN's focus had metamorphosed from only political and security concerns towards greater economic cooperation. Later, four other Asian countries acceded to ASEAN: Vietnam in 1995, Laos and Myanmar in 1997, and Cambodia in 1999.

Because it is a South–South trading agreement, AFTA was not strictly obliged to liberalize 'substantially all' sectors. AFTA follows a negative list approach for liberalizing tariffs using the Common Effective Preferential Tariff (CEPT) Scheme. In the CEPT, concessions are granted on a reciprocal, product-by-product basis and at various speeds. There are four lists under the CEPT Scheme – the inclusion list (IL), temporary exclusion list (TEL), sensitive list (SL, and HSL for highly sensitive items) and general exceptions list (GEL).

Only products on the IL enjoy tariff concessions from other countries. Products in the IL were targeted to have their tariffs reduced to between 0% and 5% by 2002 for Brunei, Indonesia, Malaysia, the Philippines, Singapore and Thailand (ASEAN6), by 2006 for Vietnam, by 2008 for Laos and Myanmar and by 2010 for Cambodia.

Products on the TEL do not enjoy concessions from other ASEAN partners until transferred to the IL, which ASEAN countries were obliged to do in equal batches up to the year 2000. Once on the IL, the transferred products are granted the same rate of tariff reduction as other products.

Different timeframes apply to sensitive and highly sensitive products for phasing them into the CEPT Scheme as well as ending their tariff rates. The SL is for some unprocessed agricultural products whose tariff rates will be phased down to final rates of 0% to 5% by 2010. Highly sensitive items may have final rates higher than 5%, and for Malaysia and Indonesia, the final rates are 20%.

AFTA initially excluded unprocessed agricultural products from tariff liberalization but subsequently incorporated them into the CEPT, allowing for flexibilities like adding new SL and HSL categories. All products on the sensitive lists of ASEAN members are from Chapters 1 to 24 of the Harmonized System (HS code), except Myanmar which listed additional products from Chapters 50 to 52 (silk worm cocoons and cotton yarn, and so on). To date, however, only a handful of tariff lines remain on the sensitive list while the rest have been liberalized or are on track for eventual tariff reduction to 0% to 5%.

AFTA is an example of how step-by-step tariff reductions, phased transitions and other flexible arrangements eventually achieve agricultural liberalization which was considered impossible only a decade ago. Although there were a number of difficulties in liberalizing some agricultural products, for example rice for Indonesia and the Philippines, the majority of the agriculture sector is now included in ASEAN regional liberalization.

7.5.2   China–ASEAN (CAFTA)[6]

China and ASEAN signed the Framework Agreement on Comprehensive Economic Cooperation in 2002, which covers tariff elimination for goods, services, investments, trade facilitation, special and differential treatment, and expansion of cooperation in various areas. With regard to liberalization of goods, CAFTA provides for three tracks: early harvest, normal track, and sensitive track.

The normal track follows a positive list approach, that is, countries list products for liberalization on their own accord and set targets from January 2005 up to January 2010 for phased reduction to 0% of tariffs for ASEAN6 and 2015 for others. The sensitive track follows the same positive list approach but, as yet, has no negotiated timelines for liberalization.

The early harvest program (EHP) has both a negative list (for Chapters 1–8 of the HS) and a positive list for other products from other chapters. The aim is an accelerated tariff reduction for these products to 0% starting January 2004 and no later than January 2006 for ASEAN 6 (2010 for others). CAFTA emphasizes reciprocity for the products that are to be liberalized, whereby China matches the concessions for exactly the same products.

Chapters 1 to 8 contain approximately 10% of the tariff lines in the HS classification. The products belong to categories such as live animals, meat and edible meat offal, fish, dairy produce, other animal products, live trees, vegetables, fruits and nuts. In addition, a small list of additional products from other chapters is included in the early harvest program.

The significant difference in CAFTA is that, while other FTAs skirt around agriculture, CAFTA instead negotiated it up front by having an early harvest program which covers a significant portion of agricultural products as per the Harmonized System chapters.

The usual flexibility applies via an exclusion list. However, it appears that, except for the Philippines which opted for a positive list, the other ASEAN countries are eager to engage China with more open agricultural trade, as shown by the relatively few excluded products.

Because of the strong reciprocity condition placed on market access, the willingness to allow Chinese unprocessed agricultural products access to ASEAN markets also reflects ASEAN interest in making inroads in the large Chinese market. In contrast, the Philippines, by liberalizing mainly products that are not significantly produced domestically, also signals its relative lack of interest in penetrating the Chinese agricultural market.

7.5.3   Japan–Mexico EPA

The FTA with Mexico was Japan's second FTA, following the one with Singapore, and it was concluded after arduous negotiations. The negotiations started in November 2002 and reached a peak in October 2003 with the visit of President Fox to Japan. However, negotiations broke down on tariff-free quotas for pork and orange juice. As a result, an agreement in principle was not reached until March 2004.

Mexico ranks among the countries that have assumed a very positive stance towards FTAs. For this reason, Mexico has gained a hub position in a series of FTAs. Because of NAFTA and the EU–Mexico FTA, North American and European companies have established tariff-free access to Mexican markets. By comparison, Japanese companies were at a clear disadvantage prior to the Japan–Mexico EPA. When Japanese manufacturers built production facilities in Mexico, their competitive position was undermined by tariffs that applied to the importation from Japan of parts and components to be used in these factories. These adversely affected Japanese companies, which had a strong interest in the conclusion of a Japan–Mexico EPA.

Mexico hoped to increase its exports to Japan by reducing the high tariff rates that applied to agricultural and food products, affecting 23% of its exports to Japan. During the course of the negotiations, Japan proposed to eliminate tariffs on approximately 300 agricultural products. However, negotiations became deadlocked on the subject of pork, Mexico's leading agricultural export product to Japan.

Japan has adopted a differential tariff system for the importation of pork. For import prices within a certain price range, a tariff is levied that is equal to the difference between the import price and a certain base price. For the importation of pork carcasses, this price range is set between 48.9 yen per kilogram (floor price for application of specific duty) and 393 yen per kilogram (ceiling price). For all pork imported in this price range, a tariff is charged that is equivalent to the difference between the import price and a base price of 410 yen per kilogram.

The bilateral negotiations on pork were eventually settled on terms that closely approximated the original Japanese proposal. In exchange for this, a tariff-rate quota for orange juice, which had not been on the agenda, was introduced, and tariff-rate quotas were also established for the first five years of the agreement for beef, poultry and fresh oranges.

7.5.4   Japan's EPAs with East Asian Countries

Japan's first FTA (EPA), with Singapore, took effect in November 2002. Using the WTO Agreement as a shield, Japan adopted strategies to effectively exclude the agricultural sector from liberalization under this agreement. Specifically, Japan was prepared to eliminate all tariffs that were already effectively at zero (duty free), but, for all other tariffs, refused to make concessions exceeding the commitments made in the WTO Agriculture Agreement. As a result, out of a total of 2,277 agricultural, forestry and fishery products, only 486 products were covered in the Japan–Singapore agreement.

In FTA negotiations with the Philippines, an agreement in principle was reached in November 2004. (For the contents of the agreement, see Box 7.2.) Turning next to the Japan–Malaysia FTA (EPA), an agreement in principle was reached in May 2005, and the agreement came into force in 2006. Over a 10-year period after the enforcement of the agreement, tariffs on motor vehicles, steel and other industrial products are to be eliminated, as will tariffs on agricultural, forestry and fishery products. In the agricultural sector, tariffs on mangos, durians and certain other products were eliminated immediately, and the agreement also provides for an annual 1,000-ton tariff-free quota on bananas. The two countries did not reach an agreement on plywood, a product of export interest to Malaysia. The decision was made to hold further negotiations on this item after the enforcement of the agreement.

In August 2005, an agreement in principle was reached on the conclusion of an FTA with Thailand. A key point in the negotiations was the reduction of tariffs on motor vehicles. Failing to reach an agreement on this matter, the two countries decided to hold further negotiations in the future. One of the factors contributing to the stalemate in motor vehicle negotiations was Japan's inadequate level of liberalization in the agricultural sector. Rice was excluded from the liberalization negotiations from the start, and negotiations on sugar were postponed until a later date. The tariff rate for boneless chicken was reduced from 11.9% to 8.5%, while the tariff rate for processed chicken meat was reduced from 6% to 3%. These concessions do not signify a high-quality FTA.

In its EPA negotiations with ASEAN, Japan reached an agreement in principle in May 2007. Japan is committed to eliminating its tariffs on 92% of its imports (on a value basis) within 10 years and reducing its tariffs by 5% to 50% on another 7% of imports. The remaining 1% of imports, which includes rice, is expected to be excluded from liberalization. The negotiations cover a total of 5,223 items, which includes manufactured products and forestry and fishery products. This greatly exceeds

BOX 7.2   DO YOU EAT APPLES INSTEAD OF
          BANANAS?

Japan has concluded a number of EPAs, as discussed in the chapter. In its FTA negotiations with the Philippines, an agreement in principle was reached in November 2004. Here again, the treatment of agricultural products remains inadequate in the resulting Japan–Philippines EPA. Such products as rice, wheat, barley, dairy products (state trading items), beef, pork, raw sugar, starch and canned pineapple have either been excluded from the agreement or have been identified as items for renegotiation. On the subject of bananas, a priority item for the Philippines, Japan agreed to eliminate its tariffs on dwarf bananas (monkey bananas) over a period of 10 years. For regular bananas, Japan's current tariff rate of 10% during the summer season (20% during the winter season) will be reduced to 8% (18%) over a 10-year period.

Given that Japan's domestic production of bananas is very nearly zero, why are bananas subject to an import tariff in the first place, and why does the tariff rate go up during the winter season? The reason given is that the availability of inexpensive bananas adversely affects the sales of domestic fruits. In particular, the tariff rate is raised as apples reach the market during the winter. In the choice of consumption, would you consider substituting bananas for apples by price? This is a rhetorical question that causes consumers to smile wryly. As long as Japan adheres to these types of policies, there is little hope for the achievement of true globalization and the adoption of policies that put the consumer first. By the way, would you eat fewer apples if the price of bananas declined by 10%?

the 1,332 items covered in the WTO agricultural negotiations, and the 1% exclusion results in the exclusion of only 52 items from liberalization negotiations.

7.5.5   Lessons from Past FTA Negotiations

Creation of a regional FTA in East Asia is a necessary step toward regional integration; however, multiple issues must be resolved before a regional FTA can be realized. Needless to say, some of the most intricate issues are to be found in the agricultural sector; agriculture entails many complex problems that have necessitated attention in past FTA negotiations. What can be learned from past FTA negotiations regarding the treatment of agriculture in regional integration?

In Japan's case, for example, all the FTAs concluded in the past have excluded Japan's principal agricultural products, which has resulted in the creation of a series of low-quality FTAs. However, the global network of FTAs is growing at an accelerating pace, and so it is not possible for Japan to continue avoiding FTA negotiations with major exporters of agricultural products.

In the East Asian region, there are both food exporting and importing countries. China and Thailand are major food exporters, while Japan and Korea are major importers in the region. Once the negotiations for the regional FTA start, there is no doubt that the exporters will press for further liberalization of the importers' priority agricultural products, such as rice, beef and pork. In contrast to past FTA negotiations, it is unlikely that food importing countries such as Japan and Korea will be able to successfully conclude an agreement with food exporting countries like China and Thailand while steadfastly refusing to liberalize these markets. The critical issue in the negotiations will be the form of market liberalization to be hammered out in the region. As previously discussed, no country has ever been able to treat agricultural products in the same way that it treats manufactured goods, so a possible solution would be to adopt exceptional measures for some sensitive agricultural products.

7.6 THE DIRECTION OF AGRICULTURAL POLICY FOR ECONOMIC INTEGRATION IN EAST ASIA

The agricultural sector has been heavily protected in some countries in East Asia, such as Japan and Korea. A large amount of political energy seems to be required to change the system and to conduct reform in the agricultural sector that will lead towards East Asian economic integration. If the above examples from the past are any indication, a variety of further arrangements for agricultural products will be necessary.

It is important to avoid the exclusion of sensitive agricultural products from the scheme of integration. Various options can be considered for the treatment of agricultural products. One option is to place agriculture on its own track. For instance, timetables could be negotiated for tariff reductions of agricultural products that are different from those of manufactured goods. Alternatively, instead of committing to tariff elimination within a given timeframe, goals for tariff reduction could be set, with renegotiation once the goals had been achieved. It is desirable for the countries in the region to examine the treatment of agriculture in previous FTAs and to make every effort to conclude high-quality integration.

If integration comes into effect among the countries in East Asia, agricultural trade is expected to increase, particularly in fruits, vegetables, floriculture and some livestock products. At the same time, intra-industry trade with product differentiation would be promoted, and every country in the region would have opportunities to increase its agricultural exports. The primary effects of the economic integration will be realized through tariff reduction and abolition, but further effects could be realized by also taking into account non-tariff barriers such as quarantine regulations.

The key to success in negotiations on agriculture is to seek commodities that have comparative advantages in each country and to promote the so-called intra-industry trade. Rice is a good example. The inclusion of rice will lead to dramatic changes in domestic agriculture, which lags furthest behind in the implementation of structural reforms in the region. It must be borne in mind that China, Thailand and other East Asian countries have a very keen interest in increasing rice exports. On the other hand, rice is now highly differentiated in quality, and rich consumers are willing to pay for high quality rice. It appears that the demand for Japonica varieties of rice is increasing rapidly in East Asian countries as incomes rise. Japan may have a comparative advantage in exporting high quality rice to some countries, in addition to rice exports to China which are already underway. It is important to search for comparative advantages beyond the traditional classification of agricultural products and to find strategies for exports. For this purpose, FTAs/EPAs that include the agricultural sector should be established among the East Asian countries.

7.6.1 Lessons from the Common Agricultural Policy in the EU

In considering economic integration in East Asia, the experiences of the European Union provide some insights. A review of the Common Agricultural Policy (CAP) for the treatment of agriculture in the integration will be particularly useful.

The CAP was set forth in the Treaty of Rome of 1957, a treaty which defined the general objectives of a common agricultural policy. The principles of the CAP were laid out at the Stresa Conference in July 1958. The CAP mechanisms were adopted by the six founding member states of France, West Germany, Netherlands, Italy, Belgium and Luxembourg in 1960, and two years later in 1962, the CAP came into force. By this time, three major principles had been established to guide the CAP: market unity, community preference, and financial solidarity. Since then, the CAP has been a central element in the European institutional system.

In the course of implementing the CAP, the six member states individually intervened strongly in their agricultural sectors, in particular with regard to the selection of which commodities to produce, the price supports for products, and the farming organization. These interventions posed obstacles to free trade in the Common Market, while the rules continued to differ from state to state. Some member states, in particular France, and all professional farming organizations wanted to maintain strong state interventions in agriculture. This could, however, only be achieved if policies were harmonized and transferred to the European Community level.

The most powerful measure protecting farmers in the region was the price supports for individual commodities coupled with a high level of border protection. Market unity was established with the common market prices which were supported by the intervention prices guaranteed to farmers. To maintain the high regional prices, variable levies were charged on agricultural imports, in which the difference between a certain fixed price and the import price was charged regardless of the import price. The costs for the price supports were financed by the EAGGF (European Agricultural Guidance and Guarantee Fund) established in 1962.[7]

A major criticism of the Common Agricultural Policy centered on this market intervention because the high support prices inevitably led to distortions in production, with over-production being the usual result. One example of the consequences was creation of grain and butter 'mountains', which were huge stores of unwanted grains and milk bought directly from farmers at prices set by the CAP well in excess of the market.

Also, subsidies allowed many small, outdated, or inefficient farms to continue to operate which otherwise would not have been viable. It would have been better to allow the market to find its own price levels and for uneconomic farming to cease. Resources used in farming would then have been switched to a myriad of more productive operations, such as infrastructure, education or healthcare. If it is necessary to protect farmers for some reason, direct payment is the correct measure to implement because it does not distort the market mechanisms.

It was in the 1990s that CAP reforms actually started. In 1992, the MacSharry reforms (named after the European Commissioner for Agriculture, Ray MacSharry) were created to limit rising production, while at the same time adjusting to the trend toward a freer agricultural market. Since the MacSharry reforms, cereal prices have been closer to the equilibrium level; there is also greater transparency in the costs of agricultural supports, and the 'decoupling' of income supports from production supports has begun. The MacSharry reforms were not sufficient by themselves to correct the CAP but led to further reforms under Agenda 2000,

Decoupling 2003, sugar regime reform, and other recent policy reforms in the EU.

What lessons were learned from the experience with the CAP for East Asian economic integration? Firstly, market unity should be achieved without market intervention. The CAP for price supports created costs not only for consumers but also for producers in the form of less efficient resource allocation. Also, the price supports delayed structural reform in the EU and resulted in an export subsidy war with the US in the 1980s. The CAP was notorious for its protectionism and regionalism.

Secondly, it is necessary to shift agricultural policy towards decoupling from price policy. There is a worldwide trend towards abandonment of price policy and adoption of decoupling; however, it is necessary to carry out structural reform prior to introduction of a decoupling policy. It is dangerous to introduce a decoupling policy before structural reform because it freezes the current agricultural structure. A decoupling policy does not give farmers incentives to change their scale of production nor to improve their efficiency. It is more effective to keep the current conditions of agriculture and maintain its multi-functionality, which is one purpose of decoupling in the EU. However, it should be remembered that the EU has experience with structural reform under the MacSharry reforms, which reduced the protection level.

Thirdly, it is important to revise the reform plans periodically. It took more than 30 years to start correcting the CAP under the MacSharry plan of 1992. Furthermore, it took another decade to implement the reform plans. When implementing East Asian economic integration, reforms should be carried out swiftly and effectively. For more drastic reforms in particular, the time schedule should be prepared as carefully and efficiently as possible.

7.7   CONCLUDING REMARKS

Despite the difficulties involved, the agricultural sector should be included in the list of tariff reductions and other treatment in the East Asian economic integration. It is also a good opportunity for the countries in the region to reform agriculture to make it viable in international competition and to cope with globalization in general. The first step towards integration is the formation of FTAs/EPAs among the countries in the region. Next, integration should be approached stepwise to create a free trade area in East Asia. The agricultural sector in each country should prepare for globalization through reform.

Agricultural policy is tending to shift worldwide toward a decoupled policy (that is, one that decouples income supports from production supports), providing direct payments to protect farmers if necessary. In addition to domestic treatments, the introduction of decoupled agricultural policy throughout the region may become an important policy arrangement. The governments should also promote the search for comparative advantages in the agricultural sector for intra-regional trade by assisting information gathering and investment in research and development.

East Asia should learn the experiences of the EU with the CAP. The history of the CAP teaches lessons on the cost of government market interventions and the importance of structural reform before introducing decoupling or a direct payment policy. Thus, the CAP is a useful reference when considering agricultural policy reform for the purposes of East Asian economic integration.

It would be desirable to establish a forum of East Asian countries to discuss the agricultural issues jointly. Not only the issue of tariff reductions but also many other issues relating to the agricultural sector need to be considered jointly in order to establish a path toward integration of an East Asian community or union. For encouraging agricultural trade in Asia, harmonization of the SPS (sanitary and phytosanitary) measures is vital. This is discussed in the SPS Agreement of the WTO, but the achievements in enforcing effective discipline lag far behind expectations.[8] In particular, developing countries have failed to participate in the implementation of the agreement as equal partners. It would be more effective for East Asian countries to provide a scheme to treat the problem jointly, by providing mutual technical and financial assistance for participation in SPS harmonization in East Asia.

In addition to the SPS issues, many other agricultural and food problems should be discussed in a multi-country framework in the East Asian region. Food security in the region is one such issue. Strong demand for food in Brazil, Russia, India and China (the so-called BRICs) and rapid increases in bio-fuel production caused world grain prices to soar in 2006–08. The world grain markets are in an unstable condition, which may cause problems in food availability for the people in the region. East Asia may need to establish a scheme for regional food security through a common grain reserve program, for example. Food safety issues are another example. East Asia should have a dispute settlement body to deal with safety problems in the food trade in the region.

As mentioned above, these issues should be discussed in a regional forum on a multi-country basis. The forum could be called 'Agricultural Partnership in East Asia' to indicate its purpose in promoting broad cooperation on agricultural policy and agricultural resource management. Japan, Korea, China and ASEAN countries should take serious steps towards economic integration, and such a forum for agricultural issues would be an important step forward.

NOTES

1. Brunei and Myanmar are excluded from Table 7.1 due to the unavailability of relevant data.
2. It should be noted that the amount of agricultural land per capita of agricultural population in East Asia is very small compared with countries in other regions. For example, the United States and Australia possess 30.6 ha and 57.2 ha, respectively. In Europe, France and Germany possess 11.8 ha and 7.0 ha, respectively (World Bank, 2007).
3. Specific duties are applied mostly to highly protected products because a specific duty softens the effect of price changes in international markets. For example, 400 yen/kg in specific duty and 400% in *ad valorem* duty are equivalent when the import price is 100 yen/kg, and both result in 500 yen/kg in the domestic market. However, if the import price declines to 50 yen/kg, the specific duty changes the domestic price just to 450 yen/kg while the *ad valorem* duty changes it to 250 yen/kg.
4. For a review of FTAs and agriculture in the East Asian region, see Pasadilla (2006), Mangabat and Natividad (2007) and Honma (2005).
5. This part mainly draws on Pasadilla (2006).
6. This part also draws heavily on Pasadilla (2006).
7. EAGGF was abolished and two funds (EAGF and EAFRD) were newly created in 2007.
8. For the SPS issues and developing countries, see, for example, Athukorala and Jayasuriya (2003) and Finger and Schuler (2002).

REFERENCES

Anderson, Kym, Yujiro Hayami and Masayoshi Honma (1986), 'The growth of agricultural protection', in K. Anderson and Y. Hayami with associates, *The Political Economy of Agricultural Protection: East Asia in International Perspective*, London and Sydney: Allen and Unwin, Chapter 2.

Athukorala, Prema-chandra and Sisira Jayasuriya (2003), 'Food safety issues, trade and WTO rules: a developing country perspective', *World Economy*, **26**(9), 1395–416.

Finger, J. Michael and Philip Schuler (2002), 'Implementation of WTO commitments: the development challenge', in Bernard Hoekman, Aditya Mattoo and Philip English (eds), *Development, Trade and the WTO: A Handbook*, Washington DC: World Bank, pp. 493–503.

Honma, Masahoshi (1994), *The Political Economy of Agricultural Problems* (in Japanese), Tokyo: Publishing Bureau of The Japan Economic Journal.

Honma, Masahoshi (2005), 'Agricultural issues on Japan–Korea FTA', in Choong Yong Ahn, Inkyo Cheong, Yukiko Fukagawa and Takatoshi Ito (eds), *Korea–Japan FTA: Toward a Model Case for East Asian Economic Integration*, Korean Institute for International Economic Policy, pp. 218–32.

Honma, Masayoshi and Yujiro Hayami (1986), 'Structure of agricultural protection in industrial countries', *Journal of International Economics*, **20**(1/2), pp. 115–29.

Mangabat, Minda C. and Antonette P. Natividad (2007), 'Agricultural trade in the Asian region: challenges for enhancing cooperation and integration', *International Journal of Economic Policy Studies*, **2**:47–67.

Pasadilla, Gloria O. (2006), 'Preferential trading agreements and agricultural liberalization in East and Southeast Asia', Working Paper Series, No. 11, Asia-Pacific Research and Training Network on Trade (ARTNet).

World Bank (2007), *World Development Report 2008*, Washington, DC: World Bank.

APPENDIX   TREATMENT OF AGRICULTURE IN NAFTA, THE US–AUSTRALIA FTA AND US–KOREA FTA

7A.1   North American Free Trade Agreement (NAFTA)

NAFTA is not directly related to East Asian integration or potential FTAs/EPAs in the region, but it is a pertinent example that shows how to reach a compromise when faced with conflicting national interests to achieve economic integration. NAFTA was launched in 1994 with the participation of the United States, Canada, and Mexico. The elimination of existing tariffs was scheduled to take place, depending on the product, either immediately, within five years, within ten years, or within fifteen years from the enforcement of the agreement. Agricultural products were scheduled to be implemented by 2008. Under NAFTA, trade liberalization in agricultural products comes under the following three bilateral agreements: the US–Canada Agreement, which represents a modification of the Canada–US Free Trade Agreement (CUSTA) that came into force in 1989; a newly formed US–Mexico Agreement; and a newly formed Canada–Mexico Agreement.

Under the US–Canada Agreement, almost all tariffs on agricultural products were removed by 1998. On the other hand, tariff-rate quotas were applied to the following products that previously were subject to quantitative restrictions: US exports of dairy products, poultry, eggs and margarine, and Canadian exports of dairy products, peanuts and peanut butter, sugar and products containing sugar, and cotton. Furthermore, the above products have been exempted from tariff elimination. In Canada, provincial marketing boards manage the supply of dairy products, poultry, and eggs and maintain prices by adjusting production. Canada did not concede on the liberalization of these products.

In contrast, the US–Mexico Agreement allows for no exceptions and adopts a four-stage schedule for elimination of existing tariffs to take place, depending on the product, either immediately, within five years, within ten years, or within fifteen years of the enforcement of the agreement. However, NAFTA does contain safeguard provisions for designated agricultural products whereby short-term protective measures automatically take effect when imports reach a certain level. The United States has applied this special safeguard system to the importation of onions, tomatoes, eggplants, chili peppers, squash and watermelons. Mexico has applied it to the importation of live hogs and almost all pork products, apples and potato products.

The Canada–Mexico Agreement allows the two countries to maintain tariffs on the following products and exempt them from tariff elimination: dairy products, poultry, eggs and egg products, and sugar and products containing sugar. The Canada–Mexico Agreement also includes safeguard provisions similar to those contained in the US–Mexico Agreement.

While the elimination of import barriers is a fundamental principle in these agreements, not all agricultural products are subject to tariff elimination. In particular, many exceptions to tariff elimination are found in the area of livestock products. Furthermore, it is noteworthy that the exceptions vary considerably among the three bilateral agreements.

7A.2   US–Australia FTA

Among the various FTAs created in recent years, the US–Australia FTA concluded in February 2004 attracted special attention. As the two signatories were both major worldwide exporters of agricultural products, attention was focused on how agricultural products would be treated in this agreement.

The US–Australia FTA provides for the immediate elimination of all tariffs on agricultural imports by Australia. On the other hand, the United States was allowed to maintain protective measures on priority agricultural products. Specifically, the United States excluded sugar from tariff elimination and adopted an 18-year schedule for the gradual lowering of tariffs on beef. The United States immediately eliminated tariffs on only about 66% of agricultural products. Tariffs are scheduled to be eliminated on a further 9% (including some priority products, such as fruit juices and certain types of mutton) within four years. Tariffs on wine are scheduled to be eliminated within 11 years.

Tariff-rate quotas on beef started at 378,000 tons and were to be increased by 15,000 tons within two years of the enforcement of the FTA. Thereafter, additions to the tariff-rate quota on beef are to be gradually increased to reach 70,000 tons by the eighteenth year. In-quota tariffs were immediately eliminated. An over-quota tariff rate of 26.4% is scheduled to be gradually lowered over an 18-year period following the enforcement of the FTA. Tariff-rate quotas also apply to various other agricultural products.

Australia applies particularly strict sanitary and phytosanitary (SPS) measures to imports of animal and plant products. As a result, imports of US poultry, pork and whole grains are banned on the grounds that they do not meet Australian SPS standards. US agricultural organizations have complained that these constitute non-tariff barriers, but Australia has refused to take ameliorative measures on the grounds that its SPS measures under the FTA are backed by scientific evidence.

Thus, the US–Australia FTA contains various exceptions and exemptions in the area of agricultural products. The fact that the two countries did arrive at an agreement points to their realization that an FTA would generate crucial benefits in important sectors other than agriculture.

7A.3   US–Korea FTA

In the conclusion of the US–Korea FTA in April 2007, while rice was excluded from liberalization, Korea virtually agreed to restart the importation of US bone-in beef that had been halted due to BSE. Korea also committed to eliminating its 40% tariff on beef over a 15-year period. Five products are recognized as priority items, including potatoes, soybeans, powdered skim milk, and powdered whole milk. These products will remain subject to tariff-rate quotas and current tariff rates will be maintained. Oranges will remain subject to the current 50% tariff rate that applies during the September–February season for Korean citrus products. A 30% tariff will apply during other months of the year but will be eliminated after seven years.

The US–Korea FTA also establishes trigger levels for safeguard (emergency import restriction) measures for a total of 30 major sensitive agricultural products, including beef and pork. Similar criteria have not been established for other agricultural products. Tariffs will be immediately eliminated on 37.9% of all agricultural items accounting for 55.8% of Korea's total imports of agricultural products from the United States. Within five years, tariff elimination will extend to about 68% of all agricultural products.

As in the case of beef, tariffs will be gradually eliminated on 30 items over a period of 15 years. These products include pork, corn, garlic, apple, peppers, onions, ginseng and barley. When imports of these products exceed a certain level, Korea is permitted to introduce a tariff surcharge. For beef, the trigger level for safeguard measures is set at 270,000 tons in the initial year of the FTA. Thereafter, the level will be raised by 6,000 tons per year to reach 354,000 tons in the fifteenth year.

Bilateral negotiations on tariff-rate quotas (TRQ) continued right up to the release of the text of the agreement. It was finally agreed that a variety of methods would be adopted for individual products, such as a first-come, first-served basis, an auction system for import rights, and licensing of historical importers. Oranges will remain subject to the current 50% tariff rate that applies during the September–February season for Korean citrus products. In exchange for this, a tariff-free quota of 2,500 tons will be introduced and will be increased annually at a rate of 3%.

8. Services trade and investment liberalization

Christopher Findlay

8.1 INTRODUCTION

The argument has been made that, in the case of one ASEAN member,

> the service sector is the oil in the engine of the economy that determines more than most people realize the course of Indonesia's growth and its economic efficiency and international competitiveness.[1]

This notion of services as the 'oil in the engine of the economy' is pursued in this chapter. The scope of the chapter is to examine the factors that help or hinder services playing that role. The chapter has a particular focus on the extent of international integration of the service sector in the East Asian economies and on how an open service sector performs better itself and how it contributes to better performance in other parts of the economy, which in turn may lead to greater integration of other sectors of the economy as well. That is, tackling factors which affect integration in services has not only direct effects in that sector but also important indirect effects in the rest of the economy.

The first part of the following section considers the scope of the service sector. The significance of the sector in the economy is then reviewed, and the phenomenon of a rising services share of output is discussed. A discussion follows of the nature of trade and investment in services and of barriers to trade in services. The significance of those barriers is examined and progress on liberalization in East Asia is reviewed, followed by a look at routes to reform.

A case study of the logistics sectors and their contribution to gains in trade facilitation illustrates some of the key points of the chapter.

The last section examines steps which, it is argued, would support a services reform program. The focus in that discussion is on how to introduce competition into markets for services, which in turn will have the effect of contributing to integration.

8.2   SERVICES IN THE ECONOMY

Hill (1977) defined a service as

> a change in the condition of a person, or of a good belonging to some economic
> unit, which is brought about as the result of the activity of some other economic
> unit, with the prior agreement of the former person or economic unit.

This definition applies to car repairs, education, consulting and dentistry,
for example, as well as the larger banking, telecommunications, insurance
and transport sectors.

Hill (1999) later warned against the danger of treating services as if they
were intangible goods, noting that a service typically consists of some kind of
an improvement to an existing entity, rather than the creation of a new entity
(p. 428). Gadrey (2000) reviews and suggests an extension of Hill's definition
to accommodate a wider range of activities normally regarded as services.

Key features that follow from this view of a services transaction are its
simultaneity of consumption and production: a good which is the subject
of a services transaction does not change ownership in the process. The
simultaneity condition has important implications for trade in services.
There is also the inability to store services outputs (instead it is the capacity to produce services which is stockpiled), the scope for differentiation,
and the likelihood therefore that services markets are less than perfectly
competitive. These have important implications for regulation, and therefore for trade and investment, in this sector.

The service sector is a relatively large share of the economy at all stages
of development. Figure 8.1 shows the service sector share of GDP at five-
year intervals in the ASEAN+6 economies. Values lie in the range from
30 to 70 percent of GDP and for most economies the trend over time is
positive.

A common trend is that the size of the service sector increases with the
level of development. In Figure 8.2, the service sector shares of GDP are
plotted against real (PPP) income levels for 2005. The figure shows the
general tendency but also the variation around the trend.

Drivers of this development include the following (reviewed in Inman,
1989). One is the relationship between the demand for services and the
growth in income. It was thought that services would be highly income
elastic, and if so demand for services would grow faster than real incomes,
in which case their share in consumption and in production would rise as
incomes increased. More recent studies have however found a wider range
of elasticity values (Falvey and Gemmell, 1996).

The second factor identified by Inman (1989) was the reorganization of

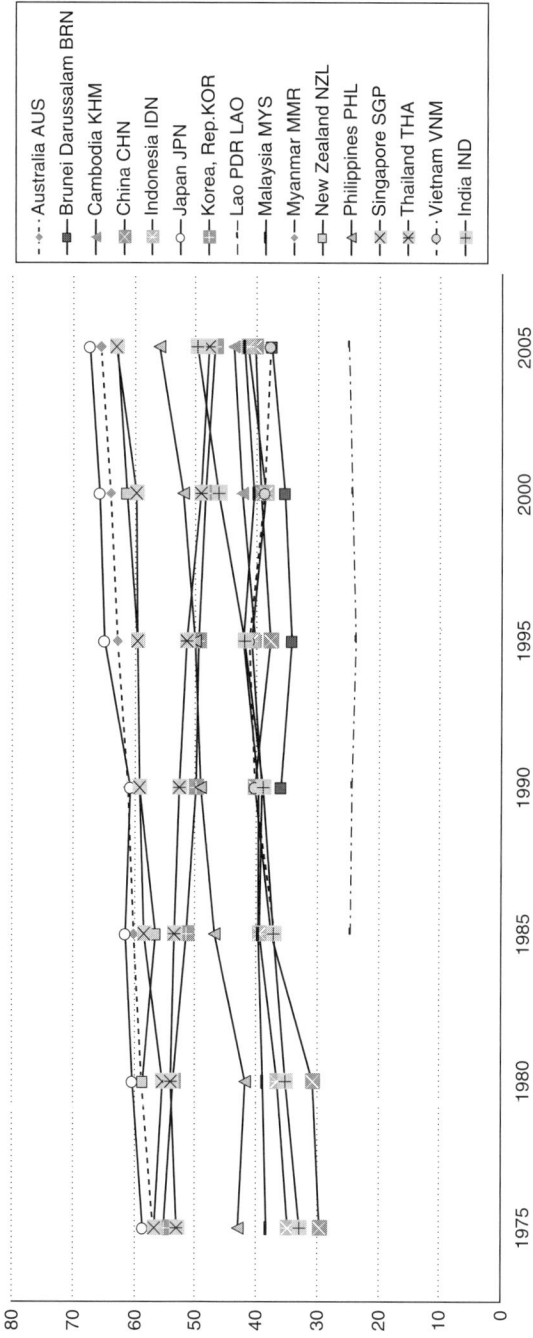

.... Australia AUS
——■— Brunei Darussalam BRN
——+— Cambodia KHM
——▲— China CHN
——×— Indonesia IDN
——○— Japan JPN
——⊞— Korea, Rep.KOR
— — Lao PDR LAO
——▲— Malaysia MYS
——◆— Myanmar MMR
——▢— New Zealand NZL
——▲— Philippines PHL
——×— Singapore SGP
——✳— Thailand THA
···○··· Vietnam VNM
——+— India IND

Figure 8.1   Service sector share of GDP (%)

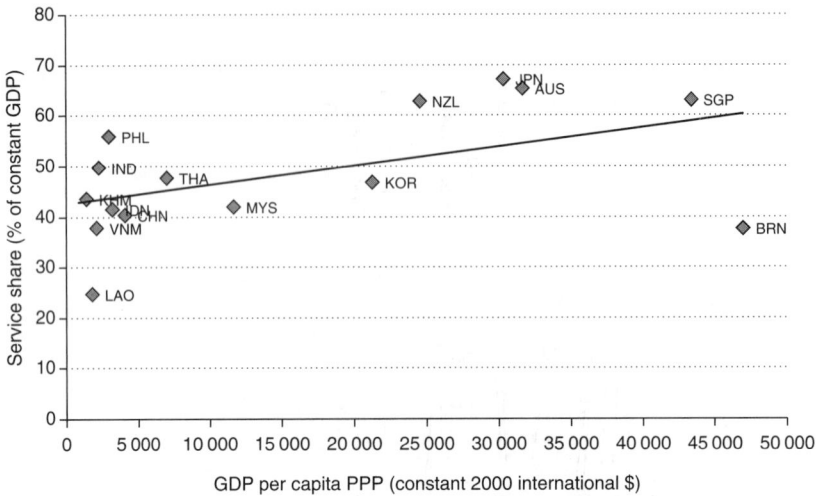

Figure 8.2   Size of service sector and GDP per capita (PPP), 2005

production. As an economy developed, and as real wages and the density of markets increased, the scope to gain from contracting out activities previously done in-house by both firms and households would increase. Manufacturing businesses for example would hire in transport services rather than run their own trucks. Households would buy in services previously provided at home as their real incomes rose and the cost of spending time in home duties increased. The contractors also had the advantage of the gains from specialization and scale. This explanation is also stressed by Shugan (1994).

One concern about the trend to a larger services sector was that it would slow down growth in the economy as a whole, because services were expected to be characterized by low productivity growth. Slower productivity growth combined with rising demand would also account for the growing size of the sector within the economy (as also discussed by Inman, 1989).

Productivity increased in the earlier stages of development with the transition of labour out of agriculture into manufacturing. The accumulation of capital and its application in labour intensive activities added to labour productivity and drove up real wages. The abundance of labour provided opportunities for productive investment. But could this process occur in the service sector, which appeared to be labour intensive?

The pessimism about services productivity could have been due to problems in measuring services output (see Diewert et al., 1999). That pessimism might also have ignored the gains from productivity that may be available not from the application of capital but from the process of reorganization of production processes, which as already noted is associated with the measured growth of the sector.

More recent research has found substantial potential for productivity growth in services. For example, in Australia, the Productivity Commission, while summarizing a substantial body of research which it has led, found that

> In the 1980s, service industries explained only one-third of market sector productivity growth – this rose to almost two-thirds in the 1990s. So far this decade almost all of the growth in market sector productivity has occurred within services. The distributive trade services (wholesale, retail and transport and storage) contributed to the 1990s surge, as did the then recently deregulated and rapidly expanding industries of finance and insurance and communications. Some of the traditional 'engines of growth', such as manufacturing, did not. (Productivity Commission, 2008, p. 9)

The questions are what policy environment drives this performance and more specifically how important is trade and investment in services? The Productivity Commission assessment links productivity growth to policy reform (see also Parham, 2004, for an assessment of the sources of the productivity in Australia, including in services). Before returning to these questions, the next step is to review the nature of trade and investment in services.

8.3 SERVICES TRADE AND INVESTMENT

Because of the nature of the transaction there is a variety of forms in which services can be traded. In the language of the WTO, these are called the four modes of supply (where 'Member' refers to a member of the WTO).[2]

- Mode 1: Cross-border supply is defined to cover services flows from the territory of one Member into the territory of another Member (for example banking or architectural services transmitted via telecommunications or mail);
- Mode 2: Consumption abroad refers to situations where a service consumer (for example tourist or patient) moves into another Member's territory to obtain a service;
- Mode 3: Commercial presence implies that a service supplier of one Member establishes a territorial presence, including through ownership or lease of premises, in another Member's territory to provide a service (for example domestic subsidiaries of foreign insurance companies or hotel chains); and

Table 8.1   International services transactions worldwide by mode of supply

Mode of supply	Estimate (US$b)
Cross border supply	1000
Consumption abroad	500
Commercial presence	2000
Movement of natural persons	50
Total	3550

Source: Data from Karsenty (2000).

- Mode 4: Presence of natural persons consists of persons of one Member entering the territory of another Member to supply a service (for example accountants, doctors or teachers). The Annex on Movement of Natural Persons specifies, however, that Members remain free to operate measures regarding citizenship, residence or access to the employment market on a permanent basis.

As Findlay (2005) discusses, while the data on the relative importance of the various modes of supply are difficult to confirm, some estimates of the scale of transactions of different types have been developed in the WTO and these are summarized in Table 8.1. Sales through commercial presence are the most important.

What is regarded as trade in services would normally include only the first and second modes that are listed in this table. Table 8.2 shows services transactions by these modes for a sample of East Asian economies for which the details are available.[3]

Outsourcing can be thought of as an example of mode 1 trade in services. Bhagwati et al. (2004) argue that 'outsourcing is fundamentally just a trade phenomenon' (p. 94) but they note how new technological possibilities convert previously nontraded services into items which can be traded at arm's length. They also review the impacts of outsourcing on jobs, wages and productivity.

Figure 8.3 shows the net export ratios, $(X - M)/(X + M)$, for this group of economies over time. This ratio, which provides some indication of comparative advantage overall in this sector, is generally lower for developing countries than for developed countries. However the indicator can range from minus to plus one, and countries shown lie in a narrower range. This result highlights the extent to which services sectors are both importers and exporters.

It is useful not only to examine trends in trade over time but also normalize services trade by the size of the economy. Figure 8.4 shows the

Table 8.2   Trade in services by category of service 2006 (USD million)

Service		Australia	China	India	Indonesia	Japan	Korea	NZL
Transportation	Exports	6356.3	21015.3	7628.8	2102.0	37652.1	25858.1	1663.4
	Imports	11321.8	34369.0	12449.3	8179.5	42838.7	23393.8	2593.9
Travel	Exports	17840.0	33949.0	8934.0	4448.0	8467.8	5322.4	4750.1
	Imports	11669.7	24321.7	7351.8	3599.6	26877.3	18241.0	2529.1
Communication	Exports	640.8	737.9	2191.1	1102.5	435.9	466.3	–
	Imports	656.6	764.1	899.1	571.1	732.6	778.3	195.2
Construction	Exports	97.1	2752.6	402.9	456.4	8990.6	126.1	–
	Imports	0.0	2049.7	905.7	984.1	6201.3	3.1	49.3
Insurance services	Exports	530.1	548.2	1115.9	32.2	1575.3	365.6	27.2
	Imports	677.7	8831.1	1247.7	383.7	4568.4	908.8	215.9
Financial services	Exports	756.0	145.4	2071.0	181.2	6151.4	2557.2	79.1
	Imports	451.8	891.5	1315.8	362.7	2988.8	616.0	75.2
Comp. & info	Exports	1049.0	2957.7	29186.3	117.8	966.5	239.9	183.5
	Imports	921.7	1738.9	2198.7	595.9	3125.6	773.4	269.8

215

Table 8.2 (continued)

Service		Australia	China	India	Indonesia	Japan	Korea	NZL
Royalties/	Exports	609.2	204.5	111.6	13.5	20104.2	2010.6	122.6
license	Imports	2205.6	6634.1	949.0	869.7	15496.3	4487.3	487.0
Other	Exports	4002.3	28972.5	23197.6	2563.9	30695.0	13070.6	820.3
business	Imports	2823.9	20605.3	21453.3	5736.0	29768.1	19904.9	1242.5
Personal and	Exports	506.8	137.4	217.8	73.7	140.2	368.5	153.0
other	Imports	852.4	121.5	117.6	123.9	1301.0	680.3	40.2
Government,	Exports	649.9	578.7	297.2	427.2	2158.2	1488.2	97.3
n.i.e.	Imports	619.0	506.4	483.8	218.9	1653.5	849.6	99.2
Total services	Exports	33037.6	91999.2	75354.2	11518.3	117337.2	51873.6	8067.8
	Imports	32200.3	100833.0	49371.9	21625.0	135552.3	70636.5	7797.4

Source: OECD.

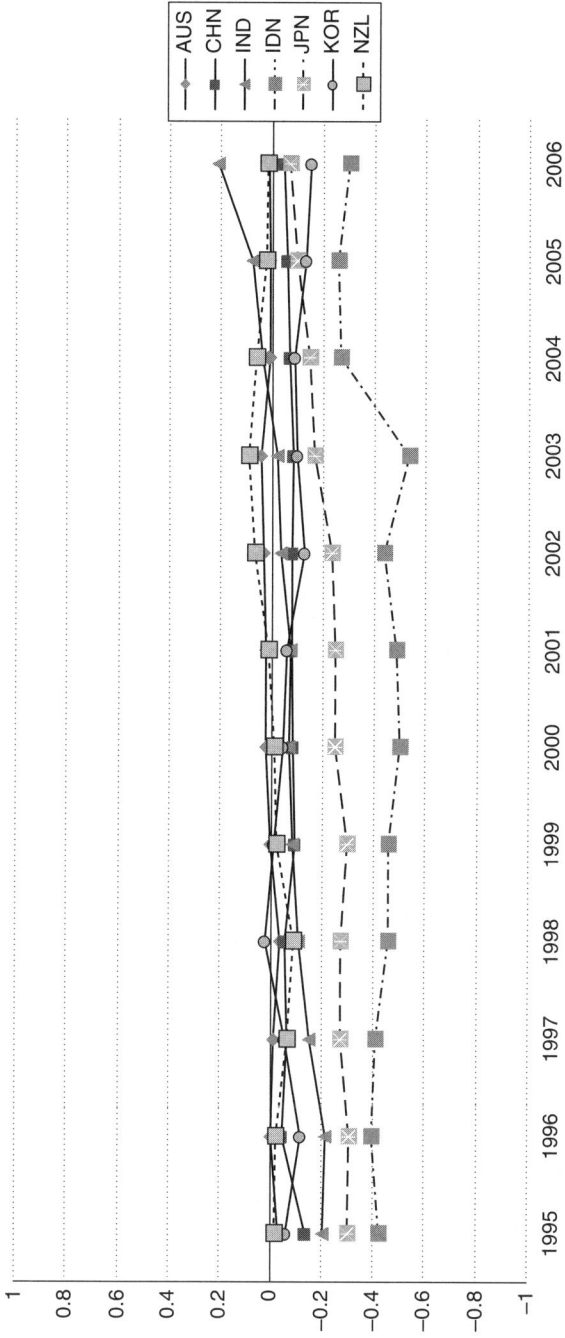

Figure 8.3 Net export ratio

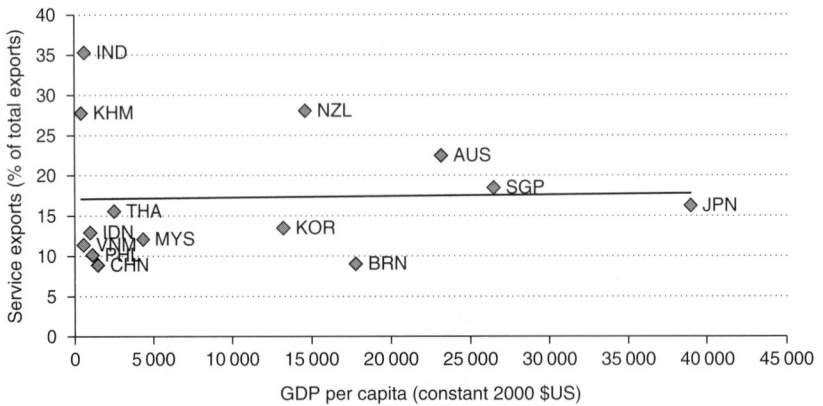

Figure 8.4   Size of service exports and GDP per capita, 2005

share of services exports of these types in total exports, plotted against real (PPP) income for a larger set of economies.

The share of services exports in the total in this group of economies is between 15 and 20 percent, slightly below the world average which is closer to 20 percent. Again, there is considerable variation in the group, with India in particular having a share higher than might be expected. The chart indicates those economies which might take a strong interest in services trade issues, but this interpretation is also qualified because, as noted, data of this type from the Balance of Payments refers only to the first and second modes of supply. Transactions in mode 3 are likely to be even more important, as suggested by the data in Table 8.1.

Data on FDI flows in services are more difficult to obtain at country level. In global terms, services are estimated to account for about 60 percent of global FDI flows. Data available for Australia and Japan are shown in Figure 8.5.

In Japan, services have accounted for a rising share of FDI inflows, 60 percent or more since 2000. The pattern is more variable in Australia.

It is useful to explore the linkages between the modes of supply of services. Services, like goods, are produced in processes in which labour and capital are employed in varying proportions, so the forces driving flows of trade would be expected to be similar to those applying to goods. Countries relatively endowed with labour might be exporting labour intensive services.

The patterns of trade are complicated, however, by the availability of alternatives for doing business internationally. A labour rich country might attract FDI and then export the services in association with the foreign investor, which is another example of international outsourcing.

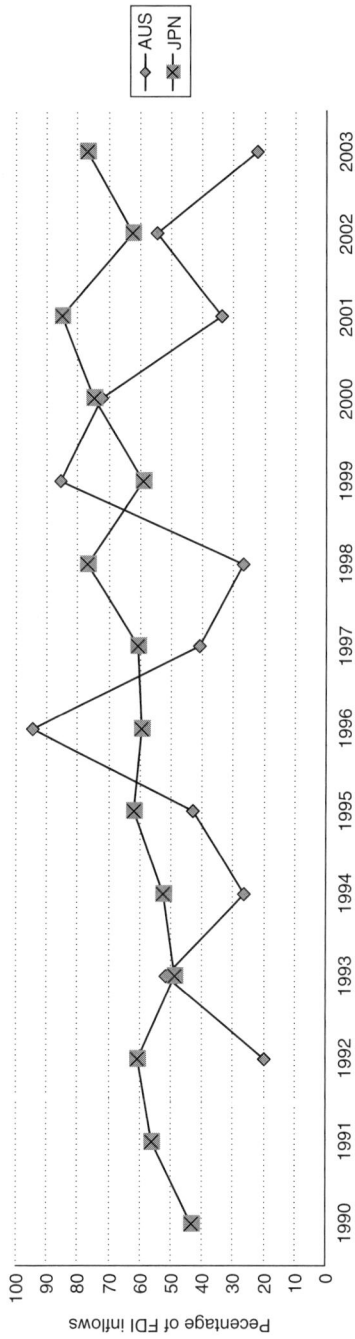

Figure 8.5   Percentage of tertiary industry to FDI inflow

219

Baldwin and Robert-Nicoud (2007) present a model of offshoring in the presence of technology transfer.

In some cases, there is an input which is specific to the services which drives the international business: tourism is an example. Finally, there are gains from variety and these too will be present in services transactions: countries will be observed to be both exporters and importers in the same service sector where the transactions are driven by the differentiation provided by suppliers in different locations. This is evident in the net export ratio data shown above.

8.4   BARRIERS TO TRADE AND INVESTMENT[4]

Given the nature of the transactions, and because of the options for international business in services, there are many barriers to trade and investment in services. Most often, though, barriers to services trade and investment operate behind the border and take the form of regulatory measures.

The barriers may be one of two types. First, they may be barriers which specifically discriminate against foreigners. These might be rules applying to the conditions under which foreigners can enter a market, or rules applying to their operations. For example, foreigners might have a cap on the extent of their investment in a local business, and their operations might be limited to certain activities or locations.

Other barriers are more wide ranging. These apply to all suppliers, both domestic and foreign, again affecting either the terms of entry or the methods of operation. A licensing scheme which applies to all suppliers is an example of the former, and the imposition of limits on banks on the forms of business in which they can participate is an example of the latter.

The General Agreement on Trade in Services (GATS) within the WTO allows for this distinction. It lists a number of measures under its market access heading which are not discriminatory, and lists these measures as items which can be the subject of negotiation. The GATS also includes measures which are limited in their application to foreign providers (and refers to these as 'derogations from national treatment').

By their nature, services are a sector where imperfect competition and other market failures (related to information problems) can occur as noted earlier. Furthermore, natural monopoly is a feature at least at some point in the production processes of network industries, for example, in the provision of bottleneck facilities. Regulatory processes are important to avoid the abuse of this market power. A feature of professional services is the difference in the amount of information about quality available to producer and consumer. Regulation has a role to play here, as it does in dealing with prudential issues in the banking system.

Governments have the right to regulate, which the GATS recognizes. A policy which is regarded as 'restrictive' would be one which is more burdensome than necessary to solve the market failure problem. The nature of this test is a key talking point in the current round of negotiations.

There is another important distinction between types of policies applying to services. Some have the effect of adding to the rents of incumbent suppliers. They limit entry (for example a licensing system) which protects incumbents from competition and allows them to earn rents which may then be capitalized into the value of their business. The removal of these barriers eliminates the rent transfer and in the process generates welfare gains from the reduction in the price of the service. These barriers are like tariffs in the composition of the effects of their reform, except that the transfers involve the protected incumbent rather than governments, which in the case of tariffs on goods lose tariff revenue.

Other measures add to costs. Their removal creates a bigger welfare gain, because it saves on resources as well as capturing the benefits of the price reduction. Reform in this case adds to productivity and saves real resources. Reform could even increase the profitability of incumbents, as well as lower costs to consumers of the service.

8.5   PROGRESS OF LIBERALIZATION

Dee and Findlay (2007) present a framework for assessing the effects of reform. To understand the economic effects of services trade barriers, and to work out policy priorities, they propose that it is critical to know three things:

- the 'height' of the trade barrier, that is, the extent of the vertical shift in supply curves;
- the 'incidence' of the barrier – whether it applies only to foreign suppliers, or whether it also applies to domestic operators; and
- the 'impact' of the barrier – whether the barrier has created rents or raised real resource costs.

There is a growing body of literature devoted to the first two aspects, but less clarity on the third.

A standard methodology is now to collect data on the scope of the policy measures applying in the sector, and make an assessment of their significance, and to link that assessment to some performance indicators in the sector, in a way that allows a link back to an assessment of an effect on prices. For example, for telecommunications, a scoring system has been used to assess the degree of restrictiveness of the licensing schemes in various countries, and then econometric methods are used to link those measures to penetration rates for various services. Assuming values for price elasticities of demand, it is possible to convert the impact on penetration rates to an equivalent price effect (Warren, 2000). There are also studies of air transport (Doove et al., 2001, and see Gregan and Johnson, 1999, for a different methodology), distribution (Kalirajan, 2000) and banking (Kalirajan et al., 2000). All the studies of this type have been reviewed by Dee (2005) and the case study on logistics reported below provides an example of the application of this methodology. Key results include the following (Dee and Findlay, 2007).

The Height of the Barrier

- in banking and telecommunications, services trade barriers are typically much higher in developing than in developed countries and in most cases the remaining barriers in the developed world are low or negligible;
- in the professions, the distribution sector (wholesale and retail trade) and electricity generation, the barriers still tend to be higher in the developing than the developed countries, but the barriers in the latter countries are often non-trivial;
- In other sectors, barriers are as high in the developed as in the developing world – air transport is an example;
- for a few services sectors, the barriers are higher in at least some developed countries than in some developing countries. Maritime transport is an example.

The Incidence of the Barrier

There is more variability among both developed and developing countries in whether barriers discriminate against foreign services providers, or also affect domestic operators. It is very rare to have a significant barrier to foreign entry and/or operations with no barrier affecting domestic new entrants.

The Impact of the Barrier

The impact of the policy depends on whether it is cost or rent creating. Rents are more likely to be created by quantitative and other barriers that limit entry and red-tape measures may add to resource costs (Dee and Findlay, 2007, p. 63). In summary, in banking and telecommunications, where explicit barriers to entry are rife, barriers appear to create rents. In distribution services, where indirect trade restrictions also apply, barriers appear to increase costs. In air passenger transport and the professions, barriers appear to have both effects. And theoretical arguments suggest that barriers in maritime and electricity generation primarily affect costs. (Dee and Findlay, 2007, p. 65)

8.6 ROUTES TO REFORM

What progress is being made in negotiations on these policy measures by the economies of interest, either in the WTO or in preferential agreements (PTAs)?

Roy et al. (2007) compared offers in the Doha round of negotiations with earlier commitments. Countries whose offers significantly improve on their pre-Doha commitments include Australia, Indonesia, Japan, Korea, Malaysia, New Zealand, and Singapore. Those with little change are China and Thailand.

On the question of preferential agreements and their contribution to liberalization, Trewin et al. (2008) have updated earlier work by Fink and Molinuevo (2008). They found that (p. 10):

- preferential agreements have increased the number of committed sectors beyond the GATS and for some countries beyond commitments offered in Doha, but there is considerable variation in this result;
- it is not clear that additional commitments have led to actual liberalization, compared to liberalization 'on paper';
- there is reasonable uniformity in excluded sectors: many agreements have separate chapters on investment (though differences exist with services provisions and it may not be clear which hold precedence), and MFN obligations (to extend commitments to other trading partners) are soft;
- some preferential agreements cover measures not in negotiation in the Doha round, including competition policy, government procurement, mutual recognition of qualifications and wider coverage of mode 4 movements than in GATS;
- Australia and India made offers in Doha which were close to those in their preferential agreements.

Ochiai et al. (2009) review a sample of free trade agreements in the Asia Pacific.[5] They stress that the agreements include sectoral exclusions in their specific commitments. This ratio is relatively low for the agreement between Australia and New Zealand but is much higher for other agreements. Some sectors are included but are associated with reservations or restrictions. Financial services, telecommunications and transport are more likely to attract reservations. Tourism, travel and construction show smaller levels of reservations. While commitments on sectors are 'wider ranging' in free trade agreements than those already made in the GATS, these commitments are also constrained by other horizontal commitments. The free trade agreements on the other hand offer wider coverage on domestic regulation, mutual recognition, subsidies, repatriation of funds, transparency, and anti-competitive practices.

Ochiai et al. (2009) review some of the structural features of agreements. Some of their conclusions are that

- agreements adopting a template which follows the NAFTA (negative list) model are generally more liberal in the scope for future negotiation, general provisions on national treatment and market access, and coverage of liberalizing measures;
- the actual effectiveness of agreements is diminished by sectoral reservations, regardless of the form of agreement;
- the degree of liberalization of trade in services is relatively low in the regional agreements between developing countries;
- agreements between developed and developing countries are relatively liberal (even compared to agreements between developed countries) but sectoral exclusions in those agreements are relatively large, which reduces their impact.

Roy et al. (2007) point out that the big countries such as China, Japan and India tend not to have agreements with each other, so for them the WTO remains the main route to services liberalization commitments. While many PTAs go further than the GATS, Dee and Findlay (2007) argue that PTAs have tended to be selective. This is not only because they have been preferential but because they tend to target only provisions that discriminate against foreigners. The latter, they argue, follows from the former, since 'the only provisions that can feasibly be liberalised on a preferential basis are those that discriminate against foreigners'.

There are other political economy forces that tend to limit concession in PTAs, not only the threat to sovereignty but also the negotiating process. Dee and Findlay (2007) note that PTAs are negotiated using a request-and-offer modality.

> Under this modality, countries are asked to contemplate, not just reforms that are in their own best interests, but reforms that are in their trading partners'

best interests. It will tend to be in a trading partner's best interests to target only those provisions that explicitly discriminate against foreigners – in this way, the foreign market share is maximised. Foreign producers would generally have little interest in unleashing competition from promising domestic new entrants. They would rather join a cartel on a far more selective basis! And in these circumstances, the liberalising countries risk simply handing monopoly rents to foreigners. (p. 69)

Regulatory regimes are always complex but the regulations that will tend to be visible to potential foreign entrants are those that discriminate against them. It is those barriers that they will seek to have reduced (Dee and Findlay, 2007, p. 70).

Modelling results (Dee, 2007) show that the gains from such PTAs are small compared to a moderately successful completion of the Doha Round, and even smaller compared to a comprehensive program of unilateral regulatory reform which aims to remove the non-discriminatory and behind-the-border restrictions on competition. Therefore, PTAs which focus on measures that discriminate against foreigners are not concentrating on the trade barriers that matter most in an economic sense (Dee and Findlay, 2007, p. 70).

Many of the studies referred to here raise the question of the origins of the interest in the PTA route to reform. Trewin et al. (2008) search for political economy factors. Roy et al. (2007) also review their costs and benefits. Mattoo and Fink (2002) compare the effects of 'sequential entry' to 'simultaneous entry' and they stress how a PTA negotiation might give a first mover advantage to a supplier who is not competitive in world terms. A country offering a concession in a trade negotiation may permit preferential entry to a second-class supplier who is difficult to unseat, not only keeping prices high but also transferring some rents out of the host country.

8.7 CASE STUDY: SERVICES AND TRADE FACILITATION

Logistics services are a key contributor to the movement of goods across borders and the performance of trade facilitation systems. Hollweg and Wong (2009) have documented the extent of regulatory restrictions applied to the logistics services and examined the linkages of the policy environment in the logistics sector with assessments of its performance. The policies covered in the index include the customs system, investment policy, policy applying to the movement of people, and aspects of the regulation of air, land and sea transport.

Figure 8.6 shows their evaluation of the degree of restrictiveness of

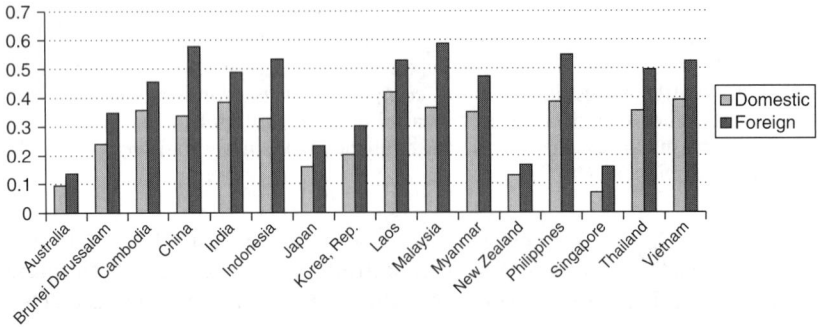

Figure 8.6   Regulatory restrictiveness indices for logistics

measures applying to the provision of logistics services in the ASEAN+6 countries.

Scores may range from zero to one in this system, and higher scores indicate a higher degree of restrictiveness. The methodology covers measures that apply to all suppliers (the domestic index value) and those applying to foreigners (the foreign index value). The different between the two scores is a measure of the degree of discrimination in the application of policy. Dee and Findlay (2007) argue that it is the extent of discrimination which is the focus of PTA negotiations whereas more significant benefits are available from lowering index values overall.

The results in Figure 8.6 show that countries with relatively high scores are Malaysia, China, Indonesia, Lao PDR, the Philippines and Vietnam, while Singapore, Australia, Japan and New Zealand have relatively open regimes.

Is this policy regime related to the performance of the logistics system? The World Bank has developed a logistics performance index (LPI) (Arvis et al., 2007) which is based on the assessments of survey respondents to questions about the quality of logistics services in their economy. Seven areas are covered: customs, infrastructure, international shipments, logistics competence, tracking and tracing, domestic logistics costs, and timeliness. A lower LPI score indicates a worse logistics sector performance. The LPI is based on the perceptions of the respondents whereas the index is based on analysis of policy information.

Hollweg and Wong (2009) compare the values of their index (the foreign index values) against the LPI values. This relationship is plotted in Figure 8.7.

The vertical axis is the foreign restrictiveness index of Hollweg and Wong (2009) (higher values are more restrictive) and the horizontal axis is

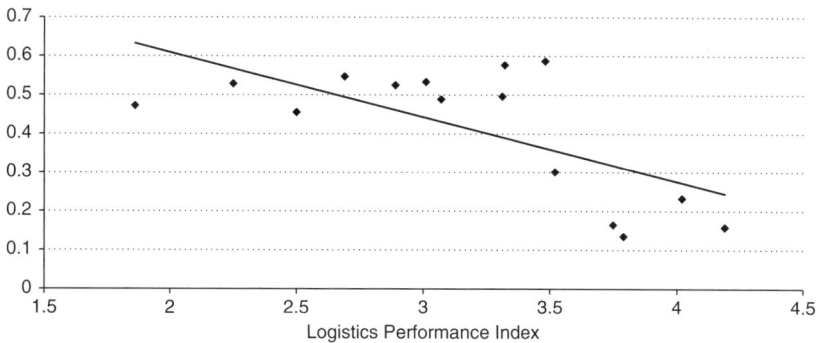

Figure 8.7   Restrictiveness index values (foreign) vs LPI

the LPI values for the ASEAN+6 countries (higher values show a better performance). Overall the relationship is negative, as might be expected, although the relationship may not be linear. That is, a similar restrictiveness index value is associated with a range of LPI values but where the restrictiveness index value falls below 0.4 the assessment of performance is more likely to be high.

Hollweg and Wong (2009) also calculated a special index of policy measures that affect the operations of the customs system. They compare this to LPI assessments of customs services and in that case they find a close negative and linear relationship between the two sets of scores.

This case study highlights the point made earlier about the likely impact of services reform – that reform will have significant impacts not just in the reforming sector but also, through its better performance, on the competitiveness of other sectors in the economy. Further, the significant gains are likely to be linked to reform programs which introduce competition, not just those which remove discrimination against foreigners. The latter run the risk of simply redistributing rents available in protected markets.

8.8 CONCLUSION[6]

Services trade and investment flows are impeded by a variety of barriers, removal of which, especially those which add to costs, could lead to significant gains in welfare. The largest gains to reform are likely to follow from the addition of competition, that is, likely to come from removing the unnecessary non-discriminatory restrictions on competition that affect both foreigners and domestic new entrants.

International commitments serve a number of purposes, such as avoiding backsliding and clarifying expectations of investors about the policy environment in markets of interest. They can also help break domestic political constraints on reform. However, there are different routes to services reform involving international commitments.

Progress in the multilateral system on services has been slow, other than for countries like China that have participated in accession negotiations. This lack of progress contributes to an interest in smaller group negotiations. Comparison of activities in the multilateral system compared to bilateral preferential agreements finds wider sectoral coverage in the latter in some cases and a wider coverage of issues, including rules and regulation. However many sectoral agreements have a high level of exclusions (this is especially the case in ASEAN), or reservations. The extent of these varies between sectors. Financial services, telecommunications and transport are more likely to attract reservations.

Agreements involving only developing countries are likely to show a lower level of liberalization, and those involving developed and developing countries generally show a higher level of liberalization although this result is qualified since they may also show more exclusions. Big countries tend not to have agreements with each other, so for them the WTO remains the main route to reform.

Additional pressure from other countries that arises during the negotiation of international commitment can help a country to overcome its own domestic political constraints to reform. But relying on those forces runs a risk of acceding to foreign requests that are not in the interests of the reforming country. An example would be providing discriminatory access to foreign providers in a market which continues to be highly regulated.

There are other ways in which international cooperation can contribute to services reform. Services reform requires a large domestic work program in which the different political economy forces that support reform can be mobilized. For example, there are often far more immediate and significant producer interests in services reform outside the sector being reformed, because of the impact of what has been described here as the indirect or intersectoral effects.

The priority in a services reform agenda is transparency followed by review and evaluation (Dee and Findlay, 2007). Given the complex nature of the policy barriers, documenting existing policy, thereby contributing to transparency, is an important first step. There will be gains from international cooperation through capacity building to provide support for this activity in developing countries where the cost of the bureaucratic resources is high.

While a preferential approach may not be sufficient for these purposes, does the WTO have a role to play? WTO principles matter and can be used to drive the reform program. While WTO members can contribute to capacity building for policy transparency and policy review, the WTO through the structure of the GATS provides valuable guidance on the information that should be collected and reported in these stages. The relevant policy information is not simply the treatment of foreigners, but the policy applied to all potential entrants into a market. The GATS references to market access, national treatment and domestic regulation issues provide a structure for this information (Dee and Findlay, 2007, p. 71).

NOTES

1. Personal communication from David Parsons, Trade Policy Adviser, Indonesian Chamber of Commerce and Industry, Jakarta.
2. http://www.wto.org/english/tratop_e/serv_e/gatsqa_e.htm.
3. Bilateral flow data for trade and FDI are difficult to find for a large group of countries and therefore it is also difficult to assess the extent of regional integration in services markets.
4. This section is based on Dee and Findlay (2007).
5. Their review includes AFTA, AFTA–China, Australia–US, CER, Chile–Korea, Japan–Mexico, Japan–Singapore, Korea–Singapore, and US–Singapore agreements.
6. For further detail of the next steps, see Dee and Findlay (2007).

REFERENCES

Arvis, Jean-François, Monica A. Mustra, John Panzer, Lauri Ojala and Tapio Naula (2007), *Connecting to Compete: Trade Logistics in the Global Economy*, Washington, DC: World Bank.

Baldwin, Richard E. and Frédéric Robert-Nicoud (2007), 'Offshoring: general equilibrium effects on wages, production and trade', CEP Discussion Paper No. 794, May.

Bhagwati, Jagdish Arvind Panagariya and T.N. Srinivasan (2004), 'The muddles over outsourcing', *Journal of Economic Perspectives*, **18**(4), 93–114.

Dee, Philippa (2005), 'A compendium of barriers to services trade', prepared for World Bank, available at http://www.crawford.anu.edu.au/pdf/Combined_report.pdf.

Dee, Philippa (2007), 'East Asian economic integration and its impact in future growth', *World Economy*, **30**(3), 405–23.

Dee, Philippa and Christopher Findlay (2007), 'Monitoring trade policy: a new agenda for reviving the Doha Round', *Trade Policy Monitoring Paper 1*, Kiel Institute for the World Economy and CEPR, www.ifw-kiel.de/konfer/2007/trade-policy-monitoring-center/mon_trade_pol.pdf.

Diewert, W. Erwin, Alice O. Nakamura and Andrew Sharpe (1999), 'Introduction and overview', *Canadian Journal of Economics*, Special Issue on Service Sector Productivity and the Productivity Paradox, **32**(2), v–xxvii.

Doove, Samantha, Owen Gabbitas, Duc Nguyen-Hong and Joe Owen (2001), 'Price effects of regulation: telecommunications, air passenger transport and electricity supply', 16 October, Productivity Commission Working Paper No. 1682.

Falvey, Rod and Norman Gemmell (1996), 'Are services income elastic? Some new evidence', *Review of Income and Wealth*, **42**(3), 257–69.

Findlay, Christopher (2005), 'Trade in services: policy options and implications for Australia-Asia relations', Melbourne Asia Policy Papers, 6.

Fink, Carsten and Martin Molinuevo (2008), 'East Asian free trade agreements in services: key architectural elements', *Journal of International Economic Law*, 1–49.

Gadrey, Jean (2000), 'The characterization of goods and services: an alternative approach', *Review of Income and Wealth*, **46**(3), 369–87.

Gregan, Tendai and Martin Johnson (1999), 'Impacts of competition enhancing air services agreements: a network modelling approach', Productivity Commission Staff Research Paper, Ausinfo, Canberra.

Hill, Peter (1999), 'Tangibles, intangibles and services: a new taxonomy for the classification of output', *Canadian Journal of Economics*, **32**(2), 426–46.

Hill, T.P. (1977), 'On goods and services', *Review of Income and Wealth*, **23**, December, 315–38.

Hollweg, Claire and Marn-Heong Wong (2009), 'Measuring regulatory restrictions in logistics services', ERIA Discussion Paper Series, May.

Inman, Robert P. (1989), *Managing the Service Economy: Prospects and Problems*, Cambridge: Cambridge University Press.

Kalirajan, Kaleeswaran (2000), 'Restrictions on trade in distribution services', Productivity Commission Staff Research Paper, Ausinfo, Canberra.

Kalirajan, Kaleeswaran, Greg McGuire, Duc Nguyen-Hong and Michael Schuele (2000), 'The price impact of restrictions on banking services', in Christopher Findlay and Tony Warren (eds), *Impediments to Trade in Services: Measurement and Policy Implications*, London and New York: Routledge, pp. 215–30.

Karsenty, Guy (2000), 'Assessing trade in services by mode of supply', in P. Sauve and R. Stern (eds), *GATS 2000: New Directions in Services Trade Liberalisation*, Washington DC: Brookings Institution.

Mattoo, Aaditya and Carsten Fink (2002), 'Regional agreements and trade in services: policy issues', World Bank Policy Research Working Paper 2852, June.

McGuire, Greg and Christopher Findlay (2005), 'Services trade liberalisation strategies for APEC member economies', *Asian-Pacific Economic Literature*, May, **19**(1), 18–41.

Ochiai, Ryo, Philippa Dee and Christopher Findlay (2009), 'Services in free trade agreements', in Christopher Findlay and Shujiro Urata (eds), *Free Trade Agreements in the Asia Pacific*, Singapore: World Scientific.

Parham, Dean J. (2004), 'Sources of Australia's productivity revival', *Economic Record*, **80**(249), 239–57.

Productivity Commission (2008), *Annual Report 2007–08,* Annual Report Series, Canberra: Productivity Commission.

Roy, Martin, Juan Marchetti and Hoe Lim (2007), 'Services liberalization in the new generation of preferential trade agreements (PTAs): how much further than the GAT', *World Trade Review*, **6**(2), 155–92.

Shugan, Steven M. (1994), 'Explanations for the growth of services', in Ronald T. Rust and Richard L. Oliver (eds), *Service Quality: New Directions in Theory and Practice*, Thousand Oaks: Sage.

Trewin, Ray et al. (2008), 'East Asian free trade agreements in services: facilitating free flow of services in ASEAN?', REPSF Project 07/004, Final report, May.

Warren, Tony (2000), 'The impact on output of impediments to trade and investment in telecommunications services', in Christopher Findlay and Tony Warren (eds) *Impediments to Trade in Services: Measurement and Policy Implications*, London and New York: Routledge.

9. Economic integration and international migration in East Asia

Tomohiro Machikita

9.1 INTRODUCTION

Economic disparity between two countries stimulates international migration from the relatively poor to the relatively rich country. Increasing access to schooling in relatively poor countries can also lead to international migration from poor to rich countries. Countries in East Asia experience increasing economic disparity within each country and decreasing economic disparity between countries (Hill 2002 and Chapter 15 of this book). Rural–urban inequality within each country plays a key role in internal migration from peripheral to core areas in East Asia. Internal migration can lead to rapid changes in urban landscape in terms of economic activities, and labor migration relocates labor expenditures to their working places, that is, agglomeration force is magnified (Nishikimi 2008). Megacities have emerged in East Asia due to inequality within each country and access to global opportunities for economic activities. Global megacities are also concentrated in East Asia (World Bank 2008a, 2008b).

Decreasing economic disparity between countries can lead to lower rates of international migration from relatively poor to relatively rich countries in East Asia, but access to schooling in relatively poor countries facilitates out-migration from poor to rich countries. Rapid urbanization in relatively poor countries can also lead to higher rates of international migration from poor to rich countries, because skills accumulated in urban areas could be transferable to relatively rich countries. Countries in East Asia still have large income gaps with developed countries such as the USA. This significant disparity can lead to higher rates of international migration from East Asia.

Finally, there is the EPA or FTA-driven demand for immigrants, especially now with the globalization of the care industry (Yeates, 2009). Japan, also, has recently accepted the immigration of medicare and health professionals, and it awards certificates for medicare and health professionals under the conditions of the EPA. The reason for this is two-fold: (1) the labor shortage of care workers in Japan's aging society; and (2) the experiences of

Indonesia in the export of care workers to Taiwan (about 100,000 workers). The Philippines also exports care workers to Hong Kong (over 20,000 workers). In Japan, 208 medicare and health profession candidates (104 nurses and 104 care workers) arrived from Indonesia in the summer of 2008 and started training in medicare and health work and the Japanese language. Japan will accept at most 600 candidates for medicare and health workers from the Philippines in 2009 and 2010 (*Mainichi Shimbun*, 14 December 2008). The government of Japan has decided that the certification of medicare and health professionals will be of a high standard. The examination for foreign medicare and health professionals will be taken in Japanese.

The aim of this chapter is to discuss the fundamental framework for interpreting the causes and consequences of international migration and to show some of the implications of the relationship between economic integration and immigration from recent trends in East Asia. We will examine evidence for and the framework of international migration by defining two layers within regions: the pair-country level and the international level. Ananta and Nurvidya Arifin (2004), Chia (2006), and Hugo and Young (2008) provide us with new insights to understand the relationship between economic integration and labor mobility in East Asia. Compared with these previous important works, the main contribution of this chapter is twofold: (1) we will also move from the more aggregate level to the local workplace, cluster, and regional levels within each country; (2) we provide not only remarkable empirical evidence of international labor mobility in East Asia but also use recent economic theories to interpret different patterns of international labor mobility by different skill types.

The next section shows the basic facts about immigration in East Asia. A theoretical framework will be discussed in section 9.3. First, we verify the causes of international migration for the sending countries. Second, we discuss the impact on the labor market of international migration for the receiving countries, to focus on enhancing the capacity of East Asia to make it a world center for innovation. Section 9.4 describes the causes and consequences of international migration in East Asia at various levels. We will explain two pieces of evidence. Section 9.5 provides a conclusion. We also discuss policy implications and directions for future research.

9.2   BASIC FACTS ABOUT IMMIGRATION IN EAST ASIA

We briefly review the basic facts on immigration and emigration in East Asia here. The stock of immigrants and emigrants in East Asia is shown in Table 9.1. This table provides clear-cut evidence on which countries

Table 9.1 Stock of immigrants and emigrants across countries in East Asia, 2005

ASEAN + 3	Stock of immigrants	Stock of immigrants as % of population	Stock of emigrants	Stock of emigrants as % of population	Emigration rate of tertiary educated (%)	Stock of emigrant physicians	Emigration of physicians among physicians trained in the country (%)
Brunei	124193	33.2	12623	3.4	21	37	9.9
Cambodia	303871	2.2	348710	2.5	6.8	75	3.7
Indonesia	159731	0.1	1736717	0.8	2	434	1.3
Lao PDR	24646	0.4	413379	7	13.8	33	1
Malaysia	1639138	6.5	1458944	5.8	10.4	2211	11.9
Myanmar	117435	0.2	426860	0.8	3.4	625	4.2
Philippines	374458	0.5	3631405	4.4	14.8	9796	9.3
Singapore	1842953	42.6	230007	5.3	15.2	607	9.7
Thailand	1050459	1.6	758180	1.2	2.2	630	3.3
Vietnam	21105	0.03	2225413	2.6	39	2443	5.6
China	595658	0.1	7258333	0.6	4.2	2407	0.1
Korea	551193	1.2	1609206	3.4	7.9	1686	1.9
Japan	2048487	1.6	940028	0.7	1.5	461	0.2

Source: Migration and Remittances Factbook 2008, World Bank.

specialize in receiving and sending out migrants. Japan has the largest stock of immigrants in East Asia, namely 2.048 million in 2005. This is almost 3.5 times of stock of immigrants in China or Korea. The top five countries which are the sources of immigration into Japan are Korea (1st, Table 9.2), China (2nd), Brazil (3rd), Korea DPR (4th), and the Philippines (5th). Table 9.2 shows the six East Asian countries which are among the top ten source countries of immigration into Japan: Korea, China, Philippines, Thailand (8th), Indonesia (9th), and Vietnam (10th). There are strong ties to Japan from the above countries in East Asia.

Singapore has the largest proportion of immigrants, 42 percent of the population in 2005. Four out of every ten people in the total population is a foreigner in Singapore. This immigration is mainly from Malaysia (1st, Table 9.2), China (2nd), India (3rd), and Indonesia (4th). In Malaysia, the proportion of immigrants in the total population is 6.5 percent. This value is also larger than the median in East Asia. This immigration mainly comes from other countries in East Asia: Indonesia (1st), the Philippines (2nd), China (3rd), Singapore (5th), and Thailand (6th). The number of migrants in the 'Indonesia–Malaysia' migration corridor is 0.7 million.

The stock of emigrants differs from immigration patterns. The overseas Chinese population was 7.258 million in 2005. This is the largest pool of emigrants in East Asia. The main destinations of overseas Chinese are the USA (1st), Singapore (2nd), Japan (3rd), Canada (4th), and Thailand (5th). The US is also the preferred destination for migrants from the Philippines and Vietnam. Table 9.3 suggests that the main destinations for emigrants from these countries are concentrated outside East Asia. In Malaysia, the share of emigrants of the total population was 5.8 percent in 2005. Evidence from Malaysia indicates a 'Malaysia–Singapore' migration corridor. The number of migrants in this corridor is one million.

A comparison of Tables 9.2 and 9.3 shows a clear asymmetry between immigration and emigration in East Asia. The top 10 source countries of emigrants to receiving countries are concentrated in East Asia. On the other hand, the top 10 destination countries of immigrants from source countries are concentrated outside East Asia. In East Asia, poor countries receive immigrants from proximate countries while relatively rich countries receive immigrants from more geographically diversified countries. Poor and relatively rich countries also push emigrants into even richer countries outside East Asia, such as the USA, Australia, and Canada. For many countries in East Asia, there is a small cost of geographic movement in terms of emigration. The cases of Indonesia, Malaysia, and Singapore are unusual in that the emigration is geographically restricted between the three countries.

In summary, the basic facts about immigration in East Asia suggest that

Table 9.2 *Top 10 source countries across receiving countries in East Asia*

		Brunei	Cam- bodia	Lao PDR	Malay- sia	Myan- mar	Philip- pines	Singa- pore	Thai- land	Korea	Japan
ASEAN +3	Brunei				1						
	Cambodia										
	Indonesia	5					7	4	4	5	9
	Lao PDR		5								
	Malaysia	1	7					1	3		
	Myanmar			4							
	Philippines	2	8		2				2	3	5
	Singapore	9	10		5						
	Thailand	3	2	3	6						
	Vietnam		1	1					9	8	8
	China	8	3	2	3	1	2	2	1	6	10
	Korea										2
	Japan		9				5			1	
Other Asia	Nepal	4							7		
	India	6			4	2	9	3	5	2	
	Sri Lanka	10			9			8	8		
	UK	7					3		6		

Destination									
Pakistan		9		5		3	7		
Bangladesh		7		6		4	8		
Hong Kong				9					
Korea, DPR	4								
Other Countries									
France					1				4
US				7					6
Australia			10					5	
Canada				10					
Angola					10				
Bahrain					4				
Antigua and Barbuda					6				
Brazil					8				3
Peru									7

Note: Source countries are not applicable for Indonesia, Vietnam, and China.

Source: *Migration and Remittances Factbook 2008*, World Bank.

237

Table 9.3 Top 10 destination countries across origin countries in East Asia

		Brunei	Cambodia	Indonesia	Lao PDR	Malaysia	Myanmar	Philippines	Singapore	Thailand	Vietnam	China	Korea	Japan
ASEAN +3	Brunei								9					
	Cambodia				8						3			
	Indonesia									2				
	Lao PDR		9											
	Malaysia			1				3	1	3		6		
	Myanmar											7		
	Philippines	4												
	Singapore			4		1						2		
	Thailand		3		2				10		10	5		8
	Vietnam						1							
	China			7	6	9		10		9	7		8	
	Korea		7	7	6	9	6	10		9	7	8		3
	Japan		8	8	6	9	6	5		5	9	3	2	

238

Asia and Middle East	India		7		2		6				2			
	Saudi Arabia	2		2	10	7		7						
Other Countries	Canada	1	5	10	4	6	7	2	4	5	7	2	4	3	6
	UK	2	4	6	5	5	5	9	2	8	8	8	8	5
	Australia	3	1	6	5	2	4	7	3	6	3	4	4	7
	US	5	1	5	3	4	4	3	1	4	1	1	1	1	1
	Nethe-lands	6		3						8	4			
	NZ	7	6	9	9	8	10	10		7	7		7	5
	Germany	8	10	9	7	10	8		4	4	11	6	5	4
	France	9	2		3	10	8			5		5	6	9
	Switzerland	10	8		10		9							
	Italy										10			10
	Guam							6						
	Sweden							8		10			9	
	Denmark								10				10	
	Brazil													2

Source: Migration and Remittances Factbook 2008, World Bank.

countries in East Asia have faced a large influx of immigrants, and have become not only senders of a labor force to the developed countries but also receivers of immigrants from countries nearby.

9.3 IMMIGRATION ECONOMICS

This section discusses the several theoretical frameworks of the causes and consequences of international migration. Firstly, we review a gravity model of international migration for explaining and forecasting global patterns of international population flows. Secondly, we briefly introduce a theoretical framework to explain the causes of immigration, that is, economic incentives for international migration are shown. In the final sub-section, we briefly explain a cutting-edge theory of knowledge creation to enhance innovation capacity through labor mobility. This provides an example of the consequences of immigration; that is, the impact on the labor market of immigration is discussed in terms of skill levels. The impact on the labor market of immigration for the receiving country has already been the subject of empirical research (Card 1990, Borjas 2003, and Cortes 2008), and the chapter does not focus on this.

9.3.1 Gravity Model for Explaining Aggregate Patterns

In international trade literature, gravity models have been used to predict the characteristics of global migration. The most recent contribution to gravity models of international migration, Cohen et al. (2008) used 43,653 migrants from 228 origins in 11 countries of migration emigrating to 195 destinations during the period 1960 to 2004 as the dependent variable. As a result, the number of migrants per year from origin to destination was positively proportional to the population of origin (.86) and the population of destination (.36), and negatively proportional to the area of origin (−.21) and distance between origin and destination (−.97) under controlling year and fixed non-random effects of origins and destinations. Parentheses indicate estimates of regression. This result suggests that the number of emigrants from an origin is affected by both its population and its population density. This result can explain migration patterns in East Asia. As we saw, among the countries in East Asia, China and Indonesia have large populations within their countries, and so account for large numbers of emigrants. Since Singapore has over 6000 people per square kilometer, Singapore also has many emigrants leaving for Malaysia or North America. Since Korea and China are geographically close to Japan, Japan accepts many more immigrants from these two countries than from other East Asian countries. However, although the gravity model can explain the aggregate patterns of international migration, the following economic theories provide the causes and consequences of international migration for sending and receiving countries. Immigration economic theory and its empirical contributions have policy implications for both local and global development. Mayda (2008) is the latest research on the determinants of bilateral flows and considers not only skill levels, and push and pull factors in each country, but also the role of changes in immigration policy in destination countries. To study flows of migrants toward developed countries and bilateral flows within developed countries, she uses data on yearly immigrant inflows into fourteen OECD countries by country of origin for the period 1980 to 1995. The result is mixed: (1) The pull factor, income opportunity in the destination country, increases the size of emigration rates; and (2) The push factor, per worker GDP in the origin country, is negative or the size of the effect is smaller than the pull factor. Migration quotas in destination countries affect the patterns of international migration in OECD countries.

9.3.2 Selectivity and Sorting Effects in International Migration

Who are the immigrants? Standard economic models based on self-selection try to explain this question. Understanding the characteristics of immigrants is a first step to shaping migration policy and estimating the welfare effects of immigration. This is not only a policy debate but also a large academic debate in the USA. Based on the self-selection model (Roy model), Borjas (1987) tests the negative-selection hypothesis that if the returns to skill in the origin country are higher than in the destination country, the less skilled (below average productive worker) immigrate. Chiquiar and Hanson (2005) test the positive-selection hypothesis that although the returns to skill are higher in Mexico than in the US, Mexican immigrants in the US would earn a higher wage on average if they returned than those who stayed in Mexico. Fernández-Huertas Moraga (2008) attributes the reason for the difference between these two previous studies to an under-count of unskilled workers and the omitted unmeasured productivity in Borjas (1987). To correct these pitfalls using a new dataset from the Mexican quarterly labor survey, the negative-selection hypothesis is not rejected among Mexican migrants to the USA.

On the other hand, there is an alternative theory for studying the determinants of who immigrates and who returns. Rosenzweig (2006a, 2006b, 2007) suggests two competing theories of international student flows: a school-constrained model and a migration model. The former, school-constrained model explains why there is a large outflow from countries with high returns to education, but with few domestic chances to invest in education. The latter migration model explains why students from countries with low returns to education do not return and remain abroad (that is, a brain drain). If the returns to education (skill-price) increase in the student's home country, more students will choose education abroad and finally return home to enjoy the higher skill-price in the school-constrained model (that is, brain circulation), but fewer students will choose education abroad in the migration model. Rosenzweig (2006a, 2006b, 2007) and Irwin (2006) suggest that these two competing models have different implications for educational prevalence in the home country. If the education system in the home country is upgraded, fewer students will choose to go abroad in the school-constrained model and more students will choose to go abroad in the migration model. The migration model implies that there is no brain circulation back to the home country. The implication of the skill-price migration model is that one must try to revise the first deficiency above. Firstly, higher-skilled persons always have greater gains from emigration (out-migration), compared with lower-skilled persons for a given skill-price gap. This means selectivity. Secondly, the higher the domestic skill price, the lower the gain from out-migration. Thus, there will be fewer immigrants from high-skill-price countries. Thirdly, schooling acquired in the destination country may increase the probability of obtaining a permanent destination-country job. Thus, this increasing access to obtaining a job also facilitates migration and skill transferability. Finally, the lower the domestic skill price, the more an increase in skill increases the gain from migrating. Thus, increasing access to schooling in low skill-price countries can lead to higher rates of out-migration.

9.3.3   The Impact of Brain Circulation on Enhancing Innovation

The microeconomic mechanism of knowledge creation and for enhancing innovation has been discussed. This has also been related to the literature on labor mobility. Berliant and Fujita (2008) are representative in this new field. They formally describe the relationship between knowledge creation, spillovers between heterogeneous populations, and the process by which different types of individuals become similar. The production of tacit and explicit knowledge spillovers is the key to explaining this similarity between initially different persons. Tacit knowledge is produced and shared during an explicit knowledge creation process. Thus tacit knowledge becomes similar during the process of long-term cooperation. If one person moves and changes partners, the tacit and explicit knowledge spillovers are achieved anew. This principle is extended by introducing mobility to explain sustained economic growth. In detail, the writers assume that heterogeneity among people with regard to their state of knowledge is essential for the creation of new knowledge. They also assume that a cooperative process of knowledge creation affects this heterogeneity through the exchange of knowledge among the people involved. The formation of groups is also endogenously modeled. The optimal size of a group depends on the heterogeneous nature of the knowledge at the beginning of the process of knowledge creation.

Berliant and Fujita (2008) move on to the relationship between long-term economic growth and knowledge diversity. Based on a microeconomic model of knowledge creation, they introduce interactions among a group of R&D workers into the growth model. They analyze the extent to which long-term economic growth is achieved through both the effectiveness of knowledge exchange among R&D workers and the effectiveness in the transmission of public knowledge. The social value of human capital could be changed if we are more open to an integration of the labor market in East Asia. Not only the spatial expansion of human capital externalities but also the level of competition could change private returns on education and human capital. Lange and Topel (2006) provide a clear-cut framework of spatial equilibrium in labor markets.

The core idea for sustained economic growth is the frequency with which knowledge workers move. The study of the micro foundation of knowledge creation also suggests a framework of migration policy for stimulating knowledge creation in wider East Asia. The geographic extent of mobility in East Asia provides an appropriate level of common knowledge and initial heterogeneity. China has played an important role in developing and spreading similar cultures and literatures in East Asia, for example, through Chinese characters. The countries in East Asia already share a common cultural background for the exchange of knowledge between themselves and the creation of new ideas. Overseas Chinese independently play a role in developing and spreading new technology and commercial schemes, and in business creation.

9.4   IMMIGRATION IN EAST ASIA

In this section, we investigate the causes and consequences of international migration at various levels: the international level, the bilateral level, and the local level. Case studies from the Indonesia–Malaysia corridor, the labor market impact of immigration in Japan, and overseas Chinese workers are examined. Immigration economics will assist in the understanding of these case studies.

9.4.1   Indonesian Workers in ASEAN and East Asia

We review the situation concerning Indonesian workers in Malaysia in order to study selectivity and the labor market impacts of immigration in the origin and destination countries. The Indonesia–Malaysia corridor is one of the major migration corridors of the world. The number of migrants from Indonesia to Malaysia is 0.7 million (World Bank, 2008a, 2008b). The Mexico–United States corridor is the world's largest corridor (10.3 millions), and there is no corridor of this magnitude within East Asia. However, the Malaysia–Singapore corridor, in which Singapore has been independent from Malaysia since 1965, is also one of the world's major migration corridors (1.0 million), although the degree of labor mobility is still at a lower level in East Asia than in other areas.

Why do we study the Indonesia–Malaysia corridor? There are three reasons for studying this corridor to understand the labor market impact of low-skilled worker immigration. Firstly, pull factors in Malaysia are concentrated in specific sectors. Secondly, push factors in Indonesia are also geographically concentrated in specific local areas. Thirdly, even though Malaysian natives and immigrants from Indonesia share similar languages, substitution parameters may be higher than in the case between Malaysian natives and immigrants from Bangladesh. Both countries share not only similar characteristics in language, culture, and religion but also national borders, namely, Borneo Island (Kalimantan in Indonesia). The Malay Peninsula for Malaysia (Semenanjung Malaysia in Malay) and Sumatra Island for Indonesia (Pulau Sumatera in Indonesia) are divided by the Straits of Malacca. The two countries share the longest border between any two countries in East Asia. These geographical features affect interactions between two countries, especially immigration from Indonesia to Malaysia. The population is distinctively different, the population of Indonesia being 223 million, and that for Malaysia 26 million in 2006. The difference in population density is also apparent, 123 people per square km for Indonesia and 78 people per square km for Malaysia. There is also large discrepancy in urbanization, 49 percent for Indonesia and 58 percent for Malaysia in 2006. The relative per capita income is over four times as large ($5,490 for Malaysia and $1,420 for Indonesia in 2006), and the poverty level also differs between the two countries. The poverty head count ratios at the national poverty line are quite different, 5.4 percent for Indonesia and almost 0 percent for Malaysia. In the Indonesia–Malaysia corridor, there is the particular feature of international migration from less developed to more developed countries compared to the Malaysia–Singapore corridor.

Following Wiyono (2008), Table 9.4 presents the number and percentage

Table 9.4 Number and ratio of Indonesian migrant workers by destination countries, gender, and type of work, 2005

	Formal				Informal				Total	Ratio of total emigrants
	Male	Ratio	Female	Ratio	Male	Ratio	Female	Ratio		
Malaysia	126672	0.6274	57023	0.2825	34	0.0002	18158	0.0899	201887	0.6791
Singapore	0	0.0000	0	0.0000	0	0.0000	25087	1.0000	25087	0.0844
Brunei	5	0.0010	2	0.0004	2407	0.4835	2564	0.5151	4978	0.0167
Hong Kong	0	0.0000	6	0.0005	2	0.0002	12135	0.9993	12143	0.0408
Korea	4020	0.8921	484	0.1074	0	0.0000	2	0.0004	4506	0.0152
Japan/Europe/USA	102	0.8947	12	0.1053	0	0.0000	0	0.0000	114	0.0004
Taiwan	3704	0.0763	829	0.0171	346	0.0071	43697	0.8996	48576	0.1634
Total	134503	0.4524	58356	0.1963	2789	0.0094	101643	0.3419	297291	1

Source: Ministry of Manpower and Transmigration, Government of Indonesia.

of Indonesian migrant workers by destination countries, gender, and type of work. In 2005, Indonesia sent 201,887 migrant workers to Malaysia. Informal workers, who take the types of job that are not covered by law in the destination countries, such as domestic workers, private nurses, and private drivers, amounted to 9 percent. The other 91 percent of Indonesian migrant workers were engaged in formal work, which includes all types of jobs that are covered by law, such as construction and factory workers, doctors/nurses for hospitals, and engineers. There is a clear contrast between males and females arising from the destination countries. Female Indonesian migrant workers concentrate in Singapore, Hong Kong, and Taiwan, where there is demand for care workers in households, while male Indonesian migrant workers concentrate in Malaysia and Korea, where there is demand in plantation, construction, and manufacturing workplaces. Local level demands for Indonesian migrant workers are concentrated in the low-wage sector in Malaysia. Economic development in Malaysia has caused the younger generation to avoid working in the low-wage sector, young and educated Malaysians especially avoiding work in the agricultural and plantation sector. Local demand for rubber as an input in the auto sector in Malaysia has, however, not decreased, and thus there is a local labor demand for Indonesian migrant workers to work in plantations in Borneo and the Malay Peninsula. Since Malaysia's auto sector also utilizes geographic proximity to access cheap rubber, the demand for cheap labor in plantations has not decreased.

There is also a clear contrast arising from destination countries between males and females by formality. Table 9.4 shows that the share of formal work for males relative to the total number of Indonesian migrants is 45.2 percent. Male workers who have formal jobs are the majority of Indonesian migrant workers. The share of female workers who have informal jobs is 34.1 percent of Indonesian migrant workers. The demand for formal male jobs and informal female jobs accounts for almost 80 percent of the labor demand for Indonesian migrant workers. Wiyono (2008) explains that the lower educational level for females in Indonesia is related to the high number of female migrants working abroad as informal workers. Thus, there is local concentration of labor demand by geography and gender.

On the other hand, we also discuss here the supply of immigrants. Table 9.5 presents the geographic distribution of origin of Indonesian migrant workers. The share of Jakarta-origin workers is 61 percent of all Indonesian migrant workers in 2008. Table 9.5 suggests that migrant workers come from specific areas in Indonesia, and the emigration impacts are concentrated in selected areas. As Wiyono (2008) states, female migrants from Jakarta are recruited by overseas labor agencies through brokers and field

Table 9.5   Number and percentage of Indonesian migrant workers by place of origin, gender, 2008

	Male	Ratio	Female	Ratio	Total	Ratio of total emigrants
Jakarta	7963	0.0811	90260	0.9189	98223	0.6089
Kupang	190	0.0780	2247	0.9220	2437	0.0151
Mataram	5570	0.5145	5257	0.4855	10827	0.0671
Medan	180	0.1641	917	0.8359	1097	0.0068
Nunukan	12690	1.0000	0	0.0000	12690	0.0787
Pekanbaru	840	0.6442	464	0.3558	1304	0.0081
Pontianak	1362	0.9877	17	0.0123	1379	0.0085
Semarang	231	0.0533	4100	0.9467	4331	0.0268
Surabaya	5342	0.4471	6605	0.5529	11947	0.0741
Tanjung Pinang	962	0.1250	6733	0.8750	7695	0.0477
Yogjykarta	269	0.7154	107	0.2846	376	0.0023
Others	191	0.0212	8825	0.9788	9016	0.0559
Total	35790	0.2219	125532	0.7781	161322	1

Source: Ministry of Manpower and Transmigration, Government of Indonesia.

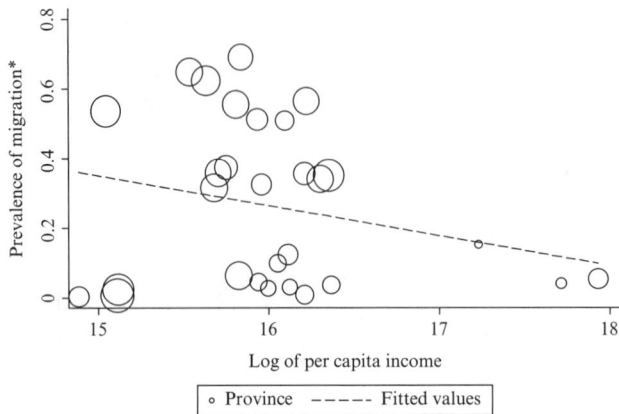

Notes:
Circle size corresponds to % of province population under poverty line. Province data excluding Papua.
* Prevalence is calculated as number of villages sending migrants to Malaysia divided by total number of villages in province.

Figure 9.1   The relationship between income and out-migration from Indonesia to Malaysia

workers to go abroad to work. The broker receives a fee from the intermediate agencies and works independently from the field workers. Nunukan in Kalimantan (Borneo Island) is the second largest location from which migrants are sent abroad, specifically to Sabah (East Malaysia), to which Nunukan has suitable geographic proximity. Immigrants into Sabah through Nunukan are almost all male agricultural and plantation workers, originating from various poor provinces in Indonesia such as East Nusa Tenggara, West Nusa Tenggara, and South Sulawesi.

Let us turn to the push effects of out-migration to foreign countries in Indonesia. There are several reasons for out-migration for households: income, poverty, and geographic proximity are all supply side effects of immigration. To take into account geographic proximity, we restrict our attention to migration from each province in Indonesia to Malaysia. There are unique datasets of international migration from Indonesia to foreign countries by province (*Statistik Potensi Desa Indonesia 2005*, Village Potential Statistics of Indonesia 2005). We add income and poverty variables to the dataset of province-level international migration (*Statistik Indonesia 2007*, Statistical Yearbook of Indonesia 2007). Figures 9.1 and 9.2 confirm the relationship between the push impacts of each province in Indonesia and Malaysia. In order to understand the situation of

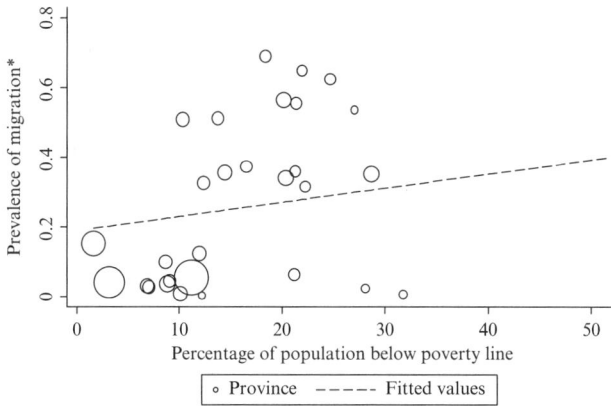

Notes:
Circle size corresponds to per capita income for province. Province data excluding Papua.
* Prevalence is calculated as number of villages sending migrants to Malaysia divided by total number of villages in province.

Figure 9.2   The relationship between poverty and out-migration from Indonesia to Malaysia

out-migration in each province, we calculate the number of villages in each province which send emigrants to Malaysia. We divide this into the number of villages in each province and we get the percentage of villages in each province from which people migrate to Malaysia. We call this the 'prevalence' of out-migration to Malaysia. Figure 9.1 finds the negative relationship between prevalence of out-migration of each province and per capita income of each province. Each circle represents a province and its radius corresponds to the below-poverty line population in the province. Indonesia has thirty provinces and we exclude Papua from province data. Papua province does not have many villages from which people moves to Malaysia. This prevalence measure suggests that low-income provinces push households and individuals from more villages into Malaysia than higher-income provinces. There are several implications in Figure 9.1. First, poorer provinces have more villages from which people move to Malaysia. This is consistent with the gravity model of international migration. If we interpret the per capita income in each province as a proxy of average skill difference between provinces, migrants from poorer provinces would concentrate into lower-skill or lower-wages sectors in Malaysia. The evidence from Table 9.4 and Table 9.5 confirms that Indonesian migrants in Malaysia are concentrated in the lower-skill population. Figure 9.1 is also consistent with selectivity and sorting effects of international migration.

Second, there is large variation of prevalence among provinces even though two provinces have the same per capita income. For example, where the log of per capita income equals 16 in Figure 9.1, there are some provinces which have almost no villages of out-migration to Malaysia, and other provinces in which 70 percent of villages send migrants to Malaysia. This suggests that there are other important reasons for out-migration from Indonesia to Malaysia.

To take account of another push effect of international migration, we examine the differences in populations living below the poverty line. Figure 9.2 considers the effects of poverty on out-migration. Figure 9.2 finds a positive relationship between the prevalence of out-migration to Malaysia and populations of poverty. The radius of each circle corresponds to per capita income for each province. Figure 9.2 suggests provinces with more population below the poverty line have more villages which send migrants to Malaysia. There is also heterogeneity among provinces even though two provinces have same populations of poverty. Some provinces with 10 percent of population below the poverty line have almost zero villages which send migrants, and others have 50 percent of villages which send migrants. However, it appears that richer provinces (with higher per capita income) are less likely to send migrants to Malaysia than poorer provinces.

Finally, we compare the Indonesia–Malaysia corridor with out-migration from Indonesia to other East Asia. From the evidence of out-migration to Hong Kong and Singapore, we do not find any similar patterns in Malaysia. There is not only a negative relationship between prevalence of out-migration to Hong Kong or Singapore for each province and per capita income but also no positive relationship between prevalence of out-migration and populations of poverty. These results suggest that other factors explain patterns of immigration into Hong Kong and Singapore, such as skill and occupations. As a result, since push effects are heterogeneous within the country, the destination countries also vary. As in the demand for immigrants, there is also local concentration of labor supply by geography and gender. Therefore, the impact of remittances is also concentrated in specific areas in Indonesia.

9.4.2   The Immigrant Technologist: Overseas R&D Returnees

In order to understand the production of immigration-based international knowledge, we review two topics that are related to the overseas Chinese. First, we show the impact of overseas Chinese returnees on a firm's performance in Beijing, China. Second, we also introduce the occupational specificity and subjective perception of Chinese students in Japanese workplaces to derive policy implications for the invitation to new talent. The most prominent cases, that is, the impact on local innovation of brain circulation between Silicon Valley and Taiwan (Hsinchu) or India are documented by Saxenian (2006, 2007, and 2008). In addition to her seminal works, this section provides clear-cut evidence of brain circulation and a bottleneck in the production of international knowledge.

Since the number of overseas Chinese students has grown since the 1980s, China has presented pros and cons for returning overseas Chinese students. The chief drawback for overseas Chinese returnees is youth unemployment in China. Youth unemployment is concentrated in students who study foreign languages, literature, humanities, and social sciences. Since studying abroad (especially in the UK, Canada, or US) is costly, their reservation wage is higher than that of local students even though they have similar skill levels, so that it is not easy for overseas Chinese students to get a job. The duration of the job-seeking period is longer for overseas Chinese students than local students (*People's Daily*, 2004). This has led to social debate suggesting that government should help them to get a job. But this is unlikely to be solved by government intervention.

On the other hand, the situation of overseas Chinese students who study science and technologies is better. The main advantage for returning overseas Chinese students is in the international connection between overseas knowledge (work experience and networking) and knowledge about the local market. In China, the effect of overseas knowledge on a local firm's performance could be higher during the transition periods. Many students with scientific knowledge and technologies have come back to Beijing and Shanghai, especially to science parks near the large Peking and Tsinghua universities. Zhongguancun Science Park (hereafter ZSP) is the one of the largest science parks in China. Many firms and industries hire local students from Peking or Tsinghua University and collaborate with both universities. There are many anecdotes and interview-based case studies about the impacts of overseas Chinese returnees on local growth in ZSP. The returnee's career path is twofold in ZSP. First, overseas Chinese returnees enter foreign firms or joint venture firms. Then they seek a startup opportunity after getting information about the local market and network. Second, returnees become entrepreneurs directly. The former case is dominant in ZSP. Li et al. (2008) present evidence of the impacts of returnee-technologists on firms' performance in ZSP. The empirical question of this paper is whether returnee entrepreneurs from overseas perform better than their homegrown counterparts. To solve this question and quantify the impacts of returnee entrepreneurs, they detect the venture ownership (legal person) in firm-level datasets in Beijing's ZSP. They then construct a pooled time series of observations over nine years (1995–2003), 45,244 firm-year observations. After constructing a sample of homegrown entrepreneurs from the firm-level dataset, they regress the firm's performance measure (the log of output and sales for firm at time) on production function inputs (capital, labor, and other inputs), with a returnee entrepreneur dummy variable equal to one if the legal representative (the highest level executive of the venture) was a returnee from overseas. The finding is impressive: on average, new ventures headed by returnee entrepreneurs outperform those headed by homegrown entrepreneurs. In particular, returnee entrepreneurs who experience FDI penetration also outperform those headed by homegrown counterparts or returnee entrepreneurs without FDI penetration. Li et al. interpret these results as consistent with the resource-based view of industrial organization. The intangible assets of returnee entrepreneurs and a foreign network with FDI penetration affect the firm's performance in emerging economies. This study also finds that returnee entrepreneurs in private ventures outperform returnee entrepreneurs in state-owned or collectively owned ventures. These results suggest that returnee entrepreneurs can raise the productivity of the host country (China) by connecting foreign and local knowledge. This is also a good example of successful brain circulation. The result based on brain circulation is consistent with the international knowledge production based theory of Berliant and Fujita (2008) and Saxenian (2006), which points out the importance of diversity for creating new knowledge.

Let us turn to the evidence from Chinese students in Japanese workplaces. What is the workplace situation for Chinese in Japan? JILPT (2008) surveyed 902 foreign workers who graduated from university in Japan. The sample is mainly Chinese (80 percent), and under 30 years old (90 percent), including the categories 'specialist in humanities/international services' (50 percent), 'engineer' (30 percent), and less than three years of labor market experience in Japan (60 percent). Their reasons for choosing their current firms were threefold: (1) interest in current job characteristics (66 percent); (2) competence in Japanese language, studied in Japan (48.9 percent); and (3) competence in specific field of knowledge, studied at university in Japan (35.5 percent for all and 49.1 percent for 'engineers'). On the other hand, the main reasons for hiring foreign students were twofold: (1) internationalization of current business (37.1 percent); and (2) competence in foreign language (36.4 percent). Unfortunately for foreign students, the following were not major hiring reasons: (1) utilizing the foreigner's specific knowledge and creativeness (9.4 percent); and (2) utilizing the foreigner's specialties in the future (15.5 percent).

What are the expectations of foreign workers concerning their future careers? The answers were as follows: (1) to become manager of a local subsidiary (31.6 percent); (2) to become professional and skilled personnel (51.4 percent for 'engineers'); and (3) to become a manager in the head office (14.7 percent). On the other hand, the expectations of employers concerning the future careers of the foreign worker included the following: (1) foreign employees are expected to become managers of a local subsidiary (3 percent); (2) foreign employees are expected to become professional and skilled personnel (15.5 percent); and (3) foreign employees are expected to become workers similar to Japanese workers (48.9 percent). There is a gap between the expectations of the employees and the employers.

Two-thirds of foreign employees want to move to other firms or work in another country: (1) want to work in current firm in Japan (33.6 percent); (2) want to work in Japan but not in current firm (28.4 percent); (3) want to return to country of origin (28.9 percent); and (4) want to work abroad, but neither in Japan nor in country of origin (5.9 percent). However, although there is a good match in terms of foreign language competence between employees and employers, there is a large discrepancy concerning future expectations. This may stimulate job-hopping by foreign employees in Japan. Employers do not always expect foreign students to be temporary workers, and may consider foreign students to be permanent workers similar to Japanese workers. There is no special option for foreign employees. The apparent gap in expectations in the future employment status is difficult to solve. The human resource management practice (hereafter HRMP) is one of the complex production components in a firm. If the HRMP for foreign employees is changed, the whole organizational design could be affected. The benefit of diversity in workplaces and the costs of changing the 'status quo' play key roles in organizational changes in integrated economies.

9.5 CONCLUSION

This chapter has investigated international migration across countries at different skill levels. We stand on the industrial divide of immigration. At the global level, we can observe that migrants also tend to move out from and move into East Asia, compared with the EU and the USA. Despite geographic proximity between countries in East Asia, most of the migrants, perhaps most skilled migrants, move to the EU or North America from East Asia. However, there are also other streams, especially the strong ties between Indonesia and Malaysia, between Malaysia and Singapore, and between China and Japan. Thailand is also a magnet for unskilled immigrants from surrounding countries, Myanmar, Laos, Cambodia, and Vietnam. Sorting migrants between and within regions is more common to East Asian integration of trade and factor markets. Why do migration streams vary so much across skills and countries? Immigration economics has several tools which help to explain mainstream, upstream, downstream, and streamlets of global migration. Firstly, an income gap between countries stimulates out-migration from a relatively poor or peripheral country to a relatively rich or core country within a region. This inequality between two countries affects the whole population in a relatively poor country. To create heterogeneity in migration streams, we need to present the following theoretical framework. Secondly, self-selectivity matters. Thirdly, skill transferability also stimulates out-migration from a poor to a rich country. Fourthly, not only income gaps but also skill-price differentials have a direct affect on individuals. Finally, increasing access to schooling in low-skill price countries stimulates the educated to move to other countries.

The case study of the Indonesia–Malaysia corridor, especially the migration of unskilled immigrants from Indonesia to Malaysia, implies that Malaysia has a demand for cheap labor in order to maintain the production of cheap rubber in plantations or manufactured goods. The local-driven supply of emigrants has been able to respond to the labor shortage in specific sectors in Malaysia. Therefore, the labor market impact of immigration is difficult to estimate. From the case study on Japan, it is seen that Japan has also experienced labor shortages in specific regions and sectors. These local-driven demands for foreign workers have been examined using several cases. The case study on Japan also provides answers as to why success in international knowledge production is difficult. This issue could be related to immigration policy in East Asia. From the case study concerning overseas Chinese, we investigated the brain drain and brain circulation problem. We ask to what extent is international mobility of the highly educated better than no mobility at all for less developed countries.

To summarize this chapter, we present the possible future direction of international migration in East Asia through the lens of economic integration. For comparison, Box 9.1 examines the experience of the EU with Immigration Policies for skilled and unskilled workers. First, we can see a large influx of immigrants from relatively poor countries to rich countries within East Asia because we still have large income differences across countries in East Asia. Even though the economies in East Asia have integrated, there remains large income inequality, and the speed of convergence is still quite a bit slower than in the EU region. Second, countries in East Asia may experience not only brain drain, brain gains, and brain waste but also brain circulation, which provides greater leverage

BOX 9.1   EU IMMIGRATION POLICY AND CHALLENGES

When Romania and Bulgaria were integrated into the EU in 2004, the extent of labor market integration also became an important issue. Only Sweden and Finland opened their labor market to immigrants from Romania and Bulgaria. The UK and Ireland imposed a migration quota on immigrants from Romania and Bulgaria. France and Belgium permitted only labor-shortage industries, such as the construction sector, to accept immigrants from the two countries. Boeri and Van Ours (2008) present the reasons why immigration policy exists. They also compute the strictness of migration policies in the countries of the EU with the largest immigration. According to Boeri and Van Ours (2008), migration policies are essentially redistribution policies. This prevents income inequality and avoids tougher competition between low-skilled natives and foreign workers. Low-end skill distribution supports these policies, but such policies do not usually lead to efficiency. A few countries, mainly southern European countries (Italy, Portugal, and Spain), have adopted an explicit immigration quota system. They are facing a potentially large influx of immigrants from North Africa, and have a higher index of strictness of migration policies. During the period 1990 to 2005, these indices for Italy, Portugal, and Spain increased, showing that immigration policies have become increasingly strict for these countries. Because the labor market integration of low-skilled workers is not an easy problem to solve in EU economic policy, the EU has a priority to maintain plans for skilled migration between countries in order to compete with North America and East Asia.

Von Weizsacker (2008) summarizes the current policy priority in the area of high-skilled migration and points out the shortcomings of inviting skilled migrants, and especially strengthening the attractiveness of European universities. According to his analysis, creation of a European Blue Card policy for high-skilled immigrants is recognized as an important step for participation in the global talent competition. The shortcomings of a European Blue Card system are two-fold. Firstly, there is a low degree of guaranteed portability of the Blue Card within the EU. It would be almost as difficult to transfer to a second member state with Blue Card acquired in the first member state as it would be to apply for a fresh

Blue Card in the second member state. The second drawback is the short initial validity period of the Blue Card compared to the US Green Card and the special H1B Visa for high-skilled immigrants, which has generous extension systems.

The key instrument for attracting high-skilled migrants is to concentrate on strengthening the attractiveness and competitiveness of European universities. To compete with the US academic and job market for talent, the EU recognizes the possibility of introducing the 'Blue Diploma' on the basis of the Blue Card. This allows foreign-born graduates with a Master's degree or equivalent from a participating university to find a job in the EU without the strict salary threshold of the Blue Card. This could lead to the increased scientific openness and competitiveness of European universities, and help to attract foreign talent to the European labor market. He concludes that the top 100 non-European universities should also be included in this scheme to start with.

---

for policies concerning innovation at the national level and for extending business opportunities in East Asia.

For skilled workers, almost all countries in East Asia welcome skilled immigrants. Unskilled workers face higher hurdles in order to move between countries. Cross-country income gaps will remain because labor mobility will never be perfect. Even though countries are more open to East Asian integration of trade and labor mobility, less skill transferability across countries will hamper labor market integration. Thus, the policy arena needs to consider how to foster human capital transferability between countries in the face of economic integration. A possible suggestion is to introduce certification of specific skills. This certification should be common across all countries within East Asia. This certification system may work to avoid information asymmetry between employers and immigrants. Another possibility is to stimulate brain circulation, as Section 9.3 of this chapter has suggested. Taking advantage of geographic proximity, many skilled immigrants from less developed countries would return at some point or mix periods at home and abroad. Portable pension plans within East Asia may be a useful instrument for institutional upgrading. Country-wide government coordination of portable pension plans would help migration-based knowledge creation in East Asia.

Economic integration in East Asia seeks to enhance the innovation of East Asia and make it a world center for innovation through labor mobility. Designing immigration policy plays a key role in this. In particular, the shaping of immigration policy with regard to the productivity of and welfare for workers needs to be clarified. Each country with a different size of market faces two different problems: the labor complementarities between the native population and the immigrants, and the magnitude of the cultural friction between the natives and the immigrants. As Fujita and Weber (2004) suggest, two developed countries may play a non-cooperative game with each other when they attract immigrants, by stipulating an immigration quota and by setting wages for international migrants. They show that even though the larger country attracts more immigrants, it stipulates a lower quota than its smaller counterpart. It is important to examine the welfare implications of the choices of countries for refining immigration policy and argue that coordinated and harmonized immigration policies may improve workers' welfare. Finally it is also important to verify whether East Asia has any inclination to enhance its capacity to innovate and become a world center for innovation at the regional level.

REFERENCES

Ananta, Aris and Evi Nurvidya Arifin (2004), *International Migration in Southeast Asia*, Institute of Southeast Asian Studies (ISEAS), Singapore.

Berliant, Markus and Masahisa Fujita (2008), 'Knowledge creation as a square dance on the Hilbert cube', *International Economic Review*, **49** (November), 1251–95.

Boeri, Tito and Jan van Ours (2008), *The Economics of Imperfect Labor Markets*, New Jersey: Princeton University Press.

Borjas, George (1987), 'Self-selection and the earnings of immigrants', *American Economic Review*, September, 531–53.

Borjas, George (2003), 'The labor demand curve is downward sloping: reexamining the impact of immigration on the labor market', *Quarterly Journal of Economics*, **118**(4), November, 1335–74.

Card, David (1990), 'The impact of the Mariel boatlift on the Miami labor market', *Industrial and Labor Relations Review*, **43** (October), 245–57.

Chia, Siow Yue (2006), 'Labor mobility and East Asian integration', *Asian Economic Policy Review*, **1**, 349–67.

Chiquiar, Daniel and Gordon Hanson (2005), 'International migration, self-selection, and the distribution of wages: evidence from Mexico and the United States', *Journal of Political Economy*, **113** (April), 239–81.

Cohen, Joel E., Marta Roig, Daniel C. Reuman and Cai GoGwilt (2008), 'International migration beyond gravity: a statistical model for use in population projections', *PNAS* (*Proceedings for National Academy of Sciences of the United States of America*), 7 October 2008, **105**(40), 15269–74.

Cortes, Patricia (2008), 'The effect of low-skilled immigration on US prices: evidence from CPI data', *Journal of Political Economy*, **3**(116), 381–422.

Fernández-Huertas Moraga, Jesús (2008), 'New evidence on emigrant selection', mimeograph.

Fujita, Masahisa and Shlomo Weber (2004), 'On labor complementarity, cultural frictions and strategic immigration policies', IDE Discussion Paper, No.8.

Hill, Hal (2002), 'Special disparities in developing East Asia: a survey', *Asian-Pacific Economic Literature*, **16**(1), 10–35.

Hugo, Graeme J. and Soogil Young (eds) (2008), *Labour Mobility in the Asia-Pacific Region*, Institute of Southeast Asian Studies (ISEAS), Singapore.

Irwin, Douglas A. (2006), 'Comments on global wage differences and international student flows', Brookings Trade Forum.

JILPT (Japan Institute for Labour Policy and Training) (2008), 'Survey on hiring foreign students who graduated from school in Japan'.

Lange, Fabian and Robert Topel (2006), 'The social value of education and human capital', Eric Hanushek and Finis Welch (eds), *Handbook of Education Economics*, Vol.1, Amsterdam: North-Holland.

Li Haiyang, Y. Zhang, Zhou Li-An, and Zhang Weiying (2008), 'Feel as a stranger at home? Performance differential between returnee and homegrown entrepreneurs in China's technology industry', mimeo, Rice University and Peking University.

Mayda, Anna Maria (2008), 'International migration: a panel data analysis of the determinants of bilateral flows', *Journal of Population Economics*, forthcoming.

Nishikimi, Koji (2008), 'Trade, agglomeration and growth under economic integration: a survey of spatial economic approach', in Koji Nishikimi (ed.), *Economics of East Asian Integration* (Midterm Report), Institute of Developing Economies (IDE-JETRO).

People's Daily, (2004), '"Sea turtles" losing job race', 25 June.

Rosenzweig, Mark R. (2006a), 'The circulation migration of the skilled and economic development', Federal Reserve Bank of Dallas.

Rosenzweig, Mark R. (2006b), 'Global wage differences and international student flows', Brookings Trade Forum, 57–86.

Rosenzweig, Mark R. (2007), 'Higher education and international migration in Asia: brain circulation', prepared for the Regional Bank Conference on Development Economics (RBCDE) – Beijing 'Higher Education and Development', January.

Saxenian, AnnaLee (2006), *The New Argonauts, Regional Advantage in a Global Economy*, Cambridge and London: Harvard University Press.

Saxenian, AnnaLee (2007), 'Brain circulation and regional innovation', in K. Polenske (ed.), *The Economic Geography of Innovation*, Cambridge: Cambridge University Press.

Saxenian, AnnaLee (2008), 'The international mobility of entrepreneurs and regional ugprading in India and China', in A. Solimano (ed), *The International Mobility of Talent: Types, Causes, and Development Impact*, Oxford University Press.

von Weizsacker, Jacov (2008), *Division of Labour: Rethinking Europe's Migration Policy*, Bruegel Brueprint Series, Volume 7, Belgium: Bruegel.

Wiyono, Nur Hadi (2008), 'Indonesian women migrant workers and the impact of remittances', mimeo, University of Indonesia.

World Bank (2008a), *World Development Report 2009: Reshaping Economic Geography*, Washington, DC: World Bank.

World Bank (2008b), *World Development Report 2009: Reshaping Economic Geography in East Asia*, Washington, DC: World Bank.

Yeates, Nicola (ed.) (2009), *Globalizing Care Economies and Migrant Workers: Explorations in Global Care Chains*, Palgrave Macmillan.

10. Monetary integration in East Asia

Eiji Ogawa and Kentaro Kawasaki

10.1 INTRODUCTION

This chapter examines the costs and benefits of monetary integration as well as theories and empirical studies on Optimum Currency Areas (OCAs). It also takes a look at the lessons learned from the Asian currency crisis of 1997 with regard to monetary integration and the necessary steps for creating a currency union. To date, no such monetary integration plans have been implemented in East Asia, although it is a topic that some scholars have discussed. Considering that, this chapter outlines how monetary integration could be realized in East Asia in a future state rather than in its current incarnation. Proposals here will contribute to possible monetary integration in East Asia in a similar fashion to how the introduction of the euro was based on the active discussion of proposals regarding monetary integration in Europe.

It is very useful to study costs and benefits for East Asian economies in the current economic situation where there is integration in terms of trade, production, and finance, even if a currency union in East Asia may be only a dream at present. It is important to note that there was no regional monetary and financial cooperation in East Asia before the crisis. After the crisis, the Chiang Mai Initiative (CMI) was launched, along with the Asian Bond Market Initiative (ABMI) and the Asian Bond Fund (ABF) initiative, and consequently regional cooperation has begun to develop. This momentum may lead to the first steps towards a future currency union in East Asia.

As the European experience of monetary integration suggests, there can be several developmental stages in the creation of a currency union (a 'multi-step' approach). It is well known that the European Monetary System (EMS) played the most important role in establishing monetary integration. The EMS included the European Currency Unit (ECU) as a regional monetary unit for coordinating exchange rate policies among the countries of Europe. It would be a natural step for East Asia to emulate the European experience and calculate its strategy accordingly. Thus, this could be a first step for the countries of East Asia in introducing a regional monetary unit for coordinated exchange rate policies in order to proceed with monetary integration in the future.

The next section briefly explains the costs and benefits of monetary integration. Section 10.3 reviews the lessons learned from the Asian currency crisis, where the double mismatch on balance sheets of local financial institutions in terms of currency and maturity can be pinpointed as the most significant problem. In particular, the *de facto* dollar peg that the monetary authorities in East Asian countries adopted can be regarded as a result of a coordination failure in exchange rate policy.

Section 10.4 explains the regional monetary unit for coordinated exchange rate policies related to currency swap arrangements under the CMI, and surveillance based on a regional monetary unit is focused on as an instrument for preventing currency crises. This is expected to play a role in future coordinated exchange rate policies. Section 10.5 examines empirical research on an Optimum Currency Area for East Asia, where researchers have focused on the economic shock correlations among East Asian countries and how they synchronize. Section 10.6 considers the necessary steps on the road to monetary integration, and towards further regional monetary cooperation in East Asia from a common currency basket system to an Asian Currency Union. Finally, Section 10.7 concludes the chapter.

10.2 ESSENTIAL ECONOMICS FOR MONETARY INTEGRATION

10.2.1 Benefits of Monetary Integration

Introducing a single currency into a region means that there are no exchange rate movements among the currencies in the region, and therefore no exchange rate risks. Decreasing the number of currencies in a region and eliminating exchange rate risks bring each of the countries in the region numerous benefits in their real and financial economic sectors and also in economic policies.

The greatest advantage in the adoption of a single currency is that economies can obtain more efficiency in cross-border transactions by saving on transaction costs in the foreign exchange-rate market, and this efficiency will enhance all of the economies in the region.[1]

The differences in prices and wages among the target countries can be expected to narrow with the elimination of transaction costs. This facilitates competition among the companies in the affected regions.

Because exporters/importers will lose the advantage of 'jump-up' competitive power from the depreciation/appreciation of the home currency, enterprises will enter into intense competition with others in the region. Facilitation of competition will bring a consumer's surplus to households. Both the elimination of exchange rate uncertainty and the facilitation of competition may also stimulate the flow of capital and promote foreign direct investment (FDI) and indirect investments through securities. Enhancing capital transactions also contributes to market efficiency and leads to the formation of an integrated financial market. Therefore, the single currency will have higher credibility than the previous individual currencies as an international currency.

10.2.2   Costs of Monetary Integration

It is also clear that decreasing the number of currencies in the region and permanently fixing the exchange rates among the countries will force each economy to pay costs in addition to the initial cost of adopting the common currency.

The largest cost for each nation is the fact that their central banks will lose independence in monetary policies. This is because introducing a single currency is in effect to adopt a 'one size fits all' monetary policy by a central bank in the region. Additionally, potential systemic risks may have an effect on the region's entire financial market. Once a financial problem occurs, some local banks might face a liquidity problem. However, the nation's central bank can no longer act as a 'lender of last resort' to protect each economy's domestic financial system. The unified central bank cannot assure an optimal monetary policy for all of the participating countries.

In the case of an asymmetric economic disturbance among member states, differences in response to economic shock may result in economic disparities among the member states. Before the adoption of a single currency, these differences in response to economic shock or business cycles among the countries are adjusted for in the exchange rate as depreciation/appreciation of the currency and can help the economy increase/decrease trade surplus. This may be referred to as a beggar-thy-neighbor policy in some cases, but once member states agree to abolish each of their national currencies they lose one tool to make adjustments among the economies of each country.

Hence, member states may find it necessary to pay relatively large adjustment costs related to fiscal policies compared to the monetary policies they paid into before. With these costs comes the drawback that member states' economies will always be at risk from the effect of another's fiscal expense and, therefore, that member states might face excess fiscal discipline that they cannot accept politically. In the transition to 'an optimum currency area', the member states may sometimes need further expansion of expenditures as a fiscal transfer to others instead of exchange rate policies. This could result in larger, additional initial costs than previously expected.

10.3   LESSONS LEARNED FROM THE ASIAN CURRENCY CRISIS

10.3.1   The Double Mismatch Problem

In the Asian currency crisis of 1997, a double mismatch (both currency and maturity mismatches) on the balance sheets of local financial institutions contributed to the currency crisis as well as a financial crisis in Asian countries. In particular, the dollar-peg system widened fluctuations in effective exchange rates among East Asian currencies against their trade partners' currencies even as it stabilized the bilateral exchange rates of the currencies in terms of the US dollar. The fluctuations in effective exchange rates at times weakened price competitiveness of home products and, in turn, worsened trade accounts among the countries. On one hand, the dollar-peg system made local financial institutions less cautious about foreign exchange risks against the US dollar, while on the other hand they had double mismatches on their own balance sheets in terms of currency. In other words, they were borrowing US dollars from US investment banks and lending domestic currency to local enterprises in their own country.

One lesson learned from the Asian currency crisis was that local financial institutions in East Asian countries should not have had such double mismatches on their balance sheets. The monetary authorities of East Asian countries have taken two initiatives related to Asian bond markets in order to foster and develop bond markets as solutions for the double mismatch problem. In their first attempt, the ASEAN+3 (ASEAN plus Japan, China, and Korea) launched the Asian Bond Market Initiative (ABMI), which focuses on the supply side or infrastructure of bond markets, including clearing and settlement systems, rating agencies, and denomination currencies. In terms of denomination currencies, the ABMI aims at creating a bond denominated in an Asian currency basket. To that end, the EMEAP (Executives' Meeting of East Asia and Pacific Central Banks) launched the Asian Bond Fund (ABF) initiative to activate investment in Asian bonds from the demand side of the Asian bond market. It includes the ABF1 (a fund of US dollar-denominated bonds) and the ABF2 (a fund of local currency-denominated bonds).

Another lesson learned is that the monetary authorities of East Asian countries should not have adopted a formal or a *de facto* dollar-peg system. The monetary authorities should have taken into account their partners in international trade and financial transactions in choosing their own exchange rate systems. Some have proposed that it would be desirable for East Asian countries to adopt a currency basket system, in which the monetary authorities target their home currency to a currency basket consisting of, for example, the US dollar, the Japanese yen, and the euro.

10.3.2   Controversy over the Exchange Rate System in East Asian Countries

The controversy over the exchange rate system, especially the fixed versus flexible exchange rates system, has been ongoing for many years. However, the focus of the controversy has shifted from 'fixed versus flexible' to 'two-corner solutions versus intermediate regimes' since the Asian currency crisis. By examining the merits and demerits of a currency basket system from the experience of the Asian currency crisis we can judge what type of exchange rate system East Asian countries had really adopted.[2]

Calvo and Reinhart (2000) analyzed the exchange rates, foreign reserves, monetary base, and interest rates in Asian countries. They concluded that although some of the Asian countries announced that they were adopting a floating exchange rate system, their currencies had strong linkages with the US dollar and the exchange rates were not floating so freely. McKinnon (2000) analyzed how the daily changes in the exchange rates of nine East Asian currencies had a strong relationship with the US dollar. He showed that the movements of East Asian currencies were highly correlated with the movements of the US dollar before 1997. These two papers suggest that most Asian countries were not in fact floaters and that some of them had adopted a *de facto* dollar-peg system, which is classified as an intermediate exchange rate system. Williamson (2000) explains this 'revealed preference' of Asian countries as follows: 'They see gains in an intermediate regime that they believe outweigh the costs in terms of greater vulnerability to crises and having less simple policy rules to follow.' Williamson (2000) believes that the primary benefit of an intermediate exchange rate system is that it allows policy to be directed to limiting misalignments of exchange rates. Overvaluation of home currencies would weaken the competitiveness of tradable goods industries while undervaluation would cause overheating and import inflation. Thus, the benefit of a basket currency system would have been significant for Asian countries following export-oriented growth strategies.

The clearest benefit of a currency basket system compared with the dollar-peg system is its contribution to keeping effective exchange rates or trade competitiveness relatively stable. If the export destination is only one country and there is no competitor other than the destination country, it is enough to peg the currency to that of the export destination country to maintain trade competitiveness. Some empirical research studies (Ito et al. 1998, Ogawa and Sun 2001, Yoshino et al. 2004) found that a currency basket system would contribute to stabilizing trade balances and capital flow for East Asian countries.

10.3.3   Coordination Failure in Exchange Rate Policies

McKinnon (2000) and Ogawa (2002) pointed out that after the Asian currency crisis, linkages of East Asian countries to the US dollar, in fact, returned to levels as high as before the crisis. One reason the monetary authorities are unwilling to adopt a currency basket peg system is related to a kind of coordination failure.[3]

Ogawa and Ito (2002) used a two-country model in a game theoretical framework to analyze how an East Asian country's choice of exchange rate system (or weights in the currency basket) is dependent on similar choices made by their neighboring countries. The dollar weights in the currency baskets of the two countries are determined as a Nash equilibrium. Generally, there are multiple equilibria and, moreover, a 'coordination failure' may result in the following situation. Suppose that all of the monetary authorities among various East Asian countries have kept a *de facto* dollar-peg system. As a consequence, the exchange rates of their home currencies *vis-à-vis* the US dollar have been kept almost fixed while the exchange rates of the home currencies *vis-à-vis* other major currencies have been fluctuating. If the monetary authorities of a country then shift their exchange rate policy from that of a *de facto* dollar-peg system to a currency basket peg system, the currency basket peg system will increase fluctuations in the exchange rate of the home currency *vis-à-vis* the US dollar.

With uncertainty over the future movements in the exchange rate of the US dollar *vis-à-vis* other major currencies, a tendency toward 'coordination failure' may increase. Suppose that alone the monetary authorities of a country shift the exchange rate policy to the currency basket peg system while the monetary authorities of neighboring countries keep the dollar-peg system. The currency of the country that adopted the currency basket peg system would appreciate against the other currencies if the US dollar depreciates against other major currencies. Under such uncertainty, monetary authorities tend to work out a strategy of 'wait and see' if they are averse to risk.

As previously stated, all of the monetary authorities are likely to implement this 'wait and see' strategy if they are risk averse, resulting in a so-called 'prisoner's dilemma' in game theory. All of the monetary authorities cannot help but choose to keep the dollar-peg system, creating a Nash equilibrium, even though they know that there is a better cooperative solution. Coordination among at least some of the monetary authorities in East Asia is necessary to initiate a shift from a Nash equilibrium to a cooperative solution.

10.4   A REGIONAL MONETARY UNIT FOR COORDINATED EXCHANGE RATE POLICIES

10.4.1   Chiang Mai Initiative

The monetary authorities of East Asian countries, especially ASEAN+3, have strengthened their regional monetary cooperation since the Asian currency crisis. The ASEAN+3 Ministers' Meeting decided upon the Chiang Mai Initiative (CMI) in May 2000. It was to establish a network of bilateral swap arrangements for managing a currency crisis in any member country as shown in Figure 10.1. The total of the network of currency swap arrangements under the CMI amounts to USD 90 billion.

Under the CMI, monetary authorities conduct a surveillance process aimed at preventing a future currency crisis. However, the monetary authorities have no standing institution to carry out any kind of surveillance in East Asia. Instead, they regularly hold an Economic Review and Policy Dialogue (ERPD) in the ASEAN+3 Deputy Ministers' Meeting for surveillance over their macroeconomic performance – although they focus only on domestic macroeconomic variables that include GDP, inflation, and soundness of the financial sector. The monetary authorities of East Asian countries must pay attention to biased changes in relative prices caused by misalignments of intra-regional exchange rates among East Asian currencies. Exchange rates among the intra-regional currencies affect the economic activities of each country in East Asia through intra-regional trade, foreign direct investments, and international capital flows. Therefore, monetary authorities must conduct surveillance over the intra-regional exchange rates as well as the domestic macroeconomic variables.

10.4.2   Surveillance Based on Regional Monetary Units

Regional surveillance over intra-regional exchange rates is indispensable in crisis prevention and for promoting policy coordination in areas such as

as of Apr. 2009

ASEAN Swap Arrangement (ASA)
US$ 2 bil

Thailand

Brunei

Malaysia

Cambodia

Philippines

Lao PDR

Myanmar

Indonesia

Vietnam

Singapore

US$ 9 bil
Japan ⇒ Thailand $ 6 bil
— Thailand ⇒ Japan $ 3 bil

US$ 6.5 bil
Japan ⇒ Philippines $ 6 bil
— Philippines ⇒ Japan $ 0.5 bil

US$ 1 bil
(Japan ⇒ Malaysia $ 1 bil)

US$ 2 bil
Korea ⇒ Thailand $ 1 bil
— Thailand ⇒ Korea $ 1 bil

US$ 12 bil
(Japan ⇒ Indonesia $ 12 bil)

US$ 4 bil
Japan ⇒ Singapore $ 3 bil
— Singapore ⇒ Japan $ 1 bil

US$ 2 bil
(China ⇒ Thailand $ 2 bil)

US$ 1.5 bil
(China ⇒ Malaysia $ 1.5 bil)

eq. US$ 2 bil[2]
(China ⇒ Philippines eq. $ 2 bil)

US$ 4 bil
(China ⇒ Indonesia $ 4 bil)

US$ 3 bil
Korea ⇒ Malaysia $ 1.5 bil
— Malaysia ⇒ Korea $ 1.5 bil

US$ 4 bil
Korea ⇒ Philippines $ 2 bil
— Philippines ⇒ Korea $ 2 bil

US$ 4 bil
Korea ⇒ Indonesia $ 2 bil
— Indonesia ⇒ Korea $ 4 bil

eq. US$ 21 bil
① Japan ⇒ Korea eq. $ 10 bil
   Korea ⇒ Japan eq. $ 5 bil
② Japan ⇒ Korea eq. $ 3 bil[4][5]
   Korea ⇒ Japan eq. $ 3 bil

Total: US$ 90.0 bil[6]

Japan

China

Republic of Korea

eq. US$ 6 bil[1]
Japan ⇒ China eq. $ 3 bil
— China ⇒ Japan eq. $ 3 bil

eq. US$ 8 bil[3]
China ⇒ Korea eq. $ 4 bil
— Korea ⇒ China eq. $ 4 bil

1. Local currency swap between Japanese yen and Chinese yuan.
2. Local currency swap between Chinese yuan and Philippines peso.
3. Local currency swap between Chinese yuan and Korean won.
4. Local currency swap between Japanese yen and Korean won.
5. The maximum amount is increased to US$ 20 billion equivalent until the end of October 2009.
6. The sum of US$ 90.0 bil does not include the ASEAN Swap Arrangement (ASA).

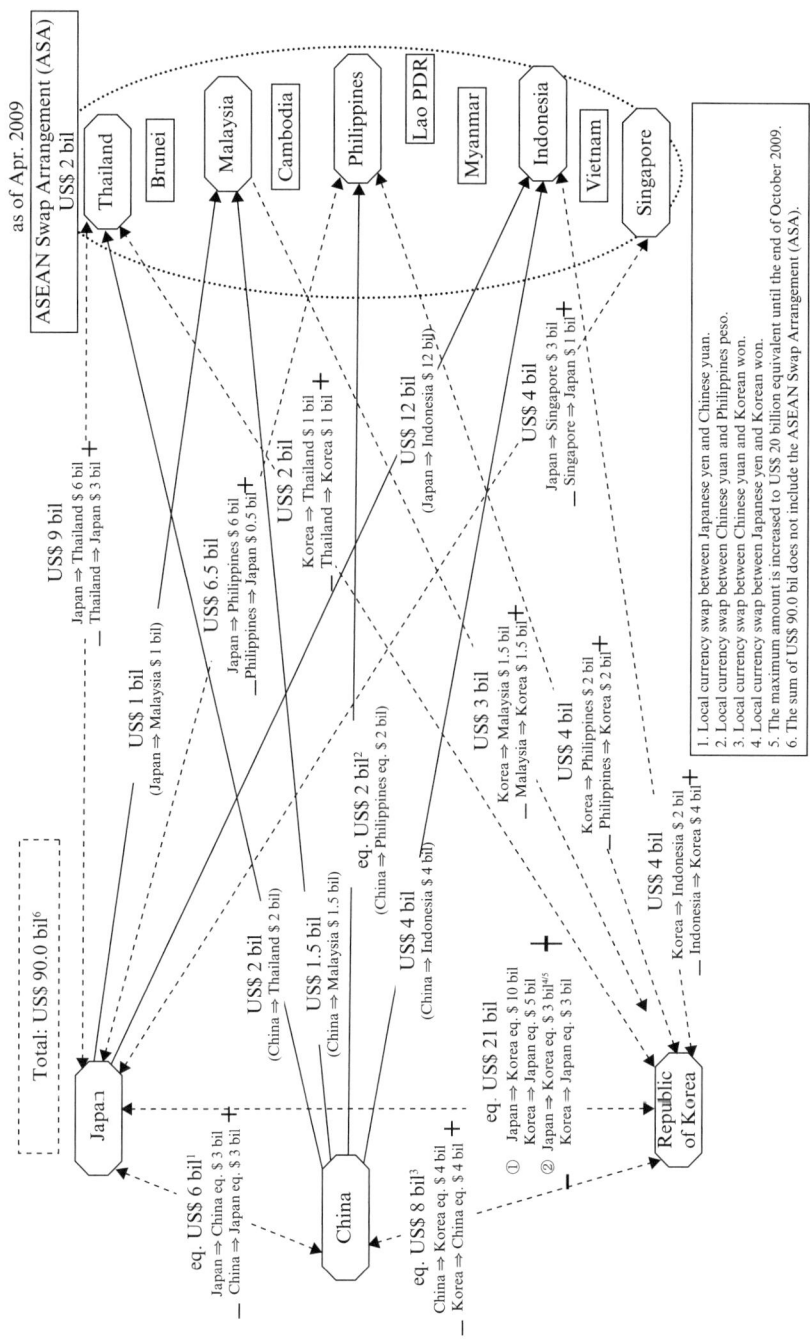

Source: Ministry of Finance, Japan.

Figure 10.1 Bilateral currency swap agreements under the Chiang Mai initiative

the exchange rate policy in East Asia. The ASEAN+3 Ministers' Meeting established a research group to conduct a study titled, 'Toward greater financial stability in the Asian region: measures for possible use of regional monetary units for surveillance and transaction' in 2007.

Monitoring the Regional Monetary Unit (RMU) and RMU Deviation Indicators (DIs), in addition to the main economic and financial indicators and those used for early warning systems such as the ratio of short-term external debt to foreign reserves, will make regional surveillance more effective. However, in order to allow regional surveillance to function well in East Asia, it should be noted that several Asian countries still have problems to be solved, such as *de facto* plural exchange rate systems, high inflation rates, and dollarized economies. With respect to the relationship between IMF surveillance and regional surveillance in East Asia, the IMF's framework for bilateral surveillance and its supplementary schemes including FSAP (Financial Sector Assessment Program) could be drawn upon for the ERPD (Economic Review and Policy Dialogue) in East Asia as well. Important to note here is that there are several things that the IMF cannot do, but that regional surveillance by ASEAN+3 likely could: monitoring cross-border transmissions of macroeconomic risks in the region; solving problems stemming from coordination failure in exchange rate policy; and dealing with problems arising from the access limit to IMF lending. Both the RMU and RMU DIs are expected to play an important role in these areas of regional surveillance in East Asia.[4]

The RMU and RMU DIs are based on the Asian Monetary Unit (AMU) and AMU DIs suggested by Ogawa and Shimizu (2006), and by Kawai (2009) based on a similar proposal for an Asian Currency Unit (ACU). Here the AMU and AMU DIs are explained and their updated data are shown. Ogawa and Shimizu (2006) proposed the creation of an AMU and AMU DIs for East Asian currencies as one part of the new surveillance criteria. These would contribute to coordinated exchange rate policies in East Asia, thereby enhancing the monetary authorities' surveillance capabilities. The AMU (Figure 10.2) would be calculated as a weighted average of East Asian currencies[5] according to the method used to calculate the European Currency Unit (ECU) adopted by EU countries under the European Monetary System (EMS) prior to the introduction of the euro.

The AMU DIs for each East Asian currency are measured to show the degree of deviation from the benchmark rate in terms of the AMU. The AMU DIs include both nominal AMU DIs on a daily basis (Figure 10.3) and real AMU DIs, which are adjusted for differences in inflation on a monthly basis (Figure 10.4). Conducting surveillance on the real AMU DIs is more appropriate for examining the effects of changes in exchange

US$-euro/AMU

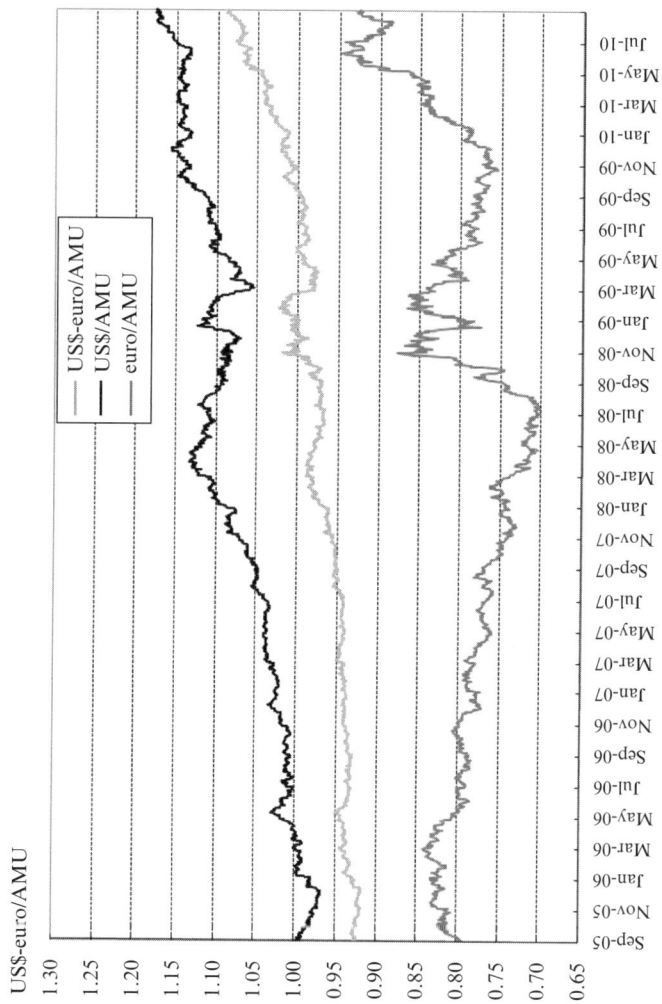

Note: Benchmark year = 2000–01, basket weight = 2004–06.

Source: Research Institute of Economy, Trade and Industry http://www.rieti.go.jp/users/amu/en/index.html#figures.

Figure 10.2   AMU in terms of USD-EURO

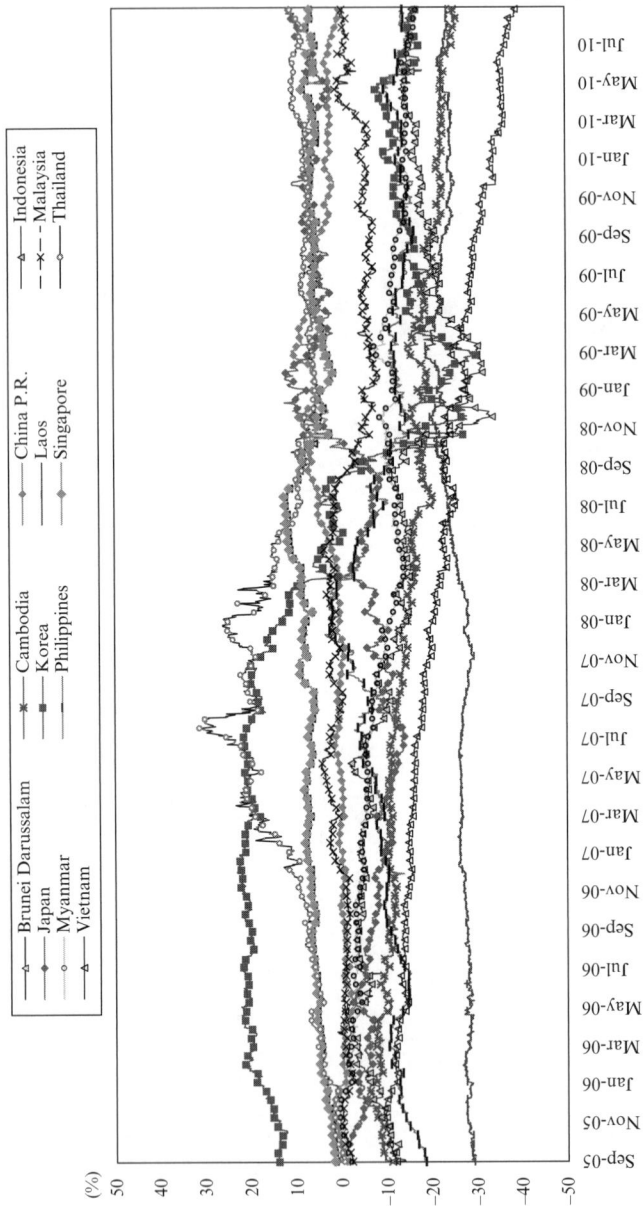

Note: Benchmark year = 2000/2001, basket weight = 2004–06, daily.

Source: Research Institute of Economy, Trade and Industry http://www.rieti.go.jp/users/amu/en/index.html#figures.

Figure 10.3 Nominal AMU deviation indicators

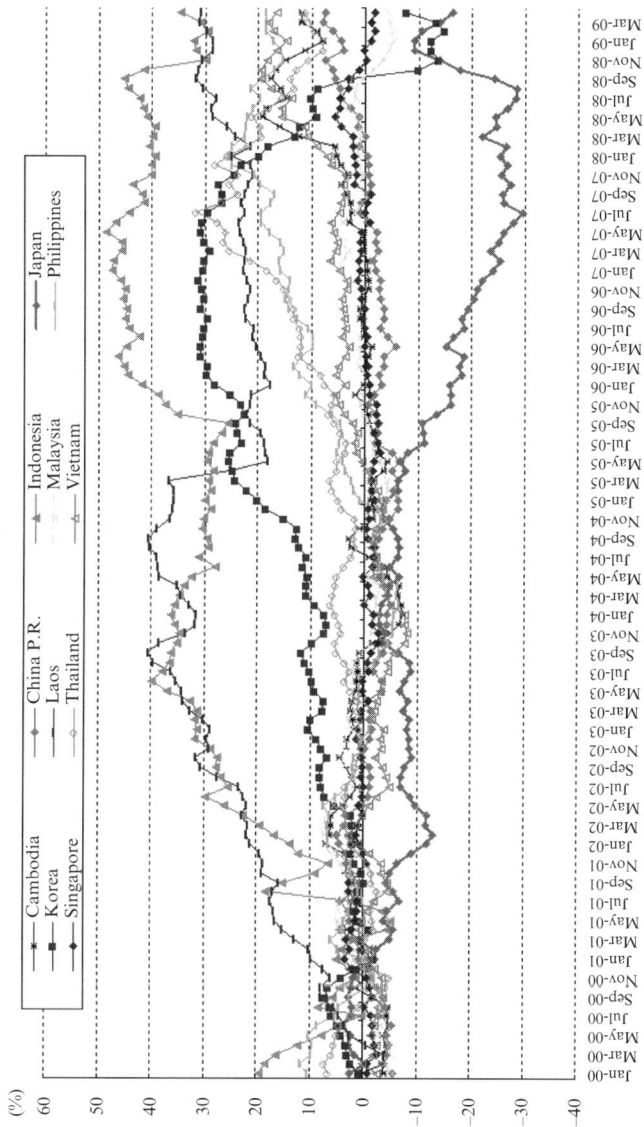

Note: Benchmark year = 2000/2001, basket weight = 2004–2006, monthly.

Source: Research Institute of Economy, Trade and Industry (http://www.rieti.go.jp/users/amu/en/index.html#figures).

Figure 10.4 Real AMU deviation indicators

rates on the real economy, while monitoring the nominal AMU DIs is more useful for day-to-day deviations from the AMU.

The nominal AMU DIs are available in terms of daily data so that we can monitor the real-time situation without any time lag. On the other hand, the real AMU DIs are more important in providing measurements on the effects of exchange rates on trade, production, and so on. However, the real AMU DI data are only available on a monthly basis because monthly data on price indexes are needed to calculate them. It is suggested that the monetary authorities should use both of these for their surveillance over their own currencies because each has different merits and demerits.

10.5   OPTIMUM CURRENCY AREA

10.5.1   What is an Optimum Currency Area?

How much each of the economies must pay for a possible monetary integration would depend on the applicability of conditions for integration. As mentioned above, various trade-offs exist. In monetary integration, policymakers should balance the savings in transaction costs against the consequences of diminished policy autonomy from losing the exchange rate and monetary policy as instruments to respond to economic shocks. If there exists an effective adjustment process or an instrument for detecting disturbance besides exchange rates, economies would not need to pay any political or economic costs for the maintenance of a common currency union. Mundell (1961) supposed that there should exist a minimum economic unit composed of the countries' currencies that should be tied to each other by fixed exchange rates. This minimum unit tied with a single currency is referred to as the theory of 'optimum currency area' (OCA).

One can ask whether the region is an optimum currency area or not, but his original developments in the theory of OCA explained that the region could be called an 'optimum currency area' if there is factor mobility, and that regions should be separated from other regions or countries that share factor immobility. Therefore, the theory insists that feasibility of a common currency area depends on 'factor mobility'.

Various factors have been pointed out that can determine an optimum currency area. Mundell (1961) presented mobility of labor as a necessary condition for a common currency area. McKinnon (1963) regarded openness of the economies as another necessary condition. Frankel (1999) suggests that a high degree of capital mobility, rather than nominal exchange rates, allows asymmetric shocks among countries to adjust their economies. Hence, it is thought that the concept of 'factor mobility' includes cross-border mobility of labor, capital, and technology as well as trade.

Moreover, fiscal transfer among countries to adjust out of the disequilibrium is essential to support the currency union. If a member state can agree to spend on a fiscal transfer to help another member state, this political adjustment channel may work as well as exchange rates. In the transition to a deepening of integration, countries may need fiscal transfer from one another even if factor mobility exists. In Mundell's original work, however, there is no detailed discussion about the speed of adjustment towards equilibrium. Therefore, it is still ambiguous whether or not conditions for OCA should be met in the short term or in the long term. Hence, this is regarded as a necessary condition in the feasibility of realizing a common currency area.

10.5.2   Feasibility of OCA in Empirical Studies

Following the discussion of the previous section, the most important criterion in the theory of an 'optimum currency area' is similarity in economic structure among each economy in the region, which could be brought about by the synchronization of business cycles and high bilateral trade intensity in the region.

Hence, Bayoumi and Eichengreen (1993) point out that the feasibility of a common currency area depends on whether countries share a symmetric response to economic shocks. Since the countries in the region do not need to make intra-regional adjustments for economic shocks, they can form a common currency union that satisfies the conditions for an OCA. They identify each country's supply shocks by using the Structural Vector Autoregressive (S-VAR) approach, developed by Blanchard and Quah (1989), and calculate the coefficient of correlations in the response of economic shocks among the countries in the region. They reported that the highest coefficient of correlation was at 0.68 between Germany and Denmark and that the second highest was at 0.62 between Germany and Belgium.[6] Bayoumi et al. (2000) apply the same methodology to the East Asian region. They obtained an empirical result that correlations are relatively high among Malaysia, Indonesia, and Singapore. Correlation is also relatively high between Singapore and Thailand. The paper concludes that these ASEAN countries might be able to form a common currency area. Supply shocks in Japan have a positive correlation with Taiwan, Korea, and Australia. However, they have a lower correlation with ASEAN countries except for Thailand.

Zhang et al. (2004) also apply a similar VAR approach to East Asian countries. Zhang et al. recent works focus more on the short-term synchronization of business cycles among countries.

The S-VAR approach applied to empirical studies for OCA theory is implemented by comparing the fluctuation patterns of output. However, symmetric response to supply shocks is only a sufficient condition for an optimum currency area. Asymmetric shocks will cause a disturbance to the formation of a currency union or in the support of a fixed exchange rate system. Nevertheless, other factors, such as factor mobility, economic openness to other countries, and capital mobility, can remedy disequilibria caused by these asymmetric shocks. Therefore, broader conditions should be considered necessary for an OCA rather than simply the condition of a symmetric response to economic shocks. As long as these factors work well in the region, the condition of the symmetric response to economic shocks may not be a necessary and sufficient condition for implementing a common currency area.

In the transition towards equilibrium, namely a currency union, countries must pursue policy coordination, since the adjustment process is expected to be very slow and nominal rigidities are expected to exist in the short run. Note that these total costs should not exceed the total benefit achieved from monetary integration in the long run.

Whether or not countries meet the OCA criteria depends on the assumptions of the researcher involved. In the decision to join a currency, strict criteria can be defined such as that countries should not pay any additional costs to adjust for asymmetric economic shocks in the region. However, if countries are allowed to pay related expenditures or losses as initial costs and opportunity costs to join a single currency, while the adjustment process may take some time, broader conditions can be adopted as the OCA criteria. The flowchart in Figure 10.5 shows steps for determining whether a region can be considered an OCA or not.

10.6   STEPS TO MONETARY INTEGRATION

10.6.1   From a Common Currency Basket to an Asian Currency Union

East Asian countries should aim to resolve coordination failures in exchange rate policies. One solution is for East Asian countries to form a currency union wherein economic agents use a common currency basket as a single common currency unit. A common currency basket might be composed of currencies of trading partner countries, given that the objective is to stabilize its real effective exchange rate and, in turn, its trade balances.[7] Considering the trading partners, a common currency basket for East

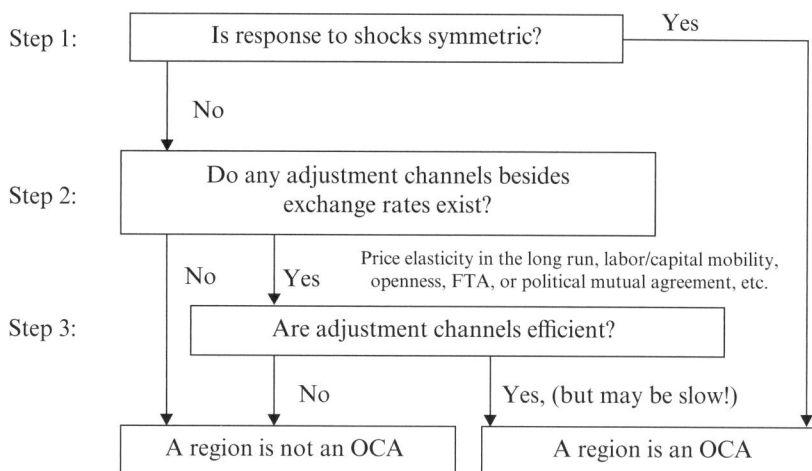

Source: Authors.

Figure 10.5 Is a region an OCA?

Asian countries might be in fact composed of the US dollar, the Japanese yen, the euro, and neighbor country currencies. Under a common currency basket system, the monetary authorities of a given country will peg or target their home currencies to a common currency basket.

In a rigid system where monetary authorities peg their home currencies to a common currency basket, the currencies are effectively pegged to each other. In a more flexible system where they target their home currencies within an exchange rate band around a central parity rate against the common currency basket, the currencies are linked to each other within an exchange rate band. Thus, if they adopt a common currency basket system, their currencies would be linked with each other at a parity rate or within a band around a central parity rate.

It is more tractable for monetary authorities to link their home currencies to a common currency unit that is equivalent to the common currency basket. For East Asian countries, a common currency unit might be composed of the US dollar, the Japanese yen, and the euro as well as the home currencies of the participating countries (Ito et al. 1998). The EU countries adopted the European Monetary System in which their home currencies were linked to a common currency unit, called the ECU, during the period from 1979 to 1998. The ECU was composed of only the home currencies of the EMS member countries. Their home currencies were linked to the ECU with an exchange rate band. The monetary authorities had an obligation to intervene in foreign exchange markets in order to keep the exchange rates of the home currency against the other EMS currencies within an exchange rate band. On the other hand, the ECU was floating against other major currencies including the US dollar and the Japanese yen.[8]

The method for adopting a common currency basket system is as follows. At first, a common currency unit such as the ECU, which consists of the home currencies of member countries, is created. Then, they link their home currencies to the common currency unit. Moreover, they link the common currency unit to a currency basket comprised of the US dollar, the Japanese yen, and the euro. This is the two-stage linkage method.

The monetary authorities of the participating countries have an obligation to intervene in foreign exchange markets in order to link their home currencies to the common currency unit and, in turn, link their home currencies to each other. At the same time, the monetary authorities of the participating countries might coordinate to intervene in foreign exchange markets in order to link the common currency unit to a currency basket that is comprised of the US dollar, the Japanese yen, and so on. Such an intervention is complicated for monetary authorities. Additionally, if the participating countries establish an intra-regional institution it could intervene in foreign exchange markets in order to link the common currency unit to a currency basket on behalf of the monetary authorities of the participating country.

Another method is for a common currency unit to be created consisting of outside currencies such as the US dollar and the euro as well as regional home currencies. These link the home currencies directly to the common currency unit. This is the direct linkage method. The monetary authorities of the participating countries have an obligation to intervene directly in foreign exchange markets in order to link their home currencies to the common currency unit. In this case it is more difficult to calculate a common currency unit comprised of the US dollar, the Japanese yen, and the euro as well as their regional home currencies.

The two methods might be, in theory, equivalent to each other. However, which method should be adopted depends on the implementation. It is easier for the monetary authorities of each country to implement the two-step linkage method if they can establish an intra-regional institution for the participating countries. The monetary authorities of the participating countries will target the home currency to the common currency unit.

The next step is for the East Asian economy to proceed towards a currency union, as long as its benefits are expected to overcome the shortcomings associated with the conditions for an optimum currency area as explained in the previous section.[9]

East Asian countries have their own home currencies that monetary authorities must link to the currency unit before they achieve a regional monetary integration. This step implies that a possibility is left for the monetary authorities to realign the exchange rates of the home currencies *vis-à-vis* the common currency unit or to break the link of their home currencies to the common currency unit. This possibility might cause speculators to make speculative attacks against weaker currencies. One option for the monetary authorities is to make a strong commitment to link their own home currencies to the common currency unit.

The strongest commitment is to participate in a currency union where the monetary authorities of the participating countries have no exit option. This kind of commitment contributes to the stability of exchange rate systems because the monetary authorities build up their confidence from private economic agents. The monetary authorities can make this strong commitment to solve the so-called 'peso problem', meaning that the future possibility of exchange rate collapse increases domestic interest rates in terms of their home currencies through expected depreciation and risk premium. Accordingly, a currency union contributes to a decrease in domestic interest rates in terms of the home currencies.

Moreover, in recent years, the world economy has followed a trend in making bilateral and regional free-trade agreements in parallel to the WTO system. Movements toward a free trade area contribute to the elimination of some trade obstacles, including tariffs and non-tariff barriers. However, economic agents regard exchange rate risks as an important trade obstacle after free-trade agreements are concluded with several countries. Even though forward contracts are used to avoid exchange rate risks, some costs must be paid to avoid those risks; this is one kind of transaction cost. In this situation agents would face an increased necessity to eliminate exchange rate risks and the related transaction costs. Economic agents would face no exchange rate risks if there is a strong commitment to maintaining a common currency union that links their home currencies to their neighbor countries' currencies.

10.6.2 Steps Toward Further Regional Monetary Cooperation in East Asia

We must consider the necessary steps toward further regional monetary cooperation in East Asia as it would be difficult for East Asia to jump from its current situation to a common currency basket system and, in turn, the Asian Currency Union.[10]

As a first step, the monetary authorities of ASEAN+3 might initiate policy dialogue concerning exchange rates and exchange rate policies. At that time, the RMU and RMU deviation indicator should be used to conduct surveillance on the exchange rates and exchange rate policies as well as domestic macroeconomic policies at the Economic Review and Policy Dialogue (ERPD) of the ASEAN+3 Financial Deputy Ministers' Meeting. The surveillance process based on the RMU must be conducted by all of ASEAN+3, which includes Japan. Accordingly, the Japanese yen should be included in the RMU.

In the second step, the monetary authorities of ASEAN+2 (China and Korea) will adopt a managed floating exchange rate system with reference to their own individual G3 currency baskets (the US dollar, the euro, and the Japanese yen) for managed floating countries. On one hand, the monetary authority of Japan might not be included in adopting a G3 currency basket system because it is difficult for it to have effective intervention in such a thick foreign exchange market such as the dollar/yen market. At the same time, the monetary authorities of ASEAN+3 should continue to conduct the surveillance process using the RMU Deviation Indicators.

In the third step, the monetary authorities of ASEAN+2 will shift to a managed floating exchange rate system with reference to a common G3 currency basket for managed floating countries. At the same time, the monetary authorities of ASEAN+3 should continue to conduct surveillance using the RMU Deviation Indicators. In the second and third steps, the Japanese yen should be one of the G3 currencies that the monetary authorities of ASEAN+2 will target in conducting their exchange rate policies.

In the fourth step, some ASEAN+3 countries (what we call 'core countries') would peg to a common regional currency basket, the RMU, in order to stabilize intra-regional exchange rates. They should conduct coordinated monetary policies in order to stabilize intra-regional exchange rates. At that time, the core countries should be limited to those that adopt the RMU peg system.

In the fifth step, some of ASEAN+3 would introduce a bilateral grid method based on the RMU to conduct a certain amount of intervention in foreign exchange markets of the relevant intra-regional exchange rates. An Asian Exchange Rate Mechanism should be established for the coordinated intervention. This would be similar to the Exchange Rate Mechanism under the EMS prior to the introduction of the euro.

In the fourth and fifth steps, the currency basket should include the Japanese yen as an anchor currency. In this case, the Japanese yen would be a regional key currency in terms of its being a main international currency with convertibility and conducting a disinflationary stance of monetary policy. East Asian currencies should be linked to a regional anchor such as the Japanese yen to stabilize their value and prevent a currency crisis. During the course of future monetary unions in East Asia, the composition currencies of RMU should be convertible not only for their current account transactions, but also their capital account transactions. In addition, their trade volumes or liquidity in foreign exchange markets should also be relatively high. At the moment, the Japanese yen is the only currency that can be freely traded for non-resident investors without any restrictions. Both the foreign exchange markets of the Japanese yen and the Japanese yen-denominated bond markets in Japan have higher liquidity compared with those in other East Asian countries.

It is expected that the RMU could be used not only by the monetary authorities but also by private sectors. Dammers and McCauley (2006) and Iwata (2005) indicated that development in private ECU in the financial field began in the early 1980s and developed rapidly. Similar to the ECU, the RMU might be used to denominate regional capital transactions. Iwata (2005) indicated that there was still room for a private RCU composed of main Asian currencies to develop.[11] Then, an RMU composed of only core currencies in the region could be started if an RMU could be used in a similar role to the ECU. If it is named 'core-RMU,' the criteria for being a composition currency of 'core-RMU' should be considered.

For example, Ogawa and Shimizu (2005) proposed an Asian Monetary Unit (AMU) as a weighted average of thirteen East Asian currencies (ASEAN10, Japan, China, and Korea) to enhance the monetary authorities' surveillance capacity in East Asia.[12] At the same time, Ogawa and Shimizu (2006) created a core-AMU currency basket, which is composed of some regional currencies with convertibility in both current and capital accounts, for private usage especially in Asian bond markets. Among core-AMU currencies, the Japanese yen's share is 58 percent, which is the highest basket weight. The core-AMU is expected to be a denomination currency of Asian bonds, which might play an important role for investment diversification in the region. Since the core-AMU denominated Asian bond is supposed to be a stable investment choice especially for Japanese investors we expect that the Japanese yen and Japanese investors will play an important role in creating and promoting a core-AMU denominated Asian bond market.

10.7 CONCLUSION

This chapter explained the costs and benefits of monetary integration, and theories and empirical studies on an optimum currency area (OCA), as well as the lessons learned from the Asian currency crisis of 1997 to consider the possibility of monetary integration and the steps necessary for moving towards a currency union. It has been argued that the double mismatch of financial institutions' balance sheets in terms of maturity and currency made the adverse effects of the currency crisis much more severe after they experienced the Asian currency crisis in 1997. For this reason, the monetary authorities of East Asian countries launched two kinds of initiatives in the 2000s. The CMI included both regional currency swap arrangements for managing a currency crisis and a surveillance process over member countries' economies for preventing it. On the other hand, the ABMI and ABF have an objective to foster and develop bond markets in East Asia as a way to solve the double mismatch problem. The initiatives are regarded as the first step to regional monetary and financial cooperation in East Asia. This is expected to develop into a regional monetary coordination and then a possible regional monetary integration in the future.

At the moment, it seems difficult for the East Asian economy to pursue regional monetary integration. However, we should understand the merits and demerits of monetary integration for the East Asian economy where production networks have already been established and trade and *de facto* financial transactions tend to be integrated. A stepwise process towards deepening and widening monetary integration should be adopted because currently East Asia includes countries in different stages of development. Among these phases, it is regarded as an important first step to introduce a Regional Monetary Unit as a measurement for surveillance of the ASEAN+3 Financial Deputy Ministers' ERPD.

NOTES

1. De Grauwe (1992) summarized the merits and demerits of international monetary integration.
2. Ogawa et al. (2004).
3. Bénassy-Quéré (1999) and Ohno (1999) analyzed how the monetary authorities peg the home currency to the US dollar as a result of a coordination failure.
4. IIMA (2008).
5. The ASEAN10+3 currencies are chosen as the component currencies of the AMU. The ASEAN10+3 is composed of Brunei, Cambodia, Indonesia, Laos, Malaysia, Myanmar, the Philippines, Singapore, Thailand, Vietnam, Japan, Korea, and China.
6. They employ 15 EU countries' annual GDP data and prices from 1969 to 1989.
7. One of the objectives is to stabilize the real effective exchange rate (Lipschitz and Sundrarajan 1980). The objective implicitly implies that the trade balance is stable as long as the monetary authorities keep the exchange rate stable around the equilibrium. Another objective is to keep the balance of trade or current accounts at an optimal level, or to stabilize the trade or current balances (Flanders and Helpman 1979, Flanders and

Tishler 1981). Turnovsky (1982) proposed that the objective was to stabilize domestic income, which is a more general one of economic policy. For domestic income stabilization, there are policy options other than the currency basket weights. Bhandari (1985), building on Turnovsky (1982), considered four criteria or a combination thereof at the same time. The four criteria are domestic price-output stability, stability of the domestic prices, reserve stock stability, and stability of an external competitiveness. See more detailed discussions in Kwan (2001).

8. Kim et al. (2000) suggested that the Asian Currency Unit be composed of only the East Asian currencies including the Japanese yen.
9. Eichengreen (2006) proposed a parallel currency approach for regional monetary cooperation in East Asia.
10. Ogawa and Shimizu (2007).
11. Iwata (2005) explained that the reason for this prospect was a lack of convergence of interest rates and inflation rates within Asia and some restrictions of capital movements in some Asian countries. He indicated that these circumstances were similar to those in the early development of a private ECU between 1979 and 1987.
12. The AMU data are published on the website of the Research Institute of Economy, Trade and Industry (RIETI, http://www.rieti.go.jp/users/amu/en/index.html).

REFERENCES

Bayoumi, Tamim and Barry Eichengreen (1993), 'Shocking aspects of European monetary integration', in Francisco Torres and Francesco Givavazzi (eds), *Adjustment and Growth in the European Monetary Union*, Cambridge: Cambridge University Press, pp. 193–229.

Bayoumi, Tamim, Barry Eichengreen and Paolo Mauro (2000), 'On regional monetary arrangements for ASEAN', *CEPR Discussion Paper*, No. 2411.

Bénassy-Quéré, Agnes (1999), 'Optimal pegs for East Asian currencies', *Journal of the Japanese and International Economies*, **13**, 44–60.

Bhandari, Jagdeep S. (1985), 'Experiments with the optimal currency composite', *Southern Economic Journal*, **51**(3), 711–30.

Blanchard, O. and D. Quah (1989), 'The dynamic effects of aggregate demand and supply disturbances', *American Economic Review*, **79**, 655–73.

Calvo, Guillermo A. and Carmen M. Reinhart (2000), 'Fear of floating', (mimeo).

Dammers, Clifford R. and Robert N. McCauley (2006), 'Basket weaving: the euromarket experiences with basket currency bonds', *BIS Quarterly Review*, March 79–92.

De Grauwe, Paul (1992), *The Economics of Monetary Integration*, Oxford: Oxford University Press.

Eichengreen, Barry (2006), 'The parallel-currency approach to Asian monetary integration', *American Economic Review*, **96**(2), 432–6.

Flanders, June M. and Elhanan Helpman (1979), 'An optimal exchange rate peg in a world of general floating', *Review of Economic Studies*, 533–42.

Flanders, June M. and Asher Tishler (1981), 'The role of elasticity optimism in choosing an optimal currency basket with applications to Israel', *Journal of International Economics*, **11**, 395–406.

Frankel, Jeffrey A. (1999), 'No single currency regime is right for all countries or at all times', National Bureau of Economic Research Working Paper Series, 7338.

Frankel Jeffery A. and Shang-Jin Wei (1994), 'Yen bloc or dollar bloc? Exchange rate policies of the east Asian economies', in Takaboshi Ito and Anne O. Krueger (eds), *Macroeconomic Linkage: Savings, Exchange Rates and Capital Flows*, Chicago: University of Chicago Press, pp. 295–355.

IIMA (Institute for International Monetary Affairs) (2008), Research Papers and Policy Recommendations on 'Toward greater financial stability in the Asian region: measures for possible use of regional monetary units for surveillance and transaction', January.

Ito, Takatoshi, Eiji Ogawa and Yuri Nagataki Sasaki (1998), 'How did the dollar peg fail in Asia?', *Journal of the Japanese and International Economies*, **12**, 256–304.

Iwata, Kenji (2005), 'Formation of regional financial and currency area: some lessons from Europe to Asia', 3rd Conference of EUSA-AP, 10 December.

Kawai, Masahiro (2009), 'The role of an Asian currency unit', in Koichi Hamada, Beate Reszat and Ulrich Volz (eds), *Towards Monetary and Financial Integration in East Asia*, Cheltenham, UK and Northampton, MA, USA: Edward Elgar.

Kim, T., J. Ryou and Y. Wang (2000), *Regional Arrangements to Borrow: A Scheme for Preventing Future Asian Liquidity Crises*, Seoul: Korea Institute for International Economic Policy.

Kwan, C.H. (2001), *Yen Bloc: Toward Economic Integration in Asia*, Washington, DC: Brookings Institution Press.

Lipschitz, Leslie and V. Sundrarajan (1980), 'The optimal basket in a world of generalized floating', *IMF Staff Papers*, **27**(1), 80–100.

McKinnon, Ronald I. (1963), 'Optimum currency area', *American Economic Review*, **53**, 717–25.

McKinnon, Ronald I. (2000), 'After the crisis, the East Asian dollar standard resurrected: an interpretation of high-frequency exchange rate pegging', Working paper, 00-013, Stanford University.

Mundell, Robert A. (1961), 'A theory of optimum currency areas', *American Economic Review*, **51**, 657–65.

Ogawa, Eiji (2002), 'Should East Asian countries return to a dollar peg again?', in P. Drysdale and K. Ishigaki (eds), *East Asian Trade and Financial Integration: New Issues*, Asia Pacific Press, pp. 159–84.

Ogawa, Eiji and Takatoshi Ito (2002), 'On the desirability of a regional basket currency arrangement', *Journal of the Japanese and International Economies*, **16**(3), 317–34.

Ogawa, Eiji and Junko Shimizu (2005), 'AMU deviation indicator for coordinated exchange rate policies in East Asia', RIETI Discussion Paper, no.05-E-017.

Ogawa, Eiji and Junko Shimizu (2006), 'The core-AMU denominated Asian bonds for local investors in East Asia', APEA Conference, July.

Ogawa, Eiji and Junko Shimizu (2007), 'Progress toward a common currency basket system in East Asia', RIETI Discussion Paper Series, 06-E-038.

Ogawa, Eiji and Junko Shimizu (2008), 'A role of the Japanese yen in a multi-step process toward a common currency in east Asia', *Fukino DP Series*, Hitotsubashi University, 3.

Ogawa, E, and Lijian Sun (2001), 'How were capital inflows stimulated under the dollar peg system?', in T. Ito and A.O. Krueger (eds), *Regional and Global Capital Flows: Macroeconomic Causes and Consequences*, Chicago: University of Chicago Press, pp. 151–90.

Ogawa, Eiji, Takatoshi Ito and Yuri Nagataki Sasaki (2004), 'Cost, benefits, and constraints of the currency basket regime for East Asia', in Asian Development

Bank (ed.), *Monetary and Financial Integration in East Asia: The Way Ahead, Volume 2*, Palgrave Macmillan, pp. 209–39.

Ohno, Kenichi (1999), 'Exchange rate management in developing Asia: reassessment of the pre-crisis soft dollar zone', ADB Institute, Working Paper Series, No. 1, January.

Turnovsky, Stephen J. (1982), 'A determination of the optimal currency basket', *Journal of International Economics*, **12**, 333–54.

Williamson, John (2000), *Exchange Rate Regimes of Emerging Markets: Reviving the Intermediate Option*, Washington, DC: Institute for International Economics.

Yoshino, Naoyuki, Sahoko Kaji and A. Suzuki (2004), 'The basket-peg, dollar-peg, and floating: a comparative analysis', *Journal of the Japanese and International Economies*, **18**, 183–217.

Zhang, Zhaoyong, Kiyotaka Sato and Michael McAleer (2004), 'Is a monetary union feasible for East Asia?', *Applied Economics*, **36**(10), 1031–43.

PART IV

Drivers of Integration

11. Institution building for economic integration in East Asia: a brief history

Jiro Okamoto

This chapter reviews the historical development of institution building in East Asia and suggests prospects for the future. After World War II, the central theme of the newly independent states became the maintenance of national sovereignty, territorial integrity and policy autonomy; economic integration was not sought until the 1990s. Economic globalization and the end of the Cold War first encouraged ASEAN members to form AFTA, which served as a precedent for subsequent East Asian economic integration processes. The Asian financial crisis, along with other factors such as the stagnation in APEC and the WTO, acted as a trigger for East Asian regionalism in the form of the ASEAN+3 process. Since the turn of the century, a number of initiatives, agreements and frameworks have proliferated in and around East Asia. At this point in time, it seems that economic integration in the region is better understood when the processes are viewed as a whole, with a distinct nature that is flexible, inclusive and multi-layered.

11.1 THE END OF THE PACIFIC WAR AND THE CREATION OF ECONOMIC ASSISTANCE AND COOPERATION FRAMEWORKS

11.1.1 Decolonization and the Emergence of the Cold War Structure

The end of the Pacific War brought epoch-making changes to the East Asia region both regionally and internationally. What produced the changes was not just the defeat of Japan as the aggressor in the region but also the region-wide decolonization that followed the end of the war. The principles embodied in the United Nations (UN) Charter, such as the right of self-determination and the responsibility of colonial powers for guiding colonial peoples to political and economic independence, were applied in East Asia. In Southeast Asia, the Philippines became independent of the United States in 1946. Burma followed suit in 1948, gaining its independence from the United Kingdom. Nationalist movements were also active in Indochina, Malaya and Indonesia.

The drive for national independence in East Asia could not escape from the Cold War structure that emerged in the region soon after the war. The difficulties faced by the former colonies in achieving independence, and in nation building after independence, were inevitably caught up in this structure. While Japan was occupied by the Allied Forces until 1952, the People's Republic of China (China) was established in 1949, pushing out the Republic of China government to Taiwan. The Korean Peninsula was divided into north and south. The Republic of Korea (South Korea) was established in August 1948 and the Democratic People's Republic of Korea (North Korea) in the next month of the same year. Reflecting the ideological tensions, these two Korean states started a 'hot' war (the Korean War, 1950–53) that involved many other states, including the United States, the United Kingdom, France, Australia, China, and the Soviet Union, among others, directly or indirectly.

The Cold War structure became evident in Southeast Asia when the withdrawal of the colonial powers (the United Kingdom, France and the Netherlands) gained momentum in the 1950s. The emergence in Indonesia of the nationalist Sukarno government with strong Chinese influence and the spread of armed conflicts within Indonesia were seen as evidence of communist penetration in the region. Soon after the fall of Dien Bien Phu in May 1954, the Southeast Asia Collective Defence Treaty (South East Asian Treaty Organization, SEATO) was signed in Manila in September of that year. The war in Indochina, nevertheless, escalated and continued well into the 1970s. Following the decision of the United Kingdom to withdraw military forces from the area east of Suez, the Five Power Defence Arrangement agreed to by Australia, New Zealand, the United Kingdom, Malaysia and Singapore came into existence in 1971.

Decolonization, independence and the Cold War structure set the basic tone for international relations in East Asia. For newly independent states who had suffered a long history of colonial rule, national sovereignty, territorial integrity and the equality of all races and nations were important principles in the UN Charter. Their inclination towards nationalism was reflected in the declaration of the 1955 Bandung Conference, for which representatives of 29 Asian and African states gathered. They were reluctant to move towards any 'integration', be it bilateral or regional, political or economic, which might undermine their sovereignty and autonomy. The divisive influence of the Cold War, on top of nationalist tendencies, continued to have strong effects until the 1990s when the conventional Cold War structure and mentality virtually ceased to exist in the region.

11.1.2   Regional Frameworks for Development Cooperation

The intention to create inter-governmental economic frameworks in Asia was present soon after the end of the war, yet the goals of these institutions were generally economic cooperation and assistance, rather than economic integration. For many, the economic development of newly independent countries was thought to be the key both to achieving stability in the region and to creating a stronger countervailing power against communist penetration. In the early post-war period, the creation of the Economic Commission for Asia and the Far East (ECAFE) in 1947 and the Colombo Plan for Cooperative Economic and Social Development in Asia and the Pacific in 1951 were notable events.

The United Nations Economic and Social Council decided in 1947 to establish ECAFE. The founding members of ECAFE included Australia, the Republic of China (Taiwan), India, the Philippines and Thailand, as well as France, the Netherlands, the Soviet Union, the United Kingdom and the United States. Other states in the region, such as Burma (Myanmar), Cambodia, Ceylon (Sri Lanka), Indonesia, Japan, South Korea, Laos, Malaysia and South Vietnam, later joined the organization. ECAFE was reorganized in 1974 as the Economic and Social Commission for Asia and the Pacific (ESCAP). In 2004, ESCAP had 53 members and nine associate members from South, Southeast, Northeast and Central Asia, the Middle East and South Pacific, as well as some from North America and Western Europe.

At the British Commonwealth Conference in Colombo in January 1950, the creation of a scheme that would provide economic assistance to developing Commonwealth members in South and Southeast Asia was proposed. As a result, the Colombo Plan was formally launched in July 1951. The Colombo Plan began as a British Commonwealth scheme, but non-Commonwealth states joined it soon after the launch, both as donors and as recipients. By the mid-1960s, members of the plan had expanded to include Afghanistan, Australia, Bhutan, Burma (Myanmar), Cambodia, Canada, Ceylon (Sri Lanka), India, Indonesia, Japan, Korea, Laos, Malaysia, the Maldives, Nepal, New Zealand, Pakistan, the Philippines, Thailand, the United Kingdom, the United States and South Vietnam. The Colombo Plan was a framework for bilateral arrangements involving foreign aid and technical assistance for economic and social development. Under the plan, the donor members provided recipient members with development projects, technical assistance and scholarships for administrative and vocational training.

11.2   THE ESTABLISHMENT OF ASEAN

The Association of Southeast Asian Nations (ASEAN) was established in 1967 mainly to promote regional political stability – peaceful relations among the members as well as security in the region as a whole. This was thought necessary for each member's national development. All Southeast Asian states had had hostile experiences with their neighbors,[1] and the leaders of these states resolved that regional hostility should end to allow for concentration on national development.

Complex political developments in Southeast Asia after the war explain this emphasis on internal and regional security. The process of the establishment of Malaysia caused serious conflicts with Indonesia over the possession of Sarawak and with the Philippines over Sabah, which eventually led to the escalation of the 'confrontation' policy of Indonesia's President Sukarno. In the early 1960s, conflicts among these states destroyed the short-lived regional cooperation initiatives of the Association of Southeast Asia (ASA)[2] and MAPHILINDO.[3] A UN investigation mission was sent to Sabah and Sarawak in August 1963 to confirm the will of the residents. The result of the mission was favorable to Malaya and, in September, Malaysia was established with Sabah and Sarawak (and Singapore) as part of its sovereign territory. When newly established Malaysia was voted onto the Security Council of the UN for a term beginning in January 1965, the Indonesian government announced in December 1964 that it would withdraw from the UN.

Under its self-imposed isolation from the world, the Sukarno government approached China and the influence of the Indonesian Communist Party (PKI) grew. The Indonesian political scene changed drastically in September 1965 when a 'pro-communist' uprising occurred but was suppressed by the military. Major-General Suharto eventually took control of national politics, and in March 1966, he made the PKI illegal. From that month, negotiations between Indonesia and Malaysia to normalize their relationship gained momentum.

While the reconciliation of these states set up a favorable environment for the establishment of ASEAN, individual members had their own reasons for participating in such a regional organization. After the change in leadership, Indonesia needed to end its isolation in order to receive development assistance from developed Western states. Thailand was maintaining a close strategic/military relationship with the United States and was under heavy pressure to take a stand against communism. It also needed to ensure that it would receive the support of other Southeast Asian states when it faced a direct threat from Vietnam. After Ferdinand Marcos was elected President in 1965, the Philippines discarded the anti-US policy of the previous government. Marcos also suspended the Philippines' claim to Sabah and tried to pursue the institutionalization of regional cooperation. As a small island state that had gained independence from Malaysia only in August 1965, Singapore needed to make friends in the region. It expected to be recognized as an independent and equal partner in the region by participating in ASEAN. In this way, Singapore could also avoid being viewed as an outpost of China and could confirm its friendship with its neighbors. After having had conflicts with every founding member of ASEAN, Malaysia was also interested in pursuing better relations in the region, especially with Indonesia.

The common understanding of members was that it was crucial for each member's domestic political and economic development that regional stability be maintained and that to maintain this stability some form of cooperative organization was necessary. The Bangkok Declaration of 1967 announced the basic principles of ASEAN and stated that the organization's aim was 'to accelerate economic growth, social progress and cultural development in the region through joint endeavors'. Members were to be united in their opposition to external interference and all foreign military bases in the region were to be regarded as temporary. This allowed members of the Non-Aligned Movement and Western allies in the region to stay in the same organization.

It is important to note that the common ground among ASEAN members was to oppose external interference in, and influence on, their domestic affairs so that they could achieve national development. Policy autonomy was crucial for all ASEAN founding members. As members of an organization that was established in the middle of the Vietnam War, they saw communist penetration as the most immediate threat in the region. But it was not necessarily the only threat. This was clearly shown in ASEAN's Zone of Peace, Freedom and Neutrality (ZOPFAN) Declaration in 1971, which stated:

> . . . inspired by the worthy aims and objectives of the United Nations, in particular by the principles of respect for the sovereignty and territorial integrity of all states, abstention from threat of use of force, peaceful settlement of international disputes, equal rights and self-determination and non-interference in the affairs of states, [ASEAN recognizes] the right of every state . . . to lead its national existence free from outside interference in its internal affairs, as

this interference will adversely affect its freedom, independence and integrity. (AMM 1971)

Since its establishment in 1967, ASEAN has made it clear that regional 'integration', be it economic or political, was not the objective of the organization and, in practice, the term has been carefully avoided as a goal in its regional cooperation schemes (Blomqvist, 1993: 57). Political or economic integration was regarded as being too close to the European experience and therefore alien to Southeast Asia where most of the states had recently achieved independence after long years of colonial rule (Dosch and Mols, 1998: 175). In fact, ASEAN had to wait until the 1990s before it began to forge regional cooperation activities explicitly aimed at economic integration.

11.3 THE EMERGENCE OF ECONOMIC COOPERATION FRAMEWORKS IN THE ASIA PACIFIC

11.3.1 Deepening Economic Interdependence

Economic interdependence among the economies in the Asia Pacific region has developed steadily since the 1960s. Drysdale (1988) identified some of the factors behind this development. One was the impact of Japan's economic growth. Japan was the first country in East Asia to start developing its national economy and, by the 1980s, its GDP had become one of the world's largest. Rapid economic growth in Japan brought about a huge increase in its demand for mineral resources, energy and foodstuffs from the region. At the same time, Japanese exports of manufactured goods, as well as the flow of capital and technology transfers to other economies in the region experienced unprecedented growth.

Another major factor was the development of other East Asian economies. Resource-rich economies such as Indonesia, Malaysia, Thailand and Australia enjoyed large growth in export earnings, while others like South Korea, Taiwan, Hong Kong and Singapore followed the Japanese path by adopting outward-looking, trade-oriented industrial strategies. By the late 1960s, Southeast Asian states were intent on emulating their success. Their economies developed steadily throughout the 1970s and began to grow rapidly in the latter half of the 1980s.[4] Flows of capital, including foreign direct investment, from Japan, South Korea, Taiwan, Hong Kong and Singapore to Southeast Asian economies increased sharply in the 1980s. Southeast Asian economies also started to invest overseas during this period.

11.3.2   The Early Development of Economic Cooperation Forums

The search for an institutional basis for economic cooperation within the Asia Pacific region dates back to the 1960s. Based on the rapid economic development of Japan and out of concern over exclusion from the European market because of the formation of the EEC, Kiyoshi Kojima, Professor at Hitotsubashi University in Japan, called for the creation of a Pacific Free Trade Area (PAFTA) and supported the creation of an Organization for Pacific Trade and Development (OPTAD) in the mid-1960s. These proposals were rejected by policy analysts in the United States, who considered such regionalism counter to US policy preferences for multilateralism and the global trade system at the time (Patrick, 1997: 10).

Kojima's initiative, nevertheless, created the momentum for regional economic cooperation. In 1968, the first Pacific Trade and Development (PAFTAD) conference was organized by the Japan Economic Research Center, bringing together a group of economists from five developed countries in the region: Australia, Canada, Japan, New Zealand and the United States. Subsequently, academics from major developing countries in the region have participated in PAFTAD conferences that have been organized every one to two years since then. In 1967, led mainly by Japanese and Australian businesses, the Pacific Basin Economic Council (PBEC) was formed as a commercial component for regional economic cooperation. In May 1968, the first formal meeting of PBEC was held in Sydney with the participation of business representatives from, again, the developed countries – Australia, Canada, Japan, New Zealand and the United States. While it started as an organization for developed economies, PBEC has attracted the participation of various Asian and Latin American developing economies.[5]

The end of the 1970s saw another development in the institutionalization of Asia Pacific economic cooperation. The US Senate commissioned a Pacific regional trade organization feasibility study. The result of the study published in 1979 (Drysdale and Patrick, 1979) engaged the policy attention of the US administration on this issue. In the same period, the Japanese and Australian Prime Ministers, Masayoshi Ohira and Malcolm Fraser, supported the idea of establishing an association for economic cooperation in the Pacific basin. In 1979, Ohira commissioned a group of Japanese bureaucrats, academics and others from the private sector to study the issue and a report was released in 1980 (Study Group on Pacific Basin Cooperation, 1980). These moves culminated in the joint Japan–Australia initiative for the Canberra Seminar in September 1980, which became the first meeting of the Pacific Economic Cooperation Conference (later Council, PECC). This time, both developed and developing economies in the region participated in the first meeting of PECC, thus involving themselves in the new regional economic cooperation process.[6]

11.3.3   The Formation of Policy Networks and the Diffusion of Policy Ideas

In several important ways, the PECC process in the 1980s built the basis for the further development of Asia Pacific economic cooperation.

First, it was agreed that PECC should stay as an informal and independent regional consultation mechanism to advance economic cooperation and market-driven integration. PECC introduced a 'tripartite' structure in which business leaders, policy-oriented academics and government officials could participate (the latter in their private capacity). On the one hand, this informal character, along with its non-exclusive approach, made it possible to avoid the intrusion of 'large–small' or 'North–South' dimensions into its activities. Thus, smaller and/or non-aligned states could participate without feeling much threat of domination by the powers. This also made the subsequent participation of the 'three Chinas' (China, Hong Kong and Taiwan) possible. On the other hand, the participation of government officials, even in their private capacity, contributed to an acknowledgement of the need for greater economic cooperation among politicians and senior bureaucrats in the respective governments.

Second, along with PAFTAD and PBEC, the PECC process created strong policy networks among business leaders, academics and government officials in the region. In fact, individual participants in PAFTAD and PBEC often overlapped with those in PECC. Direct and frequent meetings enabled them to learn about each other's problems, whereas they did not know each other well and were not familiar with each other's economic policies in the 1960s.

Third, these close personal networks helped facilitate the convergence of ideas on regional economic cooperation and foster broad-based support for it (Harris, 1994: 384). Through the PAFTAD, PBEC and PECC processes, more and more policy ideas were being shared among policy-makers from the member states by the end of the 1980s (Ravenhill, 1998: 280). They can be summarized as follows:

- Individual states need to keep developing open and outward-looking domestic economic regimes in order to maintain dynamism in economic development.
- Regional cooperation is required to encourage and assist efforts by these states towards trade and investment liberalization.

- Regional economic cooperation needs to be a gradual process towards long-term goals, based on consensus among participants. There is diversity among the region's countries in almost every aspect, for example, their history, culture, political systems and levels of economic development.

Furthermore, the global nature of international economic transactions by countries in the region suggested that it was more advantageous for them to proceed with regional economic integration in a non-discriminatory manner. In other words, any regional attempts to reduce or eliminate trade and investment barriers should be implemented on an MFN basis then automatically applied to extra-regional countries. This concept, which was often called 'open regionalism' and became a distinctive attribute of Asia-Pacific Economic Cooperation (APEC) activities in the 1990s, had also been developed in the previous PAFTAD and PBEC processes and consolidated in the PECC process (Garnaut, 1994).

11.4   REGIONAL RESPONSES TO CHANGES IN THE INTERNATIONAL ENVIRONMENT

11.4.1   Changes in the International Environment

After the worldwide recession in the early 1980s, the East Asian economies recovered strongly through further structural change. The realignment of international currencies following the Plaza Accord in September 1985 was one of the main factors driving this change. Because of the rapid appreciation of their respective currencies against the US dollar, which aggravated already increasing costs of production (such as rises in wages and land prices), manufacturers in Japan and the Newly Industrializing Economies (NIEs: Hong Kong, South Korea, Singapore and Taiwan) relocated many of their production and export bases to ASEAN members, while, by the early 1980s, most ASEAN members had adopted an export-oriented economic strategy in which they introduced various investment incentives for exporters.[7] It was this currency realignment and the subsequent relocation of production bases within the East Asian region that promoted economic globalization and significant structural change in ASEAN economies.

The international trade regime (the GATT regime), nevertheless, was fragile in the late 1980s and early 1990s. The failure of the 1982 GATT Ministerial Meeting to launch a new round caused a major shift in US foreign economic policy. After the meeting, the United States announced that it would no longer confine itself to pursuing only multilateral trade agreements: it would pursue *both* multilateral and bilateral negotiations (Snape et al., 1998: 369). US bilateralism meant that, on the one hand, it would pursue bilateral free trade agreements (FTAs) with its main trade partners. On the other hand, it meant that the United States would negotiate the market access issue directly with individual trade partners. In this kind of bilateral negotiation framework, the United States could use its influence directly on partners to realize its demands. Indeed, from the latter half of the 1980s, the United States put strong pressure on those of its trade partners whom it identified as conducting 'unfair' trade practices to comply with US demands. The enactment of the Omnibus Trade and Competitiveness Act 1988 that contained 'Super 301' and 'Special 301' provisions[8] and the subsequent use of these provisions mainly against Japan and some NIEs, with which the United States had been recording large trade deficits, characterized the 'aggressive unilateralism' of the United States during this period.[9]

When the Uruguay Round, which was finally launched in 1986, soon reached a deadlock, the United States prioritized its bilateralist policies. It opted for the creation of an FTA with Canada, in effect from January 1989, and subsequently extended this to Mexico as the North American Free Trade Agreement (NAFTA), from January 1994. The United States suggested that other bilateral and regional arrangements could follow. The EC advanced its program of creating a single market by 1993 through the Single European Act of 1987. The Treaty on European Union (the Maastricht Treaty) in 1992 led to the creation of the EU in the following year and advanced political and economic union issues. These economic groupings involving economic powers like the United States and the EU made outsiders very cautious.

During the same period, the end of the Cold War in the late 1980s provided ASEAN members with both opportunities and challenges. On the one hand, it gave ASEAN a valuable opportunity to resolve the protracted problem of the communist threat to its members, one of the main factors leading to the foundation of the organization. On the other hand, there was concern in ASEAN that the significant reduction in the direct and imminent threat might weaken ASEAN's cohesiveness. In other words, the end of the Cold War in Southeast Asia posed ASEAN members with a question of how they could maintain the relevance of the organization in a new global and regional environment.

Furthermore, the end of the Cold War saw an acceleration in the transition of former centrally planned economies into market economies and their participation in global and regional economic activities. In East Asia, China had, from the end of the 1970s, already undertaken its 'reform and opening-up' policy under the strong leadership of Deng Xiaoping. Vietnam also started to implement its 'renovation' policy in 1986 when economic (and military) assistance from the Soviet Union was significantly reduced. As a result, by the early 1990s, China and Vietnam, as well as some other East European economies, emerged as attractive new FDI destinations for Japan, the United States, the EC (EU) and the NIEs. For each ASEAN member, whose rapid economic development was heavily reliant on FDI inflows and the subsequent increase in manufactured exports, the entry of Chinese, Vietnamese and East European economies into the global economy meant the beginning of more severe competition for FDI.

Regional responses to these changes in the international environment took two directions. One was to strengthen economic cooperation in the Asia Pacific along the lines of the PAFTAD, PBEC and PECC processes by creating a new forum in which governments in the region formally participated. The other was the formation of a free trade area by ASEAN members. These two directions were distinctly different from one another. While the former response, which culminated in the establishment of APEC in 1989, was based on an open regionalism principle and sought cooperation on a voluntary basis, the latter aimed at the creation of a legally binding institution for regional economic integration, which would inevitably discriminate against outsiders.

11.4.2 APEC

While the idea that international cooperation was necessary to ensure outward-looking domestic and regional economic regimes was increasingly shared in PAFTAD, PBEC and PECC circles, they judged, under the changed environment, that formal political involvement was necessary to develop regional consensus building on policy issues such as trade liberalization, trade facilitation and the creation of an investment code, because in most cases these would require changes in domestic arrangements (Elek, 1991: 324).

Even before Australia's formal initiative in 1989, there had been various proposals for, and studies on, forming an inter-governmental regional institution for economic cooperation. For instance, Australian Prime Minister Bob Hawke made an announcement in November 1983 in Bangkok, in which he proposed the creation of an association consisting of 'Western Pacific' states to develop a united regional approach to multilateral trade negotiations. In March 1988, former Japanese Prime Minister Yasuhiro Nakasone called for a Pacific forum for the promotion of economic, cultural and general information exchanges. In July 1988, US Secretary of State George Shultz floated the idea of establishing a 'Pacific Basin Forum' in which intergovernmental exchanges on sectoral/

structural policies could be expected. In December 1988, Bill Bradley, a US Senator, called for a Pacific Coalition on Trade and Development for economic cooperation in areas such as agricultural trade, exchange rates stabilization and developing countries' debt. These US moves were followed up in early 1989 by Alan Cranston, a US Senator, who introduced a resolution into the US Congress calling for a permanent 'Pacific Basin Forum'.

Although the United States proposed these regional economic cooperation frameworks, it also intended to establish bilateral FTAs with Japan and other Asia Pacific states as part of its bilateral trade policy. Learning of US intentions, Japan's Prime Minister, Noboru Takeshita, ordered the Ministry of International Trade and Industry in January 1988 to study the regional economic cooperation issue (Funabashi, 1995: 59). The report of the study, which was published in June 1988, concluded that the promotion of Asia Pacific economic cooperation was required to prevent the US bilateralism that could lead to a closed economic bloc in the region. The report pointed out the relative decline in the capacity of the United States to support the global economic order and that, without sharing the economic burden of the United States, the multilateral trade regime that had helped Japan, NIEs and ASEAN members develop their economies could not be sustained. The report recommended that regional cooperation should be based on the ideas that had been developed through the PECC process. In particular, it should be advanced gradually on a consensus basis and conducted under the principle of open regionalism (Krauss, 2000: 476–77).

The Australian government responded enthusiastically to this report and began working closely with Japan to persuade other states of the necessity for a formal regional economic cooperation framework. After seeing a deadlock at the Montreal mid-term review of the Uruguay Round in December 1988, Hawke, in January 1989, proposed the creation of a new inter-governmental economic cooperation framework in the Asia Pacific (Snape et al., 1998: 534–6). In the short term, a new regional forum at the ministerial level could put pressure on other states at the negotiating tables of the Uruguay Round to move more quickly towards a successful conclusion. At the same time, such a forum with an open regionalism principle was expected to ease the trade tension between Japan and the United States and resolve the bilateral problems in a way that did not harm the interests of other states in the region. In the longer term, the activities of the forum for policy cooperation and coordination in areas such as trade, investment, industrial development, communications, finance and other services, and food and energy security would significantly increase regional interdependence, which would lead to an improved economic performance for potential members of the forum. Furthermore, increased economic interdependence in the region was expected to encourage a more stable and cohesive political environment (Harris, 1989: 17).

Australia's intensive diplomatic efforts, along with those of Japan, proved to be effective. The inaugural APEC Ministerial Meeting was held in Canberra in November 1989, with ministers from 12 regional economies participating: all six ASEAN members and Australia, Canada, Japan, South Korea, New Zealand and the United States. After the first meeting in 1989, the annual APEC Ministerial Meeting announced its support for a timely and successful conclusion of the Uruguay Round and the commitment of its members to this cause. APEC's continual pressure in the Uruguay Round negotiation was an important, if not the main, factor leading to the successful completion of the negotiations at the end of 1993 (Petri, 1999: 15). Since its establishment, China, Hong Kong and Taiwan (1991), Mexico and Papua New Guinea (1993), Chile (1994) and Peru, Russia and Vietnam (1998) have all joined APEC. The expansion in membership reflected the globalization of national economies and the effects of the end of the Cold War that encouraged former centrally planned economies to engage in the dynamics of regional and global economic activities.

11.4.3 AFTA

At the time of APEC's early development, ASEAN decided to aim for the creation of its own free trade area, the ASEAN Free Trade Area (AFTA), to counter moves in North America and Europe to form preferential trade areas as well as to enhance its attractiveness as an FDI location and market. In addition, ASEAN leaders felt intensified pressure from the increasing globalization of business operations, and they resolved that, through freer intra-regional trade and investment, private firms in ASEAN must acquire international competitiveness in both regional and foreign markets (Parreñas, 1998: 236). The ASEAN Summit in Singapore in 1992 declared that AFTA, under which ultimately effective intra-regional tariff rates would range from zero to 5 per cent, would be established within a time frame of 15 years, starting from January 1993. Considering the unimpressive history of ASEAN's regional economic cooperation, AFTA was a bold initiative.

It was not until the mid-1970s that ASEAN made any concrete moves towards regional economic cooperation. The limited coverage in terms of products and tariff and non-tariff barrier reductions agreed in the Preferential Tariff Agreement (PTA) in 1977 resulted in discord among the members. By the mid-1980s, although more than 18,000 items were listed as eligible for tariff reductions of at least 20 per cent, most of these items were little traded among ASEAN members. Subsequent attempts were made to improve the scheme, such as adding textiles, chemicals, rubber, cement, food, beverages and some other products to the tariff reduction list, but the PTA continued to have only a marginal effect on intra-regional trade, covering an estimated 2 per cent and 5 per cent of intra-ASEAN trade in 1980 and 1986 respectively (Pangestu et al., 1992: 335).

The implementation of the ASEAN Industrial Projects (AIP) scheme was also troubled. A total of five projects were proposed with one to be located in each member state, but most of them had feasibility problems including infrastructure and marketing.[10] The most serious problem, however, was that members pursued their own national interests rather than regional interests.[11] Generally, when one ASEAN member's AIP products competed with the domestic products of another member, the latter was reluctant to give preferential trade treatment to those products, despite its being essential for the successful implementation of the AIPs.

Learning from the unsatisfactory results of previous cooperation schemes, ASEAN created the ASEAN Industrial Joint Ventures (AIJV) scheme in 1983. The AIJV scheme had several new characteristics. First, a project under the scheme could proceed with at least two private sector partners, provided that the ASEAN component was more than 51 per cent (later reduced to 40 per cent). Second, the investors could choose the location of the project in any of the participating ASEAN members. Third, as an investment incentive, participating ASEAN members were to grant a 90 per cent tariff reduction for four years on goods produced by the AIJVs. In the 10 years after the establishment of the scheme, 26 products, including automobile parts, chemicals and food products, were granted AIJV status, but the scheme had a negligible impact on intra-ASEAN trade and investment.

AFTA represented a clear departure from previous economic cooperation schemes. Not only did it aim for more comprehensive trade liberalization, both with regard to the extent of tariff reductions and in the range of products covered, but also in the way in which ASEAN intended to realize the initiative. Although the Common Effective Preferential Tariff (CEPT) scheme, the main mechanism for intra-regional tariff reduction, allowed members some discretion, both in selecting products that would not be covered by the scheme and in setting schedules for tariff reductions, the room for such flexibility was much less than in any other previous cooperation schemes.

AFTA was also an important turning point for ASEAN economic cooperation because it openly aimed for regional economic 'integration'. The AFTA initiative showed changes in approach and attitude among ASEAN's leaders. They began to realize that in the era of economic globalization, it was critical for small states to join forces to enhance their collective position and increase the gains they could get from regional integration, in contrast to individual states discretely pursuing their own interests (Soesastro, 1995: 477; Dosch and Mols, 1998: 176). The change in attitude and approach on the part of ASEAN members did not necessarily mean that they would always prioritize regional interests over national ones, but the idea that a regional approach provided a basis for national development seemed to be widely shared.

11.5   BUILDING INSTITUTIONS FOR ECONOMIC INTEGRATION

11.5.1   The Stagnation of Multilateral Trade and Investment Liberalization

Since APEC's establishment, trade and investment liberalization in the region has been listed as one of its main objectives. Nevertheless, in the early stages, it did not have any concrete measures or goals. Rather, the intention of APEC members to liberalize regional trade was used as a lever to encourage the promotion of the Uruguay Round. It was around the same time as the completion of the Uruguay Round that APEC turned more substantively to regional trade liberalization.

The first APEC Leaders Meeting in 1993 produced the 'Economic Vision Statement' that contained, among other objectives, a vision for creating a 'community' of Asia Pacific economies whose dynamic economic growth would contribute to an expanding world economy and support an open international trading system where trade and investment barriers would continue to be reduced (APEC Leaders Meeting, 1993). The second Leaders Meeting adopted the 'Bogor Declaration' in November 1994, which set the goal of APEC liberalization as 'free and open trade and investment in the region by 2010 for developed members and by 2020 for developing members'. Subsequently, the modality for the APEC liberalization process was established in 1995 in the Osaka Action Agenda. In 1996, the first Individual Action Plans (IAPs) – each member's voluntary trade liberalization and facilitation plans – were presented by all members and, with the Collective Action Plan, compiled as the 'Manila Action Plan for APEC'. Although trade liberalization under the APEC framework looked to be going well in the mid-1990s, the first IAPs submitted in 1996 were, in fact, not much more than what the members had already committed to in the Uruguay Round (Okamoto, 2004a: 1).

The Early Voluntary Sectoral Liberalization (EVSL) initiative of APEC

(1997–99) was an ambitious attempt to stimulate APEC liberalization as a whole by opening up selected sectors earlier than others. Yet the results of EVSL, which had become clear by November 1998, were much less than initially expected. Although liberalization schedules for some sectors were consolidated, participants in the EVSL consultations could not agree on tariff reductions under the APEC framework because of their different understandings of the concept of 'voluntary liberalization'. The Ministerial Meeting in November 1998 decided to leave liberalization of EVSL sectors in the hands of the WTO in the form of the 'Accelerated Tariff Liberalization' (ATL) initiative (Okamoto, 2004b: 50–1). The WTO Ministerial Conference in Seattle in December, nevertheless, virtually collapsed and failed to launch a new round of trade negotiations, the so-called 'Millennium Round'.

11.5.2   The Asian Financial Crisis and the Emergence of the 'ASEAN+3' Framework

While the EVSL initiative was heading towards failure, the Asian financial crisis hit East Asia. The financial crisis occurred first as a disastrous currency depreciation in Thailand in July 1997 and consequently plunged many East Asian economies, Indonesia and South Korea in particular, into economic turmoil (and in some cases political confusion).

After the outbreak of the crisis, East Asian states found renewed motivation for building their own economic cooperation framework. Of the emergency loan package for Thailand worth US$ 17 billion, for instance, the IMF provided less than 25 per cent but enforced strict 'conditionalities'. The United States and EU members did not participate in the package. These circumstances led East Asian states, especially Japan, to realize that a future currency crisis in any East Asian economy, which would be highly transmissible to others, had to be dealt with primarily within the region. For the purpose of preventing currency crises in the region, Japan proposed the establishment of the Asian Monetary Fund (AMF) shortly after the outbreak of the crisis, only to be turned down by the IMF, the United States and China. The next response from Japan was the 'New Miyazawa Plan' in October 1998, the main feature of which was bilateral financial cooperation, without aiming for the creation of a regional institution.

Though China had first reacted to Japan's AMF proposal negatively, it shared with other East Asian states the view that an East Asian economic cooperation framework was desirable. The heads of governments of ASEAN members, China, Japan and South Korea held a meeting in November 1997 to discuss regional financial and economic cooperation.

After the inaugural Summit, this East Asian regional cooperation (often called the 'ASEAN+3' or APT) process began to evolve. The third Summit in December 1999 identified eight broad areas for APT cooperation, which included the economy, currencies and finance, human resources and other forms of development cooperation, as well as political and security cooperation (APT Summit, 1999). In 2000, the APT process saw agreement on the 'Chiang Mai Initiative', which was a network of bilateral currency swap agreements among East Asian states. Also in 2000, the idea of creating an Asian bond market was floated. The APT Financial Ministers Meeting in 2003 agreed on the Asian Bond Market Initiative, which aimed to develop efficient and liquid bond markets in Asia and enable better use of Asian savings for Asian investments.

11.5.3 The Proliferation of FTAs and Multilateral Economic Cooperation Frameworks in and around East Asia

While the APT process was evolving, efforts to build institutions for economic integration by East Asian states have been more evident in initiatives to negotiate and conclude bilateral, sub-regional or cross-regional FTAs, or economic partnership agreements (EPAs). Table 11.1 shows how FTAs/EPAs have been proliferating in East Asia in the 2000s.

Over the last decade, FTAs seem to have become almost synonymous with the concept of institutional economic integration in East Asia. In Table 11.1, AFTA (indicated by an asterisk) is quite prominent. As explained earlier, the intra-regional trade liberalization process within ASEAN, which marked the beginning of institutional economic integration in East Asia, started in 1993. By 2003, the five original members (Indonesia, Malaysia, the Philippines, Singapore and Thailand) and Brunei had achieved intra-regional tariffs of 5 per cent or less, with a small number of exceptions. These members are to eliminate all regional tariffs by 2010 and others (Cambodia, Laos, Myanmar and Vietnam) are to do so by 2015.

The development of FTAs between ASEAN members and Japan is also notable. Starting with Singapore in 2001, Japan has negotiated FTAs with seven out of the ten ASEAN members. The number of Chinese and South Korean bilateral FTAs with ASEAN members is small compared to Japan's because they have preferred to negotiate FTAs with ASEAN as a whole. As a result, the FTAs between China and ASEAN and between South Korea and ASEAN have come into effect earlier than the one between Japan and ASEAN.

Although Table 11.1 does not explicitly show this, there has been an initiative to establish an FTA among APT members. The reports of the East

Table 11.1   FTAs/EPAs of East Asian states/regions (as of November 2010)

	Japan	China	(Hong Kong)	(Macau)	South Korea	Taiwan	Mongolia	Indonesia	Malaysia	Philippines	Singapore	Thailand	Brunei	Cambodia	Laos	Myanmar	Vietnam	ASEAN	India	Bangladesh	Sri Lanka	Nepal	Bhutan	Pakistan	United Sates
Japan	–	● ●†			△ ●†		△	☆	☆ ◇*	☆	☆ ◇*	☆ ◇*	☆				☆ ◇*	☆	○						◇*
China	● ●†	–	☆	☆	● ●† ⊙	◎#	●				☆	☆			⊙			☆	● ⊙	⊙	⊙			☆	
(Hong Kong)		☆	–																						
(Macau)		☆		–																					
South Korea	△ ●†	● ●† ⊙			–						☆	△			⊙			☆	☆ ⊙	⊙	⊙				◎
Taiwan		◎#				–					▲														
Mongolia	△	●																							
Indonesia	☆							–	*	*	*	*	*	*	*	*	*	–	●						▲
Malaysia	☆ ◇*							*	–	*	* ◇*	*	* ◇*	*	*	*	* ◇*	–	△					☆	△ ◇*
Philippines	☆							*	*	–	*	*	*	*	*	*	*	–							▲
Singapore	☆ ◇*	☆			☆	▲		*	* ◇*	*	–	*	* ◇	*	*	*	* ◇*	–	☆					△	☆ ◇*
Thailand	☆ ◇*	☆						*	*	*	*	–	*	*	*	* □	*	–	☆	□	□	□	□	●	△
Brunei	☆ ◇*							*	* ◇*	*	* ◇*	*	–	*	*	*	* ◇*	–							▲ ◇*
Cambodia								*	*	*	*	*	*	–	*	*	*	–							
Laos		⊙			⊙			*	*	*	*	*	*	*	–	*	*	–	⊙	⊙	⊙				
Myanmar								*	*	*	*	* □	*	*	*	–	*	–	□	□	□	□	□		
Vietnam	☆ ◇*							*	* ◇*	*	* ◇*	*	* ◇*	*	*	*	–	–							◇*
ASEAN	☆	☆			☆			–	–	–	–	–	–	–	–	–	–	–	☆						▲

Canada				△							
Mexico	☆			△							
Honduras					☆						
El Salvador					☆						
Guatemala					☆						
Nicaragua					☆						
Costa Rica		◎								△	△	
Dominican Republic					☆						
Panama					☆			☆		☆		
Colombia							△					
Chile	☆ ◇*	☆		☆	▲		◎ ◇*	●	☆ ◇	●		◇
Peru	△ ◇*	☆		△		▲	△ ◇*		☆ ◇*	◎		◇*
Australia	△ ◇*	△	◎	△	△	△	△ ◇*		☆ ◇*	☆		◇*
New Zealand	▲ ◇*	◎	◎	△	▲	☆	☆ ◇*		☆ ◇	☆		◇
South Africa	▲	△		●					△	▲		
SACU		△		●					△	☆		
Egypt				△								
Jordan						☆						
Bahrain												
GCC	△	△		●	▲		◎					
Israel				△		△						
Turkey												
Ukraine	☆					△	△					
Switzerland		●										
Norway		△		●								
Iceland		△		☆								
Russia				●			△					△
EFTA				☆			☆					
EU	△		◎	◎								△

Table 11.1　　(continued)

Notes:
☆ = in effect, ◎ = signed, ○ = agreed, △ = under negotiation/agreed to start negotiations, ● = under feasibility studies/completed feasibility studies, ▲ = proposed, ⊙ = Asia-Pacific Trade Agreement (APTA formerly known as Bangkok Agreement, in effect since 1975. China joined in 2001), ✳ = AFTA, ◇ = Trans-Pacific Strategic Economic Partnership Agreement (TPP, in effect since 2006. * Australia, Malaysia, Peru, the United States and Vietnam started accession negotiations in 2010, and Japan has shown its interest in joining in 2010), □ = BIMSTEC FTA (agreed in July 2009), # = China–Taiwan Economic Cooperation Framework Agreement (ECFA: signed in June 2010), † = China–Japan–Korea FTA feasibility study.
Other multilateral FTA initiatives include:
East Asian Free Trade Agreement (EAFTA: 10 ASEAN members, China, Japan and Korea) = under feasibility study.
Comprehensive Economic Partnership in East Asia (CEPEA: 10 ASEAN members, China, Japan, Korea, Australia, India, New Zealand) = under feasibility study.
Free Trade Area of the Asia-Pacific (FTAAP: 21 APEC members) = APEC is exploring possible pathways.

Asia Vision Group and the East Asia Study Group, which were formed for a limited time as advisory groups for the APT Summit Meeting, recommended the creation of an East Asia Community in the future and proposed the formation of the East Asian Free Trade Area (EAFTA) as a mid- to long-term measure for the realization of the Community (EAVG, 2001; EASG, 2002). Following the proposal, the APT Economic Ministers Meeting in 2006 agreed to form a specialist working group in each government and start inter-governmental consultations on the issue. Also at this meeting, the schedule to start formal FTA negotiations in 2009, to reach agreement by 2011, and to eliminate tariffs on general product items by 2016 was endorsed.

Another point which should be mentioned is that most East Asian states are looking to 'extra-regional' FTA partners as well as 'intra-regional' ones. Japan's FTAs with Mexico and Chile have already entered into force. Japan has also concluded negotiations with Switzerland, and negotiations with India and Australia are underway at the time of writing. China has negotiated or is negotiating FTAs with Chile, Pakistan, Australia and New Zealand, as well as with Costa Rica, Peru, the Gulf Cooperation Council (GCC), Iceland and others. South Korea also has extra-regional FTAs with Chile and the European Free Trade Association (EFTA), has signed an agreement with the United States and is negotiating with the EU, Australia, New Zealand, Canada, Mexico and the GCC among others. Singapore and Thailand have attempted to 'run faster' in trade and investment liberalization than other ASEAN members by concluding bilateral FTAs with extra-regional states. These two states have sought FTAs with partners from South Asia, the Americas, Oceania, Africa, the Middle East and Europe.

Malaysia and Indonesia were initially critical of the Thai and Singaporean position, arguing that FTAs with non-ASEAN members would undermine the effectiveness of AFTA. Nevertheless, by the end of 2002, Malaysia had changed its stance on bilateral FTAs and, along with the Philippines and Thailand, decided to enter into negotiations with Japan. Indonesia followed suit in 2005. Since then, Malaysia has entered into FTA negotiations with the United States, India, Pakistan, Australia, New Zealand and Chile.

Table 11.2 shows the major multilateral cooperation frameworks in and around East Asia. ASEAN, ADPS, APEC and ASEM already existed before the Asian financial crisis, but other frameworks emerged after the crisis. As explained, the APT framework was created in the midst of the financial crisis, at first for the purpose of financial cooperation, but the areas of cooperation have been extended significantly since then. BIMSTEC is mainly a Thai and Indian initiative for economic cooperation across the Bay of Bengal. The members of BIMSTEC also negotiated their own FTA and have reached agreement in July 2009. Australia, India and South Africa lead the IOC-ARC framework, which focuses on cooperation in trade liberalization and facilitation, investment, science and technology, and tourism, among others. The SCO started as a security cooperation framework among members, especially between China and Russia, and remains so primarily, but it also intends to expand efforts to economic cooperation areas. ACMECS focuses on cooperation for economic development in a part of Southeast Asia, which is a sub-region of East Asia. The East Asia Summit (EAS) is an economic cooperation framework for the wider 'East Asian' region (it includes APT members, plus Australia, New Zealand and India). Japan proposed at the second East Asia Summit in January 2007 to work on a study of the Comprehensive Economic Partnership for East Asia (CEPEA), an FTA (or EPA) in which all 16 EAS members would participate.

11.6 THE NATURE OF ECONOMIC INTEGRATION IN EAST ASIA

11.6.1 Characteristics of East Asian Economic Integration Processes

From observing what has been happening in and around East Asia since the turn of the century, it is clear that the economic integration processes in the region possess several characteristics.

First, the institutions, or cooperation frameworks, for economic integration in East Asia remain area-based and function-based. For instance, FTAs and EPAs typically exhibit function-based integration, which

Table 11.2   Multilateral cooperation frameworks involving East Asia (as of November 2010)

	East Asia																		South Asia					
	Northeast Asia							Southeast Asia																	
	Japan	China	(Hong Kong)	South Korea	North Korea	Taiwan	Mongolia	Indonesia	Malaysia	Philippines	Singapore	Thailand	Brunei	Cambodia	Laos	Myanmar	Vietnam	PNG	Timor Leste	India	Bangladesh	Sri Lanka	Nepal	Bhutan	Pakistan
ASEAN (1967–)								☆	☆	☆	☆	☆	☆	☆	☆	☆	☆	○	○						
ADPS (1972–)	☆	☆		☆				☆	☆	☆	☆	☆	☆	☆	☆	☆	☆	○	○	☆					☆
APEC (1989–)	☆	☆	☆	☆		☆		☆	☆	☆	☆	☆	☆				☆	☆							
GMS (1992–)		☆										☆		☆	☆	☆	☆								
ARF (1994–)	☆	☆		☆	☆		☆	☆	☆	☆	☆	☆	☆	☆	☆	☆	☆	☆	☆	☆	☆	☆			☆
ASEM (1996–)	☆	☆		☆				☆	☆	☆	☆	☆	☆	☆	☆	☆	☆			☆					☆
ASEAN+3 (1997–)	☆	☆		☆				☆	☆	☆	☆	☆	☆	☆	☆	☆	☆								
BIMSTEC (1997–)												☆				☆				☆	☆	☆	☆	☆	
IOR-ARC (1997–)	○	○						☆	☆		☆	☆								☆	☆	☆			
CAREC (1997–)		☆					☆																		☆
SCO (2001–)		☆					○													○		○			○
ACD (2002–)	☆	☆		☆				☆	☆	☆	☆	☆	☆	☆	☆	☆	☆			☆	☆	☆		☆	☆
ACMECS (2003–)												☆		☆	☆	☆	☆								
EAS (2005–)	☆	☆		☆				☆	☆	☆	☆	☆	☆	☆	☆	☆	☆			☆					

	Central Asia						Americas					Oceania		Russia	Middle East									Africa						Europe		
							North America			South America																						
	Azerbaijan	Kazakhstan	Kyrgyzstan	Tajikistan	Turkmenistan	Uzbekistan	United States	Canada	Mexico	Chile	Peru	Australia	New Zealand	Russia	Afghanistan	Iran	Bahrain	Kuwait	Oman	Qatar	Saudi Arabia	UAE	Yemen	Kenya	Madagascar	Mauritius	Mozambique	South Africa	Tanzania	France	United Kingdom	EU
							☆	☆				☆	☆	☆																		☆
							☆	☆	☆	☆	☆	☆	☆	☆																		
							☆	☆				☆	☆	☆																		☆
												☆	☆	☆																☆	☆	☆
												☆			☆				☆			☆	☆	☆	☆	☆	☆	☆	☆	○	○	
	☆	☆	☆	☆	☆	☆									☆																	
	☆	☆	☆			☆									☆	○																
	☆	☆	☆			☆									☆		☆	☆	☆	☆	☆	☆	☆									
							☆					☆	☆	☆																		

Table 11.2   (continued)

Notes:
☆ = members/signatories, ○ = observers/dialogue partners.
ASEAN (Association of Southeast Asian Nations), ADPS (ASEAN Dialogue Partners
System), APEC (Asia-Pacific Economic Cooperation), GMS (Greater Mekong Subregion),
ARF (ASEAN Regional Forum), ASEM (Asia-Europe Meeting), BIMSTEC (Bay of
Bengal Initiative for Multi-Sectoral Technical and Economic Cooperation), IOR-ARC
(Indian Ocean Rim Association for Regional Cooperation), CAREC (Central Asia
Regional Economic Cooperation), SCO (Shanghai Cooperation Organization), ACD
(Asian Cooperation Dialogue), ACMECS (Ayeyawady–Chao Phraya–Mekong Economic
Cooperation Strategy), EAS (East Asian Summit: Russia and the United States to join in
2011).

usually includes the liberalization of trade in goods and services, investment, government procurement and the movement of natural persons, as
well as trade facilitation measures and the protection of intellectual property rights. Yet the detailed contents of FTAs are each different, reflecting
the policy preferences of each FTA party. Efforts in regional integration,
or cooperation, in areas such as finance, structural reform, energy security,
food security and the environment have been made within different frameworks. It seems that there have not been any serious attempts to 'integrate'
these integration efforts.

Second, bilateral and multilateral processes coexist and are function-
ally integrated over the same issues and in the same area. This characteristic is illustrated by the FTAs involving Southeast Asian states. The
ASEAN members base their foreign economic policies on AFTA, which
is a regional FTA, but most of them have been seeking FTAs with non-
ASEAN states at the same time. Moreover, ASEAN as a whole has negotiated FTAs as well, resulting in the emergence of a number of ASEAN+1
FTAs: with China, South Korea, Japan and Australia/New Zealand. As
mentioned earlier, the creation of an EAFTA and CEPEA have also been
discussed. In the area of finance, a network of bilateral currency swap
agreements among APT members (the Chiang Mai Initiative) is in force.
On top of this, in 2007, APT members have basically agreed to create a
mechanism that pools a certain amount of members' foreign reserves and
accommodates members with a loan during times of emergency.

Third, it is not uncommon for extra-regional states to participate in
East Asian integration processes. In Tables 11.1 and 11.2, 'East Asia' is
tentatively placed within the thick-line frame. It is quite obvious that many
'outsiders' have been involved in function-based integration. Some of the
most active 'intruders' include Australia, Chile, India, New Zealand, Peru
and the United States.

In sum, East Asian integration processes have a 'flexible', 'inclusive' and 'multi-layered' nature. They are flexible because they are area- and function-based. They allow some integration/cooperation efforts to make progress faster than others, even in the same area. They are inclusive, as they involve 'extra-regional' states not as exceptions but rather as rules. They are multi-layered, because bilateral, minilateral (sub-regional) and multilateral frameworks coexist in the processes.

11.6.2　Why Do East Asian States Seek Flexible, Inclusive and Multi-layered Processes for Economic Integration?

Why has East Asian economic integration as a whole shown a flexible, inclusive and multi-layered nature? There are several reasons.

First, it seems that East Asian states are searching for pragmatic benefits from integration processes. In other words, they are seeking concrete economic gains from the combination of bilateral, minilateral and multilateral integration/cooperation frameworks. Due to the substantial economic globalization that has been underpinned by innovation in information and communication technologies since the 1990s, individual firms have become more able to aim for optimal production, distribution and sales of their goods and services across borders. The governments in East Asia are trying to support such individual firms' activities through institutional economic integration efforts. The space for optimal economic activities is not necessarily confined to any geographical area. As long as they can expect such benefits, the stage for integration/cooperation activities can be 'sub-regional' (that is, Southeast Asia), 'regional' (that is, East Asia) or 'cross-regional' (that is, the Asia Pacific).

Second, the lesson learnt by East Asian governments, especially those of ASEAN members, from the experience of the financial crisis, was that it was crucial to restore the confidence of the market in their political and economic governance and to maintain this confidence in order to realize stable management of the national economy. In addition, the fact that Southeast Asia was increasingly seen as one of the main regions for international terrorist operations after the September 11 terrorist attacks in the United States in 2001 has induced for the governments of ASEAN members to recognize the urgent need to enhance their governance capabilities and demonstrate them to the world. ASEAN governments have sought every opportunity to rebuild their reputations for strong governance and to ensure stable investment conditions. Their bilateral and multilateral FTA negotiations with East Asian and extra-regional partners can be seen as part of their attempts to achieve this purpose.

Third, for most East Asian economies, economic relations with extra-regional countries are still crucial. While intra-regional trade and investment have increased substantially in the last decade, due mainly to the economic rise of China, the value of extra-regional trade still occupies about half the total. The United States and the EU have been important export destinations for East Asia's final products and they are likely to remain so at least in the near future. In addition, there is no country in the region that can meet its total domestic demand for raw materials and energy by itself. Thus, most East Asian economies have to rely on extra-regional countries for the supply of these goods. The FTAs and economic cooperation activities of China with African and South American states and those of Japan with Australia and the GCC can be viewed as typical in this respect.

Fourth, East Asian states seem to be concerned about any specific state exerting its influence in order to dominate the integration processes. The traditional division between 'East' and 'West' in the region disappeared after the end of the Cold War, and the emergence of fully fledged economic globalization has made the line between 'domestic' and 'foreign' economic policies increasingly blurred. Yet, for East Asian states, national sovereignty and policy autonomy seem to maintain great significance.

To balance influences, East Asian states not only check relations among themselves but also utilize extra-regional states' involvement. As in the APEC process, ASEAN as a whole is concerned about the marginalization of the organization in the process of East Asian cooperation, integration and community building. While it was reiterated at the APT and East Asia Summits in 2005 that 'ASEAN integration and the ASEAN Community' were the important basis of an East Asian community (APT Summit, 2005; East Asia Summit, 2005), ASEAN has been trying to balance the influence of powers in the region, namely China and Japan, in the APT process. This has been expressed in its efforts not only to establish FTAs with China, Japan and South Korea concurrently, but also to negotiate FTAs with extra-regional states such as India, Australia, New Zealand and the EU. ASEAN has also expressed its intention to negotiate FTAs with the United States in the near future.

The decision on orginal membership of the East Asia Summit was also a product of these 'checks-and-balances' within East Asia. Since the realization of an East Asian Community appeared on the APT agenda in 2001 as a long-term goal, China, Malaysia, Myanmar and some others, who wanted to prevent any external influence on the community building process, argued that membership should be limited to the participants in the APT process. Japan, on the other hand, maintained that East Asian cooperation should be expanded to include Australia and New Zealand, who had been Dialogue Partners of ASEAN since the mid-1970s and had

BOX 11.1   BUILDING AN ASEAN COMMUNITY BY 2015

During the first 20 years of its history, ASEAN's most significant achievement as a regional organization was in the area of political and security cooperation. The member states have not experienced major military confrontations with each other since the establishment of ASEAN. This is especially noteworthy considering that all Southeast Asian states had varying degrees of instability in their political relations with neighbors even in the years just before 1967.

As a response to challenges posed by changes in the international and regional environment in the late 1980s and early 1990s, ASEAN began to seek regional economic integration more seriously and the process to establish AFTA started in 1993. The outbreak of the Asian financial crisis caused ASEAN to further its efforts at regional integration in order to build a more robust regional framework that could prevent a recurrence of severe capital flight and take advantage of economic globalization. The ASEAN Summit, held in the midst of the crisis in December 1997, adopted the ASEAN Vision 2020, which declared its will to create an ASEAN community by 2020. The vision covered wide-ranging regional economic integration and cooperation activities such as trade, investment and financial liberalization and facilitation, the development of small and medium enterprises, human resources, technology and infrastructure, and food and energy security, as well as the creation of a socially cohesive community with a common regional identity. The Summit in December 1998 approved the Hanoi Plan of Action, which set a mid-term (from 1999 to 2004) guideline for activities to realize the broad vision.

Since the turn of the century, ASEAN's efforts at regional integration have accelerated. The Declaration of ASEAN Concord II (Bali Concord II), adopted by the ASEAN Summit in 2003, stated that ASEAN now aimed to establish an ASEAN Community consisting of the Security Community, the Economic Community and the Socio-Cultural Community. The Vientiane Action Programme of November 2004, which succeeded the Hanoi Plan of Action, provided a list of activities to be implemented during the period between 2004 and 2010 to develop the three Communities. At the ASEAN Summit in January 2007, the target year for realizing the

ASEAN Community was brought forward five years to 2015. The Declaration on the ASEAN Economic Community Blueprint, which focused on the economic cooperation part of the Vientiane Action Programme and proposed more concrete integration activities with target years for completion, was endorsed by the ASEAN Summit in November 2007. Furthermore, the Charter of the Association of Southeast Asian Nations (ASEAN Charter), which was designed to provide ASEAN with a legal and institutional framework for the first time since its establishment in 1967, was signed at the November 2007 Summit. The Charter came into force in December 2008.

In addition to having the potential of becoming able to more effectively address, through concerted collective action, the region's political, economic and social issues such as democracy, human rights, development gaps and the environment, ASEAN is seeking to build a strengthened position in its political and economic relations with extra-regional actors through the realization of an ASEAN Community by 2015. ASEAN is explicitly expecting a cohesive community to ensure and enhance its 'centrality' in the development of wider 'East Asian' integration and cooperation frameworks, such as the ASEAN Regional Forum in the area of security cooperation, and the APT and East Asia Summit processes in the area of economic integration.

substantial political and economic relations with East Asian countries. Japan did this partly because it wished to allay the impression of an exclusive community, taking into account the US response to the summit's formation.[12] More importantly, though, Japan was also concerned with the possible domination of the community building process by China, with which it did not totally share basic values such as democracy, the rule of law, human rights and a market economy.[13] As Japan saw such values, along with 'openness' and 'inclusiveness', as the principles for community building in East Asia (MOFA 2006: 61), it wished Australia and New Zealand, who shared these values more than other East Asian states, to be involved in the regional community building process. To varying degrees, Indonesia, Singapore, Vietnam and some others shared Japan's concern about Chinese influence. The end result was to extend invitations to Australia, New Zealand and India, but not to Russia and the United States, to the East Asia Summit. This was a compromise between the two groups.

11.7 SUMMARY

Decolonization, the independence movement and the emergence of the Cold War structure formed an undercurrent in the East Asian region after the war. The maintenance of national sovereignty, territorial integrity and policy autonomy became central themes for the newly independent states. While bilateral and multilateral frameworks for economic development were established in the region, they did not aim for economic 'integration'.

Thus, in East Asia, institution building specifically aimed at economic integration is a relatively recent phenomenon. First, economic globalization and the end of the Cold War encouraged ASEAN members to form AFTA, which served as a precedent for subsequent East Asian economic integration processes. The Asian financial crisis, along with other factors such as the stagnation of APEC and the WTO, acted as triggers for East Asian regionalism in the form of the APT process.

Since the turn of the century, a number of initiatives, agreements and frameworks have proliferated in and around East Asia. Now it seems that economic integration in East Asia is better understood when the processes are viewed as a whole, with a flexible, inclusive and multi-layered nature.

From the analysis in this chapter, several implications for the prospects of East Asian economic integration processes can be drawn.

- East Asian integration processes are likely to have a pragmatic and realistic focus. Rather than formulating a 'grand design' for the future of East Asia and moving towards the realization of this grand design, it is more likely that integration processes will be the accumulation of many cooperative initiatives that are seen as realizing individual and concrete economic benefits.
- Because policy preferences among East Asian countries are likely to remain diversified, multiple integration and cooperation frameworks on the same issue are also likely to continue to exist.
- Extra-regional states' participation in such multiple frameworks will not be blocked, as long as the realization of concrete and mutual benefits for both regional and extra-regional states is realistically to be expected.
- If integration processes proceed as now, the geographical concept of 'East Asia' as a space for regional economic integration will become increasingly vague. The nature of East Asian economic integration suggests a lack of direction in terms of the power and purpose of the 'region'. Thus, at least for some time, East Asia will continue to mean different things in different circumstances.

BOX 11.2   THE REGIONAL LEADERSHIP ISSUE

The initiatives to build institutions for economic integration in East Asia have been flexible, inclusive and multi-layered. In other words, they have lacked a clear sense of direction. This is more evident in the proliferation of FTA projects than in any other area of economic integration/cooperation. What has emerged since the turn of the century in the region is a complicated web of different rules for international economic activities that are applied to the participants of different FTAs.

FTAs by multiple states have also emerged in the form of ASEAN+1. ASEAN's FTAs with China and South Korea have already come into force, its FTAs with Japan, India and Australia/ New Zealand have been signed, and ASEAN is negotiating an FTA with the EU. Institutions for wider regional economic integration, which cover all APT members (EAFTA), East Asia Summit participants (CEPEA) and even APEC members (the Free Trade Area of the Asia Pacific, FTAAP), have been proposed and studied. Nevertheless, these frameworks, as they are currently implemented or planned, would not solve the problems of having complicated rules, as they are not intended to dissolve existing and overlapping FTAs.

At least in theory, this economic situation is far from the optimum for supporting the international activities of any firms of any states in the region. The lack of a sense of direction has been mainly due to the lack of political leadership in East Asia. The political (not hegemonic) leadership of major East Asian states (most likely China and/or Japan) is required to sort out this messy situation. To do this, the leaders need to build and maintain cooperative political and economic relations with extra-regional states, especially the United States, as the effects would not be confined to East Asia in this era of economic globalization. Furthermore, such leadership is also needed to counter the protectionist tendencies that have emerged not only in East Asia but also elsewhere in the world after the global financial crisis.

NOTES

1. Besides the major disputes among Indonesia, Malaya and the Philippines over the possession of Sabah and Sarawak, Thailand and Malaysia had armed border conflicts, and Singapore's independence in 1965 caused a deterioration in its relationship with Malaysia.
2. ASA was created in 1961 by Malaya, the Philippines and Thailand to promote broad regional cooperation (the economy, culture, education, science, and so on). Non-aligned states in the region like such as Indonesia did not join because ASA was seen as a pro-Western, anti-communist organization. Two years after its establishment, ASA virtually came to an end when conflicts between Malaya and the Philippines intensified.
3. In fact, MAPHILINDO itself was a product of conflicts. After Malaya set the date for the establishment of Malaysia on 31 August 1963, the heads of government from Indonesia, the Philippines and Malaya met in Manila and agreed to form a federation of Malay nations called MAPHILINDO. They also agreed to postpone the establishment of Malaysia and ask for UN intervention to resolve the Sabah/Sarawak problem. Despite the agreement, when Malaya went on to form Malaysia in September, MAPHILINDO naturally broke down.
4. For instance, in 1988, 1989 and 1990, Thailand's real GDP grew at a rate of 13.2 per cent, 12.2 per cent and 11.6 per cent respectively. Malaysia's and Indonesia's real GDPs also grew rapidly in the same period: at a rate of 8.9 per cent, 9.2 per cent and 9.7 per cent in the case of Malaysia, and 5.8 per cent, 7.5 per cent and 7.2 per cent in the case of Indonesia (International Monetary Fund, *International Financial Statistics*, various issues).
5. PBEC currently consists of business representatives from 20 states: Australia, Canada, Chile, China, Colombia, Ecuador, Hong Kong, Indonesia, Japan, Korea, Malaysia, Mexico, New Zealand, Peru, the Philippines, Russia, Singapore, Taiwan, Thailand and the United States.
6. The first PECC meeting had participants from five developed economies (Australia, Canada, Japan, New Zealand and the United States), six developing economies (five ASEAN members (Indonesia, Malaysia, the Philippines, Singapore and Thailand) and Korea), as well as delegations representing the South Pacific Island states (Papua New Guinea, Fiji and Tonga), the Asian Development Bank, PBEC and PAFTAD.
7. These incentives included exemptions from corporate tax for several years after starting operations, and customs duties exemptions on raw materials and intermediate goods provided that the final products were to be exported.
8. Section 301 of the Trade and Tariff Act 1974 gave the President discretion to act against the unfair trade practices of other states. The Omnibus Trade and Competitiveness Act 1988 amended this provision and introduced 'Super 301' and 'Special 301'. Super 301 transferred the authority for action to the USTR and made action against unfair trade practices virtually mandatory if identified states did not comply with US-imposed deadlines. 'Special 301' applies similar provisions to intellectual property rights issues (Snape et al., 1998: 458 n11).
9. Negotiations between the United States and Japan on the Semiconductor Agreement (originally signed in 1986) and those under the frameworks of the 'Market-Oriented, Sector Selective' (MOSS, started in 1985) and the 'Structural Impediments Initiative' (SII, started in 1989) were symbolic acts of US bilateralism and aggressive unilateralism.
10. The industrial projects proposed were: urea/nitrogenous fertilizer for Indonesia and Malaysia; rock salt and soda ash for Thailand; phosphoric fertilizer for the Philippines; and diesel engines for Singapore.
11. Singapore's AIP was a typical case. Other ASEAN members, especially Indonesia, opposed the production of low-horsepower diesel engines (mainly for agricultural use) under the scheme. After prolonged negotiations, Singapore decided to withdraw from the project in 1978, and to fund other members' AIP with a nominal 1 per cent share in

the equity. Japan agreed to provide 70 per cent of each AIP's funds as official development assistance. ASEAN was responsible for the remaining 30 per cent, 60 per cent
of which was to be paid by the host member and 10 per cent by other members. After
Singapore's withdrawal from the project, the allocation of funds for non-host members
changed to 1 per cent for Singapore and 11 per cent in total for the other members
(Suriyamongkol, 1988: 203–7).

12. In May 2005, Japan suggested that the United States should be invited to the East Asia
     Summit as an observer.
13. In a document released in October 2002 (MOFA 2002), the Ministry of Foreign Affairs
     of Japan stated that: 'there is no question, for Japan as well as for the stable develop-
     ment of the region, as to the importance of building an economic system in East Asia
     that should be initiated under Japan's leadership' (italics added).

REFERENCES

AMM (ASEAN Ministerial Meeting) (1971), 'Zone of Peace, Freedom and
    Neutrality Declaration', Kuala Lumpur, November (http://www.aseansec.
    org/3629.htm, accessed on 25 December 2008).
APEC Leaders Meeting (1993), 'APEC Leaders Economic Vision Statement',
    20   November   (http://www.apec.org/apec/leaders_declarations/1993.html,
    accessed on 27 December 2008).
APT Summit (ASEAN+3 Summit) (1999), 'Joint Statement on East Asia
    Cooperation', 28 November (http://www.aseansec.org/5469.htm, accessed on
    26 December 2008).
APT Summit (2005), 'Kuala Lumpur Declaration on the ASEAN Plus Three
    Summit', 12 December (http://www.aseansec.org/18037.htm, accessed on 26
    December 2008).
Blomqvist, Hans C. (1993), 'ASEAN as a model for Third World regional eco-
    nomic cooperation?', *ASEAN Economic Bulletin*, **10**(1), 52–67.
Dosch, Jörn and Manfred Mols (1998), 'Thirty years of ASEAN: achievements
    and challenges', *Pacific Review*, **11**(2), 167–82.
Drysdale, Peter (1988), *International Economic Pluralism: Economic Policy in East
    Asia and the Pacific*, North Sydney: Allen & Unwin.
Drysdale, Peter and Hugh Patrick (1979), 'An Asian-Pacific regional economic
    organization: an exploratory concept paper', The Committee of Foreign
    Relations, US Senate, Washington DC, reprinted in John G. Crawford and
    G. Seow (eds), (1981), *Pacific Economic Cooperation: Suggestions for Action*,
    London: Selangor Heinemann, pp. 63–82.
EASG (East Asia Study Group) (2002), 'Final Report of the East Asia Study
    Group', November (http://www.aseansec.org/viewpdf.asp?file=/pdf/easg.pdf,
    accessed on 24 December 2008).
East Asia Summit (2005), 'Kuala Lumpur Declaration on the East Asia Summit',
    14 December (http://www.aseansec.org/18098.htm, accessed on 26 December
    2008).
EAVG (East Asia Vision Group) (2001), 'Towards an East Asian community:
    region of peace, prosperity and progress', November (http://www.mofa.go.jp/
    region/asia-paci/report2001.pdf, accessed on 24 December 2008).
Elek, Andrew (1991), 'The challenge of Asian-Pacific cooperation', *Pacific Review*,
    4(4), 322–32.

Funabashi, Yoichi (1995), *Asia Pacific Fusion: Japan's Role in APEC*, Washington DC: Institute for International Economics.

Garnaut, Ross (1994). 'Open regionalism: its analytic basis and relevance to the international system', *Journal of Asia Economics*, **5**(2), 273–90.

Harris, Stuart (1989), 'Regional economic cooperation, trading blocs and Australian interests', *Australian Outlook*, **43**(2), 16–24.

Harris, Stuart (1994), 'Policy networks and economic cooperation: policy coordination in the Asia-Pacific Region', *Pacific Review*, **7**(4), 381–95.

Krauss, Ellis S. (2000), 'Japan, the US, and the emergence of multilateralism in Asia', *Pacific Review*, **13**(3), 473–94.

MOFA (Ministry of Foreign Affairs of Japan) (2002), 'Nihon no FTA Senryaku', (Japan's FTA Strategy) October (http://www.mofa.go.jp/mofaj/gaiko/fta/senryaku_05.html, accessed on 5 January 2008).

MOFA (2006), *Diplomatic Blue Book 2006*, April.

Okamoto, Jiro (2004a), 'Introduction', in Jiro Okamoto (ed.), *Trade Liberalization and APEC*, London and New York: Routledge, pp. 1–5.

Okamoto, Jiro (2004b), 'The development of EVSL consultations and setting the research questions', in Jiro Okamoto (ed.), *Trade Liberalization and APEC*, London and New York: Routledge, 33–64.

Pangestu, Mari, Hadi Soesastro and Mubariq Ahmad (1992), 'A new look at intra-ASEAN economic cooperation', *ASEAN Economic Bulletin*, **8**(3), 333–52.

Parreñas, Julius Caesar (1998), 'ASEAN and Asia-Pacific economic cooperation', *Pacific Review*, **11**(2), 233–48.

Patrick, Hugh (1997), 'From PAFTAD to APEC', Discussion Paper 2, APEC Study Center, Columbia University.

Petri, Peter A. (1999), 'APEC and the Millennium Round', Paper presented to the twenty-fifth PAFTAD conference, 'APEC: its challenges and tasks in the 21st century', 16–18 June, Osaka.

Ravenhill, John (1998), 'Adjusting to the ASEAN way: thirty years of Australia's relations with ASEAN', *Pacific Review*, **11**(2), 267–89.

Snape, Richard H., Lisa Gropp and Tas Luttrell (1998), *Australian Trade Policy 1965–1997: A Documentary History*, St Leonards: Allen & Unwin.

Soesastro, Hadi (1995), 'ASEAN and APEC: do concentric circles work?', *Pacific Review*, **8**(3), 475–93.

Study Group on Pacific Basin Cooperation (1980), 'Kantaiheiyo Rentai no Koso' (Pacific Basin Cooperation Concept), Report of a policy study group commissioned by Prime Minister Masayoshi Ohira, No. 4.

Suriyamongkol, Marjorie L. (1988), *Politics of ASEAN Economic Co-operation: The Case of ASEAN Industrial Projects*, Singapore: Institute of Southeast Asian Studies/Oxford University Press.

12. Institutions and policy coordination for further integration

Daisuke Hiratsuka

12.1 INTRODUCTION

With the most-favored nation (MFN) tariff rates remaining at a significant level, the majority of East Asian countries have implemented investment promotion schemes which grant import tax exemptions to intermediate goods intended for export. The import tax exemption scheme, however, is cumbersome for firms because they are compelled to employ persons to prepare documents. Also, the scheme is suspicious because it appears to be in opposition to the General Agreement on Tariffs and Trade (GATT), Article I, General Most-Favoured-Nation Treatment, in which the MFN tariffs are to be accorded unconditionally to the products originating in and destined for all parties to the agreement.

East Asia must put into practice the WTO's consistent, transparent and nondiscriminatory trade-related measures. One such measure is to extend regional trade agreements (RTAs), one of the WTO's consistent trade liberalization tools. Until the end of the 1990s, however, there were no RTAs in East Asia, except the ASEAN Free Trade Area (AFTA) and the Closer Economic Relations (CER) between Australia and New Zealand. Subsequently, the Singapore–Japan Economic Partnership Agreement opened up the path for RTAs to spearhead trade liberalization in the region. Currently in fact, there are more than thirty RTAs enforced involving East Asia, of which fourteen are intra-regional RTAs, either bilateral agreements or plurilateral agreements.

So, a question arises. Will the proliferation of FTAs be good for East Asia? To rephrase this, will East Asia benefit from the proliferation of FTAs? This chapter aims to identify the problems arising from East Asia's regionalism, evaluate the ongoing regionalism in East Asia, and suggest a proper regional cooperation framework from the regional perspective of East Asia.

Our discussion covers sixteen countries, including ten ASEAN countries plus Australia, China, Japan, India, the Republic of Korea, and New Zealand. This coverage corresponds to the member countries of the East Asia Summit (EAS) or the so-called ASEAN+6. Australia, New Zealand and India are enhancing their economic relations with ASEAN, China, and the Republic of Korea in diverse ways including FTAs. The next section reviews tariffs, non-tariff trade, and service trade barriers in East Asia, and asserts that those barriers in East Asia are rather high. Section 12.3 introduces the recent development of FTAs in the region and describes how East Asian FTAs have been led by ASEAN. Section 12.4 evaluates the existing FTAs and identifies the problems arising from the proliferation of FTAs in the region, appending a warning that the so-called spaghetti bowl phenomenon is appearing in the region. Section 12.5 discusses the utilization of East Asia's FTAs and finds that the FTAs in the region are utilized for specific industries such as the automobile and textile industries. The last section discusses the perspectives of region-wide cooperation processes such as the ASEAN+3 and the EAS processes. It is emphasized that the benefits from FTAs go to a limited number of firms and industries, thereby suggesting that the elimination of MFN tariffs should be pursued.

12.2 TRADE BARRIERS TO GOODS AND SERVICES

12.2.1 Goods

Ando and Kimura (2003) argued that most of the East Asian economies have traditionally applied a 'dual track approach,' which aims to foster both import-substituting industries and export-oriented industries at the same time.

Indeed, the East Asian countries have employed schemes for import tax exemption on intermediate goods for export production purposes. JETRO's Survey of Japanese-Affiliated Firms in ASEAN and India in 2007 (2008a) stated that the percentage of companies in ASEAN as a whole that reported 100% duty-free imports reached 32.6%, out of the 590 valid responses. By country in ASEAN, the figure was highest in the Philippines (53.0%), followed by Malaysia (43.0%) and Singapore (39.2%). On the other hand, the 100% duty-free imports amounted to only 11.8% in Thailand and 15.0% in Indonesia. By industry, 100% duty-free imports were high particularly in electric and electronic parts and components (87.5%) and non-ferrous metals (83.3%) in the Philippines, and in electric machinery and electronic equipment (68.4%) and electric and electronic parts and components (62.5%) in Malaysia. The JETRO survey result suggests that ASEAN countries have implemented the import tariff exemption scheme to promote exports, and firms in those countries, in particular in electronics, are actually using the import tariff exemption scheme.

On the other hand, import-substitution policies have also been adopted by East Asian countries, and regional economic integration has been hindered by trade protection measures. This is obvious from the findings of Freudenberg and Paulmier (2006) with regard to East Asia's tariff structure in 2002. The average East Asian tariff rate for all products was 7.4% for the East Asia exporters, which is slightly higher than that for the EU exporters, at 7.2%, but significantly higher than that for NAFTA exporters, at 5.5%. As a result, East Asian exporters are subject to higher import tariffs than those from the EU and NAFTA. In other words, East Asia is discriminating against itself. Freudenberg and Paulmier (2006) argued that Thailand, China, and Vietnam practiced an 'offensive protectionism' as an instrument of export promotion, in which high tariffs were imposed on goods that can be exported. On the other hand, Japan, Korea, the Philippines, Brunei and Malaysia practiced a 'defensive protectionism' as an instrument either for national security or to protect infant or inefficient domestic industries. Myanmar, Laos, Taiwan, Indonesia and Cambodia applied the 'wide-ranging protectionism' which combines defense of competitive and uncompetitive industries.

12.2.2   Services

In addition, barriers in service industries are high in East Asia. It is normal in developed countries to have liberalized more than 100 service sectors out of the total of 155 sectors, but many East Asian countries have made concessions in less than half of the sectors. According to the WTO concession report as summarized in Figure 12.1 which plots the number of GATS (General Agreement on Trade in Services) service sectors with commitments by WTO members in East Asia, the concession sectors number 75 in Thailand and Malaysia, only 51 in the Philippines, and 47 for Indonesia. These low numbers of GATS service sectors with commitments reflect that these countries have protected their domestic service industries.

High barriers are reflected in the ranking of the overall 'ease of doing business' by the World Bank. The World Bank's 'Doing Business 2009' report ranks Laos and Cambodia in 'ease of cross-border' trade at 165 and 122, respectively, among the 182 countries surveyed (from which Myanmar is excluded). Bureaucratic red tape, regulations, and lack of legal systems seem to be factors contributing to high non-tariff barriers and lack of ease of trade.

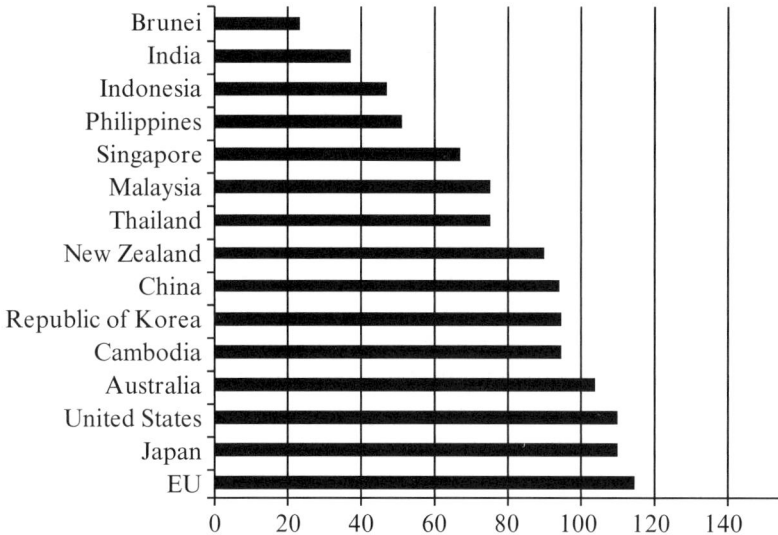

Source: Compiled by the author from the WTO statistical database.

Figure 12.1 Number of GATS service sectors with commitments

For instance, transportation costs in Laos are very high. It is often claimed that, since Laos is a small, landlocked economy, one-way trucking, for example, from Bangkok to Vientiane, is more expensive. However, the high trucking costs may be largely attributable to what is essentially a cartel operation controlling the transportation business in Laos. A Japanese affiliate producing shirts in Vientiane has suffered from charges on container trucks that are double the charges initially expected. The affiliate rents a container truck between Bangkok and Vientiane to transport materials from Bangkok to Vientiane and shirts from Vientiane to Bangkok by the same truck. However, the transportation charge for the short drive of approximately 30 kilometers from the Thanaleng truck terminal in Vientiane to the affiliate's factory in Vientiane is the same as the charge for the 640-kilometer trip from Bangkok to the terminal in Vientiane. In addition, all the truck container operators offer the same rates. This high transportation cost inside Laos may be due to the cartel-like operation by the Transport Association of Laos because the Laotian legal system is not yet well established.

Another example is the high charge for air cargo space due to the aviation agreement between Laos and Thailand. The agreement limits the number of seats permitted to each country to 2,100 seats per week.

To conform, Thai Airways operates small aircraft between Bangkok and Vientiane, and consequently some passengers have to use Lao Airlines. The aviation agreement helps to boost the utilization of seats for Lao Airlines, but on the other hand, it raises the cost of air cargo due to lack of cargo space between Bangkok and Vientiane. Although the Thai government has asked to relax the restriction on the number of seats allowed between the two cities, the Laotian government has refused the proposal, to protect its own domestic airline.

As shown by the above examples, services are frequently regulated for numerous reasons because countries have different national policy goals. East Asia is fairly restrictive with regard to services: there are significant barriers in banking, telecommunication, and business services (Dee 2005). NZIER (2008) finds that Vietnam, Brunei, India, Indonesia, Thailand and Malaysia are the most restrictive on trade of business services, and the Philippines, Thailand, India, and Indonesia are very restrictive on trade of maritime services.

12.3   PROLIFERATION OF RTAS

In spite of the fact that there are numerous trade barriers in East Asia, until the end of the 1990s, the institutionalization of regional cooperation had not progressed in tempo with the developments of *de facto* economic integration. Figure 12.2 plots the number of RTAs involving the EAS region countries and the number of intra-EAS RTAs as of December 2008 by using the WTO database, showing that, indeed, there were only a few RTAs in the EAS region. The first RTA enforced involving the EAS region was the CER between Australia and New Zealand in 1983, followed by Laos–Thailand in 1991, which was a partial-scope agreement that liberalized trade from Laos to Thailand, whereby Thailand aimed to enhance its relationship with Laos.

In 1992, ASEAN signed an agreement to actualize AFTA (ASEAN Free Trade Area) within fifteen years; however, the start of the actual tariff elimination was delayed until 1993. It was in 1999, following the eruption of the Asian currency crisis in 1997, that tariff elimination was accelerated. In September 1999, ASEAN agreed to eliminate import duties on all products by the year 2015 for the six original members of ASEAN (ASEAN6: Brunei, Indonesia, Malaysia, the Philippines, Singapore, and Thailand) and by the year 2018 for the new members of ASEAN. The ASEAN Summit in November 1999 decided to eliminate all import duties by 2010, ahead of the original schedule, for ASEAN6, and to advance the schedule from 2018 to 2015 for the new

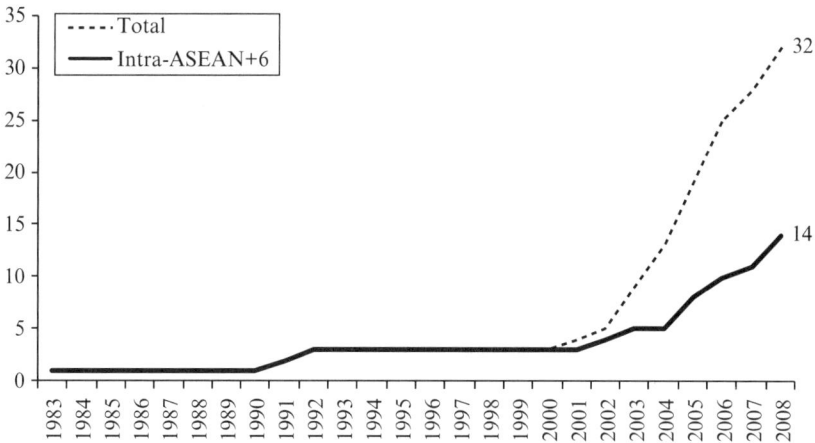

Source: Compiled by the author using the WTO RTA database (http://www.wto. org/ english/tratop_e/region_e/region_e.htm, 8 January 2009).

Figure 12.2   Regional trade agreements involving ASEAN+6 of which the GATT/WTO has been notified (cumulative)

members, but it allows some sensitive products to follow the original date of 2018.

It was the Japan–Singapore FTA in 2002 that led to the RTA movement in East Asia. Following that FTA, four RTAs were enforced in 2003 and 2004, six RTAs in 2005 and 2006, three RTAs in 2007, and four RTAs in 2008. As of December 2008, in total, thirty-two RTAs existed in the EAS region. On the other hand, as shown in Figure 12.2, the number of intra-EAS RTAs has also been increasing. After 2003, one RTA was enforced in 2003, followed by three RTAs in 2005, two RTAs in 2006, one RTA in 2007, and three RTAs in 2008. In total, there are fourteen intra-EAS RTAs in existence.

In addition to the RTAs, of which the GATT/WTO was notified as of 15 December 2008, at least three RTAs are scheduled to be enforced. They are the ASEAN–Korea FTA, the ASEAN–Japan FTA, and the ASEAN–CER FTA. The ASEAN–Korea FTA came into force in June 2007, but at that time, Thailand refused to sign due to the failure of negotiations with Korea on trade liberalization. Korea did not open up its market to major Thai agricultural products, namely rice, frozen and processed chicken, canned tuna, and fresh fruit. Thus, the Thai government, in October 2008, approved two protocols: one for trade in goods and the other for trade in services under the ASEAN–Korea FTA. These protocols have been forwarded to the joint session of Thailand's House of Representatives and Senate for approval (BOI, 2008). The Japan–ASEAN Comprehensive Economic Partnership Agreement already became partially effective in December 2008, among Japan, Singapore, Laos, Vietnam and Myanmar, and in January 2009 in relation to Brunei (MOFA, 2008). The ASEAN-CER FTA was signed in August 2008 and is scheduled to be enforced in 2009. In terms of the number of RTAs, economic integration in the EAS region has been rapidly institutionalized. East Asia is no longer delayed in *de jure* integration.

12.4   FEATURES AND LEVEL OF FTAS IN ASIA

12.4.1   Scope and Coverage of East Asia's FTAs

An RTA that considers only border protection measures is described as mere 'shallow integration', while an RTA that does much more than remove restrictive border policies is called 'deep integration'. Recent RTAs tend to be characterized by 'deep integration'. What characteristics do East Asia's RTAs display under this definition? Do they simply reduce tariffs, creating mere 'shallow integration'? Or, do they contain elements such as trade facilitation, liberalization of services, government procurement, intellectual property rights that establish a single production base and market areas in goods and services?

Table 12.1 presents a summary of RTAs by type. Most of the RTAs are free trade agreements (FTAs) under GATT Article XXIV, which stipulates liberalization of substantially all goods. A few RTAs are FTAs under the Enabling Clause which permits developing countries to enter into preferential trade agreements which do not meet the strict criteria laid out in GATT Article XXIV for regional free-trade agreements. This clause allows developing countries to cover a very limited range of products.

East Asia is launching RTAs on trade in services. As shown in Table 12.1, among thirty-two RTAs, twenty-five RTAs have agreements on services. Obviously, liberalization of service is a significant part of 'deep' integration. Only seven RTAs, those of Laos–Thailand, AFTA, India–Sri Lanka, SAFTA, India–Bhutan, Chile–China, and Pakistan–China, have no agreement on trade in services. As for AFTA, however, ASEAN is going to realize service liberalization by 2015 in the ASEAN Economic Community (AEC).

Taking into consideration the fact that East Asia's FTAs have agreements on services, East Asia's RTAs seem to have characteristics of 'deep integration'. Plummer (2007) evaluates East Asia's FTAs, putting forward

Table 12.1   Regional trade agreements of which the GATT/WTO has been notified and which are in force by date

Agreement	Goods			Services		
	Date of entry into force	Related provi-sions	Type of agree-ment	Date of entry into force	Related provi-sions	Type of agree-ment
CER	1-Jan-83	GATT Art. XXIV	FTA	1-Jan-89	GATS Art. V	EIA
Laos–Thailand	20-Jun-91	Enabling Clause	PS			
AFTA	28-Jan-92	Enabling Clause	FTA			
India–Sri Lanka	15-Dec-01	Enabling Clause	FTA			
Japan–Singa-pore	30-Nov-02	GATT Art. XXIV	FTA	30-Nov-02	GATS Art. V	EIA
EFTA–Singa-pore	1-Jan-03	GATT Art. XXIV	FTA	1-Jan-03	GATS Art. V	EIA
ASEAN–China	1-Jul-03	Enabling Clause	PS	1-Jul-07	GATS Art. V	EIA
Singapore–Austra-lia	28-Jul-03	GATT Art. XXIV	FTA	28-Jul-03	GATS Art. V	EIA
China–Macao, China	1-Jan-04	GATT Art. XXIV	FTA	1-Jan-04	GATS Art. V	EIA
China–Hong Kong, China	1-Jan-04	GATT Art. XXIV	FTA	1-Jan-04	GATS Art. V	EIA
United States–Singa-pore	1-Jan-04	GATT Art. XXIV	FTA	1 Jan 04	GATS Art. V	EIA
Korea–Chile	1-Apr-04	GATT Art. XXIV	FTA	1-Apr-04	GATS Art. V	EIA

Table 12.1   (continued)

Agreement	Goods			Services		
	Date of entry into force	Related provisions	Type of agreement	Date of entry into force	Related provisions	Type of agreement
Thailand–Australia	1-Jan-05	GATT Art. XXIV	FTA	1-Jan-05	GATS Art. V	EIA
United States–Australia	1-Jan-05	GATT Art. XXIV	FTA	1-Jan-05	GATS Art. V	EIA
Japan–Mexico	1-Apr-05	GATT Art. XXIV	FTA	1-Apr-05	GATS Art. V	EIA
Thailand–New Zealand	1-Jul-05	GATT Art. XXIV	FTA	1-Jul-05	GATS Art. V	EIA
India–Singapore	1-Aug-05	GATT Art. XXIV	FTA	1-Aug-05	GATS Art. V	EIA
Jordon–Singapore	22-Aug-05	GATT Art. XXIV	FTA	22-Aug-05	GATS Art. V	EIA
SAFTA	1-Jan-06	Enabling Clause	FTA			
Korea–Singapore	2-Mar-06	GATT Art. XXIV	FTA	2-Mar-06	GATS Art. V	EIA
Japan–Malaysia	13-Jul-06	GATT Art. XXIV	FTA	13-Jul-06	GATS Art. V	EIA
Panama–Singapore	24-Jul-06	GATT Art. XXIV	FTA	24-Jul-06	GATS Art. V	EIA
India–Bhutan	29-Jul-06	Enabling Clause	FTA			
EFTA–Korea	1-Sep-06	GATT Art. XXIV	FTA	1-Sep-06	GATS Art. V	EIA

Table 12.1   (continued)

Agreement	Goods			Services		
	Date of entry into force	Related provisions	Type of agreement	Date of entry into force	Related provisions	Type of agreement
Chile–China	1-Oct-06	GATT Art. XXIV	FTA			
Pakistan–China	1-Jul-07	GATT Art. XXIV	FTA			
Chile–Japan	3-Sep-07	GATT Art. XXIV	FTA	3-Sep-07	GATS Art. V	EIA
Japan–Thailand	1-Nov-07	GATT Art. XXIV	FTA	1-Nov-07	GATS Art. V	EIA
Pakistan–Malaysia	1-Jan-08	Enabling Clause	FTA	1-Jan-08	GATS Art. V	EIA
Japan–Indonesia	1-Jul-08	GATT Art. XXIV	FTA	1-Jul-08	GATS Art. V	EIA
Brunei Darussalam–Japan	31-Jul-08	GATT Art. XXIV	FTA	31-Jul-08	GATS Art. V	EIA
Japan–Philippines	11-Dec-08	GATT Art. XXIV	FTA	11-Dec-08	GATS Art. V	EIA

Source: Compiled by the author using the WTO RTA database (http://www.wto.org/english/tratop_e/region_e/region_e.htm, 8 January 2009).

10 criteria: (1) comprehensive goods coverage, (2) comprehensive services coverage, (3) low local content requirement and symmetrical rules of origin (ROOs), (4) best practices in customs procedures and related measures, (5) strong trade-related intellectual property rights, (6) national treatment of FDI, (7) transparent and fair antidumping procedures and dispute resolution, (8) open and nondiscriminatory government procurement policies, (9) competition policies to create a level playing field, and

(10) nondiscriminatory and transparent technical barriers. He then scored eleven FTAs involving Asia (AFTA, India–Singapore, Japan–Mexico, Japan–Singapore, Korea–Chile, Korea–Singapore, Singapore–Australia, Singapore EFTA, Singapore–New Zealand, Singapore–United States, and Thailand–United States), from 'A' (generally conforms to best practices) to 'C' (does not conform and could be inward-looking) for each of the above ten criteria. Plummer (2007) concludes that Asia's FTAs are generally more outward-oriented and conform better to best practice rules than FTAs in other regions, although shortcomings exist, notably in their ROOs.

12.4.2   Open Toward Outside Entities but Closed Against Inside Entities

East Asia's RTAs appear 'deep' at first glance. However, East Asia's RTA-FTA regionalism is problematic on several points. First, East Asia's FTAs tend to be open toward those outside of the region but rather closed against those inside of the region. For example, Korea and Thailand agreed on a very high-level FTA in terms of market access and other aspects with the United States; however in the ASEAN–Korea FTA, they placed many of each other's products on sensitive lists. Harrigan et al. (2006) pointed out the tendency for intra-Asian bilateral FTAs to offer less favorable treatment than extra-Asian FTAs.

12.4.3   Rules of Origin (ROOs)

Second, East Asia's RTAs are FTAs which require rules of origin (ROOs). Operational certificate procedures to identify whether goods are products of an agreement country are cumbersome. AFTA has employed the cumulate value content (VC) rule wherein, if at least 40% of their content originates from other member states, the goods are regarded as being of ASEAN origin.

The regional value content rule adopted by AFTA is becoming a standard for other FTAs involving ASEAN, such as the ASEAN–China FTA and ASEAN–Korea FTA; however, the value content rule itself is very cumbersome for firms. First, the calculation of value content requires all the invoices. Nevertheless, the value of materials changes frequently according to market conditions, which may create occasions where the 40% value content requirement is not met. Sometimes, the invoices contain confidential information for manufacturers, such as those in chemical and electronics industries. Obviously, the change in the tariff code (CTC) rule works better when preparing documents, since firms normally have the 'Bill of Materials' (BOM) which describes in flow-chart form the production process of the materials.

East Asia's ROOs are problematic in that East Asia's FTAs employ a third party certification system in which an exporter submits documents to a third-party organization to prove that its export products satisfy the rules of origin, and a certificate of origin is issued by the third-party organization for each export. The third party certificate system is demanding for exporters, while the benefits go to importers. However, this third party system that benefits importers is utilized for intra-firm trade but is not utilized for arm's length trade. In addition, the third party certificate system requires time, which does not fit with the 'just in time' production system used in global competition.

In August 2008, ASEAN revised the ROOs system from the 40% value content rule to an option system where applicants can chose either a value content rule or a change in tariff classification (CTC). The CTC rule determines the country of origin when the tariff code changes between procurement and shipment at a certain Harmonized System level. Moreover, the ASEAN–Japan FTA employs the option system. The recent trend toward favoring the option system may encourage the utilization of FTAs. In this regard, East Asia's FTAs are evolving toward better practices.

12.4.4   The Spaghetti Bowl Phenomenon Caused by the Proliferation of FTAs

Third, the proliferation of FTAs in East Asia has caused the so-called spaghetti bowl phenomenon. As of December 2008, AFTA, ASEAN–China FTA, ASEAN–Korea FTA, and ASEAN–Japan FTA had become effective, and ASEAN–CER (Australia and New Zealand) is to be implemented in 2009. Each FTA sets several tariff levels, such as a 0% tariff, 0% to 5% tariff, 50% tariff and so on, and each FTA has a different phase-out tariff elimination schedule. ROOs vary by products and by FTA. Kawai and Wignaraja (2007) showed the different ROOs applied on automobile and auto parts. Consequently, exporters are faced with different tariffs, phase-out schedules and ROOs on a product depending on the destination. Baldwin (2008) pointed out that the degree of market access available to an AFTA exporter of any particular product varies according to the ASEAN destination market concerned, meaning AFTA is not a single FTA but is composed of forty-five $((10 \times 9)/2=45)$ bilateral FTAs. So, as long as each country can freely set tariffs on products, ASEAN+3 potentially produces 78 different bilateral FTAs $((13 \times 12)/2=78)$, and ASEAN+6 produces 120 different bilateral FTAs $((16 \times 15)/2=120)$, even if ROOs are harmonized.

12.5   FTA UTILIZATION

The proliferation of FTAs raises a question as to whether they are actually well utilized by firms and bestow equal benefits on firms. By using the Asian International Input–Output Tables for 1990 and 2000, Kuroiwa (2008) calculated the local content ratios, ASEAN cumulative regional content ratios, and ASEAN–China cumulative regional contents ratios. These ratios are 84.2%, 85.7%, and 86.5%, respectively, for Indonesia, 65.1%, 69.7%, and 70.3% for the Philippines, 67.4%, 71.3%, and 72.9% for Thailand, 57.1%, 67.7%, and 69.2% for Malaysia, and 51.4%, 59.9%, and 62.0% for Singapore. These figures suggest that firms in those countries can potentially utilize FTAs well because high local and regional content ratios satisfy the local and regional local content requirements.

So, are East Asia's FTAs actually well utilized? Thailand and Malaysia have released the values of their trade utilizing FTAs, and these values are basic data for evaluating the status of FTA utilization in Asia. The total value of Thai exports taking advantage of AFTA amounted to 30.9% of the total value of exports in 2007, while that figure for Malaysia was 19.1%; these are the highest figures on record since 1998 (JETRO, 2008b). As for the ASEAN–China FTA, the value of Thai exports to China in 2007 that took advantage of preferential tariffs accounted for only 11.1% of the total. The figures were 6.7% in 2005 and 12.3% in 2006. Those figures for Malaysia are 2.9% in 2005, 8.9% in 2006 and 10.5% in 2007. As for the ASEAN–Korea FTA, the agreement has not become effective between Thailand and Korea. Hence, an evaluation is possible only of Malaysia and Korea. Malaysia's exports to Korea that utilized the ASEAN-Korea FTA accounted for 11.1% of Malaysia's total exports to Korea.

How should these figures be interpreted? First, the AFTA utilization of Thailand, at 30.9%, and that of Malaysia, at 11.1% are sufficiently high considering that trade within ASEAN is composed mainly of intermediate goods intended for export products which are exempted from import taxes due to import tax exemption schemes or the Information Technology Agreement (ITA). Second, the difference in utilization of FTAs between Thailand and Malaysia arises from the fact that Thailand utilizes automobile exports to Malaysia, the Philippines, and Indonesia, and on the other hand, Malaysia mainly exports electronics whose tariffs are exempted due to the ITA and the import tariff exemption scheme for export purposes. Third, the ASEAN–China FTA and the ASEAN–Korea FTA have not been well utilized compared to AFTA, reflecting the fact that, due to the elimination of phase-out tariffs, the margins between preferential tariffs and the MFN tariffs are currently small. The utilization rates will increase proportionately with the progress of phase-out tariff elimination.

Looking at the actual items utilizing FTAs, automobiles and automotive parts account for the major share in exports from Thailand to other ASEAN countries. Malaysia utilized AFTA in exports of palm oil, air conditioners, non-alloy steel and resins, and Malaysia's exports to Korea that utilized the ASEAN–Korea FTA are rubber, textile products, boilers and electric machinery. The utilization of FTAs tends to be concentrated in specific industries such as automobiles and textiles. This leads to another question. How intensively are FTAs involving East Asia utilized in terms of the number of firms? JETRO conducted a large sample survey in late 2006 to check the utilization of FTAs by Japanese firms. Among the responding firms, only 5.1% (37 firms) are currently utilizing preferential FTA tariff schemes. Chia (2008) presents 2007 survey results in which, of the 83 Singapore firms that responded, only 14.5% utilized FTAs; 8.4% utilized one FTA, 6.0% utilized two FTAs, and no firms utilized three FTAs. She concluded that the FTA utilization rate is low in Singapore and that East Asia's FTAs have inherent problems.

Hiratsuka et al. (2008) interviewed 37 Japanese firms during the period from July 2007 to May 2008 and identified a problem in East Asia's FTAs wherein the administrative costs borne by the exporter for preparation of documents to obtain a certificate of origin are high, but the benefits go to the importer.

12.6   A WAY FORWARD

12.6.1   Enhancement of the ASEAN Hub FTA Structure

East Asia will enhance the hub-and-spoke FTA structure with ASEAN as the hub and other East Asian countries as the spokes. As summarized in Table 12.2, AFTA will eliminate import duties on all products placed on the normal track by 2010 for ASEAN6. Tariffs between ASEAN6 and China, and between ASEAN6 and Korea, will be eliminated on products placed on the normal track in the ASEAN–China FTA and ASEAN–Korea FTA, respectively. Furthermore, the ASEAN–Japan FTA came into partial force in December 2008, and the ASEAN–CER FTA will be enforced in 2009. FTA networks with ASEAN as the hub are expanding rapidly in East Asia.

In contrast, East Asia's region-wide FTAs are still at the idea stage. In the ASEAN+3 process, the East Asia Study Group (EASG) proposed the East Asian Free Trade Area (EAFTA) as one of the nine long-term measures proposed at the eighth ASEAN+3 Summit in November 2004. A feasibility study on the proposed EAFTA conducted by a Track Two study

Table 12.2   Tariff elimination schedules of ASEAN-related FTAs

	AFTA			
	ASEAN6	Vietnam	Laos, Myanmar	Cambodia
Normal track to be 0%	2010	2015	2015	2015
Sensitive lists to be 0–5%	2010	2013	2015	2017

	ASEAN–China FTA		
	ASEAN6 and China	Vietnam	Cambodia, Laos, Myanmar
Normal track to be 0%	2010	2015	2015
Sensitive lists to be 0–5%	2018	2020	2020
Highly sensitive lists to be not more than 50%	2015	2018	2018

	ASEAN–Korea FTA		
	ASEAN6 and Korea	Vietnam	Cambodia, Laos, Myanmar
Normal track to be 0%	2010	2016	2018
Sensitive lists to be 0–5%	2016	2021	2024
Group A: not more than 50%	2016	2021	2024
Group B: to be not less than 20%	2016	2021	2024
Group C: reduction by 50%, to be not less than 50%	2016	2021	2024
Group D: tariff rate quotas			
Group E: exempted from elimination			

	ASEAN–Japan FTA		
Japan	ASEAN6	Vietnam	Cambodia, Laos, Myanmar
Elimination to be 0% for 90%	2018	2023	2026

Note: Japan liberalized 90% of products in 2008. Tariffs are to be eliminated not later than 1 January of the corresponding commitment years.

Source: Prepared by the author.

(an academic expert group study) chaired by a Chinese national was presented in brief at the 2006 ASEAN+3 Economic Ministers Meeting. The ASEAN ministers, however, insisted on the necessity of expeditiously concluding ASEAN+1 FTAs before concluding an EAFTA. The ASEAN+3 Summit in January 2007 welcomed Korea's proposal to conduct a Phase II EAFTA study focusing on a sector-by-sector analysis, and on the other hand, the summit leaders decided to examine other possible FTAs, such as the Comprehensive Economic Partnership in East Asia (CEPEA) to cover the ASEAN+6 countries, proposed by Japan. The EAS in January 2007 agreed to launch a Track Two study on CEPEA and requested the ASEAN Secretariat to prepare a time frame for the study. Study group meetings on CEPEA have already been held several times with Japan as chair, and participants have been assigned to report on issues related to CEPEA. At the strong request of ASEAN, the ASEAN-hub and six-countries-spoke FTAs are progressing before the region-wide FTAs such as EAFTA and CEPEA.

Harrigan et al. (2006) evaluated East Asia's FTAs such as AFTA, ASEAN+3, ASEAN+6, the ASEAN-hub+3 spokes (China, Japan and Korea), and the ASEAN-hub+ 6 spokes (ASEAN FTA plus PRC, Japan, Korea, India, Australia, and New Zealand). The results show that region-wide FTAs, such as ASEAN+3 (liberalization among +3 countries) or ASEAN+6 (liberalization among +6 countries), are likely to generate greater benefits for global economies than other FTAs. According to Harrigan et al. (2006), ASEAN can reap the largest benefit from the ASEAN-hub+6 spokes, which is an ongoing process, and ASEAN is emphasizing it in its FTA strategy. However, it should be remembered that the ASEAN+6 FTA means 120 (16*15/2=120) bilateral FTAs and the ASEAN-hub+6 spoke FTAs means 60 bilateral FTAs, as long as each country is free to set sensitive lists and phase-out tariff elimination schedules, even if the common ROOs are adopted. Considering this, region-wide FTAs should have equal preferential tariff rates, that is, 0% tariffs, at least on all manufactured products. If such a region-wide EAFTA or CEPEA is realized, firms will have to prepare documents to use FTAs, which may exclude SMEs from the utilization of FTAs. In the end, the elimination of the MFN tariffs under the WTO is the trade liberalization instrument needed for East Asia to escape from the spaghetti bowl problem and generate more equal benefits for all.

12.6.2 Necessity of Region-wide Cooperation

Nevertheless, region-wide cooperation, in particular in the EAS process, will be essential for spreading the benefits more widely. In regional cooperation, ASEAN has taken the lead in East Asia. In 2007, the ASEAN Summit agreed to the ASEAN Economic Community (AEC) Blueprint, which presents a roadmap leading towards the AEC. The AEC consists of four pillars of (a) a single market and production base, (b) a highly competitive economic region, (c) a region of equitable economic development, and (d) a region fully integrated into the global economy (ASEAN Secretary, 2007a). An ASEAN single market and production base comprises five core elements: (i) free flow of goods; (ii) free flow of services; (iii) free flow of investment; (iv) freer flow of capital; and (v) free flow of skilled labor (ASEAN Secretary, 2007b). An economic region competition policy consists of consumer protection, intellectual property rights, infrastructure development such as a transport network and enhancement of transport facilitation and logistic services, taxation, and e-commerce. Policies relevant to equitable economic development cover SME development and initiatives for ASEAN integration through collective efforts toward narrowing development gaps, which will provide more equal benefits to the countries and provinces. For full integration into the global economy, a region aims to integrate into the global economy with a coherent approach toward external economic relations and enhanced participation in global supply networks. The AEC Blueprint presents a detailed schedule of implementation for realizing the AEC. Such broad regional integration of ASEAN by the AEC will bring benefits not only to ASEAN but also to areas outside of ASEAN, in particular to the neighboring areas in East Asia.

Other regional cooperation processes are growing slowly but steadily in East Asia. As mentioned in Chapter 11, to cope with the Asian currency crisis that erupted in Thailand in 1997, the ASEAN+3 leaders met together and started bilateral swap arrangements among the ASEAN+3 countries (known as the Chiang Mai Initiative) to manage regional short-term liquidity problems and to facilitate the work of other international financial arrangements and organizations like the IMF. Regional financial cooperation in East Asia is proceeding with unprecedented intensity. The developments in financial cooperation include voluntary monthly exchanges among the ASEAN+3 countries of short-term data in 2001, two Asian Bond Funds in 2003 and 2004, and an Asian Bond Markets Initiative in 2004. The ASEAN+3 process has evolved; the ASEAN+3 Summit has been regularized, and various instances of functional cooperation on trade, energy, environment, tourism, labor, and so forth have started.

The EAS process, which consists of regional cooperation by ASEAN, China, Japan, Korea, Australia, New Zealand, and India, started in 2005 at the initiative of Japan. The function of the EAS is to discuss regional and global issues. In January 2007, the EAS approved a study by CEPEA for the establishment of the Economic Research Institute for ASEAN and East Asia (ERIA). ERIA was established in Jakarta in June 2008 and received international organization status from the ASEAN member countries in December 2008. ERIA's role includes providing input to the EAS to contribute to further economic integration, narrowing of development gaps, and sustaining of the economic growth of the region through its activities of research, capacity building programs, and tripartite seminars among researchers, the business sector, and government sector. Currently, ERIA is proposing the East Asia Industrial Corridor project which will develop the continent from India to the CLMV countries.

Obviously, a sense of regional cooperation is being fostered through the regional cooperation processes of ASEAN, ASEAN+3, and EAS, and this will contribute to the realization of the AEC, for which a detailed time frame has been established.

12.7 SUMMARY

This chapter discusses the recent developments in institution and policy coordination in East Asia by examining ASEAN, China, Japan, Korea, Australia, New Zealand, and India. In East Asia, import tax exemption schemes on some intermediate goods for export purposes as well as the Information Technology Agreements, which allow 0% tariffs on most electronics products among the contracting members under the WTO, have been employed. On the other hand, tariffs on manufactured products remain at significant levels. Also, there are many non-tariff barriers in East Asia. Well-utilized import tax exemption schemes are suspected of being in opposition to the GATT, Article I, General Most-Favored-Nation Treatment, in which the MFN tariffs are to be accorded unconditionally. So, East Asia needs to establish WTO-consistent trade arrangements, and RTAs represent one such WTO-consistent trade arrangement.

Currently, however, East Asia has more than thirty RTAs, including intra-regional RTAs. All of these RTAs are in the form of FTAs, which entail cumbersome procedures and benefit the importers only. Indeed, the actual utilization rates of FTAs are not high. FTAs are well utilized in the garment, automobile and chemical industries but not by other industries. Also, the users of FTAs are limited to specific firms. It is possible that SMEs might not obtain benefits from FTAs. Furthermore, the proliferation of FTAs has raised concerns over the so-called spaghetti bowl phenomenon. Each country freely sets tariff rates and lists for exclusions from tariff elimination. As a result, due to the proliferation of FTAs, an exporter faces various tariff levels, tariff elimination schedules, and differing rules of origin for each product depending on its destination, and this spaghetti bowl phenomenon discourages exporters from utilizing FTAs. Even if a region-wide FTA is established, the spaghetti bowl phenomenon will not disappear as long as current FTAs continue to exist. The only way to escape this problem is to eliminate MFN tariffs, at least on all manufactured products.

Because of the proliferation of FTAs, region-wide cooperation, in particular in the EAS process which covers the widest area, is necessary to manage the proliferating FTAs in the region. In addition, region-wide cooperation is essential to facilitate trade and investment. So far, ASEAN has taken the lead in regional cooperation with its blueprint to establish the ASEAN Economic Community (AEC), which will be composed of a single market and production base with progressive and equitable development measures to provide more equal benefits to the countries and provinces. The ASEAN+3 process and the EAS (ASEAN+6) process are progressing concurrently. The ASEAN-related ministerial and summit meetings are held frequently, contributing to the promotion of the AEC and the facilitation of trade and investment in East Asia.

REFERENCES

Ando, Mitsuyo and Fukunari Kimura (2003), 'The formation of international production and distribution networks in East Asia', National Bureau of Economic Research, Working Paper 10167.

ASEAN Secretary (2007a), Chairman's Statement of the 13th ASEAN Summit, 'One ASEAN at the Heart of Dynamic Asia', Singapore, 20 November (http://www.aseansec.org/21093.htm, 10 January 2009).

ASEAN Secretary (2007b), ASEAN Economic Community Blueprint (http://www.aseansec.org/21083.pdf, 10 January 2009).

Baldwin, Richard (2008), 'The East Asian noodle bowl syndrome', in Hiratsuka and Kimura (eds), *East Asia's Economic Integration: Progress and Benefit*, London: Palgrave Macmillan.

Board of Investment, Thailand (BOI) (2008), 'Thailand's trade liberalization with South Korea under the ASEAN–Korea Free Trade Agreement Framework', press release, 4 November (http://www.boi.go.th/japanese/how/press_releases_detail.asp?id=2962, 10 January 2009).

Chia, Siou Yue (2008), 'Singapore case study on FTA impact on business', ADB Research Workshop Bangkok, 31 January.

Dee, Philippa (2005), 'A competition of barriers in services trade', mimeo, prepared for the World Bank.

Freudenberg, Michael and Thierry Paulmier (2006), 'A comparison of *de jure* economic integration in East Asia: is East Asia discriminating against itself?', in Hiratsuka (ed.), *East Asia's De Facto Economic Integration*, London: Palgrave Macmillan.

Harrigan, Frank, William James, Michael Plummer and Fan Zhai (2006),

'Bilateralism or regionalism: alternative scenarios for Asian trade liberalization', Paper presented at the conference Shaping the Future: Prospects for Asia's Long-term Development Over the Next Two Decades, ADB Resident Mission, Bangkok, December.

Hiratsuka, Daisuke, Ikumo Isono, Hitoshi Sato and So Umezaki (2008), 'Escaping from FTA trap and spaghetti bowl problem in East Asia: an insight from the enterprise survey in Japan', in ERIA (ed.), *Deepening Economic Integration*, IDE-JETRO: Japan.

JETRO (2008a), '2007 survey of Japanese-affiliated firms in ASEAN and India', Overseas Research Department.

JETRO (2008b), 'White Paper on International Trade and Foreign Direct Investment, JETRO, Overseas Research Department.

Kawai, Masahiro and Ganeshan Wignaraja (2007), 'ASEAN+3 or ASEAN+6: which way forward?', ADBI, Discussion Paper No. 77, Tokyo: ADBI.

Kuroiwa, Ikuo (2008), 'Rules of origin, local content and cumulative local content in East Asia: application of an international input–output analysis', in Hiratsuka and Kimura (eds), *East Asia's Economic Integration: Progress and Benefit*, London: Palgrave Macmillan.

MOFA (Ministry of Foreign Affairs of Japan) (2008), 'Notification of the entry into force of the Japan–ASEAN comprehensive economic partnership agreement by Brunei', (http://www.mofa.go.jp/announce/announce/2008/12/1185514_1080.html. 10 January 2009)

NZIER (2008), 'Service liberalization in East Asia: business, postal/courier, and maritime services', ERIA JRP Series.

Plummer, Michael G. (2007), 'Best practices in regional trading arrangements: an application to Asia', *World Economy*, **30**(12), 1771–96.

13. Economic integration and the expansion of trade and transport networks

Ikumo Isono

13.1 INTRODUCTION

Freight transport in East Asia has been developing extremely rapidly in recent decades. This is the result of a great expansion in demand for international trade. Transport networks, which have a variety of routes, modes, speed and quality, have evolved to offer faster, more extensive and more accurate services to meet industry needs. At the same time, manufacturing firms have been changing their behavior regarding the utilization of transport networks. Trade volume has grown dramatically as markets have become integrated and production bases have dispersed to several countries according to the different products and production processes.

On the other hand, there are several unsolved bottlenecks remaining in East Asia, where there are great differences in the level of transport development as well as in the level of economic development. To find the remaining bottlenecks, it is necessary to determine what factors affect transport costs and trade patterns. Thus, this chapter discusses how transport networks have been improved, what factors affect transport costs and trade patterns, and what issues and bottlenecks remain unsolved, especially in East Asia.

Figure 13.1 shows the basic framework for transport networks, transport costs and other factors in this chapter. We describe transport networks as the all-shipping routes and modes available, or the total reticulated 'trails' in a figurative sense. Moving goods leaves trails in roads, railroads, sea and air, like animal trails. Manufacturing and logistics firms utilize preferable routes many times, so that certain routes become beaten and more usable.[1] Manufacturing and logistics firms also seek new routes. As a result, self-organized reticulated trails or transport networks in the region are being deepened on particular routes, thickened in existing areas, and expanded into surrounding regions.

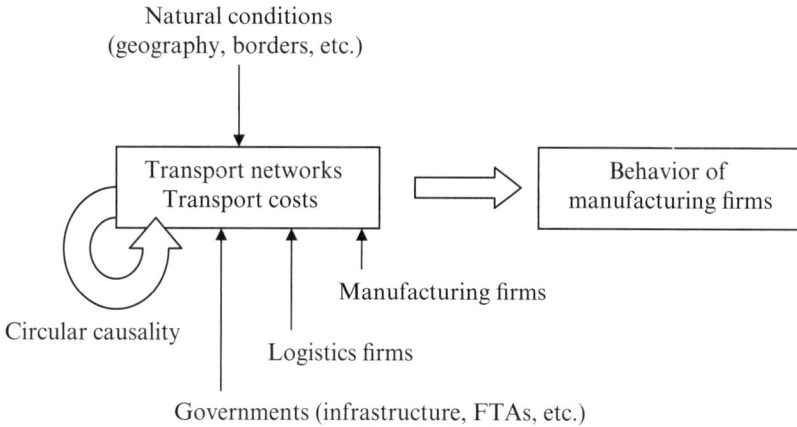

Source: IDE-GSM team.

Figure 13.1   Basic framework for transport networks/costs and other factors

Transport networks are affected by the following factors. First, natural barriers or impediments such as distance, seas, mountains and rivers define the basic conditions of transport networks. National borders may also be considered as natural conditions, as discussed in more detail below. We define transport costs as 'broadly defined' transport costs. Broadly defined transport costs include not only transport costs in a restricted sense, such as loading, carrying, collecting, storing, transshipping, unloading, sorting, distributing and delivering, but also the costs for the movement of people and information, tariffs and non-tariff barriers, language and cultural differences and other costs related to selling to different places.

Governments, logistics firms and manufacturing firms have been attempting to overcome natural conditions and impediments and decrease broadly defined transport costs. Governments in East Asian countries have been improving their trunk roads, international ports and airports. They have also been promoting Free Trade Zones (FTZ) or Export Processing Zones (EPZ) and inviting multinational firms. Preferential trade arrangements and FTAs have proliferated. Customs procedures have been improved in individual countries and within bilateral and multilateral frameworks.

Logistics firms have also had important roles in eliminating impediments. They have handled international intermodal freight transport, and they have made international Just-in-Time (JIT) operations available in developed countries and more advanced developing countries such as Japan, Korea, China, Singapore, Malaysia and Thailand. They have pursued high-volume carrying and storing to reduce unit costs, whereas they have also pursued small lot shipments such as Less-Than-Truckload (LTL) and Less-Than-Container Load (LCL) to meet their customers' needs and to differentiate themselves from other logistics firms.

Manufacturing firms have been pursuing the reduction of transport costs through optimal production, distribution, and location choice of factories. They have not only been saving on transport costs, but optimizing expenses for transport costs. Moreover, as Fujita and Mori (2005) have noted in their article on the new economic geography, the existence of scale economies in transport services yields a kind of circular causality. If larger and more frequent services are offered on a transport link, shippers are attracted. Increasing numbers of shippers also attract services providers, because the demand for shipping increases. It is said that this kind of circular causality leads to evolutionary change in transport networks.

This chapter is organized as follows. In Section 13.2, we outline the performance of transport networks in East Asia. In Section 13.3, we summarize several factors influencing transport costs and factors influencing changes in transport costs. In Section 13.4, we review new trends in logistics in East Asia. We also discuss unresolved issues. Finally, we conclude with Section 13.5.

13.2 RAPID EXPANSION OF TRADE AND TRANSPORT NETWORKS IN EAST ASIA

Transport networks in East Asia have been developing extremely rapidly in recent decades. This has resulted from the great expansion of demand for international trade. In other words, the development of transport networks as well as lowering tariffs enabled the great expansion of international trade in East Asia (see Chapter 1). First of all, we can see a rapid increase in interregional and intraregional trade. One of the most prominent actors is China, whose imports and exports have significantly increased. In 1995, China imported 22 billion dollars worth of goods from Japan, 9 billion dollars from ASEAN countries, 9 billion dollars from Korea, and 0.4 billion dollars from Taiwan.[2] In 2005, these figures had increased by 265%, 675%, 664% and 10729%, respectively, compared to 1995. From 1995 to 2005, China's exports increased from 28 billion dollars to 84 billion dollars worth of goods to Japan, from 10 billion dollars to 55 billion dollars to ASEAN, from 7 billion dollars to 35 billion dollars to Korea and from 3 billion dollars to 18 billion dollars to Taiwan.

The trade in intermediate parts and components is one of the main factors in the rapid increase in intraregional trade. We saw explosive growth in the trade of intermediate parts and components in China and ASEAN countries, as Ozeki (2008) clearly pointed out. We found that China and ASEAN countries imported large amounts of intermediate parts and components, and exported large amounts of final goods to the world. In 2005, the share of parts and components in imports to China from Japan and Korea was more than 30%, and more than 40% from ASEAN. The share of parts and components in ASEAN imports was more than 30% from China and the EU15, and more than 40% from Japan, Korea and NAFTA. However, the shares of parts and components in imports to NAFTA, the EU and Japan were relatively low. That to NAFTA was less than 20% from China and the EU15, and less than 30% from Japan, Korea, and ASEAN. That to the EU was less than 20% from China and less than 30% from Japan, Korea, ASEAN, and NAFTA. That to Japan was also relatively low.

East Asia's reliance on ocean freight transport has been increasing faster than trade. This is because Chinese and Southeast Asian ports handle relatively cheap, heavy and bulky goods and the products are transshipped at the hub ports. In 2005, Singapore, Hong Kong, Shanghai, Shenzhen, Busan and Kaohsiung are the top six container handling ports in the world. In fact, about 60% of sea freight containers in the world departed from or arrived at East Asian ports in 2004. From 1980 to 2005, container traffic handled in Singapore, Hong Kong, Shanghai, Busan and Kaohsiung increased by 2,430%, 1,430%, 36,800%, 1,770% and 870%, respectively (American Association of Port Authorities). About 80% of loadings in Singapore were transshipped in 2003 (Shibasaki et al. 2005).

Meanwhile, Japanese ports have been losing importance in recent decades. From 1980 to 2005, container traffic handled in Kobe, Yokohama and Tokyo increased by 50%, 300% and 500%, respectively. During this period, they have fallen from 4th to 32nd, from 12th to 27th and from 18th to 21st, respectively, in the rankings of global container handlers. There were three main reasons for this. First, Japanese ports had relatively smaller container terminals (Table 13.1). Second, higher costs and longer times were involved in freight handling. Costs to handle one 40-foot container in Tokyo port were about 55% higher than in Busan and Kaohsiung ports. Third, the industrial structure of the Japanese economy has been changing to small-lot, high value-added and time-conscious products. In Japan, almost 50% of the money value of exports was carried by air in 2004 (Japan customs).

We can find an agglomeration of freight handling in a small number of ports (Figure 13.2). Singapore, Hong Kong, and Shanghai have become the transport hubs of the region. They enjoy large-scale economies in

Table 13.1   Scale of container terminals

	Minami Honmoku (Yokohama)	Pasir Panjang (Singapore)	HIT (Hong Kong)	Shinsundae (Busan)
Container yard area (ha)	35	84	77	104
Berth length (m)	700	2145	3300	1200
Gantry crane (units)	5	24	32	11

Source: Compiled by the author using data from the Ministry of Land, Infrastructure, Transport and Tourism, Japan.

freight transport. Hong Kong and Shanghai have developed to fill an increasing transport demand in China. Singapore became a key junction of transshipment between large mother ships and small feeder ships using the Strait of Malacca. Furthermore, they have future development plans. The first phase of the development of Yangshan deep-water port in Shanghai was completed with five berths in 2005, handling 3.1 million TEU in the first year. In contrast to the other existing ports in Shanghai, Yangshan could host world-class size vessels because it was in a small island off the coast of Shanghai. After the completion of the entire project with the expansion of the island in 2020, Yangshan deep-water port will have 60 berths with capacity of 25 million TEUs along a 22-kilometer waterfront (Yang and Lionel 2006).

We also find dispersion within agglomeration, as in Chapters 2 and 3. From 1996 to 2005, container traffic handled in Shenzhen increased 2,650%. Hong Kong and Shenzhen ports are seeking ways to differentiate from each other. The port of Tanjun Pelapas in Johor, Malaysia became one of the top 20 container handling ports in the world, though it handled only 0.02 million TEUs in 1999. It has taken over a portion of Singapore's freight handling. More than 95% of containers handled in the port of Tanjun Pelapas in 2003 were only for transshipment purposes (Shibasaki et al. 2005).

Air cargo volume in airports in East Asia has also been increasing in importance. The global share of air freight tons within Asia increased from 16% in 1994 to 21% in 2003 (Kimura et al. 2007). In 2005, five airports were in the top ten cargo handling airports in the world. Hong Kong, Seoul, Shanghai and Singapore in addition to Tokyo became important hubs in air cargo transport (Figure 13.3).

On the other hand, there are several unsolved bottlenecks remaining in East Asia. There are great differences in the level of transport networks as well as time required to export and import. The World Bank (2007)

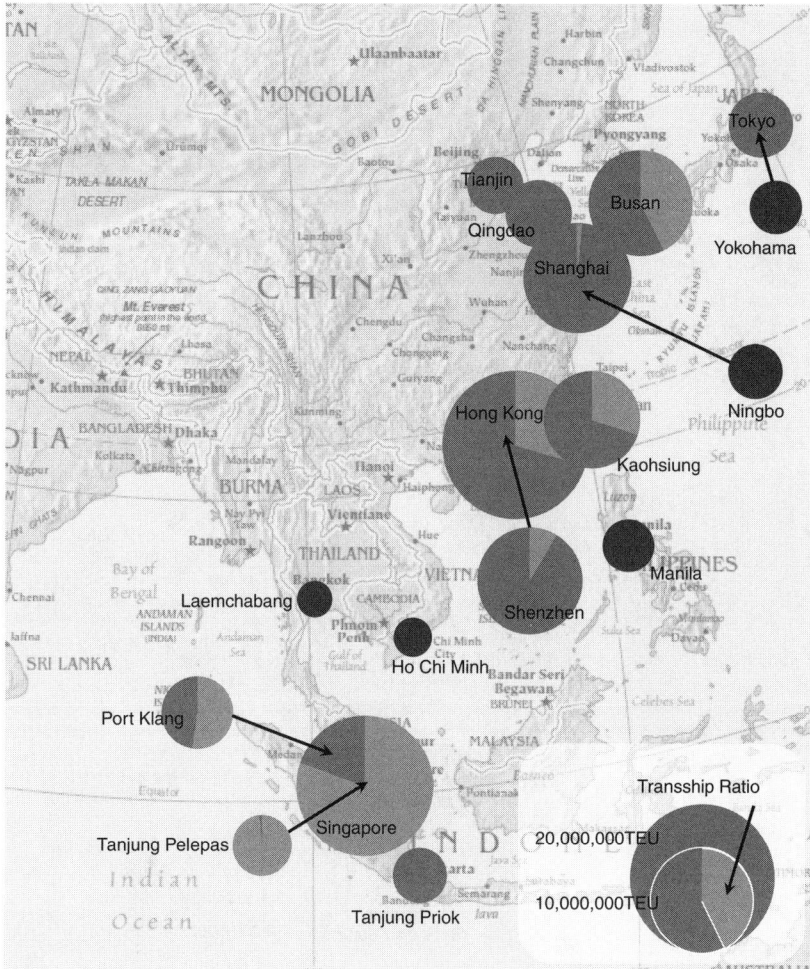

Source: Compiled by the author from Shibasaki et al. (2005). The map was obtained from the World Factbook.

Figure 13.2   *Ports by container traffic in East Asia (2003)*

has developed the Logistics Performance Index, which includes the level of customs, infrastructure, international shipments, logistics competence, tracking, domestic logistics costs and timeliness. Of 150 countries in the world, Singapore took first place while Laos ranked 117th and Myanmar was 147th in logistics performance (Figure 13.4). It took 50 days[3] to both export and import to Vientiane, Laos[4] while it takes only a few days in

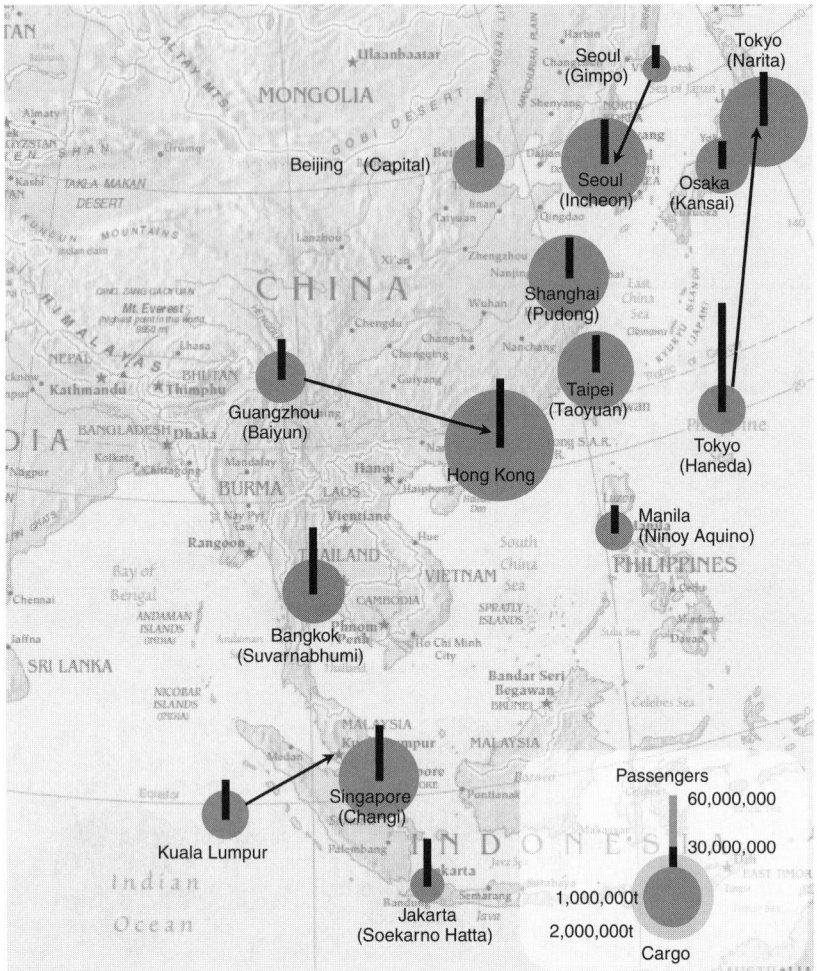

Source: Compiled by the author using data from the Airports Council International. The map was obtained from the World Factbook.

Figure 13.3   Airports by cargo volume and passengers (2005)

Singapore (Figure 13.5 and 13.6). Great differences exist especially in documentation time.

For Laos, the days to export includes procedures from packing the goods at the factory in Vientiane to departure from Laemchabang port in Thailand. Therefore, being a landlocked country, Laos has inherent disadvantages for trade.

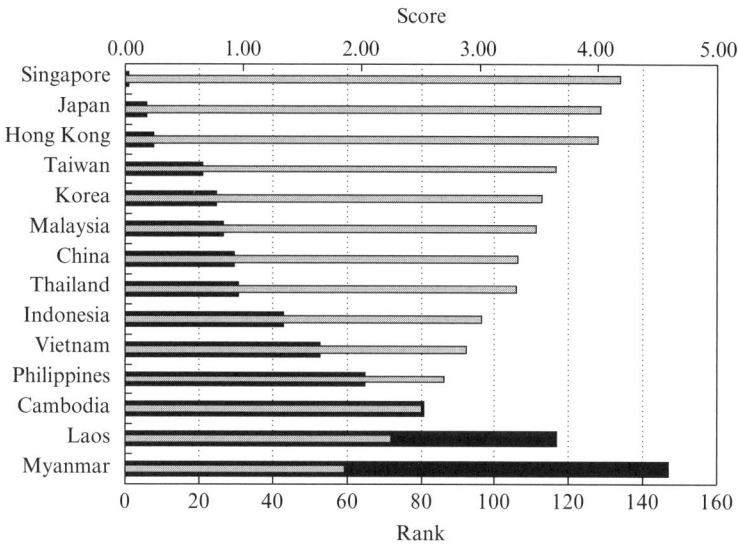

Source: Compiled by the author from World Bank (2007).

Figure 13.4 Scores and ranks of the logistics performance index

13.3 FACTORS INFLUENCING TRANSPORT COSTS

We have seen that trade and transport networks in East Asia have been developing in parallel and extremely rapidly in recent decades. We also noticed that transport networks in East Asia leave much room for improvement. To find the remaining bottlenecks, it is necessary to determine what factors affect transport costs and trade patterns. Now, we review the factors and characteristic estimation results as well as anecdotal material in the literature.

We define transport costs as 'broadly defined' transport costs. In addition to prices, manufacturing firms and logistics firms also consider time, frequency, accuracy and reliability. Considering these factors, manufacturing firms and logistics firms pursue cost-reduction, quick delivery, and minimization of stock-out risk. The broadly defined transport costs include not only transport costs in a restricted sense, such as loading, carrying, collecting, storing, transshipping, unloading, sorting, distributing and delivering, but also the costs for the movement of people and information, tariffs and non-tariff barriers, language and cultural differences and other costs related to selling to different places.

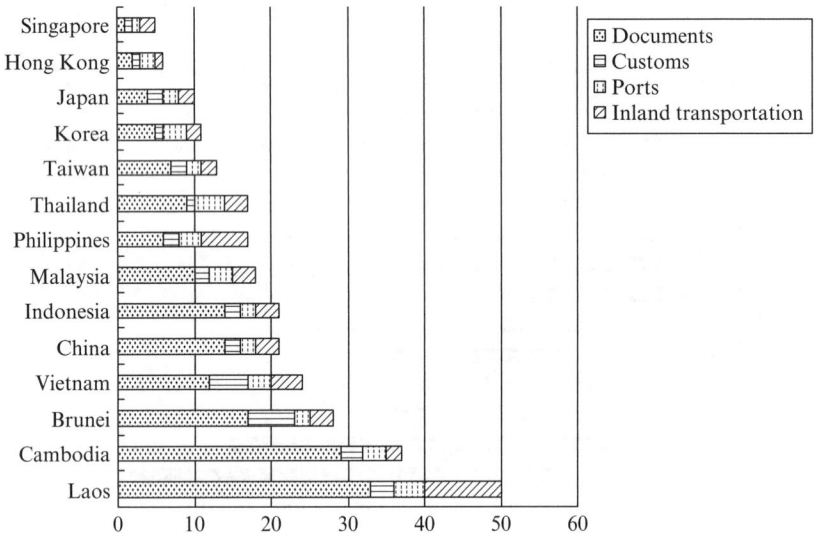

Legend:
- ⊠ Documents
- ⊟ Customs
- ▢ Ports
- ▨ Inland transportation

Source: Compiled by the author from www.doingbusiness.org (accessed on 3 December 2007).

Figure 13.5   Time to export (days)

Anderson and van Wincoop (2004) estimated that tax equivalent trade costs between two developed countries amount to 170% of the product price. This can be broken down into 21% for transport costs, 44% for national border costs and 55% for the domestic distribution costs of retail and wholesale (1.21 * 1.44 * 1.55 − 1=1.7). The 44% for national border costs can be roughly divided into 8% for policy barriers, 7% for language barriers, 14% for currency barriers, 6% for information cost barriers, and 3% for security barriers.

Decreasing broadly defined transport costs increases trade volume. Baier and Bergstrand (2001) claimed that 67% of the growth of world trade was attributed to income growth, 25% to decreasing tariffs and 8% to decreasing transport costs.

13.3.1   Shipping Expenses

First of all, transport costs are incurred basically as shipping expenses. The prices for freight transport services are decided by logistics firms or by negotiation between manufacturing firms and logistics firms. The prices vary according to several factors and the situation at the time. The level of

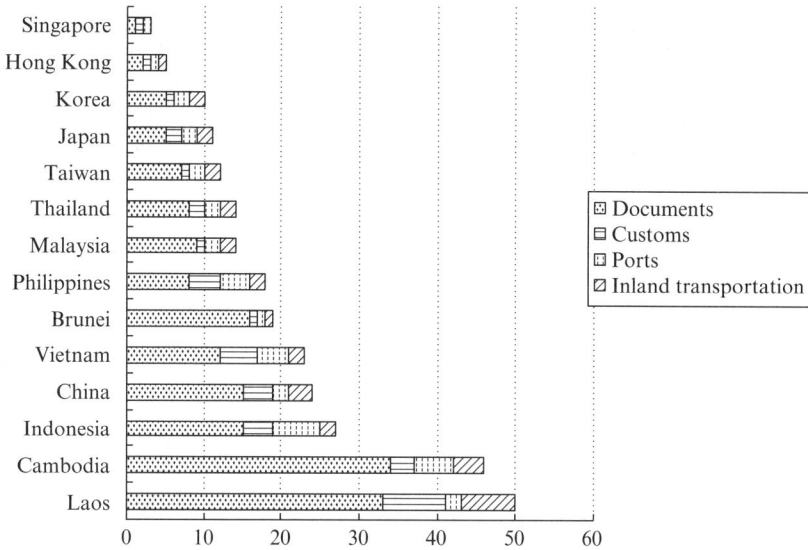

Source: Compiled by the author from www.doingbusiness.org (accessed on 3 December 2007).

Figure 13.6   Time to import (days)

transport costs depends on whether there are appropriate routes, ports, or airports. Manufacturing firms pay service fees to logistics firms, while logistics firms also pay service fees to expressway operators, air carriers, terminal operators, and maritime companies. They also bear fuel costs, labor costs, maintenance costs for trucks, and so on. Hummels (2006) has pointed out that trade has become lighter and less transport sensitive per dollar shipped.

13.3.2   Distance Still Matters

Distance is the basic factor in transport costs. Transport costs increase with distance. Hummels (1999, 2006) revealed that overall freight costs associated with increased distance have declined. He devised an index to show that ocean freight rates measured in terms of quantity or value shipped have increased. Air rates have declined and the transport costs for longer routes have declined rapidly. When we compared a longer route (9,000 km) and a shorter route (1,000 km) for ocean-shipped goods, the longer route was 59% more expensive than the shorter route in 1974, but the difference declined to 32% in 1998. For shipments by air, the longer route was 200% more than the shorter route in 1974, but only 68% more expensive in 1998.

Although transport costs have declined, distance still matters. Disdier and Head (2008) showed an interesting result using 1,467 distance effects estimated in 103 papers. On average, a 10% increase in distance decreases bilateral trade by about 9%. They also showed that distance effects decreased slightly in the first half of the 20th century and then rose after the 1950s.

13.3.3   Borders

It is said that national borders increase transport costs and thus reduce trade. McCallum (1995) claimed that trade volumes between Canadian provinces are 20 times higher than between a province in Canada and a state in the United States by using gravity equations. Anderson and van Wincoop (2003) threw doubt on McCallum's claim and estimated that borders reduced trade between developed countries by about 20–50%. Overman et al. (2003), Redding and Venables (2004), and Behrens et al. (2008) also estimated border costs based on the theory of new economic geography. Behrens et al. (2008) measured border effects and divided them into pure border effects, relative and absolute wage effects, and selection effects.

13.3.4   Time

The time cost itself is one type of transport cost. Delivery time, quality, congestion and capacity of infrastructure are crucial for firms. Firms also take procedure time into account, including not only from loading to unloading, but also documentation before actual shipment. For instance, current FTAs require a certificate of origin. If firms need to change purchasing sources at short notice, the time needed to obtain a new certificate of origin will place a burden on firms. We may consider language or other cultural costs to be types of time costs, because it takes time for firms to adjust their products to the market.

Hummels (2001) revealed that each day saved in shipping time is worth 0.8% *ad valorem* per day of the value of the manufactured goods. That is, an average length ocean voyage of 20 days is equivalent to a 16% tariff. Djankov et al. (2008) argued that each additional day that a product is delayed reduces trade by more than 1% and it is equivalent on average to a distance of about 70 km. Evans and Harrigan (2005) found that growth for time-sensitive apparel products in the USA was much faster from proximate countries such as Mexico than from East Asia and South Asia.

On the other hand, landlocked countries have a disadvantage. Limao and Venables (2001) found that median landlocked countries have transport costs that are about 50% higher and about 70% lower trade volumes than median coastal countries. Radelet and Sachs (1998) also claimed that landlocked countries face great cost disadvantages.

13.3.5 Density and Hubs

Volume and frequency may change transport costs. Due to the existence of scale economies, shipping larger volumes at one time, storing in one place, and introducing the same system at different places will decrease unit transport costs. We note that there are economies of density when unit transport costs are declining as demand or users for a means of transport increase. Mori and Nishikimi (2002) reported that the transport cost per container decreases by 0.31% given a 1% increase in ship size in maritime transportation. Hummels (1999) stated that containerization would lead to transport savings of as much as 50–60% relative to conventional cargo ships. World-class size cargo ships are designed to reach the maximum size that will enable them to pass through the Suez Canal (Suezmax), or Panama Canal (Panamax).

Caves et al. (1984) and Brueckner and Spiller (1994) stated that the cost differences between trunk and local routes in airline services mainly depends on differences in density. Hendricks et al. (1997) claimed that deregulation in the airline industry and economies of density can explain the emergence of hub and spoke networks.[5] Braeutigam et al. (1984) discussed economies of density for the railroad industry and found that a 1% increase in effective track miles contributes to a 0.277% decrease in variable costs. Takahashi (2006) succeeded in incorporating economies of density in the transport sector into the model endogenously.

Scale economies at nodes also play a large role, because loading, unloading and reshipping many times and storing large amounts in one place reduces unit costs. Hub ports and highly developed container terminals around ports also reduce transport costs. Mori and Nishikimi (2002) cited the transport costs from Japan to a non-hub port as being 22.6% higher than to a hub port in Southeast Asia. Krugman (1993) and Fujita and Mori (1996) explained that a region with a transport hub attracts firms and consumers due to its better access.[6]

Establishing industrial estates is also a useful way to pursue scale economies in electricity, water supply, gas, and high quality roads. Industrial estates are also useful to logistics firms. A high-frequency shipment service will decrease unit transport costs. High-frequency service also contributes to reducing inventory costs and the efficiency of JIT operations.

13.3.6 Competition and Efficiency

The existence of sound price competition among logistics firms will decrease transport costs. Hummels et al. (2007) argued that if shipping firms face fewer competitors shipping prices will increase significantly. Exporters with two shippers in Latin America incur 22–23% higher shipping rates than exporters with eight shippers. A 1% tariff increase results in a 1–2% increase in transport costs due to a loosening of price competition.

High efficiency in ports and airports decreases transport costs. Micco and Serebrisky (2004) estimated that in air transport an improvement in airport infrastructure from the 25th to 75th percentiles reduces transport costs by 15%. Clark et al. (2004) found that improvement of port efficiency from the 25th to the 75th percentile reduces shipping costs by 12%. De (2007) found that poor infrastructure as well as tariffs and distance will increase trade costs in East Asia. Improvement of infrastructure by 10% in both export and import countries will contribute to an increase in imports of 5.9% in import countries and exports of 1.5% in export countries.

Reliability and alternatives are significant for logistics services. Time accuracy is rapidly gaining significance. If a truck runs on low-quality roads, its speed diminishes, delivery time will become uncertain, or goods may be damaged. Security issues within a region, within a country or within an industry may greatly increase transport costs. All Indonesian airlines, including Garuda Indonesia, were banned from flying to EU airports in 2008 because it was thought that they had safety concerns.

13.3.7 Product-specific Factors and Business Relationships

The characteristics of products may influence transport costs. The shape and weight of products have an effect on the usage of modes of transport and thus transport costs. Leinbach and Bowen (2004) have estimated that the mean period of time from order to delivery is 17.1 days for manufacturing firms that always use air transport and 46.6 days for firms that use air transport only in emergencies. Chen (2004) found that technical barriers and product-specific information costs raise border effects.

Ability to manage divided or fragmented production processes depends on several factors. It includes product-specific factors, geographical and business relationships among processes, and efficiencies of firms. Thus the design of production processes also influences transport costs (see Kimura and Ando 2005 and Chapter 4).

13.4 KEY ISSUES AND NEW TRENDS IN TRANSPORT NETWORKS

In this section we will look at key issues and new trends in transport networks in East Asia. First, further development is required in the more advanced developing countries to meet the needs of firms that are optimizing expenses for transport costs and utilizing their production networks. Second, we discuss recent infrastructure development in the Indochina Peninsula. Third, we review the issues of back-hauling and other remaining issues.

13.4.1 Further Development of Transport Networks

In East Asia, the development of transport networks has benefited manufacturing firms in their search to expand production networks. However, further development is required in the more advanced developing countries such as Singapore, Malaysia, Thailand and China to meet the needs of firms that are optimizing expenses for transport costs and utilizing their production networks. Now, we look at two contrasting anecdotes concerning how transport networks and production networks are interrelated.

The first example is the case of a hard disk drive assembler in Thailand. In the hard disk drive industry, merger and exit have been occurring in succession and only a few companies have survived either as assemblers or parts makers. This is because the hard disk drive industry requires high technology and large economies of scale. In 2005, almost all hard disk drives were assembled in China and Southeast Asia.

One hard disk drive assembler in Thailand has adopted the 'multiple supplier procurement system' (Hiratsuka 2006). That is, it procures the same parts from different suppliers in different countries. For example, it procures disk media from Malaysia, Singapore, Japan and the USA. Trade from the USA is intra-firm trade, but the remainder is inter-firm trade. The firm procures heads from China, the USA and Mexico. In the case of heads, the trade from the USA and China is intra-firm trade. There are four main reasons for adopting a multiple supplier procurement system. First, the firm can utilize zero-tariff trade and international JIT. Due to exemptions for intermediate products and ITA (Information Technology Agreement) schemes, the firm is not required to pay customs duties. All parts suppliers and the assembler adopt the same inventory management system that was developed by an international logistics company, and this logistics company delivers the parts for the assembler on an exclusive basis. Second, it is hoping to maintain its bargaining power *vis-à-vis* the parts makers. In the hard disk drive industry, parts makers also have relatively strong bargaining powers because few companies have survived even as parts makers, as we have stated. The assembler firm and another hard disk drive assembler in Thailand procure parts such as top clamps, disks, suspensions and spindle motors from the same parts makers. If the firm procures a component from one source, bargaining power will be reduced. Third, it can manage short-term variations in demand. By procuring from other parts makers when demand is high, excessive capacity in production is not required. Fourth, the firm wants to have parts and factories maintain their price-competitiveness by engaging in competition.

The shakeout of firms and the multiple supplier procurement system should contribute to growth in the demand for transport. Further, firms with a good transport network are likely to survive and firms with a poor transport network are more likely to exit. And thus, further development is required to meet demands of the firms.

The second example is the case of a PC distributor/assembler in Singapore. Its Singapore factory is a distribution base of PC parts as well as an assembling base for personal computers. One may think that assembling PCs in Singapore is strange, because assembling PCs is a relatively labor-intensive activity and labor costs in Singapore are too high to operate labor-intensive production processes. However the company has made this possible through a 'global pipeline distribution model.'

In 2006, the company had factories in Singapore, Hong Kong, Dubai, Los Angeles, Amsterdam and Miami. The Singapore factory was a five-minute car ride from Changi Airport. It procured PC parts in bulk when the price was low, and distributed them among the six logistics hubs to absorb short-term variations in demand, just as the flow of water in connected pipelines adjusts itself to the same level. This is the exact opposite of JIT operations.

The global pipeline distribution model was made possible partly because the firm has highly efficient distribution networks. Proportions of logistics costs and labor costs to total sales were only 0.15% and 0.35% for the company, while those for its competitors were on average 1.5% and 2%, respectively. The company was able to minimize the logistics costs by locating logistics hubs around the world, enjoying the low handling charges, high frequency and high efficiency of the hub airports, and utilizing its distribution networks.

Therefore, having highly efficient distribution networks can change the shape of production networks. Although it is a special case, the further development of transport networks will encourage the development of such kinds of highly differentiated innovative production networks.

13.4.2   Fostering the Utilization of FTAs

Lowering tariffs by FTAs is a way of decreasing broadly defined transport costs. However, in reality, the utilization of FTAs has not been so high. For example, we review the case of Japan. As of 2008, among the top ten trade partners of Japan, only Thailand has signed an FTA with Japan. There are several tariff exemption schemes, such as the benefits given by BOI (Board of Investment of Thailand) or the ITA scheme. Furthermore, FTAs request troublesome Rules of Origin (ROO) (see Chapter 11), and might not be worth the expense since all the documents have to be prepared by the exporters, while the benefits of the FTAs will go to the importers.[7]

Utilization of FTAs was not so high even in the auto industry, especially among the auto parts makers, where it was said that tariffs in the auto industry were relatively high and so FTAs would be beneficial for the auto firms. Regarding the auto industry, Japanese auto assemblers and auto-parts makers made their products not only in Japan, but also in foreign countries. In the automobile industry, many auto-parts factories have already located near the final assemblers' factories. They have been pursuing local production in foreign countries and international specialization of products. If a part has a large trade volume, the firm will try to move the production process to local production. If a part has a small trade volume, the benefit of utilizing FTAs will diminish because it requires the tasks of preparing documentation. The firm will not utilize the FTA. In particular, it is difficult for small parts makers to even learn about FTAs, because they have to read all the provisions involved.

It is thought that the centralized procurement system will become a best practice. In the case of an automobile affiliate group in Thailand, the trading company in the group in Japan procures steel sheets and coils in bulk and exports to the same company in Thailand under the Japan–Thailand EPA (Economic Partnership Agreement). The trading company in Thailand sells sheets and coils to the key affiliate parts-makers. The amount is more than 80% of the total use of them for all the affiliate companies in Thailand. The system has two benefits. First, the benefit of FTAs will remain within the group because it is intra-firm trade within the affiliate trade company. Second, parts-makers need not be concerned with cumbersome international transactions. The trading company centralizes the procurements, documentation procedures, and risks management, including the foreign exchange risk. Centralizing procurements and documentation procedures will decrease the unit costs of utilizing FTAs, and so we can think of it as a sort of benefit of economies of density.

13.4.3   Reducing Border-related Costs in the Mekong Region

The development of infrastructure and reducing border-related costs are the key development policies in East Asia, especially in the Mekong region, because they will contribute to reducing economic gaps in the region. The road networks between Thailand, Laos, Cambodia and Vietnam have been less developed than those between Thailand, Malaysia and Singapore due to poor security and poor infrastructure. There are now signs that things may be changing. The second Mekong Bridge, linking Savannakhet and Mukdahan, was opened on 20 December 2006. There are plans to establish the first Special Economic Zone at Savannakhet. In 2006, Savannakhet received more FDI approvals than the sum of its FDI approvals from 1992 to 2005. Now a route for shipping goods 7,000 km from Shanghai to Singapore by road is coming into service.

We can find other national and international facilitations. In the Greater Mekong Subregion (GMS) program, there are several Cross-Border Transport Agreements (CBTA) that are being tested and implemented. These include single-stop/single-window customs inspection, cross-border movement of transport operators, exemptions from physical customs inspection, exchanges of commercial traffic rights, and infrastructure design standards. In the first phase, seven border points, at Mukdahan–Savannakhet, Lao Bao–Dansavanh, Aranyaprathet–Poipet, Bavet–Moc Bai, Hekou–Lao Cai, Myawaddy–Mae Sot and Mae Sai–Tachilek have been selected (see Chapter 14).

It is expected that the Bangkok–Hanoi surface route using the East–West Economic Corridor will become an alternative mode to the maritime transport route. JETRO (2008) conducted trial runs from Bangkok to Hanoi for surface, sea and air transport (Figure 13.7 and Table 13.2). Many logistics firms cooperated or exhibited an interest in the trial runs because they might benefit from the development of the surface transport route between Bangkok and Hanoi.

JETRO reported that it cost US$2,650 and required three nights/four days for the surface transport. The time did not include documentation time. This reflected the reality that the logistics firms brought forward the documentation before they actually transported the goods while the firms expected it would take some time to process the documents. Logistics firms also adjusted the departure time from Bangkok so that vehicles would reach Mukdahan during customs operating hours.

The time for surface transport in the trial run required four customs clearing events; that is, export customs clearance at Mukdahan, transit customs clearance at Savannakhet, another transit customs clearance at Dansavanh, and import customs clearance at Lao Bao. The time also

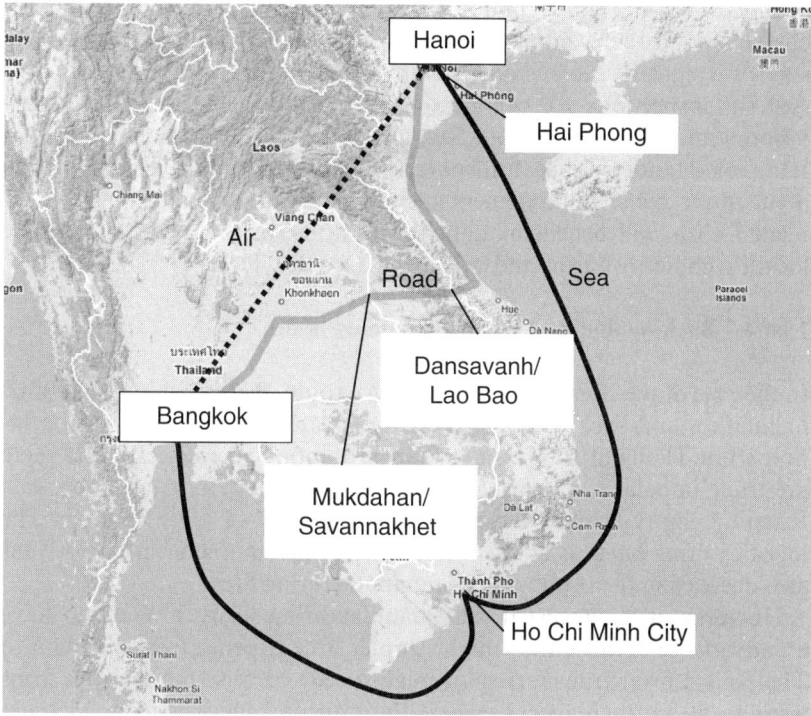

Source: Compiled by the author from the ASEAN Logistics Network Map 2008, JETRO. The map was obtained from Google™ Map.

Figure 13.7 Routes from Bangkok to Hanoi

Table 13.2 Time and expenses from Bangkok to Hanoi

	Time	Expense(US$)
Road	70 hours 48 minutes	2,650
Sea	212 hours 52 minutes	2,660 (40ft)
		1,740 (20ft)
Air	28 hours 16 minutes	46,750 (20ft)

Note: Waiting time at Mukdahan is assumed to be one hour for road transport.

Source: Compiled by the author from the ASEAN Logistics Network Map 2008, JETRO.

included 14 hours and 30 minutes waiting time at Dansavanh because the customs point there did not offer a 24-hour service and the truck had to stay overnight at the customs point. Because single-stop/single-window customs inspections are being tested at those borders and it took only 5 hours and 30 minutes from Savannakhet to Dansavanh, the time for Bangkok–Hanoi surface transport left room for improvement to two nights/three days. Improvement of infrastructure and reducing border-related costs will benefit manufacturing firms, or may even change the location choices of firms and consumers (see Box 13.1).

13.4.4   Back-hauling and Other Remaining Issues

In the case of the Bangkok–Hanoi surface route, there exist issues of trade imbalances and back-hauling. There are greater demands for transportation from Thailand to Vietnam than in the opposite direction. If there are trade imbalances, logistics firms have to run empty trucks one way. Running empty trucks decreases the profitability of logistics firms. The logistics firms have to charge higher rates to manufacturing firms, thus also decreasing the profitability of manufacturing firms.

However, it is suggested that manufacturing firms in Vietnam have an advantage because they might ship at little expense from Vietnam to Thailand. Lower transport rates might occur because the logistics firms want to fill up their trucks even if the transport charges from Vietnam to Thailand are reduced. A good solution was reported in the case of a logistics firm in Hanoi. It is also said that Vietnam has a large demand for intermediate parts and components from China, while there is a trade imbalance in land transport for manufactured goods between China and Vietnam. The logistics firm succeeded in starting up regular surface shipment services between Hanoi and South China, by contracting with Canon for shipment of finished Canon printers from Hanoi to South China.

Regular surface shipment services will provide manufacturing firms with alternative choices. If there are regular freight services and the firms' products are not so time-conscious, the firms can shift the loading to a time when freight fees are not expensive. This is because there are fluctuations in freight fees according to demand.

There are other problems in back-hauling. Table 13.3 shows the courier service costs from Vientiane and from Bangkok. The fee from Vientiane to Bangkok, the direction in which trade volume was lower, was higher than in the opposite direction although it was expected that logistics firms would reduce the transport charges from Vientiane to Bangkok. This situation arose because customers in Vientiane usually order delivery to

BOX 13.1 GEOGRAPHICAL SIMULATION MODEL

We have seen great developments in infrastructure in East Asia. We have also found that logistics firms and even manufacturing firms affect the level of transport costs. Lowering transport costs will benefit manufacturing firms, or may even change the location choices of firms and consumers. We will now investigate how transport networks contribute to economic growth and vitality in East Asia.

Kumagai et al. (2008) have been developing the IDE/ERIA Geographical Simulation Model (GSM). IDE/ERIA-GSM is a simulation model based on spatial economics (Krugman 1991, Fujita et al. 1999), which predicts the effects of economic integration in a region, especially with the development of transport infrastructure and reductions in border costs. Box Figure 13.1 shows the

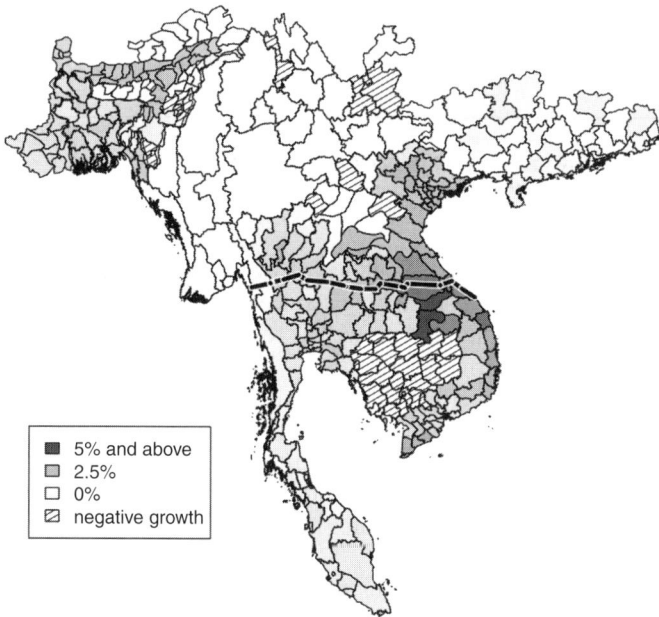

- ■ 5% and above
- ▨ 2.5%
- □ 0%
- ▨ negative growth

Source: Author.

Box Figure 13.1 Economic impacts of East–West economic corridor (2025) economic effects of the East–West Economic Corridor on GDP. In this figure, the economic effect for Savannakhet in Laos is 23%. It means that if we improve the East–West Economic Corridor and minimize related border costs along the corridor, the GDP of Savannakhet will become 23% higher than the baseline in 2025. We found that Malaysia, Bangkok, Hanoi and the Ho Chi Minh area also benefit. IDE/ERIA-GSM says that the development of transport infrastructure should be accompanied by making trade easier to conduct across borders, because these two changes have a multiplier effect.

Table 13.3   Courier service costs from Vientiane and from Bangkok (US$ for 10kg)

From	To	Vientiane	Bangkok	Singapore	Beijing	Tokyo	New York
Vientiane			113	141	182	223	288
Bangkok		65		43	65	65	78

Source: Compiled by the author from *Facts and Figures: Cost of Investing and Doing Business in ASEAN*, 2001 edition.

logistics firms in Vientiane, which have low handling volume and low efficiency. We need to foster matching services between manufacturing firms and international freight firms as well as to strengthen the competitiveness of domestic logistics firms.

There are several other issues that remain unsolved. First, the development of a Thailand–Myanmar route is proposed, but is difficult to realize. The Bangkok to Yangon surface route through the border takes less than three days. However, ocean-going ships have to travel around the Indochina Peninsula via Singapore, taking about one month for the trip (JETRO 2008).

Second, corruption in customs and other charges in surface transport have become recognized as a serious problem. Oraboune (2008) pointed out that firms are often asked to pay tolls under the table during surface transport. These costs account for a certain percentage of the total transport costs, but they are difficult to estimate or quantify, because the amounts depend on the particular officials in the transit process who ask for these charges.

Third, we have to consider safety issues. In Cambodia, Laos, Myanmar and Vietnam, large numbers of motorcycles, tractors, schoolchildren on bicycles and even cows run along and across the national trunk roads. These can cause delays in shipment and serious accidents.

13.5 CONCLUSIONS

Freight transport in East Asia has been developing extremely rapidly because of the great expansion of demand for international trade. About 60% of sea freight containers in the world departed from or arrived at East Asian ports in 2004. Logistics and manufacturing firms have been attempting to overcome natural impediments and utilize preferred routes. The logistics firms have made the best use of economies of density to reduce unit costs, but they have also pursued small lot shipping to meet their customers' needs and differentiate themselves from other logistics firms. The manufacturing firms have been optimizing expenses for transport costs, given their circumstances. The governments have been developing infrastructure, making customs procedures easier and lowering tariffs to support logistics and manufacturing firms.

We emphasized the importance of several factors influencing transport costs, especially the importance of economies of density. Due to the existence of scale economies, shipping larger volumes at one time, storing in one place, and introducing the same system at different locations helps to decrease unit transport costs. Economies of density foster hub and spoke networks in air and maritime transport. Tanjun Pelapas, in which more than 95% of loadings are trans-shipped, is a fine example.

We also found that there are great differences in the level of transport development, and several issues remain. Among the 150 countries in the world in the Logistics Performance Index, Singapore took first place while Laos ranked 117th and Myanmar was 147th. Courier service costs from Vientiane to Bangkok are higher than those from Bangkok to New York. Transport networks in East Asia leave much room for improvement. In East Asia, we have no customs union, quarantine standards or liberalization in the movement of people, like the Schengen Agreement in EU, so there is still a need for border crossing procedures such as customs, immigration and quarantine, even for intra-regional transactions. Lowering economic gaps through infrastructure projects and trade facilitations will benefit not only newcomer countries like Cambodia, Laos and Myanmar, but also manufacturing firms, logistics firms, and thus all people in countries in East Asia.

NOTES

1. In this chapter, we redefine it as the economies of density.
2. Data were obtained from the World Trade Matrix, JETRO. This was based on export data or FOB value.
3. The World Bank report compiled all requirements for exporting and importing a standardized cargo of goods by ocean transport, including all documents required. For the export of goods, it includes procedures from packing the goods at the factory in the country's most populated city to departure from the port. For the import of goods, it includes procedures from the arrival of a ship at the port to the delivery at the factory warehouse.
4. In reality, the days to export and import were totally different between companies. In the case of the border between Vientiane, Laos and Nong Khai, Thailand, in our interviews, one firm answered that it took less than four hours to cross the border. Another firm replied that it took more than 50 days to cross the same border. Firms like the former one have succeeded in crossing the border many times, brought forward the documentation before they actually transported and even devised ways of loading a container for ease of inspection.
5. Barla (1999) explained that if airline companies face demand uncertainty, they may choose hub and spoke type networks.
6. Ago et al. (2006) showed disadvantages of the hub due to fierce price competition by using the model of Ottaviano et al. (2002).
7. The exporters may obtain some benefits from FTAs thanks to increased demand.

REFERENCES

Ago, Takanori, Ikumo Isono and Takatoshi Tabuchi (2006), 'Locational disadvantage of the hub', *Annals of Regional Science*, **40**(4), 819–48.

Anderson, James E. and Eric van Wincoop (2003), 'Gravity with gravitas: a solution to the border puzzle', *American Economic Review*, **93**(1).

Anderson, James E. and Eric van Wincoop (2004), 'Trade costs', *Journal of Economic Literature*, **42**(3), 691–751.

Baier, Scott L. and Jeffrey H. Bergstrand (2001), 'The growth of world trade: tariffs, transport costs, and income similarity', *Journal of International Economics*, **53**, 1–27.

Barla, Philippe (1999), 'Demand uncertainty and airline network morphology with strategic interactions', Cahiers de recherche 9907, Université Laval – Département d'économie.

Behrens, Kristian, Giordano Mion, Yasusada Murata and Jens Suedekum (2008), 'Trade, wages, and productivity', IZA Discussion Paper No. 3682.

Braeutigam, Ronald, R. Andrew, F. Daughety and Mark A. Turnquist (1984), 'A firm specific analysis of economies of density in the US railroad industry', *Journal of Industrial Economics*, **33**(1), 3–20.

Brueckner, Jan K. and Pablo T. Spiller (1994), 'Economies of traffic density in the deregulated airline industry', *Journal of Law and Economics*, **37**(2), 379–415.

Caves, Douglas W., Laurits R. Christensen and Michael W. Tretheway (1984), 'Economies of density versus economies of scale: why trunk and local service airline costs differ', *RAND Journal of Economics*, **15**, 471–89.

Chen, Natalie (2004), 'Intra-national versus international trade in the European Union: why do national borders matter?', *Journal of International Economics*, **63**, 93–118.

Clark, Ximena, David Dollar and Alejandro Micco (2004), 'Port efficiency, maritime transport costs, and bilateral trade', *Journal of Development Economics*, **75**(2), 417–50.

De, Prabir (2007), 'Impact of trade costs on trade: empirical evidence from Asian countries', in *Trade Facilitation Beyond the Multilateral Trade Negotiations: Regional Practices, Customs Valuation and other Emerging Issues*, UNESCAP.

Disdier, Anne-Célia and Keith Head (2008), 'The puzzling persistence of the distance effect on bilateral trade', *Review of Economics and Statistics*, **90**(1), 37–48.

Djankov, Simeon, Caroline Freund and Cong S. Pham (2008), 'Trading on time', forthcoming in *Review of Economics and Statistics*.

Evans, Carolyn and James Harrigan (2005), 'Distance, time, and specialization: lean retailing in general equilibrium', *American Economic Review*, **95**(1), 292–313.

Fujita, Masahisa and Tomoya Mori (1996), 'The role of ports in the making of major cities: self-agglomeration and hub-effect', *Journal of Development Economics*, **49**, 93–120.

Fujita, Masahisa and Tomoya Mori (2005), 'Frontiers of the new economic geography', *Papers in Regional Science*, **84**(3), 377–405.

Fujita, Masahisa, Paul Krugman and Anthony J. Venables (1999), *The Spatial Economy: Cities, Regions, and International Trade*, Cambridge, MA: MIT Press.

Hendricks, Ken, Michele Piccione and Guofu Tan (1997), 'Entry and exit in hub-spoke networks', *RAND Journal of Economics*, **28**(2), 291–303.

Hiratsuka, Daisuke (2006), 'Vertical intra-regional production networks in East Asia: a case study of the hard drive industry', in Daisuke Hiratsuka (ed.), *East Asia's De Facto Economic Integration*, Palgrave Macmillan.

Hummels, David (1999), 'Have international transportation costs declined?', University of Chicago, mimeo.

Hummels, David (2001), 'Time as a trade barrier', GTAP Working Paper No. 18.

Hummels, David (2006), 'Transportation costs and trade over time', in *Transport and International Trade*, ECMT Round Tables No. 130, OECD.

Hummels, David, Volodymyr Lugovskyy and Alexandre Skiba (2007), 'The trade reducing effects of market power in international shipping', NBER Working Paper No. 12914.

JETRO (2008), *ASEAN Logistics Network Map 2008*, JETRO (forthcoming in English).

Kimura, Fukunari and Mitsuyo Ando (2005), 'Two-dimensional fragmentation in East Asia: conceptual framework and empirics', *International Review of Economics and Finance*, **14**, 317–48.

Kimura, Fukunari, Yuya Takahashi and Kazunobu Hayakawa (2007), 'Fragmentation and parts and components trade: comparison between East Asia and Europe', *North American Journal of Economics and Finance*, **18**, 23–40.

Krugman, Paul (1991), 'Increasing returns and economic geography', *Journal of Political Economy*, **99**(3), 483–99.

Krugman, Paul (1993), 'The hub effect: or, threeness in international trade', in Wilfred J. Ethier, Elhanan Helpman and J. Peter Neary (eds), *Trade Policy and Dynamics in International Trade*, Cambridge: Cambridge University Press, pp. 29–37.

Kumagai, Satoru, Toshitaka Gokan, Ikumo Isono and Souknilanh Keola (2008), 'Predicting long-term effects of infrastructure development projects in continental South East Asia: IDE Geographical Simulation Model', ERIA Discussion Paper Series No. 2008-02.

Leinbach, Thomas R. and John T. Bowen, Jr (2004), 'Air cargo services and the electronics industry in Southeast Asia', *Journal of Economic Geography*, **4**, 299–321.

Limao, Nuno and Anthony J. Venables (2001), 'Infrastructure, geographical disadvantage, and transport costs', *World Bank Economic Review*, **15**(3), 451–79.

McCallum, John (1995), 'National borders matter: Canada–US regional trade patterns', *American Economic Review*, **85**(3), 615–23.

Micco, Alejandro and Tomas Serebrisky (2004), 'Infrastructure, competition regimes, and air transport costs: cross-country evidence', World Bank Policy Research Working Paper No. 3355.

Mori, Tomoya and Koji Nishikimi (2002), 'Economies of transport density and industrial agglomeration', *Regional Science and Urban Economics*, **32**, 167–200.

Oraboune Syviengxay (2008), 'Infrastructure development in Lao PDR', in Nagesh Kumar (ed.), *International Infrastructure Development in East Asia*, ERIA Research Project Report 2007, No. 2, Chiba: IDE-JETRO.

Ottaviano, Gianmarco I.P., Takatoshi Tabuchi and Jacques-Francois Thisse (2002), 'Agglomeration and trade revisited', *International Economic Review*, **43**, 409–36.

Overman, Henry G., Stephen J. Redding and Anthony J. Venables (2003), 'The economic geography of trade, production and income: a survey of the empirics', in E.K. Choi and J. Harrigan (eds), *Handbook of International Trade*, vol. I, London: Basil Blackwell.

Ozeki, Hiromichi (2008), 'Development of de facto economic integration in East Asia', in Hadi Soesastro (ed.), *Deepening Economic Integration in East Asia: The ASEAN Economic Community and Beyond*, ERIA Research Project Report 2007, No.1–2, Chiba: IDE-JETRO.

Radelet, Steven and Jeffrey Sachs (1998), 'Shipping costs, manufactured exports and economic growth', mimeo.

Redding, Stephen J. and Anthony J. Venables (2004), 'Economic geography and international inequality', *Journal of International Economics*, **62**(1), 53–82.

Shibasaki, Ryuichi, Tomihiro Watanabe, Takashi Kadono and Yasuo Kannami (2005), 'Estimation methodology and results on international maritime container OD cargo volume mainly focused on East Asian area', research report of National Institute for Land and Infrastructure Management 25 (in Japanese).

Takahashi, Takaaki (2006), 'Economic geography and endogenous determination of transport technology', *Journal of Urban Economics*, **60**(3), 498–518.

Takahashi, Takaaki (2007), 'Asymmetric transport costs and economic geography', CSIS Discussion Paper No. 87, University of Tokyo.

World Bank (2007), *Connecting to Compete: Trade Logistics in the Global Economy*, World Bank.

Yang Mu and H.O. Lionel (2006), 'Shanghai's Yangshan deep water port: an international mega port in the making', EAI Background Briefs No. 290.

14. Infrastructure connectivity for East Asia's economic integration[1]

Biswa Nath Bhattacharyay

14.1 INTRODUCTION

The current global financial and economic crisis, which was initially triggered by the rising defaults on sub-prime mortgages in the United States and has spread to other industrialized countries, is a serious concern for East Asia. The prospect of prolonged weak demand for developing East Asia's goods from these advanced countries could slow down its exports and foreign direct investment (FDI) inflows, reducing Asia's production and economic growth. At this juncture, enhancing trade and economic integration is essential for boosting intra-regional trade and regional demand, thus offsetting the reduced export prospect from industrialized countries.

The past decades have seen a remarkable growth and dynamism in Asia as well as a period of economic and financial turbulence. The Asian financial crisis of 1997 was a wake-up call for policymakers of the region that regional economic cooperation and integration can maximize the benefits of globalization while minimizing the costs. East Asia is again facing a severe global financial and economic crisis.

Regional cooperation and integration in trade, investment, and infrastructure development can foster outward-oriented development and generate large economic and social benefits. Integration will bring reduced transaction costs, greater productive infrastructure services, lower trade barriers, faster communication of ideas, goods and services, and rising capital flows. The East Asian economic cooperation is more crucial in this difficult period. Enhanced cross-border or regional physical connectivity between economies through high quality environment-friendly infrastructure can strengthen trade and economic integration.

In these trying times, cross-border infrastructure development across East Asia can enhance intra-regional trade and investment promotion and deepen the economic fabric; and thus can be instrumental in generating jobs and supporting quick economic recovery. If the crisis is prolonged, demand from advanced economies for East Asian exports is expected to decelerate, hence slowing production. This calls for gearing national and cross-border infrastructure to support East Asia's production networks and supply chains for intraregional trade, and to sustain the expected rise in regional demand.

This chapter looks at the role of infrastructure connectivity in East Asia's economic integration and associated issues and challenges. The chapter is organized as follows: Section 14.2 reviews infrastructure and its functions in East Asia's growth and integration as well as the trends in the quality and quantity of national and cross-border infrastructures, particularly transport and logistics in East Asian economies and their relationship in enhancing trade, economic growth, and global competitiveness. Section 14.3 examines the role of regional cooperation in cross-border infrastructure development in East Asia's connectivity and economic integration, and the role of policies and institutions using the case of the Greater Mekong Subregion (GMS). Section 14.4 presents investment requirements for infrastructure development and discusses the ways and means and the current response to the ongoing global financial crisis. The conclusion is provided in Section 14.5.

14.2   OVERVIEW AND ROLE OF INFRASTRUCTURE IN EAST ASIA'S TRADE, GROWTH AND ECONOMIC INTEGRATION

Infrastructure such as roads, railways, airports, seaports, harbors, and communication systems are crucial to spatially connect people, cities and towns to one another. These infrastructures facilitate the movements of goods, services, people and ideas locally, nationally, regionally and internationally.

14.2.1   East Asia's Trade Expansion and Transport Networks

Table 14.1 shows the national average distance to capital city of each economy in East Asia as well as the available transportation network and indicators of how these networks are used. Given the geographical nature of the countries in East Asia, only Singapore is compact, with a very accessible capital city. In comparison with China, Korea, and Japan, many countries are lagging behind in terms of percentage of roads that are paved, ranging from as low as 6.3% and 25.1% only. Moreover, Indonesia and the Philippines, which have some similarities with the archipelagic nature of Japan and Korea, also lag behind Korea and Japan in the number of airports with a paved runway as well as number of ports. This shows the wide disparity in the quantity and quality of transport infrastructure in East Asian economies.

Table 14.1 Distances to capital city and transport infrastructure indicators

East Asian countries/economies	National ave. distance to capital city (kms)	Roads, total network per 10,000km*	Roads, paved (% of total roads)*	Rail lines (total route-km, per 10,000km)*	Air transport, freight (million tons/km)*	Air transport, passengers carried per 1000 pop*	Airports with paved runway (number)	Ports and terminals (number)
	2000	2005	2005	2005	2005	2005	2007	2007
Brunei	NA	2010.0	34.7	NA	134.1	2615	NA	NA
Indonesia	1519.0	1934.1	58.0	193.06	439.8	122	159	9
Malaysia	873.0	2993.9	81.3	60.23	2577.6	804	37	9
Philippines	555.0	6667.9	21.6	15.97	322.7	97	83	6
Singapore	11.0	45608.0	100.0	0.00	7571.3	4087	9	1
Myanmar	619.0	413.3	11.4	38.30	2.7	30	21	3
Cambodia	206.0	2113.2	6.3	35.90	1.2	12	6	2
Thailand	428.0	1118.7	98.5	79.00	2002.4	294	66	4
Vietnam	646.0	6746.0	25.1	81.11	230.2	66	26	2
Lao PDR	311.0	1318.0	14.4	21.21	2.5	50	9	0
China	1668.0	2011.4	82.5	64.80	7579.4	105	403	7
Korea	187.0	10102.7	86.8	33.03	7432.6	702	69	5
Japan	531.0	31154.0	77.7	555.88	8549.2	800	145	10

Note: Hong Kong, Taiwan China and Mongolia were excluded due to lack of data.

Source: World Bank, (2009), *World Bank in CD Rom (2008).

Table 14.2   Trends in trade logistics indicators in East Asian countries

East Asia countries/ economies	Index of shipping difficulties (2008)	Average tariffs and custom duties, % of import value (2005)
Brunei	36.0	NA
Indonesia	41.0	3.0
Malaysia	21.0	5.6
Philippines	57.0	20.4
Singapore	1.0	0.1
Myanmar	NA	2.3
Cambodia	139.0	21.6
Thailand	50.0	6.2
Vietnam	63.0	NA
Lao PDR	158.0	NA
ASEAN (average)	62.9	8.5
China	42.0	NA
Korea	13.0	3.4
Japan	18.0	NA

Note: NA – not available.

Source: World Economic Forum (2008a, 2008b, 2008c).

Table 14.2 exhibits the trends in trade logistic indicators in selected East Asian countries. There is a wide variation in shipping difficulties and average tariff and customs duties as a proportion of the total import value of goods. This shows the huge potential for improving soft or facilitating infrastructure in several East Asian countries. The index of shipping difficulties varies from 1.0 in Singapore to as high as 158.0 in Lao PDR.

Trade expansion and foreign investment depend on improving trade facilitation and road transport services. Recently, the World Economic Forum (WEF, 2008c) has turned its attention to trade facilitation through the Global Enabling Trade Report (WEF, 2008b) which introduced the concept of a new index called the Enabling Trade Index (ETI). ETI[2] measures the factors, policies and services facilitating the free flow of goods over borders and to destinations. The data in this report was utilized to compare the performance of East Asian economies. Table 14.3 provides a snapshot of how East Asian economies have fared in terms of market access, border administration, transport and communication, and business environment. The ASEAN member countries demonstrate a poor average rating in transport and communication (3.87) and market access (3.91). This average rating is consistently below the more developed

Table 14.3 *East Asia's Enabling Trade Index*

East Asia economy/country	Market access		Border administration		Transport & communication infrastructure		Business environment		Overall ranking	
	Score	Ranking	Score	Ranking	Score	Ranking	Score	Ranking	Score	Ranking
Brunei										
Indonesia	5.03	22	3.96	63	3.13	74	4.97	32	4.27	47
Malaysia	4.09	68	5.23	24	4.62	27	5.07	27	4.75	29
Philippines	3.86	80	3.54	82	2.95	83	3.93	95	3.57	87
Singapore	4.99	27	6.51	1	5.53	1	5.82	7	5.71	2
Cambodia	2.62	108	2.74	107	NA	NA	NA	NA	NA	113
Thailand	4.25	62	4.07	56	3.93	41	4.49	61	4.18	52
Vietnam	2.50	112	3.60	76	3.08	75	4.48	62	3.42	91
ASEAN(8)	3.91		4.24		3.87		4.79		4.32	
China	4.07	71	4.51	43	4.15	36	4.28	77	4.25	48
Korea	4.07	72	5.49	18	5.23	19	5.02	30	4.95	24
Japan	5.86	4	5.55	17	5.42	13	4.9	35	5.43	3
Hong Kong, China	6.66	1	5.99	7	5.66	4	5.84	2	6.04	1
Taipei, China	4.83	38	5.27	22	5.37	15	5.13	22	5.15	21
Mongolia	4.08	69	2.58	113	2.89	87	3.98	91	3.38	93

Note: There are no available data for Myanmar and Lao PDR and data for Cambodia is incomplete. The overall ranking is among the 118 countries surveyed based on the computed index score. Score ranges from 1 (poorly developed and inefficient) to 7 (among the best in the world).

Source: World Economic Forum (2008a, 2008b, 2008c).

Table 14.4   Growth rate and infrastructure investment in selected countries in East Asia, 2005

Country	GDP Growth Rate	Infrastructure investment, GDP %
Cambodia	13.3	0–4
Indonesia	5.7	
Philippines	5.0	
Lao PDR	6.8	4–7
Mongolia	7.3	
China	10.4	More than 7
Thailand	6.3	
Vietnam	7.8	

Source: ADB, JBIC and WB (2005); WB PPI Database 2005; ADB and ADBI (2009).

economies such as Korea, Hong Kong, China and Japan. Transport infrastructure services remain uneven across East Asia, as exhibited by the wide variation in performance across the region.

14.2.2   Growth and Infrastructure Investment in East Asia

Infrastructure connectivity such as ports, roads, and rail within countries as well as between countries in East Asia and with the rest of the world is a significant determinant of economic performance. Within countries, connectivity plays a critical role in the country's growth performance. For example in China and Vietnam, where gross fixed capital formation has averaged about 40% of GDP and 30% of GDP respectively, much of this growth can be attributed to infrastructure development (ADB, JBIC and WB, 2005). Table 14.4 shows the relationship between infrastructure investment and growth.

The faster growing developing countries of the region manage substantial infrastructure assets and in many instances, the stock of these assets has grown, and the capability to generate services has also increased at remarkable rates. In fact, sustained investment and efficiency have helped some economies in the region, specifically Thailand and Malaysia, to achieve considerable competitive advantage across infrastructure sectors (ADB, JBIC and WB, 2005).

For comparative purposes, the total road network and electricity generating capacity as well as the corresponding growth for selected East Asian countries over a ten-year period are shown in Table 14.5. It shows that the growth of roads and electricity had a strong relationship

Table 14.5 Total road network and electricity generating capacity in selected countries in East Asia, 1990–2000

East Asia	Total road network (km)			Electricity generating capacity (GW)			Annual ave
	1990	2000	Growth (%)	1990	2000	Growth (%)	GDP Growth %
Indonesia	288 727	355 951	23.0	13	25	98.0	4.2
Lao PDR	13 971	23 922	71.0	0	0	92.0	6.3
China	1 028 348	1 679 848	63.0	127	299	136.0	10.1
Philippines	161	201 994	26.0	7	12	81.0	3.0
Rep. of Korea	56 715	86 990	53.0	20	50	150.0	1.7
Thailand	52 305	60 354	15.0	8	19	125.0	4.5
Vietnam	165 557	215 628	104.0	2	6	180.0	7.6

Notes: GW – giga watts.

Source: Adapted from ADB, JBIC and WB (2005).

with economic growth during 1990–2000. East Asia has developed infrastructure better than other regions in Asia, but there is much room for improvement, and supply needs to keep pace with rapidly rising demand. The rapid growth in several economies, particularly China, Vietnam and Thailand, has put visible pressure on existing infrastructure.

14.2.3   Overall Evaluation: East Asia's Infrastructure and Global Competitiveness

As previously noted, East Asia's trade expansion has been facilitated and motivated by the development of supporting infrastructure which includes the physical (hard) and facilitating (soft) infrastructure, such as policies, regulations, systems and procedures. Infrastructure investment's quantity, infrastructure services' quality and coordination of those services are influential factors in trade performance (Limao and Venables, 2001; Clark et al., 2004).

A fundamental driver of competitiveness is the presence of an extensive and efficient infrastructure. The quality and extensiveness of infrastructure networks significantly impact economic growth and reduce income inequalities and poverty in a variety of ways. The Global Competitiveness Index (GCI) measures national competitiveness capturing the microeconomic and economic foundations, and defines competitiveness as the set of institutions, policies and factors that determine the level of productivity of a country. Well-developed infrastructure reduces the effect of distance between regions by truly integrating national markets and connecting them to markets in other countries and regions.

Table 14.6 shows the scores in global competitiveness and in infrastructure assessment of the economies in East Asia. The average infrastructure score of East Asia has increased marginally from 4.46 in 2006 to reach 4.60 in 2009, whereas the GCI remains stagnant at 4.75. The latest data (2008–09) showed that Singapore leads with the GCI score of 5.53 and infrastructure score of 6.39 while Cambodia remains at the bottom at 2.80 and 3.50, respectively. The mean score at the sub-regional level also confirms that much infrastructure is needed for GMS countries to improve their global competitiveness rating.

Moreover, it confirms the strong relationship between competitiveness and infrastructure quality.[3] This indicates the essential part of infrastructure improvement in maintaining and further increasing the competitiveness of East Asia.

Table 14.6   Global competitiveness and infrastructure service quality indexes of East Asian countries

East Asia Economy/Country	2006–07		2007–08		2008–09	
	GCI	Infrastructure	GCI	Infrastructure	GCI	Infrastructure
Brunei	NA	NA	NA	NA	4.50	4.40
Indonesia	4.18	2.81	4.24	2.74	4.25	2.95
Malaysia	5.15	5.34	5.1	5.29	5.04	5.25
Philippines	3.98	2.64	3.99	2.7	4.09	2.86
Singapore	5.46	6.35	5.45	6.36	5.53	6.39
Cambodia	3.44	2.42	3.48	2.68	3.50	2.80
Thailand	4.76	4.68	4.7	4.85	4.60	4.67
Vietnam	4.09	2.61	4.04	2.8	4.10	2.86
Korea	5.07	5.21	5.4	5.55	5.28	5.63
Japan	5.51	6.16	5.43	5.98	5.38	5.80
PRC	4.6	3.73	4.6	3.97	4.70	4.20
Taipei, China	5.35	5.34	5.25	5.38	5.22	5.46
Hong Kong, China	5.37	6.22	5.37	6.24	5.33	6.32
East Asia (ave)	4.75	4.46	4.75	4.55	4.75	4.60
ASEAN (ave)	4.44	3.84	4.43	3.92	4.45	4.02
GMS 3 (ave)	4.10	3.24	4.07	3.44	4.07	3.44

Notes:
On the computed scores: 1 (poorly developed and inefficient) – 7 (among the best in the world).
ASEAN is composed of Indonesia, Malaysia, Philippines, Singapore, Cambodia, Thailand, Vietnam.
GMS is composed of Cambodia, the People's Republic of China (PRC, specifically Yunnan Province and Guangxi Zhuang Autonomous Region), Lao People's Democratic Republic (Lao PDR), Myanmar, Thailand and Vietnam. China is excluded as data are not available separately for its two provinces.

Source: The Global Competitiveness Reports: 2006–07, 2007–08 and 2008–09 (World Economic Forum, 2007, 2008a, 2008c).

14.3 TOWARDS EAST ASIA'S CONNECTIVITY AND INTEGRATION: REGIONAL COOPERATION IN CROSS-BORDER INFRASTRUCTURE DEVELOPMENT

Related studies have indicated that infrastructure difference accounted for about one third of the difference in output per worker between Latin America and East Asia (Calderon and Serven, 2004). The 1994 World Development Report 'Infrastructure for Development' compared the performance of East Asia with the sub-Saharan region and concluded that higher Asian growth was due to improvements in infrastructure access. However, not all infrastructure services have seen enough growth. Transport sector is lagging behind other infrastructure sectors in East Asia, and is less than what is required. The assessment of infrastructure quality and quantity also indicates the wide gap between the developed economies and the developing economies. It also suggests that connectivity for the inclusive development of the East Asian region is quite low.

14.3.1 Subregional Infrastructure Cooperation

There are various subregional infrastructure cooperation efforts for physical connectivity and integration in Asia. These include overlapping subregional initiatives related to infrastructure programs such as ASEAN, Bay of Bengal Initiative for Multi-Sectoral Technical and Economic Cooperation (BIMSTEC), Central Asia Regional Economic Cooperation (CAREC), BIMP-EAGA (Brunei, Indonesia, Malaysia and the Philippines–East ASEAN Growth Area), GMS, and IMT-GT (Indonesia–Malaysia–Thailand Growth Triangle). The progress of these programs is rather limited with the exception of GMS. On the other hand, some of these subregional programs can integrate or link East Asia with other sub-regions such as South Asia and Central Asia, for example, BIMSTEC and CAREC. Table 14.7 shows subregional infrastructure programs containing East Asian countries.

ASEAN is the oldest among the sub-regional cooperation initiatives. It was established in 1967 with the objectives of accelerating growth, social progress and cultural development in the region, and promoting regional peace and stability through abiding respect for justice and the rule of law in the relationship among countries in the region and adherence to the principles of the United Nations Charter (ASEAN, 2009). In contrast, GMS includes several ASEAN member countries and a part of China, and was formed through the assistance of the Asian Development Bank

Table 14.7   Subregional cooperation programs in East Asia

	Member countries	Major infrastructure sector thrust
ASEAN	Brunei Darussalam, Cambodia, Indonesia, Lao PDR, Malaysia, Myanmar, Philippines, Singapore, Thailand and Vietnam	Transport and Energy
BIMSTEC	Bangladesh, Bhutan, India, Myanmar, Nepal, Sri Lanka and Thailand	Transport
BIMP-EAGA	Brunei Darussalam plus provinces in Indonesia, Malaysia and Philippines	Transport
CAREC	Afghanistan, Azerbaijan, Kazakhstan, Kyrgyz Republic, Mongolia, Tajikistan, Uzbekistan plus the Xinjiang Uygur Autonomous Region and the province of Inner Mongolia of China	Transport and energy
GMS	Cambodia, Lao PDR, Myanmar, Thailand, Vietnam plus Guangxi and Yunnan provinces of China	Transport, energy and telecommunications
IMT-GT	Provinces in Indonesia, Malaysia and Thailand	Transport

Source: Bhattacharyay (2010).

(ADB) in 1992 to enhance economic relations among its member countries (ADB and ADBI, 2009). BIMP-EAGA was launched in 1994 by four governments with the objective of enhancing economic development through regional cooperation. It is eyed as a major location in ASEAN of high value added agro-industry, natural resource-based manufacturing, and high-grade tourism as well as non-resource-based industries (ADB and ADBI, 2009). IMT-GT was launched as a cooperation program in 1993 to accelerate the subregion's economic transformation through exploiting complementarities and comparative advantages, enhancing competitiveness for investment and exports, promoting tourism, lowering transport and transaction costs and reducing production and distribution costs through scale economies (ADB and ADBI, 2009).

BIMSTEC is composed of countries in South Asia and one country in East Asia, and has a goal of economic integration through free trade agreements. CAREC involves six countries in Central Asia plus Mongolia and provinces of Xinjiang Uygur Autonomous Region and Inner Mongolia of

China, and generally aims for regional integration in trade with infrastructure (transport and energy) as one of its major functions.

The existence of these overlapping subregional infrastructure initiatives suggests that East Asian infrastructure connectivity can be achieved through coordination and integration, using these initiatives as building blocks.

14.3.2   ASEAN Infrastructure Program

On the 30th anniversary of ASEAN, the ASEAN Vision 2020 was adopted by the ASEAN leaders. It envisions Southeast Asian nations as outward looking, living in peace, stability and prosperity, bonded together in partnership in dynamic development in a community of caring societies. By 2003, ASEAN leaders decided to establish the ASEAN community which looked at the security, the economy and the socio-cultural dimensions of achieving its vision. The goal is to change ASEAN into a stable, prosperous and highly competitive region with economic development (ASEAN, 2009). To achieve this, regional cooperation and integration must complement the initiatives at the country level. Thus, by working together, the members of ASEAN countries can open its vast economic potential, achieve rapid and sustained growth and reduce poverty.

While ASEAN has already decided to establish the ASEAN Economic Community (AEC) to strengthen economic integration, the regional economic cooperation and integration cannot stop at policy measures, cutting tariffs, removing non-tariff barriers, reducing obstacles to investment and easing restrictions on trade in services. It must bind ASEAN members through infrastructure in energy, transport and communications like lifeblood and the nervous system of an integrated economy. This is important to make capital flows and trade in goods and services possible, and because infrastructure availability and efficiency encourage entrepreneurship and investment. Construction and operation of ASEAN infrastructure is expected to stimulate economic activity, connecting with other sub-regions and the rest of the world.

Infrastructure development is crucial to the realization of ASEAN economic integration as well as to its success, especially in the face of the ongoing global financial crisis. Accelerating the development of infrastructure, enhancing physical connectivity and sharing resources such as energy, water, capital and services become more important than ever.

Given the region's geographic and economic diversity, achieving regional infrastructure integration is one of ASEAN's major challenges. Due to ongoing financial crisis, ASEAN member countries must primarily depend on their own national resources to build up infrastructure.

ASEAN's role then, is to ensure cooperation and coordination of its members' infrastructure projects, harness shared resources such as capital, energy services and technology, harmonize cross-border rules and regulations, and facilitate exchange of good practices on institutions and policies. Cooperation can occur in building regional infrastructure and in financing infrastructure development (Bhattacharyay, 2009).

At present, there are four long-term flagship regional projects for integrating ASEAN's infrastructure. These projects, mainly in the transport and energy sectors, are aimed at integrating member countries' transport and energy systems.

Transport infrastructure

The ASEAN Highway Network Project consists of 23 designated routes totaling 38,400km and is being implemented in three stages. The first stage is the network configuration and designation of national routes. The second stage is the installation of road signs for all designated national routes, upgrading to Class III standards, building missing links in the national routes and designating cross-border points. The last stage is the upgrading to at least Class I of all designated national routes, with Class II standards acceptable for low traffic non-arterial routes. In the highway classification, Class III is regarded as the minimum desirable standard, with two lanes and double bituminous treatment for paving. Class III is upgraded to Class II when asphalt or cement concrete is used for paving. A highway is classified as Class I when there are four or more lanes and when asphalt or cement concrete is used for paving (UNESCAP, 2009).

The Singapore–Kunming Rail Link Project is one of the core transport projects under the ASEAN Mekong Basin Development Cooperation. The 7,000 km railway line is expected to link major cities in eight countries including Singapore, Malaysia, Thailand, Cambodia, Vietnam, Lao PDR, Myanmar and China.

Energy infrastructure
The major energy projects, namely the ASEAN Power Grid (Box 14.1) and the Trans-ASEAN Gas Pipeline (Box 14.2) are aimed at linking the power systems of neighboring ASEAN countries. Their objective is to ensure greater security and sustainability of regional energy supplies through diversification, development and conservation of resources, the efficient use of energy and the wider application of environmentally sound technologies (Roberts and Cull, 2003).

The current challenges that ASEAN infrastructure is facing include

---

BOX 14.1   ASEAN POWER GRID

The ASEAN Power Grid consists of 14 interconnection projects and the system is expected to enable ASEAN countries to share reserve margins through electrical interconnections. However, only two have been carried out and are under operation. Eleven still require feasibility studies or identification of funding sources, with one just revived. The two operational projects are (i) the Peninsular Malaysia-Thailand Interconnection developed in 1981, which allows maximum power transfer of 80 megawatts (currently being upgraded to 300 megawatts), and (ii) the Peninsular Malaysia-Singapore Interconnection constructed in 1985, which improved resilience of the two power systems and has enabled them to help each other. These projects will provide interconnections between Singapore and Batam Island in Indonesia; Sarawak and West Kalimantan; southern Philippines and Sabah; Sarawak, Sabah and Brunei Darussalam; Thailand and Lao PDR; Lao PDR and Vietnam; Thailand and Myanmar; Vietnam and Cambodia; Lao PDR and Cambodia; and Thailand and Cambodia. At present, only the Sarawak project is being revived.

Source: ASEAN (2008).

---

geographical diversity and different levels of development. The infrastructure of less developed members such as Cambodia, Lao PDR, Myanmar and Vietnam lags behind that of more developed countries. Some countries are separated by sea making linkages between them expensive. These challenges of developing port facilities for sea connections and roads for land links present huge infrastructure investment needs. Other issues include ensuring the symmetric distribution of the costs and benefits of regional infrastructure across participating countries, and synchronizing national and sub-regional planning and financing of infrastructure.

14.3.3   GMS Infrastructure

The GMS Economic Cooperation Program started in 1992 and aims to facilitate efficient cross-border transportation infrastructure to enhance regional economic development and regional cooperation as well as to promote the freer flow of goods and people in the sub-region. The

---

BOX 14.2   TRANS-ASEAN GAS PIPELINE

This is part of ASEAN's Plan of Action on Energy Cooperation 1999–2004 which aims to ensure reliability of gas supply, encourage the use of environment-friendly fuel, attract multinational companies to invest in gas exploration and reduce the region's dependence on crude oil. To date, the identified gas pipeline interconnecting routes are (1) Malaysia–Singapore; (2) Myanmar (Yadana) to Thailand (Ratchaburi); (3) Myanmar (Yetagun) to Thailand (Ratchaburi); (4) Indonesia (West Natuna) to Singapore; (5) Indonesia (West Natuna) to Malaysia (Duyong); (6) Indonesia (Grissik) to Singapore; (7) Thailand (Joint Development Area) to Malaysia; (8) Indonesia (South Sumatra) to Malaysia; (9) Indonesia (Arun) to Malaysia; (10) Indonesia (East Natuna and West Natuna) to Malaysia (Kerteh) and Singapore; (11)Indonesia (East Natuna) to Thailand (JDA-Erawan); (12) Indonesia (East Natuna) to Malaysia (Sabah) and the Philippines (Palawan-Luzon); and (13) Malaysia-Thailand (JDA) to Vietnam (Block B).

Source: AMEM (2004).

10-year strategic framework for enhancing connectivity, competitiveness and a sense of community in the subregion was endorsed by the GMS ministers in 2001. GMS programs include transport and energy cooperation.

Transport infrastructure
The strategic thrust of the GMS Transport Cooperation (1992–2005) is to create cross-border access and facilitate cross-border traffic. In response to this thrust, the principles involved in selecting, prioritizing and designing projects include prioritizing the improvement of existing infrastructure over construction of new facilities, emphasizing trade generation and implementing in sections.

GMS has planned 73 transport projects with an estimated cost of $18.3 billion, 32 energy projects needing $6 billion, 35 trade and facilitation projects requiring around $453 million and 26 telecommunication projects needing around $356 million (Bhattacharyay, 2010).

To date, eleven GMS flagship programs have been identified, including three economic corridors to connect infrastructure development with economic and investment activities. These include the (i) North–South

Economic Corridor, (ii) East–West Economic Corridor, (iii) Southern Economic Corridor, (iv) Telecommunications backbone, (v) Regional Power Interconnection and Trading Arrangement, (vi) Facilitating Cross-border Trade and Investment, (vii) Enhancing Private Sector Participation and Competitiveness, (viii) Development of Human Resources and Skills Competencies, (ix) Strategic Environment Framework, (x) Flood Control and Water Resource Management and (xi) GMS Tourism Development (ADB, 2006).

The three economic corridors are intended to promote trade, investment and economic development in and among the areas connected by the new transport infrastructure. The East–West Economic Corridor (EWEC) runs from Da Nang, Vietnam through Lao PDR and Thailand to Myanmar. The North–South Economic Corridor (NSEC) covers the major routes from Kunming through Chiang Rai to Bangkok or Nanning through Hanoi to Haipong. The Southern Economic Corridor (SEC) runs through the southern parts of Thailand, Cambodia and Vietnam. These corridors are presented in Figure 14.1.

To facilitate free movement of traded goods through cross-border transport infrastructure, the GMS has created a forum for discussing transport strategies and exchanging information in order to develop a common approach through a Cross Border Transport Agreement (CBTA) as highlighted in Box 14.3.

Appropriate policy, regulatory and financing initiatives are required to transform the transport corridors into complex but more rewarding economic corridors. For example, in the Southern Economic Corridor, the Thai–Cambodia Joint Development Study for Economic Cooperation (ADB, 2005) has identified programs and investments in infrastructure, agro-industry, fisheries, light manufacturing and industry, and tourism and trade.

These economic corridors have generated significant benefits. For example, recent studies showed some improvement in the socio-economic conditions of the community. For instance in the East–West Economic Corridor on Savannakhet Province, the number of households living below the poverty level decreased from 37,282 in 1998 to 24,400 in 2004. In Savan-Seno Special Economic Development Zone (Lao PDR), FDI increased to US $207 million for the period 2001–05 from US$17.9 for the period 1995–2000. Moc Bai Special Economic Development Zone attracted seven domestic investors with 38 projects totaling a capital of US$350 million for the period 2005–06 (ADB, JICA and WB, 2005).

For developing an effective transport corridor and converting it to an economic corridor, effective institutions, policies, regulations and cross-border agreements need to be created.

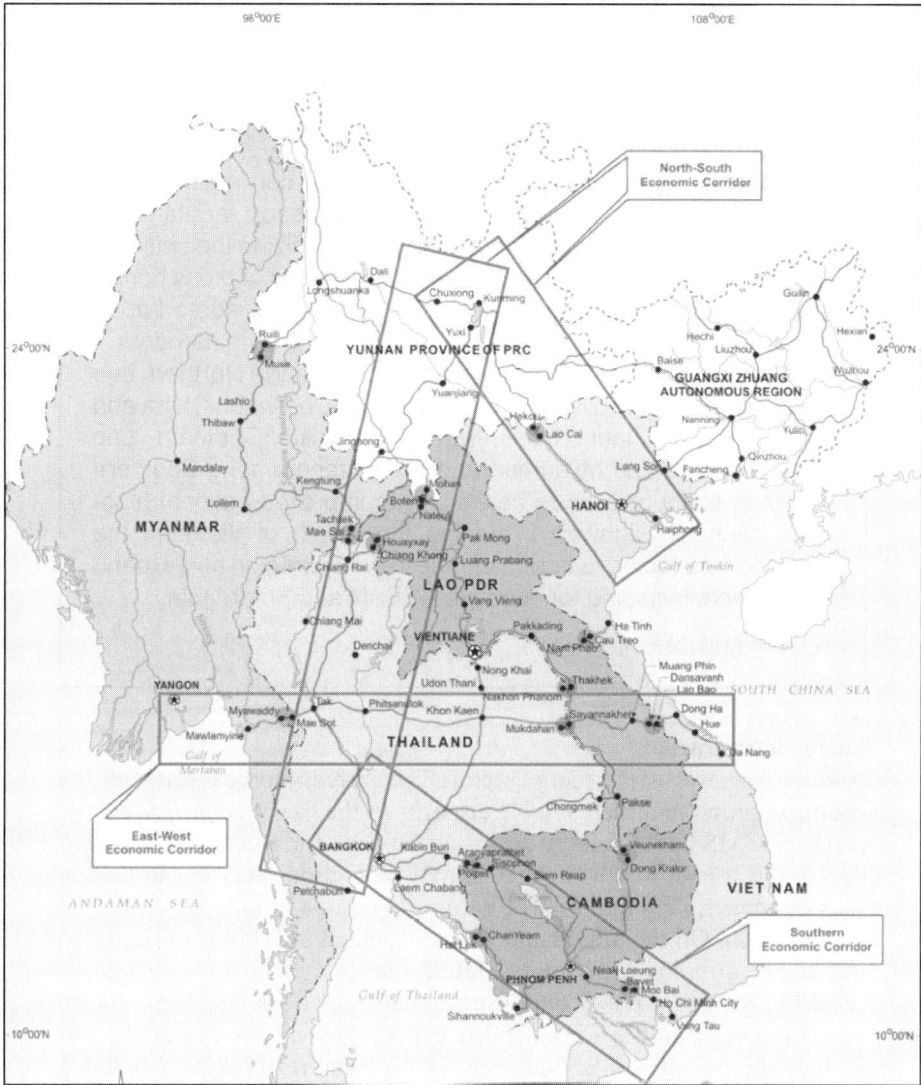

Source: ADB and ADBI (2009).

Figure 14.1 GMS economic corridors and border crossing points

---

BOX 14.3   CROSS BORDER TRANSPORT AGREEMENT (CBTA)

The CBTA is a multilateral instrument approved by all GMS countries and includes references to international conventions. This covers all relevant issues of cross-border transport facilitation in one document. It is an important step in harmonizing the software relating to infrastructure use. It covers key aspects of cross border facilitation and applies to selected and mutually agreed-upon routes and points of entry and exit of selected growth corridors.

These growth corridors are expected to transform Northern Lao PDR and Yunnan Province into vital gateways between China and Southeast Asia, launch east–west trade linking Vietnam, Lao PDR, Thailand and Myanmar, and boost trade among Southern Vietnam, Cambodia and Thailand. With improved national highways such as Highway 1 running the length of Vietnam, the network is projected to facilitate trade in the subregion and expand trade reach, including for example ASEAN and South Asia.

Source: ADB (2008c).

Energy infrastructure

Another key area is the energy sector. The current physical status of the countries shows that there is a big disparity in the size of countries' energy markets. GMS has an energy exporting capacity for at least the next two decades. It is endowed with 330,000 MW of hydropower, 59,340 million tons of coal, 1,378 billion m^3 of natural gas and 478 million tons of oil (ADB, 2005). On the other hand, energy demand in GMS is projected to increase by around 8% per year (ADB, 2008b).

GMS provided a policy and institutional framework (see Box 14.4) to promote opportunities for extended cooperation in power trading and is developing a grid interconnection infrastructure through a building block approach allowing the cross-border dispatch of power (see Figure 14.2). These facilities are being accomplished through appropriate institutions, such as the Electric Power Forum and Experts Group on Power Interconnection and Trade (ADB, 2008b).

A recent study showed that GMS regional cooperation in energy could save the region US$200 billion. The gains are possible because of the expected large increases in energy demand over the coming years, the uneven resource endowments across the region and the potential for

---

BOX 14.4   GMS ENERGY COOPERATION PROGRAM

In 2002, GMS members signed an Inter-Governmental Agreement (IGA) on regional power trade. Article 4 of the IGA deals with the institutional framework, defining the role and responsibility of the Regional Power Trade Coordination Committee (RPTCC). So far around 52 energy projects have been identified. Several projects are under construction for the GMS power transmission such as the first high-voltage transmission line between Cambodia and Vietnam. The transnational hydropower projects such as Theun Hinboun are already able to internationally draw income. Other GMS power generation projects include Lao PDR Nam Theun 2 which has private sector investment developing a 1070 MW power plant on Nam Theun River, a tributary of the Mekong. It exports power to Thailand (95%) and the rest is for domestic use. There are two projects in Cambodia. The Offshore Gas Resource Development, costing US$800 million, is a power transmission and distribution system project within Cambodia and is for potential sale to Thailand and Vietnam. The other one is the Lower Sre Pok II Hydropower Project, costing US$400 million to construct and operate a 200 MW low head hydroelectric generating facility on the Sre Pok River, with potential sale of electricity to Vietnam.

Source: ADB (2008b).

---

countries to meet demand by importing energy from their neighbors, which may be the least-cost option (ADB, 2008c).

The process of developing cross-border or regional infrastructure projects is very complex. Regional infrastructure planning involves many difficult issues because planners are often faced with several constituencies, numerous and often conflicting objectives, lack of an overarching legal framework and lack of a single decision making body. There is need for appropriate policies and institutions for developing regional projects as exemplified by GMS, particularly in its transport and energy projects.

The GMS is a good benchmark in evaluating successful subregional and cross-border cooperation. It has steadily evolved from a varying collection of cautious neighbors into a highly effective collaboration in numerous infrastructure investments directly attributed to GMS initiative. It has accomplished this with a largely informal approach using the self-selection

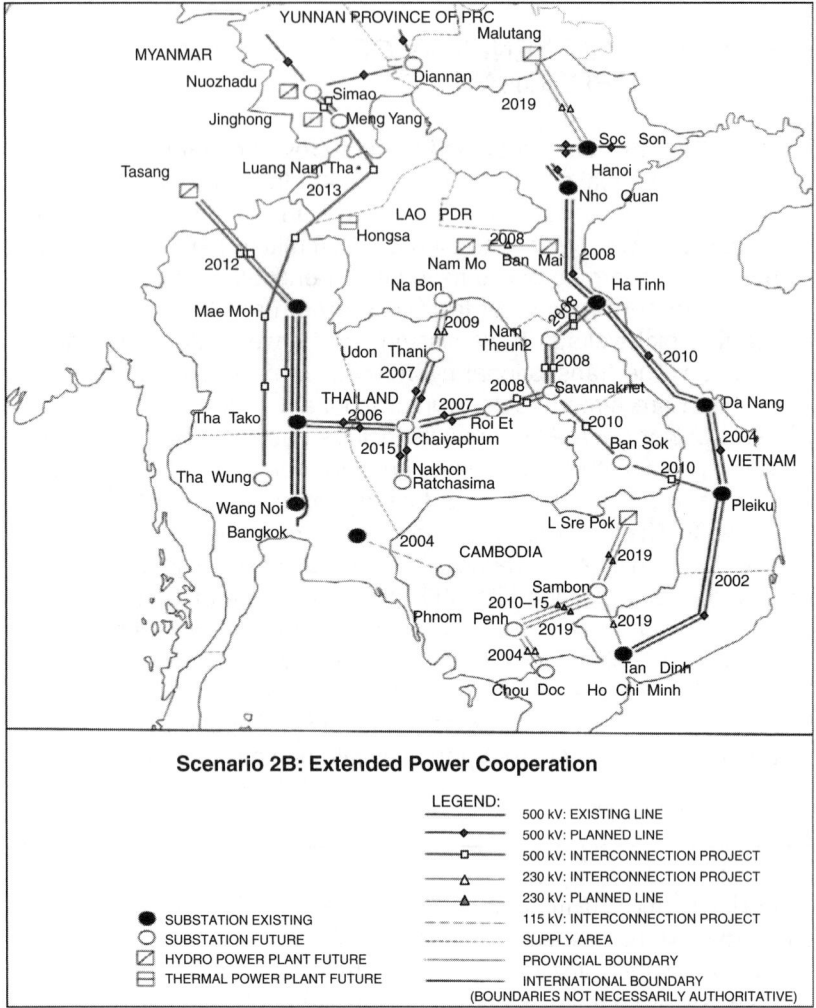

Scenario 2B: Extended Power Cooperation

LEGEND:
- 500 kV: EXISTING LINE
- 500 kV: PLANNED LINE
- 500 kV: INTERCONNECTION PROJECT
- 230 kV: INTERCONNECTION PROJECT
- 230 kV: PLANNED LINE
- 115 kV: INTERCONNECTION PROJECT
- SUPPLY AREA
- PROVINCIAL BOUNDARY
- INTERNATIONAL BOUNDARY
- (BOUNDARIES NOT NECESSARILY AUTHORITATIVE)

- SUBSTATION EXISTING
- SUBSTATION FUTURE
- HYDRO POWER PLANT FUTURE
- THERMAL POWER PLANT FUTURE

Source: ADB (2008b).

Figure 14.2   Regional master plan on power interconnection in GMS: a scenario

formula whereby those who involve themselves in a particular undertaking are bound by that agreement. There are no pressures to participate nor does it stop those who wish to proceed within their own territories and at their own speed. With a multilateral development bank – Asian Development Bank (ADB) – acting as a secretariat, GMS members were able to adopt nine priority sectors: transport, telecommunications, energy, tourism, human resources development, environment, agriculture, trade and investment. In particular, there were individual subregional sectoral forums for electric power, telecommunications and transport. GMS has established several sectoral institutions and policies for effective planning and implementation of projects.

In addition, ADB plays the role of an honest broker by bringing together various countries and getting involved in a neutral way and providing loans and technical assistance for high priority projects. Regional cooperation helped in providing knowledge and expertise to ensure effective implementation of projects. It acted as coordinator in facilitating the involvement of other development partners (Bhattacharyay, 2009).

14.3.4 Linking to Other Regions: Role of BIMSTEC and CAREC

As previously mentioned, there are subregional initiatives that have plans to link East Asia to other subregions in Asia which could eventually establish a Pan-Asia connectivity. The BIMSTEC Trilateral Highway (BTH) project plans to link Myanmar and Thailand with a total length of 1,360km and could link East Asia to India through Myanmar (RIS, 2008).

On the other hand, CAREC has planned a project for developing a transport corridor through the western region of Mongolia connecting Yarant at the China border to Ulaanbaishint at the Russian Federation border via Hovd and Olgivy, the 'aimag' (provincial centers). It makes up a portion of Asian Highway 4 and a component of the larger Asian Highway Network under the auspices of UNESCAP. The project supports Mongolia's priority development plans of building roads for the Asian Highway under the national development strategy as well as strengthening Mongolia's transport links to China, the Russian Federation and other countries. This project can link East Asia to central Asia (ADB, 2008d).

These overlapping subregional and pan-Asia infrastructure projects could create a pan-Asia connectivity through proper coordination and cooperation.

14.4 FINANCING INFRASTRUCTURE DEVELOPMENT

East Asia's infrastructure demand is expected to grow rapidly in the next decades. Infrastructure investment has played an important part in East Asian growth. However, the increasing demands related to growth have

Table 14.8   Sector-wise overall national infrastructure investment needs in selected countries of East Asia, 2010–20 ($ billion in 2008 prices)

Country name	Energy	Transport	Tele-commu-nication	Total	% of the sub-total	Annual Ave
Brunei	NA	0.1	NA	0.1	–	–
Cambodia	2.3	0.9	4.6	7.8	0.2	0.8
China	2396.8	849.7	563.1	3809.5	79.6	380.9
Indonesia	122.5	222.2	113.8	458.4	9.6	45.8
Lao PDR	–	1.6	2.4	4.0	0.1	0.4
Malaysia	58.0	76.4	8.2	142.7	3.0	14.3
Mongolia	–	1.1	0.8	1.9	–	0.2
Philippines	41.1	15.3	32.7	89.1	1.9	8.9
Thailand	80.9	43.3	31.1	155.3	3.2	15.5
Vietnam	58.3	15.0	40.9	114.1	2.4	11.4
Sub-total	2759.8	1225.6	797.7	4783.0	100.0	478.3

Note: NA – not available; – negligible.

Source: ADBI (2009) and Bhattacharyay (2010).

also highlighted shortfalls in the quantity and quality of infrastructure. This is increasingly seen as a binding constraint on accelerating further growth. Mobilizing large levels of finance for infrastructure is one big challenge as a number of East Asian countries do not have adequate fiscal space to expand investment levels in a short period of time. This situation calls for mobilizing private savings from the capital market.

14.4.1   Financing Requirement

Mobilizing funds for financing infrastructure requires deep, and integrated financial markets and innovative financial instruments which will allow free movement of capitals across the region. This needs to be achieved at the national level as well as at the regional level through strong regional cooperation. A recent ADB and ADBI study (2009) 'Infrastructure for Seamless Asia' provided an estimation of the indicative infrastructure investment needs of developing Asia. Based on the projections in this study, Table 14.8 presents the overall national infrastructure investment needs of East Asian countries during 2010–20 for energy, transport and telecommunications.

The estimates were obtained using a two-step procedure. The first step uses appropriate econometric models to estimate demand for new physical infrastructure capacity needs by each sector for each year between 2010 and 2020. The models estimate the demand from major determinants, such as income per capita, shares of agriculture and manufacturing in GDP, urbanization, and population density. The second step values the estimated demands for infrastructure stock of new capacity using appropriate unit costs. Then the investments required to maintain and/or replace the current capacity at the end of its useful life are estimated based on the assumption that replacement investments would be around 2% of the investments required for new capacity for transport and energy, and 8% for telecommunications (ADBI, 2009; Bhattacharyay, 2010b).

Addressing current shortfalls in infrastructure and meeting additional requirements to support future economic growth will require massive investments over the next decade. As shown in Table 14.8, the major developing economies in East Asia need $4,783 billion during 2010–20. This total investment includes investment for new capacity and for maintenance or replacing of existing infrastructure capacity. Of this projected amount, more than half, or around $2,759.8 billion (58%) will be needed for energy projects. Transport projects will require $1,225.6 (25%) and telecommunication projects around $797.7 (17%) (ADBI, 2009, Bhattacharyay, 2010).

China accounts for a major portion (80%) of total need of around $3,809 billion. This is followed by major ASEAN countries, namely Indonesia with an investment need of $458 billion, Thailand with $155 billion, Malaysia with $143 billion, Vietnam with $114 billion and the Philippines with $89 billion. East Asia on average needs to spend $478 million per year from 2010 to 2020, with China spending more than three times the rest of the aggregate total in selected countries in East Asia. With the exception of China, governments of East Asian countries may not be in a position to meet this large demand (ADBI, 2009; Bhattacharyay, 2010).

Meeting this financing requirement will need greater coordination between the public and private sectors. The use of public private partnership (PPP) in infrastructure development needs to be enhanced. Towards this end, the public sector needs to (i) provide the enabling environment for private sector participation and funding; (ii) develop 'bankable' projects, with proper consideration of various associated risks; (iii) improve financial intermediation functions by increasing banking sector efficiency; and (iv) strengthen and link domestic bond markets to mobilize Asia's massive savings.

*Table 14.9   Domestic savings and foreign exchange reserves in Asia, 2007
            ($ billion)*

Country/region	GDP	Savings	Reserves
China	3 239	1 384	1 434
Japan	4 403	1 311	923
East Asia 5	9 173	3 207	3 034
ASEAN 5	1 091	457	409
Asia 11	11 349	3 992	3 710

Note: East Asia 5 = China; Hong Kong, China; Japan; Republic of Korea; Taiwan,
China; ASEAN 5 = Indonesia, Malaysia, Philippines, Singapore, Thailand; ASIA11 = East
Asia 5, ASEAN5 and India.

Sources: Bhattacharyay and Krueger (2008), ADB (2007, 2008a), IMF (2008) and World
Bank (2008).

14.4.2   Developing Bond Markets

Asia's large foreign exchange reserves and savings represent a huge, untapped resource for financing regional infrastructure (Table 14.9). The Asia 11 countries (China; Hong Kong, China; Japan; Republic of Korea, Taiwan, China; ASEAN5; and India) alone have savings worth $3,992 billion, and foreign exchange reserves amounting to $3,710 billion in 2007.

In order to meet the huge financing requirements for infrastructure, especially for cross-border infrastructure in East Asia through utilizing regional savings, a strong regional financial cooperation is required to develop domestic and regional capital markets, harmonize rules and regulations and create innovative financial instruments to meet investment requirements. Traditionally, East Asian infrastructure financing has been met through short-term or medium-term bank loans which create a maturity mismatch for long-term infrastructure projects.

East Asia needs to further develop bond markets as an alternative source of funding to bank loans, as learned from the 1997 Asian financial crisis. As measures to ensure the availability of long-term domestic currency funding (and prevent maturity and currency mismatches), policy makers have already started the development of regional bond markets through various national and regional efforts. One of the widely known regional efforts is the Asian Bond Markets Initiative (ABMI) endorsed by the finance ministers of ASEAN and China, Japan and Republic of Korea (ASEAN+3). The Asian central banks through the Executives Meeting of the East Asia-Pacific Central Banks (EMEAP) in June 2003 also launched the Asian Bond Fund (ABF). Promoting issuance of new infrastructure bonds can assist in developing both primary and secondary bond markets while at the same time widening the issuer base and available products for investors. For strengthening bond markets, East Asian policy makers should undertake various measures such as (i) building sufficient sovereign bond issuance to establish market benchmarks; (ii) constructing an effective regulatory environment for the region's financial institutions to issue bonds to meet their financing requirements; (iii) creating markets for asset-backed securities and other relatively new products, (iv) increasing issuance of multilateral development banks and government agencies and (v) expanding local currency bonds and introducing currency-basket bonds. The East Asian bond market has already witnessed some progress. The local bond markets in ASEAN+3 have grown three times with total outstanding bond issues in emerging East Asian currencies totaling $3.9 trillion as of June 2008. Several markets – Indonesia, Philippines and Vietnam – instituted new rules aimed at bolstering bond issuance from revenue-generating sectors such as local government public utilities (ADB and ADBI, 2009).

Furthermore, additional regional initiatives are needed to address certain structural issues which have led to chronic underinvestment in infrastructure. These include (i) high risk premiums associated with infrastructure projects in low-income or highly indebted countries; (ii) uncertainties due to long tenures and the requirements for government guarantees; (iii) foreign exchange risks, including currency mismatch arising from long tenures; and (iv) the weak capacity of domestic financial institutions and markets. Other impediments include high costs and limited insurance facilities; process inefficiencies and lack of capacity to manage projects; limited information and coordination; and market and regulatory restrictions (Goh, 2008).

The development of an appropriate East Asia infrastructure financing mechanism for developing and financing bankable projects and financing facilities, particularly for cross-border projects, is crucial for enhancing physical connectivity within the region. An East Asia Infrastructure Bond Fund should be created to utilize the vast savings and reserves of major East Asian countries. Other East Asian countries can join this regional collaborative effort subsequently. Integrating East Asian financial markets will also be necessary for effective intermediation of the region's savings. Such regional-level approaches should be complemented by domestic initiatives to strengthen local currency bond markets.

Enhanced private sector participation through PPP should be encouraged for meeting the financing requirement as well as for ensuring efficient project implementation. In this regard, there is a need to (i) provide the enabling environment for private sector participation and funding; (ii) develop 'bankable' projects, with proper consideration of managing various associated risks; (iii) improve financial intermediation functions by increasing financial sector efficiency; and (iv) strengthen and link domestic bond markets to mobilize Asia's massive savings.

14.4.3   The Global Financial Crisis and Fiscal Stimulus

The current global financial crisis has major repercussions for East Asia. Singapore and Thailand are already in recession and other countries are experiencing the effect of the ongoing crisis.

To mitigate the medium-term effects of the crisis, East Asia should place greater emphasis on increasing regional demand. Hence, it should gear its national and regional infrastructure to support regional production networks and supply chains for enhancing intraregional trade. In addition, regional infrastructure projects which connect smaller East Asian markets to larger markets like China as well as to large markets in other subregions like India can play an important role in this difficult time. Therefore, the current global financial crisis presents an opportunity for developing regional infrastructure to connect isolated areas to major economic and financial centers.

During the 1997–98 Asian crisis, public and private infrastructure investments were substantially reduced in many Asian economies. In fact, infrastructure programs were among the first to be cut in Indonesia and the Philippines and to a lesser extent Malaysia. Indonesia and the Philippines are still suffering from large infrastructure deficit due to collapse of investment after the 1997 financial crisis, and poor infrastructure has kept growth rates below their potential (Greenwood, 2006). Amid weak global demand, countries in East Asia need to rely more on national and regional demand to sustain growth. Several countries have been making efforts to stimulate domestic demand, and alleviate the further impact of the spiraling crisis, by setting aside resources for infrastructure investment under their stimulus packages.

China is leading the infrastructure stimulus with a fiscal package that is 13.3% of its GDP, with a big portion of investment for infrastructure. The State Council of China has approved RMB2.0 trillion ($292 billion) in railway investment under the new stimulus package of RMB4.0 trillion (*China Business Review*, 2009). Singapore, whose economy is projected to be strongly hit by the current crisis, plans to spend between $11.9 and $13.2 billion on infrastructure projects (such as a new cruise liner terminal, new roads and parks, and upgrading of schools, sports facilities and public housing estates) in 2009 (Nopporn, 2009).

It is important to enhance infrastructure investment now, because a high return can be expected in terms of sustaining demand, creating jobs and raising long-term growth. At this juncture enhanced regional cooperation has the potential to be an important platform in complementing country-level efforts. If these country-level efforts can be coordinated to connect major economic centers of East Asian countries with hinterland, large benefits in terms of income gain can be achieved.

14.5   CONCLUDING REMARKS

Infrastructure development, especially at cross-border level, is an important factor for a successful economic integration in East Asia. The effective development of cross-border infrastructure is crucial particularly in narrowing the development gap among East Asian economies. This can be achieved by improving the region's physical connectivity as well as by harmonizing and enhancing policies which can give access to larger markets and production networks and supply chains. Infrastructure development can accelerate economic integration in the region as physical linkage can address the diversity and complementarities across countries. Infrastructure can bind the countries in East Asia to be committed in stimulating economic activity through sharing of scarce resources such as water and electricity, and through the symmetric distribution of costs and benefits of regional infrastructure across participating countries.

East Asia has witnessed good progress in infrastructure development. Over the last 16 years, East Asian countries have worked to build infrastructure links among themselves through several subregional programs. Improvement in connectivity has paid off as some of the most dynamic growth in trade in East Asia has been in the GMS region through the implementation of its regional infrastructure development program. It is important that follow-ups are made for such initiatives.

However, the increasing demands for infrastructure related to growth in East Asia also show that the quantity of infrastructure initiatives in the region are not enough to meet the recruirements, nor does the quality match the required standards. Meeting additional infrastructure requirements to support future economic growth is projected to require massive investments. The financing requirements for infrastructure, especially for cross-border infrastructure, have ample space for enhancing regional financial cooperation to develop domestic and regional capital markets, harmonize rules and regulations and create innovative financial instruments to meet investment requirements. Integrating financial markets is necessary to utilize the available savings of the region especially in view of the ongoing financial crisis.

There is an urgent need to develop an appropriate East Asia infrastructure financing mechanism for developing and financing bankable projects, particularly cross-border projects, for enhancing physical connectivity within the region. An East Asia Infrastructure Bond Fund could be established to utilize the vast savings and reserves of major East Asian countries.

Private sector participation in infrastructure development through PPP is crucial to meet huge infrastructure financing needs as well as to improve the efficiency of project implementation. The governments of East Asian economies need to create proper business environments conducive to private sector participation.

NOTES

1. The views expressed in this chapter are those of the author and do not reflect the views and policies of the Asian Development Bank (ADB), Asian Development Bank Institute (ADBI), its Board of Directors, or the governments they represent. ADBI does not guarantee the accuracy of the data included in this chapter and accepts no responsibility for any inconsistencies of their use. Terminology used may not necessarily be consistent with ADB/ADBI official terms. The usual disclaimers apply.
2. ETI are calculated based on the 'hard data' and 'survey data'. The latter is derived from the responses to the World Economic Forum's Executive Opinion Survey and range from 1 to 7. Survey Data from World Bank's Logistics Performance Index (LPI) Survey have also been included and hard data were collected from various sources. Computations, especially the standard formula for converting each hard data variable to the 1-to-7 scale, are found in the technical notes of the 'Global Enabling Trade Report', WEF 2008b.
3. Correlation coefficient is 0.95, calculated based on the pooled data (2008–09).

REFERENCES

ADB (Asian Development Bank (2005), *GMS Flagship Initiative: East-West Economic Corridor*, Manila: ADB.

ADB (2006), 'Greater Mekong Subregion: regional cooperation strategy and program update', Manila.

ADB (2007), 'Cross-border infrastructure: a tool kit', Manila: ADB. Available at http://www.ppiaf.org/documents/toolkits/Cross-Border-Infrastructure-Toolkit/Cross-Border%20Compilation%20ver%2029%20Jan%2007/cross-border%20booklet%2029%20jan%2007.pdf.

ADB (2008a), *Key Indicators for Asia and the Pacific 2009*, Manila: ADB.

ADB (2008b), 'About Greater Mekong Subregion', available at http://www.adb.org/GMS/about.asp.

ADB (2008c), 'About Greater Mekong Subregion', available at http://www.adb.org/Documents/Events/Mekong/Proceedings/SEF2-Annex4-ADB-Presentation.pdf.

ADB (2008d), 'Implementation Action Plan for the Transport and Trade

Facilitation Strategy', Prepared report for consideration at the 7th Ministerial Conference on Central Asian Regional Economic Cooperation, Baku, Azerbaijan, 19–21 November.

ADB and ADBI (2009), *Infrastructure for Seamless Asia*, ADB Institute, Tokyo (forthcoming).

ADB, JBIC (Japan Bank for International Cooperation), and WB (World Bank) (2005), *Connecting East Asia: A New Framework for Infrastructure*, Manila.

ADBI (ADB Institute) (2009), 'Demand for infrastructure financing in Asia 2010–2020', *ADBI Internal Report* (prepared by Centennial Group Holdings, LLC, Washington DC), Tokyo.

ASEAN (Association of Southeast Asian Nations) (2008), 'ASEAN infrastructure', available at http://www.aseansec.org/10367.htm.

ASEAN (2009), 'ASEAN Updates', available at http://www.aseansec.org/.

ASEAN Ministers of Energy Meeting (AMEM) (2004), ASEAN Plan of Action for Energy Cooperation 2004–2009, June, Manila: ADB.

Bhattacharyay, Biswa Nath (2009), 'Infrastructure development for ASEAN economic integration', ADBI Working Paper 138, Tokyo: Asian Development Bank Institute, available at http://www.adbi.org/working-paper/2009/05/27/3011.infrastructure.dev.asean.economic/.

Bhattacharyay, Biswa Nath (2010), 'Estimating demand for infrastructure in energy, transport, telecommunications, water and sanitation in Asia and the Pacific: 2010–2020', No. 248, ADBI Working Paper, September Tokyo: ADBI.

Bhattacharyay, Biswa Nath and Russell Krueger (2008), 'Modes of Asian financial integration: financing Asia's infrastructure', Background paper for the study Infrastructure and Regional Cooperation, Tokyo: ADBI.

Calderon, Cesar A. and Luis Serven (2004), 'The effects of infrastructure development on growth and income distribution', World Bank Policy Research Working Paper No. WPS 3400, Washington, DC: World Bank.

Clark, Ximana, David Dollar and Alejandro Micco (2004), 'Port efficiency, maritime transport costs and bilateral trade', *Journal of Development Economics*, **75** (2): 417–50.

Goh, Ching Yin (2008), 'ASEAN infrastructure financing mechanism: concepts and progress', Paper presented at the ASEAN Infrastructure Financing Mechanism Conference, Kuala Lumpur, Malaysia, 10 November.

Greenwood, C.L. (2006), 'Sustaining growth through infrastructure investment', speech prepared for the Asian Pacific Infrastructure Congress, Hong Kong, 5 September.

IMF (2008), *International Financial Statistics (IFS), 2008*, Washington, DC: International Monetary Fund.

Limao, Nuno and Anthony J. Venables (2001), 'Infrastructure, geographical disadvantage, transport costs and trade', *World Bank Economic Review*, **15**, 451–79.

Nopporn, Wong-Anan (2009), 'Singapore: $12 billion spending on infrastructure this year', Interactive Investors, available at http://www.ii.co.uk/news/?type=afx news&articleid=7230714&action=article.

RIS (Research and Information System for Developing Countries) Policy Brief (2008), 'Deepening regional cooperation in the Bay of Bengal: agenda of the BIMSTEC Summit', No. 38, November, available at http://www.ris.org.in/pb38.pdf.

Roberts, Peter and Alex Cull (2003), 'Building the Trans-ASEAN gas pipeline', *Asia Pacific Review*, July, 15–20.

United Nations Economic and Social Commission for Asia and the Pacific (UNESCAP) (2009), 'Asian highway classification, design and standards', available at http://www.unescap.org/ttdw/common/tis/ah/AnnexII-E.pdf.

WEF (World Economic Forum) (2008a), *The Global Competitiveness Report 2007-2008*.

WEF (World Economic Forum) (2008b), 'The global enabling trade report', available at http://www.weforum.org/documents/get08 browser/index.html.

WEF (World Economic Forum) (2008c), *The Global Competitiveness Report 2008–2009*.

World Bank (2008), *World Development Indicators CD-ROM 2008*, Washington DC: World Bank

World Bank (2009), *World Development Report 2009: Reshaping Economic Geography*, Washington DC: World Bank.

PART V

Cohesion and Sustainability

15. Economic integration and regional disparities in East Asia

Nobuaki Hamaguchi and Wei Zhao

15.1 INTRODUCTION

Compared to North America and Europe, East Asia contains countries with substantially different income levels. In 2007, the per capita gross national income of Japan was about 67 times larger than those of the Lao PDR and Cambodia. By contrast, the per capita national income disparity between the United States and Mexico was 5.5 times, while among 27 member states of the EU, the difference between Ireland (the highest except for Luxembourg) and Romania (the lowest) was about ten times. On the other hand, it is believed that income inequality within each country of East Asia is relatively small, compared, for example, with Latin America.

Even so, there is plentiful evidence to suggest that societies in East Asian countries are becoming increasingly unequal. Only a part of each country is effectively incorporated into the successful nexus of East Asian economic integration, leaving other regions unaffected by the dynamic process that is at work in East Asia as a whole. A conspicuous feature is that the division between prosperous groups and bypassed ones often has a spatial dimension (World Bank 2008), signifying pronounced regional inequality. Regional inequality is just one facet of income inequality within a country where there are many other kinds of inequality in, for example, education levels, ethnic composition of the population, gender, formal and informal types of economic activity, and rural and urban lifestyles. Yet, issues of regional inequality are given great attention by policy makers because of organized voting behavior or because of the threat that fierce conflicts, arising in the context of regions where people share common local interests, can pose for the stability of ruling national governments.

This chapter aims to give a regional interpretation of trends in East Asia by discussing some of the underlying forces that are responsible for the emergence of regional income inequality. In this, it is important to recognize that a region is a flexible concept that can be applied to areas that span national borders as well as to areas within them. The chapter will analyze inequality by defining regions in various layers: in the international sphere, as geographical groupings within each country, and as purely local divisions.

The chapter is organized as follows. In the next section, we will review some conceptual issues related to the possible influence of trade integration on the emergence of income inequality among countries and among regions within a country. By encouraging the location of production to develop internationally and by emphasizing the importance of scale economies, trade integration tends to narrow income inequalities among countries while widening inequalities among regions within a country. Such concurrent change can be explained from the viewpoint of the new economic geography. In section 15.3 of the chapter, we will trace the evolution of regional income inequality in Japan and will relate this phenomenon to the transformation of Japan's industrial structure. We will also examine the contention that the concentration of income in primate cities is a strongly persistent trend in Asian developing countries. Section 15.4 presents an analysis of China's regional inequality and shows the need to adopt a viewpoint that takes into account the differences in the responses of Chinese regions to institutional transition from a centrally planned to a market economy. Section 15.5 draws the various threads of the discussion into a conclusion.

15.2   CONCEPTUAL ISSUES

15.2.1   Trade and International Income Inequality

First, we need to consider East Asia as a region and pay attention to inequality across countries. According to the neoclassical economic model, economic growth leads each country towards a long-run income level, or steady state. If countries share the same steady state, we might expect a convergence of income level in which poorer countries in the initial stages should grow faster than richer ones. Thus, many empirical works investigate the existence of a negative relationship between the initial per capita GDP and the growth of per capita GNP across countries, or in other words absolute or unconditional convergence (Barro and Sala-i-Martin 1991).

If empirical regression analysis shows income convergence only after controlling for additional factors that affect the steady state level, the process is called conditional convergence. In this case, each country travels towards its own steady state independent of the others, a development that does not necessarily mean that poorer countries are catching up with richer ones, and one that explains the persistence of income gaps across countries. In a slightly different context, Ben-David (1995) points out the emergence of convergence clubs where income convergence is prevalent at both ends of the income spectrum while the middle group vanishes. Ben-David (1996, 1998) also shows that high income countries that trade extensively with one another show convergence while the low income club represents the poverty trap in which people lack a basic productive capability and survive by depleting their initial endowment. In this case, the gap between the rich and poor economies should be widening. If so, will poor countries leap out of poverty if they can be integrated into the international trade system? Although the answer to this question is not quite clear within the framework of the neoclassical model of constant returns to scale (see Slaughter 2001), it is likely that poor countries also gain from trade because the payments to unskilled labor will increase as a result of being intensively employed in activities relating to the exports of the country concerned.

On the assumption that industrial goods are characterized by increasing returns to scale (IRS) technology, Krugman and Venables (1995) showed that globalization (the reduction of trade costs across nations) first intensifies the concentration of industrialization in richer countries which have better access to consumer markets and input suppliers. Since workers are not mobile across nations, agglomeration of industries raises wages in countries with IRS industries, widening the gap between them and poor countries that have no IRS industries. Redding and Venables (2004), meanwhile, found support for the hypothesis that access to markets and suppliers explains cross-country variations in per capita income. However, Krugman and Venables (1995) assert that if trade costs become sufficiently low, firms will be highly sensitive to wage differentials, and will relocate to lower wage countries, and wage disparities will be narrow. Hence, the model based on IRS industries implies that the effect of trade on international income inequality depends on how well poor countries are integrated.

While we usually assume that labor cannot move easily across countries, capital is fairly mobile even internationally, as shown by the increasing presence throughout the world of multinational firms. Foreign direct investment generates local industrial employment related to trade, mobilizing workers from the rural sector, and thus contributes to the catching-up process of the poorer countries. In East Asia, foreign direct investment has functioned as a catalyst in the process known as the 'flying geese' pattern of economic development (Fujita and Hamaguchi 2008, and Kumagai, in the Introduction to this volume). The wide disparity in income levels across the nations of the region has served as the basis

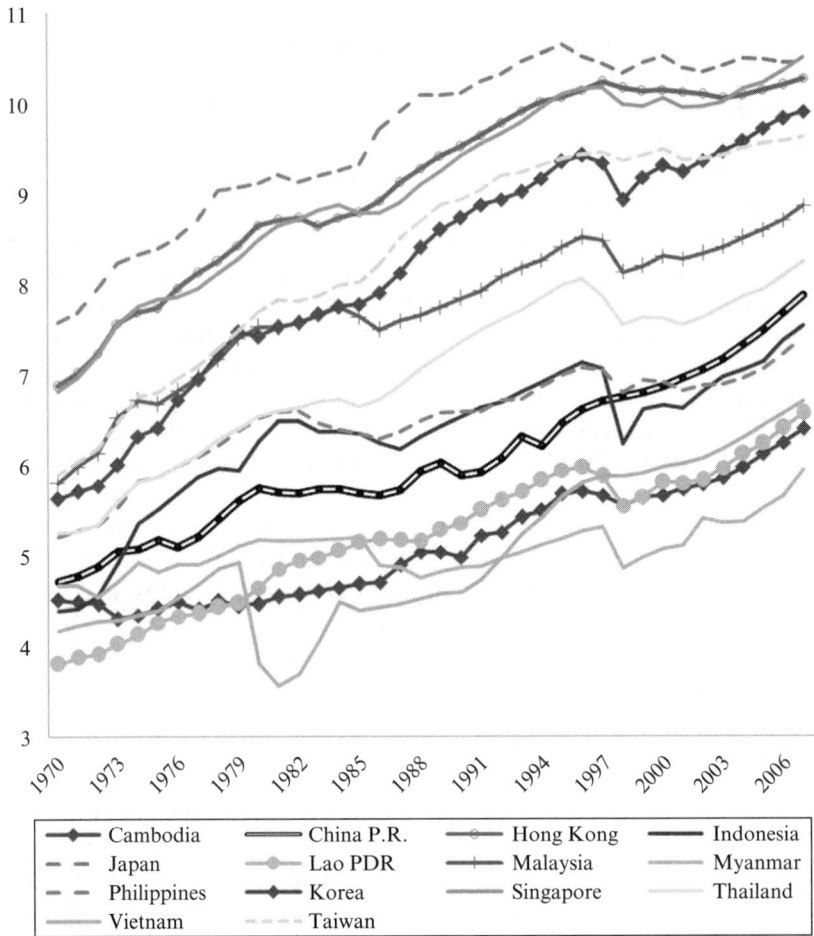

Note: Vertical axis: log of per capita GDP.

Source: United Nations National Accounts Database (http://unstats.un.org/unsd/snaama/selectionbasicFast.asp).

Figure 15.1   Growth of per capita GDP of the East Asian countries

for the formation of productive linkages by multinational firms which fragment their productive processes (Kimura and Ando 2005), allowing late-industrializing economies to embark on industrialization based on the abundant availability of cheap labor.

Figure 15.1 reveals the tendency for international income convergence

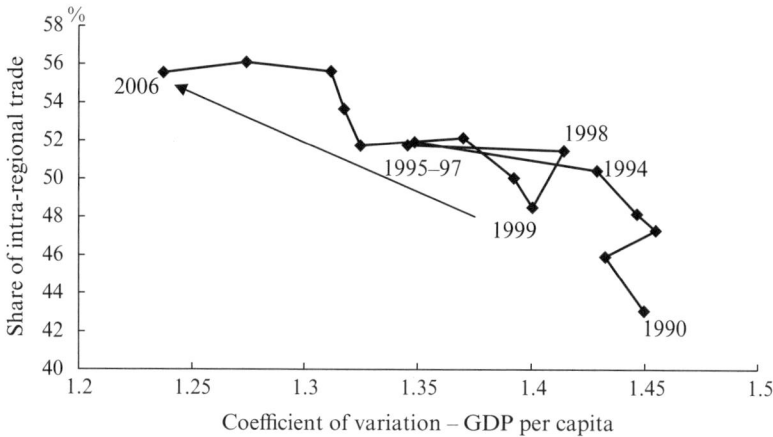

Source: GDP per capita from United Nations National Accounts Database (http://
unstats.un.org/unsd/snaama/selectionbasicFast.asp) and Taiwan National Statistics (http://
www1.stat.gov.tw); share of intra-regional trade from ADB-Asia Integration Center (http://
aric.adb.org/indicator.php).

Figure 15.2   Regional integration and income inequality among countries

to occur in East Asia. At the top, the income levels of Japan and that of the
four NIEs (Korea, Singapore, Hong Kong, and Taiwan) are converging,
whereas Korea and Taiwan, which were poorer initially, grew faster than
the others and are now approaching the top group. The lowest income
group consisting of Cambodia, Lao PDR, Myanmar, and Vietnam also
shows convergence among the countries concerned, Vietnam being the
group's star performer in recent years. The middle income group is more
dispersed but also shows a tendency towards convergence from the 1980s
to the present. Within this group, the ASEAN4 countries (Indonesia,
Malaysia, the Philippines, and Thailand) were more seriously affected by
the economic crises of the 1980s and by the financial crisis of 1997–98,
while China maintained economic growth throughout.

   Although the growth trajectories of countries in the region show considerable variety, we can observe international income convergence in the
East Asian region as a whole, and the economy of the region has exhibited
a deepening integration. This can be seen in Figure 15.2. In this figure, with
respect to the annual situation in the same 15 countries, we plot the coefficient of variation of per capita GDP as a measure of international income
disparity, and the share of intra-regional trade as a measure of regional integration. The diagram shows that deepening of regional trade integration is
associated with a reduction of international income inequality in East Asia.

15.2.2   Regional Income Inequality Within a Country

Next, let us turn to income inequality among regions within a country. In a seminal work, Williamson (1965) found an inverted-U shaped pattern between economic development and regional inequality. That is, regional inequality increases as the economy develops from the low- to middle-income stage, and then decreases in the later stages of development.

In order to understand this process, it is essential to consider the role of migration. In the neoclassical framework which assumes decreasing marginal product of labor, workers move from a labor-abundant location to a labor-scarce one, attracted by higher wages. Since the migration leads to factor price equalization, this implies faster and more complete income convergence (Magrini 2004). Thus, as a higher proportion of population migrates to the urban sector, regional inequality will decrease in the later development stage. Although this paradigm describes the process from concentration to dispersion, it cannot explain why industries agglomerate in the first place, unless it can rely on a priori assumptions of lumpiness of geography such as existence of a port (or any other transportation advantage) and access to the source of a non-ubiquitous input.

Without introducing such ad hoc assumptions, new economic geography (NEG) models standardized by Fujita et al. (1999) provide an alternative interpretation. When trade costs are very high, firms will produce near consumers, and by so doing, firms will disperse. When trade costs are reduced to a reasonable level, IRS firms will relocate to a bigger market, without losing many sales in the smaller market, by delivering with cost. Because IRS firms are more profitable in the bigger market, they offer higher wages, and this induces workers to move to the location with a larger number of firms. This, in turn, increases scale economies in the bigger market and attracts even more IRS firms. This cumulative process leads to the concentration of firms and workers in a particular location. When trade costs are reduced to an extremely low level, market access is no longer a concern for firms, and they move from a high cost industrial agglomeration to a lower cost periphery. In this way, dispersion occurs. NEG models show that regional income disparity increases with agglomeration and then equalizes with dispersion, a finding that is consistent with Williamson (1965).

We can broadly characterize the current situation of regional income inequality and urbanization in East Asia as follows. As shown by Table 15.1, the gap between the richest and the poorest regions varies from country to country. In some countries, the gap is significantly large, exceeding a factor of ten. Next, using the agglomeration index[1] of the World Bank (2008), we can assemble the following groups by degree of

Table 15.1   Difference in per capita gross regional domestic product (GRDP) between the richest and the poorest local units

	Richest	Poorest	Richest/poorest per capita GRDP ratio	Year
Japan	Tokyo	Okinawa	2.36	2005
China	Shanghai	Guizhou	9.97	2006
Malaysia	Kuala Lumpur	Kelantan	4.55	2005
Philippines	Metro Manila	Muslim Mindanao	11.24	2007
Indonesia	DKI Jakarta	Gorontalo	15.16	2005
Thailand	Bangkok & Vicinities	Northeast	7.88	2007
Lao PDR	Vientiane	Huaphanh	6.28	2006–7

Source: Official statistics of each country, except for Malaysia, whose data are taken from the Eighth Malaysia Plan.

urbanization: high (80–100) – Hong Kong, Japan, Korea, Singapore, Taiwan; medium high (60–80) – Malaysia; medium low (40–60) Indonesia, the Philippines, and Vietnam; and low (less than 40) – China, Thailand, Cambodia, Myanmar, and the Lao PDR. Inspection of these data reveals that regional income inequality is larger in countries belonging to the medium low and low urbanization groups. This suggests that the movement of a higher proportion of the population into the urban sector might reduce regional inequality. This proposition is supported by the theoretical analysis of Puga (1999) using an NEG model that further develops Krugman and Venables (1995) by introducing the variable of labor mobility. Puga has shown that the free relocation of workers should eliminate wage differentials as a result of the agglomeration of industries. Thus, if people decide to live in rural areas because of factors that impede mobility, we might expect a persistence of the income gap. See the case of the regional policy introduced in the European integration process (Box 15.1).

Two policy issues need to be raised regarding factors that generate serious regional inequality. One possible explanation of inequality is the existence of restrictions imposed on migration, such as is the case in China. Meanwhile, Zhang and Zhang (2003) provide evidence to support the view that regional income inequality in China reflects segmentations of factor markets (labor and capital), as a result of which the benefits of China's integration with the global economy are distributed across regions in a highly uneven manner.

Another possible explanation for regional inequality is the lack of

---

BOX 15.1   EU REGIONAL POLICY

When Greece, Spain and Portugal became members of the EU, the resulting expansion of European integration required explicit regional policy because of the increased voting power of the poorer members (Baldwin and Wyplosz 2004). Under the aegis of the Directorate General for Regional Policy, the European Union (EU) administers two special funds (Structural Funds and Cohesion Funds) for three objectives: convergence of living standards through promoting growth-enhancing conditions in poor regions, regional competitiveness and employment through the improvement of accessibility to technology and human capital development, and European territorial cooperation to strengthen cross-border cooperation through joint local and regional initiatives. Structural Funds are composed of a Regional Development Fund (ERDF) aimed at infrastructure development, and a European Social Fund (ESF). The ERDF pays particular attention to infrastructure building for innovation, telecommunications, transportation, and energy, while ESF targets unemployment aid. The Cohesion Fund is only for poorer countries whose GDP per capita is below 75% of the EU average. In the 2008 budget, 36% of the total budget of the EU went to supporting structural and cohesion policy. About 22% of the population of the member states is covered by the EU's regional policy funds (http://ec.europa.eu/regional_policy/objective1/index_en.htm).

According to Puga (2002), income differences across member states have shrunk, but inequalities between regions within each member state have widened. Midelfart-Knarvik and Overman (2002) found that regional policy aid has helped recipients to attract R&D-intensive industries, even though such industries are not necessarily suited to underdeveloped regions which are not abundantly endowed with highly skilled labor. In other words, EU regional policy tends to promote technology intensive industries but is distortional in terms of resource allocation efficiency.

---

an infrastructure adequate enough to sustain the growth of the urban sector. By way of an example, let us consider a region of a country that is integrated to the East Asian production network. This region potentially enjoys the achievement of significant scale economies because it is connected to the global market. However, it soon reaches a growth limit if its infrastructure is poorly developed, and if for example it lacks a transport network capable of serving surrounding areas and if its circumstances do not allow the development of industrial concentrations, an electricity grid, housing estates, and the like. People may still migrate to rich regions attracted by the wage gap, but the urban sector cannot properly accommodate them, resulting in an expansion of slums and the growth of an informal economy, an adverse development that is known as the 'Todaro paradox'. In such cases, we may argue that existing agglomerations are too small to let the people in poor regions escape out of poverty.

15.3   REGIONAL INCOME INEQUALITY IN EAST ASIA

15.3.1   Transformation of the Japanese Regional Economy in a Nutshell

In order to understand the relationship between the integration of a country with the global economy and regional income inequality, it is instructive to start with an overview of the historical process of economic growth in Japan, a country which has undergone a substantial transition from underdevelopment to the developed economy stage.

During the high growth period of the Japanese economy (between the late 1950s and the early 1970s), there was steady population migration from non-metropolitan areas to the three largest metropolitan areas (MAs): Tokyo, Osaka, and Nagoya. During this period, the income inequality depicted by Figure 15.3 (using Theil's index) exhibited an inverted-U shape. Fujita and Tabuchi (1997) noted that migration in this period was a consequence of the income differentials, but that the reverse is not true. This implies that the migration from the non-MAs to the MAs increased the labor supply in the latter and reduced it in the former, narrowing the income disparities between the two. Figure 15.3 shows that the decline of inequality between non-MAs and MAs accounted for most of the decrease in total inequality that had occurred by the mid-1970s.

The two energy crises of the 1970s seriously affected the Osaka and Nagoya MAs, both of which had developed a strong specialization in heavy and chemical industries. Moreover at this time, the Japanese economy underwent a transition towards the service and financial sectors, and towards R&D-intensive high technology production and related producer services. As part of this process, an increasing concentration of corporate headquarters and R&D activities in the Tokyo MA, together with an agglomeration of highly skilled workers, paved the way for the emergence of the 'Tokyo monopolar system' (Tabuchi and Fujita 1997). Since

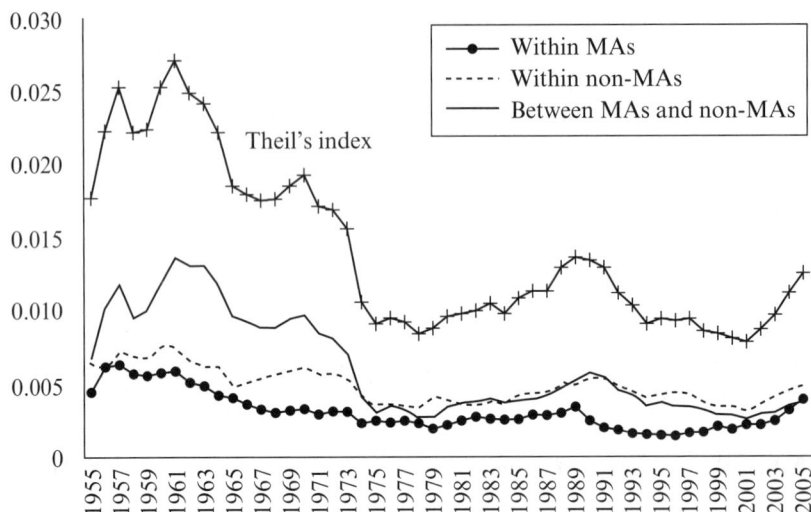

Note: Metropolitan Areas (MAs) include: Tokyo MA (Tokyo, Kanagawa, Chiba, Saitama); Nagoya MA (Aichi, Gifu, Shizuoka, Mie); and Osaka MA (Osaka, Kyoto, Hyogo, Nara).

Source: Cabinet Office, http://www.esri.cao.go.jp/jp/sna/toukei.html#kenmin.

Figure 15.3   Japan: decomposition of Theil's index of interregional per capita GRP

the mid-1970s, net population inflows into the Osaka and Nagoya MAs have become stagnant, and the two regions have even undergone some net outflow. By contrast, net migration to the Tokyo MA grew throughout the 1980s and continued until 1992. It should be noted that this monopolar population growth was accompanied by a widening regional per capita income disparity,[2] which was propelled mainly by the difference between MAs and non-MAs. This provided the basis for the development of a real estate bubble, because the increase in the number of workers earning higher incomes in a narrower space intensified the demand for land.

When the bubble burst, thrusting the economy into a prolonged financial crisis, net population inflow into the Tokyo MA dropped sharply between 1993 and 1996 and then resumed vigorously as the economy gradually recovered from the recession. Inequality of prefectural per capita GDP began to rise again after 2001. It should be noted that in this process, although the difference between MAs and non-MAs has been losing importance, the influences of the difference within non-MAs and within MAs are continuing to rise. The increasing difference within non-MAs is attributable to the encroachment of industrial areas into the non-MA prefectures surrounding the MAs, and in these new industrial areas, incomes have grown faster than in the country's peripheral prefectures. The rise in inequality within the group of MAs, on the other hand, reflects reinforcement of the preeminent position of the Tokyo MA in the current knowledge-intensive industrial economy of Japan.

The recent history of Japanese regional inequality suggests that the process of the rise and fall of regional inequality is not a monotone but rather a phenomenon that can repeat itself as the economy changes its structure, influenced by agglomeration and the dispersion of economic activities and providing support in a Japanese context for the contentions advanced by NEG models. Japan's experience, and in particular the widening income inequality between Tokyo MA and the rest of the country, also shows that the shift to a knowledge-based economy can alter the economic geography of a country from a multi-centric pattern to a monocentric one. The reduction of trade costs related to the emergence of knowledge-intensive activities, accompanied by savings in travel time and the development of information and communication technology, may have accelerated this process.

15.3.2 Regional Inequality in Developing East Asia

In developing countries in East Asia, regional income inequality remains high and is becoming ever more conspicuous, reflecting the sustained agglomeration of industries and the migration of workers to the main economic centers. This is partly the result of the transition of industrialization in each country from import-substitution types of industrial production to export-oriented ones. During the import-substitution phase, a preference for market access induced firms to concentrate in large cities. This process left its mark on the export-oriented industrialization era because industries were attracted by the better infrastructure quality offered by traditional economic centers.[3]

Figure 15.4 shows the recent trend of per capita gross regional domestic product comparing Metro Manila and the rest of the Philippines. The figure makes it clear that Metro Manila has grown faster than the rest of the country in recent years and that the disparity between the two is now widening. Metro Manila enjoys a dominant position and in recent years has come to account for about one-third of national GDP in recent years. Balisacan et al. (2008) point out the high cost of domestic mobility, and especially that of labor, not only because of the country's archipelagic geography but also because serious underinvestment in infrastructure for national integration has created spatial disparities in welfare levels.

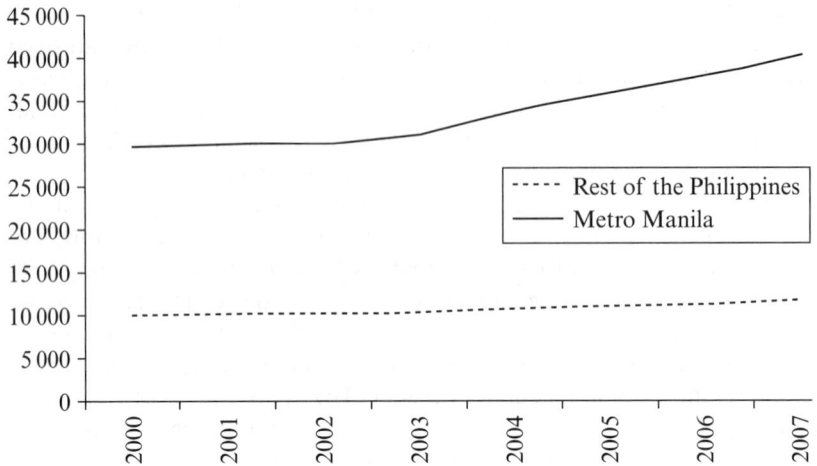

Note: Vertical axis 1985 price peso.

Source: National Statistical Coordination Board.

*Figure 15.4   Regional income inequality: GRDP per capita for Metro
Manila and the rest of the Philippines, 2000–07*

As is shown by Figure 15.5, regional inequality in Indonesia has shown
a slight rise and fall since the 1990s but remains at a very high level. This
figure needs to be interpreted with caution because of the influence of the
oil sector on resource-rich regions such as East Kalimantan whose per
capita private consumption share in the national total is much lower than
that of per capita gross regional domestic product (Hill 2008). Moreover
the inequality figure can be misleading because it is influenced by the oil
price. In fact, as a result of concentration in Jakarta and its surrounding
urban sprawl, the dominance of West Java has intensified. Thus the metropolitan region's share of GDP increased from 28.9% in 1990 to 34% in
2004.

Although they contain regions such as Riau (connection with Singapore),
Bali (tourism) and Cebu (an export processing zone) that have achieved a
comparatively high degree of integration with the world market, both
Indonesia and the Philippines exhibit geographical patterns of economic
activity that are strongly centralized.

Turning to Thailand, a quick inspection of Theil's index as depicted
by Figure 15.6 shows that regional income inequality is rising sharply.
Decomposition of the Theil index reveals that inequality between the metropolitan and non-metropolitan areas was what basically drove the rise in

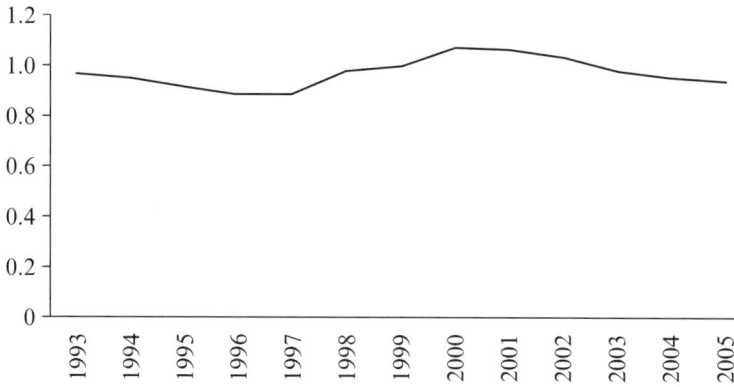

Note: Vertical axis is for the coefficient of variation of provincial GRDP.

Source: Statistics Indonesia (BPS).

Figure 15.5 Provincial income inequality in Indonesia (1993–2005)

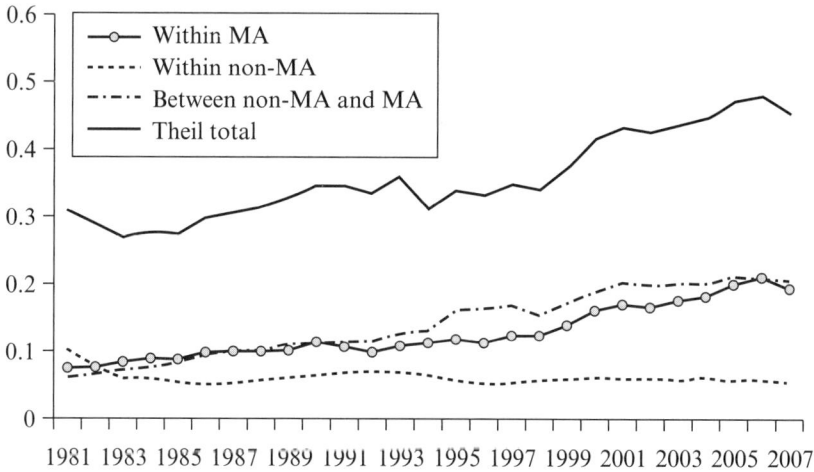

Note: Metropolitan Area (MA) includes Bangkok and vicinities, Eastern, and North regions.

Source: National Economic and Social Development Board.

Figure 15.6 Thailand (1981–2007): decomposition of inequality of per capita GRDP using Theil's index

inequality until the end of the 1990s. Since 2000, however, there has been little change in this difference and instead, it has been mainly inequality within the provinces of the MA that has caused the gap to widen. Closer inspection of the data reveals a remarkable increase in the regional GDP of Rayong province in the Eastern region, where the automobile industry is rapidly agglomerating in the Eastern Seaboard industrial estates.

Finally, the question of regional income inequality in China has been the focus of much attention in recent years. Since China exhibits a complex spatial system, we will discuss this issue at greater length in the following section.

15.4   REGIONAL INCOME DISPARITY IN CHINA

15.4.1   Understanding the Structure of Regions in China

'Regions' in China can be defined and classified in terms of several layers in accordance with the different dimensions that result from the characteristics of political, economical and geographical divisions and the governing structure related to them. The four layers below are usually considered appropriate for dividing Mainland China into economic regions.

The first layer is that of the 'national economy', which since mid-1980s has been officially classified into three broad areas: the East area consisting of nine provinces and the three municipalities that are directly ruled by central government (Beijing, Tianjin, and Shanghai), the Middle area, consisting of nine provinces, and the West area, consisting of nine provinces and one government-administered municipality (Chongqing).

The second layer is that of the provincial economies: in Mainland China there are 31 provinces and provincial level metropolitan regions (hereafter abbreviated as 'municipalities'). Most provinces in China have a population of between 30 million and 60 million and a land coverage ranging from 150,000 to 300,000 square kilometers, although the larger ones are even more than double these totals, in terms of either population size or land coverage and are comparable to big EU member states.[4]

The third layer is that of the prefectures and the prefecture-level municipalities (PLMs). Currently, there are 332 prefectures and PLMs in Mainland China. In the past, and especially during the period of the centrally planned economy, prefectural governments used to function as the representative agencies of provincial governments, but with the opening up of China and the reforms that have occurred during the last thirty years, they have been gradually transformed into units of local government with real administrative power. In the administrative hierarchy, they occupy a position that is intermediary between provincial governments and county ones.

The fourth layer is that of the counties. Each prefecture or PLM usually consists of six to twelve counties. A representative county in the coastland areas has a population of between one million and one and a half million and a land coverage of between 1,000 and 2,000 square kilometers. Big counties in China[5] are comparable to a big administrative province in France or an upper-middle-sized prefecture in Japan. Judicially, a county has enough power within its territory to administer a comparatively independent local economic system.

The intensification of regional income inequalities in China that has accompanied the remarkable economic growth that followed the introduction of market reforms has attracted much attention. As will become apparent below, discussions among academics and policy makers have overwhelmingly focused on the higher layers of the four-layer model (in other words on the first and second layers). However for a country like China which is large and geographically diverse, the real situation cannot be adequately depicted without considering circumstances in the units that make up the lower layers (that is, the prefectures and counties). We refer the reader to Box 15.2 for additional insights.

15.4.2 Regional Income Disparity in China: The Upper-layer Regions

In the first layer of regions, or in other words at the level of the national economy, there are substantial regional income disparities among the three broad regions, namely the East, the Middle and West areas. The official statistics show that in 1996, per capita GDP in the East area was 53% higher than the national average, while in the Middle and West areas, it was 19.5% and 37.3% lower respectively. Ten years later, the advanced East Area had extended its lead still further, with a per capita GDP that was 66.8% higher than the national average. Meanwhile the relatively lowly position of the two backward areas remained almost unchanged (see Table 15.2).

As regards the second layer of regions, namely the provinces (see Figure 15.7), we here compare the per capita GDP of all the provincial economies (throughout this chapter, we include in this layer the autonomous regions of minorities, and municipalities administered directly by central government). We can classify provinces into four groups according to the following criteria. Table 15.3 exhibits those ranked at the top, the middle, and the bottom in each group in terms of income level.

Group A This group consists of the most developed provinces, which can be defined as those whose regional per capita GDP is over double the

BOX 15.2 LOWER-LAYERED REGIONS VIEW ON REGIONAL INCOME DISPARITY IN CHINA

In Section 15.4.2, we showed that regional income disparities within Mainland China are conspicuous in the higher layer regions, especially among provinces and province-level municipalities. In the lower layer regions that consist of prefectures and counties, the extent of inequality is quite diverse. This seems natural considering the vast size and geographical diversity of China, and taking into account the fact that local governments are empowered to make practical decisions as the central government is often too remote from prefectures and counties to impose direct influence. Since such lower-layered regional inequalities constitute a significant part of the gap between the rich and poor regions, it is not enough to depict the real circumstances of regional income disparity in China without considering the lower echelons of the regional hierarchy, namely the prefecture and county layers.

For illustration, we have chosen two similar geographical units in terms of average income and we compare regional income distribution within each geographical unit. The units concerned are Zhejiang and Guangdong provinces, both of which belong to Group B in Table 15.3, and we examine the two provinces in terms of inter-prefecture inequality. Zhejiang forms part of the Yangzi River Delta area while Guangdong is located in the Zhu Jiang (Pearl River) Delta area. The two provinces have often been seen as models in studies of Chinese regional economic development in the last thirty years, although they have followed different paths so far as institutional transformation and opening up of the regional economy have been concerned (Zhao 2001, 2005). As is well known, Guangdong was the first part of China to benefit from the opening-up of the economy and at an early stage it became dependent on foreign direct investment in a single highly concentrated region, whereas the development of Zhejiang's economy has been based on clusters of small and medium-size local private enterprises emerging within the province.

As reported in Box Table 15.1, there exists a similarly big difference in per capita regional GDP between the richest prefecture and the poorest one in both provinces. There is notable difference in the distribution. Zhejiang province's 11 prefectures are almost evenly split into five above the provincial average (37,128 Yuan) and six below it. In contrast, the twelve typical prefectures that we chose from the 21 prefectures of Guangdong province are polarized between the two richest, with a per capita GDP of over 70,000 Yuan, and the others, which are below the provincial average (32,713 Yuan in 2007). The difference in per capita GDP between the richest prefectural region and the poorest one is as much as 7.6 times in Guangdong province, which is much bigger than that in Zhejiang (3.3 times bigger). Thus, although their average income level is similar, the prefectures display a contrast in income disparity, which is much more pronounced in Guangdong than in Zhejiang.

The example of the contrasting situations in these two coastal provinces shows us the importance of different patterns of regional industrialization in shaping the formation of regional disparities. Recent research (Zhao 2009) suggests that the two provinces took different paths in terms of capital formation and investment flow in their regional industrialization. In Guangdong

Box Table 15.1   Income disparities at prefectural level: Zhejiang and Guangdong (2007)

A. Within Zhejiang				B. Within Guangdong			
	Per capita GDP (Yuan)	As % of provincial average	As % of bottom		Per capita GDP (Yuan)	As % of provincial average	As % of bottom
Hangzhou	51878	139.7	329.6	Shenzhen	79614	243.4	761.9
Ningbo	51460	138.6	326.9	Guangzhou	72274	220.9	691.6
Jiaxing	40206	108.3	255.4	Fuoshan	61255	187.2	586.2
Shaoxing	38540	103.8	244.9	Zhongshan	48729	149.0	466.3
Zhoushan	34682	93.4	220.3	Dongguan	46690	142.7	446.8
Huzhou	29527	79.5	187.6	Huizhou	28857	88.2	276.1
Jinhua	27108	73.0	172.2	Jiangmen	26650	81.5	255.0
Taizhou	26026	70.1	165.3	Shanwei	17089	52.2	163.5
Wenzhou	24390	65.7	155.0	Zhaoqing	16818	51.4	160.9
Lishui	18644	50.2	118.4	Chaozhou	15312	46.8	146.5
Quzhou	15740	42.4	100.0	Shanwei	10521	32.2	100.7
				Jieyang	10450	31.9	100.0

Source: Zhejiang Provincial Bureau of Statistics, 2008.

Source: Guangdong Provincial Bureau of Statistics, 2008.

province, especially in the Pearl River Delta area, investment was at first heavily concentrated in the metropolitan area, and then flowed out to the towns and the countryside, while in Zhejiang, the opposite occurred. In Zhejiang, to begin with, medium-size industrial clusters were formed, at first in a dispersed pattern, and some of these are now expanding with the further opening up of the economy. This difference of industrial capability among towns and villages can reasonably explain the different circumstances of income disparity between the two provinces, suggesting the importance of factors that result from the diversity of institutions at the prefectural layer of regions in transition in an economy such as the Chinese one.

Turning now to the income difference among counties within the prefectures of the group which we classified as the lowest layer, let us choose two prefectures from Jiangsu province in the Yangzi River delta. Jiangsu has become famous in recent years for combining township industries with foreign direct investment. The two prefectures we chose are Suzhou and Yangcheng which are respectively ranked in the top and bottom positions in the province in terms of per capita regional GDP, the former's being 5.5 times the size of the latter's. According to Box Table 15.2, among the five

Box Table 15.2   Economic differences at county level: two Jiangsu prefectures compared

Counties	GDP per capita (Yuan)	As % of prefecture average	As % of bottom county	Counties	GDP per capita (Yuan)	As % of prefecture average	As % of bottom county
Suzhou Prefecture Counties	91 911	100.0		Yancheng Prefecture Counties	16 987	100.0	
Kunshan	171 068	186.1	218.9	Dafeng	23 864	140.5	249.8
Zhangjiagang	117 927	128.3	150.9	Dongtai	19 455	114.5	203.6
Taican	95 173	103.5	121.8	Jianhu	17 376	102.3	181.9
Changshu	91 847	99.9	117.5	Sheyang	14 992	88.3	156.9
Wujiang	78 149	85.0	100.0	Funing	11 004	64.8	115.2
				Xiangshui	10 454	61.5	109.4
				Binghai	9 554	56.2	100.0

Source: Jiangsu Provincial Bureau of Statistics, Statistical Yearbook of Jiangsu, 2008.

counties (or county-ranked municipalities) in Suzhou prefecture, the difference in per capita GDP of the richest county (Kunshan) and the poorest (Wujiang) is just 2.2 times, whereas among the seven counties of Yangcheng prefecture, the per capita GDP of Dafeng (the richest) is about 2.5 times bigger than that of Binhai (the poorest). Thus, income disparities appear to be less accentuated among counties and the magnitude is almost the same regardless of the average income level of the prefectures to which they belong.

Table 15.2   Per capita GDP difference among China's East, Middle, and West areas (1996, 2006)

	1996		2006	
	Average per capita GDP (Yuan)	As % of national average	Average per capita GDP (Yuan)	As % of national average
National	6079	100	16113	100
East	9299	153	26882	166.8
Middle	4893	80.5	12737	79.0
West	3810	62.7	10298	63.9

Source: National Bureau of Statistics of China (1998, 2007).

national average. All the three coastland municipalities, namely Shanghai, Beijing and Tianjin, clearly belong to this group. The top and the bottom positions are held by Shanghai and Tianjin respectively, while Beijing is in the middle. Official statistics in 2006 showed that Shanghai's per capita GDP amounted to 57,695 Yuan (approximately US$7,389[6]), whereas Beijing and Tianjin were not far behind, their per capita GDP being respectively 87.5% and 71.3% of that of Shanghai.

Group B   This group consists of the relatively developed provinces whose provincial per capita GDP is above the national average but not greater than double the average. Nine provincial regions can be put into this group. The per capita GDP of the province at the top of this group (Zhejiang, with 31,874 Yuan, approximately US$4,082) is almost twice as large as that of the bottom province, Heilongjiang, with 16,195 Yuan (about US$ 2,074), while the middle-ranking Shangdong has about

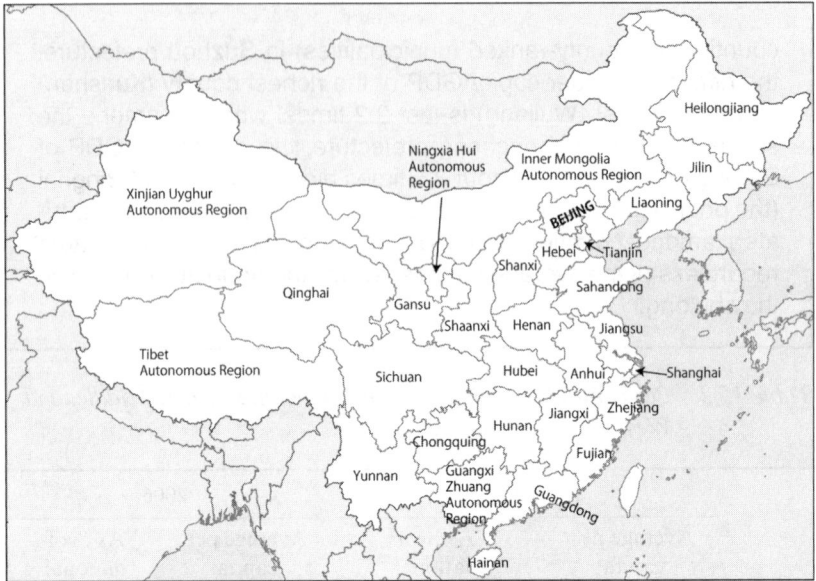

Figure 15.7   Mainland China

two-thirds of the per capita GDP of Zhejiang province. Income levels of most provinces in this group are similar to that of Shangdong.

Group C   This group consists of the relatively underdeveloped regions whose provincial GDP per capita is between 70 and 99% of the national average. Ten provincial regions come into this category. The topmost and lowest ranking members of this group are Jilin and Qinghai respectively. The income level of the former is about four times that of the latter – a gap that is larger than in the other regional groups. Per capita GDP of the middle rank province in this group is roughly 80% of that of the topmost member of the group.

Group D   This group consists of the least developed provinces whose provincial per capita GDP is less than 70% of the national average. Eight provinces belong to this group. The topmost province of the group is Jiangxi whose per capita GDP (10,798 Yuan, about US$ 1,382) is nearly double the size of that of the bottom-ranked Guizhou province (5,787 Yuan, about US$ 741). Per capita GDP of the middle rank province in this group is only 8,970 Yuan (US$1149), which is about 83% of that of Jiangxi.

The above regional outline leads us to the following conclusion. The

Table 15.3 China: per capita GDP difference at provincial level (2006)

Sample regions		GDP per capita (Yuan)	As % of national average	As % of the group top	As % of national top	Other provinces in the group
Group A*						
top	Shanghai	57 695	358.1	100.0	100.0	–
middle	Beijing	50 467	313.2	87.5	87.5	
bottom	Tianjin	41 163	255.5	71.3	71.3	
Group B						
top	Zhejiang	31 874	197.8	100	55.2	Jiangsu, Guangdong, Hebei, Liaoning, Fujian, Inner Mongolia.
middle	Shandong	23 794	147.7	74.7	41.2	
bottom	Heilon-gjiang	16 195	100.5	50.8	28.1	
Group C						
top	Jilin	15 720	97.6	100.0	27.2	Xinjiang, Hainan Shanxi, Shan'xi, Hunan, Hubei, Ningxia, Chongquing
middle	Henan	13 313	82.6	84.7	23.1	
bottom	Qinghai	11 762	73.0	74.8	20.4	
Group D						
top	Jiangxi	10 798	67.0	100.0	18.7	Sichuan, Tibet, Guangxi, Anhui, Gansu
middle	Yunnan	8 970	55.7	83.1	15.5	
bottom	Guizhou	5 787	35.9	53.6	10.0	

Note: *This group consists of municipalities administered by the central government.

Source: National Bureau of Statistics of China (2007).

division between the East area (the coastlands of China) and other two areas (the inland regions) basically coincides with the division of Groups A and B as opposed to Groups C and D. Table 15.3 shows that only one province (Hainan) that originally belonged to the East area, is included in Group C, which mainly consists of non-East area provinces. But regions belonging to the Middle area and West area are mixed together in Groups C and D. Table 15.2 shows that even the poorest West area province has an average per capita regional GDP that is about 40% of that of the East area in both 1996 and 2006. There are much clearer income differences between Group A and the other provinces. Thus Zhejiang, the province at the top of Group B, has a per capita GDP that is only 55.2% of that of Shanghai, while the per capita GDP totals of the middle-ranking provinces in Groups B, C, and D amount respectively to only 41.1%, 23.1% and 15.5% of that of Shanghai, and the per capita GDP of the poorest province, Guizhou, is just one tenth of that of Shanghai. We can therefore say that the income inequality that is apparent in the second layer is much greater than that in the first layer.

15.4.3 Unbalanced Progress of Institutional Reform and Regional Policies

The remarkable gaps in wealth among the Chinese regions, especially at national and provincial levels, have been one of the main concerns of economic researchers and governmental policy makers since the late 1990s. The Chinese central government has launched a series of policies in the form of strategic initiatives such as the 'West Area Development Strategy' and 'Constructing a Harmonized Society' and so on. It is, however, either too difficult or too early to evaluate the actual effects of the governmental policies and strategies on regional disparities that have been launched so far. In fact researchers remain very much divided as to whether or not the disparities have slowed down or have even gone into reverse during the last few years.

The Chinese economy is in the midst of a multi-faceted transition consisting of marketization, industrialization and internationalization. For this reason, it could well be misleading to examine regional disparities in present-day China and evaluate regional policies in the same way as we do with mature free-market-based industrial economies, without taking into account the heterogeneous nature of the Chinese economic transition. Earlier research (Zhao 2005, 2006) suggests that the economic disparities among the major regions (the three areas and the provincial regions) are evidently related to the unbalanced progress of institutional transformation and the opening up of regions. Although the central government pursues income redistribution policies such as infrastructure investment in less developed regions, the key barriers might still be inefficient institutional arrangements and incomplete integration of regions with the rest of the domestic market. For example, recent reforms of the property rights of production have included measures such as giving local residents usage-rights over forest lands in some backward areas. More so than government infrastructure investment, seemingly modest policies such as this have proved to be much more effective in increasing the family income of peasants and per capita GRDP in the regions.

This being the case, it is doubtful whether industrial relocation and the preferential allocation of infrastructure investment in favor of backward regions is an effective way of increasing productive jobs and income in such regions in an attempt to reduce regional inequalities. In fact for the Chinese economy, which is still in the midst of unfinished industrialization, productive capital and workers can be more efficiently utilized by concentrating on the developed areas, taking advantage of agglomeration economies, and thus creating more jobs and higher incomes in the long run. On balance, this may be a better way of achieving progress than redirecting labor and other resources to unproductive regions for the short-sighted purpose of immediate income redistribution.

15.5   CONCLUDING REMARKS

This chapter has examined income inequality across East Asia's geographical space at different levels. At the broadest level, we can observe a tendency toward income convergence among the East Asian countries, especially those that are more open to regional integration of trade and investment. We also find that in several countries the fruits of regional integration are enjoyed only within the limited geographical spaces in which industries agglomerate. The concurrence of international income convergence on the one hand and widening interregional income disparities within a country on the other, is related to the deepening of regional production linkages that have allowed finer vertical disintegration of the production process across the countries of the region and the formation of industrial agglomerations in which such globally linked production is concentrated, as has been discussed extensively in other chapters of this volume. We are led to the view that growing regional inequality is to some extent inevitable as the mobility of goods and productive factors increases with regional integration, because the strengthening of linkages with the international market and the promotion of agglomeration economies help countries to grow. Lack of labor mobility and insufficient urban infrastructure will prevent agglomerations becoming large enough to allow people in poor regions to migrate out of poverty, resulting in persisting and widening regional income inequality.

From the Chinese case study, it is between provinces that we find the most striking disparities although regional income inequalities are substantial at all levels of regional classification. Relatively richer provinces are concentrated in the East area. This has come about not only because of the natural advantages of the coastal area for international trade but also because there is a gap in progress toward institutional reform between China's developed and underdeveloped provinces. Beside the lack of agglomeration economies, in the Chinese context, policies to redirect investment to underdeveloped regions can be even more problematic and less productive than harmonizing institutional quality.

Taking the foregoing discussion into account, the following policy implication can be drawn. If it is the case that poor infrastructure is retarding the development of those industrial agglomerations that are integrated to the global market through the East Asian production network, priority should be given to investment in infrastructure development in such regions, and the population migration from the poor regions should be encouraged. In many developing countries, industrialization in agglomerations is as yet an unfinished agenda. Looked at another way, it may even be counter-productive to encourage industries to move to backward regions.

In reality, however, factor mobility will never be perfect. Since people will not move for many reasons including non-economic ones, regional inequality is likely to persist. Thus, policy makers should be concerned with how to narrow the gap between the prosperous regions and the bypassed ones. Development strategy at local level should aim at promoting scale economies by creating connections to the nearest node of the East Asian regional integration network. Thus, agglomerations will be linked as conceptualized in Chapters 2 and 3. If such a node is found in a different country, coordination may be necessary at national government level to facilitate cross-border locality-to-locality integration.

Finally, for localities whose natural conditions are disadvantageous for transportation development, product differentiation, or branding, is one way of overcoming economic distance (Fujita 2007). If activities such as agriculture and tourism take advantage of locally abundant resources, such as land, cheap labor, climate, and natural beauty, and produce products and services that are highly differentiated from generic competitors, such regions will be able to obtain access to the market even though they are in remote locations.

NOTES

1. See World Bank (2008), pp. 54–7 and Table A2.
2. In the interpretation of regional inequality, a caveat must be noted because these figures do not take into consideration inter-regional income transfers.
3. A notable exception is Malaysia where export industries have developed in regions far from the Selangor-Kuala Lumpur region. Such zones include the northern district of Penang, which has a good transportation infrastructure, and Johor, in the south, which enjoys close links with Singapore.
4. The latest census shows that out of 31 provinces and municipalities, nine have populations that are over 50 million, eleven are between 30 million and 50 million, seven between 10 million and 30 million, and only four have populations that are below 10 million. In the European Union, only four member countries, that is, Germany, France, Britain and Italy, have populations of over 50 million, two have populations of between 30 and 50 million, and six have populations of between 10 million and 30 million.
5. The three most populated counties in China are Puning in Guangdong province, Lingquan in Anhui province and Shuyang in Jiangsu province. In 2005, they had populations of 2.12 million, 2 million and 1.76 million respectively.
6. The exchange rate of the US dollar to the RMB Yuan was $1=¥7.8087 at the end of 2006.

REFERENCES

Baldwin, Richard and Charles Wyplosz (2004), *The Economics of European Integration*, New York: McGraw Hill.

Balisacan, Arsenio M., Hal Hill and Sharon Faye Piza (2008), 'Spatial disparities and development policy in the Philippines', in Yukon Huang and Alessandro Magnoli Bocchi (eds), *Reshaping Economic Geography in East Asia*, Washington, DC World Bank.

Barro, Robert J. and Xavier Sala-i-Martin (1991) 'Convergence across states and regions', *Brookings Papers on Economic Activity*, **1**, 107–82.

Ben-David, Dan (1995), 'Convergence clubs and diverging economies', Foelder Institute Working Paper, 40–95.

Ben-David, Dan (1996), 'Trade and convergence among countries', *Journal of International Economics*, **40**, 279–98.

Ben-David, Dan (1998), 'Convergence clubs and subsistence economies', *Journal of Development Economics*, **55**, 153–69.

Fujita, Masahisa (2007), 'Spurring economic development by capitalizing on brand agriculture: turning development strategy on its head', in François Bourguignon and Boris Pleskovic (eds), *Annual World Bank Conference on Development Economics 2007, Global: Rethinking Infrastructure for Development*, World Bank (forthcoming).

Fujita, Masahisa and Nobuaki Hamaguchi (2008), 'Regional integration in East Asia: perspectives of spatial and neoclassical economics', in Masahisa Fujita, Satoru Kumagai and Koji Nishikimi (eds), *Economic Integration in East Asia: Perspectives from Spatial and Neoclassical Economics*, Cheltenham, UK and Northampton, MA, USA: Edward Elgar, pp. 13–42.

Fujita, Masahisa and Takatoshi Tabuchi (1997), 'Regional growth in postwar Japan', *Regional Science and Urban Economics*, **27**, 643–70.

Fujita, Masahisa, Paul Krugman and Anthony Venables (1999), *The Spatial Economy: Cities, Regions, and International Trade*, Cambridge, MA: MIT Press.

Hill, Hal (2008), 'Globalization, inequality, and local-level dynamics: Indonesia and the Philippines', *Asian Economic Policy Review*, **3**, 42–61.

Kimura, Fukunari and Mitsuyo Ando (2005), 'Two-dimensional fragmentation in East Asia: conceptual framework and empirics', *International Review of Economics and Finance*, **14**, 317–48.

Krugman, Paul, and Anthony Venables (1995), 'Globalization and the inequality of nations', *Quarterly Journal of Economics*, **110**, 857–80.

Magrini, Stefano (2004), 'Regional (Di) Convergence', in J. Vernon Henderson and Jacques-François Thisse (eds), *Handbook of Regional and Urban Economics*, Volume 4, Amsterdam: Elsevier, pp. 2741–96.

Midelfart-Knarvik, Karen and Henry G. Overman (2002), 'Delocation and European integration: is structural spending justified?', *Economic Policy*, **35**, 322–59.

National Bureau of Statistics of China (various years), *China Statistical Yearbook*, China Statistical Press.

Puga, Diego (1999), 'The rise and fall of regional inequalities', *European Economic Review*, **43**, 303–34.

Puga, Diego (2002), 'European regional policies in light of recent location theories', *Journal of Economic Geography*, **2**, 373–406.

Redding, Stephen and Anthony Venables (2004), 'Economic geography and international inequality', *Journal of International Economics*, **62**, 53–82.

Slaughter, Matthew (2001), 'Trade liberalization and per capita income convergence: a difference in difference analysis', *Journal of International Economics*, **55**, 203–28.

Tabuchi, Takatoshi and Masahisa Fujita (1997), 'Regional growth in postwar Japan', *Regional Science and Urban Economics*, **27**, 643–70.

Williamson, Jeffery G. (1965), 'Regional inequality and the process of national development', *Economic Development and Cultural Change*, **13**, 3–45.

World Bank (2008), *World Development Report 2009: Reshaping Economic Geography*, Washington, DC: World Bank.

Zhang, Xiabo and Kevin Zhang (2003), 'How does globalization affect regional inequality within a developing country? Evidence from China', *Journal of Development Studies*, **38**, 47–67.

Zhao, Wei (2001), 'Regional opening up: China's peculiar way and its trend in near future' (in Chinese), *Zhejiang Academic Journal*, **2**, 76–80.

Zhao, Wei (2005), *The Economic Opening Up of the Regions in China: Patterns and Trend* (in Chinese), Economic Science Press.

Zhao, Wei (2006) 'Opening up of the regional economies in China: a multi-layered and multi-dimension checking' (in Chinese), *Social Science Frontier*, 12–19.

Zhao, Wei (2009), 'Zhejiang pattern: a multifold transitional way of the Chinese regional economies' (in Chinese), *Zhejiang Social Sciences*, **2**, 22–31.

16. Economic integration and poverty

Hosaki Kono

16.1 INTRODUCTION

For the last two decades, East Asian countries have experienced a move toward globalization and regional economic integration. While governments, industry and international institutions have promoted this move, it has been the target of NGO protests at every high-level international meeting on trade liberalization or globalization. Globalization, NGOs argue, benefits only the rich, leaving the poor behind.

Theoretically, economic integration can create opportunities for employment and economic activities through economic development induced by agglomeration and concentrated dispersion (Chapters 2 and 3), increases in foreign direct investment (FDI, Chapter 5), and the expansion of trade (Chapter 13). However it is also possible that the inflow of more inexpensive products, resulting from concentrated dispersion, increases in FDI, and trade expansion, may lead to the defeat of local producers and have adverse effects on the poor. In the long-run when all the adjustment has been completed, those who lost their jobs or suffered significant income losses will find new opportunities and gain from economic development induced by economic integration, which can reduce aggregate poverty. However, in the short run, the adverse effects may dominate the economic development effects and economic integration may actually increase aggregate poverty, as argued by NGOs. There is also no guarantee that poor people in remote areas can enjoy the fruits of economic development.

In this chapter, we present the existing empirical evidence on economic integration (especially trade expansion and increased FDI inflows) and poverty reduction with the purpose of facilitating discussion between advocates and critics of economic integration. The available data show that trade expansion and increased inflows of FDI have no significant impact on aggregate poverty rates. Though aggregate poverty rates do not change, the expansion of trade creates winners and losers. In order to mitigate the adverse effect on losers, we offer some policy suggestions, which may also help reduce political barriers against further economic integration, contributing to economic development and prosperity in the long run.

Section 16.2 presents an overview of poverty in East Asian countries. Section 16.3 gives a survey of the literature and an empirical analysis of economic integration and poverty reduction. Section 16.4 offers policy implications. The final section presents conclusions.

16.2 POVERTY IN EAST ASIA

This section presents an overview of poverty in East Asia and the education indicator in the respective countries, since education is a proxy for human capital.

Table 16.1 and Figure 16.1 show the GDP per capita of East Asian countries from World Development Indicators, in constant (2000) dollars. Information for Myanmar is not available, but as of year 2006, it can be seen that the CLMV countries (Cambodia, Lao PDR, Myanmar and Vietnam) are among the poorest countries in this region. Since Japan, Korea and Singapore have high GDP per capita, more than 10,000 US$, and the poverty issue for them is less relevant than for other countries, no further information on these three countries is given in this section.

Table 16.1   GDP per capita (constant 2000 US$)

	1985	1995	2005	2006
Cambodia	n.a.	225	408	445
China	290	658	1451	1598
India	265	372	588	634
Indonesia	474	827	942	983
Japan	27012	35439	38962	39824
Korea, Rep.	4386	9159	13240	13865
Lao PDR	218	274	415	439
Malaysia	2081	3471	4360	4535
Mongolia	477	419	584	626
Myanmar	n.a.	n.a.	n.a.	n.a.
Philippines	821	913	1117	1154
Singapore	10866	19359	25968	27125
Thailand	956	2086	2494	2601
Vietnam	202	305	539	576

Source: World Development Indicators 2008.

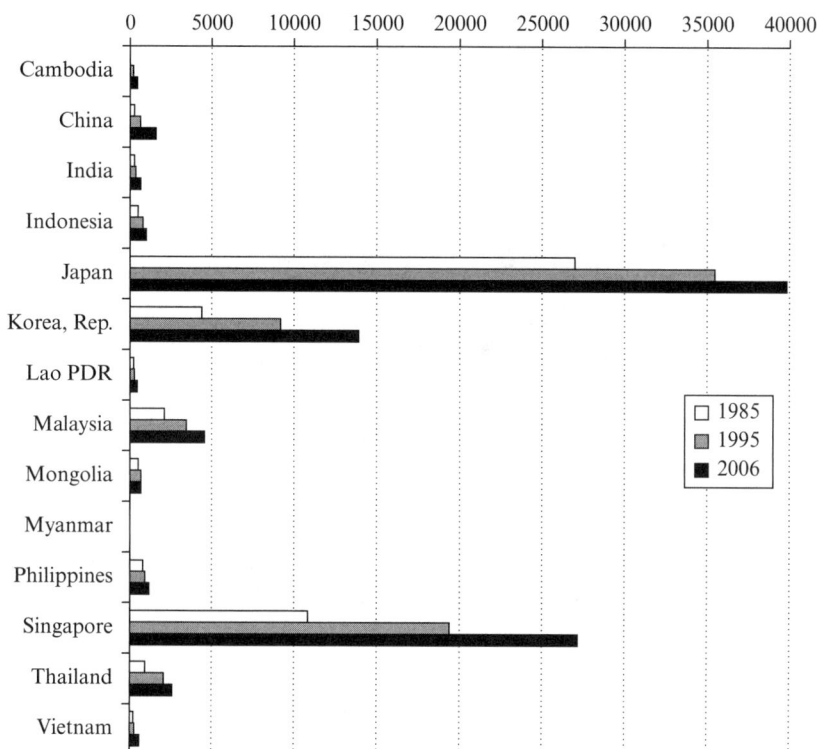

Source: World Development Indicators 2008.

Figure 16.1   GDP per capita (constant 2000 US$)

Figure 16.2 gives the latest available information from World Development Indicators on poverty headcount ratio (hereafter *poverty rate*) in East Asian countries, poverty rate being defined as the proportion of the national population whose incomes are below the official thresholds set by the national government. Due to the scarcity of recent data, the poverty rates in China, Philippines and Thailand, are those from before year 2000. The information on Malaysia is from the 9th Malaysia Plan (p. 330, Table 16.1) because of no recent data is available in World Development Indicators. As in the case of GDP per capita, we have no information on poverty rates for Myanmar. It can be seen that countries with low per capita GDP, such as Cambodia, India, Lao PDR, Mongolia, and Vietnam, have a high incidence of poverty. The poverty rates for the Philippines are also high, partly a reflection of the fact that the figures are for the year 1997. A common feature throughout the region is that rural

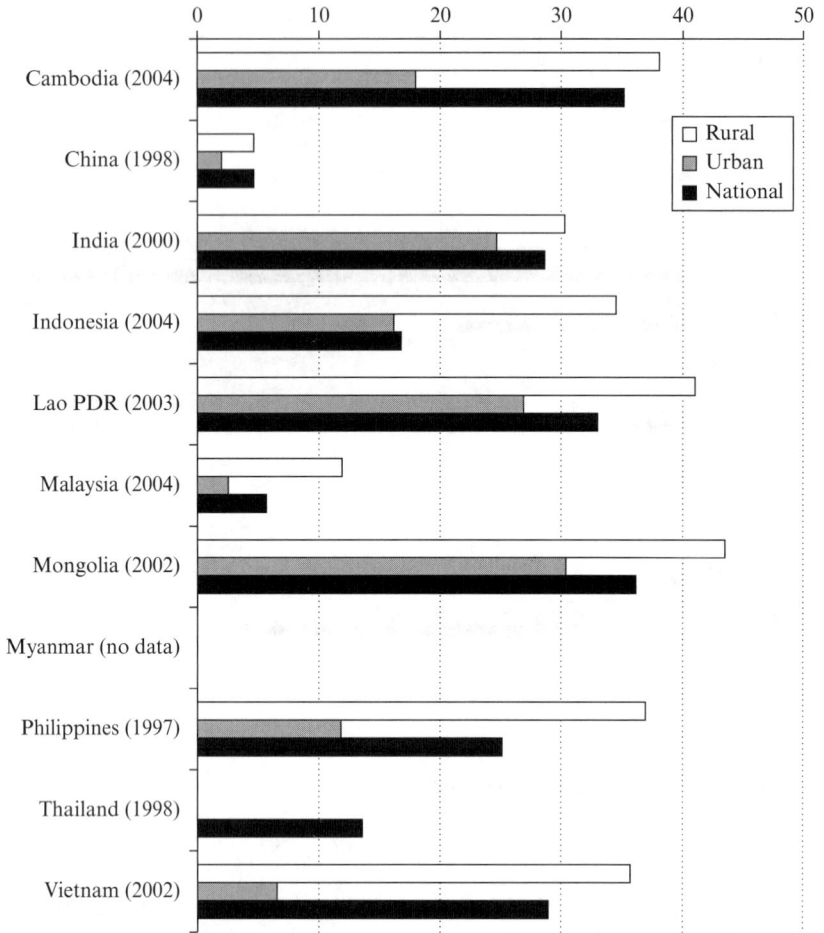

Note: The urban and rural poverty headcount ratios in Indonesia and Lao PDR are for 1999 and 1998, respectively.

Source: World Development Indicators 2008, 9th Malaysia Plan (p. 330, Table 16-1).

Figure 16.2   Poverty headcount ratio measured by the national poverty line (% of population), rural poverty line (% of rural population), and urban poverty line (% of urban population)

poverty rates are higher than urban ones, indicating that poverty is concentrated in rural areas. This suggests the importance for poverty reduction of the way in which economic integration affects poor rural households.

More frequent data is available from the World Bank's PovcalNet.[1] Figure 16.3 shows the time-series data of the poverty rates in each country. Here poverty lines are set at 1.25 dollars a day at 2005 Purchasing Power Parity (PPP) exchange rates.[2] Remarkable progress in poverty reduction can be seen in China, Indonesia, Thailand and Vietnam. Poverty reduction in the Philippines and Mongolia is rather stagnant. Lao PDR and Cambodia have not yet started rapid progress in poverty reduction.

As we argue in the next section, the impact of economic integration can be different across educational levels and occupations. Low levels of human capital may prevent poor people from starting new activities or expanding their existing production when new opportunities arrive due to economic integration, making it difficult for them to appropriately cope with the losses that also accompany economic integration. Low levels of human capital also discourage international firms from investing in these countries. All of these factors affect the impact of economic integration on poverty. The literacy rates and school enrollment rates in East Asian countries are given in Figure 16.4 and Figure 16.5, respectively.

Figure 16.4 shows that even though most East Asian countries record very high literacy rates, the literacy rates in Cambodia and Lao PDR are rather low, especially for females. India is on a par with these two countries. Since female literacy rates among youth are somewhat higher than the overall female literacy rates in these countries, we can conjecture that the illiteracy rates among older women are fairly high.

Figure 16.5 shows that while almost all East Asian countries have nearly achieved universal primary education, secondary school enrollment rates greatly vary and are low in Cambodia, Lao PDR, and Myanmar. But compared to Cambodia and Lao PDR, Myanmar's education indicators are fairly good, indicating potential for economic growth if economic integration and other policies are appropriately implemented. Mongolia and Vietnam record rather high secondary school enrollment, given their levels of per capita GDP.

16.3   EVIDENCE ON ECONOMIC INTEGRATION AND POVERTY REDUCTION

Economic integration has various aspects, including goods market integration (international trade), capital market integration (foreign direct and indirect investment), and labor market integration

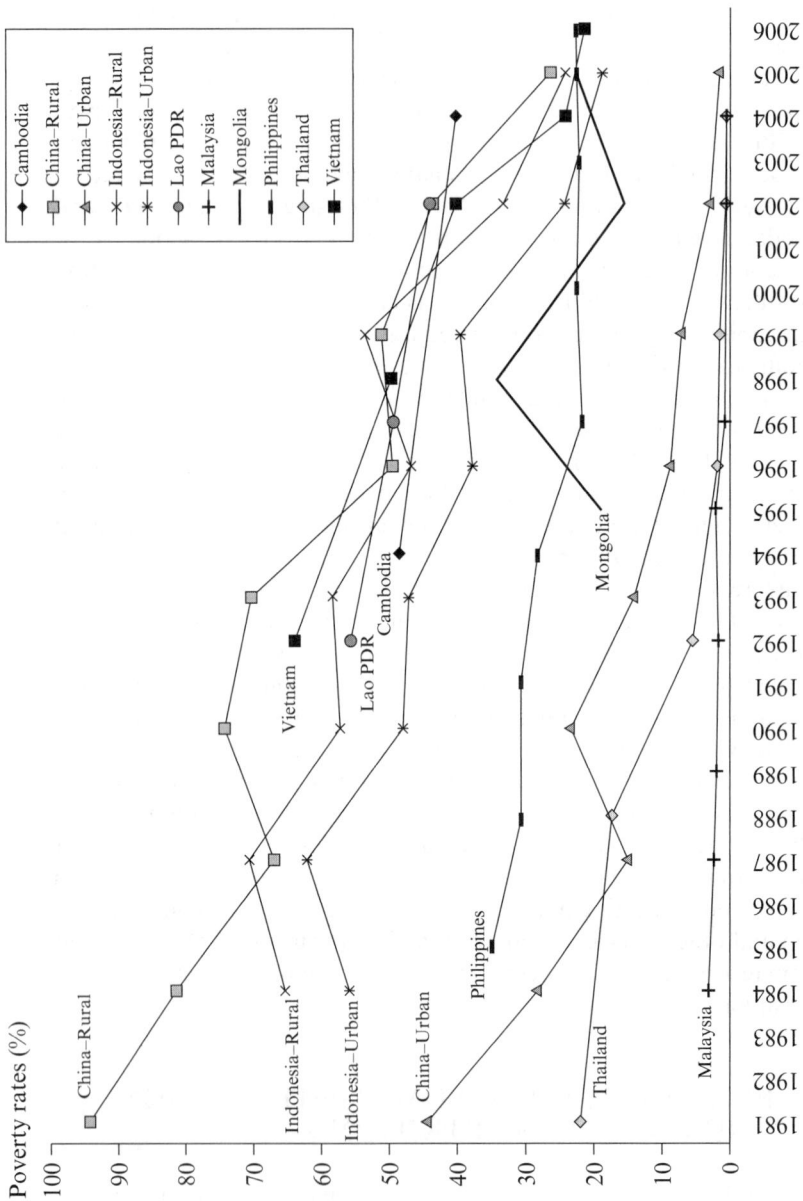

Poverty rates (%)

China–Rural

Indonesia–Rural

Indonesia–Urban

China–Urban

Philippines

Thailand

Malaysia

Vietnam

Lao PDR

Cambodia

Mongolia

Source: PovcalNet, http://iresearch.worldbank.org/PovcalNet/jsp/index.jsp.

Figure 16.3   Trend in the poverty headcount ratio (below US$1.25 per day)

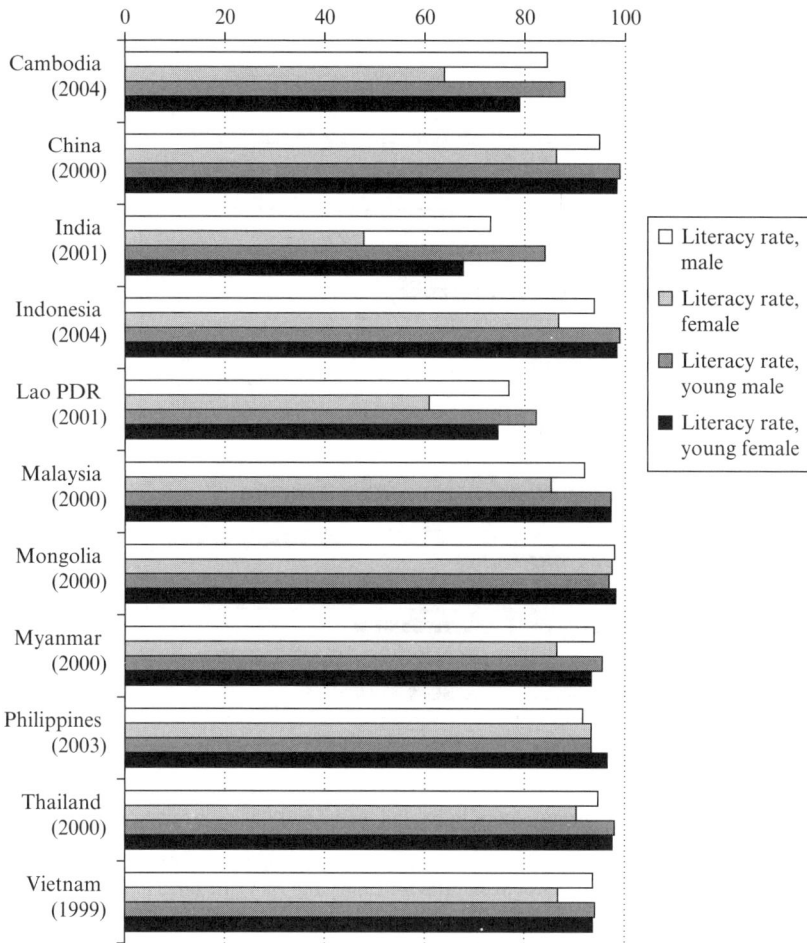

Notes:
a   Percent of literate males and females aged 15 and above.
b   Percent of literate males and females aged 15–24.

Source: World Development Indicators 2008.

Figure 16.4   Literacy rates[a] *and youth literacy rates*[b]

(immigration). In this section, we focus on the impact of trade expansion and FDI inflows on poverty. The issues of indirect investment or portfolio investment and immigration are not dealt with due to the lack of sufficient data.

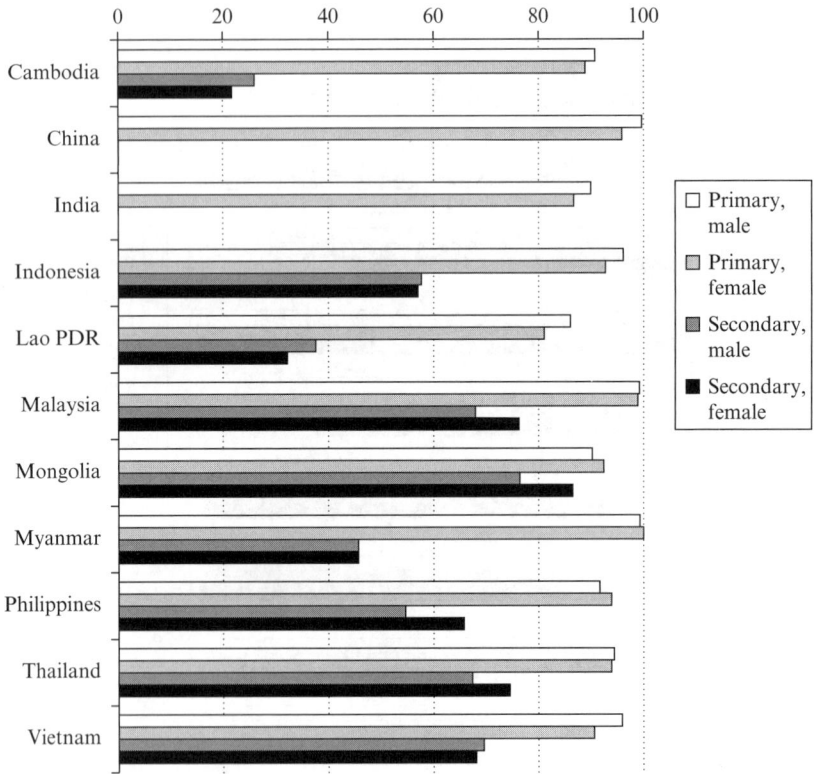

Note: The school enrollment rates of India, Indonesia, and Philippines, and secondary school enrollment rates of Cambodia are for 2005. Those of China and Malaysia are for 1991 and year 2004, respectively. The primary school enrollment rates of Vietnam are for 2001. The secondary school enrollment rates for China and India are not available.

Source: World Development Indicators 2008.

Figure 16.5   School enrollment rates in 2006

We first note that economic growth has contributed to poverty reduction, implying that economic integration, which is expected to enhance economic growth, will contribute to poverty reduction in the long run. However, in the short run, the increased inflow of inexpensive goods through expanded imports or FDI may hurt local producers. The following part shows that trade expansion and FDI increases do not have a significant impact on aggregate poverty rates. Finally we see the heterogeneous impacts of economic integration on the living of poor people.

16.3.1 Economic Growth is Good for Poverty Reduction

Economic growth is a powerful driving force for alleviating poverty. Continuous rapid economic growth in China and Vietnam, for example, has substantially contributed to poverty reduction in these countries in the last two decades. Using cross country time series data, Ravallion (2001) estimated that a 1 percent increase in mean income resulted, on average, in a fall of 2.0–2.5 percent in the proportion of people in absolute poverty. Using data for 92 countries, Dollar and Kraay (2002) show that the mean income of the poor (bottom 20 percent of the income distribution) moves proportionally with mean income. Thus it is quite widely accepted that economic growth is, on the average, good for the poor.

Figure 16.6 is the East Asia version of Ravallion's (2001) analysis. It shows the relationship between the change in GDP per capita in PPP and the change in the proportion of people who are below the poverty line of US$1.25 in PPP, using the PovcalNet data presented in the previous section. The slope of the fitted line is negative and significantly different from zero, indicating that economic growth has contributed to poverty reduction in East Asia as well. The fact that the magnitude of the coefficient here is higher than Ravallion's (−0.758 vs. −0.2) implies that, in East Asia, economic growth was more pro-poor than the world average.

16.3.2 Poverty Reduction Impact of Trade Expansion: Macro Evidence

It is widely argued that export-oriented strategies and the expansion of production networks in East Asia have contributed to economic growth in this region, which will contribute to poverty reduction in the long run. On the other hand, the increased inflow of inexpensive import goods can harm local producers and may have an adverse impact on poverty. For example, it is often said that the huge inflow of Chinese manufacturing goods threatens the survival of domestic producers. However, it is also possible that inflows of inexpensive input goods, say, fertilizers, help farmers increase their income. It may also be the case that the poor cannot take advantage of new opportunities created by the expansion of exports, possibly due to a lack of skills, lack of access to financing, lack of market access, and lack of the qualifications (such as education) required to be hired by export-oriented manufacturing firms. Thus the relationship between trade expansion and poverty reduction is not unambiguous.

The existing empirical literature does not find a clear relationship between trade expansion and poverty. While there is no robust evidence that trade expansion reduced poverty, there is also no evidence that trade liberalization generally had an adverse impact on poverty (Winters et

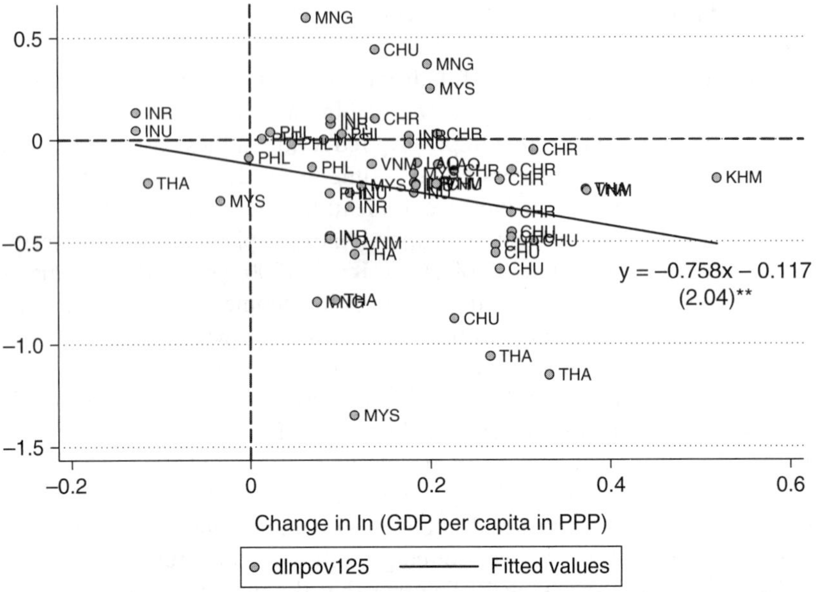

Note: The horizontal axis shows the change in ln (GDP per capita in PPP) and the vertical axis the change in ln (poverty rate with a poverty line of US$1.25 in PPP). The fitted line shows the fitted values, and the absolute t-value associated with the coefficient of the horizontal variable is in parentheses. Country names are coded as follows: Cambodia KHM; China rural CHR; China urban CHU; Indonesia rural INR; Indonesia urban INU; Lao PDR LAO; Malaysia MYS; Mongolia MNG; Philippines PHL; Thailand THA; Vietnam VNM.

Figure 16.6   *Change in poverty rates and GDP per capita in East Asian countries*

al., 2004). Ravallion (2006), analyzing cross country data and the experience of China, shows that there is no correlation between changes in poverty and the growth of trade. In China, a rapid reduction of poverty was achieved in the early 1980s. However, most trade reforms were not introduced until the late 1980s, and the poverty rate slightly *increased* in the late 1980s and early 1990s. He attributes poverty reduction in China to growth in agricultural output induced by other economic reforms, such as the introduction of the 'household responsibility system' and agricultural pricing policies which raised procurement prices. The cross-country analysis performed by Milanovic (2005) shows that trade expansion reduces the income share of poor and middle-income groups and expands inequality,[3] especially in poorer countries. Barro (2000) and Ravallion (2001) report similar results and state that in some of the formulations, an increase in

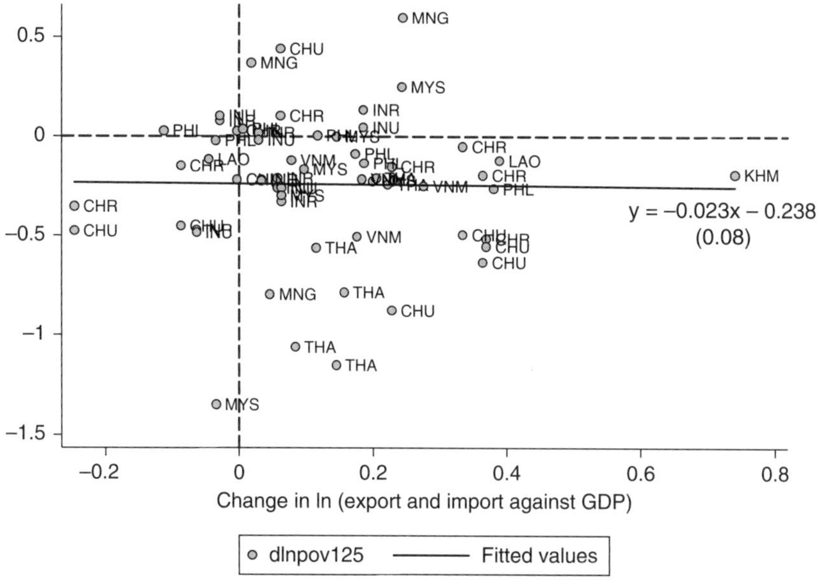

Note: The horizontal axis shows the change in ln (export and import against GDP) and the vertical axis the change in ln (poverty rate with a poverty line of US$1.25 in PPP). The fitted line shows the fitted values, and the absolute t-value associated with the coefficient of the horizontal variable is in parentheses. Country names are coded as follows: Cambodia KHM; China rural CHR; China urban CHU; Indonesia rural INR; Indonesia urban INU; Lao PDR LAO; Malaysia MYS; Mongolia MNG; Philippines PHL; Thailand THA; Vietnam VNM.

Figure 16.7   Change in poverty rates and trade openness (trade/GDP) in East Asian countries

trade volume has a negative impact on the income level of the poor. The increased inequality offsets the economic growth effect of trade expansion on poverty reduction.[4]

Figure 16.7 shows the relationship between changes in openness (measured by the ratio of exports and imports to GDP) and changes in poverty rates in East Asian countries. By focusing on the changes, we can reduce the estimation bias due to time-invariant country characteristics and time trends.

It is shown that trade expansion has no statistically significant effect on poverty reduction in East Asian countries. A closer look at the figure reveals that increases in trade volume seem to have had a positive impact on poverty reduction in Thailand, while China experienced a reduction in poverty irrespective of changes in trade volume. But even if we control

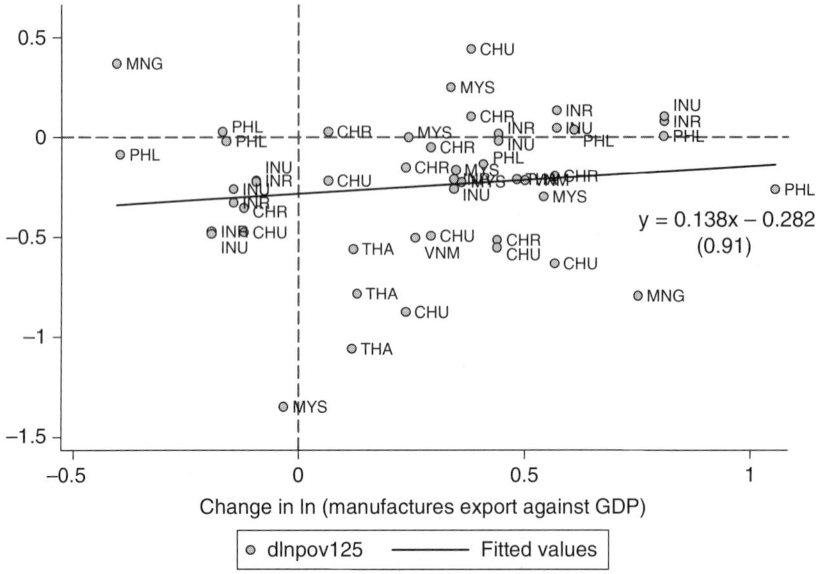

$$y = 0.138x - 0.282$$
$$(0.91)$$

Change in ln (manufactures export against GDP)

| ○ dlnpov125 | ——— Fitted values |

Note: The horizontal axis is the change in ln (manufactures export against GDP) and the vertical axis is the change in ln (poverty rate with a poverty line of US$1.25 in PPP). The fitted line shows the fitted data, and the absolute t-value associated with the coefficient of the horizontal variable is in parentheses. Country names are coded as follows: Cambodia KHM; China rural CHR; China urban CHU; Indonesia rural INR; Indonesia urban INU; Lao PDR LAO; Malaysia MYS; Mongolia MNG; Philippines PHL; Thailand THA; Vietnam VNM.

Figure 16.8   Change in poverty rates and manufactures exports relative to GDP in East Asian countries

the China effect, the estimation results are similar. Notice that many of the observations lie in the fourth quadrant, where the changes in trade volume are positive and the changes in poverty rates are negative. Many East Asian countries have experienced poverty reduction along with trade expansion, which may tempt one to conclude that trade expansion has contributed to poverty reduction in East Asia. However, the figure shows that greater changes in the trade ratio do not result in greater changes in the poverty rate, which renders the correlation between changes in trade volume and changes in poverty rates insignificant.

Next we examine the relationship between manufacturing exports and poverty in order to investigate whether the development of the manufacturing export sector has contributed to poverty reduction. Figure 16.8 shows the results. The increase in the expansion of manufactures exports has no statistically significant impact on poverty reduction. We also used

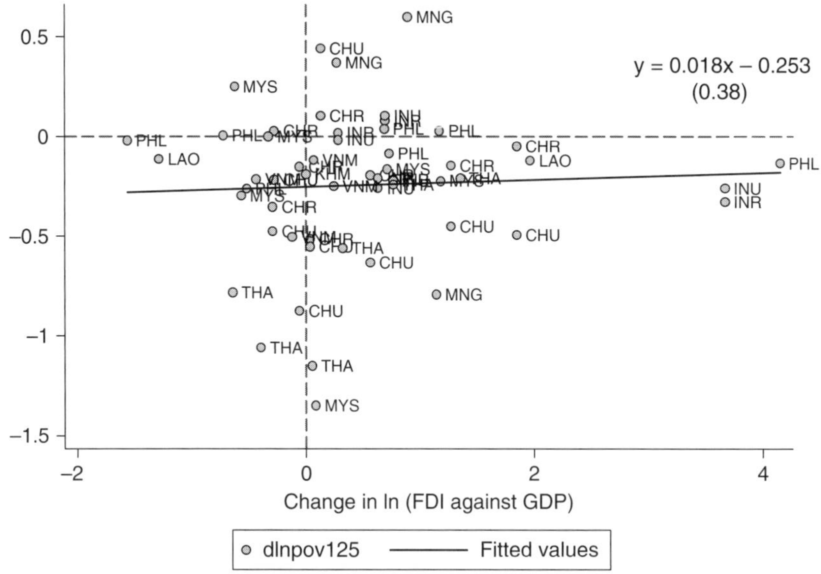

Note: The horizontal axis is the change in ln (FDI against GDP) and the vertical axis is the change in ln (poverty rate with poverty line of US$1.25 in PPP). The fitted line is depicted and the absolute t-value associated with the coefficient of the horizontal variable is in parentheses. Country names are coded as follows: Cambodia KHM; China rural CHR; China urban CHU; Indonesia rural INR; Indonesia urban INU; Lao PDR LAO; Malaysia MYS; Mongolia MNG; Philippines PHL; Thailand THA; Vietnam VNM.

Figure 16.9   Change in poverty rates and change in FDI in East Asian countries

other measurements of trade or export but can find no significant effect on poverty. In sum, the available data show that trade or export expansion has not affected aggregate poverty, at least in the short run.

16.3.3   FDI and Poverty Reduction: Macro Evidence

Next we examine the impact of FDI on poverty reduction by a way analogous to Figures 16.7 and 16.8. It is often argued that, especially in Southeast Asia, FDI has played an important role in letting the host countries take off and recording high growth rates. However, Figure 16.9, which depicts the relationship between change in FDI relative to GDP and change in poverty rates shows that FDI has had no statistically significant impact on poverty reduction in East Asian countries, at least in the short run. Controlling other factors, including lagged variables of FDI, does not alter the result. As with Figures 16.7 and 16.8, many of the observations lie in the fourth quadrant. Many East Asian countries have witnessed both poverty reduction and increased FDI at the same time. However, there are also many countries which saw reduced poverty despite negative changes in FDI. In addition as with Figures 16.7 and 16.8, a greater change in FDI does not result in greater changes in the poverty rate. These render the correlation between changes in FDI and changes in poverty rates insignificant.

One possible reason for the lack of significance of the impact of FDI on poverty is that FDI has heterogeneous impacts. Since most foreign firms employ educated people who are not poor, FDI may have little impact on the living of the poor. It is also possible that poor countries derive less benefit from FDI. Borensztein et al. (1998) conducted cross-country growth regressions and found that FDI inflows enhanced economic growth only in countries with high educational levels, not in those with low educational levels, possibly because populations with low educational levels have weak skill absorption capacity and cannot learn the new technologies embedded in FDI.[5] In any case, the data do not lend support to the assertion that FDI has contributed to poverty reduction.[6]

16.3.4   Heterogeneous Impact on Households

Even if the expansion of trade does not affect aggregate poverty, it often faces fierce opposition because it inevitably creates 'winners' and 'losers.' This is because trade expansion entails an increase in flows of imports and exports, affecting the prices of domestic goods. A huge inflow of cheap electronic goods made in China had a large effect on the domestic price of electronic goods, which often had an adverse effect on domestic electronic goods producers. On the other hand, an increase in rice exports contributed to an increase in the rice price in the domestic market in some countries, to the benefit of rice producing farmers, but also raised the cost of living for nonagricultural sector workers. Which goods are influenced and to what extent depends on which countries participate in the economic integration. It is politically important to know what characterizes individuals who will become losers so that the governments can implement complementary targeting policies to offset the adverse effects of trade expansion. As FDI has a smaller impact than trade expansion on domestic prices, here we focus on the impact of trade expansion at the household level.

The effect of price changes on households depends on whether they are net producers or net consumers of the goods involved. If a household is a net producer of, say, rice, then an increase in the price of rice will benefit that household. On the other hand, if a household is a net consumer of rice (which would include the case of a rice-producing household if its rice production was insufficient to meet its demand for rice, necessitating the purchase of rice at market prices), it would suffer from a rice price increase and its real income would decrease. It is also possible that a household that was initially a net consumer produces more rice in response to the rice price increase and becomes a net producer. In this case, the positive impact of a rice price increase is more subtle but is nevertheless calculable.

The characteristics of households that are net consumers or net producers of a certain product can be identified from household survey data. Thus the winners and losers are predictable to some extent. Ravallion and van de Walle (1991), for instance, consider a hypothetical Indonesian rice reform and report that the very poor are net consumers of rice and so suffer from the price rises induced by the reform, and that farmers just below the standard poverty line are net producers and hence benefit and gain an increased chance to escape from poverty. This kind of research should be conducted in the preparatory stages of economic integration so that policies to protect losers can be implemented along with the progress of economic integration. This in turn will alleviate the political conflicts that often accompany economic integration, and contribute to long-run poverty alleviation through economic growth.

Another route of price change impact is via the creation or loss of employment. If a domestic sector (for example, the textile sector) has produced relatively cheaper than other countries in the region, economic integration will result in export expansion and employment expansion in this sector. On the other hand, if an increasing inflow of imports brings down domestic goods' prices, then some firms will cut production and employment, or even exit from the market. In this case, economic integration leads to job losses in the sector, which will affect the livelihood of workers and exacerbate poverty in the country. According to the basic Stolper-Samuelson theorem, where wages are flexible, there is no unemployment, and there are only two goods and two factors (labor and capital or skilled labor and unskilled labor), labor-abundant or unskilled-labor-abundant countries like East Asia will experience an increase in the price of the labor-intensive or unskilled-labor-intensive good, which in turn will increase the real wage of labor or unskilled labor, resulting in reducing poverty. However in their survey of the literature, Goldberg and Pavcnik (2007) find a tendency for globalization to increase the wage gap between more- and less-skilled workers in developing countries, a finding which contradicts the prediction of the basic Stolper-Samuelson theorem. Winters et al. (2004) conclude from their extensive literature survey that it is not guaranteed that the least-skilled workers, and thus those most likely to be poor, will be the most intensively used factor in the production of exportable goods. This can be attributed to (1) the fact that export goods are usually of relatively higher quality and thus require a certain level of skilled labor and (2) the existence of large, labor-abundant countries like China. Thus the key is (1) whether expanding sectors increase employment of unskilled labor and (2) whether the goods produced by the sectors with a high ratio of unskilled labor are competitive to the substitutable goods made in China.

16.3.5   CGE Analysis and Heterogeneous Response to Economic Integration

Looking only at net consumers and net producers may not be adequate for capturing the overall effect of trade liberalization, since trade liberalization also affects macroeconomic performance through (possibly) economic growth and the reallocation of domestic resources, presumably toward more efficient allocation. Computable General Equilibrium (CGE) analysis can deal explicitly with the general equilibrium effects of trade liberalization. CGE models usually consist of a number of sectors and inputs, including several types of workers, and assume that markets are perfect, labor and other inputs are mobile between sectors and there is no unemployment. Assuming perfect factor mobility and zero unemployment may overstate the impact of efficiency improvements through resource reallocation but can predict the response of the economy to economic integration *in the long run* when the adjustment has been completed.

It should be noted that the results of CGE analysis depend critically on the specifications and assumptions of the model, and the predictions of some CGE models contradict the results of empirical studies that use actual observational data. Researchers should make efforts to reconcile the results of CGE simulations with empirical results in order to improve the reliability of the model. Well-constructed CGE models can clarify points and facilitate policy discussions.

Ezaki and Nguyen (2008) constructed a global CGE model to predict the impact of East Asian economic integration, including trade liberalization and foreign investment, on Vietnam, China, Thailand and Indonesia. According to their simulation, the impact of East Asian economic integration on growth is positive for all these countries. East Asian economic integration does not have great merit for China, at least in terms of the growth effect. China would benefit more from wider integration with the EU and the US, as this would lead to a substantial increase in its exports.

Though some of their simulation results are plausible, some contradict the existing empirical literature or other CGE analyses, which serves as a good example of how the predictions of CGE models depend on the specification of the model. For instance, they predict that East Asian economic integration or a wider economic integration would lead to a dramatic reduction of the urban–rural income disparity in China. On the other hand, Chen and Ravallion's (2004) simulation of the impact of WTO accession on China finds that it will have a negligible effect on poverty in the aggregate, that rural households will suffer losses after the accession, and that there will be substantial negative impacts on the very poorest rural households due to a drop in the wholesale prices of most farm products, while urban households will gain. This difference in the results of these two analyses is due to the fact that Ezaki and Nguyen neglect the differences in the composition of consumption and production at the household level between rural and urban areas.

When constructing CGE models, one should take into consideration the fact that the response of the poor might differ from that of the non-poor due to credit constraints, poor infrastructure, low educational levels, and so on. For example, López et al.'s (1995) empirical study on Mexico shows that farmers with low levels of capital inputs (which may be correlated with other factors, such as lack of access to credit, poor land quality and low education) were less responsive to price incentives than those with higher levels. Balat et al. (2009) find that while export crop production reduces poverty in Ethiopia, households in regions with higher export marketing costs are less likely to be engaged in export crop production and hence are more likely to be poor. Deininger and Olinto (2000) study Zambia over the period 1993/94–1994/95 and show that for many households a major constraint on improvements in agricultural productivity following external liberalization was the absence of key productive assets such as draft animals and implements. These findings indicate that poor households are constrained in responding to the new opportunities generated by economic integration and that support policies such as better infrastructure, information distribution, skill training, credit provision, and removal of regulations on entry and production are important in enabling poor households to realize gains from trade. It is also possible that households in regions with poor infrastructure, less educated households and households that lack access to credit cannot protect themselves from price decreases for their products, since their situation makes it difficult for them to switch to other activities. These concepts should be included in the CGE models to make them more reliable and to enable them to simulate the impact of accompanying policies. Chen and Ravallion (2004) move in this direction as they combine CGE models with household survey data.

CGE modeling can also be used for the selection of geographical targeting areas. Fujii and Roland-Holst (2008) combine a CGE model with a small area estimation of the incidence of poverty and examine how

Vietnam's accession to the World Trade Organization changed the provincial level poverty rates. They find that the impact is heterogeneous across provinces and that the northwestern area and some other mountainous areas are likely to lag behind (see Figure 16.10). This information can help the government to identify regions on which to focus national poverty reduction strategies.

In sum, although the predictions produced by CGE models depend on the structure of the model, CGE models provide a good starting point for political discussion on economic integration. Currently, many CGE models neglect market imperfections, and as a result poor households appear to be relatively responsive to price changes induced by economic integration, a result which is not consistent with some empirical studies. The ignorance of market imperfections can also make CGE models irrelevant to examinations of the short-run impact of economic integration on poverty, which should be the main matter in discussions on economic integration and poverty. Researchers should improve CGE models by incorporating market imperfections and market frictions to contribute to the policy discussion.

16.4   HOW CAN WE MAKE ECONOMIC INTEGRATION MORE PRO-POOR?

The previous section shows that economic integration creates winners and losers and that poorer households are likely to have limited ability to take advantage of new opportunities and protect themselves against adverse effects. In order to make economic integration more pro-poor, complementary policies which strengthen social protection for losers and enhance the ability of poorer households to exploit potentially beneficial changes are required. This section lists a set of the policies which make economic integration more pro-poor and lower the political barriers to economic integration.

16.4.1   Improving Infrastructure

Balat et al. (2009) find that higher export marketing costs prevent farmers from exploiting the benefits of international trade opportunities and hinder them from escaping poverty. Better infrastructure will enable farmers and local producers in remote areas to sell their goods in export markets and the growing urban markets. A reduction in transportation costs thanks to infrastructure improvement may also attract investment projects which take advantage of low labor costs in rural and remote areas (see also Chapter 15 for arguments on the importance of domestic integration through better infrastructure). On the other hand, Gisselquist and Grether

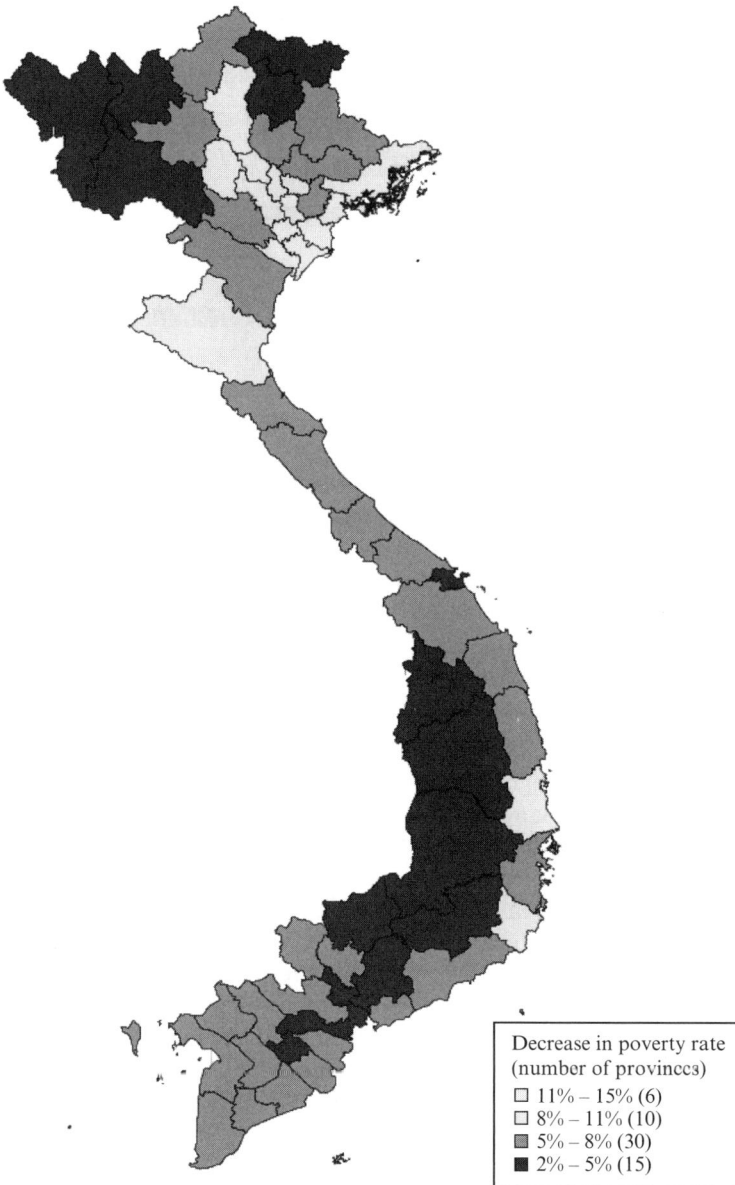

Decrease in poverty rate
(number of provinces)
☐ 11% – 15% (6)
☐ 8% – 11% (10)
▨ 5% – 8% (30)
■ 2% – 5% (15)

Source: Fujii and Roland-Holst (2008).

*Figure 16.10   Utilization of CGE model for geographical targeting in
Vietnam*

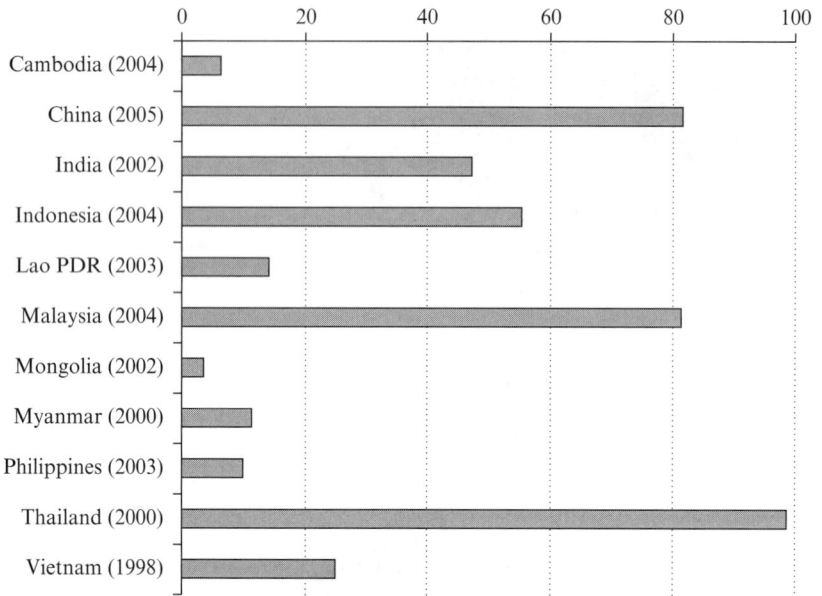

Source: World Development Indicators 2008.

Figure 16.11   Ratio of paved roads in East Asian countries

(2000) report that a significant direct benefit of liberalization for agricultural producers in Bangladesh was the increased availability of inputs, and Deininger and Olinto (2000) point out that the absence of a key productive asset constrained improvements in agricultural productivity after external liberalization in Zambia. Better infrastructure facilitates access to necessary inputs by reducing transportation costs. Thus, improvements in infrastructure make rural households more responsive to the price changes and new opportunities generated by economic integration.

Figure 16.11 shows the ratio of paved roads in East Asian countries. Compared to other countries, Cambodia, Lao PDR, Mongolia, the Philippines, and Vietnam have low ratios, leaving households in rural and remote areas behind in the dynamics of economic integration. Improving infrastructure in these countries should be given priority in this region.

16.4.2   Reducing Market Frictions

In the existing CGE model and static analysis of economic integration, it is assumed that those who lose their jobs in 'losing sectors' can immediately find jobs in 'winning sectors', and thus that economic integration benefits most people. But in reality, labor mobility across sectors is not very high, at least in the short run. It is usually very difficult for rural farmers or uneducated casual workers to find new jobs in booming sectors. Support for the acquisition of new skills and for job searches would alleviate the pains of job losses and income losses due to economic integration. Since low education is often a barrier for poor people seeking jobs in export sectors, making education more accessible and attractive to poor people is also important, especially in countries with low secondary school enroll-ment such as Cambodia, Indonesia, Lao PDR, and Myanmar (see Figure 16.5). If labor mobility (and capital mobility as well) is highly limited and difficult to improve, a strategy of gradual economic integration should be considered to alleviate the short-term pain of structural changes.

Market frictions are sometimes generated by government regulations in areas such as labor and investment. When frictions are non-negligible, firms tend to lower investment and employment levels, since employment and capital stocks cannot be quickly reduced when firms face difficulties. Aghion et al. (2008) analyze the impact of liberalization on firm entry and production activities in India and find that industries located in states with pro-employer labor regulations (that is, less friction in the labor market) grew more quickly than those in pro-worker environments. They also find that unemployment is lower in states with pro-employer environments. These findings imply that reducing market frictions through appropriate deregulation can make economic integration more pro-poor.

16.4.3 Microcredit

Credit constraints are also a form of market friction. Even though eco-nomic integration creates new profit opportunities, without access to affordable interest credit, poor people and small enterprises who lack sufficient funds for new investments cannot take advantage of the new opportunities. Recently, microcredit programs have been expanded in most developing countries to improve the credit access of the poor.

Microcredit has drawn the attention of both policymakers and academ-ics mainly because of its high repayment rates, averaging over 95 percent. Historically, many governments in developing countries have tried to provide inexpensive credit to poor households, especially small rural farmers. The repayment rates, however, were dismal in most cases, typi-cally being less than 50 percent.

The characteristics of microcredit are: (1) the small value of the loans made (which is why it is called 'microcredit'), (2) the targeting of poor households, (3) repayment through frequent installments at group meetings, (4) availability of larger loans after full repayment of the current loan, (5) group lending where all members are jointly liable for each other's loans and prospective borrowers are required to form groups by themselves. In group lending, if any member does not repay, all the members are punished, often in the form of denial of future credit access. Armendariz De Aghion and Morduch (2005) and Kono and Takahashi (2010) elaborate how these characteristics have contributed to achieving high repayment rates.

Although microcredit has spread throughout the world and there are now more than 100 million people who have obtained microcredit loans, the impact of microcredit on borrowers' economic status is still in dispute. Some studies find that microcredit has a positive impact on borrowers' incomes, expenditures and assets (Pitt and Khandker, 1998; Chemin, 2008), while others do not (Coleman, 1999; Banerjee et al., 2009; Karlan and Zinman, 2009; Roodman and Morduch, 2009). But since the impact of microcredit, or access to credit, can be expected to increase with the arrival of new opportunities such as a product price increase induced by economic integration, promoting microcredit activity along with economic integration will benefit the poor.

However, one caution is in order. Increasing competition among microcredit institutions can make the situation worse, because it provides borrowers with a way out when they default, which undermines the incentive to repay. McIntosh and Wydick (2005, 2007) suggest the necessity of credit bureaus to facilitate information sharing among microcredit institutions so that defaulting borrowers cannot access further credit from other microcredit institutions.

16.4.4   Boosting the Agricultural Sector

Since a substantial portion of poor people reside in rural areas, boosting the agricultural sector is important for poverty reduction. World Bank (2007) calculates that at least 81 percent of the reduction in rural poverty is due to the reduction of poverty among rural residents and that the contribution of migration to poverty reduction is small. In East Asia, nearly all the decline in rural poverty is because of a genuine decline in poverty in rural areas and about a half of overall poverty reduction is attributable to the reduction of rural poverty. Thus boosting the agricultural sector through economic integration can make economic integration more pro-poor.

Economic integration may create new opportunities for the agricultural sector through agricultural trade liberalization. As Tokarick's (2008) international CGE analysis of agricultural trade liberalization suggests, an import tariff will inflict a larger efficiency loss on an economy than will a production subsidy. In addition, it finds that the removal of production subsidies by developed countries will on average harm developing countries by increasing the prices of the products which were subsidized, since developing countries are on average net importers of these products. Thus, agricultural trade liberalization should focus on the reduction of tariffs on agricultural products. Technical and technological cooperation in the region and support for nonfarm business development through better infrastructure and better access to credit should also be considered. Readers should refer to Chapter 7 for further issues involving agriculture.

16.4.5 Targeting

Household-level analysis and CGE analysis clearly show that economic integration produces winners and losers. By combining these two analytical methods to predict the impact of economic integration on different categories of households, governments can prepare policies, such as targeted transfers and skill training, to alleviate the adverse impact of economic integration. Ravallion (2006) suggests the usefulness of this approach. Fujii and Roland-Holst (2008) suggest the possibility of utilizing these two types of analysis to implement geographical targeting policies which concentrate policy resources on regions which gain little, or even lose out, from economic integration.

Economic integration creates losers and winners. But if the aggregate gains are larger than the losses, then economic integration will benefit all through compensation for the losers from the winners' gains. However, losers may be concentrated in one country and the losses may dominate the gains in that country. In this case, target transfers across countries should be implemented. The Initiative for ASEAN Integration, which aims to assist the newer members of ASEAN in four priority areas (infrastructure, human resource development, information and communications technology, and regional economic integration), is expected to play this role.

16.5 CONCLUSION

Although economic integration is expected to have positive impacts on poverty alleviation in the long run by promoting economic growth, some argue that globalization only benefits the rich and is harmful to the poor, at least in the short run. However, the existing data show that economic integration has not significantly affected aggregate poverty in the short run. Economic integration is not harmful to the poor in aggregate.

We should note that the impact of economic integration is heterogeneous across households and sectors and that it creates winners and losers. In the long run, when all the adjustment has been done, losers will find jobs in developing sectors or start new activities which take advantage of the new opportunities created by economic integration, but at least in the short run, the losers can experience a significant drop in income. By utilizing household survey data and CGE analysis, we can predict the characteristics of households and sectors that will suffer losses. Unlike predictions using the basic Stolper-Samuelson Theorem, it is not guaranteed that the least-skilled poor workers will be the most intensively used factor in the production of exportable goods.

In order to make economic integration more pro-poor, policies which mitigate the negative effects of economic integration on loser households and which help poor farmers take advantage of new opportunities are required. Better infrastructure will enable farmers and local producers in remote areas to take more advantage of the new opportunities by giving them better access to export markets, growing urban markets and necessary inputs. Reducing market frictions through education and skill training, support for job searches, provision of credit at affordable interest rates including microcredit, and appropriate deregulation will help people avoid the negative impacts and take advantage of the new opportunities. Boosting the agricultural sector in rural areas, where the majority of the poor reside, and poverty reduction among rural residents, are important in order to reduce poverty in rural areas. Household survey data and CGE analysis will also be useful for implementing targeted transfer and geographical targeting. Since economic integration generates losers and winners across countries, target transfers across countries and regional cooperation such as the Initiative for ASEAN Integration are required for facilitating economic integration.

NOTES

1. http://iresearch.worldbank.org/PovcalNet/jsp/index.jsp.
2. Ravallion et al. (2008) propose $1.25 a day at 2005 PPP as the new international poverty line.
3. Though Dollar and Kraay (2002) argue that increases in trade volume have little effect on the income share of the poor, Milanovic (2005) points out that their measurement of trade volume increases (PPP base) substantially underestimates the levels and changes of trade openness in poor countries, resulting in failure to detect a significant relationship between openness and inequality.
4. Dollar (1992), Edwards (1998), and Frankel and Romer (1999) find that trade expansion has a positive impact on economic growth, but their analyses suffer from econometric problems (Rodriguez and Rodrik, 2001). An increase in trade volume may be the result

of economic growth, and these studies may simply be capturing the reverse causal effect. Further, trade reforms are usually executed along with other policies, such as investment promotion policies, domestic reforms and deregulation, making it difficult to isolate the effect of the trade volume increases from those of associated policies. Though these econometric problems are serious, it is also true that there is no credible empirical evidence that a trade volume increase is bad for economic growth.

5. Carkovic and Levine (2005) cast doubt on the results of Borensztein et al. They point out the possibility of reverse causality (positive correlation between growth and FDI being generated by the fact that FDI is usually made in fast growing countries). Serious consideration of this issue shows that there is little support for a positive effect of FDI on economic growth.

6. It is also possible that FDI increases inequality, which reduces the impact of FDI on poverty reduction, as in the argument on trade expansion in the previous subsection. However, Milanovic (2005) finds that, unlike trade expansion, FDI does not statistically significantly change the income share of any group.

REFERENCES

Aghion, Philippe, Robin Burgess, Stephen Redding and Fabrizio Zilibotti (2008), 'The unequal effects of liberalization: evidence from dismantling the license raj in India', *American Economic Review*, **98**(4), 1397–412.

Armendariz De Aghion, Beatriz and Jonathan Morduch (2005), *The Economics of Microfinance*, Cambridge, MA: MIT Press.

Balat, Jorge, Irene Brambilla and Guido Porto (2009), 'Realizing the gains from trade: export crops, marketing costs, and poverty', *Journal of International Economics*, **78**(1), 21–31.

Banerjee, Abhijit, Esther Duflo, Rachel Glennerster and Cynthia Kinnan (2009), 'The miracle of microfinance? Evidence from a randomised evaluation', Poverty Action Lab Working Paper 101.

Barro, Robert (2000), 'Inequality and growth in a panel of countries', *Journal of Economic Growth*, **51**(1), 5–32.

Borensztein, Eduardo, Jose De Gregorio and Jong-Wha Lee (1998), 'How does foreign direct investment affect economic growth?', *Journal of International Economics*, **45**(1), 115–35.

Carkovic, Maria and Ross Levine (2005), 'Does foreign direct investment accelerate economic growth?', in Theodore Moran (ed.), *The Impact of Foreign Direct Investment on Development: New Measurements, New Outcomes, New Policy Approaches*, Washington DC: Institute of International Economics.

Chemin, Matthieu (2008), 'The benefits (and costs) of microfinance: evidence from Bangladesh', *Journal of Development Studies*, **44**(4), 463–84.

Chen, Shaohua and Martin Ravallion (2004), 'Welfare impacts of China's accession to the World Trade Organization', *World Bank Economic Review*, **18**(1), 29–57.

Coleman, Brett E (1999), 'The impact of group lending in Northeast Thailand', *Journal of Development Economics*, **60**(1), 105–41.

Deininger, Klaus and Pedro Olinto (2000), 'Asset distribution, inequality, and growth', World Bank Policy Research Working Paper 2375.

Dollar, David (1992), 'Outward-oriented developing economies really do grow more rapidly: evidence from 95 LDCs, 1976–1985', *Economic Development and Cultural Change*, **40**(3), 523–44.

Dollar, David and Aart Kraay (2002), 'Growth is good for the poor', *Journal of Economic Growth*, **7**(3), 195–225.

Edwards, Sebastian (1998), 'Openness, productivity, and growth: what do we really know?', *Economic Journal*, **108**(447), 383–98.

Ezaki, Mitsuo and Tien Dung Nguyen (2008), 'Regional economic integration and its impacts on growth, income distribution and poverty in East Asia: a CGE analysis', http://ir.lib.oita-u.ac.jp/dspace/handle/123456789/13271.

Frankel, Jeffrey A. and David Romer (1999), 'Does trade cause growth?', *American Economic Review*, **89**(3), 379–99.

Fujii, Tomoki and David Roland-Holst (2008), 'How does Vietnam's accession to the World Trade Organization change the spatial incidence of poverty?', in Machiko Nissanke and Erik Thorbecke (eds), *Globalization and the Poor in Asia: Can Shared Growth be Sustained?*, Basingstoke: Palgrave Macmillan, pp. 47–89.

Gisselquist, David and Jean-Marie Grether (2000), 'An argument for deregulating the transfer of agricultural technologies to developing countries', *World Bank Economic Review*, **14**(1), 111–27.

Goldberg, Penny and Nina Pavcnik (2007), 'Distributional effects of globalization in developing countries', *Journal of Economic Literature*, **45**(1), 39–82.

Karlan, Dean and Jonathan Zinman (2009), 'Expanding microenterprise credit access: using randomized supply decisions to estimate the impacts in Manila', BREAD Working Paper No. 235.

Kono, Hisaki and Kazushi Takahashi (2010), 'Microfinance revolution: its effects, innovations, and challenges', *Developing Economies*, **48**(1), 15–73.

López, Ramón, John Nash and Julie Stanton (1995), 'Adjustment and poverty in Mexican agriculture: how farmers' wealth affects supply response', World Bank Policy Research Working Paper 1494.

McIntosh, Craig and Bruce Wydick (2005), 'Competition and microfinance', *Journal of Development Economics*, **78**(2), 271–98.

McIntosh, Craig and Bruce Wydick (2007), 'Adverse selection, moral hazard, and credit information systems', presented at the 2007 Northeast Universities Development Consortium Conference, Harvard University.

Milanovic, Branko (2005), 'Can we discern the effect of globalization on income distribution? Evidence from household surveys', *World Bank Economic Review*, **19**(1), 21–44.

Pitt, Mark and Shahidur Khandker (1998), 'The impact of group-based credit programs on poor households in Bangladesh: does the gender of participants matter?', *Journal of Political Economy*, **106**(5), 958–96.

Ravallion, Martin (2001), 'Growth, inequality and poverty: looking beyond averages', *World Development*, **29**(11), 1803–15.

Ravallion, Martin (2006), 'Looking beyond averages in the trade and poverty debate', *World Development*, **34**(8), 1374–92.

Ravallion, Martin and Dominique Van de Walle (1991), 'The impact on poverty of food pricing reforms: a welfare analysis for Indonesia', *Journal of Policy Modeling*, **13**, 281–99.

Ravallion, Martin, Shaohua Chen and Prem Sangraula (2008), 'Dollar a day revisited', World Bank Policy Research Working Paper 4620.

Rodriguez, Francisco and Dani Rodrik (2001), 'Trade policy and economic growth: a sceptic's guide to the cross-national evidence', *NBER Macroeconomics Annual 2000*, Cambridge, MA: MIT Press, pp. 261–324.

Roodman, David and Jonathan Morduch (2009), 'The impact of microcredit on the poor in Bangladesh: revisiting the evidence', Working Paper No. 174, Center for Global Development.

Tokarick, Stephen (2008), 'Dispelling some misconceptions about agricultural trade liberalization', *Journal of Economic Perspectives*, **22**(1), 199–216.

Winters, L. Alan, Neil McCulloch and Andrew McKay (2004), 'Trade liberalization and poverty: the evidence so far', *Journal of Economic Literature*, **42**(1), 72–115.

World Bank (2007), *World Development Report 2008: Agriculture for Development*, Washington, DC: World Bank.

17. Energy bottlenecks and cooperation

Nobuhiro Horii

17.1 INTRODUCTION

The purpose of this chapter is to explore the issue of whether energy supply will become a bottleneck that hampers the economic development of Asian nations, and, if that is the case, to also explore what kinds of measures should be taken. This in turn leads to the question of whether measures for regional energy cooperation are feasible, and if so, how to promote them. We will explore what measures the Asian nations should take to safeguard their energy supply subsequent to the recent changes and increasing price volatility in the energy market.

In Section 17.2, the author will analyse the energy structure in the Asian region based on macro data and explore the necessity of energy cooperation. In Section 17.3, the author will evaluate the ongoing progress of energy cooperation within the Asian region and issues associated with such cooperation. In Section 17.4, based upon the developments in the emerging economies as represented by China, which is the second largest energy consumer, the author will explore a new situation for energy cooperation in Asia following the drastic price fluctuations in the energy market. In Section 17.5, I will analyse the high tensions among the Asian countries caused by China's overseas investments in its efforts to secure its energy supply, and expound on the necessity of high-level energy cooperation in Asia. To conclude, the author will propose recommendations toward the needed energy cooperation.

17.2 ENERGY STRUCTURE IN THE ASIAN REGION

17.2.1 Past and Current Energy Supply and Demand in the Asian Region

As shown in Figure 17.1, overall global energy consumption has been increasing steadily and the growth of the ASEAN+3 countries in the share

Million tons oil
equivalent

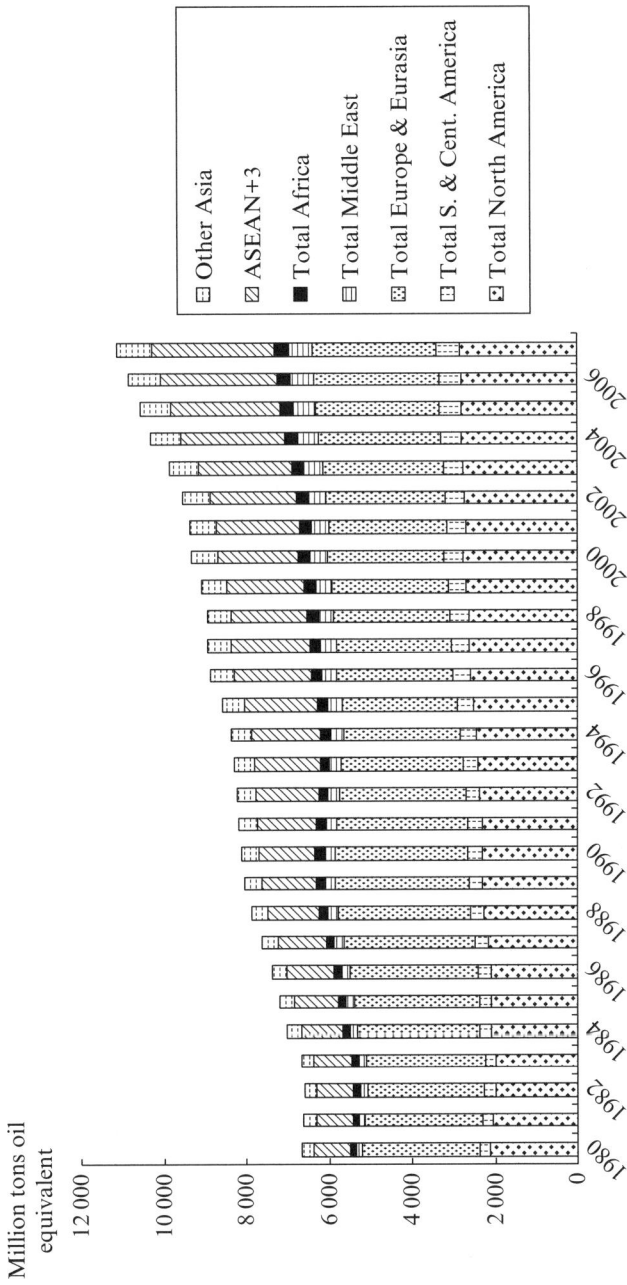

Legend:
- ⊞ Other Asia
- ▨ ASEAN+3
- ■ Total Africa
- ⊞ Total Middle East
- ⊠ Total Europe & Eurasia
- ⊡ Total S. & Cent. America
- ⊡ Total North America

Note: Energy consumption of Cambodia, Laos, Myanmar, and Vietnam is included in 'Other Asia' not in 'ASEAN+3' because of data category in data source.

Source: **BP** (2008).

Figure 17.1 Changes in energy consumption, 1985–2007

of world energy consumption is outstanding. In 1980, the energy consumption of the ASEAN+3 countries occupied 13.3% of the global total, and by 2007, it had grown to 26.8%. From 1980 to 2007, the increase in net global energy consumption amounted to 4.5 billion tons (oil equivalent), of which the demand from ASEAN+3 countries accounted for 46.9%, or 2.1 billion tons. Especially during 2000 to 2007, the energy consumption of the ASEAN+3 countries went up sharply as a share of the total energy consumption structure, and 57.0% of the extra global energy demand came from countries in ASEAN+3.

Strong economic momentum drove the rapid expansion of energy demand in the ASEAN+3 countries. In particular, starting in the 1980s, China gradually became the center of energy demand in Asia, due to the rapid economic growth unleashed by its reforms and openness policies. Figure 17.2 reflects the energy consumption in the main countries of ASEAN+3. As shown in the figure, China's consumption reached 62.6% of the total, by far dominating the energy consumption in the region, followed by Japan at 17.4% and Korea at 7.9%. The combined energy consumption of these three countries accounted for 87.8% of all consumption in ASEAN+3. China's energy consumption quadrupled from 417 million tons in 1980 to 1,863 million tons in 2007, and her share of energy consumption in ASEAN+3 also grew from 46.9% to 62.6%.

Figure 17.3 focuses on the changes in the degree of self sufficiency in oil, natural gas and coal within the Asian region, which demonstrates the necessity of energy cooperation there. Obviously the degree of self sufficiency in oil and natural gas within the region has been decreasing, particularly that of oil. In 1981, the self sufficiency rate of oil within the region was 58.0%, and by 2007, it had declined to 30.7%. With regard to natural gas, the self sufficiency rate of natural gas within the region reached its historic high of 97.2% in 1987. In 2007, it fell to 84.3%. Over the past few years, the self sufficiency rate of both oil and natural gas has fallen further, to reach historically low levels in 2007. On the other hand, the self sufficiency rate of coal within the region, which had been stable over the years, rose in 2000 to hit a historically high level of 94.3% in 2005 before dropping slightly to 91.9% in 2007.

Although the self sufficiency rate of oil and natural gas within the region both fell, looking at Figure 17.3, we can observe that there are differences. The oil production, which had been basically stable, began to fall after it reached its highest point in 1997, as the oil production of two oil exporters – Indonesia and Malaysia – dropped substantially due to resource exhaustion. Oil is traded as a commodity in the international markets, but considering the fluctuations in the international oil market over the last few years and the turbulence in the oil producing regions including the Middle East,

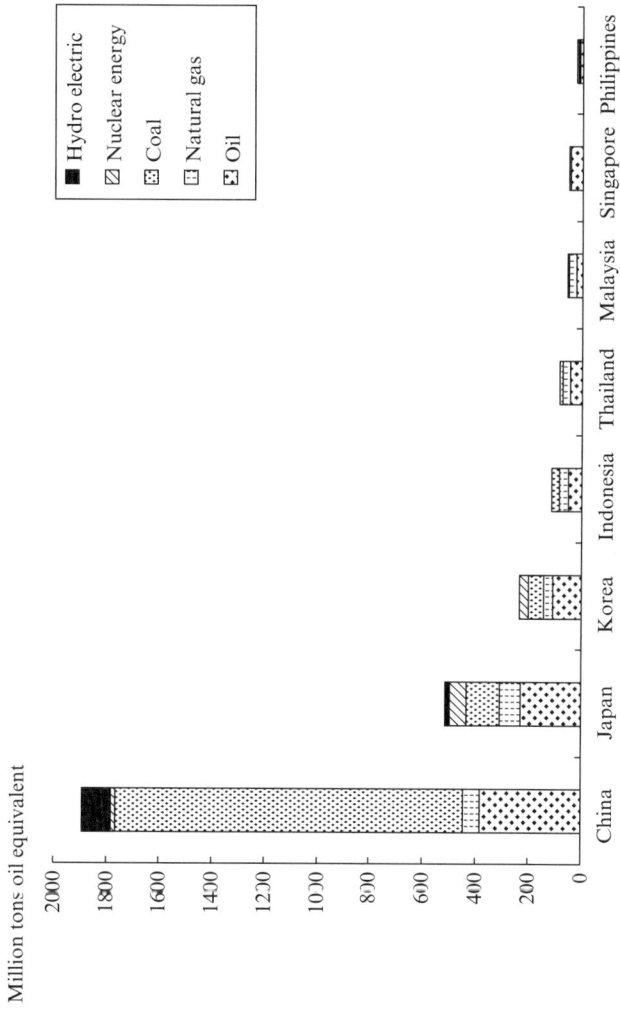

Million tons oil equivalent

Legend:
- ■ Hydro electric
- ▨ Nuclear energy
- ▦ Coal
- ⊞ Natural gas
- ⊡ Oil

Countries: China, Japan, Korea, Indonesia, Thailand, Malaysia, Singapore, Philippines

Note: See Figure 17.1.

Source: See Figure 17.1.

Figure 17.2 Structure of energy consumption in the Asian region by country (2007)

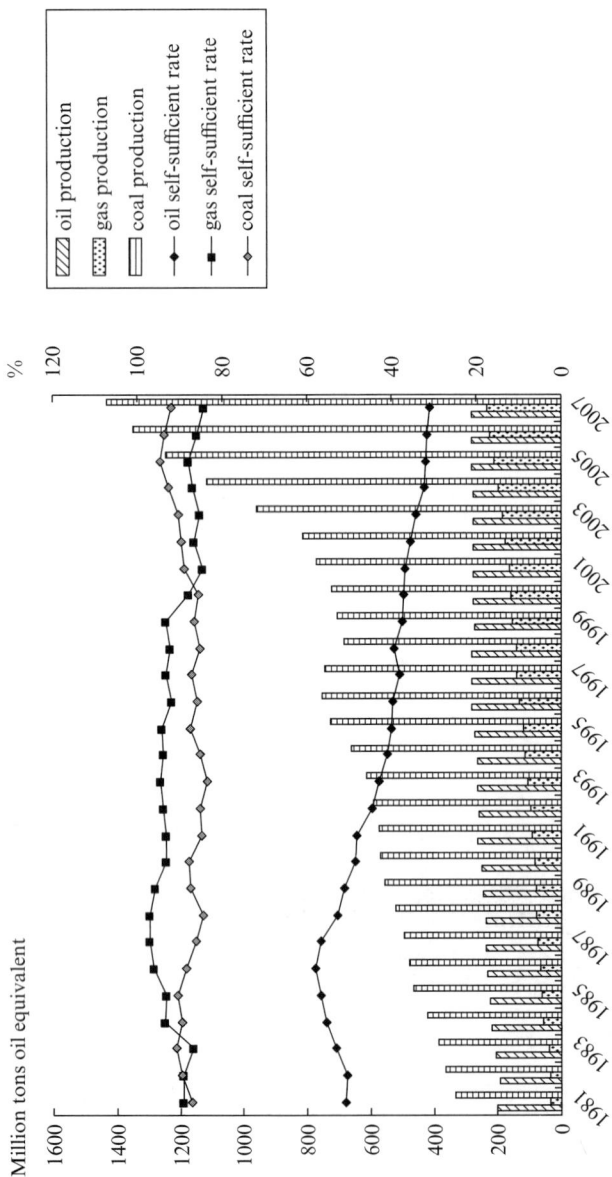

Million tons oil equivalent

Legend
▨ oil production
▧ gas production
▤ coal production
◆ oil self-sufficient rate
■ gas self-sufficient rate
◇ coal self-sufficient rate

Note: 'Self-sufficient rate' is not the actual rate of self sufficiency calculated from trade volume; instead it is the theoretic rate of self sufficiency found by dividing output by consumption in the region.

Source: See Figure 17.1.

Figure 17.3   Changes in the degree of energy sufficiency rate in the Asian region (1981–2007)

Latin America, and Africa, a decreasing oil self sufficiency rate within Asia could negatively affect the future economic growth of Asian nations, and therefore appropriate measures need to be adopted to address it.

In contrast to oil, the production of natural gas increased significantly, but a decrease in the self sufficiency rate in the region was caused by even stronger growth in energy consumption, as supply was unable to keep pace with demand. Natural gas differs from oil as its means of transportation are limited and it is a regional commodity rather than an international commodity.[1] Therefore, the decrease in the regional self sufficiency rate could be attributed to underdeveloped transportation infrastructure, in spite of the existing production potential within the region. It may be possible to supply natural gas to the countries within the region at lower prices than liquified natural gas (LNG) by developing the pipeline network within the region. However, this would involve massive initial costs to build the pipelines, and policy support and involvement are also necessary.

The regional self sufficiency rate for coal is quite high. By comparison with oil and natural gas in Figure 17.3, coal has played a very important role in satisfying the rapidly growing demand for energy in Asia. Coal production grew dramatically starting especially from 2002 (mainly in China), which significantly helped to satisfy the ever-growing appetite for energy as the global economy expanded. As shown in Figure 17.2, for Asia and particularly for China, coal serves as the primary source of energy. However, the high dependence on coal causes serious air pollution, and in addition, it also creates a heavy obligation to take measures against global warming. Therefore, it is necessary to organize regional cooperation in order to popularize relevant solutions and achieve the goal of sustainable utilization of coal.

17.2.2 Future Prospects for Energy Supply and Demand in the Asian Region

Next, let us take a look at the future prospects for the world's and Asia's energy supply and demand, based on the IEA (International Energy Agency) forecast[2] (IEA 2007). The world's primary energy needs are projected to grow by 55% between 2005 and 2030, at an average annual rate of 1.8% per year. Very importantly, the share of energy consumed by various countries is projected to change drastically during these 25 years, and developing countries will contribute 74% of the increase. As a result, developing countries will comprise 47% of the global energy market in 2015 and more than half in 2030, compared with only 41% in 2005. Among those developing countries, the increase in China's energy demand will be particularly huge, accounting for 45% of the developing countries' increase and 33% of the world's increase. China will continue to be the key player in increases in energy demand in the future.

Another important prediction in the IEA forecasts is the shift in the composition of the energy sources. Oil will remain the single largest fuel, though its share in global demand will fall from 35% to 32%. Coal will experience the largest increase, jumping by 73% between 2005 and 2030 and pushing its share of total energy demand up from 25% to 28%. The reason why the share of coal will increase in spite of negative motivational influences such as global warming is that most of the increase in coal use will arise in China and India. China's coal demand is projected to increase by 1.3 billion tons between 2005 and 2030, which is equal to 62% of the total coal demand increase in the entire world.

China, which is predicted to be the largest energy-consuming country even in 2015, is projected to import oil in the amount of 13.1 mb/d (millions of barrels per day) in 2030, up from 3.5 mb/d in 2005, and China's share of imported oil will rise from 50% to 80% of the total. Even for coal, China's main energy source now and in the future, China's net imports will reach 3% of its demand and 7% of the global coal trade in 2030.

So, how about supply side? The critical question is whether such a large demand increase can be satisfied by increasing the supply or not. The IEA forecast concludes that world oil resources are estimated to be sufficient to meet the projected growth in demand up to 2030, although production will become more concentrated in OPEC countries. The inter-regional oil and gas trade will grow rapidly, with a widening of the gap between intrar-egional production and demand in every consuming region. The volume of oil trade will expand from 41 mb/d in 2006 to 51 mb/d in 2015 and 65 mb/d in 2030. The Middle East, Africa and Latin America will export more oil, and OPEC's share of the world oil supply will jump from its current 42% to 52% in 2030.

As indicated in the IEA forecast, reduced geographic diversity in the supply increases the risk of heightened short term energy insecurity for consuming countries. With such a strong global energy demand, all regions will be faced with higher energy prices in the medium to long term in the absence of a concomitant increase in supply side investment or stronger policy action to curb demand growth in all countries. The IEA projection is formulated based on the assumption that the necessary investment is forthcoming. However, the increasing concentration of the world's remaining oil reserves in a small group of countries, notably Middle Eastern members of OPEC and Russia, will increase their market dominance and may put at risk the required rate of investment in production capacity. Therefore, it is very important to build and maintain the incentive system to keep capital flowing to the oil industry and to other energy industries as well. Higher energy prices would be especially burdensome for developing countries which are still seeking to protect their consumers through subsidies.

17.3 CURRENT ENERGY COOPERATION IN THE ASIAN REGION

Within the Asian region, there are such frameworks as APEC, ASEAN and ASEAN+3 which could serve as platforms to promote energy cooperation. In this section, the author will survey the current energy cooperation under those international frameworks within the region.

17.3.1 Energy Cooperation under APEC

In 1990, APEC set up the Energy Working Group (EWG) to promote energy cooperation, as one of the 11 working groups for different sectors. In 1992, EWG held a ministerial meeting in Seoul, and EWG was upgraded to ministerial level.

In the following decade, EWG worked on the following (APEC EWG Secretariat 2002): (1) serving as a platform for issues related to collaboration for securing an energy supply for the region, (2) exchanging views on coordination of energy policies, (3) supporting the development of IPPs (Independent Power Producers), (4) promoting environmental protection in the power sector, (5) promoting the construction of gas infrastructure, (6) supporting the connection of power grids in countries within the region, (7) unifying energy standards, and (8) promoting energy conservation.

Since 2000, the modality of the APEC EWG cooperation has turned to focus on energy security, environmental protection, reforms of the energy market within the region, setting up of specific strategies and execution of those strategies. Specific achievements have included the APEC Energy Security Initiative and the Type II Partnership Initiative proposed at the 2002 Sustainability World Summit. To translate these two initiatives into action, EWG worked out a 2005 Action Plan, including the following main items (APEC EWG Secretariat 2005).

Firstly, the mission of EWG is: (1) to prevent interruptions in the energy supply, (2) to promote energy investment, (3) to improve energy efficiency, (4) to expand energy options, and (5) to strengthen capital investment for technological advancements. Since crude oil prices have skyrocketed on the international market, EWG has set the following areas for short- and long-term cooperation, respectively.

Short-term cooperation includes: (1) sharing of oil data, (2) security of sea lanes, (3) establishment of a real-time emergency information sharing system, (4) contingency plans for emergencies in the energy supply, and (5) research on the impact of soaring oil prices. The following have been selected for long-term cooperation: (1) energy investment, (2) energy conservation, (3) trade of natural gas, (4) nuclear energy, (5) methane hydrate, (6) clean fossil energy, (7) renewable energies, (8) hydrogen, fuel cells and alternative fuel for transportation, and (9) upgrading of refining infrastructures. The long-term cooperation is focused on diversifying energy sources and enhancing the stability of the energy supply as a whole while simultaneously addressing environmental issues.

17.3.2   Energy Cooperation under ASEAN

ASEAN has established mechanisms such as the Energy Senior Officials Meeting and Ministerial Meeting as well as the consultation platform for energy cooperation. In order to advance substantive cooperation, ASEAN has set up the ASEAN Energy Center, ASEAN Oil Committee, and ASEAN Power Forum, and at the same time, has established oil, power, coal, energy conservation, renewable energy, and non-conventional energy research forums under the ASEAN Science and Technology Committee.

On energy cooperation, ASEAN prepared an ASEAN Plan of Action for Energy Cooperation (ASEAN Secretariat 2004). The plan set out the five years from 1999 to 2004 as Phase 1 to execute specific projects. Phase 1 focused on the connection of power grids and the connection of gas pipelines within the region.

In addition, ASEAN also proposed advancing energy security and integrating infrastructure within the region, initiating structural reforms in the energy sector, working on market liberalization and cooperating on environmental protection. What was achieved in Phase 1 included finalization of the master plan for connecting gas pipelines and power grids within ASEAN and working out of the roadmap on institutional facilities needed to execute the plans. Furthermore, ASEAN also worked out programs to unify energy efficiency standards,[3] organized workshops to popularize energy conservation technologies, worked on projects to promote CCT (Clean Coal Technology) and renewable energies, set up energy databases within the region, and engaged in capacity building related to energy security policies and research on the energy policies in various countries within the region.

In Phase II of the ASEAN Plan of Action for Energy Cooperation outlined for 2004 to 2009, projects in the following six cooperation fields are to be implemented: (1) connection of the power grids in ASEAN, (2) connection of gas pipelines within ASEAN, (3) coal, (4) improvement of energy efficiency and energy conservation, (5) renewable energy, and (6) coordination of energy policies within the region.

17.3.3 Energy Cooperation under ASEAN+3

As described above, ASEAN is seeking, through energy cooperation, to confront energy problems by establishing broad and reasonable targets.

However, cooperation under the framework of ASEAN has inherent limitations since most of the ASEAN members are producers of conventional energies who have only a very short history as energy consumers. As domestic energy production has declined, the energy producers have become consumers who need to secure an overseas energy supply and control their ever-expanding energy demand in order to prevent energy shortages. In that sense, ASEAN+3 must have more measures for promoting energy cooperation with energy consumers, including Japan, China and Korea, in its framework.

Energy cooperation under the ASEAN+3 framework includes the following: (1) building a network for mutual accommodation of oil supplies in an emergency, (2) setting up oil reserves among member countries, (3) jointly researching the oil market in ASEAN, (4) promoting natural gas development, and (5) improving energy efficiency and developing renewable energies. Since 2003, expert forums on the above five key cooperation fields have been established to continue to do relevant research.

The first Energy Ministers Meeting under the framework of ASEAN+3 was held in June 2004. The meeting called on the oil producers to take action to expand oil production in response to the tight oil supply in the market. More importantly, through the meeting, the importance of a strategic national oil reserve system was agreed upon, and the meeting made a point of setting up an oil reserve system. Under the framework of ASEAN+3, only Japan and Korea, being members of the IEA, have established their own strategic oil reserve systems. The reaching of a consensus on the absolute importance of building an oil reserve system is highly significant for safeguarding energy security within ASEAN+3. In addition to the requirement to set up oil reserve systems, the countries involved are also required to coordinate the timing of the release of oil reserves in emergencies. It is plausible that energy cooperation under the framework of ASEAN+3 will require the stakeholders to coordinate the actions of each country, possibly by coordinating the decision making of the member countries.

Energy cooperation under the framework of ASEAN+3 made a certain amount of progress in recent years. Energy cooperation projects under the framework of ASEAN+3 included the following: (1) promotion of data sharing on oil reserve policies and methods as well as on the oil reserve systems among the concerned countries, (2) holding of the 2nd Dialogue between the Oil Producers and Consumers, in May 2007 in Riyadh, (3) establishment of the Energy Conservation Cooperation Center initiated by Japan, (4) launching of the initiative on promoting natural gas trade within the region, (5) setting up of the Coal Liquefaction Support Center in Indonesia as one of the facilities to promote Clean Coal Technology (CCT) (initiated by Japan).

In addition, the ASEAN+3 Cooperation Work Plan (2007–17) was approved during the 11th ASEAN+3 Summit, held on 20 November 2007. It was proposed that the modality adopted by APEC and ASEAN should be coordinated. In the future, efforts will be made to develop additional stable energy supplies by improving the energy market efficiency under the framework of ASEAN+3, and efforts will also be made to organize research on promotion of energy conservation and diversification of renewable energy sources. In addition, the plan listed very specific measures for energy conservation, including the setting up of sectoral targets, enhancement of cooperation on emergency preparedness by fully utilizing the ASEAN+3 Energy Security Communication System for energy conservation and outlining of the measures for coordination of the energy policies of the concerned countries[4] (ASEAN Secretariat 2007).

17.3.4   Evaluation of Current Energy Cooperation in the Asian Region

To secure supply side, as shown from self sufficiency in Figure 17.3, the main issue for oil is to secure oil supply from overseas and to control the risk of disruptions in the oil supply to the region. As for natural gas, the main issue is the development of transportation infrastructure. Therefore, it is necessary to expand the natural gas production by enhancing the exploitation and development efforts, and, at the same time, more investment is needed to further develop the transportation infrastructure and pipeline network. Looking at coal, coal exports from Indonesia and Vietnam are now increasing but are expected to turn into decreasing after 2020. Consequently the share of Australian coal exports will be increased and Australia's control over market price will be further strengthened. Therefore, the Asian region needs to increase its coal production and also take measures to secure a stable supply from outside the region. In addition, it is absolutely vital to promote environmental protection technologies to tackle the negative impacts of coal. Measures need to be taken to tackle cross-border pollution caused by SO_2 emission and to minimize coal's impact on global warming in order to achieve sustainable use of coal.

Based on those needs to stabilize energy markets in the Asian region, regional cooperation under the frameworks of APEC, ASEAN and ASEAN+3 can be evaluated as flowing in the right direction; however, such cooperation has inherent limitations.

First of all, although APEC has confronted many issues faced by the Asian region, most of its work has been focused on studies and research, and few valuable practical results have been produced. This is because the role of initiator is played by few countries within the APEC framework, and there are also capital issues.

There are specific projects under the framework of ASEAN, and in particular, the master plan for the natural gas pipeline network within the region should be highly commended. This pipeline could support the expansion of energy consumption in the region by expanding natural gas output and also could help to improve the self sufficiency rate of natural gas in the region. There are also CCT projects aimed at reducing the environmental impact of coal as well as energy diversification projects which focus on renewable energy development. However, most of the projects lack substance and have not gone beyond sharing of information. The reason may be attributable to the fact that most of the ASEAN members were formerly energy producers who focused on developing and exporting energy, paying little attention to energy-saving technology.

Cooperation under the ASEAN+3 framework has made more progress, owing to the participation of Japan as a technology provider. The Energy Conservation Cooperation Center initiated by Japan has been established, and the CCT demonstration project in Indonesia will help to promote Japanese energy technology in Asia. Furthermore, ASEAN+3's efforts to build oil reserves to prevent disruptions to the oil supply and endeavors on energy policy coordination are also highly commendable. However, issues do exist; for example, most projects have resembled bilateral cooperation between Japan and other nations rather than joint efforts under the international framework, and in most cases of technology transfer, the current Japanese technologies are brought to the recipient country without any customization, failing to take advantage of the dynamic emerging technological innovation by the recipient country, especially China (further elaborated in Section 17.4).

Therefore, there are still some issues for improvement associated with regional cooperation in Asia. In Sections 17.4 and 17.5, the author will explore the measures that are needed to address such issues.

17.4   CHANGE IN MARKET STRUCTURE AND INFLUENCE ON ENERGY COOPERATION IN THE ASIAN REGION

The energy market in the last few years has been heavily influenced by the financial market, and the prices of energies have fluctuated drastically. On the other hand, the rise of Asia's manufacturing capability means that there may be potential for technological innovations in energy and environmental protection in the region. In this section, we will analyse those two changes related to energy cooperation in the Asian region.

17.4.1   Impacts Caused by the Structural Changes in the Energy Market

From early 2007 to mid 2008, energy prices shot up sharply. The prices of most energies also displayed abnormal rises of several fold within a period of a few years. At that time, the ever-expanding appetite for energy in Asia, especially in China and India, was blamed as the main factor behind the skyrocketing prices of energy and resource products. Today, we can see that it was incorrect to say that increased demand in Asia resulted in the price hike[5] and that in fact it was a consequence of the bubble in the financial world (Box 17.1). Based upon the conventional energy economics framework, that is, price is set under the balance of real (not speculative) demand and supply and few were aware of the structural changes taking place in the energy market.

The energy price level exerts a great impact on energy supply and demand. The prices affect investments poured into the energy industry and determine the future energy supply capacity. In addition, if energy prices maintain a high level, different forms of energies will be substituted for each other. As for demand, a price hike in energies will also drive the introduction of energy-saving technologies, which will reduce the energy demand. So, what kinds of impacts have price hikes exerted on the demand and supply of energy over the past few years and future?

Based upon the forecast by the IEA mentioned in Section 17.2, even under the scenario in which the developing countries headed by China and India maintain their growth momentum, the energy supply should be able to cope with the extra energy demand. However, there is one prerequisite – the necessary investment must be guaranteed. One of the critical factors that determines the future energy supply is whether the energy industry receives the needed investments. Since the 1980s, due to the low oil price, the energy sector, including crude oil, natural gas and coal, all lacked capital investment, and as a result, energy supply infrastructure (for

---

BOX 17.1   BACKGROUND TO ROLLERCOASTER OIL PRICES AFTER 2007

From 2007 to mid 2008, the crude oil price on the international market climbed to successive new highs. On 11 July 2008, the price hit the historic new high of US$147.27. Subsequently, it trended downward, and within months, on 19 November, fell to US$32.40, which was less than one-quarter of its highest value. The rollercoaster movement of the oil price in the international market over these two years was not explicable by the conventional market analysis framework based upon the real economy. The massive volatility was not determined by the conventional supply and demand theory, but instead it was driven by financial factors.

The price of crude oil started its upward move in 2003 due to the emergence of numerous commodity investment funds. At that time, there was plenty of capital; globally, there was excessive liquidity. Speculative capital, hoping to spot better investment opportunities offering higher performance than conventionally seen in the stock market, rushed into the commodities market, focusing in particular on crude oil, gold and other precious metals as well as grain. The commodity investment funds functioned as the vehicle by which to put a lot of money into the commodities markets. On one hand, the commodity investment funds could offer new money-making opportunities, and at the same time, given that commodities prices move differently from the prices of stocks and bonds, the funds were expected to reduce investment risks through diversification; hence, such funds started to absorb a large amount of investment money.

In the past, speculative capital like hedge funds has also been invested in the crude oil market. However, commodity investment funds differ from the hedge funds in the following aspects: in terms of operational style, hedge funds mainly focus on short-term buying and selling, while commodity investment funds focus more on the mid- to long-term investment, with long (buying) positions, resulting in snowballing accumulation of the capital they inject into the market.

As there were no short orders, the number of long orders continued to increase, resulting in the upward movement of the oil price. This upward trend was interpreted as the success of the commodity investment funds, which attracted more capital into such funds, and in turn such capital was injected into the commodities market, led by the crude oil market. Pension funds noticed the success of the commodity investment funds, and they also transferred part of their capital from the stock and bond markets.

Once the subprime mortgage problem in the US was exposed in the summer of 2007, investors at various levels withdrew their capital from stock markets and turned to the commodities market, which was deemed to be less risky: hence the price hike of crude oil. However, by the summer of 2008, the US government had strengthened its oversight of the futures market, and capital began fleeing from the commodities market, including the oil market, triggering the tumble from the historic high point of the oil price. Once the trend was reversed, the losses began snowballing. Then the bankruptcy of Lehman Brothers occurred, causing more people to worry that the financial crisis would spread into the real economy, and consequently, more capital fled from the oil market, further pushing down the oil price.

example, rigs for oil drilling and tankers for transportation) lagged far behind. An increasing number of people point out this as the bottleneck of the energy industry over the last few years.

However, given the high oil prices during 2007 and 2008, people began exploring how to develop those high-cost oil fields as well as unconventional oil fields like oil shale and oil sand. In the meantime, significant development was achieved in other alternative energies including coal liquification, bio-fuel, wind and solar energies. Even though some lead time is required to expand supply, the price hike certainly facilitated expansion on the supply side. Besides, different forms of energies are substitutable; therefore, if one form of energy faces resource restrictions, other forms of energy will emerge to fill the void.

At the same time, we should not neglect the increased investment in energy-saving technologies given the high energy prices. For instance, in 2006, China started to aggressively enforce energy conservation policies during its 11th five-year plan. The high price of energy improves the likelihood that China will achieve its target of reducing per unit energy consumption by 20% by 2010 using the energy consumption level in 2005 as a baseline. In addition, in the transportation sector, one of the main users of oil, the global auto manufacturers, has invested much more into

R&D to promote commercialization of electric vehicles, including plug-in hybrid vehicles.

In summary, it could be said that the energy price hike led by the oil price over the past few years helped to expand and diversify the energy supply. This is because many people believed energy prices would remain at high levels in the future, making it less risky to develop conventional energy, alternative energy and energy conservation technologies. In fact, even highly risky projects had been launched as many had very strong expectations of high energy prices in the future. However, after the oil price tumbled, such efforts also plummeted. For instance, from October to November 2008 alone, 17 oil resource development projects were delayed or cancelled, and researchers forecast that 5–10% (some said 20%) of the planned investments for capacity by 26 of the world's major oil companies would be deleted in 2009. As a result, 4% of the current production capacity is estimated to disappear in 2013, which might cause severe shortage of oil supply (LeVine 2008).

Since tumbling energy prices would result in the suspension of many projects that are aimed at expansion of the energy supply, it is quite likely that the balance of energy demand and supply will turn out to be energy shortage once demand is restored. In the author's view, if that happens, energy prices may rise to a certain degree but will not increase dramatically as in 2007 and 2008. From the perspective of healthy development of the energy business, it is necessary for prices to increase to some degree, but the rise should not be overly dramatic. In fact, when the international oil price skyrocketed between 2006 and 2008, some people called for a certain degree of government intervention in the futures market, but such calls were shelved as soon as oil prices tumbled. Nevertheless, the same issue may pop up again in the future.

17.4.2 New Situation and Influence on Energy Cooperation in Asia

The Asian nations are changing from producers to consumers. In 2004, Indonesia became a net oil importer, and oil production in Malaysia also declined. It is forecast that by 2020, all current oil exporters in Asia except Brunei will become importers, including Malaysia and Vietnam. China, the top coal producer in the world, will depend on imports to meet 3% of its total coal demand, which will amount to 7% of the global coal trade in 2030, and which will increase the needs for coal by the Asian region. In fact, in 2009, China finally imported 126 million tons of coal (103 million tons net).

Even so, these countries have not reformed systems which were developed while they were large energy producers; they continue to provide subsidies to the energy industry and subsidize imported energy products, and their citizens still enjoy energy at low prices. Since 2004, these countries have been forced to shoulder massive financial burdens due to the price hikes and subsidies, and the governments have had to significantly mark up energy prices. Policy changes are needed to minimize price intervention, which will in turn promote energy conservation. And to promote energy conservation technologies, they need to push forward institutional reforms and establish an energy pricing system that facilitates energy conservation. Therefore, Japan should also become more engaged in facilitating institutional development.

Furthermore, technological cooperation between Japan and other Asian nations also needs to be improved in accordance with the new situation, which refers to the idea of taking advantage of the increased manufacturing capabilities of Asian nations to better promote adoption of energy savings and environmental protection technologies. Due to the high costs involved, it is very difficult for developing countries (and in some cases even for developed countries) to apply energy conservation and environmentally friendly technologies. Under the situation that the control of oil and coal supply by a small number of countries is being strengthened, it is imperative for Asian countries to adopt energy conservation technologies. In addition, as analysed in Section 17.2, coal is a critical energy source for Asian nations, and to continue to utilize coal, these nations must adopt environmental protection technologies to tackle pollution, which is the largest negative aspect of coal.

In fact, the emergence of Asia (and in particular China) as the world manufacturing center could offer opportunities to innovate energy conservation and environmental protection technologies. Take the example of FGD (flue gas desulfurization), which has been rapidly deployed in China (Box 17.2). In the past, due to high cost, deployment of FGD was limited to developed countries such as Japan, the US and Germany, but by the end of 2009, 71% of the power plants in China had introduced FGD, which basically addressed the issue of SO_2 emission associated with burning coal. The key to deployment of FGD in China has been dramatic cost reduction (up to 80%) through localization of the production of FGD equipment.

We can see two important implications in the example of FGD adoption in China. Firstly, China's huge market served as a massive driving force for the development of energy conservation technology and environmental protection technology. Even after innovative technology by Chinese FGD makers cut the cost of installment of FGD to power plants by 80%, within five years, Chinese power plants had invested RMB50 billion (US$7.3 billion) at the low end, or almost RMB90 billion (US$13

BOX 17.2   BACKGROUND TO THE DEPLOYMENT OF FGD IN CHINA

By combining technology from developed countries with the demand of the local market, Chinese enterprises successfully reduced the production cost of flue gas desulfurization (FGD) by simplifying some processes and dramatically cutting back component and raw material costs. It is true that these alterations also affected the efficiency of the FGD equipment (efficiency seems to have declined by 10–20%, compared with the most advanced technology), but nonetheless such alterations made it possible to provide the equipment at astonishingly low costs. The wide adoption of FGD in China is attributable to the combined efforts of enterprises, which cut costs, and the government, which passed regulations. Some enterprises worked hard to seize this new business opportunity. It should be noted that China received the technology transfer mostly from US and European companies rather than Japanese companies, although Japanese companies had also developed advanced FGD technology just like their rivals in Germany and the US. The reason is that the US and European companies allowed more flexibility for the Chinese enterprises to transfer the technology through patent licenses, while the Japanese companies insisted on their own existing technology for production in China through joint ventures. The reality in China is that, unless the local producers find ways to vigorously cut the costs, there is little chance of acquiring a large market share for Japanese products in spite of their high quality. Therefore, to succeed, it is critical to make use of the cost-cutting ingenuity of Chinese enterprises.

---

billion) at the high end, to procure FGD equipment. Such a huge market could offer enough incentive for the enterprises to engage in R&D.[6] This shows that Asia, emerging as the growth center of energy demand, has an advantage in driving forward and promoting energy conservation technologies and environmental protection technologies: other examples are high efficient coal combustion technology (Super Critical), solar power and wind power.

It seems to be important that the government should provide incentives to encourage enterprises to drive down the costs of energy conservation and environmental protection technologies. Industrial policies aimed at protecting certain enterprises, however, do not always bear fruit. When China promoted FGD, the government only issued a regulation requiring power plants to install FGD, and aside from a small number of enterprises that participated in the national project to develop FGD technology, most companies did not enjoy any special treatment. Market competition drove the costs down, in sharp contrast to solar energy and bio-fuel, which have also been booming around the world. The adoption of solar energy is attributable to the feed-in tariff system promoted typically by the German government; the adoption of bio-fuel is attributable to the procurement targets set by the US government. In other words, the adoption of these energies was achieved only under preferential policies that entailed much higher purchase prices. Despite remarkable progress, many producers are being eliminated as people anticipate that the preferential policies will be readjusted, reflecting the tumbling energy prices and the deteriorating economic environment. If the promoted policies are not successful in encouraging enterprises to drive down their product price, the policies will not be sustainable because installment costs cannot be reduced and the overall social costs increase.

Therefore, Asian nations should take full advantage of the massive potential demand within the region, particularly in China, and attempt breakthroughs in the area of energy conservation and environmentally friendly technologies. To achieve that, environmental regulation and enforcement monitoring systems need to be developed. Effective environmental regulations can themselves create a huge market and enterprises will come to participate in the market actively.

The important thing is to reduce costs by promoting customization of technology through the market mechanism in promoting wide adoption of technologies for energy conservation and environmental protection. In contrast the Energy Conservation Cooperation Center established under the framework of ASEAN+3 merely aimed to import the existing technology from Japan to the emerging economies without any changes. Technology cooperation needs to be reconsidered: it should mean more than simply trying to copy Japanese energy-saving and environmental protection technologies in other countries.

17.5   THE NECESSITY OF COORDINATION OF ENERGY POLICIES

In Section 17.4, we discussed the impacts of structural changes in the energy market on energy cooperation and reached the following conclusion: to have effective cooperation, the market mechanism must play a role, although it is also necessary to take measures to prevent excessive price volatility which could destabilize the energy supply (since uncertainties lead to increased investment risks).

On the other hand, there remain issues that cannot be resolved simply by applying the market mechanism. One example is the friction between China and its neighbors triggered by China's overseas oil development, which has been in the spotlight in the past few years. In this section, the author will elaborate on the necessity of energy policy coordination by the countries in the region. Firstly, we will overview the reason for the friction, focusing on the key country, China.

China has an enormous appetite for energy, as shown in Section 17.2, and since domestic energy production could not keep pace with the rapid growth of demand, energy imports to China have been increasing every year. The main reason to increase energy imports is to meet the gap in oil supply caused by expanding demand. Due to the rapid development of the auto industry in the car boom of recent years, oil consumption has grown sharply. At the same time, the production of most domestic oil fields, with Daqing Oil Field as the primary example, is waning, and production growth cannot keep pace with the immense growth of consumption. To address the gap between supply and demand, China's oil imports have risen sharply.

In 1990, China imported only 2.92 million tons of crude oil. However, by 2009, imports had grown to 240.80 million tons, and from this we can imagine the size of the impact of China's oil consumption on the international oil market, although it was incorrect to regard increased demand in China as the main cause of the international price hike. As shown in Figure 17.4, the external oil dependency ratio of China had risen radically, from 2.5% in 1990 to 51.3% in 2009.

As the world's second largest energy consumer, China could realize its great energy-saving potential by improving energy efficiency. In Table 17.1, we can see that energy consumption per unit in China was much higher for most products than that in developed countries, and its energy efficiency lagged far behind the advanced level. This means that, should the advanced energy conservation technologies in Japan and other developed countries be introduced to China, future growth of energy consumption could be restrained considerably.[7] By supporting less advanced countries by providing energy efficiency technology, more advanced countries could help to dampen the growth of energy consumption in the region as a whole, and this could serve as one of the pillars of energy cooperation within the region.

Forced to import ever-increasing amounts of energy, China has worked out several strategies over the past few years. To better utilize coal, its

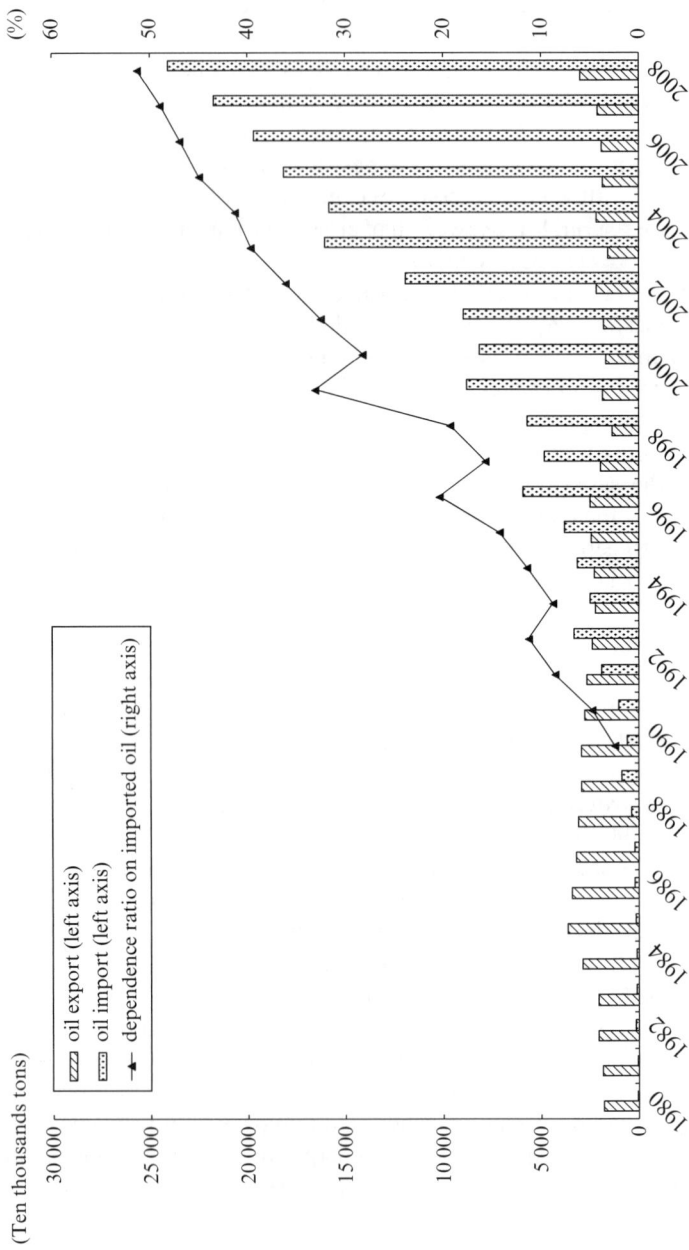

(Ten thousands tons)

oil export (left axis)
oil import (left axis)
dependence ratio on imported oil (right axis)

Source: Based on the annual *China Statistics Yearbook* and news reports.

Figure 17.4   Changes in China's oil imports and degree of imported oil dependency (1980–2009)

470

Table 17.1   Energy efficiency in China

Technology	Unit	1980	1990	2000	International frontier	Gap (%)
Thermal power generation at plant*	g-sce/ kWh	413	392	363	303	19.8
Thermal power generation at end-use**	g-sce/ kWh	448	427	392	316	24.1
Coal production	kWh/t	34.3	44	30.9	30	3.0
Steel production	kg-sce/t		997	789	646	22.1
Copper production	kg-sce/t	2028	1705	1352	820	64.9
Aluminum production	kg-sce/t		6998	6427	≦5800	
Oil refinery	kg-sce/t		20.58	20.01		
Ethylene production	kg-sce/t	2013	1580	1212	714	69.7
Ammonia production by large scale gas plant	kg-sce/t	1431	1343	1200	970	23.7
Cement production	kg-sce/t	219	201	181	126	43.7

Note: * Coal needed to produce 1 kWh power at plant; ** coal needed to send 1 kWh power to end-users, which includes transmission loss caused in the process of sending power from plants to end-users through grid.

Source: China Energy Development Report 2007.

primary energy source, China has applied great efforts to develop and deploy clean coal technology (CCT), which partially mitigates the environmental impact of coal. China has also worked hard to introduce energy conservation technology to reduce energy consumption. Especially in the 11th Five-Year Plan, energy conservation has been a key focus, and the plan establishes targets for reducing energy consumption per unit of GDP by 20% and reducing SO_2 emissions by 10% through installation of FGD devices in power plants. At the end of the year 2010, it was reported that the reduction of the energy consumption per capita GDP reached 19.1%, almost accomplishing the target. In particular, SO_2 emission was reduced by 14.3%, achieving more than the target.

In addition, to secure a source of oil imports, China is actively pursuing such strategies as purchasing overseas oil fields for proprietary development. China pursues overseas proprietary oil development through the three major state-owned overseas oil operations (Kaku 2010). As a result, China was involved in 147 overseas oil and gas projects by June 2009; PSA (agreements on sharing production) crude output reached 750 thousand barrels per day, and PSA natural gas production reached 10.1 million m^3 per day, which is equivalent to 15.6% of China's total crude imports. In comparison, Japan, which learned the lessons from the oil crisis in the 1970s and worked to obtain overseas oil assets much earlier, achieved overseas PSA crude amounting to 15.2% of its total imports at the highest point, as of the end of 1999; in 2003, this figure fell to 9.8% due to maturing of contracts and so on. We can see that China's PSA crude imports exceeded Japan's in a matter of a few years, which may be considered a great success.

However, China's activities to secure energy supply have also triggered friction with other countries. China is contending with neighboring countries in Asia, including Japan, for the rights to develop offshore oil and gas fields. Specifically, China is in dispute with Japan over the East China Sea natural gas fields and competes with ASEAN countries for the oil fields near the Spratly Islands. Furthermore, China and Japan argued over the development of Russia's gas in the Sakhalin region and the routing of the Irkutsk gas pipeline, which turned out to be a struggle in which Russia ended up as the biggest winner. Although China was not solely to blame for the above issues, China's zeal for securing resources has caused other Asian nations to become nervous and has triggered a chain reaction of distrust, as all nations wanted to grab the resources for themselves, fearing they will be grabbed by others.[8]

The frictions caused by the international expansion of Chinese oil companies are not limited to Asia; the US and European countries have also gone on alert. For example, strong opposition was displayed by US public opinion when China National Offshore Oil Corporation (CNOOC) bid for Unocal in 2005. In addition, the US and Europe intensively criticized some of China's overseas projects for helping the 'non-democratic' regimes in Africa, including Sudan and Angola, to maintain their existing administration.[9]

As shown in Figure 17.5, the overseas investment of Chinese oil companies has flowed to many countries, and African countries have been a major target. Locations with better resource conditions, such as the Middle East, had all been taken by the major international oil companies, and Chinese oil companies, as the latecomers, had limited choices. In a sense, this has been a positive factor for increasing global oil production because Chinese oil companies ventured to develop oil resources in the international market that otherwise might never have been developed.

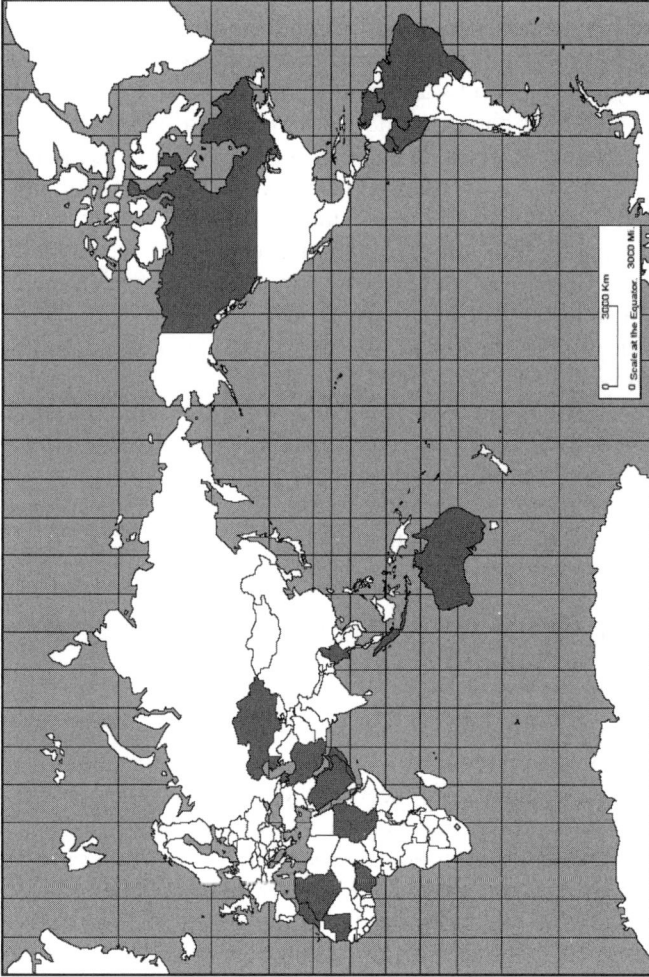

Note: The shaded countries are those in which Chinese oil companies have obtained interests in developing oil and gas fields.

Source: *China's Energy Moves – Current Status of Overseas Oil and Natural Gas/Outlook on China's Energy Industry* (JETRO 2006).

Figure 17.5 Overseas oil interests owned by Chinese oil companies (by the end of 2005)

Moreover, even if China only aimed to obtain resources, in reality it has made great contributions to infrastructure construction in African nations. The investment from China has already exceeded the balance of the loans from both the African Development Bank and the World Bank in the African region.

At the moment, Chinese oil companies' overseas investments are being monitored closely by concerned parties around the world. The Chinese government has taken note of the stern attitude adopted by other countries, particularly the US and European countries, and has initiated measures to mitigate their concerns and wariness toward the Chinese oil companies' overseas investments. It could be said that China has paid a high political price to secure overseas oil resources. In terms of economic costs alone, when competing with other countries (particularly with other Asian nations including India) in international tenders for the rights to develop resources, China has won only at very high bids, which might have damaged the interests of Chinese companies.

In summary, measures adopted by China to secure a stable energy supply triggered friction with the US, European countries and East Asian nations. Nations fell into zero-sum games as each country put maximization of its own interests first, and each acted on its own, fighting for energy without any cooperation. To overcome this situation and advance mutual interests, it is imperative to expand energy cooperation. In the conclusion, we will discuss the necessary steps toward energy cooperation within the Asian region.

17.6   CONCLUSION: TOWARD EFFECTIVE ENERGY COOPERATION

How does one promote effective cooperation, including coordination of energy policies, given the prerequisite of assigning equal importance to the overall interests of both energy producers and consumers while maximizing the interests of each nation? In the opinion of the author, it is necessary to set up another regional supranational organization, something like an energy agency for the Asian region, specifically for energy cooperation.

Certainly, it would be overly optimistic to think that such an energy agency could be established easily in a short time period, and much preparation is necessary. Some time will be required to create an environment in which Japan could play the leading role, or to set up a mechanism under which Japan, China and Russia, and other countries, could cooperate together. The process used for the Energy Charter Treaty signed in 1991 in Europe could serve as a reference for this purpose (Box 17.3).

With reference to the European experience, what procedures should

BOX 17.3   ENERGY COOPERATION: THE EUROPEAN EXPERIENCE

The Energy Charter Treaty was based upon the Energy Charter signed by 51 countries in Den Haag, the Netherlands, in 1991. The Treaty was signed in 1994 by 49 countries.[a] In 1998, it became effective in 30 of the signatory countries. One of the objectives of the treaty was to establish a formal cooperation mechanism between Western Europe, Eastern Europe and the former Soviet Union, and to safeguard investments in energy resources and transportation within the member countries. The treaty was signed against the backdrop of the period following the 1980s during which countries in Western Europe become considerably more dependent upon natural gas from the former Soviet Union and concern was on the rise over the stability of the energy supply imported to Western Europe. In the 1980s, prior to the signing of the treaty, in order to reduce such dependency, gas supplied from the former Soviet Union was capped at 35% of the total gas supply to the region. Later, the concerned parties realized that instead of capping the energy supply from the former Soviet Union, setting up a system that could help the former Soviet Union to gain more trust from its clients would generate greater benefits to all the actors involved; hence, the treaty was developed and signed.

In the 1990s, output in the former Soviet Union declined temporarily due to disorder caused by institutional changes. Subsequently, its supply capacity was greatly expanded as huge new gas reserves were discovered. In Western Europe, demand for natural gas increased drastically following the deregulation of the power industry, which includes open access of grid to IPPs (independent power producers) and stimulated the entry of small gas-fired power producers into the power industry. Given such a situation, the cooperation mechanism predicated on the Energy Charter Treaty helped to prevent disruptions to the energy supply and catered to the immense growth in both the demand and supply sides, which in turn further highlighted the importance of expanding cooperation between Western Europe and Russia as well as the benefits it could produce for the two sides.

By reviewing how Europe and the former Soviet Union (Russia) signed the Energy Charter Treaty to secure energy supplies, it becomes clear that the stakeholders must first identify common interests associated with cooperation and institutionalize various cooperation programs (Godement et al. 2004). In terms of organizational structure, the treaty is independent from the EU itself and specializes in energy cooperation; its Secretariat is able to provide information to relevant parties, and those in charge of the energy sector can organize concerned personnel for discussion sessions from time to time, which has proven beneficial.

Note: [a] In addition to the former Soviet Union and European countries, the US, Canada, Australia and Japan also signed this treaty.

be followed in order to promote energy cooperation in the Asian region? First, Japan should provide a public good for cooperation. By transferring energy conservation and other technologies, energy consumption could be reduced in the recipient countries, and ultimately energy consumption in the region as a whole could be restrained, which is in line with the national interest of Japan and is highly feasible. Of course, energy conservation technologies are owned by the private sector, and it is not usual practice to have the private sector engage in such cooperation by providing subsidies. Therefore, such technology transfers could be combined with some international scheme, such as CDM (Clean Development Mechanism) projects which help prevent global warming, so that part of the cost could be recovered through those schemes.

In fact, in 2007, the first step, initiated by Japan, was made by setting up the Asia Energy Cooperation Center. However, this center is more a tool for bilateral cooperation with Japan than a public good in the region. The public good should be supplied similarly to multi-entity cooperation schemes under the energy agency of the East Asian region, for more effective promotion of cooperation in the entire region.

NOTES

1. In most cases, natural gas is transported through pipelines, as the operational cost of pipelines is very low, even though massive initial costs are required to build them. Therefore, natural gas is highly suited to being traded as a regional commodity. Regarding other means of transportation, natural gas can also be liquified and transported by LNG tankers in the same manner as oil. In the past, liquification cost was very high and hence Japan accounted for over 50% of LNG trades. Over the last few years, the liquification cost has fallen sharply, and the US and China have also started to import LNG. To a certain extent, the decline in the regional natural gas self sufficiency ratio also reflects the increase in imports of natural gas in the form of LNG.

2. IEA (2007) suggests two scenarios approaching 2015 and 2030, one being the 'Reference Scenario' and the other being the 'Alternative Policy Scenario'. The 'Reference Scenario' can be thought of as BAU (business as usual), in which government policies are assumed to remain unchanged from mid-2007. On the other hand, the 'Alternative Policy Scenario' is based on the assumption that the governments will move on to a more sustainable economic and environmental path through stricter enforcement of existing policies and introduction of the new ones now being discussed. In this chapter, we refer to the 'Reference Scenario' as the scenario indicating maximized energy demand approaching 2030.

3. The establishment of common energy efficiency standards across Asia for equipment that consumes energy aids the advancement of energy conservation technology within the region so that such technology can be widely promoted.

4. In addition, it also promotes dialogue with Middle Eastern oil and gas producing countries to enhance mutual understanding and cooperation between oil-producing and oil-consuming countries.

5. If China's increasing energy demand were the cause, then the WTI price in 2005 should have declined since China's oil imports decreased in 2005 as its export growth slowed following the sharp increase in China's exports in 2004. Instead, WTI rose even further. The global crude oil stockpile continued to increase in 2005. According to the conventional energy economics framework, oil prices should have declined. We can see that the reason why the conventional expectations failed to materialize was because the financial world exerted a great impact on the oil price. Those who believed that higher demand from China caused the price hike arrived at their conclusion by following the conventional rule of thumb that demand drives up price, instead of conducting substantial studies on supply and demand in China, and this type of hasty conclusion should be avoided.

6. Wind power is another example. At the moment, wind power generation equipment is being installed rapidly in China, and Xingjiang Goldwind Group and Sinovel Wind Group have been quickly increasing their market share in China. Even though the technological level of both companies lags far behind their US and European counterparts, they have chosen to focus on small- and medium-sized wind power generators and have constantly improved their price advantage in the market. The reason that such latecomers as Goldwind and Sinovel could obtain such a large market share is attributable to two points: China's huge market and the number of price-sensitive customers in the market.

7. In fact, in the 11th Five-Year plan period, China succeeded in improving her energy efficiency remarkably. For example, efficiency in power generation was improved by 2.0%, in steel production by 2.7%, in cement production by 4.7%, and in ethylene production by 2.0% between 2006 and 2009. As a result of remarkable performance in these years, the energy efficiency gap between China and developed countries got smaller than in 2000, but is still substantial.

8. Japan's 'New National Energy Strategy' has been the most obvious manifestation of this mentality. In 2006, the Japanese government set a target to increase the ratio of imports of overseas proprietary oil development to 40% of total oil imports by 2030, even though just a few years before, the Japanese government had dismissed the Japan National Oil Corporation, the entity responsible for overseas oil development projects, for low efficiency. Then, more recently, the Japanese government decided to strengthen its interests in overseas oil resources through the involvement of the state, which without a doubt is a response to the anxiety caused by the initiatives of the Chinese.

9. It is undeniable that criticism against China for supporting 'undemocratic' regimes was greatly manipulated by the US. However, China seemed unable to effectively defend itself against the criticism that its aid to the Sudanese government played an important role, and was tantamount to assenting to the mass killings in Sudan, where 60% of China's overseas crude oil interests are located.

REFERENCES

APEC EWG Secretariat (2002), 'The APEC energy working group operational plan 2002', November, download from http://www.apecenergy.org.au.

APEC EWG Secretariat (2005), 'The APEC energy working group operational plan 2005', January, download from http://www.apecenergy.org.au.

ASEAN Secretariat (2004), 'ASEAN plan of action for energy cooperation (APAEC) 2004–2009', adopted by the 22nd ASEAN Ministers on Energy Meeting, 9 June, Makati City, Metro Manila, Philippines, download from http://www.aseansec.org/4948.htm.

ASEAN Secretariat (2007), 'ASEAN Plus Three cooperation work plan (2007–2017)', adopted by the Eleventh ASEAN Plus Three Leaders' Meeting, 20 November, Singapore, download from http://www.aseansec.org/21104.pdf.

BP (2008), 'BP statistical review of world energy 2008', June, downloaded from http://www.bp.com/statisticalreview.

Godement, François, Françoise Nicholas and Taizo Yakushiji (eds) (2004), *Asia and Europe: Cooperating for Energy Security*, Paris: Institute français des relations international.

IEA (International Energy Agency) (2007), *World Energy Outlook 2007*, OECD/IEA.

Kaku, Shishi (2010), 'Increased demand-supply gap and China's oil companies' overseas operation', Chapter 2 in Nobuhiro Horii (ed.), *China's Sustainable Development: Can Restriction in Resource and Environment be Overcome?* (in Japanese), Tokyo: Institute of Developing Economies-JETRO.

LeVine, Steve (2008), 'Oil majors cut back on new wells as prices fall', *Business Week*, 8 December.

18. Trade and the environment

Michikazu Kojima and Etsuyo Michida

18.1 INTRODUCTION

Continued prosperity throughout the course of economic integration in East Asia depends on the environmental consequences. If the increase in trade and investment flow results in environmental degradation that poses serious threats to health, amenities, and productivity, fear of further integration might be spawned. The growth of East Asian economies has been accompanied by pollution, global warming, waste generation, deforestation, losses in biodiversity, and so on. Does economic growth driven by increased trade necessarily magnify environmental degradation? To our surprise, we found that economic integration may work to promote improvement in some environmental issues; however, freer trade does exacerbate other issues.

To anticipate the impacts of trade on various environmental issues and adopt effective policy measures for prevention of adverse effects, it is important to reach an understanding of the trade–environment linkages by disentangling causalities and aggregating the different forces involved. Specifically, the impacts of trade on the environment through changes in industrial composition, environmental regulation and income are addressed in various studies. Although a consensus has not yet been reached, understanding of these linkages has progressed.

In practice, precautionary measures have been applied to prevent potential problems that may arise from increased cross-border transactions within free trade areas. The EU and NAFTA have established networks and organizations to monitor and prevent potential environmental problems in a systematic way, whereas Asia, in the process of economic integration, has applied precautionary measures on an ad hoc basis.

This chapter begins by showing the state of the environment in East Asia as illustrated by some indicators of pollution and resources. In order to isolate the trade effects on the environment from other forces, a simple empirical study is conducted in Section 18.3. We use East Asian data to supplement previous studies, most of which use international or US data to approach the issue. Our study finds that East Asian integration may have a beneficial effect on sulfur dioxide concentration of the region. In Section 18.4, the linkages between openness and the environment are discussed, and results from various studies are presented. Section 18.5 reviews the policy efforts of the EU and NAFTA that are predecessors in dealing with the environmental problems of economic integration. Then, the situations of the EU and NAFTA are compared with that of Asia to draw lessons for future actions.

18.2   STATE OF THE ENVIRONMENT IN EAST ASIA

The environment in East Asia has been compromised because the acceleration of economic activities has not been achieved without sacrificing it to some extent. As East Asian economies grow dynamically, pressures on the environment are becoming larger than ever. Before focusing on the trade-related effects, this section reviews the state of the environment in East Asia by presenting some key indicators.

The first indicators pertain to air quality. Sulfur dioxide is a pollutant produced from fossil fuel combustion and industrial processes. It causes problems such as respiratory disease mainly in the area where it is emitted and is also a source of acid rain, which damages areas distant from the source. Sulfur dioxide in East Asia increased by 1.4 times between 1990 and 2000, while the GDP of the region increased by 1.3 times.[1] East Asia accounted for 20% of the world's total emissions in 1990, and its share increased to 28% in 2000. Figure 18.1 shows GDP per capita and sulfur dioxide emissions per capita for East Asian economies, and uses arrows to show the changes from 1990 to 2000. More than 70% of the regional emissions are produced by China due to the usage of high-sulfur coal. The figure shows that sulfur dioxide emissions increased in most countries, although the emissions per GDP decreased.[2]

There are pollutants whose damage extends beyond national borders. An example is carbon dioxide, a greenhouse gas. Carbon dioxide emissions in East Asia increased by 1.7 times from 1990 to 2003, and East Asia accounted for 18% of the world's total in 1990 and 25% in 2003.[3] Figure 18.2 shows carbon dioxide emissions per capita and GDP per capita in 1990 and 2003. Note that the increase in the emissions does not decelerate, unlike the case of sulfur dioxide. Singapore is an exception. The total emissions of Singapore increase but the per capita emissions decrease due to population growth.

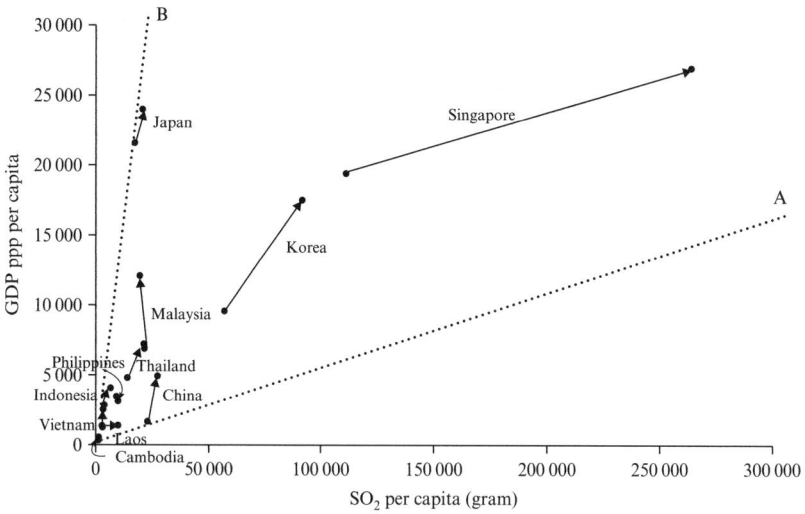

Sources: Olivier et al. (2005) and Heston et al. (2006).

Figure 18.1 SO_2 emissions for 1990 and 2000

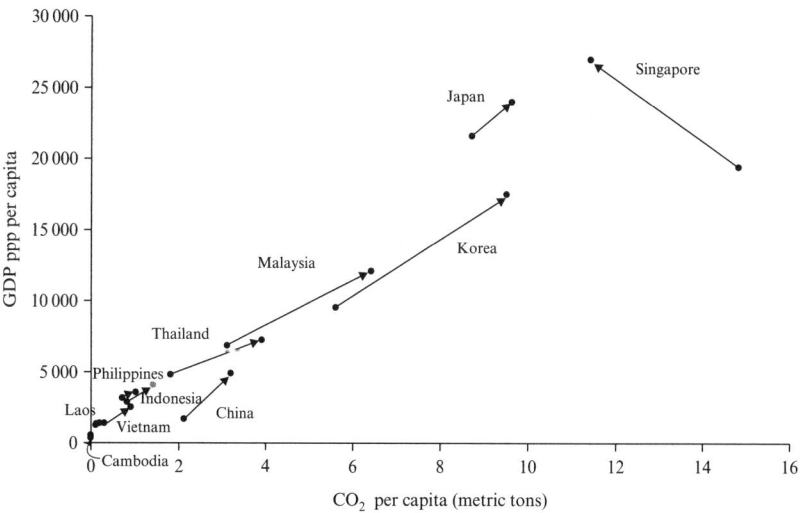

Sources: World Bank (2007) and Heston et al. (2006).

Figure 18.2 CO_2 emissions for 1990 and 2003

Table 18.1   *Emission of organic water pollutants (BOD) from industrial activities*

	Thousand kg per day	
	1990	2004
China	7038.1	6088.7
Japan	1556.6	1184.7
Korea	369.2	315.2
Philippines	228.3	
Cambodia	11.8	
Thailand	291.6	
Malaysia	104.7	183.8
Indonesia	495.6	733.0
India	1410.6	1519.8

Source: World Bank (2008).

Water pollution is a matter of concern in Asian countries. If dirtier manufacturing production increases after trade liberalization, pollution in rivers and contamination of soil will become serious. Governments are tightening regulations to reduce water pollution, but in many countries, the effort does not appear to be successful. The emission of organic water pollutants (BOD) from industrial activities increased in Malaysia, Indonesia and India between 1990 and 2004 (see Table 18.1). Firms from developed countries have access to cleaner technology because they face tighter regulation in their home countries, and it is often observed that the firms from developed countries investing in developing countries adopt cleaner technology than domestic firms (Kojima 2007). However, there are some problematic cases. For example, in 2008, a Taiwanese company in Vietnam producing monosodium glutamate polluted a river, and the Vietnamese government imposed a penalty on the company, ordering it to pay more than US$7 million.

Soil contamination has been widely observed in many Asian countries, including water pollution due to mining activities which resulted in contaminated soil. In China, Japan, Thailand and other countries, people who eat food grown in fields contaminated by heavy metals have suffered from health problems (Hata 2003). Acid deposition reduces the fertility of land, and it is reported that acid rain affects 25% of Chinese territory (OECD 2007).

Expanded trade could also harm natural resources unless resource use is properly regulated. Deforestation in Asia is an example of such harm.

Table 18.2   Deforestation in Asia (1,000 ha)

	Forest area 2000	Forest area 2005	Annual change	Annual change rate (%)
China	177001	197290	4058	2.2
Japan	24876	24868	−2	−0.0
Korea	6300	6265	−7	−0.1
Philippines	7949	7162	−157	−2.1
Vietnam	11725	12931	241	2.0
Cambodia	11541	10447	−219	−2.0
Lao	16532	16142	−78	−0.5
Thailand	14814	14520	−59	−0.4
Malaysia	21591	20890	−140	−0.7
Indonesia	97852	88495	−1872	−2.0
India	67554	67701	29	0.0

Source: FAO Forest Resource Assessment 2005, downloaded from http://www.fao.org/forestry/32033/en/.

Table 18.2 shows that deforestation in most Asian countries worsened between 2000 and 2005. In Indonesia, one of the largest areas of deforestation in the world, conversion of forest into plantations and agricultural production areas contributes to deforestation, in addition to the deforestation caused by logging activities. Increased exports of agricultural products such as palm oil and illegal timber accelerate forest conversion as well (Jones 2006). Moreover, expansion of plantations has also caused forest fires and subsequent adverse impacts on health due to the severe haze reported in Indonesia, Singapore and Malaysia.

We now turn to examples of environmental goods trade and related problems. The environmental damage caused by international recycling is a source of concern. International trade of recyclables has surged in recent years, with China as a major importer of recyclable wastes such as plastics, used paper, copper scraps and aluminum scrap. Korea, Taiwan and China are major importers of steel scrap. International recycling is expected to improve efficiency in processing recyclables, provided that it is conducted with environmentally friendly technology. However, pollution from e-waste (electronic waste) recycling, for example, has created serious problems in some locations where environmental legislation is not properly implemented (see Box 18.1).

Trade in endangered species is conducted in Asia, although the countries involved have joined the Convention on International Trade in Endangered Species of Wild Fauna and Flora (CITES). Manufacture of

BOX 18.1   HAZARDOUS WASTE TRADE AND THE
BASEL CONVENTION

In the 1980s and 1990s, shipment of hazardous wastes from
developed countries to developing countries caused serious environmental problems. In Asia, it was reported that Taiwan imported
lead waste scrap for recycling from developed countries, including
the US and Japan. Lead recycling plants without adequate pollution control caused pollution problems and affected human health.
In the case of one lead recycling plant in Keelung, Taiwan, the
mental development of kindergarten children near the plant was
delayed. In 1993, it was found that tens of shipments of plastic
waste were abandoned in several ports in Indonesia. The wastes
had been exported from developed countries, especially from the
Netherlands, which took back the containers in 1995 after being
criticized. In the mid 1990s, the Chinese government appre-
hended several illegal shipments of waste exported from the
United States.

To prevent developing countries from being dumping grounds
and to prevent pollution problems arising from the recycling of
imported waste, various trade measures were applied. Some
countries, such as China, Indonesia, and Malaysia, prohibit the
import of hazardous waste.

The Basel Convention requires a prior informed consent (PIC)
procedure for the shipment of hazardous wastes. China, which
became a major importer of recyclables, instituted standards for
imported recyclable waste and requires pre-shipment inspection.
In recent years in Asian countries, awareness has grown concerning the need for international cooperation on regulatory enforcement and for communication among authorities. The 'Asian
Network for Prevention of Illegal Transboundary Movement of
Hazardous Wastes' was established in 2004.

Source: Kojima (2005).

Chinese medicine is one of the major uses of tiger bones, rhino horns and
other items which are extracted from Asian and African countries. Furs of
wild animals such as leopards and tigers, which are used for clothing and
accessories, are also traded illegally on an international scale (Kojima et
al. 2005).

18.3   TRADE IMPACT ON THE ENVIRONMENT IN EAST ASIA

Should economic integration be blamed for the environmental deterioration? Many environmental indicators reflect not only the environmental change caused by trade or FDI but also other forces such as economic growth that are unrelated to trade. This section attempts to answer the above question by examining how the openness of economies affects air quality in East Asian countries.[4] We use sulfur dioxide concentration data from East Asian countries to conduct an empirical examination. Although it may be suspected that economic integration in East Asia has detrimental effects on the environment, it was found that openness might be beneficial to air quality. This result is consistent with studies of international data (Antweiler et al. 2001, Frankel and Rose 2005) and studies of subregional data in the US (Chintrakarn and Millimet 2006) which found positive association between openness and environmental quality.

18.3.1   Methodology

A pollution indicator is regressed on the log of GDP per capita and its square, openness represented by the ratio of nominal exports and imports to GDP and the variables of monitoring site characteristics. Our interest lies in the coefficient of openness. If the coefficient is negative, openness has favorable effects on the environment. We include the log of GDP per capita and its square because previous literature suggests environmental damage often increases as income rises but that the rate of damage decreases.[5] Our estimation equation is as follows:

$$\ln(pollution_{it}) = const + \beta_1 \ln(Income_{it}) + \beta_2 [\ln(Income_{it})]^2$$

$$+ \beta_3 \ln(Openness_{it}) + \varphi(site_i) + u_{it}$$

where $Pollution_{it}$ is sulfur dioxide concentration for site i for time t. $Pollution_{it}$ is GDP per capita for the country of monitoring site i for time t. $Income_{ot}$ are the dummy variables for site characteristics, and these are constant over time.

We first run pooled OLS.[6] As trade and GDP variables are likely to have endogeneity, openness is instrumented by estimating a gravity model. The log of bilateral export and import sum divided by nominal GDP denominated in US dollars is regressed on the log of the countries' area, the log of distance of trading countries, the log of partner country population, and

Table 18.3   Summary statistics

Variable	Obs	Mean	Std. Dev.	Min.	Max.
Mean(ppb)	100	2.73	3.52	.04	16.33
gdpcapita (I$ in 2000 constant prices)	100	1 406	9 106.83	2 283.90	24 659.93
siterural	100	.35	.48	0	1
siteremote	100	.37	.49	0	1
openness	100	.56	.43	.17	1.7

the dummy variable of common border and common language. We aggregated the exponent of the fitted values across trading partners to arrive at an instrument for openness for each country in the sample.[7]

18.3.2   Data

Table 18.3 shows summary statistics. A sulfur dioxide concentration indicator is used for our analysis as it is a pollutant emitted from fossil-fuel combustion processes and is relevant to the majority of economic activities. Data for China, Indonesia, Malaysia, Thailand, Japan and Vietnam from 2001 to 2006 was obtained from the Acid Deposition Monitoring Network in East Asia, EANET (EANET; Network Center 2008, EANET 2008). The pollution concentration data is reported with monitoring site information; the categories are urban, rural and remote sites, and these are used as the site variables. The sources of data are listed in the Appendix.

18.3.3   Results

The results are presented in Table 18.4. For the pooled OLS regression, openness of economies works to improve the environment. For the instrumental variable (IV) estimation, openness is found to have a beneficial effect on pollution, although it is statistically insignificant and the magnitude is smaller than the pooled OLS. The results indicate that increased trade might have beneficial effects on the environment in East Asia. With regard to other variables, the estimation shows a higher GDP per capita increases pollution, but the rate of increase decreases as income rises for both pooled OLS and IV.[8] As discussed in the next section, the result is consistent with other studies on the income–environment relationship. Site dummies have negative signs as expected. Overall results for IV

Table 18.4   Pooled OLS and instrumental variable (IV) estimation results

logmean	OLS			IV		
	Robust			Robust		
	Coef.	Std. Err.	t	Coef.	Std. Err.	t
lngdpcapita	7.30	1.45	3.31	1.53	1.08	1.42
lngdpcapita2	−.43	0.81	−3.49	−.10	.06	−1.63
siteremote	−.59	0.12	−4.04	−.49	.09	−5.37
siterural	−.36	0.11	−3.37	−.39	.09	−4.08
lnopenness	−.38	0.12	−3.14			
lnfittedopen				−.06	.105	−0.54
_cons	−30.50	6.44	−4.73	−5.33	4.87	−1.10

Notes:
Pooled OLS: F statistics=23.27, Prob>F=0.00, R-squared=0.55, Adj R-squared=0.53
IV: F statistics=48.21, Prob>F=0.00, R-squared=0.44, Adj R-squared=0.46.
1.   The Breusch-Pagan/Cook-Weisberg test for heteroskedasticity was performed. Homoskedasticity was rejected, and we report robust standard errors.
2.   lnopenness is instrumented, and the instruments are area, population, distance, border, and common language. Fitted values for lnopenness have a correlation of 0.8 with lnopenness.

are less significant, and the magnitude of the coefficients is smaller than the OLS estimation, although all the coefficients we obtained have the expected signs.

18.4   DISENTANGLING THE LINKAGES BETWEEN TRADE AND THE ENVIRONMENT

We are interested in the effects of various channels of trade on the environment in order to know what to expect when East Asian economies become more liberalized. The association between trade and environmental quality is decomposed into selected links.[9] Figure 18.3 shows a map of some links and causality, and we discuss each linkage below.

18.4.1   Trade–Composition–Environment Linkage

Economic integration leads to increased specialization. Freer trade and factor movement affects geographical patterns of pollution emissions because firm relocation is accompanied by environmental byproducts.[10] Some suspect pollution-intensive industries migrate to developing countries where environmental regulations are often weakly enforced. A

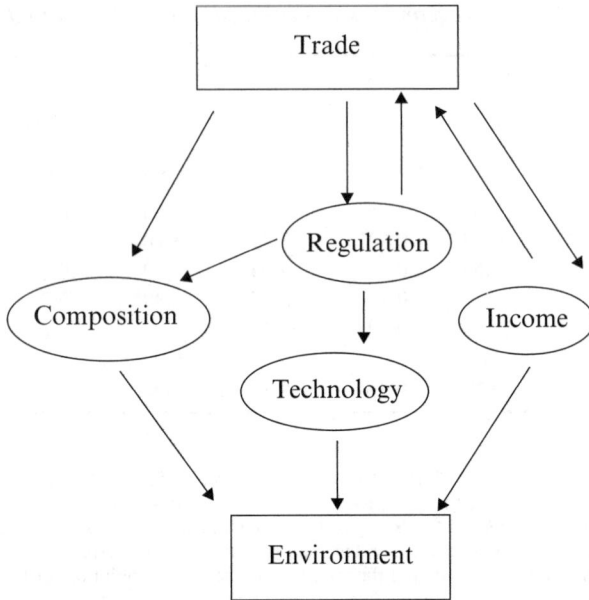

Figure 18.3   Relationship between trade and the environment

consequence is that developing countries may become more polluted due to economic integration. This concern has attracted much attention and is called the pollution haven hypothesis (PHH) (see Taylor 2004 for further discussion). A mechanism for the pollution haven hypothesis is presented by theoretical work which assumes that the sole trade motive is the difference in the stringency of environmental regulations covering pollutants causing damage locally (Copeland and Taylor 1994, Michida and Nishikimi 2003[11]). Alternatively, if capital-intensive firms are pollution-intensive at the same time, more pollution might be produced in developed countries where a comparative advantage lies in capital intensive production. The two hypotheses are examined by investigating the trade–composition–environment linkages. Empirical works find little evidence for the pollution haven hypothesis for local pollutants (for example, Ederington et al. 2004, Kahn 2003). Moreover, motives presented by the factor endowment hypothesis are found to be larger than pollution haven motives, if any (Antweiler et al. 2001). Elliott and Shimamoto (2008) examine Japanese outbound FDI toward South-East Asian countries to see if the pollution-intensive FDI is drawn to the countries with lax regulations and provide evidence counter to the pollution haven hypothesis.

18.4.2 Trade–Regulation/Technology–Environment Linkage

Conflicting views are presented on the linkages between environmental regulation, technology and the environment. One view is that, as environmental regulations require firms to allocate some resources for pollution abatement activities, additional costs are imposed on firms and competitiveness may be impaired. Do we find evidence of this?

Recent empirical works find some evidence of this, and Keller and Levinson (2002) find pollution abatement costs deter foreign direct investment. However, the effect on both trade and foreign direct investment is not as strong as other determinants such as labor costs (see Jaffe et al. 1995 and Copeland and Taylor 2004 for surveys).

Due to the possible impairment of competitiveness by regulations, it has been feared that countries with freer trade might adopt looser environmental standards in order to boost their international competitiveness, resulting in a race-to-the-bottom. However, the story may not stop there. If the population is mobile across countries and skilled workers with a preference for higher environmental quality can emigrate from polluted countries, governments may decide not to enact lax regulations (Elbers and Withagen 2004). On the contrary, Porter and Linde (1995) argue, by showing anecdotal evidence, that tighter environmental regulation could stimulate adoption and innovation of cleaner technology, making production more efficient. In reality, even though governments in developing countries may introduce optimal regulations, enforcement is often sporadic due to limited government resources for policy implementation. Empirical examinations have not yet reached a conclusion; further work is needed to understand the linkage among trade, environmental regulations, technology and the environment.

18.4.3 Trade–Income–Environment Linkage

The environmental Kuznets curve hypothesis, which claims an inverted-U-curve relationship between income and pollution, has been examined intensively since the early 1990s. The literature is important as we are interested in the effect of trade-induced income changes on the environment. Specifically, if higher income due to trade liberalization eventually leads to positive effects on environmental quality, we could enjoy win-win opportunities. Empirical studies show that there exists an inverted-U-curve relationship in which pollution emissions increase initially and then decrease as incomes rise for some local pollutants such as sulfur dioxide. Why does environmental quality deteriorate at lower incomes and improve as incomes increase? Literature explains some mechanisms: that is, a change of industrial composition from dirtier to cleaner as incomes rise, more demand for a cleaner environment accompanying higher income, and the start of pollution abatement when marginal willingness to pay for the environment becomes large enough to equal the marginal willingness to pay for goods.[12]

18.4.4 Overall Effects on Local Pollution

When the overall effect is summed up, trade appears to be good for the environment (Grossman and Krueger 1995). Antweiler et al. (2001) estimate the magnitudes and finds that composition effects are small and technique effects that have a positive impact on environmental quality outweigh negative scale effects for sulfur dioxide. Dean and Lovely (2008) examine Chinese environmental data and find production fragmentation has a positive effect on the decline in the pollution intensity of China's trade.

18.4.5 Trade Impact on Transboundary Pollution

For transboundary or global pollutants such as ozone-depleting gases and greenhouse gases, different outcomes are expected. As the environmental effects of such pollutants are less restricted to local areas, changes in industrial composition and income could lead to different results from local pollutants. Holtz-Eakin and Selden (1995) show that carbon dioxide emissions increase as income grows. Moreover, there is no turning point within a sample, and the stabilization of emissions is observed at best. Shafik (1994) argues that pollutants without local impacts (for example, carbon dioxide) have not been regulated, while pollutants with local impacts (for example, sulfur dioxide) have been subject to regulation. Reduction of greenhouse gases requires multinational coordination since a single country's effort might be offset by an emission increase in other countries. Thus, due to free-rider problems, carbon dioxide emissions do not have an environmental Kuznets curve relationship as is found for local air pollutants but have a monotonically increasing relationship. In fact, international coordination to cut greenhouse gas in the Conference of the Parties to the United Nations Framework Convention on Climate Change (COP) has progressed slowly, and corresponding domestic measures have not been fully implemented in many countries.

The emissions of global pollutants do not stay within national borders, and so concentrations of pollution intensive industries do not create pollution havens in specific locations. Copeland and Taylor (1995) show that if trading countries significantly differ in income levels, world pollution increases after trade is liberalized; however, free trade among similar income countries does not affect the levels of pollution. An empirical finding for such pollutants shows openness increases carbon dioxide emissions, although the effects are moderate (Frankel and Rose 2005).

18.5   REGIONAL ENVIRONMENTAL COOPERATION

As Asian economies become more integrated, trade–environment interaction intensifies. Production and consumption in a given home country may have large impacts on the environment in other countries via export, import and investment. Attainment of sustainable development in the region requires consideration of the environment beyond the national borders. Coordination of environmental policy among countries helps prevent environmental problems caused by trade and investment. For those countries facing difficulties implementing an appropriate environmental policy, enforcement can be strengthened by sharing experiences among the trading countries and providing technical assistance through regional cooperation. The EU and NAFTA have initiated regional cooperation to protect the environment because of concern among environmental officials, non-governmental organizations and others over the 'race to the bottom'.

18.5.1   IMPEL in the European Union[13]

The EU has issued various directives on environmental issues such as pollution control, waste management and so forth, and European countries are responsible for implementing these directives. However, the measures being taken are insufficient for preventing a 'race to the bottom' situation. To improve the effects of the directives, the enforcement level of the regulations should be standardized.

In the EU, the European Union Network for the Implementation and Enforcement of Environmental Law (IMPEL) has been formed. IMPEL was first established as an informal network of European regulators and authorities in 1992 with the objective of strengthening the implementation and enforcement of environmental law.

In recent years, IMPEL has been composed of four major clusters. The first cluster is 'Improving permitting, inspection and enforcement'. Recently, this cluster prepared a series of guidance manuals including a guidance report for planning environmental inspections. One of the source materials of the report is Recommendation 2001/331/EC of the

European Parliament and of the Council of 4 April 2001 which provides for minimum criteria for environmental inspections (RMCEI).

The second cluster is 'Transfrontier Shipments of Waste, IMPEL-TFS', which focuses on the transboundary movement of waste. If the enforcement of the regulations on transboundary movement of waste is weak in a given port, that port might become a loophole for the regulations. To prevent illegal transboundary movement of waste, inspectors need to exchange their know-how, and to facilitate this, the cluster conducted joint inspection programs and published guidance documents.

The third cluster is 'Better Regulation (practicability and enforceability)'. The cluster assesses the existing legislation from the viewpoint of practicability and enforceability in order to encourage stakeholders to pay more attention to practicability and enforceability in the process of creating regulations.

The fourth cluster is the 'AC Cluster' which was in existence until 2005. It focused on countries newly admitted to the EU. The objective of the cluster was to transfer know-how to new member countries by conducting trainer programs, performance reviews on environmental enforcement and study tours of inspection practices. The activities of this cluster were concluded in 2005 since a new program, called 'Environmental Compliance and Enforcement Network for Accession', was developed by the EU to transfer know-how to newly admitted countries.

18.5.2   Commission for Environmental Cooperation: Monitoring the Impact of NAFTA[14]

When NAFTA was established, a supplementary agreement on environmental issues, called the North American Agreement on Environmental Cooperation (NAAEC), was enacted. The NAAEC complements the environmental provisions of NAFTA.

Based on this agreement, the Commission for Environmental Cooperation (CEC) was established by the NAFTA countries (Canada, Mexico and the United States). The objectives of the commission are to address regional environmental concerns, to help prevent potential trade and environmental conflicts, and to promote the effective enforcement of environmental law. CEC is administered by a council whose members consist of ministers of each member country. A Joint Advisory Committee makes some recommendations to the council concerning the activities of CEC. Public participation plays an important role; public petitions can be submitted to the Commission and the claims of petitions are investigated by experts and the secretariat. The results of these investigations are disclosed to the public.

Some projects are implemented by CEC. Environmental information on water, biodiversity, and human influence on the environment is collected and published in the form of various maps. An ongoing Environmental Assessment of NAFTA is also conducted by CEC, and the 2008 assessment includes studies on 'pollution and international trade in services', 'tourism and the environment', 'transportation services and air quality', and 'evolution of the environmental services industries'. There are some cooperative projects in the field of air pollution control and chemical management, including capacity building for pollution prevention, monitoring of pollutants, and tracking of pollutant release and transfers in North America.

18.5.3 Regional Efforts to Solve Environmental Issues in Asia

In Asia, regional cooperation on specific environmental issues such as transboundary movement of hazardous waste, acid rain and deforestation has been conducted (see Table 18.5). Asian countries also ratified various multinational environmental agreements which regulate trade of scheduled goods related to specific environmental issues (see Box 18.2). However, compared with EU and NAFTA, the Asian approach is arbitrary; no organization oversees the situation surrounding trade and environmental issues in the region in order to identify the necessary actions. The weakness of arbitrary formulation of networks and programs is that there is no systematic assessment of the impact of trade liberalization on the environment, making it difficult to apply precautionary measures.[15]

With the aim of taking an integrated approach, efforts for regional coordination have been launched. Ministerial meetings on the environment for ASEAN+3 have been organized since 2002. Some activities related to regional environmental policies are accelerating in recent years. Among these, the Economic Research Institute for ASEAN and East Asia (ERIA), which was formally established by sixteen countries in 2008, has started several research projects. Topics include the standardization of bio-fuel, the impact of environmental policy on trade, and review of 3R (reduce, reuse, recycle) policies in the region.

Asia as a community shares a common environmental challenge, and efforts for regional coordination and cooperation have just started. However, these activities are formulated based on cooperation in an ad hoc manner, despite the fact that issues have some inter-linkages. For example, policies favoring bio-fuel, including the reduction of trade

Table 18.5   Regional networks on environmental issues

Name	Year established	Countries	Objectives
Acid Deposition Monitoring Network in East Asia	Preparatory phase 1998, regular phase: 2001	Cambodia, China, Indonesia, Japan, Lao PDR, Malaysia, Mongolia, Myanmar, Philippines, Republic of Korea, Russia, Thailand, Vietnam	(1) To create a common understanding of the state of the acid deposition problems in East Asia, (2) to provide useful inputs for decision making, (3) to contribute to cooperation
Asian Network for Prevention of Illegal Trans-boundary Movement of Hazardous Wastes	2005	Brunei, Cambodia, China, China (Hong Kong SAR), Indonesia, Republic of Korea, Malaysia, Philippines, Singapore, Thailand, Vietnam	Sharing information and creating a common understanding on the status of illegal transboundary movements of hazardous wastes
Asia Forest Partnership	2002	Australia, China, Finland, France, India, Indonesia, Japan, Republic of Korea, Nepal, Malaysia, Netherlands, Philippines, Switzerland, Thailand, UK, USA, Vietnam, EC	To promote sustainable forest management in Asia through addressing five urgent issues: control of illegal logging, control of forest fires, rehabilitation and reforestation of degraded lands, good governance and forest law enforcement, and development of capacity for effective forest management
ASOEN Haze Technical Task Force	1995	ASEAN countries	To operationalize and implement the measures recommended in the ASEAN Cooperation Plan on Transboundary Pollution relating to atmospheric pollution

Note: ASOEN stands for ASEAN Senior Officials on the Environment.

Source: Compiled from various sources.

BOX 18.2   RATIFICATION STATUS OF
MULTILATERAL ENVIRONMENTAL
AGREEMENTS WITH TRADE
RESTRICTIONS

There are a number of multilateral agreements that restrict international trade of specified goods. It is said that more than 20
international environmental treaties restrict trade of specified
goods (Rao 2000).

CITES (the Convention on International Trade in Endangered
Species of Wild Fauna and Flora) controls the international trade
of endangered species. The Montreal Protocol regulates the international trade of Ozone Depleting Substances such as CFCs
(chlorofluorocarbons). The Basel Convention regulates the transboundary movement of hazardous waste. The Cartagena Protocol
regulates the international trade of genetically modified organisms.

The following table shows the status of ratification of these
agreements by Asian countries: most of the countries have ratified

Box Table 18.1   *Ratification and accession of selected Asian*
countries to organizations and international
environmental agreements

	CITES (signature 1973, effective 1975)	Montreal Protocol (signature 1987, effective 1989)	Basel Convention (adopted 1989, effective 1992)
Japan	1980	1988	1993
ROK	1993	1992	1994
China	1981	1991	1991
Philippines	1981	1991	1993
Indonesia	1978	1992	1993
Singapore	1986	1989	1996
Malaysia	1977	1989	1993
Vietnam	1994	1994	1995
Laos	–	1998	–
Cambodia	1997	2001	2001
Thailand	1983	1989	1997
Myanmar	1997	1993	–
India	1976	1992	1992

Source: Compiled from the website of each agreement.

> these conventions. The types of trade regulations include prohibi-
> tion of trade, prior notice and consent, and certification of exporting
> countries.

barriers on palm oil, stimulate the conversion of forests into palm oil
plantations, which causes deforestation and haze problems. Therefore,
a more systematic assessment of environmental issues needs to be
conducted.

18.6 CONCLUSION

The impact of economic integration on the environment could be beneficial if the effects of tighter regulation and cleaner technology outweigh
the negative income and composition effects. However, as we illustrated
through examples, increased trade does cause environmental problems
in countries where regulations are weakly enforced. To prevent potential
problems, coordination of impact monitoring and joint implementation of
effective measures are necessary. The EU and NAFTA have started such
attempts.

In Asia, while *de facto* economic integration has been deepening
supported by trade liberalization policies, environmental policy is not
yet well coordinated. Asia, as a community, should exert intensive
efforts to protect the environment. Among the steps forward that need
to be taken are cooperation in assessing the impact of trade liberalization on the environment, application of some precautionary measures, and standardization of the enforcement level of environmental
regulation.

NOTES

1. Real GDP ppp from Penn Table 6.3 was used for calculation. East Asia in this section
   includes Cambodia, China, Indonesia, Japan, Republic of Korea, Malaysia, Thailand,
   and Vietnam.
2. Lines connecting the data and zero in the figure, such as Lines A and B, represent GDP
   per unit of sulfur dioxide emissions. Lines A and B are drawn for China in 1990 and for
   Japan in 1990, respectively. Countries on the north-east direction line are cleaner than
   those on the south-west direction line; that is, countries on Line B are cleaner than those
   on Line A.
3. The source of the CO_2 emission data is the World Bank (2007), and the source of the
   SO_2 emission data is Olivier et al. (2005).

4. The association between trade intensity and environmental quality has been examined by many studies, and most studies use international or US data.
5. The environmental Kuznets curve hypothesis suggests that there is an inverse-U curve relationship between environmental damage indicators and income per capita.
6. Pooled OLS was also run with time dummies, and time dummies are not significant at a 95% significance level.
7. For constructing the instrumental variable, see Frankel and Rose (2005).
8. This result is consistent with what the environmental Kuznets curve hypothesis suggests.
9. Copeland and Taylor (1994) and Antweiler et al. (2001) decompose the relationship between trade and the environment into scale, composition and technique effects theoretically.
10. Emissions include local, transboundary, and global pollution. Examples of local pollutants are sulfur dioxide emissions and chemicals that cause soil contamination. Transboundary pollutants include water pollution in international rivers. Global pollutants are ozone depleting substances and global warming gases.
11. Copeland and Taylor (1994) show a mechanism of PHH for a pollutant common across industries while Michida and Nishikimi (2003) use the same setting and find PHH for industry-specific pollutants with local effects.
12. Copeland and Taylor (2004) summarize the mechanisms as sources of growth, income effects and threshold effects.
13. http://ec.europa.eu/environment/impel/.
14. http://www.cec.org/.
15. This is partially because the difference in organizational settings in governments across Asian countries hampers effective cooperation. Moreover, it is possible that public participation in the process of identifying potential environmental problems is not always secured.

REFERENCES

Antweiler, Werner, Brian Copeland and M. Scott Taylor (2001), 'Is free trade good for the environment?', *American Economic Review*, **91**(4), 877–908.

Asian Development Bank (2008), *Key Indicators for Asia and the Pacific 2008*.

Chintrakarn, Pandej and Daniel L. Millimet (2006), 'The environmental consequences of trade: evidence from subnational trade flows', *Journal of Environmental Economics and Management*, **52**(1), 430–53.

Copeland, Brian R. and M. Scott Taylor (1994), 'North-south trade and the environment', *Quarterly Journal of Economics*, **109**(3), 755–87.

Copeland, Brian R. and M. Scott Taylor (1995), 'Trade and transboundary pollution', *American Economic Review*, **85**(4), 716–37.

Copeland, Brian R. and M. Scott Taylor (2004), 'Trade, growth, and the environment', *Journal of Economic Literature*, **42**(1), 7–71.

Dean, Judith M. and Mary E. Lovely (2008), 'Trade growth, production fragmentation, and China's environment', NBER Working Paper, no. 13860.

EANET (2008), 'Data report on the acid deposition in the East Asian region 2006', EANET homepage http://www.eanet.cc/, accessed on 2 November 2008.

EANET, Network Center (2008), Data sets on the acid deposition in the East Asian region 2001, 2002, 2003, 2004, 2005.

Ederington, Josh, Arik Levinson and Jenny Minier (2004), 'Trade liberalization and pollution havens', *Advances in Economic Analysis and Policy*, **4**(2), Article 6.

Elbers, Chris and Cees Withagen (2004), 'Environmental policy, population dynamics and agglomeration', *Contributions to Economic Analysis and Policy*, **3**(2), Article 3.

Elliott, Robert J.R. and Kenichi Shimamoto (2008), 'Are ASEAN countries a haven for Japanese pollution-intensive industry?', *World Economy*, **31**(2), 236–54.

Frankel, Jeffrey A. and Andrew K. Rose (2005), 'Is trade good or bad for the environment? Sorting out the causality', *Review of Economics and Statistics*, **87**(1), 85–91.

Grossman, Gene M. and Alan B. Krueger (1995), 'Economic growth and the environment', *Quarterly Journal of Economics*, **110**(2), 353–78.

Hata, Akio (2003), 'Mining and its environmental damage', in Japan Environmental Council (ed.), *The State of the Environment in Asia*, Tokyo: Springer, pp. 25–45.

Heston, Alan, Robert Summers and Bettina Aten (2006), 'Penn World Table Version 6.2', Center for International Comparisons of Production, Income and Prices at the University of Pennsylvania.

Holtz-Eakin, Douglas and Thomas M. Selden (1995), 'Stoking the fires? CO_2 emissions and economic growth', *Journal of Public Economics*, **57**, 85–101.

International Monetary Fund (2008a), *International Financial Statistics*.

International Monetary Fund (2008b), *Direction of Trade Statistics*.

Jaffe, Adam B., Steven R. Peterson and Paul R. Portney (1995), 'Environmental regulation and the competitiveness of US manufacturing: what does the evidence tell us?', *Journal of Economic Literature*, **33**(1), 132–63.

Jones, David Seth (2006), 'ASEAN and transboundary haze pollution in Southeast Asia', *Asia Europe Journal*, **4**(3), pp. 431–46.

Kahn, Matthew E. (2003), 'The geography of US pollution intensive trade: evidence from 1958 to 1994', *Regional Science and Urban Economics*, **33**(4), 383–400.

Keller, Wolfgang and Arik Levinson (2002), 'Pollution abatement costs and foreign direct investment inflows to US states', *Review of Economics and Statistics*, **84**(4), 691–703.

Kojima, Michikazu (ed.) (2005), *International Trade of Recyclable Resources in Asia*, Institute of Developing Economies, JETRO, Chiba.

Kojima, Michikazu (2007), 'Rating programme revisited: in the case of Indonesia', in Tadayoshi Terao and Otsuka Kenji (ed.), *Development of Environmental Policy in Japan and Asian Countries*, IDE-JETRO.

Kojima, Michikazu, Hisako Kiyono, Masafumi Yokemoto, Arata Izawa, Haruko Yamashita and Satoshi Tachiban (2005), 'Trade and environment: promoting environmentally friendly trade', Japan Environmental Council (ed.), *The State of the Environment in Asia 2005/2006*, Springer.

Michida, Etsuyo and Koji Nishikimi (2003), 'North-south trade and industry-specific pollutants', *Journal of Environmental Economics and Management*, **54**(2), 229–43.

OECD (2007), *OECD Performance Reviews: China*, Paris: OECD.

Olivier, J.G.J, J.A. Van Aardenne, F. Dentener, L. Ganzeveld and J.A.H.W. Peters (2005), 'Recent trends in global greenhouse gas emissions: regional trends and spatial distribution of key sources', in A. van Amstel (coord.), *Non-CO_2 Greenhouse Gases (NCGG-4)*, Rotterdam: Millpress, pp. 325–30.

Porter, Michael E. and Claas van der Linde (1995), 'Toward a new conception of the environment-competitiveness relationship', *Journal of Economic Perspectives*, **9**(4), 97–118.

Rao, P.K. (2000), *The World Trade Organization and the Environment*, Palgrave Macmillan.

Shafik, Nemat (1994), 'Economic development and environmental quality: an econometric analysis', *Oxford Economic Papers*, **46**, 757–73.

Taylor, M. Scott (2004), 'Unbundling the pollution haven hypothesis', *Advances in Economic Analysis & Policy*, **4**(2), Article 4.

World Bank (2007), *World Development Indicators 2007*, Washington, DC: World Bank.

World Bank (2008), *World Development Indicators 2008*, Washington, DC: World Bank.

APPENDIX

Table 18.A1   Trade impact on the environment: data sources

Data	Source
Sulfur dioxide	EANET 2008
Openness (Import, export, GDP)	IMF, International Financial Statistics ADB, Key Statistics for China's import and export
Exchange rate	IMF, *International Financial Statistics*, RF series
GDP ppp per capita	Penn World Table 6.2, Real GDP per capita (constant prices: Laspeyres)
Bilateral trade (import, export)	IMF, *Direction of Trade Statistics*, 2008
Distance, area, language, border	Bilateral data set from website of Andrew K. Rose (2008), http//faculty.haas.berkeley.edu/arose

19. New challenges and directions for East Asian integration

Masahisa Fujita, Ikuo Kuroiwa and Satoru Kumagai

As previous chapters have emphasized, *de facto* integration has thus far preceded *de jure* integration in East Asia. Making effective use of the heterogeneous economic conditions in the region, East Asia has developed a highly integrated export platform and has become a world factory, in which a broad range of intermediate goods are exchanged closely through intra-firm or intra-industry trade (Chapters 1, 4 and 5). This development has been attained mainly through market forces, the role of formal institutions being limited until the late 1990s (Chapters 11 and 12).

Although there is room to make East Asia a more efficient 'world factory', especially through the involvement of latecomer countries, the region has reached a critical stage where further enhancement and development will require the establishment of region-wide formal institutions. On the one hand, a number of region-wide problems of critical importance have emerged. These include the stability of the financial and monetary system, the further promotion of free trade and investment, support for less developed countries or regions, energy and environmental problems, SARS and other epidemics that have originated in East Asia, as well as various issues of regional security.

On the other hand, the current world financial crisis triggered by the collapse of the American financial market has revealed that East Asian exports have relied excessively on extra-regional demand. We need to seek a more balanced development strategy to overcome the current crisis so that growth can proceed in a sustainable manner.

In this chapter, two new challenges and directions for future East Asian integration are discussed. One challenge is that of the need to deepen economic integration, and the other is the task of shifting development orientation from an export-led growth to a more balanced growth strategy.

19.1   DEEPENING ECONOMIC INTEGRATION: DEVELOPING FORMAL INSTITUTIONS

When a sufficiently high level of region-wide economic interdependency has been achieved through trade and investment driven by MNEs, which is the case as regards East Asia today, developing formal institutions could become critical – as well as more politically feasible – for a deepening of economic integration. There are several issues for which formal institutions are required.

Managing widespread free trade agreements

Solving the 'spaghetti-bowl' problem – the confusion caused by overlapping free trade agreements – calls for the establishment of a formal project. Except for some industries, the utilization rates of FTAs are generally low. Small and medium-size enterprises (SMEs), in particular, are reluctant to use them. At some point, a region-wide institutional framework will become necessary to make more effective the numerous FTAs in the region (Chapter 12).

Financing cross-border infrastructure development

East Asia is home to a vast amount of savings, but these savings are not efficiently employed for the development of the region. In particular, there is an urgent need for an infrastructure financing mechanism. In this regard, an East Asia Infrastructure Bond Fund to finance cross-border infrastructure development would be a useful step forward (Chapter 14).

Removing stumbling blocks in agriculture

To address agricultural issues, East Asia needs a forum for the discussion of various agricultural problems that are common to the countries of the region. Harmonization of SPS (sanitary and phytosanitary) measures is vital for enhancing intra-regional agricultural trade. In addition, East Asia may need to establish a regional food security scheme under a common grain reserve program (Chapter 7).

Liberalizing services trade

Services reform requires a larger domestic agenda in which different political economy forces that support reform can be mobilized. To achieve this goal, the priority in a service reform agenda must be transparency. Documenting existing policy would be an important first step, and the WTO provides valuable guidelines on relevant policy information (Chapter 8).

Enhancing brain circulation

In order to encourage 'brain circulation', or mobility of highly skilled migrants, a regional coordination scheme, such as a portable pension plan, could play a useful role. It is also important to establish a common certification system for some professional occupations (Chapter 9).

Promoting monetary integration

Although East Asia needs to consider the pros and cons of monetary integration carefully, a formal scheme of monetary coordination will be indispensable once East Asia takes steps toward deeper integration. An important preliminary measure would be to introduce a Regional Monetary Unit as a surveillance measurement of the ASEAN+3 Financial Deputy Ministers' Economic Review and Policy Dialogue (ERPD) (Chapter 10).

Addressing inequality and poverty

The fruits of economic integration are enjoyed only within limited geographical space, where industries agglomerate, and the process of integration inevitably causes the emergence of winners and losers. The Initiative for ASEAN Integration, which aims to assist new members of ASEAN, is expected to play an important role in tackling this problem (Chapters 15 and 16).

Solving energy issues

Since East Asia is a net importer, as well as a substantial producer, of energy resources, it could gain great benefits from establishing an agency to jointly pursue energy security. Besides energy security, ensuring a transition to a 'greener' form of energy is also important. It is desirable to transfer green technologies from leading countries to latecomer countries, partly through some form of regional organization (Chapter 17).

Addressing environmental problems

Economic integration tends to cause problems in countries where regulations are weakly enforced. East Asia needs to have a coordinated mechanism for environmental impact assessment and needs to implement effective measures for environmental protection. It is also necessary to standardize the enforcement of environmental regulations across countries (Chapter 18).

As described above, there is a need for formal institutions for solving specific region-wide problems. In developing East Asia-wide formal institutions, neither the EU nor NAFTA can provide a relevant model. The regional integration of Europe has been achieved under the super-national projects of the EU, while that of North America has made progress under the aegis of NAFTA. Furthermore, in comparison with the EU and NAFTA, East Asia is a region characterized by huge diversity in many aspects and includes developing countries whose legal systems and governance remain weak in many ways.

To promote deeper integration successfully in the context of such diversity, and also in the context of complex international relations, East Asia needs to develop its own formal institutions gradually and patiently by considering the following points.

First, in promoting regional integration in East Asia, we cannot adopt the EU approach whereby expansion of membership is made gradual by the EU's insistence on rather stringent qualifying standards. If we do so, many less developed countries in Asia will be excluded from the initial political process of regional integration, making it even more difficult for them to develop. Rather, a principal aim of developing formal institutions for Asian integration must be to promote the economic development of less developed countries through active cooperation of all the countries of the region. Thus, in building the institutional framework for Asian integration, all countries and regions in East Asia need to be included from the start.

Second, this in turn means that the actual process of institution building for Asian integration must proceed gradually and patiently while working consistently toward the eventual goal. This is especially necessary in the context of the complex international relationships of Asia involving the United States, Japan and China, and increasingly also India. In practice, this means that the Asian integration process needs to be based on a functional approach in which each urgent and important task must be pursued separately in its own framework.

Third, although East Asia's huge diversity might be a burden for regional integration in the short term, it could be a great asset in the long run. The big wage differential in the region, for example, represents a huge potential in developing efficient international production systems based on complementarity and the division of labor. Furthermore, the rich diversity of culture and ethnicity in the region represents another important asset in the coming age of the brainpower society in which diversity of people will play an essential role in creating new knowledge and innovations through the synergy of unexpected combinations (Fujita 2007).

Fourth, it is essential to establish, as institutions, region-wide forums for ongoing discussions concerning research into, and the development of, common region-wide policies. For this purpose, the recent establishment by 16 countries of the Economic Research Institute for ASEAN and East Asia (ERIA), in Jakarta, marks the beginning of an intellectual contribution to regional efforts for East Asian Economic Integration over a wide range of policy areas.

Finally, needless to say, for achieving deeper and sustainable integration of Asia, the active participation of the broadest range of individuals and agents in various forms, in addition to national governments, will be indispensable.

19.2   SHIFTING THE ORIENTATION OF DEVELOPMENT

East Asia has successfully become the world's factory by developing efficient production networks. This itself is a great achievement, but for further advancement of the East Asian economy, East Asia needs to outgrow the world factory and become more innovation-driven and less dependent on demand from outside the region. It is first necessary to enhance the innovative capacity of the East Asian economies. Second, East Asia's internal demand needs to be boosted so as to absorb the greater part of East Asian production and to reduce dependency on extra-regional demand.

The current global financial turmoil has brought out a world economic crisis comparable in severity to the Great Depression of 1929.[1] From the viewpoint of spatial economics, this economic crisis is an eventual outcome of the global division of labor, which has developed over the last half-century as a result of a steady reduction of transport costs (broadly defined) for the international movement of goods and services, people, money and capital, as well as information, technology and knowledge. This reduction of transport costs has been realized through incessant improvement in transport technologies and the revolutionary development of information technologies (Chapter 13), together with continuing efforts to lower trade barriers by means of new international measures and the establishment of institutions such as the GATT, WTO and free trade agreements. This steady reduction of transport costs has come to yield a global division of labor in which East Asia has become the world's factory (Chapters 1 and 4) with the United States functioning as the world's financial center. The world factory of East Asia has been developed, as explained earlier, by combining effectively the huge and diverse population of East Asia with an advanced production technology transferred to the region from developed countries. In contrast, the United States has become the world's financial center partly because her currency (the US dollar) assumed the position of the world's key currency, dominating other currencies in global patterns of trade and investment.

This global division of labor, however, over the course of time has given

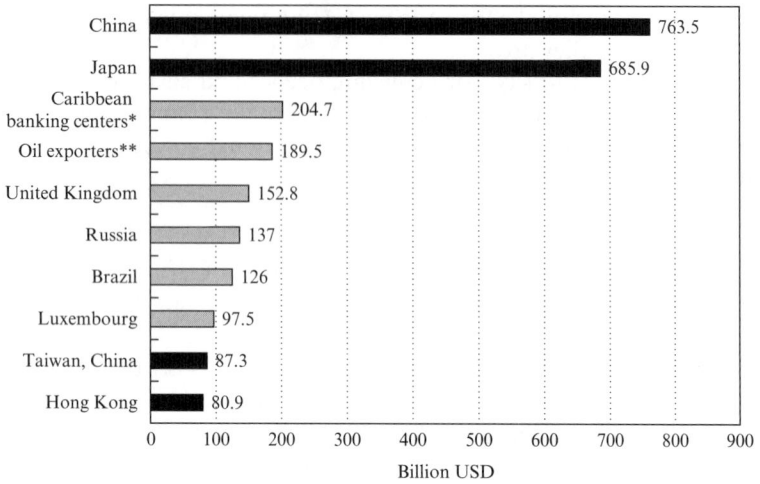

Notes:
* Includes Bahamas, Bermuda, Cayman Islands, Netherlands Antilles and Panama.
** Includes Ecuador, Venezuela, Indonesia, Bahrain, Iran, Iraq, Kuwait, Oman, Qatar, Saudi Arabia, the United Arab Emirates, Algeria, Gabon, Libya, and Nigeria.

Source: Treasury International Capital System, US Department of the Treasury.

Figure 19.1   Top 10 holders of US treasury bonds (as of April 2009)

rise to an unsustainable trade imbalance between the United States and East Asia. In other words, over the last two decades, East Asia as the global factory has continued to accumulate a huge trade surplus (which was mostly brought about through trade with the United States), while the United States has run a huge trade deficit. In turn, most of the trade surplus of East Asia (together with that of the oil producing countries) has been invested back into the financial markets in the United States (Figure 19.1 shows major holders of US treasury bonds), thus supporting the very substantial consumption demand of the United States.

This mechanism of global financial circulation worked as the engine of world economic growth until quite recently. However, the global financial crisis triggered by the explosion of the subprime loan problem in the United States in September 2008 has shown clearly that such a mechanism of world economic growth based on the global trade imbalance is no longer sustainable.

In order for the world economy to overcome today's economic crisis and start growing anew in a sustainable manner, it needs to be reshaped so that East Asia, the United States and the rest of the world are mutually balanced so far as trading relationships are concerned. This means that East Asia needs to outgrow its past export-led growth, based on abundant labor, and instead needs to become a more mature economy in which a sufficient amount of demand is created internally by stimulating regional consumption and investment.

19.2.1   Enhancing the Innovation Capacity of East Asia

In order to achieve this objective, the people of East Asia must be able to earn higher incomes through achieving higher labor productivity, while spending their annual incomes sufficiently without worrying too much about the future. For achieving such a structural change of the economy, it is essential to promote economic growth by enhancing the innovation capacity of the region. Chapter 6 argues that differences in post-1997-crisis economic performance in each East Asian economy may well depend on differences in R&D intensity (the ratio between R&D expenditure and GDP).

In fact, some countries and regions in East Asia, particularly Korea, Taiwan, Hong Kong, and Singapore, are trying in earnest to become innovation-driven, brain power societies. In such countries and regions, technological progress has been achieved through technology transfer and through R&D activities, and regional knowledge now flows within the region through increased patent citation to neighboring countries (Gill and Kharas 2007).

For example, in the Chinese government's National Plan for Scientific and Technology Development of 2006, it is announced that China will become an advanced country in science and technology by 2020, and will become a world center in science and technology by 2050. In conformity with this plan, the share of R&D expenditure in Chinese GDP has undergone a rapid increase in recent years.

It is, however, difficult to transform East Asia into a brain power society by the efforts of individual countries alone. To achieve the transformation, it is essential to utilize effectively the synergy created through the interactions among diverse groups of brain power centers that have been nurtured in the individual countries and regions of East Asia. It is also important to promote further the exchange of college and university students as well as professionals in various fields among all countries and regions of East Asia. By means of cooperation among all the region's countries, East Asia needs to develop dense networks of knowledge creation and exchange, and also needs to further strengthen the role of advanced production networks. In this way, it is hoped that East Asia will eventually become a world innovation center, comparable to the United States and Europe.

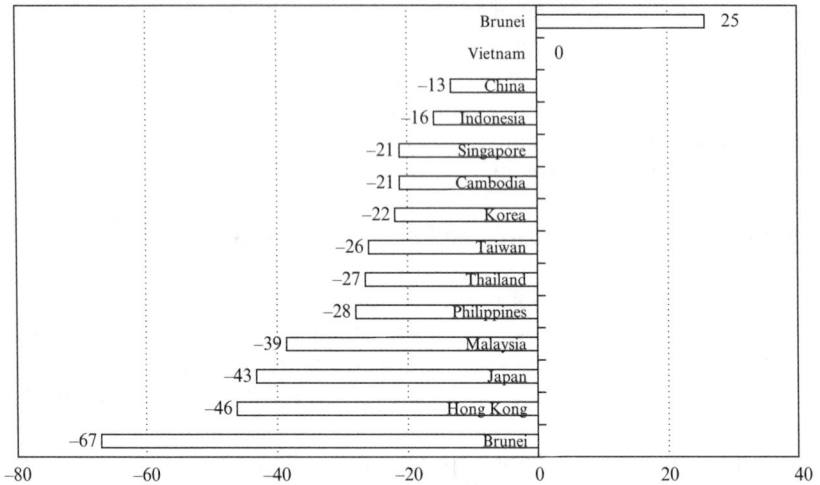

Source: USITC Interactive Trade and Tariff Database.

Figure 19.2   Rapid decline in US imports from East Asia, January–May 2009 against 2008, (%)

19.2.2   Boosting Regional Demand

The current global financial crisis has revealed the vulnerability of the East Asian economy. Although its macroeconomy and financial sector remained relatively stable, East Asia was hit hard by the downfall of the developed economies (Figure 19.2).

The East Asian economy has been heavily dependent on the American and European markets, especially as regards exports of final goods (Chapter 1). Therefore, once the Western economies went into a tailspin, East Asia lost its major markets. Its production networks then worked to the region's disadvantage and stifled industrial development. This reflects the vulnerability of the East Asian economy, which has adopted an export-led growth strategy that has led to the region becoming a world factory, highly dependent on the markets of the United States and Europe (Table 19.1). This vulnerability needs to be addressed if the current crisis is to be overcome.

As trade imbalances are reflected in macroeconomic imbalances, addressing these imbalances is crucial for the rebalancing of trade. Specifically, investment rates declined sharply in crisis-affected countries, namely in Indonesia, Korea, Malaysia, the Philippines, and Thailand. However, since the saving rates of these countries did not decline in

Table 19.1   Export market destinations for final goods, 2006 (%)

		Destination		
	East Asia	NAFTA	EU25	R.O.W
East Asia	25.9	37.1	24.0	13.0
NAFTA	10.8	60.8	16.8	11.6
EU25	5.2	11.0	69.6	14.2

Source: COMTRADE.

parallel, they began to exhibit saving surpluses, as well as current account surpluses, after the Asian crisis of 1997. China, on the other hand, continued to increase investment rates even after the Asian crisis, but Chinese saving rates increased even more. Thus, China's saving surplus as well as its current account surplus have both reached unprecedented levels (Taniuchi 2009).

It is obvious that the Asian crisis-affected countries need to increase investment, while China should attach more importance to increasing consumption. It should be noted that people do not spend much on consumption in some East Asian countries due to lack of reliable social security systems. East Asian countries need to improve their social security systems to reduce uncertainty in people's lives. To increase consumption in the region, it is also necessary to reduce income inequality and increase the number of middle-income people – against this expectation, income inequality within the East Asian countries has often widened, while income inequality between countries has shrunk (Chapters 15 and 16).

Moreover, East Asian countries have curbed the import of consumption goods through the imposition of higher tariff barriers (Chapter 1). Free trade agreements are needed to remove such barriers and encourage intra-regional trade in consumption goods. Finally, exchange rate adjustments are critically important for rebalancing trade. Exchange rates, however, affect all of the countries concerned, and thus coordinated efforts are necessary within a regional framework. It should be noted that such cooperation may lead to regional monetary coordination and thence, ultimately, to a possible regional monetary integration (Chapter 10).

19.2.3   Mobilizing Intra-regional Savings for Investment

On the other hand, investment cannot be increased without well-developed capital markets. In particular, bond markets play a vital role in raising funds for medium to long-term investment. But the fact is that only a few of the East Asian countries have well-developed bond markets. Financial cooperation schemes, such as the ABMI and ABF, can play an important part in the development of Asian bond markets, while the Chiang Mai Initiative is a positive step forward in that it will help to reduce the risks of a future currency crisis (Chapter 10). The other important factor hindering the development of financial and capital markets in the region is the weakness of its institutions. Financial institutions as well as government bodies responsible for supervising financial institutions need to strengthen their capacities, so that Asian savings can be mobilized for Asian investment.

Since many East Asian countries have a strong economic growth potential, investment can yield a higher rate of return than in developed countries. To boost investment however, the public sector needs to play a leading role. Infrastructure, especially cross-border transport infrastructure, is crucial for creating an integrated market as well as a well-functioning production platform. In East Asia, three economic corridors in the Greater Mekong Sub-region (GMS) – the East–West, North–South, and Southern Economic Corridors – have attracted great interest from investors. These have been followed by other notable projects, such as the ASEAN Highway Network Project and the Singapore–Kunming Rail Link Project (Chapters 13 and 14). Furthermore, ERIA (Economic Research Institute of ASEAN and East Asia) has recently proposed the East Asia Industrial Corridor Development which connects East Asia and India through a highway network and sea route.

In these projects, the impact of cross-border transport infrastructure will be magnified if they are linked with other transport facilities, such as ports and airports. Furthermore, the investment climate will be improved dramatically if industrial estates are set up near transport nodes. These efforts will attract private investment and will create massive regional demand. At the same time, they will increase the competitiveness of the East Asian economies.

19.3   CONCLUSION

In this chapter, we have discussed two new challenges and directions for East Asian integration, namely, deepening economic integration and changing development orientation from export-led growth to a more balanced growth strategy, emphasizing the importance of formal institutions, innovation and regional demand.

East Asia has reached a critical stage where various issues need to be tackled jointly by the region's countries acting in concert. Aiming for deeper integration, we should proceed step by step by setting a common agenda and tackling each item jointly, while strengthening mutual trust and nurturing the common identity of the East Asian community.

NOTE

1. The depth and length of the current world economic crisis is unknown at the time of writing. However, the decline in the housing price index in the US market is already deeper than that during the great depression of 1929 (Reinhart and Rogoff 2009).

REFERENCES

Fujita, Masahisa (2007), 'Towards the new economic geography in the brain power society', *Regional Science and Urban Economics*, **37**(4), 482–90.

Gill, Indermit and Homi Kharas (2007), *An East Asia Renaissance: Ideas for Economic Growth*, Washington DC: World Bank.

Reinhart, Carmen M., and Kenneth S. Rogoff (2009), 'The aftermath of financial crises', *American Economic Review*, **99**(2), 466–72.

Taniuchi, Mitsuru (2009), *Global Imbalances and Asian Economies* (in Japanese, *Gurobaru Keizai Fukinkō to Higashi Ajia Keizai*), Kyoto: Kōyo-shobō.

Index